One-Stop Internet Resources

Log on to ca.hss.glencoe.com

ONLINE STUDY TOOLS

- Study Central
- Chapter Overviews
- ePuzzles and Games
- Self-Check Quizzes
- Vocabulary e-Flashcards
- Multi-Language Glossaries

ONLINE RESEARCH

- Student Web Activities
- Current Events
- Beyond the Textbook Features
- Web Resources
- State Resources

FOR TEACHERS

- Teacher Forum
- Web Activity Lesson Plans

Also Featuring a Complete Interactive Student Edition

GLENCOE
CALIFORNIA SERIES

DISCOVERING OUR PAST

Ancient Civilizations

JACKSON J. SPIELVOGEL, PH.D.

NATIONAL
GEOGRAPHIC

McGraw Hill Glencoe

New York, New York   Columbus, Ohio   Chicago, Illinois   Peoria, Illinois   Woodland Hills, California

Authors

Jackson J. Spielvogel is associate professor emeritus of history at the Pennsylvania State University. He received his Ph.D. from The Ohio State University, where he specialized in Reformation history under Harold J. Grimm. His articles and reviews have been published in several scholarly publications. He is coauthor (with William Duiker) of *World History,* published in 1994 (3rd edition, 2001). Professor Spielvogel has won five major university-wide awards, and in 1997, he became the first winner of the Schreyer Institute's Student Choice Award for innovative and inspiring teaching.

The National Geographic Society, founded in 1888 for the increase and diffusion of geographic knowledge, is the world's largest nonprofit scientific and educational organization. Since its earliest days, the Society has used sophisticated communication technologies, from color photography to holography, to convey geographic knowledge to a worldwide membership. The Education Products Division supports the Society's mission by developing innovative educational programs—ranging from traditional print materials to multimedia programs including CD-ROMs, videodiscs, and software.

About the Cover: Throughout ancient history and across the world, people have built great monuments that still stand today. Top: The Great Pyramid of Khafre built by the ancient Egyptians c. 2520 B.C. stands 417 feet (144 m) tall. Left: This life-size terra-cotta statue of a Chinese archer was one of 7,000 figures created for the Emperor Qin Shihuangdi's tomb c. 200 B.C. Right: The Roman Colosseum held 60,000 spectators and was built in A.D. 70 during the reign of the Emperor Vespasian.

 **Glencoe**

The McGraw-Hill Companies

Send all inquiries to:
Glencoe/McGraw-Hill
8787 Orion Place
Columbus, OH 43240-4027

ISBN: 007-868874-4

Printed in the United States of America.

2 3 4 5 6 7 8 9 10 071/055 10 09 08 07 06 05

Contributing Authors, Consultants, and Reviewers

Contributing Authors

Stephen F. Cunha, Ph.D.
Professor of Geography
Director, California Geographic Alliance
Humboldt State University
Arcata, California

Douglas Fisher, Ph.D.
Professor
San Diego State University
San Diego, California

Nancy Frey, Ph.D.
Assistant Professor
San Diego State University
San Diego, California

Robin C. Scarcella, Ph.D.
Professor and Director
Academic English/ESL
University of California, Irvine
Irvine, California

Emily M. Schell, Ed.D.
Visiting Professor, San Diego State University
Social Studies Education Director
SDSU City Heights Educational Collaborative
San Diego, California

David Vigilante
Associate Director
National Center for History in the Schools
San Diego, California

Ruben Zepeda II, Ph.D.
Adviser, Instructional Support Services
Los Angeles Unified School District
Los Angeles, California

Academic Consultants

Winthrop Lindsay Adams
Associate Professor of History
University of Utah
Salt Lake City, Utah

Sari J. Bennett
Director, Center for Geographic Education
University of Maryland Baltimore County
Baltimore, Maryland

Richard G. Boehm
Jesse H. Jones Distinguished Chair in
    Geographic Education
Texas State University
San Marcos, Texas

Stephen F. Dale, Ph.D.
Department of History
The Ohio State University
Columbus, Ohio

Sheilah Clarke-Ekong
Associate Professor of Anthropology and
    Interim Dean
Evening College
University of Missouri, St. Louis
St. Louis, Missouri

Timothy E. Gregory
Professor of History
The Ohio State University
Columbus, Ohio

Robert E. Herzstein
Department of History
University of South Carolina
Columbia, South Carolina

Kenji Oshiro
Professor of Geography
Wright State University
Dayton, Ohio

Joseph R. Rosenbloom
Adjunct Professor, Jewish and Near
    Eastern Studies
Washington University
St. Louis, Missouri

Guy Welbon, Ph.D.
Department of History
University of Pennsylvania
Philadelphia, Pennsylvania

FOLDABLES **Dinah Zike**
Educational Consultant
Dinah-Might Activities, Inc.
San Antonio, Texas

Reading Consultants

Maureen D. Danner
Project CRISS
National Training Consultant
Kalispell, Montana

ReLeah Cossett Lent
Florida Literacy and Reading Excellence
    Project Coordinator
University of Central Florida
Orlando, Florida

Steve Qunell
Social Studies Instructor
Montana Academy
Kalispell, Montana

Carol M. Santa, Ph.D.
CRISS: Project Developer
Director of Education
Montana Academy
Kalispell, Montana

Bonnie Valdes
Master CRISS Trainer
Project CRISS
Largo, Florida

Teacher Reviewers

Jack Ewing
Taylor Middle School
Millbrae, California

Linda Chapel
Vista View Middle School
Fountain Valley, California

Sara Greenfield
Lincoln Middle School
Santa Monica, California

Reynaldo Macías
Mark Twain Middle School
Los Angeles, California

Mark Romo
Vista Verde Middle School
Greenfield, California

Kelly VanAllen
Pine Grove Elementary School
Santa Maria, California

Carl Vanderbosch
Orangeview Junior High School
Anaheim, California

Helen Ligh
Social Studies and Language Arts Teacher
Macy Intermediate
Montebello Unified School District
Monterey Park, CA

Barbara S. Lindemann, Ph.D.
Professor of History and Ethnic Studies
History Department Chair
Santa Barbara City College
Santa Barbara, CA

Reynaldo Antonio Macías
World History Teacher
Mark Twain Middle School
Los Angeles Unified School District
Los Angeles, CA

Jennifer Metherd
Program Coordinator
Tehama County Department of Education
Red Bluff, CA

Derrick K. Neal
Social Studies Department Chair
Patrick Henry Middle School
Los Angeles Unified School District
Los Angeles, CA

Robin C. Scarcella, Ph.D.
Professor and Director
Academic English/ESL
University of California, Irvine
Irvine, CA

Emily M. Schell, Ed.D.
Visiting Professor, San Diego State University
Social Studies Education Director
SDSU City Heights Educational Collaborative
San Diego, CA

Dale Steiner, Ph.D.
Professor of History
California State University, Chico
Chico, CA

Roy Sunada
Social Studies Teacher/AP Coordinator
Marshall Fundamental Secondary School
Pasadena Unified School District
Pasadena, CA

David Vigilante
Associate Director
National Center for History in the Schools
San Diego, CA

Ruben Zepeda II, Ph.D.
Adviser, Instructional Support Services
Los Angeles Unified School District
Los Angeles, CA

Contents

▼ Ancient Assyrian soldiers

◄ Ancient Egyptian artwork of a funeral boat

Hindu goddess Siva ▶

Contents

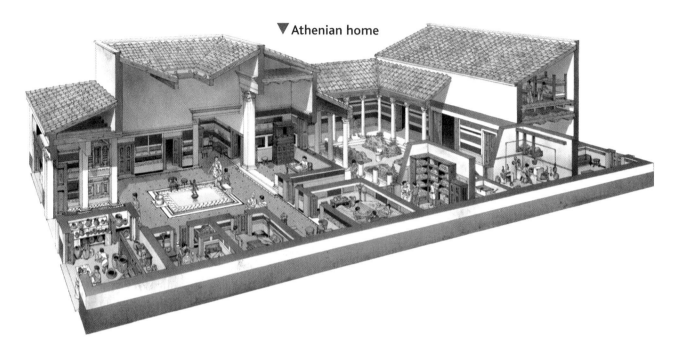

▼ Athenian home

Appendix

Trojan horse ▶

▲ Clay carving of
Trojan horse

Features

Primary Source

Analyzing Primary Sources

WORLD LITERATURE

Hatshepsut ▶

◀ Constantine

Biography

SkillBuilder Handbook

Features

▲ Students today

▲ Mesopotamian cuneiform tablet

Primary Source Quotes

| Ed. = Editor | Tr. = Translator | V = Volume |

Primary Source Quotes

Maps, Charts, Graphs, and Diagrams

National Geographic Maps

Charts and Graphs

Diagrams

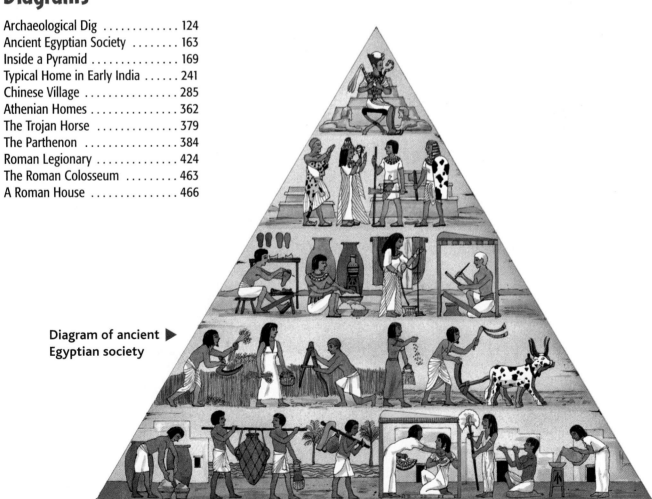

Diagram of ancient ▶
Egyptian society

A Guide to the California Standards

▼ California state capitol, Sacramento

For Students and Their Families

What are the California History–Social Science Content Standards?

The California Department of Education has developed content standards for every course at every grade level. These standards can be found on the California Department of Education website. The History–Social Science Content Standards for grade 6 are designed to measure a student's knowledge of world history between the years of the world's early ages and the fall of the Roman Empire. The content of *Discovering Our Past* matches these standards.

Why should students be aware of these standards?

In grade 8, students will be tested on what they learn in grades 6 and 7 world history courses and in their United States history course in grade 8.

Historical and Social Sciences Analysis Skills

To help you learn and understand content standards for any course you take, it is important to master the following skills. These skills focus on critical thinking, analysis, and research and will be represented like this: **CA HR1.**

Chronological and Spatial Thinking

CS1. Students explain how major events are related to one another in time.

CS2. Students construct various time lines of key events, people, and periods of the historical era they are studying.

CS3. Students use a variety of maps and documents to identify physical and cultural features of neighborhoods, cities, states, and countries and to explain the historical migration of people, expansion and disintegration of empires, and the growth of economic systems.

Research, Evidence, and Point of View

HR1. Students frame questions that can be answered by historical study and research.

HR2. Students distinguish fact from opinion in historical narratives and stories.

HR3. Students distinguish relevant from irrelevant information, essential from incidental information, and verifiable from unverifiable information in historical narratives and stories.

HR4. Students assess the credibility of primary and secondary sources and draw sound conclusions from them.

HR5. Students detect the different historical points of view on historical events and determine the context in which the historical statements were made (the questions asked, sources used, author's perspectives).

Historical Interpretation

HI1. Students explain the central issues and problems from the past, placing people and events in a matrix of time and place.

HI2. Students understand and distinguish cause, effect, sequence, and correlation in historical events, including the long- and short-term causal relations.

HI3. Students explain the sources of historical continuity and how the combination of ideas and events explains the emergence of new patterns.

HI4. Students recognize the role of chance, oversight, and error in history.

HI5. Students recognize that interpretations of history are subject to change as new information is uncovered.

HI6. Students interpret basic indicators of economic performance and conduct cost-benefit analyses of economic and political issues.

History –Social Science Standards

These content standards describe what History–Social Science Standards you should master when you complete this course.

World History and Geography: Ancient Civilizations Standards

Main Standard WH6.1 Students describe what is known through archaeological studies of the early physical and cultural development of humankind from the Paleolithic era to the agricultural revolution.

Supporting Standard WH6.1.1 Describe the hunter-gatherer societies, including the development of tools and the use of fire.

Supporting Standard WH6.1.2 Identify the locations of human communities that populated the major regions of the world and describe how humans adapted to a variety of environments.

Supporting Standard WH6.1.3 Discuss the climatic changes and human modifications of the physical environment that gave rise to the domestication of plants and animals and new sources of clothing and shelter.

▼ Golden Gate Bridge, San Francisco

Main Standard WH6.2 Students analyze the geographic, political, economic, religious, and social structures of the early civilizations of Mesopotamia, Egypt, and Kush.

Supporting Standard WH6.2.1 Locate and describe the major river systems and discuss the physical settings that supported permanent settlement and early civilizations.

Supporting Standard WH6.2.2 Trace the development of agricultural techniques that permitted the production of economic surplus and the emergence of cities as centers of culture and power.

Supporting Standard WH6.2.3 Understand the relationship between religion and the social and political order in Mesopotamia and Egypt.

Supporting Standard WH6.2.4 Know the significance of Hammurabi's Code.

Supporting Standard WH6.2.5 Discuss the main features of Egyptian art and architecture.

Supporting Standard WH6.2.6 Describe the role of Egyptian trade in the eastern Mediterranean and Nile valley.

Supporting Standard WH6.2.7 Understand the significance of Queen Hatshepsut and Ramses the Great.

Supporting Standard WH6.2.8 Identify the location of the Kush civilization and describe its political, commercial, and cultural relations with Egypt.

Supporting Standard WH6.2.9 Trace the evolution of language and its written forms.

Main Standard WH6.3 Students analyze the geographic, political, economic, religious, and social structures of the Ancient Hebrews.

Supporting Standard WH6.3.1 Describe the origins and significance of Judaism as the first monotheistic religion based on the concept of one God who sets down moral laws for humanity.

Supporting Standard WH6.3.2 Identify the sources of the ethical teachings and central beliefs of Judaism (the Hebrew Bible, the Commentaries): belief in God, observance of law, practice of the concepts of righteousness and justice, and importance of study; and describe how the ideas of the Hebrew traditions are reflected in the moral and ethical traditions of Western civilization.

Supporting Standard WH6.3.3 Explain the significance of Abraham, Moses, Naomi, Ruth, David, and Yohanan ben Zaccai in the development of the Jewish religion.

Supporting Standard WH6.3.4 Discuss the locations of the settlements and movements of Hebrew peoples, including the Exodus and their movement to and from Egypt, and outline the significance of the Exodus to the Jewish and other people.

Supporting Standard WH6.3.5 Discuss how Judaism survived and developed despite the continuing dispersion of much of the Jewish population from Jerusalem and the rest of Israel after the destruction of the second Temple in A.D. 70.

▼ San Francisco row houses

Main Standard WH6.4 Students analyze the geographic, political, economic, religious, and social structures of the early civilizations of Ancient Greece.

Supporting Standard WH6.4.1 Discuss the connections between geography and the development of city-states in the region of the Aegean Sea, including patterns of trade and commerce among Greek city-states and within the wider Mediterranean region.

Supporting Standard WH6.4.2 Trace the transition from tyranny and oligarchy to early democratic forms of government and back to dictatorship in ancient Greece, including the significance of the invention of the idea of citizenship (e.g., from *Pericles' Funeral Oration*).

Supporting Standard WH6.4.3 State the key differences between Athenian, or direct, democracy and representative democracy.

Supporting Standard WH6.4.4 Explain the significance of Greek mythology to the everyday life of people in the region and how Greek literature continues to permeate our literature and language today, drawing from Greek mythology and epics, such as Homer's *Iliad* and *Odyssey*, and from *Aesop's Fables*.

Supporting Standard WH6.4.5 Outline the founding, expansion, and political organization of the Persian Empire.

Supporting Standard WH6.4.6 Compare and contrast life in Athens and Sparta, with emphasis on their roles in the Persian and Peloponnesian Wars.

Supporting Standard WH6.4.7 Trace the rise of Alexander the Great and the spread of Greek culture eastward and into Egypt.

Supporting Standard WH6.4.8 Describe the enduring contributions of important Greek figures in the arts and sciences (e.g., Hypatia, Socrates, Plato, Aristotle, Euclid, Thucydides).

Main Standard WH6.5 Students analyze the geographic, political, economic, religious, and social structures of the early civilizations of India.

Supporting Standard WH6.5.1 Locate and describe the major river system and discuss the physical setting that supported the rise of this civilization.

Supporting Standard WH6.5.2 Discuss the significance of the Aryan invasions.

Supporting Standard WH6.5.3 Explain the major beliefs and practices of Brahmanism in India and how they evolved into early Hinduism.

Supporting Standard WH6.5.4 Outline the social structure of the caste system.

Supporting Standard WH6.5.5 Know the life and moral teachings of the Buddha and how Buddhism spread in India, Ceylon, and Central Asia.

Supporting Standard WH6.5.6 Describe the growth of the Maurya empire and the political and moral achievements of the emperor Asoka.

Supporting Standard WH6.5.7 Discuss important aesthetic and intellectual traditions (e.g., Sanskrit literature, including the *Bhagavad Gita;* medicine; metallurgy; and mathematics, including Hindu-Arabic numerals and the zero).

Main Standard WH6.6 Students analyze the geographic, political, economic, religious, and social structures of the early civilizations of China.

Supporting Standard WH6.6.1 Locate and describe the origins of Chinese civilization in the Huang-He Valley during the Shang Dynasty.

Supporting Standard WH6.6.2 Explain the geographic features of China that made governance and the spread of ideas and goods difficult and served to isolate the country from the rest of the world.

Supporting Standard WH6.6.3 Know about the life of Confucius and the fundamental teachings of Confucianism and Daoism.

Supporting Standard WH6.6.4 Identify the political and cultural problems prevalent in the time of Confucius and how he sought to solve them.

▼ Windmills

Supporting Standard WH6.6.5 List the policies and achievements of the emperor Shi Huangdi in unifying northern China under the Qin Dynasty.

Supporting Standard WH6.6.6 Detail the political contributions of the Han Dynasty to the development of the imperial bureaucratic state and the expansion of the empire.

Supporting Standard WH6.6.7 Cite the significance of the trans-Eurasian "silk roads" in the period of the Han Dynasty and Roman Empire and their locations.

Supporting Standard WH6.6.8 Describe the diffusion of Buddhism northward to China during the Han Dynasty.

Main Standard WH6.7 Students analyze the geographic, political, economic, religious, and social structures during the development of Rome.

Supporting Standard WH6.7.1 Identify the location and describe the rise of the Roman Republic, including the importance of such mythical and historical figures as Aeneas, Romulus and Remus, Cincinnatus, Julius Caesar, and Cicero.

Supporting Standard WH6.7.2 Describe the government of the Roman Republic and its significance (e.g., written constitution and tripartite government, checks and balances, civic duty).

Supporting Standard WH6.7.3 Identify the location of and the political and geographic reasons for the growth of Roman territories and expansion of the empire, including how the empire fostered economic growth through the use of currency and trade routes.

Supporting Standard WH6.7.4 Discuss the influence of Julius Caesar and Augustus in Rome's transition from republic to empire.

Supporting Standard WH6.7.5 Trace the migration of Jews around the Mediterranean region and the effects of their conflict with the Romans, including the Romans' restrictions on their right to live in Jerusalem.

Supporting Standard WH6.7.6 Note the origins of Christianity in the Jewish Messianic prophecies, the life and teachings of Jesus of Nazareth as described in the New Testament, and the contribution of St. Paul the Apostle to the definition and spread of Christian beliefs (e.g., belief in the Trinity, resurrection, salvation).

Supporting Standard WH6.7.7 Describe the circumstances that led to the spread of Christianity in Europe and other Roman territories.

Supporting Standard WH6.7.8 Discuss the legacies of Roman art and architecture, technology and science, literature, language, and law.

English–Language Arts Standards

These content standards describe what English-language arts skills you should master by the time you complete sixth grade. Items that relate to an English–Language Arts Standard will be represented like this: **CA RW1.0**

Reading

6RW1.0 Word Analysis, Fluency, and Systematic Vocabulary Development

Word Recognition

6RW1.1 Read aloud narrative and expository text fluently and accurately and with appropriate pacing, intonation, and expression.

Vocabulary and Concept Development

6RW1.2 Identify and interpret figurative language and words with multiple meanings.

6RW1.3 Recognize the origins and meanings of frequently used foreign words in English and use these words accurately in speaking and writing.

6RW1.4 Monitor expository text for unknown words or words with novel meanings by using word, sentence, and paragraph clues to determine meaning.

6RW1.5 Understand and explain "shades of meaning" in related words (e.g., *softly* and *quietly*).

6RC2.0 Reading Comprehension

Structural Features of Informational Materials

6RC2.1 Identify the structural features of popular media (e.g., newspapers, magazines, online information) and use the features to obtain information.

6RC2.2 Analyze text that uses the compare-and-contrast organizational pattern.

Comprehension and Analysis of Grade-Level-Appropriate Text

6RC2.3 Connect and clarify main ideas by identifying their relationships to other sources and related topics.

6RC2.4 Clarify an understanding of texts by creating outlines, logical notes, summaries, or reports.

6RC2.5 Follow multiple-step instructions for preparing applications (e.g., for a public library card, bank savings account, sports club, league membership).

Expository Critique

6RC2.6 Determine the adequacy and appropriateness of the evidence for an author's conclusions.

6RC2.7 Make reasonable assertions about a text through accurate, supporting citations.

6RC2.8 Note instances of unsupported inferences, fallacious reasoning, persuasion, and propaganda in text.

▼ California farmland

6RL3.0 Literary Response and Analysis

Structural Features of Literature

6RL3.1 Identify the forms of fiction and describe the major characteristics of each form.

Narrative Analysis of Grade-Level-Appropriate Text

6RL3.2 Analyze the effect of the qualities of the character (e.g., courage or cowardice, ambition or laziness) on the plot and the resolution of the conflict.

6RL3.3 Analyze the influence of setting on the problem and its resolution.

6RL3.4 Define how tone or meaning is conveyed in poetry through word choice, figurative language, sentence structure, line length, punctuation, rhythm, repetition, and rhyme.

6RL3.5 Identify the speaker and recognize the difference between first- and third-person narration (e.g., autobiography compared with biography).

6RL3.6 Identify and analyze features of themes conveyed through characters, actions, and images.

6RL3.7 Explain the effects of common literary devices (e.g., symbolism, imagery, metaphor) in a variety of fictional and nonfictional texts.

Literary Criticism

6RL3.8 Critique the credibility of characterization and the degree to which a plot is contrived or realistic (e.g., compare use of fact and fantasy in historical fiction).

Writing

6WS1.0 Writing Strategies

Organization and Focus

6WS1.1 Choose the form of writing (e.g., personal letter, letter to the editor, review, poem, report, narrative) that best suits the intended purpose.

6WS1.2 Create multiple-paragraph expository compositions:

a. Engage the interest of the reader and state a clear purpose.

b. Develop the topic with supporting details and precise verbs, nouns, and adjectives to paint a visual image in the mind of the reader.

c. Conclude with a detailed summary linked to the purpose of the composition.

6WS1.3 Use a variety of effective and coherent organizational patterns, including comparison and contrast; organization by categories; and arrangement by spatial order, order of importance, or climactic order.

Research and Technology

6WS1.4 Use organizational features of electronic text (e.g., bulletin boards, databases, keyword searches, e-mail addresses) to locate information.

6WS1.5 Compose documents with appropriate formatting by using word-processing skills and principles of design (e.g., margins, tabs, spacing, columns, page orientation).

Evaluation and Revision

6WS1.6 Revise writing to improve the organization and consistency of ideas within and between paragraphs.

Writing Applications
(Genres and Their Characteristics)

· ·

6WA2.0 Using the writing strategies of grade six outlined in Writing Standard 1.0, students:

6WA2.1 Write narratives:

- **a.** Establish and develop a plot and setting and present a point of view that is appropriate to the stories.

- **b.** Include sensory details and concrete language to develop plot and character.

- **c.** Use a range of narrative devices (e.g., dialogue, suspense).

6WA2.2 Write expository compositions (e.g., description, explanation, comparison and contrast, problem and solution):

- **a.** State the thesis or purpose.

- **b.** Explain the situation.

- **c.** Follow an organizational pattern appropriate to the type of composition.

- **d.** Offer persuasive evidence to validate arguments and conclusions as needed.

6WA2.3 Write research reports:

- **a.** Pose relevant questions with a scope narrow enough to be thoroughly covered.

- **b.** Support the main idea or ideas with facts, details, examples, and explanations from multiple authoritative sources (e.g., speakers, periodicals, online information searches).

- **c.** Include a bibliography.

6WA2.4 Write responses to literature:

- **a.** Develop an interpretation exhibiting careful reading, understanding, and insight.

- **b.** Organize the interpretation around several clear ideas, premises, or images.

- **c.** Develop and justify the interpretation through sustained use of examples and textual evidence.

6WA2.5 Write persuasive compositions:

- **a.** State a clear position on a proposition or proposal.

- **b.** Support the position with organized and relevant evidence.

- **c.** Anticipate and address reader concerns and counterarguments.

▼ California's Pacific Coast

Written and Oral English Language Conventions

. . . .

6WC1.0 Written and Oral English Language Conventions

Sentence Structure

6WC1.1 Use simple, compound, and compound-complex sentences; use effective coordination and subordination of ideas to express complete thoughts.

Grammar

6WC1.2 Identify and properly use indefinite pronouns and present perfect, past perfect, and future perfect verb tenses; ensure that verbs agree with compound subjects.

Punctuation

6WC1.3 Use colons after the salutation in business letters, semicolons to connect independent clauses, and commas when linking two clauses with a conjunction in compound sentences.

Capitalization

6WC1.4 Use correct capitalization.

Spelling

6WC1.5 Spell frequently misspelled words correctly (e.g., *their, they're, there*).

Listening and Speaking Strategies

. . . .

6LS1.0 Listening and Speaking Strategies

Comprehension

6LS1.1 Relate the speaker's verbal communication (e.g., word choice, pitch, feeling, tone) to the nonverbal message (e.g., posture, gesture).

6LS1.2 Identify the tone, mood, and emotion conveyed in the oral communication.

6LS1.3 Restate and execute multiple-step oral instructions and directions.

Organization and Delivery of Oral Communication

6LS1.4 Select a focus, an organizational structure, and a point of view, matching the purpose, message, occasion, and vocal modulation to the audience.

6LS1.5 Emphasize salient points to assist the listener in following the main ideas and concepts.

6LS1.6 Support opinions with detailed evidence and with visual or media displays that use appropriate technology.

6LS1.7 Use effective rate, volume, pitch, and tone and align nonverbal elements to sustain audience interest and attention.

Analysis and Evaluation of Oral and Media Communications

6LS1.8 Analyze the use of rhetorical devices (e.g., cadence, repetitive patterns, use of onomatopoeia) for intent and effect.

6LS1.9 Identify persuasive and propaganda techniques used in television and identify false and misleading information.

Speaking Applications
(Genres and Their Characteristics)

. . . .

6SA2.0 Speaking Applications

6SA2.1 Deliver narrative presentations:

  a. Establish a context, plot, and point of view.

  b. Include sensory details and concrete language to develop the plot and character.

  c. Use a range of narrative devices (e.g., dialogue, tension, or suspense).

6SA2.2 Deliver informative presentations:

  a. Pose relevant questions sufficiently limited in scope to be completely and thoroughly answered.

  b. Develop the topic with facts, details, examples, and explanations from multiple authoritative sources (e.g., speakers, periodicals, online information).

6SA2.3 Deliver oral responses to literature:

  a. Develop an interpretation exhibiting careful reading, understanding, and insight.

  b. Organize the selected interpretation around several clear ideas, premises, or images.

  c. Develop and justify the selected interpretation through sustained use of examples and textual evidence.

6SA2.4 Deliver persuasive presentations:

  a. Provide a clear statement of the position.

  b. Include relevant evidence.

  c. Offer a logical sequence of information.

  d. Engage the listener and foster acceptance of the proposition or proposal.

6SA2.5 Deliver presentations on problems and solutions:

  a. Theorize on the causes and effects of each problem and establish connections between the defined problem and at least one solution.

  b. Offer persuasive evidence to validate the definition of the problem and the proposed solutions.

▼ **California's state flower**

Correlation to the California Standards

Historical and Social Sciences Analysis Skills	Student Edition Pages
Chronological and Spatial Thinking	
CS1. Students explain how major events are related to one another in time.	94–95, 96–97, 131, 164, 415, 434, 521
CS2. Students construct various time lines of key events, people, and periods of the historical era they are studying.	94–95, 96–97, 195, 307, 415, 441, 451, 521
CS3. Students use a variety of maps and documents to identify physical and cultural features of neighborhoods, cities, states, and countries and to explain the historical migration of people, expansion, and disintegration of empires, and the growth of economic systems.	98–101, 102–03, 139, 147, 150, 191, 194, 212, 226, 227, 245, 270, 283, 303, 306, 316, 324, 325, 343, 370, 403, 414, 415, 425, 434, 451, 454, 491, 494, 524
Research, Evidence, and Point of View	
HR1. Students frame questions that can be answered by historical study and research.	104–05, 147, 191, 227, 245, 271, 291, 307, 371, 455, 514
HR2. Students distinguish fact from opinion in historical narratives and stories.	104–05, 194, 271, 371, 455, 525
HR3. Students distinguish relevant from irrelevant information, essential from incidental information, and verifiable from unverifiable information in historical narratives and stories.	104–05, 193, 303, 525
HR4. Students assess the credibility of primary and secondary sources and draw sound conclusions from them.	106–07, 149, 164, 253, 305, 452, 493
HR5. Students detect the different historical points of view on historical events and determine the context in which the historical statements were made (the questions asked, sources used, author's perspectives).	106–07, 141, 212, 225, 227, 267, 293, 323, 350, 357, 369, 371, 403, 405, 413, 441, 443, 455, 494, 508, 523
Historical Interpretation	
HI1. Students explain the central issues and problems from the past, placing people and events in a matrix of time and place.	108–09, 147, 151, 164, 212, 226, 227, 495
HI2. Students understand and distinguish cause, effect, sequence, and correlation in historical events, including the long- and short-term causal relations.	108–09, 131, 139, 147, 149, 164, 170, 186, 194, 205, 212, 223, 226, 253, 267, 269, 270, 271, 321, 324, 325, 367, 371, 397, 411, 414, 434, 443, 454, 483, 491, 494, 495, 508, 514, 521, 524, 525
HI3. Students explain the sources of historical continuity and how the combination of ideas and events explains the emergence of new patterns.	108–09, 150, 253, 283, 403, 441
HI4. Students recognize the role of chance, oversight, and error in history.	110–11, 150, 325, 403
HI5. Students recognize that interpretations of history are subject to change as new information is uncovered.	110–11, 151, 227, 325
HI6. Students interpret basic indicators of economic performance and conduct cost-benefit analyses of economic and political issues.	110–11, 139, 151, 303, 343, 451, 483

History–Social Science Content Standards for Grade 6	Student Edition Pages
WH6.1 Students describe what is known through archaeological studies of the early physical and cultural development of humankind from the Paleolithic era to the agricultural revolution.	122–31
WH6.1.1 Describe the hunter-gatherer societies, including the development of tools and the use of fire.	123–26
WH6.1.2 Identify the locations of human communities that populated the major regions of the world and describe how humans adapted to a variety of environments.	123–28, 129, 130–31
WH6.1.3 Discuss the climatic changes and human modifications of the physical environment that gave rise to the domestication of plants and animals and new sources of clothing and shelter.	127–28, 129, 130–31
WH6.2 Students analyze the geographic, political, economic, religious, and social structures of the early civilizations of Mesopotamia, Egypt, and Kush.	132–39, 142–47, 156–64, 165–70, 178–86, 187–91
WH6.2.1 Locate and describe the major river systems and discuss the physical settings that supported permanent settlement and early civilizations.	133–36, 157–60
WH6.2.2 Trace the development of agricultural techniques that permitted the production of economic surplus and the emergence of cities as centers of culture and power.	133–37, 138, 159–62
WH6.2.3 Understand the relationship between religion and the social and political order in Mesopotamia and Egypt.	133–37, 163–64, 166–70, 183–84,186
WH6.2.4 Know the significance of Hammurabi's Code.	138, 139, 140–41
WH6.2.5 Discuss the main features of Egyptian art and architecture.	168–70, 179
WH6.2.6 Describe the role of Egyptian trade in the eastern Mediterranean and Nile valley.	161–62, 180–81, 189–91
WH6.2.7 Understand the significance of Queen Hatshepsut and Ramses the Great.	180–81, 182, 184, 185, 186, 192–93
WH6.2.8 Identify the location of the Kush civilization and describe its political, commercial, and cultural relations with Egypt.	188–91, 192–93
WH6.2.9 Trace the evolution of language and its written forms.	123–26, 148–49, 159–60, 188
WH6.3 Students analyze the geographic, political, economic, religious, and social structures of the Ancient Hebrews.	200–05, 206–12, 213–23, 224–25
WH6.3.1 Describe the origins and significance of Judaism as the first monotheistic religion based on the concept of one God who sets down moral laws for humanity.	201–03
WH6.3.2 Identify the sources of the ethical teachings and central beliefs of Judaism (the Hebrew Bible, the Commentaries): belief in God, observance of law, practice of the concepts of righteousness and justice, and importance of study; and describe how the ideas of the Hebrew traditions are reflected in the moral and ethical traditions of Western civilization.	201–03, 210–12, 214–15, 217–18, 220–23
WH6.3.3 Explain the significance of Abraham, Moses, Naomi, Ruth, David, and Yohanan ben Zaccai in the development of the Jewish religion.	201–05, 207, 208, 209–10, 219, 220–23

History–Social Science Content Standards for Grade 6	Student Edition Pages
WH6.3.4 Discuss the locations of the settlements and movements of Hebrew peoples, including the Exodus and their movement to and from Egypt, and outline the significance of the Exodus to the Jewish and other people.	201–05, 210–12, 215–16
WH6.3.5 Discuss how Judaism survived and developed despite the continuing dispersion of much of the Jewish population from Jerusalem and the rest of Israel after the destruction of the second Temple in A.D. 70.	220–23
WH6.4 Students analyze the geographic, political, economic, religious, and social structures of the early civilizations of Ancient Greece.	336–43, 344–50, 351–57, 358–67, 376–85, 392–97, 398–403, 406–11
WH6.4.1 Discuss the connections between geography and the development of city-states in the region of the Aegean Sea, including patterns of trade and commerce among Greek city-states and within the wider Mediterranean region.	337–43
WH6.4.2 Trace the transition from tyranny and oligarchy to early democratic forms of government and back to dictatorship in ancient Greece, including the significance of the invention of the idea of citizenship (e.g., from *Pericles' Funeral Oration*).	341–42, 345–46, 348–50, 361, 364–67
WH6.4.3 State the key differences between Athenian, or direct, democracy and representative democracy.	359–60
WH6.4.4 Explain the significance of Greek mythology to the everyday life of people in the region and how Greek literature continues to permeate our literature and language today, drawing from Greek mythology and epics, such as Homer's *Iliad* and *Odyssey*, and from *Aesop's Fables*.	368–69, 377–80, 381, 382–83, 412–13
WH6.4.5 Outline the founding, expansion, and political organization of the Persian Empire.	352–53
WH6.4.6 Compare and contrast life in Athens and Sparta, with emphasis on their roles in the Persian and Peloponnesian Wars.	346–50, 354–57, 362–67
WH6.4.7 Trace the rise of Alexander the Great and the spread of Greek culture eastward and into Egypt.	399–403, 404–05, 407–10
WH6.4.8 Describe the enduring contributions of important Greek figures in the arts and sciences (e.g., Hypatia, Socrates, Plato, Aristotle, Euclid, Thucydides).	368–69, 384–85, 393–95, 396, 397, 407–10, 412–13
WH6.5 Students analyze the geographic, political, economic, religious, and social structures of the early civilizations of India.	238–45, 246–53, 259–67
WH6.5.1 Locate and describe the major river system and discuss the physical setting that supported the rise of this civilization.	239–41
WH6.5.2 Discuss the significance of the Aryan invasions.	242–43
WH6.5.3 Explain the major beliefs and practices of Brahmanism in India and how they evolved into early Hinduism.	247–48
WH6.5.4 Outline the social structure of the caste system.	243–45
WH6.5.5 Know the life and moral teachings of the Buddha and how Buddhism spread in India, Ceylon, and Central Asia.	249–50, 251, 252–53, 268–69

History–Social Science Content Standards for Grade 6	Student Edition Pages
WH6.5.6 Describe the growth of the Maurya empire and the political and moral achievements of the emperor Asoka.	260, 261, 262, 263
WH6.5.7 Discuss important aesthetic and intellectual traditions (e.g., Sanskrit literature, including the *Bhagavad Gita;* medicine; metallurgy; and mathematics, including Hindu-Arabic numerals and the zero).	242–43, 265–67, 268–69
WH6.6 Students analyze the geographic, political, economic, religious, and social structures of the early civilizations of China.	276–83, 284–91, 294–303
WH6.6.1 Locate and describe the origins of Chinese civilization in the Huang-He Valley during the Shang Dynasty.	277–81
WH6.6.2 Explain the geographic features of China that made governance and the spread of ideas and goods difficult and served to isolate the country from the rest of the world.	277–78
WH6.6.3 Know about the life of Confucius and the fundamental teachings of Confucianism and Daoism.	287–88, 289, 290–91, 292–93, 304–05
WH6.6.4 Identify the political and cultural problems prevalent in the time of Confucius and how he sought to solve them.	287–88, 289, 290–91, 292–93
WH6.6.5 List the policies and achievements of the emperor Shi Huangdi in unifying northern China under the Qin Dynasty.	295–96, 297
WH6.6.6 Detail the political contributions of the Han Dynasty to the development of the imperial bureaucratic state and the expansion of the empire.	298–300
WH6.6.7 Cite the significance of the trans-Eurasian "silk roads" in the period of the Han Dynasty and Roman Empire and their locations.	300–02
WH6.6.8 Describe the diffusion of Buddhism northward to China during the Han Dynasty.	303
WH6.7 Students analyze the geographic, political, economic, religious, and social structures during the development of Rome.	420–25, 426–34, 435–41, 444–51, 460–68, 474–83, 522–23
WH6.7.1 Identify the location and describe the rise of the Roman Republic, including the importance of such mythical and historical figures as Aeneas, Romulus and Remus, Cincinnatus, Julius Caesar, and Cicero.	421–25, 427–29, 430, 436–41
WH6.7.2 Describe the government of the Roman Republic and its significance (e.g., written constitution and tripartite government, checks and balances, civic duty).	427–29, 431
WH6.7.3 Identify the location of and the political and geographic reasons for the growth of Roman territories and expansion of the empire, including how the empire fostered economic growth through the use of currency and trade routes.	432–34, 446, 448–51
WH6.7.4 Discuss the influence of Julius Caesar and Augustus in Rome's transition from republic to empire.	438–41, 442–43, 445–46, 447, 452–53
WH6.7.5 Trace the migration of Jews around the Mediterranean region and the effects of their conflict with the Romans, including the Romans' restrictions on their right to live in Jerusalem.	500–08

History–Social Science Content Standards for Grade 6	Student Edition Pages
WH6.7.6 Note the origins of Christianity in the Jewish Messianic prophecies, the life and teachings of Jesus of Nazareth as described in the New Testament, and the contribution of St. Paul the Apostle to the definition and spread of Christian beliefs (e.g., belief in the Trinity, resurrection, salvation).	500–03, 504, 505–06, 507, 508, 522–23
WH6.7.7 Describe the circumstances that led to the spread of Christianity in Europe and other Roman territories.	478, 506, 508, 509–14, 515–21
WH6.7.8 Discuss the legacies of Roman art and architecture, technology and science, literature, language, and law.	431, 461–63, 482–83

English–Language Arts Standards for Grade 6	English–Language Arts Standards for Grade 6
Reading **6RW1.0 Word Analysis, Fluency, and Systematic Vocabulary Development**	**6RL3.3** Student page: 176, 390, 472
6RW1.2 Student page: 443	**6RL3.4** Student page: 411
6RW1.4 Student page: 283, 307	**6RL3.5** Student page: 257
6RC2.0 Reading Comprehension **(Focus on Informational Materials)** Student page: 147, 150, 191, 205, 223, 226, 283, 293, 306, 316, 324, 350, 367, 370, 403, 411, 414, 425, 434, 441, 454, 468, 495, 514, 521, 524, 525	**6RL3.6** Student page: 385
	6RL3.7 Student page: 257
6RC2.1 Student page: 271, 441, 514	**Writing** **6WS1.0 Writing Strategies** Student page: 303
6RC2.2 Student page: 191, 194, 223, 226, 270, 306, 343, 367, 370, 397, 411, 414, 454	**6WS1.1** Student page: 223, 227, 321, 350, 357, 483
6RC2.3 Student page: 147, 150, 170, 223, 245, 267, 306, 343, 385, 397, 468, 483, 495, 521	**6WS1.2** Student page: 139, 176, 195, 291
6RC2.4 Student page: 131, 151, 164, 170, 186, 191, 194, 205, 212, 245, 253, 271, 283, 316, 321, 325, 350, 357, 367, 385, 397, 403, 411, 425, 434, 441, 451, 468, 483, 491, 508, 514	**6WS1.3** Student page: 151, 186, 195, 267, 291, 303, 316, 371
	6WA2.0 Writing Applications (Genres and Their Characteristics) Student page: 371
6RC2.6 Student page: 186, 369	**6WA2.1** Student page: 195, 253, 257, 307, 411, 415, 451, 495, 525
6RC2.7 Student page: 141, 245, 270	**6WA2.2** Student page: 151, 186, 269, 291, 343, 367, 385, 425, 455, 495, 508
6RL3.0 Literary Response and Analysis Student page: 414, 472	**6WA2.3** Student page: 205, 227, 307, 325, 371, 415, 455, 525
6RL3.1 Student page: 385	**6WA2.4** Student page: 257, 390, 472
6RL3.2 Student page: 176, 390	**6WA2.5** Student page: 170, 223, 245, 271, 293, 305, 307, 324, 350, 357, 397, 405, 415, 434, 441, 443, 455, 483

Previewing Your Textbook

Follow the reading road map through the next few pages to learn about using your textbook, *Discovering Our Past: Ancient Civilizations*. Knowing how your text is organized will help you discover interesting events, fascinating people, and faraway places.

Unit Preview

Your textbook is divided into units. Each unit begins with four pages of information to help you begin your study of the topics.

WHY IT'S IMPORTANT

Each unit begins with a **preview** of important events and *Why It's Important* to read about them.

TIME LINE

A time line shows you **when** the events in this unit happened. It also compares events and people from different places.

MAP

This map shows you **where** the events in this unit happened.

PLACES TO LOCA...

You can look for thes... important places to locate as you read th... unit.

PEOPLE TO MEET

People who have made an impact on world history are highlighted throughout your text.

Unit Review

A **Unit Review** falls at the end of the unit and **compares** the content.

COMPARISON CHART

All of the different civilizations talked about in this unit are **compared** in a chart.

WORLD MAP

A **map** shows you where each civilization existed.

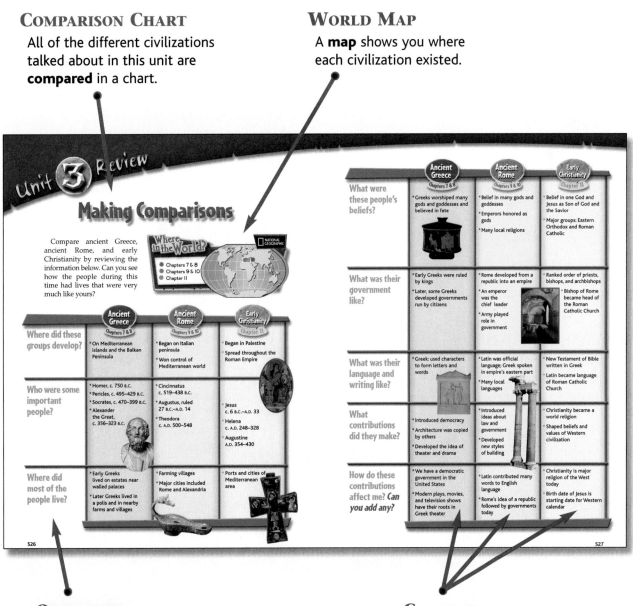

QUESTIONS

The chart answers the **same questions** about each group of people making it easier to compare them.

CHAPTERS

The most **important ideas** in each chapter are listed in the columns.

Chapters

Each unit of your textbook is divided into chapters. Each chapter starts by giving you some background information about what you will be reading.

CHAPTER TITLE
The chapter title tells you the main topic you will be reading about.

COLORFUL PHOTO
Shows you what this part of the world is like.

WHERE AND WHEN?
Here you can see where and when events in this chapter happened.

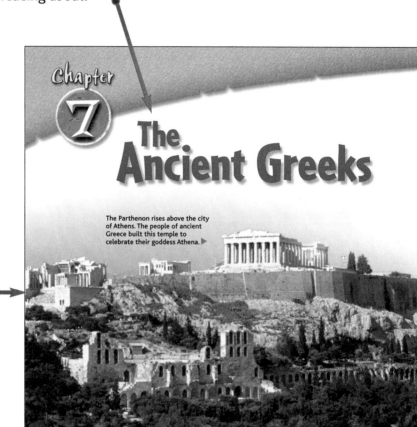

Chapter 7

The Ancient Greeks

The Parthenon rises above the city of Athens. The people of ancient Greece built this temple to celebrate their goddess Athena. ▶

NATIONAL GEOGRAPHIC **Where & When?**

700 B.C.	600 B.C.	500 B.C.	400 B.C.
c. 750 B.C. Greece's Dark Age comes to an end	c. 650 B.C. Tyrants over-throw nobles in city-states	480 B.C. Xerxes invades Greece	431 B.C. Peloponnesian War begins

Big Ideas

Throughout your text important ideas are given at the beginning of each chapter. These ideas alert you to the big themes of history that occur over and over again.

BIG IDEAS

The important ideas of each section are explained for you. ●

HISTORY ONLINE

This tells you where you can go online for more information. ●

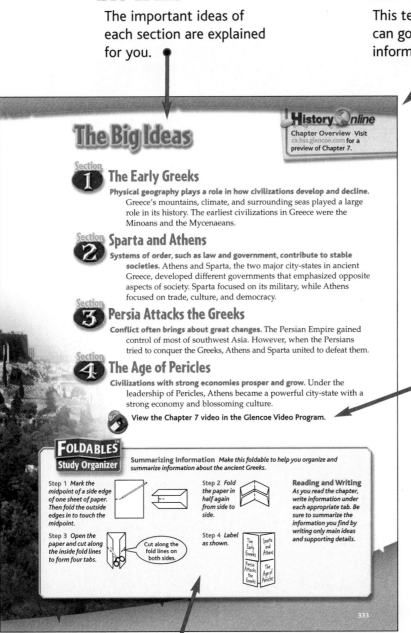

The Big Ideas

History Online
Chapter Overview Visit ca.hss.glencoe.com for a preview of Chapter 7.

Section 1 The Early Greeks

Physical geography plays a role in how civilizations develop and decline. Greece's mountains, climate, and surrounding seas played a large role in its history. The earliest civilizations in Greece were the Minoans and the Mycenaeans.

Section 2 Sparta and Athens

Systems of order, such as law and government, contribute to stable societies. Athens and Sparta, the two major city-states in ancient Greece, developed different governments that emphasized opposite aspects of society. Sparta focused on its military, while Athens focused on trade, culture, and democracy.

Section 3 Persia Attacks the Greeks

Conflict often brings about great changes. The Persian Empire gained control of most of southwest Asia. However, when the Persians tried to conquer the Greeks, Athens and Sparta united to defeat them.

Section 4 The Age of Pericles

Civilizations with strong economies prosper and grow. Under the leadership of Pericles, Athens became a powerful city-state with a strong economy and blossoming culture.

View the Chapter 7 video in the Glencoe Video Program.

FOLDABLES™ Study Organizer

Summarizing Information *Make this foldable to help you organize and summarize information about the ancient Greeks.*

Step 1 *Mark the midpoint of a side edge of one sheet of paper. Then fold the outside edges in to touch the midpoint.*

Step 2 *Fold the paper in half again from side to side.*

Step 3 *Open the paper and cut along the inside fold lines to form four tabs.*

Cut along the fold lines on both sides.

Step 4 *Label as shown.*

The Early Greeks | Sparta and Athens
Persia Attacks the Greeks | The Age of Pericles

Reading and Writing *As you read the chapter, write information under each appropriate tab. Be sure to summarize the information you find by writing only main ideas and supporting details.*

333

GLENCOE VIDEO PROGRAM

● Each **video program** highlights a unique topic in the chapter and has a Viewer's Guide.

FOLDABLES™

Use the **Foldables™** Study Organizer to **take notes.**

Previewing Your Textbook

Chapter Reading Skill

Because reading about Social Studies is different than reading a novel or magazine, every chapter of your text offers help with reading skills.

READING SKILL

This shows you what reading skill you will be learning about—**Comparing and Contrasting.**

LEARN IT!

This explains how the skill applies to the **reading** you do every day.

READING TIP

The Reading Tip tells you more about making **connections** in your reading.

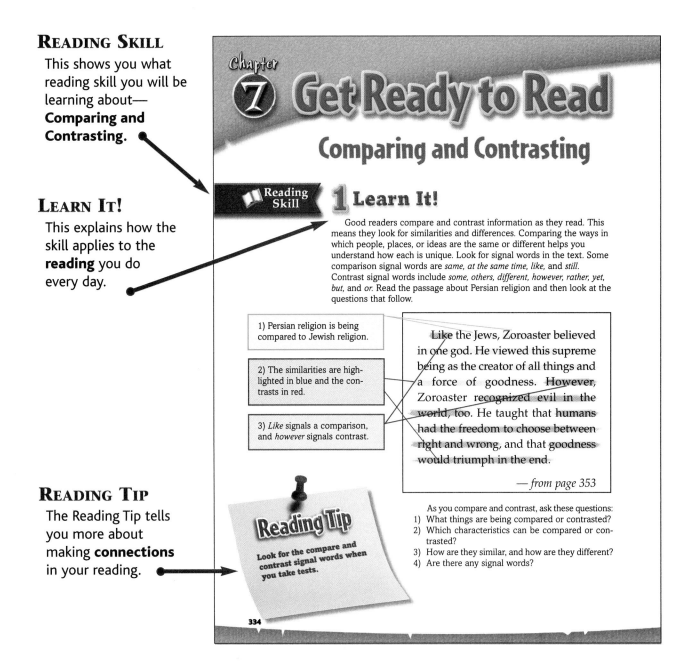

Chapter

7 Get Ready to Read

Comparing and Contrasting

Reading Skill

1 Learn It!

Good readers compare and contrast information as they read. This means they look for similarities and differences. Comparing the ways in which people, places, or ideas are the same or different helps you understand how each is unique. Look for signal words in the text. Some comparison signal words are *same, at the same time, like,* and *still.* Contrast signal words include *some, others, different, however, rather, yet, but,* and *or.* Read the passage about Persian religion and then look at the questions that follow.

1) Persian religion is being compared to Jewish religion.

2) The similarities are highlighted in blue and the contrasts in red.

3) *Like* signals a comparison, and *however* signals contrast.

Like the Jews, Zoroaster believed in one god. He viewed this supreme being as the creator of all things and a force of goodness. However, Zoroaster recognized evil in the world, too. He taught that humans had the freedom to choose between right and wrong, and that goodness would triumph in the end.

— *from page 353*

Reading Tip

Look for the compare and contrast signal words when you take tests.

As you compare and contrast, ask these questions:
1) What things are being compared or contrasted?
2) Which characteristics can be compared or contrasted?
3) How are they similar, and how are they different?
4) Are there any signal words?

334

PRACTICE IT!

Next comes an easy-to-follow **practice** activity.

WRITING

Writing about what you read will help you remember the events.

---

2 Practice It!

Read the passage and the directions below.

> Athens and Sparta, the two major city-states in ancient Greece, developed different governments that emphasized opposite aspects of society. Sparta focused on its military, while Athens focused on trade, culture, and democracy.
>
> — *from page 333*

Read Section 2 and use a chart like the one below to organize the similarities and differences between Sparta and Athens. In the first column, fill in the characteristics that you will compare and contrast. In the second and third columns, describe the characteristics of each city-state.

Characteristic	Sparta	Athens

Read to Write
Reread the passage labeled *Roles of Men and Women* in Section 4 of this chapter. Then write a short paragraph comparing and contrasting what life was like for men and women in ancient Athens.

▼ Spartan warrior

APPLY IT!

Here is an opportunity to **apply** what you have learned.

3 Apply It!

As you read the chapter, choose three pairs of subjects to compare and contrast. List the similarities and differences using a graphic organizer, such as the one above.

335

READING SKILLS HANDBOOK

Located on pages 36-45 is a handbook that is full of reading strategies to help you read your text. You can look back at this handbook as you read.

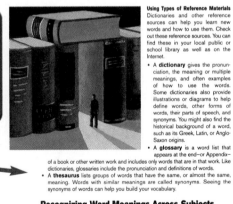

Reading Skills Handbook

Using Types of Reference Materials
Dictionaries and other reference sources can help you learn new words and how to use them. Check out these reference sources. You can find these in your local public or school library as well as on the Internet.

- A **dictionary** gives the pronunciation, the meaning or multiple meanings, and often examples of how to use the words. Some dictionaries also provide illustrations or diagrams to help define words, other forms of words, their parts of speech, and synonyms. You might also find the historical background of a word, such as its Greek, Latin, or Anglo-Saxon origins.
- A **glossary** is a word list that appears at the end—or Appendix—of a book or other written work and includes only words that are in that work. Like dictionaries, glossaries include the pronunciation and definitions of words.
- A **thesaurus** lists groups of words that have the same, or almost the same, meaning. Words with similar meanings are called synonyms. Seeing the synonyms of words can help you build your vocabulary.

Recognizing Word Meanings Across Subjects
Have you ever learned a new word in one class and then noticed it in your reading for other subjects? The word probably will not mean exactly the same thing in each class. But you can use what you know about the word's meaning to help you understand what it means in a different subject area. Look at the following example from three different subjects:

- **Social studies:** One *product* manufactured in the southern part of the United States is cotton cloth.
- **Math:** After multiplying the numbers five and five, explain how you arrived at the *product*.
- **Science:** One *product* of photosynthesis is oxygen.

CHECKING YOUR UNDERSTANDING

The following sentence does not include real English words, but you can use what you have learned about English syntax to decode the sentence. First read the sentence. Then answer the questions that follow.

The shabs smatously graled the mul-bulowed rotfabs.

1. What is the verb in the sentence?
2. What is the subject?
3. What is the object?

CHECK UNDERSTANDING

Did you understand the reading lesson?

Previewing Your Textbook

Sections

A section is a division, or part, of a chapter. The first page of the section, the Section Opener, helps you set a purpose for reading.

GUIDE TO READING
Read the **connection** between what you already know and what you are about to read.

CONTENT VOCABULARY
Points out important social studies **terms** and how to say them.

Section 1

The Early Greeks

Guide to Reading

History Social Science Standards
WH6.4 Students analyze the geographic, political, economic, religious, and social structures of the early civilizations of Ancient Greece.

Looking Back, Looking Ahead
In Chapters 1 and 2, you learned about Mesopotamia and Egypt. These civilizations grew up in great river valleys with rich soil. Greece had no great river valleys. Instead, it had mountains, rocky soil, and many miles of seacoasts.

Focusing on the Main Ideas
- The geography of Greece influenced where people settled and what they did. (page 337)
- The Minoans earned their living by building ships and trading. (page 338)
- Mycenaeans built the first Greek kingdoms and spread their power across the Mediterranean region. (page 339)
- The idea of citizenship developed in Greek city-states. (page 341)
- Colonies and trade spread Greek culture and spurred industry. (page 343)

Meeting People
Agamemnon (A•guh•MEHM•nahn)

Locating Places
Crete (KREET)
Mycenae (my•SEE•nee)
Peloponnesus (PEH•luh•puh•NEE•suhs)

Content Vocabulary
peninsula (puh•NIHN•suh•luh)
polis (PAH•luhs)
agora (A•guh•ruh)
colony (KAH•luh•nee)

Academic Vocabulary
region (REE•juhn)
culture (KUHL•chuhr)
overseas (OH•vuhr•SEEZ)
community (kuh•MYOO•nuh•tee)

Reading Strategy
Finding Details Draw a diagram like the one below. In each oval write one detail about a polis.

polis

NATIONAL GEOGRAPHIC Where & When?

2000 B.C.   1250 B.C.   500 B.C.

GREECE
Mycenae
Crete — Knossos

c. 2000 B.C. Minoans control eastern Mediterranean

c. 1200 B.C. Mycenaean civilization declines

c. 750 B.C. Greece's Dark Age comes to an end

336   CHAPTER 7 • The Ancient Greeks

WH6.4.1 Discuss the connections between geography and the development of city-states in the region of the Aegean Sea, including patterns of trade and commerce among Greek city-states and within the wider Mediterranean region.

The Geography of Greece

Main Idea The geography of Greece influenced where people settled and what they did.

Reading Connection Do you rake leaves in the fall? Do you walk uphill to school? Your answers explain how geography shapes your life. Read to learn how geography shaped life in early Greece.

If you fly over Greece today, you will see a mountainous land framed by sparkling blue water. To the west is the Ionian (eye•OH•nee•uhn) Sea, to the south is the Mediterranean Sea, and to the east is the Aegean (ih•JEE•uhn) Sea. Hundreds of islands lie offshore, stretching across to Asia like stepping-stones. Mainland Greece is a peninsula (puh•NIHN•suh•luh)—a body of land with water on three sides.

Many ancient Greeks made a living from the sea. They became fishers, sailors, and traders. Others settled in farming communities. Greece's mountains and rocky soil were not ideal for growing crops. However, the climate was mild, and in some places people could grow wheat, barley, olives, and grapes. They also raised sheep and goats.

Ancient Greeks felt deep ties to the land, but the mountains and seas divided them from one another. As a result, early Greek communities grew up fiercely independent.

Reading Check Cause and Effect How did geography discourage Greek unity?

NATIONAL GEOGRAPHIC **Ancient Greece** c. 750 B.C.

MACEDONIA
Mt. Olympus
Troy
BALKAN PENINSULA
GREECE
Ionian Sea
Aegean Sea
ASIA MINOR
Delphi
Thebes
Corinth
Mycenae
Athens
Miletus
PELOPONNESUS
Sparta
Mediterranean Sea
Sea of Crete
Knossos
Crete
Sea of Marmara

KEY
Ancient Greece

Using Geography Skills
1. Location What body of water lies directly east of the Balkan Peninsula?
2. Movement What transportation was probably most useful to the early Greeks?
Find NGS online map resources @ www.nationalgeographic.com/maps

Mountains and seas played an important role in Greek history. ▶

CALIFORNIA HISTORY–SOCIAL SCIENCE STANDARDS
Content Standards covered in this section.

MAIN IDEAS
Preview the **main ideas** of each section which are repeated in the reading.

ACADEMIC VOCABULARY
Tells you other **new words** you might not know that will come up in your reading.

24

READING CHECK

This is a **self check** question to see if you understand the main ideas.

MAPS

Large maps help you learn how **geography and history** are related.

CALIFORNIA STATE STANDARDS

The California History–Social Science standard that is covered on the pages you are about to read is listed here.

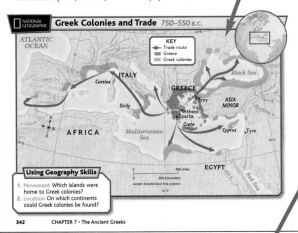

Slaves and foreign-born residents, however, continued to be excluded. Women and children might qualify for citizenship, but they had none of the rights that went with it.

What exactly were the rights of Greek citizens? They could gather in the agora to choose their officials and pass laws. They had the right to vote, hold office, own property, and defend themselves in court. In return, citizens had a duty to serve in government and to fight for their polis as citizen soldiers.

Citizens as Soldiers In early Greece, wars were waged by nobles riding horses and chariots. As the idea of citizenship developed, however, the military system changed. By 700 B.C., the city-states had begun to depend on armies of ordinary citizens called hoplites (HAHP•lyts).

Unable to afford horses, the hoplites fought on foot and went into battle heavily armed. Each soldier carried a round shield, a short sword, and a 9-foot (2.7-m) spear. Row upon row of soldiers marched forward together, shoulder to shoulder in a formation called a phalanx (FAY•langks). With their shields creating a protective wall, they gave their enemies few openings to defeat them.

Hoplites made good soldiers because as citizens, they took pride in fighting for their city-state. However, "hometown" loyalties also divided the Greeks and caused them to distrust one another. A lack of unity always existed among the Greek city-states.

✓ Reading Check Explain How did citizenship make the Greeks different from other ancient peoples?

NATIONAL GEOGRAPHIC
Greek Colonies and Trade 750–550 B.C.

KEY
→ Trade route
▪ Greece
▪ Greek colonies

ATLANTIC OCEAN
ITALY
Corsica
Sicily
AFRICA
Mediterranean Sea
GREECE
Troy
Athens
Sparta
Crete
Black Sea
ASIA MINOR
Cyprus
Tyre
EGYPT
Red Sea

500 miles
500 kilometers
Lambert Azimuthal Equal-Area projection
20°E

Using Geography Skills
1. **Movement** Which islands were home to Greek colonies?
2. **Location** On which continents could Greek colonies be found?

342 CHAPTER 7 • The Ancient Greeks

WH6.4.1 Discuss the connections between geography and the development of city-states in the region of the Aegean Sea, including patterns of trade and commerce among Greek city-states and within the wider Mediterranean region.

A Move to Colonize

Main Idea Colonies and trade spread Greek culture and spurred industry.

Reading Connection If you read labels, you know that your food and clothing come from all over the world. Read to find out where the early Greeks got their goods.

As Greece recovered from its Dark Age, its population rose quickly. By 700 B.C., city-states could no longer grow enough grain to feed everyone. As a result, cities began sending people outside Greece to start **colonies** (KAH•luh•nees). A colony is a settlement in a new territory that stays closely linked to its homeland.

Between 750 B.C. and 550 B.C., adventurous Greeks streamed to the coasts of Italy, France, Spain, North Africa, and western Asia. With each new colony, Greek culture spread farther.

Colonists traded regularly with their "parent" cities, shipping them grains, metals, fish, timber, and enslaved people. In return, the colonists received pottery, wine, and olive oil from the mainland. Overseas trade got an extra boost during the 600s B.C., when the Greeks began to mint coins. Merchants were soon exchanging goods for currency rather than for more goods.

By importing grain and other foods from their colonies, many city-states could support a much larger population. This made it very important to protect their colonies, otherwise people would starve. Trade also led to the growth of industry. As the demand for goods grew, producers had to keep pace. People in different areas began specializing in certain products. For example, pottery became popular in places with large amounts of clay.

✓ Reading Check Cause and Effect How did the founding of new colonies affect industry?

History Online
Study Central Need help understanding the importance of geography in ancient Greece? Visit ca.hss.glencoe.com and click on Study Central.

Section 1 Review

Reading Summary
Review the Main Ideas
- Geography influenced the way Greek communities developed.
- The Minoan civilization on the island of Crete built ships and became wealthy from trade.
- The Mycenaeans created the first Greek kingdoms.
- After the Dark Age, the Greeks set up colonies and trade increased.
- The idea of citizenship developed in Greek city-states.

What Did You Learn?
1. What made the Minoans wealthy?
2. How was a Greek city-state different from a city?

Critical Thinking
3. Compare Create a Venn diagram to compare the Minoans and Mycenaeans. CA 6RC2.2

   Minoan Both Mycenaean

The Big Ideas How did early Greek civilizations use their natural surroundings to prosper and grow? CA CS3.

5. Citizenship Skills Name three rights granted to Greek citizens that American citizens have today. CA 6RC2.1
6. Economics Connection Why did the use of money help trade to grow? CA HI6.
7. **Reading** Comparing and Contrasting Write an essay that compares and contrasts the Mycenaeans and the Dorians. Look for clues in the text that will help you make these comparisons. CA 6WA2.2

CHAPTER 7 • The Ancient Greeks 343

SECTION REVIEW

Here you can review the main topics and answer questions about what you have read.

STUDY CENTRAL

Here you can receive help with **homework.**

CALIFORNIA STATE STANDARDS

The oval shows the Historical and Social Sciences Analysis Skills and the English–Language Arts Content Standards covered by this question.

Previewing Your Textbook

Chapter Assessment

These pages offer you a chance to check how much you remember after reading the chapter.

VOCABULARY REVIEW

Content vocabulary is reviewed here.

MAIN IDEAS

Revisit the **Main Ideas** found in your reading.

Chapter 7 Assessment
Standard WH6.4

Review Content Vocabulary

Write the vocabulary word that completes each sentence. Write a sentence for each word not used.

a. satrap   d. direct democracy
b. agora   e. oligarchy
c. democracy   f. peninsula

1. In a(n) ___, a few wealthy people hold power.
2. The Greek mainland is a(n) ___, a body of land with water on three sides.
3. In a(n) ___, people at mass meetings make decisions for the government.
4. A(n) ___ acted as tax collector, judge, chief of police, and army recruiter.

Review the Main Ideas

Section 1 • The Early Greeks
5. How did the geography of Greece influence where people settled and how they made a living?
6. How did the building of ships affect Minoan civilization?
7. Which group built the first Greek kingdoms?
8. How did the Greek colonies help industry to grow?
9. What are Greek city-states also known as?

Section 2 • Sparta and Athens
10. Why were tyrants able to seize control from Greek nobles?
11. Who did the Spartans fear most within their city-states?
12. Describe the differences between Athens and Sparta.

Section 3 • Persia Attacks the Greeks
13. What system did Darius use to unite his large empire under one government?
14. Why did Sparta and Athens unite during the Persian Wars?

370   CHAPTER 7 • The Ancient Greeks

Section 4 • The Age of Pericles
15. How was democracy expanded during the Age of Pericles?
16. What were the main duties of women in Athens?
17. What was the result of the Peloponnesian War?

Critical Thinking

18. **Cause and Effect** How did the geography of Greece help to encourage trade? **CA CS3.**
19. **Conclude** Did the people of ancient Athens have a full democracy? Explain. **CA 6RC2.0**
20. **Explain** Do you think people would enjoy more freedom in an oligarchy or a tyranny? Explain. **CA 6RC2.2**

Geography Skills

Study the map below and answer the following questions.

21. **Place** What sea lies along the west coast of Greece? **CA CS3.**
22. **Location** Where was Knossos? **CA CS3.**
23. **Movement** If you traveled from Athens to Troy, in what direction would you be going? **CA CS3.**

NATIONAL GEOGRAPHIC   **Ancient Greece**

STANDARDS

Historical and Social Sciences Analysis Skills and English-Language Arts standards covered are listed in ovals.

26

ACADEMIC VOCABULARY

Terms are reviewed here.

WRITING ABOUT BIG IDEAS

You are reminded about the chapter **Big Ideas** here.

HISTORY ONLINE

Go to the web for a quick **self-check** quiz.

READING SKILL

Review the reading Strategy you learned at the beginning of the chapter.

REVIEW ARROWS

Look for the *Review* arrows that tell you are **reviewing** material you have learned before.

Read to Write

24. **The Big Ideas** Writing Research Reports Write an essay explaining how democracy helped create a strong and stable society in Greece. **CA 6WA2.3**

25. Using Your **FOLDABLES** Use the information from your completed chapter opener foldables to create a brief study guide for the chapter. Your study guide should include at least five questions for each section. Questions should focus on the main ideas. Exchange your study guide with a partner and answer each of the questions. **CA HR1.**

Using Academic Vocabulary

26. Separate the words below into three categories: Verbs, Nouns, and Adjectives. Keep in mind that some of the words can be placed in more than one column.

region	participate
culture	economy
overseas	vision
community	internal
enforce	framework

Linking Past and Present

27. **Making Comparisons** Choose a person mentioned in Chapter 7. Write a description of someone in the news today who has similar ideas or has acted in similar ways. List some of their similarities. **CA 6WA2.0**

Building Citizenship

28. **Analyze** Democracy is not easy to achieve or maintain. Make a chart like the one below to identify things that challenged or threatened democracy in Athens. **CA HI2.**

Challenges to Democracy

History Online

Self-Check Quiz To help you prepare for the Chapter Test, visit ca.hss.glencoe.com

Reviewing Skills

29. **Reading Skill** Comparing and Contrasting Write an essay comparing and contrasting the Persian Empire to the Greek city-states. Explain how these similarities and differences affected the result of the Persian Wars. **CA WS1.3**

30. **Analysis Skill** Facts and Opinions Reread the quotations from Xenophon (page 364) and Pericles (page 366). Determine whether these statements are facts or opinions. Write a paragraph about each quotation explaining your decision. **CA HR2.; HR5.**

Standards Practice

Read the passage below and answer the following question.

"My intent is to . . . march an army through Europe against Greece, that thereby I may obtain vengeance from the Athenians for the wrongs committed by them . . ."

31 The above words were spoken by the leader of which group of people?

A the Romans

B the Athenians

C the Persians

D the Minoans

CHAPTER 7 • The Ancient Greeks **371**

STANDARDS PRACTICE AND REVIEW

Answer practice questions to help you master the **California standards**.

Previewing Your Textbook

California Standards

In your textbook, on pages 1–18—in the **Guide to California Standards**—you will find a listing of all of the California History–Social Science standards. All of these are covered in *Discovering Our Past: Ancient Civilizations.*

TO PARENTS AND STUDENTS

Here is an explanation of what is contained in the **Guide to California Standards.**

ANALYSIS SKILLS

Here is a list of standards that relate to **thinking and research skills** you can use in all of your classroom subjects.

ENGLISH–LANGUAGE ARTS STANDARDS

Here you will find the Grade 6 English–Language Arts Standards

CALIFORNIA HISTORY–SOCIAL SCIENCE STANDARD

This is the main idea of the standard.

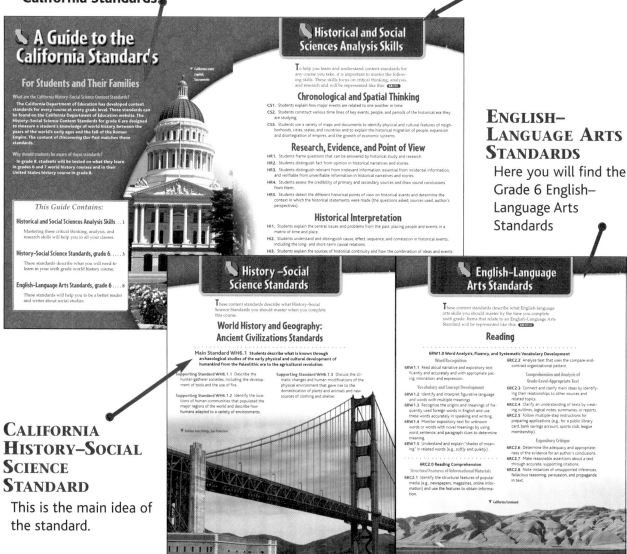

CALIFORNIA STATE SYMBOL

Look for the California state symbol and the standard top or the side of the page.

CALIFORNIA STANDARDS [SIDE]

Sometimes you will find standards covered listed in the side column of the page.

CALIFORNIA STANDARDS [TOP]

Most often the standards covered on the page will be listed at the top.

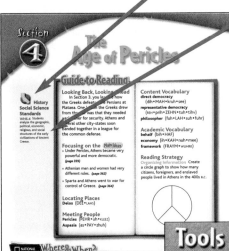

ARTIFACT

Many interesting **artifacts** are shown throughout the text.

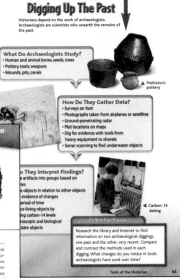

TOOLS OF THE HISTORIAN ANALYSIS SKILLS

This section gives you an overview of how historical detectives find out about the history of the world. These detectives use the Historical and Social Sciences Analysis Skills. The Historical Analysis Skills are noted for you.

THINKING LIKE A HISTORIAN

Questions help you pick out the **important information** from the reading.

Previewing Your Textbook

Standards Review Handbook

This handbook found on pages 548–561 gives you another chance to practice your understanding of the **6th grade History–Social Science Content Standards** you are required to know.

MAIN STANDARD

The chart shows the **main standards** you need to know.

WHERE CAN I FIND IT?

Tells you where in your text you can read more about this standard.

ANSWER KEY

Answers to the Practice Questions are given for you to **check yourself.**

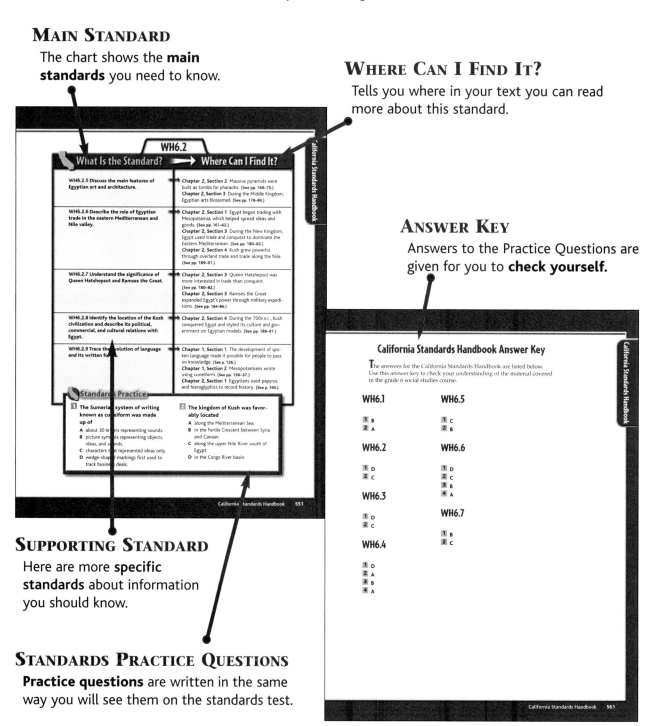

SUPPORTING STANDARD

Here are more **specific standards** about information you should know.

STANDARDS PRACTICE QUESTIONS

Practice questions are written in the same way you will see them on the standards test.

Special Features

Special Features supply more information about topics in the chapter or unit. They help history come alive. Here is a sample of the *World Literature* feature.

W☉RLD LITERATURE

ICARUS AND DAEDALUS

Retold by Geraldine McCaughrean

Before You Read

The Scene: This story takes place on the Greek island of Crete in the legendary time when both humans and gods lived in ancient Greece.

The Characters: Daedalus is the master architect for King Minos of Crete. Icarus is the son of Daedalus.

The Plot: King Minos summons Daedalus and Icarus to build him a palace and then keeps them captive in their own creation. Daedalus plans to escape.

Vocabulary Preview

labyrinth: an extremely complicated maze

luxurious: characterized by comfort or pleasure

astonishment: sudden wonder or surprise

taunt: to mock in an insulting manner

daub: to cover with a sticky matter

plume: a large and showy feather of a bird

Have you ever known someone
did
is
ho
r and

390

W☉RLD LITERATURE

I'm the first boy ever to fly! I'm making history! I shall be famous! thought Icarus, as he flew up and up, higher and higher.

At last Icarus was looking the sun itself in the face, "Think you're the highest thing in the sky, do you?" he jeered. "I can fly just as high as you! Higher, even!" He did not notice the drops of sweat on his forehead: He was so determined to outfly the sun.

Soon its vast heat beat on his face and on his back and on the great wings stuck on with wax. The wax softened. The wax trickled. The wax dripped. One feather came unstuck. Then a plume of feathers fluttered slowly down.

Icarus stopped flapping his wings. His father's words came back to him clearly now: *"Don't fly too close to the sun!"*

With a great sucking noise, the wax on his shoulders came unstuck. Icarus tried to catch hold of the wings, but they just folded up in his hands. He plunged down, his two fists full of feathers—down and down and down.

The clouds did not stop his fall.

The sea gulls did not catch him in their beaks.

His own father could only watch as Icarus hurtled head first into the glittering sea and sank deep down among the sharks and eels and squid. And all that was left of proud Icarus was a litter of waxy feathers floating on the sea.

Responding to the Literature

1. What does Daedalus build for King Minos?

2. What does King Minos do to keep Daedalus and Icarus from escaping from Crete?

3. **Drawing Conclusions** Do you think Daedalus is a concerned father? Why or why not? Support your opinion with examples. CA DR1.3.2

4. **Analyze** How does the setting of the story influence the plot? Support your ideas with details from the story. CA DR1.3.3

5. **Read to Write** Imagine you are Icarus. Would you listen to your father's advice? Write two or three paragraphs explaining what you would have done and why. CA 6WA2.4

Reading on Your Own...

 From the California Reading List

Do you want to learn more about the ancient Greeks?
If so, check out these other great books.

Nonfiction

Trade and Warfare by Robert Hull explores the history of Greece through trading and conflict. It looks at the different types of ships the Greeks used and the battles on both land and sea. *The content of this book is related to History–Social Science Standard WH6.4.*

Biography

Archimedes and the Door of Science by Jeanne Bendick follows the life of the Greek scientist Archimedes. Learn about the different discoveries and inventions of one of the greatest minds of the ancient world. *The content of this book is related to History–Social Science Standard WH6.4.*

Mythology

Adventures of the Greek Heroes by Mollie McLean and Anne Wiseman is a book written by two teachers who love the tales of action and adventure in ancient Greece. Exciting tales give the reader a glimpse into the lives of heroic Greeks. *The content of this book is related to History–Social Science Standard WH6.4.*

Mythology

D'Aulaires' Book of Greek Myths by Edgar and Ingri D'Aulaire is a retelling of the most significant stories of ancient Greece. The book is filled with adventures and stories of the gods and goddesses and men and women who influenced Greek mythology. *The content of this book is related to History–Social Science Standard WH6.4.*

391

BEFORE YOU READ

Get an idea of what the literature selection is about before you read.

DOCUMENT-BASED QUESTIONS

Respond to questions based on the reading.

READING ON YOUR OWN

Read more about this time in world history. These titles are just suggestions.

Previewing Your Textbook

ANALYZING PRIMARY SOURCES

You will be given an opportunity to judge the value and truthfulness of a variety of **primary and secondary sources.**

CALIFORNIA STANDARD

The **History–Social Science standard** covered here is noted.

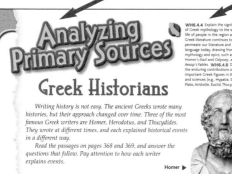

Analyzing Primary Sources

Greek Historians

Writing history is not easy. The ancient Greeks wrote many histories, but their approach changed over time. Three of the most famous Greek writers are Homer, Herodotus, and Thucydides. They wrote at different times, and each explained historical events in a different way.

Read the passages on pages 368 and 369, and answer the questions that follow. Pay attention to how each writer explains events.

Homer ▶

WH6.4.4 Explain the significance of Greek mythology to the everyday life of people in the region and how Greek literature continues to permeate our literature and language today, drawing from Greek mythology and epics, such as Homer's *Iliad* and *Odyssey*, and from Aesop's *Fables*. **WH6.4.8** Describe the enduring contributions of important Greek figures in the arts and sciences (e.g., Hypatia, Socrates, Plato, Aristotle, Euclid, Thucydides).

Reader's Dictionary

Hector: a prince of Troy
Deiphobus (day•ee•FOH•buhs): a powerful fighter from Troy
Paris: brother of Hector and a prince of Troy
Priam (PREE•uhm): father of Hector and Paris

Helen: a beautiful Greek woman who was kidnapped by Paris, causing the Trojan War.
Medea (meh•DEE•uh): a woman the Greeks had kidnapped from the Persians

The Histories by Herodotus

Herodotus often tried to provide sources for his history. Here he gives one of the reasons he believes the Greeks and the Persians did not like each other. the mythological story about how the Greeks had kidnapped the woman Medea from people in the land near Troy.

Paris, the son of **Priam,** was inspired . . . to steal a wife for himself out of Greece, being confident that he would not have to pay for the venture any more than the Greeks had done. And that was how he came to carry off **Helen.**

The first idea of the Greeks . . . was to send a demand for satisfaction and for Helen's return. The demand was met by a reference to the seizure of **Medea** and the injustice of expecting satisfaction from people to whom they themselves had refused it, not to mention the fact that they had kept the girl.

. . . [T]he Greeks, merely on account of a girl from Sparta, raised a big army, invaded Asia and destroyed the empire of Priam. From that root sprang their belief in the perpetual enmity of the Grecian world towards them—Asia with its various foreign-speaking peoples belonging to the Persians, Europe and the Greek states being, in their opinion, quite separate and distinct from them.

Such then is the Persian story. In their view it was the capture of Troy that first made them the enemies of the Greeks.

—Herodotus, *The Histories*

Thucydides' *History of the Peloponnesian War*

Thucydides took great care to analyze the causes of events and the sources for his history. In this passage, he discusses a terrible plague that hit Athens in 430 B.C.

The most terrible thing of all was the despair into which people fell when they realized that they had caught the plague; for they would immediately adopt an attitude of utter hopelessness, and, by giving in this way, would lose their powers of resistance. Terrible, too, was the sight of people dying like sheep through having caught the disease as a result of nursing others. This indeed caused more deaths than anything else. For when people were afraid to visit the sick, then they died with no one to look after them; indeed, there were many houses in which all the inhabitants perished through lack of any attention. When, on the other hand, they did visit the sick, they lost their own lives.

—Thucydides, *History of the Peloponnesian War*

▲ Thucydides

DBQ Document-Based Questions

Homer's Iliad
1. What does Hector think Athena did?
2. Why does Hector believe he is going to die?

The Histories by Herodotus
3. Why does Paris think he can get away with kidnapping Helen?
4. What does Herodotus's use of myths say about how he wrote his history?

Thucydides' History of the Peloponnesian War
5. According to Thucydides, what caused more deaths than anything else during the plague?
6. What caused people to lose their powers of resistance?

Read to Write
7. Which passage seems the most reliable? Why? How is Thucydides' approach to history different from the way Homer and Herodotus explain events? **CA 6RC2.6 CA HR5.**

CHAPTER 7 • The Ancient Greeks   369

They accepted certain duties, such as paying taxes and defending the city. They also gained certain rights, such as the ability to vote and run for office. Pericles' speech reminded Athenians of the power of democracy and gave them the courage to keep fighting. Its ideas are still important for people living in democratic nations today.

Primary Source

Pericles' Funeral Oration

Pericles was a dominant figure in Athenian politics between 461 B.C. and 429 B.C., a period historians call the Age of Pericles. In his Funeral Oration, given during the Peloponnesian War, Pericles described democracy, the importance of the individual, and citizenship.

"Our constitution is called a democracy because power is in the hands not of a minority but of the whole people. When it is a question of settling private disputes, everyone is equal before the law; when it is a question of putting one person before another in positions of public responsibility, what counts is not membership of a particular class, but the actual ability which the man possesses.

▲ Pericles

No one . . . is kept [out of government] because of poverty. And, just as our political life is free and open, so is our day-to-day life in our relations with each other."

—Pericles, as recorded by Thucydides, *History of the Peloponnesian War*

DBQ Document-Based Question
When Pericles said "everyone is equal before the law," what did he mean?

366   CHAPTER 7 • The Ancient Greeks

Why Was Athens Defeated? At the beginning of the Peloponnesian War, both Sparta and Athens thought they knew how to win. The Spartans and their allies surrounded Athens. They hoped that the Athenians would send out an army to fight. However, Pericles knew that Spartan forces could beat the Athenians in open battles. Believing his people would be safe behind the city walls, he urged farmers and others on the outskirts to move inside the city. There Athenians stayed put and had the navy deliver supplies from their colonies and allies. Because Sparta did not have a navy, it could not attack the Athenian ships.

Athens escaped serious harm for some time. Then, in the second year of the war, a deadly disease spread through the overcrowded city. It killed more than a third of the people, including Pericles himself in 429 B.C. Despite these terrible losses, the Athenians fought on. Over the next 25 years, each side won victories but did not have the strength to defeat the other city-state.

The historian Thucydides recorded what he saw:

❝ This, then, was the calamity which fell upon Athens, and the times were hard indeed, with men dying inside the city and the land outside being laid waste. ❞

—Thucydides, *History of the Peloponnesian War*

Finally, desperate to win, the Spartans made a deal with the Persian Empire. In exchange for enough money to build a navy, they gave the Persians some Greek territory in Asia Minor.

In 405 B.C. Sparta's new navy destroyed the Athenian fleet. The next year, after losing more battles on land, Athens surrendered.

DOCUMENT-BASED QUESTIONS

Following the reading, you will be asked to answer some questions based on the document—or reading—you have just completed.

MORE PRIMARY SOURCES

Shorter Primary Source selections are also included in the text.

YOU DECIDE

Two sides of an issue are presented. Imagine you were there and could give your opinion.

You Decide . . .

WH6.4.7 Trace the rise of Alexander the Great and the spread of Greek culture eastward and into Egypt.

Alexander the Great: Villain or Hero?

Villain

Was Alexander the Great really great? Or was he an evil conqueror? Those who see him as bloodthirsty and cruel give this as evidence against Alexander. They say he
- destroyed Persepolis
- attacked Tyre, killing 10,000 people and enslaving 30,000
- treated his slaves harshly
- ordered the murder of several close advisers.

Many legends about Alexander have been told. One historian found this account to support the "villain theory."

"The following is my favourite [story] which is found all the way from Turkey to Kazakhstan: Iskander [Alexander] was actually a devil and he had horns. But his hair was long and wavy and the horns were never seen. Only his barbers knew. But he feared they could not keep the secret. So, he killed them when they discovered. His last barber pretended not to notice and kept the secret. Eventually though he could bear it no longer and, as he could tell no one, he ran to a well and called down the well: 'Iskander has horns!' But in the bottom of the well were whispering reeds [used in flutes] and they echoed the story until it went round the whole world."

—Michael Wood, "In the Footsteps of Alexander the Great"

▲ Alexander the Great (at far left)

404

▲ Alexander the Great

Hero

Other historians consider Alexander the Great to be a hero. They claim he brought progress, order, and culture to each new land he conquered. In support of him, they say Alexander
- tried to promote learning
- visited all of his wounded men after each battle
- spared the lives of the queen and princess of Persia
- ... cities where others had ...

Arrian, a Greek historian who lived in the A.D. 100s, wrote about Alexander this way:

"For my own part, I think there was at that time no race of men, no city, nor even a single individual to whom Alexander's name and fame had not penetrated. For this reason it seems to me that a hero totally unlike any other human being could not have been born without the agency [help] of the deity [gods]."

—Arrian, *The Anabasis of Alexander*

On two points all historians agree: Alexander was a brilliant general and he was a brave fighter. He once boasted to his men:

"For there is no part of my body, in front at any rate, remaining free from wounds; nor is there any kind of weapon used either for close combat or for hurling at the enemy, the traces of which I do not bear on my person. For I have been wounded with the sword in close fight, I have been shot with arrows, and I have been struck with missiles projected from engines of war; and though oftentimes I have been hit with stones and bolts of wood for the sake of your lives, your glory, and your wealth, I am still leading you as conquerors over all the land and sea, all rivers, mountains, and plains. I have celebrated your weddings with my own, and the children of many of you will be akin to my children."

—Arrian, *The Anabasis of Alexander*

You Be the Historian

DBQ Document-Based Questions

1. Why do some historians view Alexander as a villain? **CA HR5**

2. Why do others view him as a hero? **CA HR5**

3. Was Alexander wicked or heroic? ... the role of a historian. Write ... essay that explains ... der t... CA2.5

405

Biography

WH6.4.2 Trace the transition from tyranny and oligarchy to early democratic forms of government and back to dictatorship in ancient Greece, including the significance of the invention of the idea of citizenship (e.g., from Pericles' Funeral Oration)

PERICLES
c. 495–429 B.C.

Pericles was born just outside Athens, to a wealthy and powerful family. He received his education from philosophers. As a young man, he was known for his skill with words. Later, when he became a political leader, he strongly supported democracy.

Although he was from a wealthy family himself, he believed that citizenship should not be limited to the few and give it to the many. However, in describing Pericles' rule over Athens, Greek historian Thucydides wrote "In name democracy, but in fact the rule of one man."

The "Age of Pericles" was Athens's Golden Age, and the city blossomed under his leadership. Pericles wanted Athens to be a model for the world. He made it a centerpiece of art, philosophy, and democracy.

Pericles' goal was to make Athens a city that Greeks could be proud of. He hired hundreds of workers to construct public buildings in Athens. The most well known is the Parthenon. Based on the value of money today, it cost about $3 billion to build. Workers hauled 20,000 tons of marble from a nearby mountain and spent almost 15 years completing it.

Pericles was a private person. He avoided being in public as much as possible. He spent most of his time alone, with family, or with close friends. He married and had three sons. In 429 B.C. Pericles died from the plague.

Pericles ▲

"Athens... is the school of Greece."
—*Pericles, as recorded by Thucydides*

▲ The Parthenon sits at the top of the Acropolis.

Then and Now
Consider what Thucydides wrote about Pericles' rule in Athens. Do research to find out how the U.S. Constitution ensures that our government is not dominated by one leader.

361

DOCUMENT BASED QUESTIONS

Here you answer questions about what you have read.

BIOGRAPHIES

Read more about important people and what they achieved.

Previewing Your Textbook

CONNECTING PAST AND PRESENT

See the **connections** between what it was like then and what it is like today.

WH6.4.2 Trace the transition from tyranny and oligarchy to early democratic forms of government and back to dictatorship in ancient Greece, including the significance of the invention of the idea of citizenship (e.g., from Pericles' Funeral Oration).
WH6.4.6 Compare and contrast life in Athens and Sparta, with emphasis on their roles in the Persian and Peloponnesian Wars.

NATIONAL GEOGRAPHIC
The Way It Was

Focus on Everyday Life

Women's Duties In ancient Athens, a woman's place was in the home. Her two main responsibilities were caring for the household and raising children. The Greek writer Xenophon (ZEH•nuh•fuhn) recorded a man's explanation of women's duties.

"Thus your duty will be to remain indoors and send out those servants whose work is outside, and superintend those who are to work indoors . . . . And when wool is brought to you, you must see that cloaks are made for those that want them. You must see too that the dry corn is in good condition for making food."

—Xenophon, Memorabilia and Oeconomicus

The second floor of each home was the women's quarters. An Athenian woman lived there with her children. She was expected to keep her children well and happy. She encouraged them to learn sports and play with toys, and taught them how to interact with friends and family members. Some boys went to school, while the girls stayed at home.

▲ Greek woman and

The Peloponnesian War

Main Idea Sparta and Athens went to war for control of Greece.

Reading Connection Have you ever tried to get people to work together and been frustrated when they will not cooperate? Read to find out how the Greek city-states' refusal to cooperate nearly led to their destruction.

As the Athenian empire became rich and powerful, other city-states, especially Sparta, grew suspicious of Athenian aims. Sparta and Athens had built two very different kinds of societies, and neither state understood or trusted the other. After the Persian Wars, both city-states desired to be the major power in the Greek world. They clashed over this goal several times between 460 B.C. and 445 B.C. In this year, Athens and Sparta signed a peace treaty.

Conflict Between Athens and Sparta In the years following the Persian Wars, Sparta suffered from a major earthquake and the revolt of the helots. Both of these events weakened Sparta for some time. Meanwhile, Athens continued gaining more control over its empire, sometimes using its military to force other city-states to pay tribute. Between 460 B.C. and 450 B.C., Athens was able to gain a land empire near Thebes and Corinth. However, these city-states were able to throw off Athenian control by 446 B.C. Both Corinth and Thebes remained distrustful of Athens and became allies with Sparta.

Although Athens had lost some of its

WH6.4.2 Trace the transition from tyranny and oligarchy to early democratic forms of government and back to dictatorship in ancient Greece, including the significance of the invention of the idea of citizenship (e.g., from Pericles' Funeral Oration).
WH6.4.6 Compare and contrast life in Athens and Sparta, with emphasis on their roles in the Persian and Peloponnesian Wars.

Athens

Main Idea Unlike Spartans, Athenians were more interested in building a democracy than building a military force.

Reading Connection When visiting a new city, does everything feel strange to you? Spartans who visited Athens probably felt the same way. Read to find out why.

Athens lay northeast of Sparta, at least a two-day trip away. The two city-states were also miles apart in their values and systems of government.

What Was Life in Athens Like? Athenian citizens raised their children very differently from Spartans. In Athenian schools, one teacher taught boys to read, write, and do arithmetic. Another teacher taught them sports. A third teacher taught them to sing and to play a stringed instrument called the lyre. This kind of instruction created well-rounded Athenians with good minds and bodies. At age 18, boys finished school and became citizens.

Athenian girls stayed at home. Their mothers taught them spinning, weaving,

Linking Past & Present

The Olympics

PAST In ancient Greece, only men could participate in and view the Olympic games. Athletes competed by themselves, not as part of a team. Contests included running, jumping, wrestling, and boxing. Each winning athlete won a crown of olive leaves and brought glory to his city.

▼ Modern Olympic athletes

PRESENT In today's Olympic games, both men and women compete. These athletes come from all over the world. They may compete in either individual or team sporting events. Olympic athletes strive to win gold, silver, or bronze medals. *What did ancient Greek Olympic winners receive? What do present-day Olympic winners receive?*

▲ A warrior's race in the ancient Olympics

WH6.7.2 Describe the government of the Roman Republic and its significance (e.g., written constitution and tripartite government, checks and balances, civic duty).
WH6.7.8 Discuss the legacies of Roman art and architecture, technology and science, literature, language, and law.

Roman Law

Main Idea The Roman Republic's legal system was based on the rule of law.

Reading Connection Have you ever heard the phrase "innocent until proven guilty"? Read to learn how Rome introduced this idea that we still use in our courts today.

One of Rome's major gifts to the world was its system of law. The legal system of the United States owes much to the Roman system.

Rome's first code of laws was the Twelve Tables, adopted about 451 B.C. Before this time, Rome's laws were not written down. As a result, plebeians claimed that patrician judges often favored their own class. They demanded that the laws be put in writing for everyone to see.

The patricians finally agreed. They had the laws carved on bronze tablets that were placed in Rome's marketplace, or the Forum (FOHR• uhm). The Twelve Tables became the basis for all future Roman laws. They established the principle that all free citizens had the right to be treated equally by the legal system.

The Twelve Tables, however, applied only to Roman citizens. As the Romans took over more lands, they realized that new rules were needed to solve legal disputes between citizens and noncitizens. They created a collection of laws called the Law of Nations. It stated principles of justice that applied to all people everywhere.

These standards of justice included ideas that we still accept today. A person was seen as innocent until proven guilty. People accused of crimes could defend themselves before a judge. A judge had to look at the evidence carefully before making a decision.

The idea that the law should apply to everyone equally and that all people should be treated the same way by the legal system is called the "rule of law." In the age of

NATIONAL GEOGRAPHIC
HISTORY MAKERS

Twelve Tables c. 451 B.C.

The Twelve Tables were laws written on tablets that described the rights of each person in the Roman Republic. The laws were the first written rules to govern Rome. Writing the laws down and putting them on public display ensured that everyone knew the laws and that judges did not apply the laws differently to different people.

The laws on the Twelve Tables explained a person's rights concerning property, wills, public behavior, family law, and court actions. The Twelve Tables were the first step toward equal rights for citizens of all classes in ancient Rome. They were also a first step toward the idea of the rule of law that we still uphold today.

Rome, the rule of law was still a new concept. In many lands, people at the top of society often had special privileges and did not have to obey the same laws or use the same courts as people lower down. In some places, people at the bottom of society did not have any legal rights at all.

The rule of law is one of the key ideas that the Romans gave to the world. It remains the basis of our legal system today.

Reading Check Identify What is the "rule of law" and why is it important?

HISTORY MAKERS

Read about history makers who changed history forever!

Scavenger Hunt

Discovering Our Past contains a wealth of information. The trick is to know where to look to access all the information in the book. If you run through this scavenger hunt exercise with your teacher or parents, you will see how the textbook is organized and how to get the most out of your reading and study time. Let's get started!

1. What civilizations are discussed in Unit 3?

2. What is the topic of Chapter 5?

3. Who is the topic of the *Biography* on page 129?

4. What *Reading Skill* will you be learning about on pages 498–499?

5. What does the *Foldables*™ *Study Organizer* on page 373 ask you to do?

6. How are the key terms in Chapter 9, Section 2, *patricians* and *plebeians*, highlighted in the text?

7. There are four types of Web site boxes in Chapter 11. One box previews the chapter, one suggests a Web activity, and one provides help with homework. What does the fourth box provide help with?

8. What is the first *Big Idea* introduced on page 235?

9. What is the topic of *The Way It Was* feature on page 464?

10. What kinds of skills are on page 2 of the *Guide to the California Standards*?

READING TO LEARN

This handbook focuses on skills and strategies that can help you understand the words you read. The strategies you use to understand whole texts depend on the kind of text you are reading. In other words, you do not read a textbook the way you read a novel. You read a textbook mainly for information; you read a novel for the story and the characters. To get the most out of your reading, you need to choose the right strategy to fit the reason you are reading. This handbook can help you learn about the following reading strategies:

- how to identify new words and build your vocabulary;
- how to adjust the way you read to fit your reason for reading;
- how to use specific reading strategies to better understand what you read;
- how to use critical thinking strategies to think more deeply about what you read; and
- how to understand text structures to identify an author's ideas.

TABLE OF CONTENTS

Identifying Words and Building Vocabulary

What do you do when you come across a word you do not know as you read? Do you skip over the word? If you are reading a novel, you use the context to understand the meaning of the word. But if you are reading for information, an unfamiliar word may get in the way of your understanding. When that happens, follow the strategies below to learn how to say the word and what it means.

Reading Unfamiliar Words

Sounding Out the Word One way to figure out how to say a new word is to sound it out, syllable by syllable. Look carefully at the word's beginning, middle, and ending. For example, in the word *coagulate,* what letters make up the beginning sound or beginning syllable of the word? *Co* rhymes with *so.* Inside *coagulate,* do you see a word you already know how to pronounce? The syllable *ag* has the same sound as the *ag* in *bag,* and the syllable *u* is pronounced like the letter *u.* What letters make up the ending sound or syllable? *Late* is a familiar word you already know how to pronounce. Now try pronouncing the whole word: **co ag u late.**

Determining a Word's Meaning

Using Syntax Like all languages, the English language has rules and patterns for the way words are arranged in sentences. The way a sentence is organized is called the syntax. If English is your first language, you have known this pattern since you started using sentences. If you are learning English now, you may find that the syntax is different from the patterns you know in your first language.

In a simple sentence in English, someone or something (the subject) does something (the predicate or verb) to or with another person or thing (the object): *The soldiers attacked the enemy.* Sometimes adjectives, adverbs, and phrases are added to add details to the sentence: *The courageous young soldiers fearlessly attacked the well-entrenched enemy shortly after dawn.*

Knowing about syntax can help you figure out the meaning of an unfamiliar word. Just look at how syntax can help you figure out the following nonsense sentence: *The blizzy kwarkles sminched the flerky fleans.* Your experience with English syntax tells you that the action word, or verb, in this sentence is *sminched.* Who did the *sminching*? The *kwarkles.* What kind of *kwarkles* were they? *Blizzy.* Whom did they *sminch*? The *fleans.* What kind of *fleans* were they? *Flerky.* Even though you don't know the meaning of the words in the nonsense sentence, you can make some sense of the entire sentence by studying its syntax.

Using Context Clues You can often figure out the meaning of an unfamiliar word by looking at its context, the words and sentences that surround it. To learn new words as you read, follow these steps for using context clues.

- Look before and after the unfamiliar word for a definition or a synonym, a general topic associated with the word, a clue to what the word is similar to or different from, or an action or a description that has something to do with the word.
- Connect what you already know with what the author has written.
- Predict a possible meaning.
- Use the meaning in the sentence.
- Try again if your guess does not make sense.

Using Types of Reference Materials

Dictionaries and other reference sources can help you learn new words and how to use them. Check out these reference sources. You can find these in your local public or school library as well as on the Internet.

- A **dictionary** gives the pronunciation, the meaning or multiple meanings, and often examples of how to use the words. Some dictionaries also provide illustrations or diagrams to help define words, other forms of words, their parts of speech, and synonyms. You might also find the historical background of a word, such as its Greek, Latin, or Anglo-Saxon origins.

- A **glossary** is a word list that appears at the end—or Appendix—of a book or other written work and includes only words that are in that work. Like dictionaries, glossaries include the pronunciation and definitions of words.

- A **thesaurus** lists groups of words that have the same, or almost the same, meaning. Words with similar meanings are called synonyms. Seeing the synonyms of words can help you build your vocabulary.

Recognizing Word Meanings Across Subjects

Have you ever learned a new word in one class and then noticed it in your reading for other subjects? The word probably will not mean exactly the same thing in each class. But you can use what you know about the word's meaning to help you understand what it means in a different subject area. Look at the following example from three different subjects:

- **Social studies:** One *product* manufactured in the southern part of the United States is cotton cloth.
- **Math:** After multiplying the numbers five and five, explain how you arrived at the *product*.
- **Science:** One *product* of photosynthesis is oxygen.

CHECKING YOUR UNDERSTANDING

The following sentence does not include real English words, but you can use what you have learned about English syntax to decode the sentence. First read the sentence. Then answer the questions that follow.

The shabs smatously graled the mul-bulowed rotfabs.

1. What is the verb in the sentence?
2. What is the subject?
3. What is the object?

Reading for a Reason

Why are you reading that paperback mystery? What do you hope to get from your history textbook? And are you going to read either of these books in the same way that you read a restaurant menu? The point is, you read for different reasons. The reason you are reading something helps you decide on the reading strategies you use with a text. In other words, how you read will depend on why you are reading.

Knowing Your Reason for Reading

In school and in life, you will have many reasons for reading, and those reasons will lead you to a wide range of materials:

- **To learn and understand new information,** you might read news magazines, textbooks, news on the Internet, books about your favorite pastime, encyclopedia articles, primary and secondary sources for a school report, instructions on how to use a calling card, or directions for a standardized test.
- **To find specific information,** you might look at the sports section for the score of last night's game, a notice on where to register for a field trip, weather reports, bank statements, or television listings.
- **To be entertained,** you might read your favorite magazine, e-mails or letters from friends, the Sunday comics, or even novels, short stories, plays, or poems!

Adjusting How Fast You Read

How quickly or how carefully you should read a text depends on your purpose for reading it. Because there are many reasons and ways to read, think about your purpose and choose the strategy that works best. Try out these strategies:

- **Scanning** means quickly running your eyes over the material, looking for key words or phrases that point to the information you are looking for. Scan when you need to find a particular piece or type of information. For example, you might scan a newspaper for movie show times.
- **Skimming** means quickly reading a piece of writing to find its main idea or to get a general overview of it. For example, you might skim the sports section of the daily newspaper to find out how your favorite teams are doing. Or you might skim a chapter in your textbook to prepare for a test.
- **Careful reading** involves reading very slowly and paying close attention with a purpose in mind. Read carefully when you are learning new concepts, following complicated directions, or preparing to explain information to someone else.

 CHECKING YOUR UNDERSTANDING

If you were working on a research paper on the American Revolution, how would you adjust the speed at which you were reading for each of the following cases?

1. You have just found a 1,200-page work that covers the entire colonial and revolutionary era of the British colonies in North America.

2. You have discovered an article in a leading history magazine that supports every point that you are trying to make.

Understanding What You Read

Reading without understanding is like trying to drive a car on an empty gas tank. Fortunately, there are techniques you can use to help you concentrate on and understand what you read. Skilled readers adopt a number of strategies before, during, and after reading to make sure they understand what they read.

Preparing to Read

It is important to set the stage before you read. Following these steps will make the reading process more rewarding.

Previewing If you were making a preview for a movie, you would want to let your audience know what the movie is like. When you preview a piece of writing, you are trying to get an idea about the piece. Follow these steps to preview your reading assignments.

- Look at the title and any illustrations that are included.
- Read the headings, subheadings, and anything in bold letters.
- Skim the passage to see how it is organized.
- Set a purpose for your reading.

Using What You Know You already know quite a bit about what you are going to read. You bring knowledge and personal experience to a selection. Drawing on what you learned in a previous class is called *activating prior knowledge,* and it can help you create meaning in what you read. Ask yourself, *What do I already know about this topic?*

Predicting *Predicting* requires using background and prior knowledge, as well as the ability to make educated guesses. Make educated guesses before you read and while you read to figure out what might happen in the story or article you are reading.

Reading the Text

Following these suggestions while you read will help ensure that you get the most out of your reading.

Visualizing Creating pictures in your mind as you read—called *visualizing*—is a powerful aid to understanding. As you read, set up a movie theater in your imagination. Picture the setting—city streets, the desert, or the moon. If you can visualize, selections will be more vivid, and you will recall them better later on.

Identifying Sequence When you discover the logical order of events or ideas, you are identifying *sequence.* Do you need to understand step-by-step directions? Are you reading a persuasive speech with the reasons listed in order of importance? Look for clues and signal words that will help you find the way information is organized.

Determining the Main Idea When you look for the *main idea* of a selection, you look for the most important idea. The examples, reasons, and details that further explain the main idea are called *supporting details.* Some main ideas are clearly stated within a passage—often in the first sentence of a paragraph, or sometimes in the last sentence of a passage. Other times, however, an author does not directly state the main idea. Instead, he or she provides details that help readers figure out what the main idea is.

Questioning By learning how to analyze questions, you will quickly learn where to look for information as you read. Questions vary in many ways. One of the ways that questions vary is by how explicit or implied the question is compared with the text. These types of questions fall into four categories:

- **Right there** questions can be answered based on a line from the text.
- **Think and search** questions can be answered by looking in a few different places in the text.
- **Author and you** questions can be answered by thinking about the text but that also require your prior knowledge.
- **On your own** questions cannot be answered by the text and rely on the reader.

Clarifying Clear up, or clarify, confusing or difficult passages as you read. When you realize you do not understand something, try these techniques to help you clarify the ideas. *Reread* the confusing parts slowly and carefully. *Look up* unfamiliar words. Simply *talk out* the part to yourself.

Monitoring Your Comprehension As you read, check your understanding by using the following strategies.

- **Summarize** what you read by pausing from time to time and telling yourself the main ideas of what you have just read. Answer the questions *Who? What? Where? When? Why?* and *How?* Summarizing tests your comprehension by encouraging you to clarify key points in your own words.
- **Paraphrase** what you have just read to see whether you really got the point. Paraphrasing is retelling something in your own words. If you cannot explain it clearly, you should probably reread the text.

CHECKING YOUR UNDERSTANDING

1. How does visualizing help you understand what you read in your textbook or when you read for pleasure?

2. How can you determine the main idea of a selection if the author never explicitly explains what it is?

3. Why is clarifying an important skill for you to develop?

Thinking About Your Reading

*S*ometimes it is important to think more deeply about what you have read so you can get the most out of what the author says. These critical thinking skills will help you go beyond what the words say and get at the important messages of your reading.

Interpreting

When you listen to your best friend talk, you do not just hear the words he or she says. You also watch your friend, listen to the tone of voice, and use what you already know about that person to put meaning to the words. In doing so, you are interpreting what your friend says. Readers do the same thing when they interpret as they read. *Interpreting* is asking yourself *What is the writer really saying here?* and then using what you know about the world to help answer that question.

Inferring

You may not realize it, but you make inferences every day. Here is an example: You run to the bus stop a little later than usual. No one is there. "I have missed the bus," you say to yourself. You might be wrong, but that is the way our minds work. You look at the evidence (you are late; no one is there) and come to a conclusion (you have missed the bus).

When you read, you go through exactly the same process because writers do not always directly state what they want you to understand. They suggest certain information by providing clues and interesting details. Whenever you combine those clues with your own background and knowledge, you are making an inference.

Drawing Conclusions

Skillful readers are always *drawing conclusions,* or figuring out much more than an author says directly. The process is like a detective solving a mystery. You combine information and evidence that the author provides to come up with a statement about the topic. Drawing conclusions helps you find connections between ideas and events and gives you a better understanding of what you are reading.

Making Connections

One way that you can remember what you have read is by making connections with the text. Your teacher often expresses these connections aloud so that you and your classmates have a model. Your teacher may also ask you to make connections with the text and share them with the class. The most common connections include:

- **Text-to-self** connections, in which you remember something from your own life that serves as a connection with what is being read. *(While reading about the Civil War, you think about a fight you had with a relative.)*
- **Text-to-world** connections, in which you remember something that is happening or has happened in the world that serves as a connection with what is being read. *(While reading about the Civil War, you remember reading a newspaper article about the civil war in Somalia.)*
- **Text-to-text** connections, in which you remember something you have read elsewhere that serves as a connection with what is being read. *(While reading about the Civil War, you recall the novel* Red Badge of Courage.)

Analyzing

Analyzing, or looking at separate parts of something to understand the entire piece, is a way to think critically about written work. In analyzing persuasive *nonfiction,* you might look at the writer's reasons to see if they actually support the main point of the argument. In analyzing *informational text,* you might look at how the ideas are organized to see what is most important.

Distinguishing Fact From Opinion

Distinguishing between fact and opinion is an important reading skill. A *fact* is a statement that can be proved. An *opinion,* on the other hand, is what a writer believes on the basis of his or her personal viewpoint. Writers can support their opinions with facts, but an opinion is something that cannot be proved.

Evaluating

When you form an opinion or make a judgment about something you are reading, you are *evaluating.* If you are reading informational texts or something on the Internet, it is important to evaluate how qualified the author is to be writing about the topic and how reliable the information is that is presented. Ask yourself whether the author seems biased, whether the information is one-sided, and whether the argument presented is logical.

Synthesizing

When you *synthesize,* you combine ideas (maybe even from different sources) to come up with something new. It may be a new understanding of an important idea or a new way of combining and presenting information. For example, you might read a manual on coaching soccer, combine that information with your own experiences playing soccer, and come up with a winning plan for coaching your sister's team this spring.

CHECKING YOUR UNDERSTANDING

1. How does making connections with what you have read help you remember more?

2. How do analyzing and synthesizing differ?

3. How do facts and opinions differ? Why is it important to differentiate between the two as you study history?

Understanding Text Structure

Good writers do not just put together sentences and paragraphs in any order. They structure each piece of their writing in a specific way for a specific purpose. That pattern of organization is called text structure. When you know the text structure of a selection, you will find it easier to locate and recall an author's ideas. Here are four ways that writers organize text.

Comparison and Contrast

Comparison-and-contrast structure shows the *similarities* and *differences* among people, things, and ideas. Maybe you have overheard someone at school say something like "He is better at throwing the football, but I can run faster than he can." This student is using comparison-and-contrast structure. When writers use comparison-and-contrast structure, they often want to show you how things that seem alike are different or how things that seem different are alike.

Signal words and phrases: *similarly, on the one hand, on the other hand, in contrast to, but, however*

Cause and Effect

Just about everything that happens in life is the cause or the effect of some other event or action. Sometimes what happens is pretty minor: You do not look when

you are pouring milk *(cause);* you spill milk on the table *(effect).* Sometimes it is a little more serious: You do not look at your math book before the big test *(cause);* you mess up on the test *(effect).*

Writers use cause-and-effect structure to explore the reasons for something happening and to examine the results of previous events. This structure helps answer the question that everybody is always asking: *Why?* A historian might tell us why an empire rose and fell. Cause-and-effect structure is all about explaining why things are as they are.

Signal words and phrases: *so, because, as a result, therefore, for the following reasons*

Problem and Solution

How did scientists overcome the difficulty of getting a person to the moon? How will I brush my teeth when I have forgotten my toothpaste? These questions may be very different in importance, but they have one thing in common: Each identifies a problem and asks how to solve it. *Problems and solutions* are part of what makes life interesting. Problems and solutions also occur in fiction and nonfiction writing.

Signal words and phrases: *how, help, problem, obstruction, difficulty, need, attempt, have to, must*

Sequence

Take a look at three common forms of sequencing, the order in which thoughts are arranged.

- **Chronological order** refers to the order in which events take place. First, you wake up; next, you have breakfast; then, you go to school. Those events do not make much sense in any other order.
  Signal words: *first, next, then, later, finally*

- **Spatial order** tells you the order in which to look at objects. For example, consider this description of an ice-cream sundae: *At the bottom of the dish are two scoops of vanilla. The scoops are covered with fudge and topped with whipped cream and a cherry.* Your eyes follow the sundae from the bottom to the top. Spatial order is important in descriptive writing because it helps you as a reader to see an image the way the author does.
  Signal words: *above, below, behind, next to*

- **Order of importance** is going from most important to least important or the other way around. For example, a typical news article has a most important to least important structure.
  Signal words: *principal, central, important, fundamental*

CHECKING YOUR UNDERSTANDING

Read the following paragraph and answer the questions about the selection's text structure below.

The Huntington City Council recently approved an increase in the city sales tax. Recognizing the need to balance the city's budget, the council president Matt Smith noted that the council had no choice. The vote ended more than a year of preparing voters for the bad news. First, the council notified citizens that there would be a public discussion last April. Then, the council issued public statements that the vote would take place in November. Finally, the council approved the increase last week even though many residents opposed it. On one hand, the increase will increase revenues. On the other hand, more taxes could lead to fewer shoppers in the city's struggling retail stores.

1. How does the writer use comparison and contrast text structure?

2. How does the writer use problem and solution text structure?

3. What signal words show that the writer is setting the chronological order of events?

REFERENCE ATLAS

 NATIONAL GEOGRAPHIC

ATLAS KEY

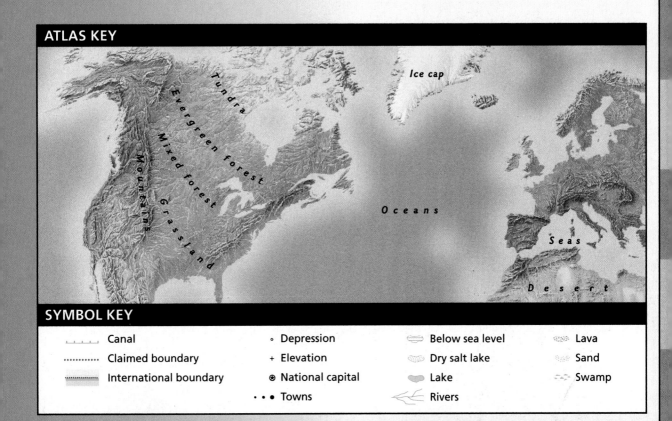

Tundra

Evergreen forest

Mixed forest

Mountains

Grassland

Ice cap

Oceans

Seas

Desert

SYMBOL KEY

⌐⌐⌐	Canal	○	Depression	⬭	Below sea level	⬮	Lava
··········	Claimed boundary	+	Elevation	⬭	Dry salt lake	⬮	Sand
▓▓▓▓	International boundary	⊗	National capital	⬭	Lake	⤳	Swamp
		• • ●	Towns	⥊	Rivers		

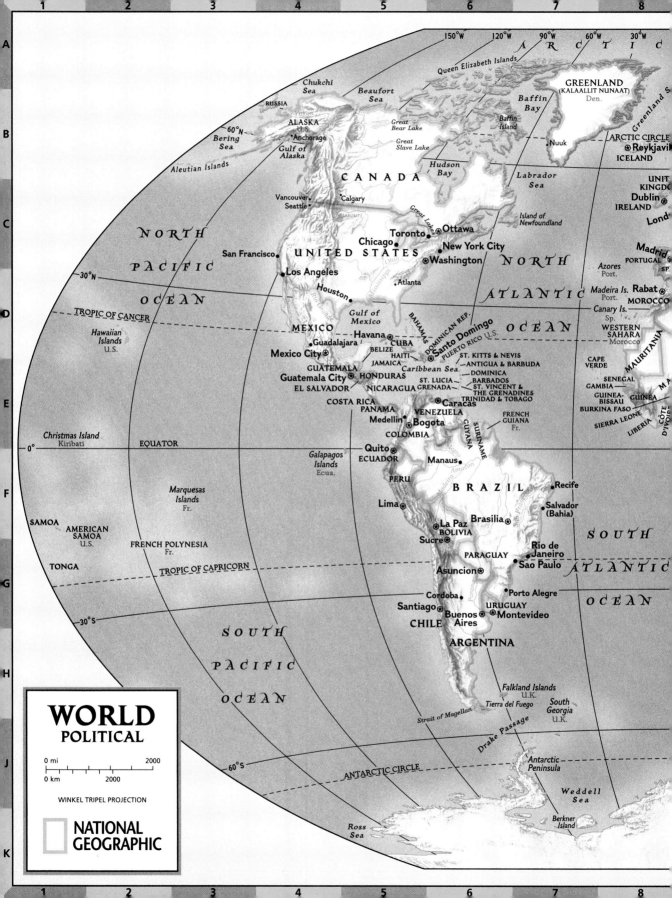

WORLD
POLITICAL

0 mi   2000

0 km   2000

WINKEL TRIPEL PROJECTION

NATIONAL GEOGRAPHIC

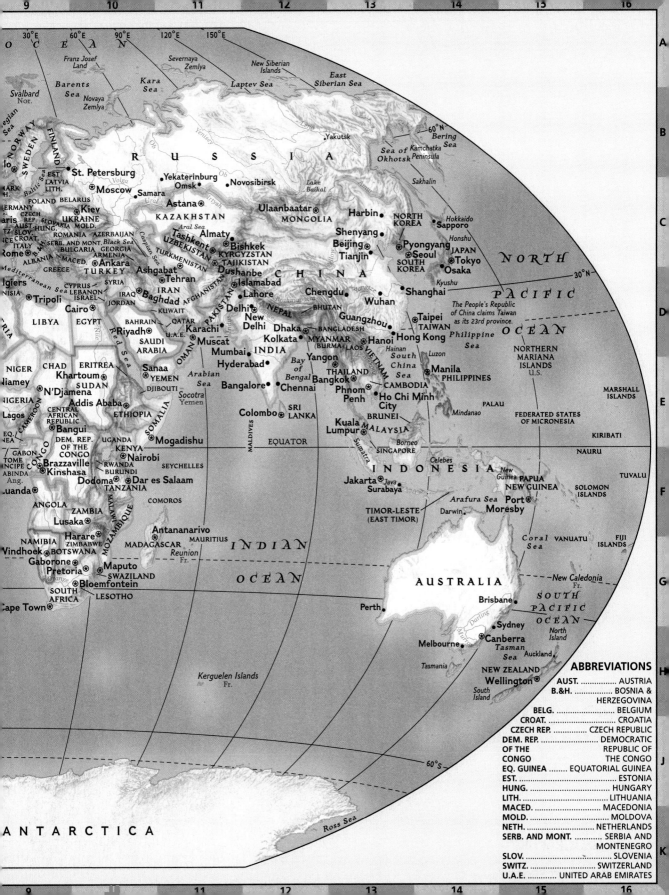

ABBREVIATIONS

AUST.	AUSTRIA
B.&H.	BOSNIA & HERZEGOVINA
BELG.	BELGIUM
CROAT.	CROATIA
CZECH REP.	CZECH REPUBLIC
DEM. REP. OF THE CONGO	DEMOCRATIC REPUBLIC OF THE CONGO
EQ. GUINEA	EQUATORIAL GUINEA
EST.	ESTONIA
HUNG.	HUNGARY
LITH.	LITHUANIA
MACED.	MACEDONIA
MOLD.	MOLDOVA
NETH.	NETHERLANDS
SERB. AND MONT.	SERBIA AND MONTENEGRO
SLOV.	SLOVENIA
SWITZ.	SWITZERLAND
U.A.E.	UNITED ARAB EMIRATES

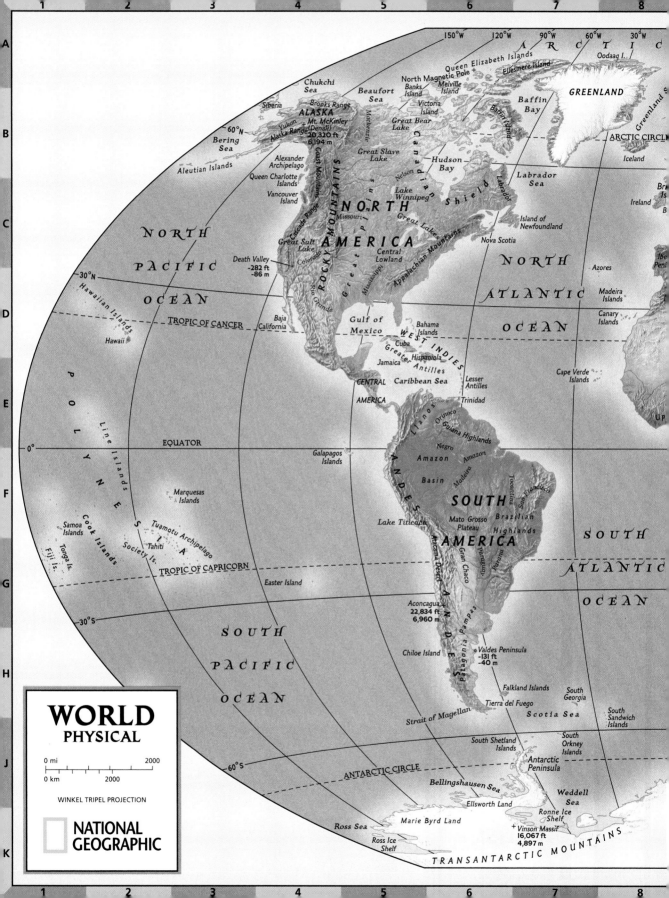

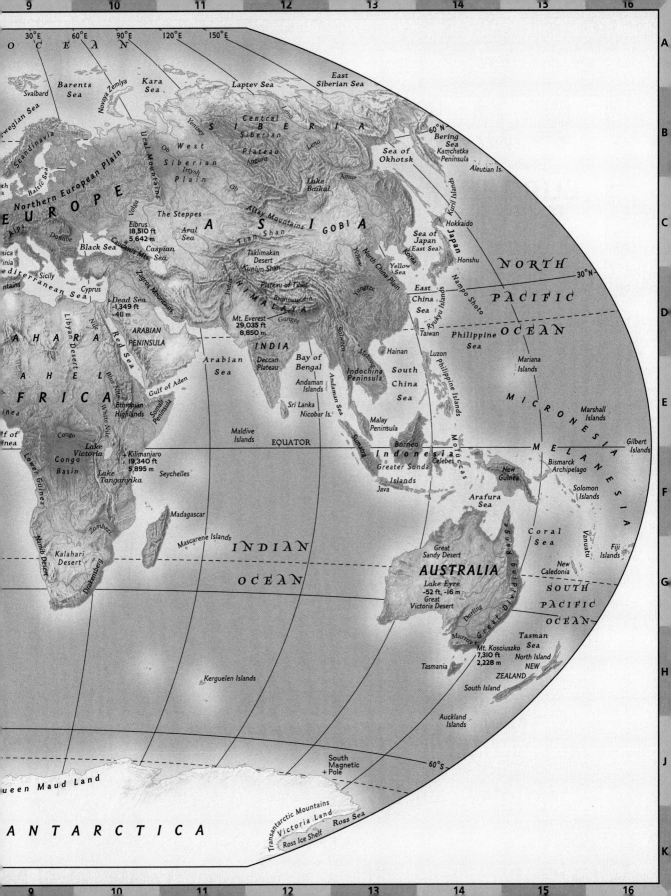

EUROPE
POLITICAL

0 mi — 400
0 km — 400

AZIMUTHAL EQUIDISTANT PROJECTION

NATIONAL GEOGRAPHIC

ATLANTIC OCEAN

ICELAND
• Akureyri
⊛ Reykjavik

Faroe Islands
Den.
• Torshavn

Rockall
U.K.

Isle of Lewis

Shetland
Islands
• Lerwick

Orkney Islands

Inverness •

UNITED
SCOTLAND
• Aberdeen
Glasgow • ⊛ Edinburgh

NORTHERN
IRELAND
⊛ Belfast

IRELAND
Dublin ⊛
Irish
Sea
• Cork

Liverpool •
• Manchester

KINGDOM
WALES
Cardiff •
ENGLAND
• Birmingham

Celtic
Sea

Land's End
London ⊛
Southampton •

English Channel

Brest •
Le Havre •

Rennes •
⊛ Paris

Nantes •

La Rochelle •
FRANCE

Bay of
Biscay
Bordeaux •
Limoges •

A Coruña •
Vigo •
Porto •
Coimbra •

PORTUGAL

Lisbon ⊛

Cape
St. Vincent

Cadiz •
GIBRALTAR
U.K.
• Malaga

Strait of Gibraltar

Bilbao •
Donostia-
San Sebastian

Toulouse •
Pyrenees

Valladolid •
ANDORRA
• Zaragoza

Madrid ⊛

SPAIN
• Barcelona

Valencia •

• Cordoba
• Seville
Murcia •
• Cartagena

Palma •
Balearic
Islands
Sp.

Norwegian Sea

MERIDIAN OF GREENWICH (LONDON)

ARCTIC CIRCLE

N

Troms

NORWAY
SWEDEN

• Are
Trondheim •
Alesund •
• Sundsvall
Bergen •
• Uppsala
Oslo ⊛
• Stockholm ⊛
Goteborg •
Gotland

Skagerrak

DENMARK
• Arhus
Copenhagen ⊛
• Malmo

Baltic

North
Sea

Stavanger •

• Kiel
• Hamburg
Gdansk •

The NETH.
Hague ⊛
• Amsterdam
Berlin •
Bydgoszcz •

GERMANY
POLAND
Lodz

Brussels ⊛
BELGIUM
• Bonn
LUX.
Frankfurt •
Wroclaw •
Prague ⊛
CZECH REP.

Strasbourg •
Bratislava ⊛
SLOVAK

Munich •
Vienna ⊛

Zurich •
LIECH
AUSTRIA
Bern ⊛
Budapest
SWITZERLAND
ALPS
SLOVENIA
HUNGA
Geneva •
• Milan
Ljubljana ⊛
• Zagreb
Lyon •
CROATIA
• Turin
Venice •
MONACO
• Genoa
SAN
BOSNIA &
MARINO
HERZEGOVIN
Nice •
Sarajevo •
Marseille •
ITALY

Corsica
Fr.
VATICAN
CITY ⊛ Rome

Sardinia
It.
Tiran
ALBAN
• Naples

• Cagliari
Tyrrhenian
Sea

Ionian
Palermo •
Messina
Sicily
• Catania

Valletta ⊛
MALTA

Mediterranean

AFRICA

Rhine
Oder

LIECH

Adriatic Sea

40°W
60°N
30°W
50°N
30°W
20°W
40°N
30°N

40°W
30°W
20°W
10°W
70°N
0°
10°E

10°W
0°
10°E

North Cape

Barents Sea

30°E

40°E

70°N

70°E

60°N

80°E

Pechora

Kola
Peninsula

White Sea

U
R
A
L

Northern Dvina

*Europe-Asia
boundary*

ASIA

F
I
N
L
A
N
D

*Lake
Region*

Lake
Onega

R U S S I A N

M
O
U
N
T
A
I
N
S

70°E

Lake
Ladoga

E
U
R
O
P
E
A
N

Kama

Volga

Ural

50°N

Helsinki ⊛

Gulf of Finland

ESTONIA

⊛ Tallinn

P
L
A
I
N

Volga

Ural

⊛ Riga

⊛ Moscow

LATVIA

C E N T R A L

Oka

Volga

KAZAKHSTAN

LITHUANIA

Vilnius ⊛

R U S S I A N

Don

C
a
s
p
i
a
n

D
e
p
r
e
s
s
i
o
n

Minsk ⊛

BELARUS

Dnieper

U P L A N D

Volga

60°E

Warsaw

Kiev ⊛

UKRAINE

Don

40°N

Dniester

Dnieper

*Sea of
Azov*

C
a
s
p
i
a
n

MOLDOVA

⊛ Chisinau

Crimea

Elbrus
18,510 ft
+5,642 m

ROMANIA

Caucasus Mountains

AZERBAIJAN

GEORGIA

⊛ Baku

Belgrade

⊛ Bucharest

S
e
a

Danube

BALKAN

Black   Sea

BULGARIA

Balkan Mountains

Sofia ⊛

PENINSULA

⊛ Skopje

MACED.

T U R K E Y

Dardanelles

*Sea of
Marmara*

*Aegean
Sea*

ASIA

⊛ Athens

Peloponnesus

Crete

Rhodes

Nicosia ⊛

30°N

CYPRUS

Sea

30°E

40°E

50°E

EUROPE

Black Sea

Sea of
Marmara

Istanbul

ANATOLIA

Ankara

TURKEY

40°N

Tunis

TUNISIA

Tripoli

Mediterranean Sea

30°N

Taurus Mountains

CYPRUS   Aleppo
             SYRIA
LEBANON—
Beirut   Damascus

ISRAEL   *Syrian Desert*

Jerusalem   Amman

Alexandria   **JORDAN**
Cairo
El Giza   *Sinai Pen.*

See inset below

LIBYA

EGYPT   *Nile R.*

SAHARA

Aswan
High Dam

Boundary claimed
by Sudan

Red Sea

Hejáz

SUDAN

30°N

AFRICA

Khartoum

30°E

Eastern Mediterranean Area

30°E

TURKEY

N

Aleppo

CYPRUS   **SYRIA**

*Mediterranean
Sea*

LEBANON

Beirut   Damascus

Sea of Galilee   Golan Heights
Jordan River

Tel Aviv–Yafo   West Bank

Suez Canal

Jerusalem   Amman

Gaza Strip

Dead Sea

ISRAEL   **JORDAN**

El Giza   Cairo

EGYPT

Nile River

Gulf of Suez

Gulf of Aqaba

**SAUDI
ARABIA**

30°N

0 mi   100

0 km   100

Red Sea

MIDDLE EAST

PHYSICAL / POLITICAL

0 mi — 500
0 km — 500

AZIMUTHAL EQUIDISTANT PROJECTION

NATIONAL GEOGRAPHIC

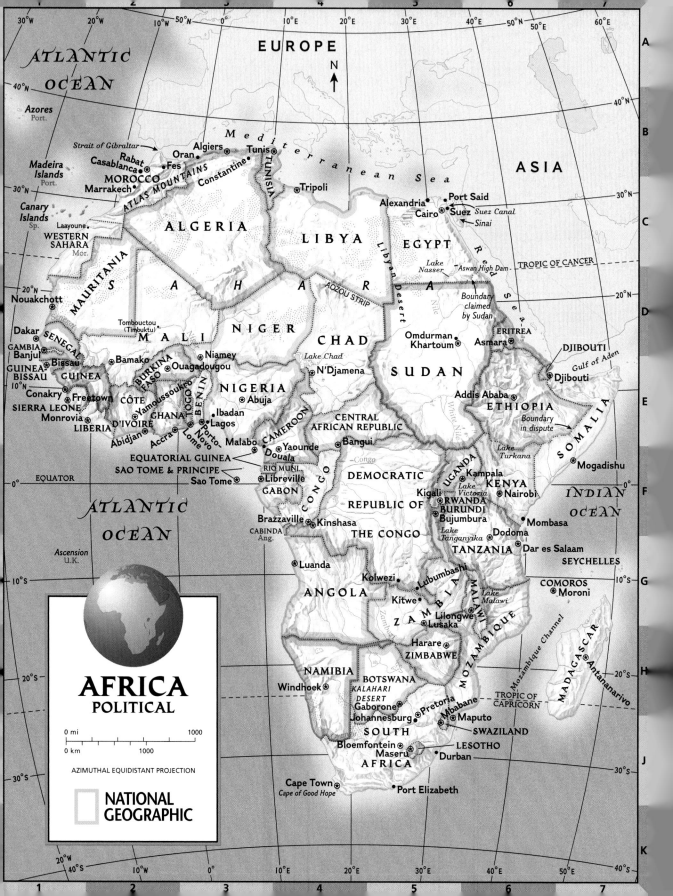

AFRICA
POLITICAL

AZIMUTHAL EQUIDISTANT PROJECTION

NATIONAL GEOGRAPHIC

0 mi   1000
0 km   1000

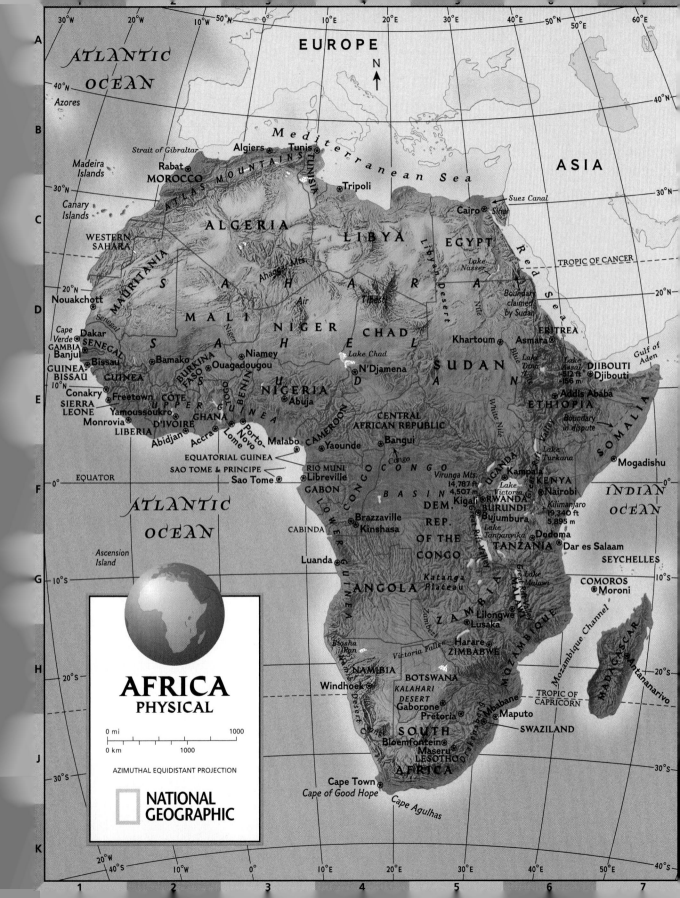

AFRICA
PHYSICAL

0 mi 1000

0 km 1000

AZIMUTHAL EQUIDISTANT PROJECTION

NATIONAL GEOGRAPHIC

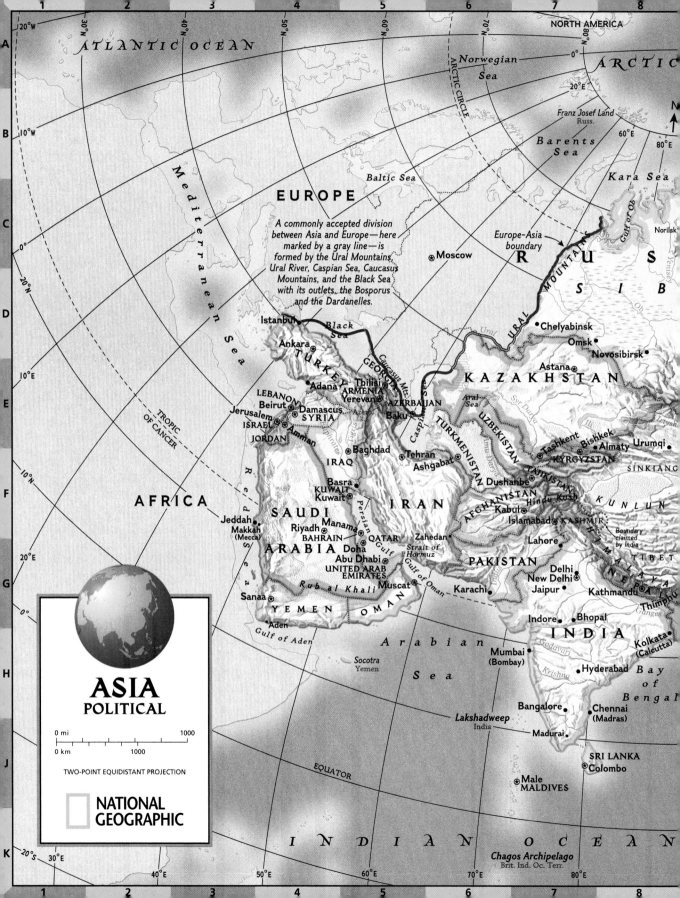

ATLANTIC OCEAN

Mediterranean Sea

EUROPE

A commonly accepted division
between Asia and Europe — here
marked by a gray line — is
formed by the Ural Mountains,
Ural River, Caspian Sea, Caucasus
Mountains, and the Black Sea
with its outlets, the Bosporus
and the Dardanelles.

*Norwegian
Sea*

NORTH AMERICA

ARCTIC

Franz Josef Land
Russ.

*Barents
Sea*

Kara Sea

Baltic Sea

⊗ Moscow

Europe-Asia
boundary

R   U   S
S
I
B

Norilsk

Istanbul
Ankara ⊗

*Black
Sea*

Chelyabinsk
Omsk ⊗
Novosibirsk ⊗

Astana ⊗

KAZAKHSTAN

Caucasus Mts.

TURKEY

GEORGIA

Adana   Tbilisi ⊗
ARMENIA
Yerevan ⊗
AZERBAIJAN
Baku ⊗

*Aral
Sea*

Syr Darya

Tashkent ⊗   Bishkek ⊗   Almaty ⊗   Urumqi ⊗

SINKIANG

TROPIC
OF CANCER

LEBANON
Beirut ⊗   Damascus
Jerusalem ⊗   SYRIA
ISRAEL ⊗   ⊗ Amman
JORDAN

Tigris

⊗ Baghdad
IRAQ

Basra
KUWAIT
Kuwait ⊗

Euphrates

TURKMENISTAN

Ashgabat ⊗

UZBEKISTAN

Amu Darya

Dushanbe ⊗
TAJIKISTAN

KYRGYZSTAN

KUNLUN

⊗ Tehrān

IRAN

AFGHANISTAN
Kabul ⊗
Hindu Kush

HIMALAYA

TIBET

Boundary
claimed
by India

AFRICA

Red Sea

Jeddah ⊗
Makkah
(Mecca)

SAUDI
Riyadh ⊗   Manama ⊗
BAHRAIN
ARABIA   QATAR   Doha ⊗
Abu Dhabi ⊗
UNITED ARAB
EMIRATES

Persian Gulf

Zahedan ⊗

*Strait of
Hormuz*

Gulf of Oman

Islamabad ⊗   KASHMIR

PAKISTAN

Lahore ⊗

Delhi ⊗
New Delhi ⊗
Jaipur ⊗

Indore ⊗   Bhopal ⊗

Indus

Kathmandu ⊗
Thimphu

Ganges

INDIA

Rub al Khali
Muscat ⊗

Sanaa ⊗   YEMEN   OMAN

Gulf of Aden
Aden

Karachi ⊗

Godavari

Krishna

Mumbai ⊗
(Bombay)

Hyderabad ⊗   *Bay
of
Bengal*

*Arabian

Sea*

Socotra
Yemen

Bangalore ⊗
Lakshadweep
India

Chennai ⊗
(Madras)

Madurai ⊗

SRI LANKA
⊗ Colombo

⊗ Male
MALDIVES

ASIA
POLITICAL

0 mi   1000

0 km   1000

TWO-POINT EQUIDISTANT PROJECTION

**NATIONAL
GEOGRAPHIC**

EQUATOR

I N D I A N   O C E A N

Chagos Archipelago
Brit. Ind. Oc. Terr.

NORTH AMERICA

Bering Strait

North Pole

OCEAN

Chukchi Sea

Wrangel I.

East Siberian Sea

North Land

New Siberian Islands

Laptev Sea

Gulf of Anadyr

Anadyr

Bering Sea

Commander Is.

Kamchatka Peninsula

Magadan

Cherskiy Range

Kolyma Range

Verkhoyansk Range

Sea of Okhotsk

Yakutsk

SIBERIA

Sakhalin

Kuril Islands

Lake Baikal

Irkutsk

MANCHURIA

Vladivostok

Changchun

Ulaanbaatar

MONGOLIA

ALTAY MTS.

GOBI

Shenyang

Beijing

Pyongyang

NORTH KOREA

Seoul

SOUTH KOREA

Hokkaido

Sapporo

Sea of Japan (East Sea)

JAPAN

Honshu

Tokyo

Kyoto

Osaka

Hiroshima

Kyushu

Marcus I. Jap.

TROPIC OF CANCER

Shijiazhuang

Qingdao

Yellow Sea

Lanzhou

SHAN

Xian

Xuzhou

East China Sea

Nanjing

Shanghai

CHINA

Ryukyu Islands

Bonin Is. Jap.

Volcano Is. Jap.

Chengdu

Nanchang

Okinawa

Guiyang

Changsha

Fuzhou

Parece Vela Jap.

Boundary claimed by China

BHUTAN

BANGLADESH

Dhaka

Kunming

Guangzhou

Hong Kong

Macau

Taipei

TAIWAN

The People's Republic of China claims Taiwan as its 23rd province.

PACIFIC OCEAN

Philippine

Hanoi

Haiphong

South

China

Luzon

Quezon City

Manila

Sea

MYANMAR (BURMA)

Vientiane

LAOS

Hainan

Da Nang

Mindoro

Samar

PHILIPPINES

Leyte

Yangon (Rangoon)

THAILAND

VIETNAM

Sea

Panay

Negros

Bangkok

CAMBODIA

Phnom Penh

Ho Chi Minh City

Palawan

Mindanao

EQUATOR

Andaman Islands India

Gulf of Thailand

Bandar Seri Begawan

BRUNEI

SABAH

Halmahera

Morotai

Biak

Jayapura

New Guinea

Andaman Sea

SARAWAK

Kepi

Merauke

Dolak

Nicobar Islands India

MALAYSIA

MALAY

Buru

Ceram

Aru Is.

Kuala Lumpur

Medan

Borneo

Celebes

Moluccas

SINGAPORE

INDONESIA

Tanimbar Is.

Sumatra

GREATER

SUNDA ISLANDS

Dili

TIMOR-LESTE (EAST TIMOR)

Mentawai Islands

Java Sea

Timor Sea

AUSTRALIA

Jambi

Jakarta

Java

Kupang

Timor

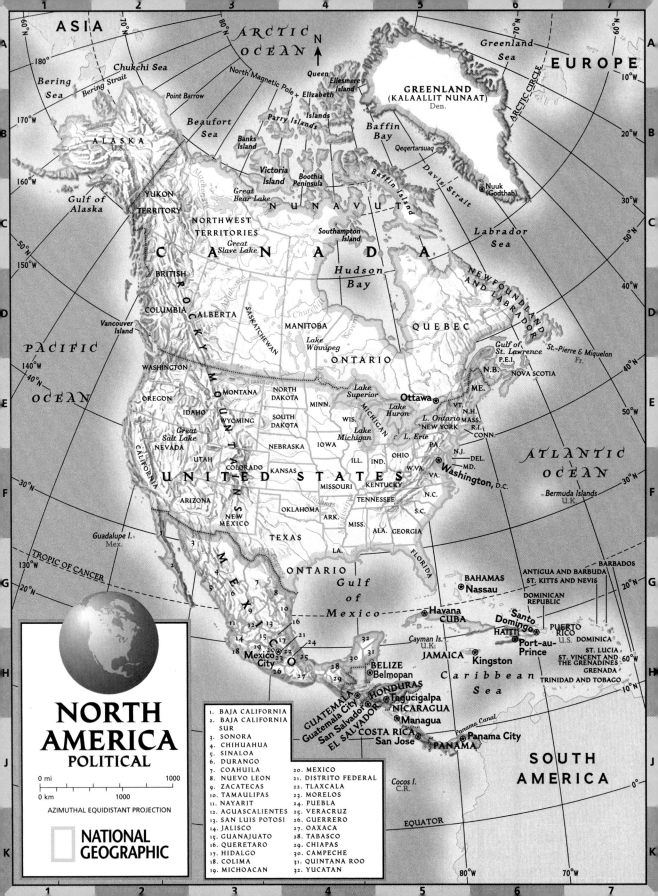

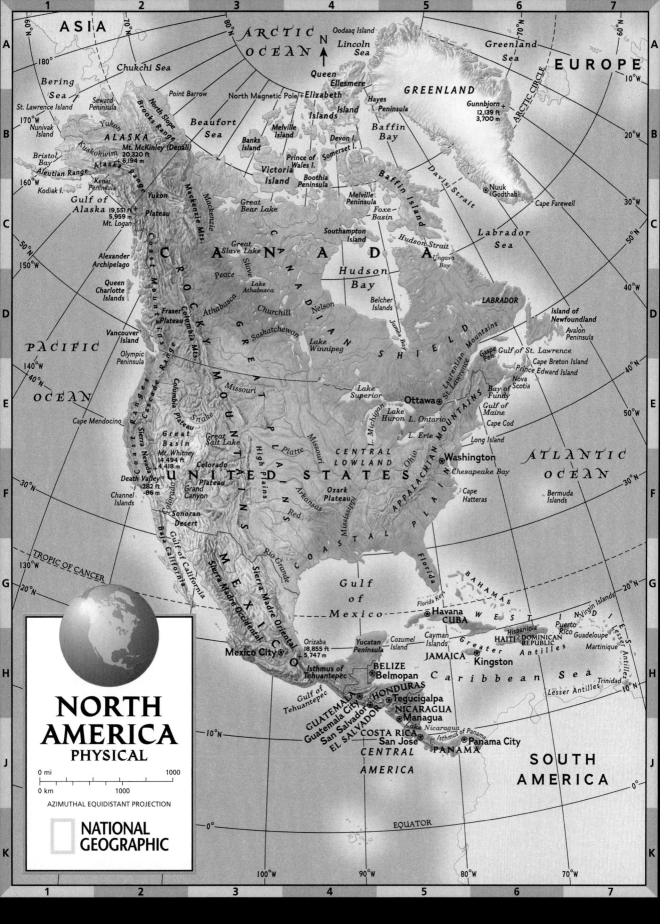

NORTH AMERICA
PHYSICAL

0 mi   1000

0 km   1000

AZIMUTHAL EQUIDISTANT PROJECTION

NATIONAL GEOGRAPHIC

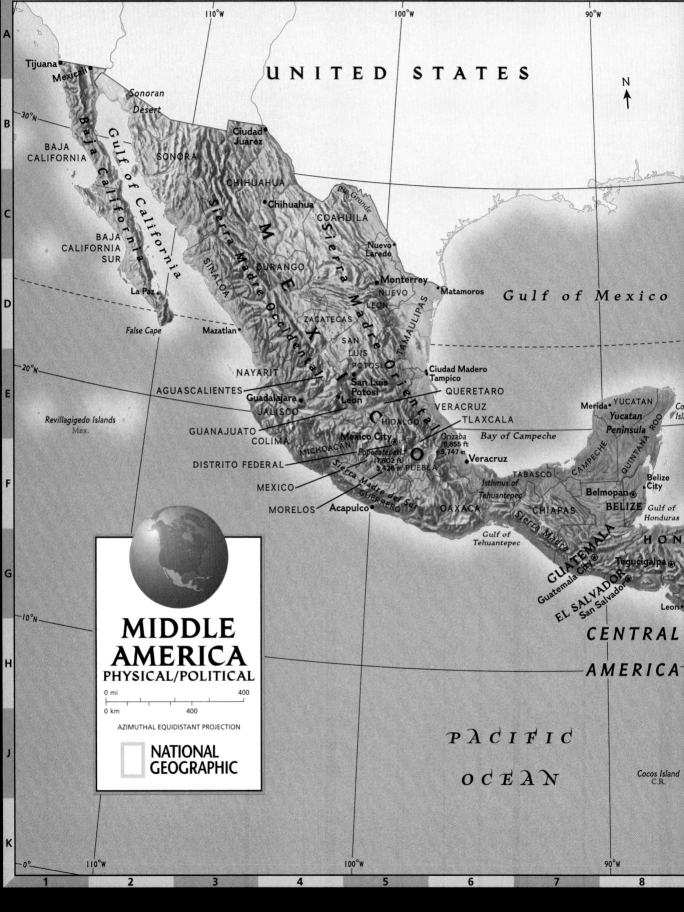

110°W   100°W   90°W

A

Tijuana
Mexicali

UNITED STATES

N

Sonoran
Desert

B
30°N

BAJA
CALIFORNIA

Gulf of California

SONORA

Ciudad
Juarez

CHIHUAHUA

Rio Grande

C

BAJA
CALIFORNIA
SUR

Chihuahua

COAHUILA

Nuevo
Laredo

Gulf of Mexico

Sierra Madre Occidental

DURANGO

SINALOA

Monterrey
NUEVO
LEON

Matamoros

La Paz

D

False Cape   Mazatlan

ZACATECAS

SAN
LUIS
POTOSI

TAMAULIPAS

M E X I C O

Sierra Madre Oriental

20°N

NAYARIT

AGUASCALIENTES

Guadalajara

JALISCO

San Luis
Potosi
Leon

Ciudad Madero
Tampico

QUERETARO

VERACRUZ

Merida   YUCATAN

Yucatan
Peninsula

Co
Isl

E

Revillagigedo Islands
Mex.

GUANAJUATO

COLIMA

MICHOACAN

Mexico City

Popocatepetl
17,802 ft
5,426 m

DISTRITO FEDERAL

TLAXCALA

HIDALGO

Orizaba
18,855 ft
5,747 m

PUEBLA

Bay of Campeche

Veracruz

CAMPECHE

QUINTANA ROO

Belize
City

F

MEXICO

MORELOS

Acapulco

Sierra Madre del Sur

GUERRERO

OAXACA

Isthmus of
Tehuantepec

TABASCO

CHIAPAS

Sierra Madre

Belmopan

BELIZE

Gulf of
Honduras

G

Gulf of
Tehuantepec

GUATEMALA

Guatemala City

EL SALVADOR

San Salvador

Tegucigalpa

HON

Leon

10°N

H

CENTRAL

AMERICA

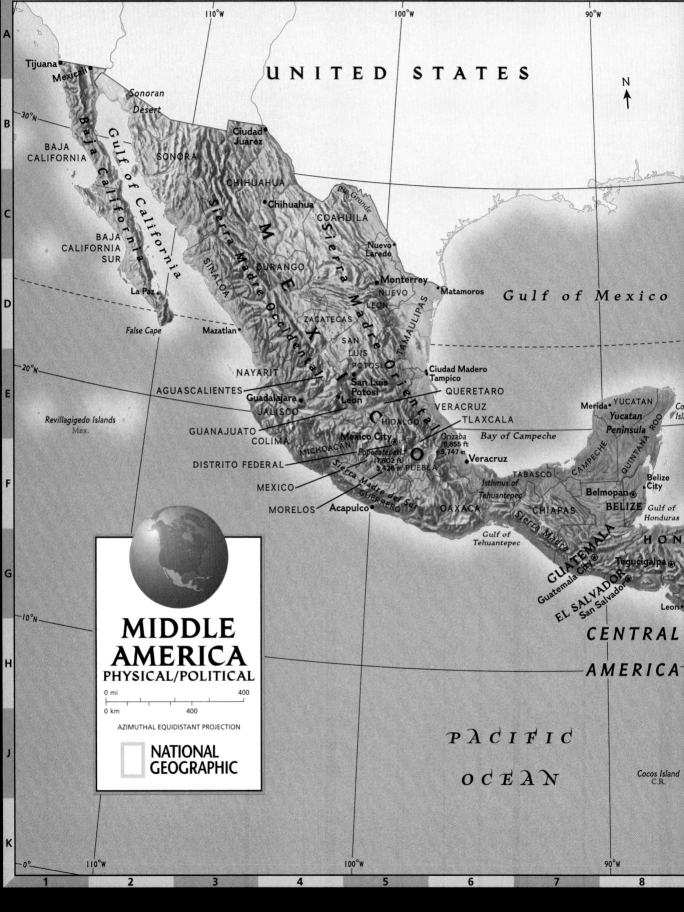

**MIDDLE
AMERICA**
PHYSICAL/POLITICAL

0 mi   400

0 km   400

AZIMUTHAL EQUIDISTANT PROJECTION

**NATIONAL
GEOGRAPHIC**

PACIFIC

J

OCEAN

Cocos Island
C.R.

K

0°

110°W   100°W   90°W

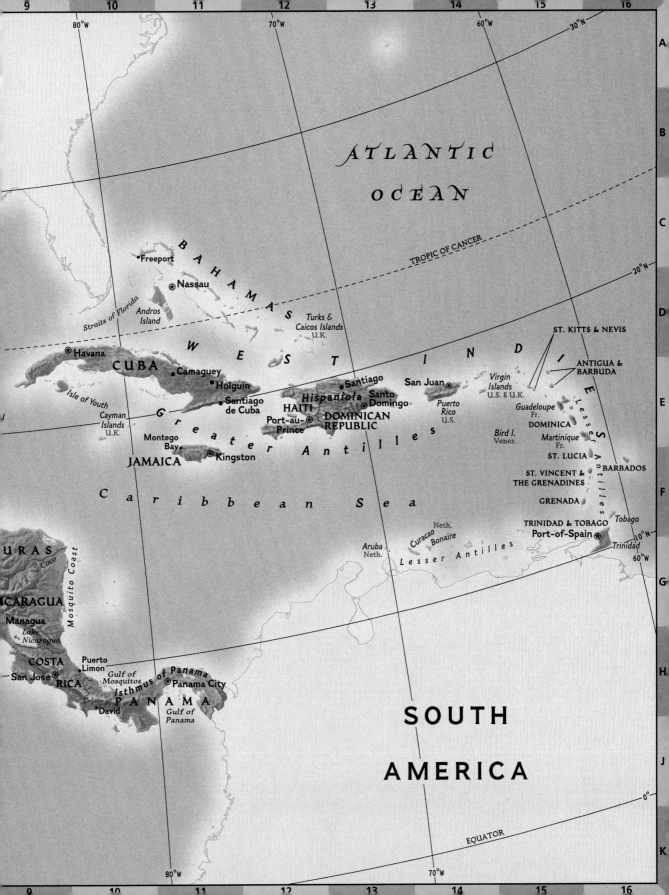

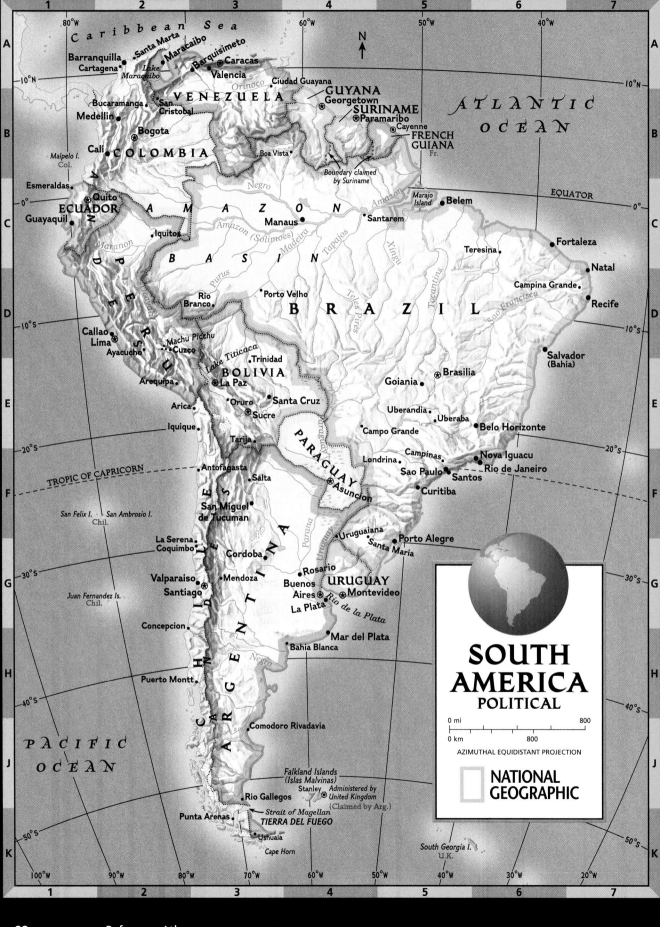

SOUTH
AMERICA
POLITICAL

0 mi   800
0 km   800

AZIMUTHAL EQUIDISTANT PROJECTION

NATIONAL
GEOGRAPHIC

SOUTH AMERICA
PHYSICAL

0 mi   800
0 km   800

AZIMUTHAL EQUIDISTANT PROJECTION

NATIONAL GEOGRAPHIC

Caribbean Sea

ATLANTIC OCEAN

PACIFIC OCEAN

VENEZUELA
COLOMBIA
ECUADOR
Quito
Bogota
Lake Maracaibo
⊗ Caracas
Orinoco
LLANOS
GUYANA
Georgetown
SURINAME
⊗ Paramaribo
Cayenne
FRENCH GUIANA
Angel Falls
Total drop
3,212 ft, 979 m
GUYANA HIGHLANDS
Boundary claimed by Suriname
Marajo Island
Amazon

AMAZON
Negro
Amazon
Selvas
Purus
Madeira
Tapajos
Xingu
Teles Pires
Tocantins
Sao Francisco
BASIN
BRAZIL
BRAZILIAN
HIGHLANDS
Ucayali
Machu Picchu
Lima ⊗
Lake Titicaca
BOLIVIA
La Paz
⊗ Sucre
Altiplano
Salar de Uyuni
MATO GROSSO PLATEAU
Brasilia

PARAGUAY
Paraguay
GRAN CHACO
Asuncion
Iguazu Falls

TROPIC OF CAPRICORN

San Felix I.   San Ambrosio I.

Juan Fernandez Is.

ANDES
ARGENTINA
PAMPAS
Parana
Uruguay
Aconcagua 22,834 ft 6,960 m
Santiago
Buenos Aires
URUGUAY
Montevideo
Rio de la Plata
Negro

-131 ft -40 m Valdes Peninsula

PATAGONIA
Chiloe Island
Taitao Peninsula
Gulf of San Jorge
Wellington I.

Falkland Islands
(Islas Malvinas)
Stanley

Strait of Magellan
Tierra del Fuego

Cape Horn   South Georgia I.

Malpelo I.

EQUATOR

10°N
10°N
0°
0°
10°S
10°S
20°S
20°S
30°S
30°S
40°S
40°S
50°S
50°S

80°W 60°W 50°W 40°W
100°W 90°W 80°W 70°W 60°W 50°W 40°W 30°W 20°W

PACIFIC
RIM
PHYSICAL/POLITICAL

0 mi   1500

0 km   1500
MILLER CYLINDRICAL PROJECTION

NATIONAL
GEOGRAPHIC

WORLD'S PEOPLE

RELIGIONS, ECONOMY, LANGUAGES, AND POPULATION DENSITY

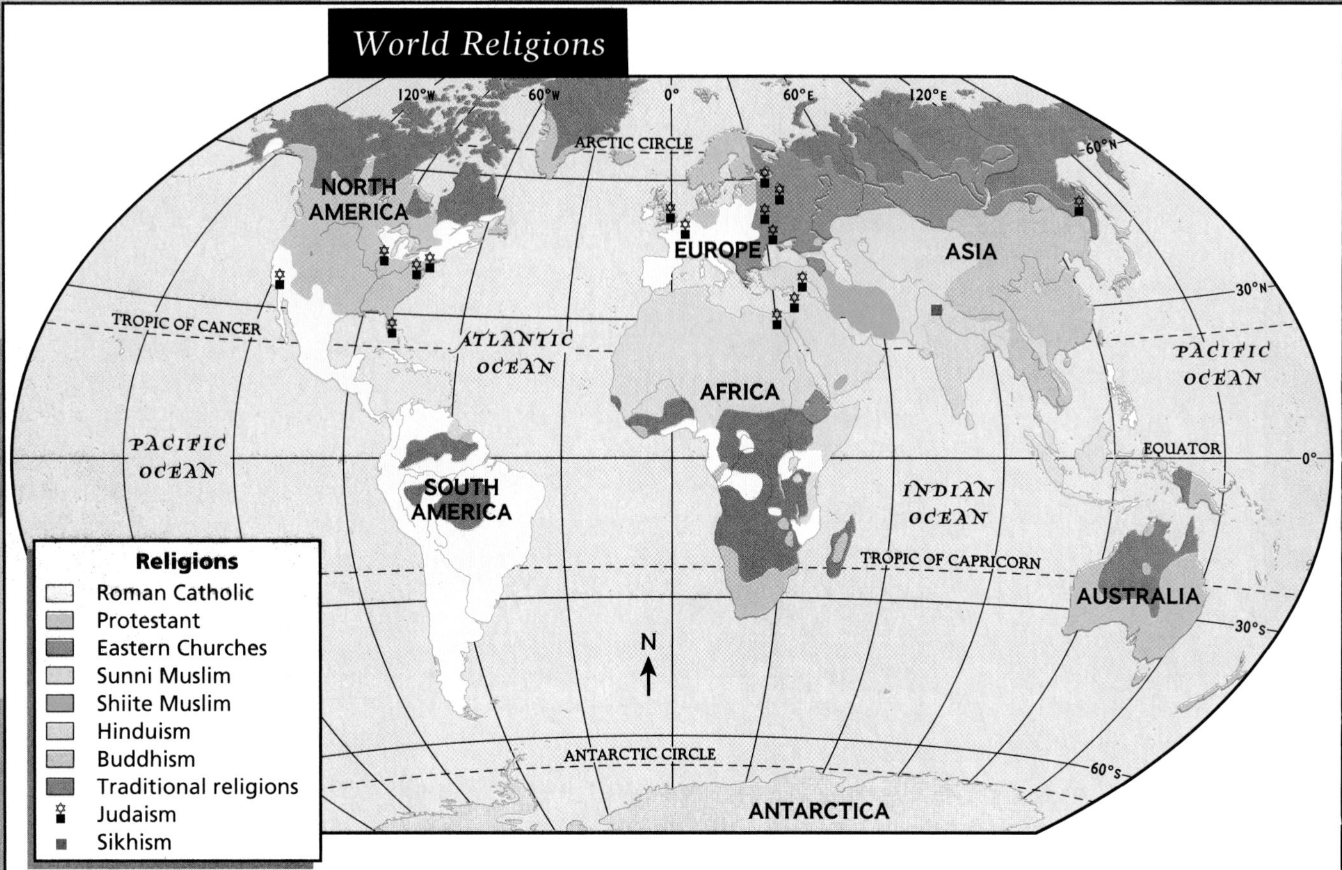
World Religions
120°W
60°W
0°
60°E
120°E
ARCTIC CIRCLE
60°N
30°N
0°
30°S
60°S
NORTH AMERICA
EUROPE
ASIA
AFRICA
SOUTH AMERICA
AUSTRALIA
ANTARCTICA
TROPIC OF CANCER
TROPIC OF CAPRICORN
EQUATOR
ANTARCTIC CIRCLE
ATLANTIC OCEAN
PACIFIC OCEAN
PACIFIC OCEAN
INDIAN OCEAN
N
Religions
Roman Catholic
Protestant
Eastern Churches
Sunni Muslim
Shiite Muslim
Hinduism
Buddhism
Traditional religions
Judaism
Sikhism

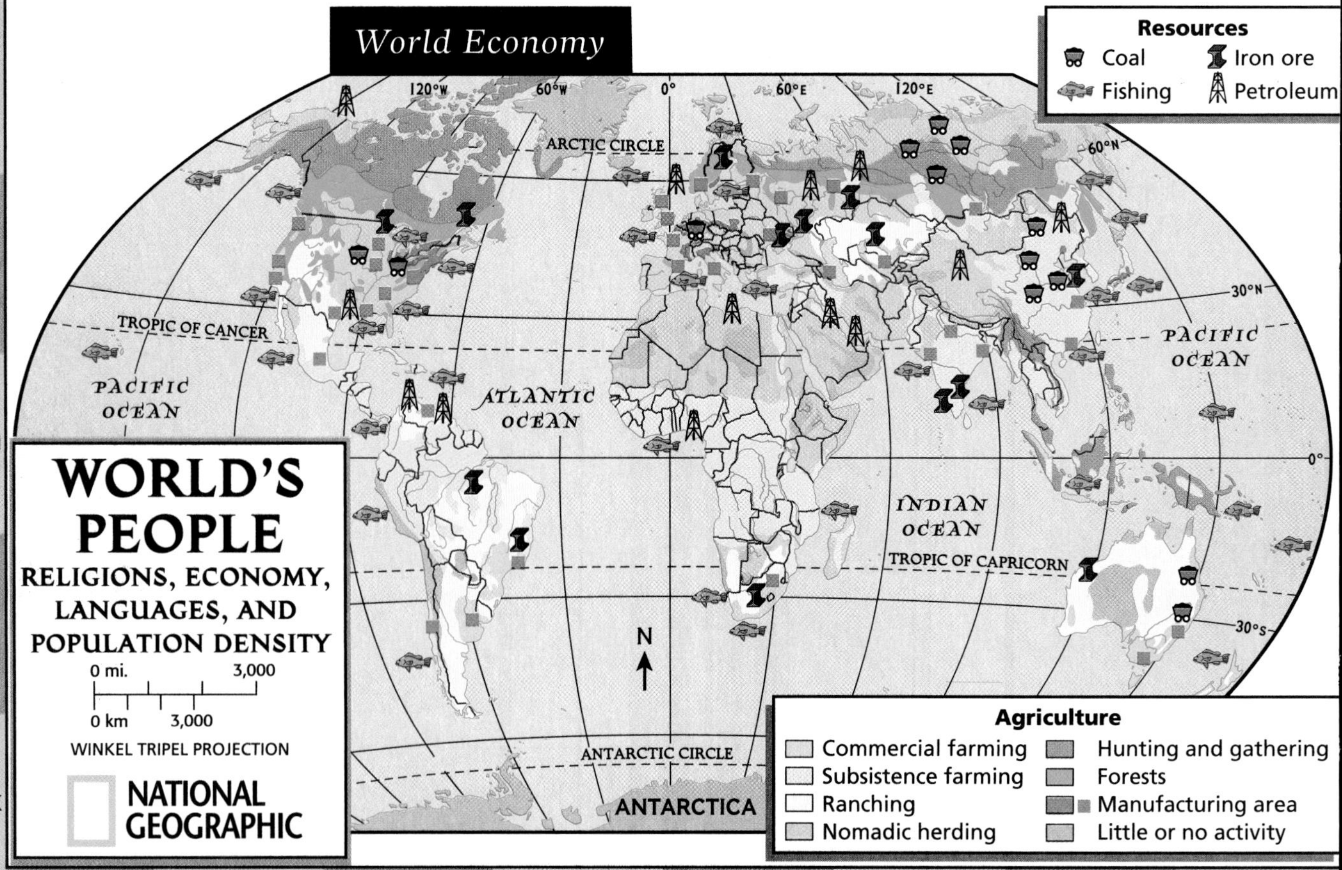
World Economy
120°W
60°W
0°
60°E
120°E
ARCTIC CIRCLE
60°N
30°N
0°
30°S
TROPIC OF CANCER
TROPIC OF CAPRICORN
ANTARCTIC CIRCLE
ATLANTIC OCEAN
PACIFIC OCEAN
PACIFIC OCEAN
INDIAN OCEAN
ANTARCTICA
N
Resources
Coal
Iron ore
Fishing
Petroleum
Agriculture
Commercial farming
Subsistence farming
Ranching
Nomadic herding
Hunting and gathering
Forests
Manufacturing area
Little or no activity

0 mi. 3,000
0 km 3,000
WINKEL TRIPEL PROJECTION

NATIONAL GEOGRAPHIC

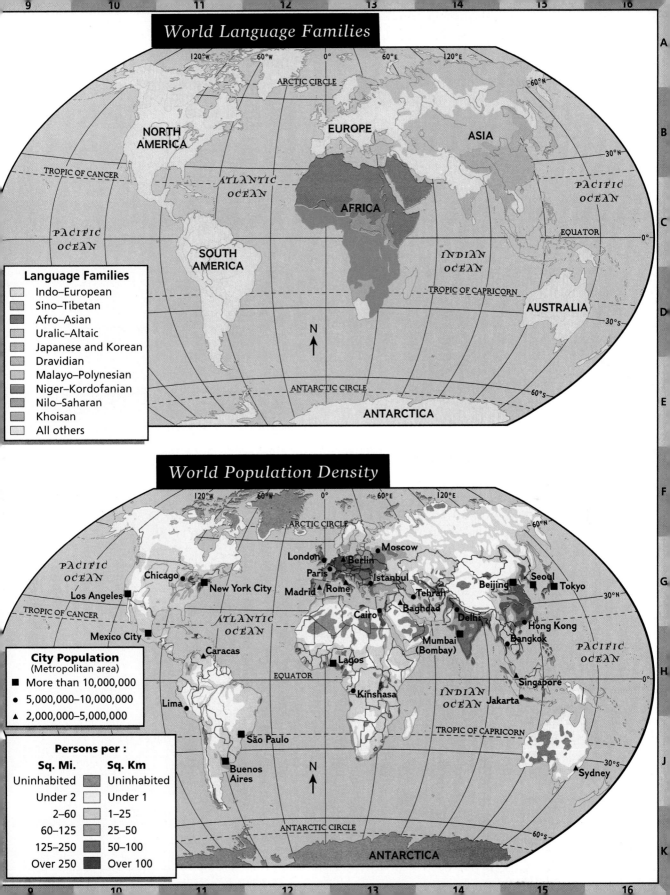

World Language Families

NORTH AMERICA

EUROPE

ASIA

AFRICA

SOUTH AMERICA

AUSTRALIA

ANTARCTICA

ARCTIC CIRCLE
TROPIC OF CANCER
EQUATOR
TROPIC OF CAPRICORN
ANTARCTIC CIRCLE

ATLANTIC OCEAN
PACIFIC OCEAN
PACIFIC OCEAN
INDIAN OCEAN

120°W · 60°W · 0° · 60°E · 120°E
60°N · 30°N · 0° · 30°S · 60°S

N

Language Families
- Indo–European
- Sino–Tibetan
- Afro–Asian
- Uralic–Altaic
- Japanese and Korean
- Dravidian
- Malayo–Polynesian
- Niger–Kordofanian
- Nilo–Saharan
- Khoisan
- All others

World Population Density

ARCTIC CIRCLE
TROPIC OF CANCER
EQUATOR
TROPIC OF CAPRICORN
ANTARCTIC CIRCLE

PACIFIC OCEAN
ATLANTIC OCEAN
PACIFIC OCEAN
INDIAN OCEAN

120°W · 60°W · 0° · 60°E · 120°E
60°N · 30°N · 0° · 30°S · 60°S

ANTARCTICA

N

Chicago, Los Angeles, New York City, Mexico City, Caracas, Lima, São Paulo, Buenos Aires
London, Paris, Madrid, Berlin, Rome, Moscow, Istanbul, Tehran, Baghdad, Cairo, Lagos, Kinshasa
Beijing, Seoul, Tokyo, Delhi, Mumbai (Bombay), Hong Kong, Bangkok, Singapore, Jakarta, Sydney

City Population
(Metropolitan area)
- ■ More than 10,000,000
- ● 5,000,000–10,000,000
- ▲ 2,000,000–5,000,000

Persons per :

Sq. Mi.	Sq. Km
Uninhabited	Uninhabited
Under 2	Under 1
2–60	1–25
60–125	25–50
125–250	50–100
Over 250	Over 100

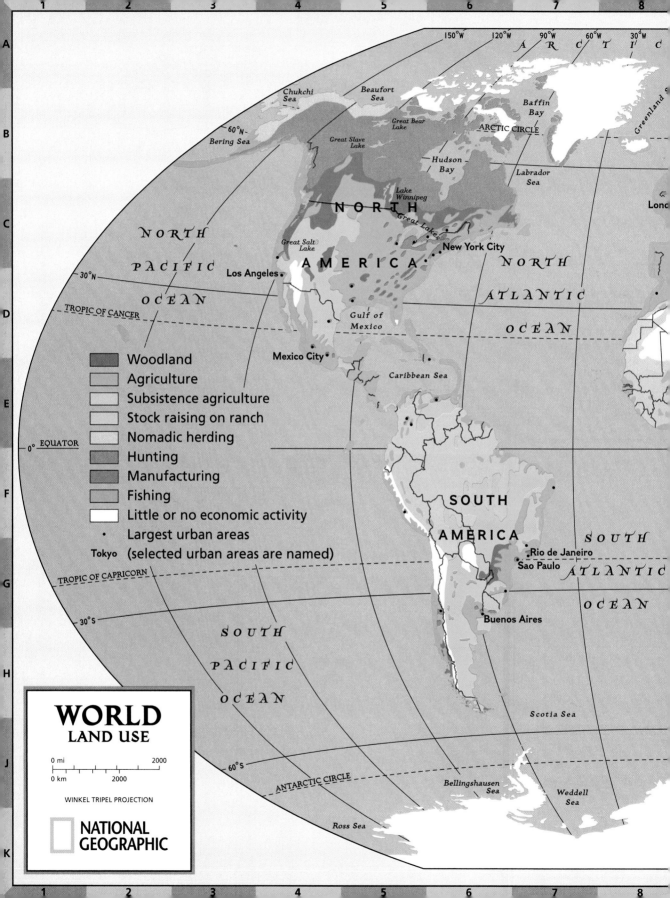

WORLD
LAND USE

Woodland
Agriculture
Subsistence agriculture
Stock raising on ranch
Nomadic herding
Hunting
Manufacturing
Fishing
Little or no economic activity
· Largest urban areas
Tokyo (selected urban areas are named)

0 mi   2000
0 km   2000

WINKEL TRIPEL PROJECTION

NATIONAL GEOGRAPHIC

ARCTIC

Chukchi Sea

Beaufort Sea

Baffin Bay

Great Bear Lake

ARCTIC CIRCLE

Greenland S

60°N
Bering Sea

Great Slave Lake

Hudson Bay

Labrador Sea

Lake Winnipeg

NORTH

Great Lakes

Lond

NORTH

New York City

PACIFIC

Great Salt Lake

AMERICA

NORTH

30°N

Los Angeles

ATLANTIC

TROPIC OF CANCER

OCEAN

OCEAN

Gulf of Mexico

Mexico City

Caribbean Sea

EQUATOR

SOUTH

AMERICA

SOUTH

Rio de Janeiro

ATLANTIC

Sao Paulo

TROPIC OF CAPRICORN

OCEAN

30°S

Buenos Aires

SOUTH

PACIFIC

OCEAN

Scotia Sea

60°S

ANTARCTIC CIRCLE

Bellingshausen Sea

Weddell Sea

Ross Sea

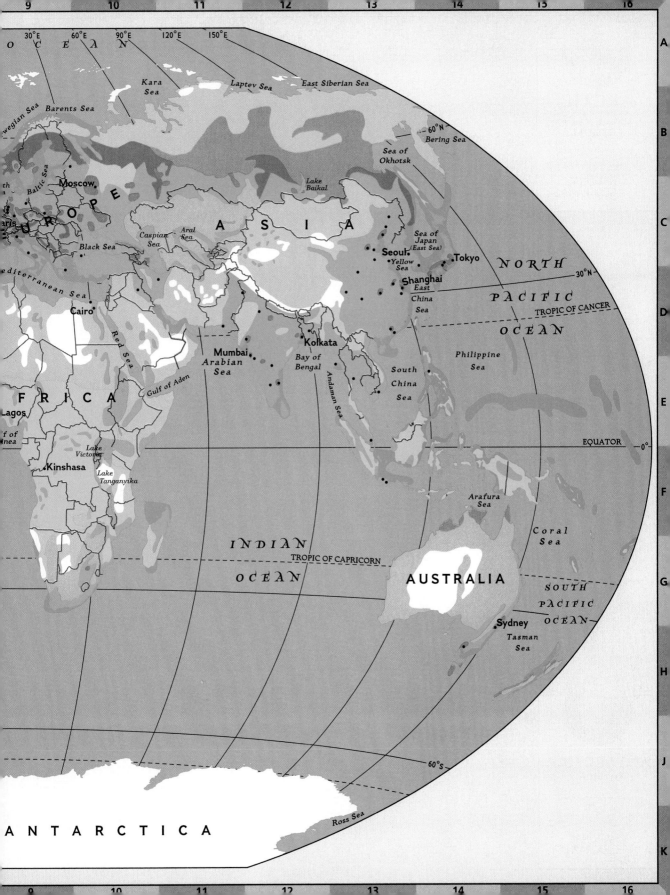

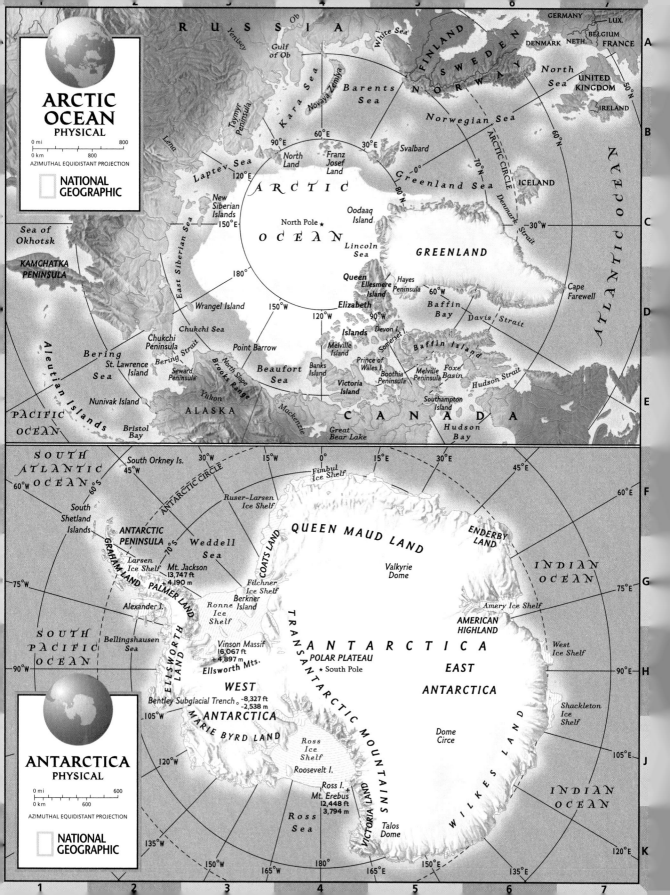

ARCTIC OCEAN
PHYSICAL

0 mi 800
0 km 800
AZIMUTHAL EQUIDISTANT PROJECTION

NATIONAL GEOGRAPHIC

RUSSIA
GERMANY   LUX.
DENMARK   NETH.   BELGIUM   FRANCE
Ob
Yenisey
Gulf of Ob
White Sea
FINLAND
SWEDEN
NORWAY
United Kingdom
IRELAND
North Sea
Norwegian Sea
Taymyr Peninsula
Kara Sea
Novaya Zemlya
Barents Sea
Svalbard
ARCTIC CIRCLE
ICELAND
Lena
Laptev Sea
North Land
Franz Josef Land
Greenland Sea
Denmark Strait
New Siberian Islands
A R C T I C
North Pole ★
O C E A N
Oodaaq Island
Lincoln Sea
GREENLAND
Cape Farewell
Sea of Okhotsk
East Siberian Sea
Wrangel Island
Queen
Ellesmere Island
Elizabeth
Hayes Peninsula
Baffin Bay
Davis Strait
KAMCHATKA PENINSULA
Chukchi Sea
Islands
Devon I.
Chukchi Peninsula
Point Barrow
Melville Island
Somerset I.
Baffin Island
Bering Strait
Bering Sea
St. Lawrence Island
Seward Peninsula
North Slope
Brooks Range
Beaufort Sea
Banks Island
Prince of Wales I.
Boothia Peninsula
Melville Peninsula
Foxe Basin
Hudson Strait
Aleutian Islands
Nunivak Island
Yukon
ALASKA
Mackenzie
Victoria Island
C A N A D A
Southampton Island
Hudson Bay
PACIFIC OCEAN
Bristol Bay
Great Bear Lake
ATLANTIC OCEAN
50°N
60°N
70°N
80°N
0°
30°E
60°E
90°E
120°E
150°E
180°
150°W
120°W
90°W
60°W
30°W

SOUTH ATLANTIC OCEAN
South Orkney Is.
ANTARCTIC CIRCLE
Fimbul Ice Shelf
Ruser-Larsen Ice Shelf
South Shetland Islands
ANTARCTIC PENINSULA
GRAHAM LAND
Weddell Sea
COATS LAND
QUEEN MAUD LAND
ENDERBY LAND
INDIAN OCEAN
Larsen Ice Shelf
Mt. Jackson 13,747 ft +4,190 m
PALMER LAND
Filchner Ice Shelf
Berkner Island
Valkyrie Dome
Amery Ice Shelf
Alexander I.
Ronne Ice Shelf
AMERICAN HIGHLAND
SOUTH PACIFIC OCEAN
Bellingshausen Sea
ELLSWORTH LAND
Vinson Massif 16,067 ft +4,897 m
Ellsworth Mts.
A N T A R C T I C A
POLAR PLATEAU
★ South Pole
West Ice Shelf
WEST
TRANSANTARCTIC MOUNTAINS
EAST ANTARCTICA
Bentley Subglacial Trench ○ -8,327 ft -2,538 m
ANTARCTICA
Shackleton Ice Shelf
MARIE BYRD LAND
Dome Circe
Ross Ice Shelf
Roosevelt I.
VICTORIA LAND
WILKES LAND
Ross I.
Mt. Erebus 12,448 ft 3,794 m
Ross Sea
Talos Dome
INDIAN OCEAN
60°S
70°S
45°W
30°W
15°W
0°
15°E
30°E
45°E
60°E
75°E
90°E
105°E
120°E
135°E
90°W
105°W
120°W
135°W
150°W
165°W
180°
165°E
150°E
75°W

ANTARCTICA
PHYSICAL

0 mi 600
0 km 600
AZIMUTHAL EQUIDISTANT PROJECTION

NATIONAL GEOGRAPHIC

NATIONAL GEOGRAPHIC

Geography Handbook

The story of the world begins with geography—the study of the earth in all of its variety. Geography describes the earth's land, water, and plant and animal life. It is the study of places and the complex relationships between people and their environment.

The resources in this handbook will help you get the most out of your textbook—and provide you with skills you will use for the rest of your life.

▼ The Gui River, Guilin, China

▲ Saharan sand dunes, Morocco

The Amazon, Brazil ▶

I Study Geography?

Six Essential Elements

Recently, geographers have begun to look at geography in a different way. They do this to understand how our large world is connected. They break down the study of geography into Six Essential Elements. You should think of these elements as categories into which to sort information you learn about the world's geography.

Being aware of these elements will help you sort out what you are learning. Examples of each of the Essential Elements detailed in maps throughout *Discovering Our Past* are explained here.

Element 2

Places and Regions

Place has a special meaning in geography. It means more than where a place is. It also describes what a place is like. It might describe physical characteristics such as landforms, climate, and plant or animal life. Or it might describe human characteristics, including language and way of life.

To help organize their study, geographers often group places into regions. **Regions** are united by one or more common characteristics.

Element 1

The World in Spatial Terms

Geographers first take a look at where a place is located. **Location** serves as a starting point by asking "Where is it?" Knowing the location of places helps you develop an awareness of the world around you.

Element 3

Physical Systems

When studying places and regions, geographers analyze how **physical systems**—such as hurricanes, volcanoes, and glaciers—shape the earth's surface. They also look at communities of plants and animals that depend upon one another and their surroundings for survival.

Element 4

Human Systems

Geographers also examine **human systems,** or how people have shaped our world. They look at political boundary lines and why people settle in certain places. A key theme is the continual **movement** of people, ideas, and goods.

Element 5

Environment and Society

What is the relationship between people and their natural surroundings? This is what the theme of **human/environment interaction** investigates. It also shows how people affect the environment.

Element 6

The Uses of Geography

Knowledge of geography helps us understand people, places, and environments over time. Knowing how to use the tools of geography prepares you for our modern society.

Five Themes

Some geographers study geography through five themes. The **Five Themes of Geography** are (1) location, (2) place, (3) human/environment interaction, (4) movement, and (5) regions. You will see these highlighted throughout *Discovering Our Past.*

How Do I Use Maps and Globes?

Hemispheres

To locate place on the earth, geographers use a system of imaginary lines that crisscross the globe. One of these lines, the **Equator,** circles the middle of the earth like a belt. It divides the earth into "half spheres," or **hemispheres.** Everything north of the Equator is in the Northern Hemisphere. Everything south of the Equator is in the Southern Hemisphere.

Another imaginary line runs from north to south. It helps divide the earth into half spheres in the other direction. Find this line—called the **Prime Meridian** on a globe. Everything east of the Prime Meridian for 180 degrees is in the Eastern Hemisphere. Everything west of the Prime Meridian is in the Western Hemisphere.

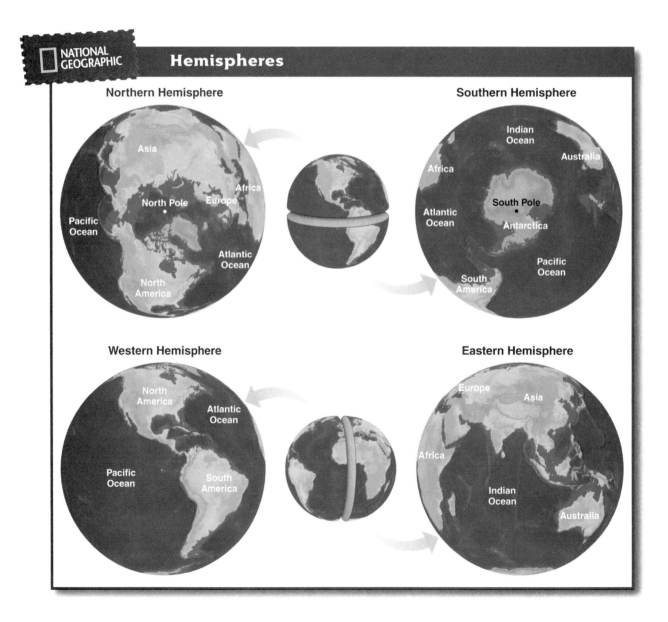

NATIONAL GEOGRAPHIC Hemispheres

Northern Hemisphere

Asia
Africa
Europe
North Pole
Pacific Ocean
Atlantic Ocean
North America

Southern Hemisphere

Indian Ocean
Australia
Africa
South Pole
Atlantic Ocean
Antarctica
Pacific Ocean
South America

Western Hemisphere

North America
Atlantic Ocean
Pacific Ocean
South America

Eastern Hemisphere

Europe
Asia
Africa
Indian Ocean
Australia

Understanding Latitude and Longitude

L ines on globes and maps provide information that can help you easily locate places on the earth. These lines—called **latitude** and **longitude**—cross one another, forming a pattern called a grid system.

Latitude

Lines of latitude, or **parallels,** circle the earth parallel to the **Equator** and measure the distance north or south of the Equator in degrees. The Equator is at 0° latitude, while the North Pole lies at latitude 90°N (north).

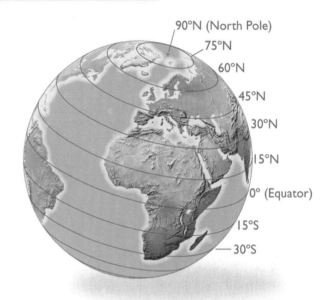

90°N (North Pole)
75°N
60°N
45°N
30°N
15°N
0° (Equator)
15°S
30°S

Longitude

Lines of longitude, or **meridians,** circle the earth from Pole to Pole. These lines measure distances east or west of the starting line, which is at 0° longitude and is called the **Prime Meridian** by geographers. The Prime Meridian runs through the Royal Observatory in Greenwich, England.

45°W
30°W
15°W
0° (Prime Meridian)
15°E
30°E
45°E

Absolute Location

The grid system formed by lines of latitude and longitude makes it possible to find the absolute location of a place. Only one place can be found at the point where a specific line of latitude crosses a specific line of longitude. By using degrees (°) and minutes (′) (points between degrees), people can pinpoint the precise spot where one line of latitude crosses one line of longitude—an **absolute location.**

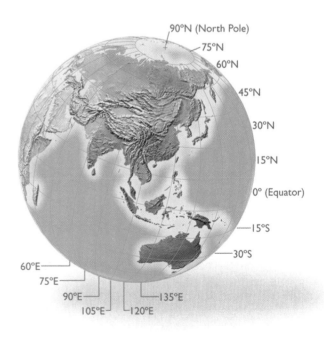

90°N (North Pole)
75°N
60°N
45°N
30°N
15°N
0° (Equator)
15°S
30°S
60°E
75°E
90°E
105°E
120°E
135°E

From Globes to Maps

*T*he most accurate way to depict the earth is as a *globe*, a round scale model of the earth. A globe gives a true picture of the continents' relative sizes and the shapes of landmasses and bodies of water. Globes accurately represent distance and direction.

A *map* is a flat drawing of all or part of the earth's surface. Unlike globes, maps can show small areas in great detail. Maps can also display political boundaries, population densities, or even voting returns.

From Globes to Maps

Maps, however, do have their limitations. As you can imagine, drawing a round object on a flat surface is very difficult. **Cartographers,** or mapmakers, use mathematical formulas to transfer information from the round globe to a flat map. However, when the curves of a globe become straight lines on a map, the size, shape, distance, or area can change or be distorted.

Great Circle Routes

Mapmakers have solved some problems of going from a globe to a map. A **great circle** is an imaginary line that follows the curve of the earth. Traveling along a great circle is called following a **great circle route.** Airplane pilots use great circle routes because they are the shortest routes.

The idea of a great circle shows one important difference between a globe and a map. Because a globe is round, it accurately shows great circles. On a flat map, however, the great circle route between two points may not appear to be the shortest distance. Compare Maps A and B on the right.

Mapmaking With Technology

Technology has changed the way maps are made. Most cartographers use software programs called **geographic information systems (GIS).** This software layers map data from satellite images, printed text, and statistics. A **Global Positioning System (GPS)** helps consumers and mapmakers locate places based on coordinates broadcast by satellites.

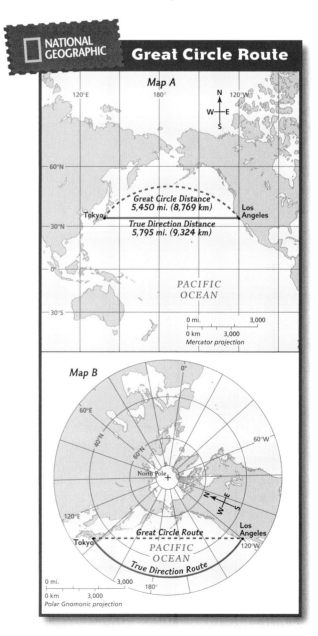

NATIONAL GEOGRAPHIC

Great Circle Route

Map A

Great Circle Distance
5,450 mi. (8,769 km)

True Direction Distance
5,795 mi. (9,324 km)

Tokyo

Los Angeles

PACIFIC OCEAN

0 mi. 3,000
0 km 3,000
Mercator projection

Map B

North Pole

Great Circle Route

Los Angeles

Tokyo

PACIFIC OCEAN

True Direction Route

0 mi. 3,000
0 km 3,000
Polar Gnomonic projection

Common Map Projections

Imagine taking the whole peel from an orange and trying to flatten it on a table. You would either have to cut it or stretch parts of it. Mapmakers face a similar problem in showing the surface of the round earth on a flat map. When the earth's surface is flattened, big gaps open up. To fill in the gaps, mapmakers stretch parts of the earth. They choose to show either the correct shapes of places or their correct sizes. It is impossible to show both. As a result, mapmakers have developed different **projections**, or ways of showing the earth on a flat piece of paper.

Goode's Interrupted Equal-Area Projection

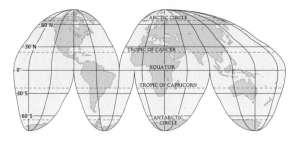

▲ Take a second look at your peeled, flattened orange. You might have something that looks like a map based on **Goode's Interrupted Equal-Area** projection. A map with this projection shows continents close to their true shapes and sizes. This projection is helpful to compare land areas among continents.

Robinson Projection

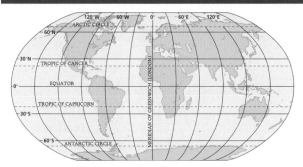

▲ A map using the **Robinson** projection has minor distortions. Land on the western and eastern sides of the Robinson map appears much as it does on a globe. The areas most distorted on this projection are near the North and South Poles.

Winkel Tripel Projection

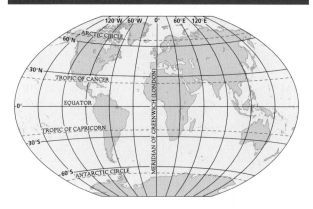

▲ The **Winkel Tripel** projection gives a good overall view of the continents' shapes and sizes. Land areas in a Winkel Tripel projection are not as distorted near the Poles as they are in the Robinson projection.

Mercator Projection

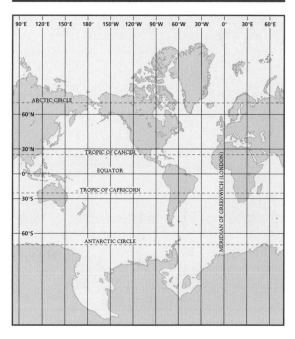

▲ The **Mercator** projection shows true direction and land shapes fairly accurately, but not size or distance. Areas that are located far from the Equator are quite distorted on this projection. Alaska, for example, appears much larger on a Mercator map than it does on a globe.

Parts of Maps

Map Key An important first step in reading a map is to note the map key. The **map key** explains the lines, symbols, and colors used on a map. For example, the map on this page shows the various climate regions of the United States and the different colors representing them. Cities are usually symbolized by a solid circle (•) and capitals by a (✪). On this map, you can see the capital of Texas and the cities of Los Angeles, Seattle, New Orleans, and Chicago.

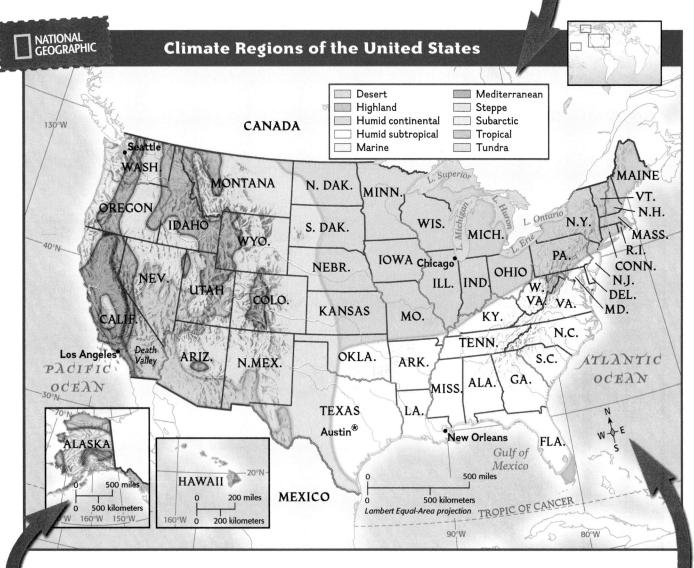

Climate Regions of the United States

Map Key:
- Desert
- Highland
- Humid continental
- Humid subtropical
- Marine
- Mediterranean
- Steppe
- Subarctic
- Tropical
- Tundra

Lambert Equal-Area projection

Scale A measuring line, often called a **scale bar,** helps you figure distance on the map. The map scale tells you what distance on the earth is represented by the measurement on the scale bar.

Compass Rose A map has a symbol that tells you where the **cardinal directions**—north, south, east, and west—are positioned.

Types of Maps

General Purpose Maps

Maps are amazingly useful tools. Geographers use many different types of maps. Maps that show a wide range of general information about an area are called **general purpose maps.** Two of the most common general purpose maps are physical and political maps.

Physical Maps

Physical maps call out landforms and water features. The physical map of Sri Lanka (below) shows rivers and mountains. The colors used on physical maps include brown or green for land and blue for water. In addition, physical maps may use colors to show **elevation**—the height of an area above sea level. A key explains what each color and symbol stands for.

Political Maps

Political maps show the names and boundaries of countries, the location of cities and other human-made features of a place, and often identify major physical features. The political map of Spain (above), for example, shows the boundaries between Spain and other countries. It also shows cities and rivers within Spain and bodies of water surrounding Spain.

Special Purpose Maps

Some maps are made to present specific kinds of information. These are called **thematic** or **special purpose maps.** They usually show themes or patterns, often emphasizing one subject or theme. Special purpose maps may present climate, natural resources, and population density. They may also display historical information, such as battles or territorial changes. The map's title tells what kind of special information it shows. Colors and symbols in the map key are especially important on these types of maps. Special purpose maps are often found in books of maps called atlases.

One type of special purpose map uses colors to show population density, or the average number of people living in a square mile or square kilometer. As with other maps, it is important to first read the title and the key. The population density map of Egypt shows that the Nile River valley and delta are very densely populated.

Some other special purpose maps such as the one of China's Defenses are not presented in color. They are printed in black and white. This is an example of a map you might find on a standardized test or in a newspaper.

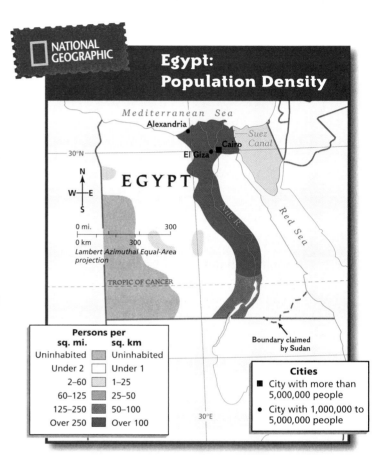

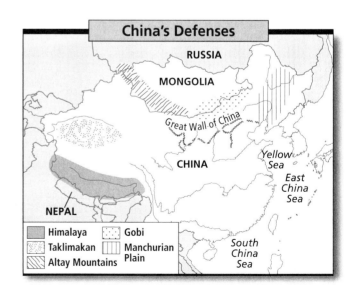

Using Graphs, Charts, and Diagrams

Bar, Line, and Circle Graphs

A graph is a way of summarizing and presenting information visually. Each part of a graph gives useful information. First read the graph's title to find out its subject. Then read the labels along the graph's **axes**—the vertical line along the left side of the graph and the horizontal line along the bottom. One axis will tell you what is being measured. The other axis tells what units of measurement are being used.

Graphs that use bars or wide lines to compare data visually are called **bar graphs.** Look carefully at the bar graph (right) that compares world languages. The vertical axis lists the languages. The horizontal axis gives speakers of the language in millions. By comparing the lengths of the bars, you can quickly tell which language is spoken by the most people. Bar graphs are especially useful for comparing quantities.

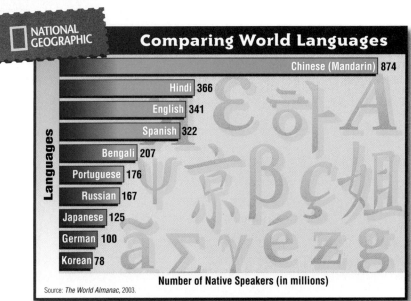

NATIONAL GEOGRAPHIC

Comparing World Languages

Language	Number of Native Speakers (in millions)
Chinese (Mandarin)	874
Hindi	366
English	341
Spanish	322
Bengali	207
Portuguese	176
Russian	167
Japanese	125
German	100
Korean	78

Source: *The World Almanac*, 2003.

Bar graph

A **line graph** is a useful tool for showing changes over a period of time. The amounts being measured are plotted on the grid above each year and then are connected by a line. Line graphs sometimes have two or more lines plotted on them. The line graph (below) shows that the number of farms in the United States has decreased since 1940.

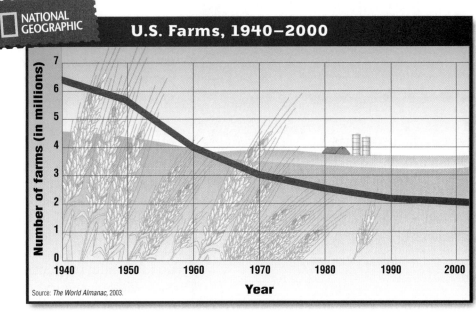

NATIONAL GEOGRAPHIC

U.S. Farms, 1940–2000

Number of farms (in millions) vs. Year

Source: *The World Almanac*, 2003.

Line graph

You can use **circle graphs** when you want to show how the whole of something is divided into its parts. Because of their shape, circle graphs are often called pie graphs. Each "slice" represents a part or percentage of the whole "pie." On the circle graph at right, the whole circle (100 percent) represents the world's population in 2002. The slices show how this population is divided among some of the most heavily populated areas of the world.

Charts

Charts present facts and numbers in an organized way. They arrange data, especially numbers, in rows and columns for easy reference. To interpret the chart, first read the title. Look at the chart on page 91. It tells you what information the chart contains. Next, read the labels at the top of each column and on the left side of the chart. They explain what the numbers or data on the chart are measuring.

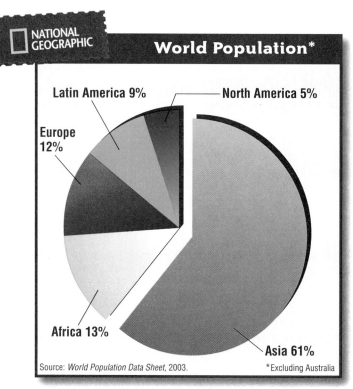

NATIONAL GEOGRAPHIC

World Population*

Latin America 9%
North America 5%
Europe 12%
Africa 13%
Asia 61%

Source: *World Population Data Sheet*, 2003.
*Excluding Australia

Circle graph

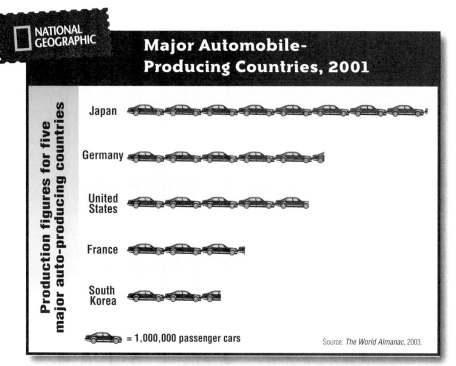

NATIONAL GEOGRAPHIC

Major Automobile-Producing Countries, 2001

Production figures for five major auto-producing countries

Japan

Germany

United States

France

South Korea

= 1,000,000 passenger cars

Source: *The World Almanac*, 2003.

Pictograph

Pictographs

Like bar and circle graphs, pictographs are good for making comparisons. **Pictographs** use rows of small pictures or symbols, with each picture or symbol representing an amount. Look at the pictograph (left) showing the number of automobiles produced in the world's five major automobile-producing countries. The key tells you that one car symbol stands for 1 million automobiles. The total number of car symbols in a row adds up to the auto production in each selected country.

Climographs

A **climograph,** or climate graph, combines a line graph and a bar graph. It gives an overall picture of the long-term weather patterns in a specific place. Climographs include several kinds of information. The green vertical bars on the climograph of Moscow (right) show average monthly amounts of precipitation (rain, snow, and sleet). These bars are measured against the axis on the right side of the graph. The red line plotted above the bars represents changes in the average monthly temperature. You measure this line against the axis on the left side.

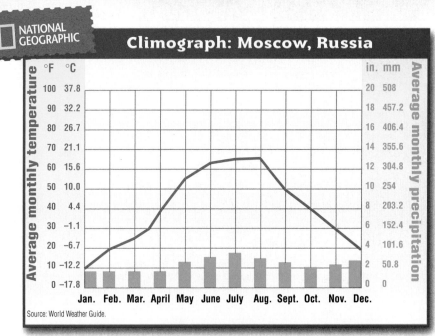

NATIONAL GEOGRAPHIC

Climograph: Moscow, Russia

Source: World Weather Guide.

Climograph

Diagrams

Diagrams are drawings that show steps in a process, point out the parts of an object, or explain how something works. An **elevation profile** is a type of diagram that can be helpful when comparing the elevations—or height—of

an area. It shows an exaggerated side view of the land as if it were sliced and you were viewing it from the side. The elevation profile of Africa (below) clearly shows sea level, low areas, and mountains.

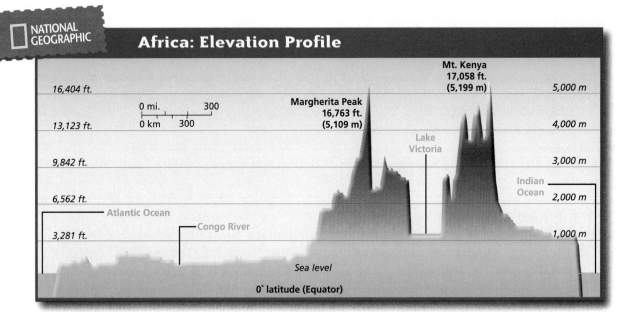

NATIONAL GEOGRAPHIC

Africa: Elevation Profile

Diagram

Geographic Dictionary

As you read about world history, you will encounter the terms listed below. Many of the terms are pictured in the diagram.

(Diagram labels: Strait, Volcano, Mountain peak, Sound, Valley, Island, Cape, Ocean, Cliff, Isthmus, Bay, Harbor, Gulf, Delta, Peninsula, Seacoast)

absolute location exact location of a place on the earth described by global coordinates

basin area of land drained by a given river and its branches; area of land surrounded by lands of higher elevation

bay part of a large body of water that extends into a shoreline, generally smaller than a gulf

canyon deep and narrow valley with steep walls

cape point of land that extends into a river, lake, or ocean

channel wide strait or waterway between two landmasses that lie close to each other; deep part of a river or other waterway

cliff steep, high wall of rock, earth, or ice

continent one of the seven large landmasses on the earth

cultural feature characteristic that humans have created in a place, such as language, religion, housing, and settlement pattern

delta flat, low-lying land built up from soil carried downstream by a river and deposited at its mouth

divide stretch of high land that separates river systems

downstream direction in which a river or stream flows from its source to its mouth

elevation height of land above sea level

Equator imaginary line that runs around the earth halfway between the North and South Poles; used as the starting point to measure degrees of north and south latitude

glacier large, thick body of slowly moving ice

gulf part of a large body of water that extends into a shoreline, generally larger and more deeply indented than a bay

harbor a sheltered place along a shoreline where ships can anchor safely

highland elevated land area such as a hill, mountain, or plateau

hill elevated land with sloping sides and rounded summit; generally smaller than a mountain

island land area, smaller than a continent, completely surrounded by water

isthmus narrow stretch of land connecting two larger land areas

lake a sizable inland body of water

latitude distance north or south of the Equator, measured in degrees

longitude distance east or west of the Prime Meridian, measured in degrees

lowland land, usually level, at a low elevation

map drawing of the earth shown on a flat surface

meridian one of many lines on the global grid running from the North Pole to the South Pole; used to measure degrees of longitude

mesa broad, flat-topped landform with steep sides; smaller than a plateau

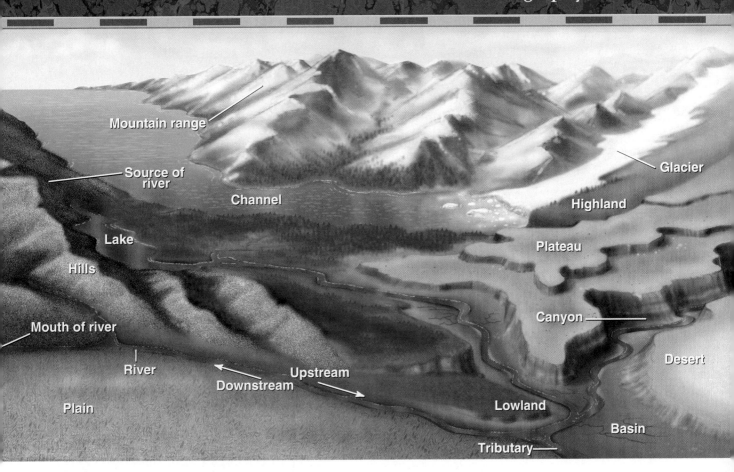

Mountain range

Source of river

Channel

Glacier

Highland

Lake

Plateau

Hills

Canyon

Mouth of river

Desert

River

Upstream

Downstream

Plain

Lowland

Basin

Tributary

---

mountain land with steep sides that rises sharply (1,000 feet [305 m] or more) from surrounding land; generally larger and more rugged than a hill

mountain peak pointed top of a mountain

mountain range a series of connected mountains

mouth (of a river) place where a stream or river flows into a larger body of water

ocean one of the four major bodies of salt water that surround the continents

ocean current stream of either cold or warm water that moves in a definite direction through an ocean

parallel one of many lines on the global grid that circle the earth north or south of the Equator; used to measure degrees of latitude

peninsula body of land jutting into a lake or ocean, surrounded on three sides by water

physical feature characteristic of a place occurring naturally, such as a landform, body of water, climate pattern, or resource

plain area of level land, usually at a low elevation and often covered with grasses

plateau area of flat or rolling land at a high elevation, about 300–3,000 feet (91–914 m) high

Prime Meridian line of the global grid running from the North Pole to the South Pole through Greenwich, England; starting point for measuring degrees of east and west longitude

relief changes in elevation over a given area of land

river large natural stream of water that runs through the land

sea large body of water completely or partly surrounded by land

seacoast land lying next to a sea or ocean

sea level position on land level with surface of nearby ocean or sea

sound body of water between a coastline and one or more islands off the coast

source (of a river) place where a river or stream begins, often in highlands

strait narrow stretch of water joining two larger bodies of water

tributary small river or stream that flows into a larger river or stream; a branch of the river

upstream direction opposite the flow of a river; toward the source of a river or stream

valley area of low land between hills or mountains

volcano mountain created as liquid rock or ash erupts from inside the earth

Tools of the Historian

A historian is a person who studies and writes about people and events of the past. Historians find out how people lived, what happened to them, and what happened around them. They look for the reasons behind events and study the effects of events.

Have you ever wondered if you could be a historian? To answer that question, you will need to find out how history is researched and written. Historians use a number of skills to research and organize information. You can learn about these skills in the next few pages. As you study this textbook, you will see that the sections listed below will help you understand world history:

Scientists looking ▶ for evidence of past civilizations

Digging Up The Past

Historians depend on the work of archaeologists. Archaeologists are scientists who unearth the remains of the past.

What Do Archaeologists Study?
- Human and animal bones, seeds, trees
- Pottery, tools, weapons
- Mounds, pits, canals

▲ Prehistoric pottery

How Do They Gather Data?
- Surveys on foot
- Photographs taken from airplanes or satellites
- Ground-penetrating radar
- Plot locations on maps
- Dig for evidence with tools from heavy equipment to shovels
- Sonar scanning to find underwater objects

How Do They Interpret Findings?
- Organize artifacts into groups based on similarities
- Compare objects in relation to other objects
- Look for evidence of changes over a period of time
- Date once-living objects by measuring carbon-14 levels
- Use microscopic and biological tests to date objects

◀ Carbon-14 dating

Do Your Own Digging

Research the library and Internet to find information on two archaeological diggings, one past and the other, very recent. Compare and contrast the methods used in each digging. What changes do you notice in tools archaeologists have used over time?

Measuring Time

Historical and Social Sciences Analysis Skills

Chronological and Spatial Thinking

CS1. Students explain how major events are related to one another in time.

CS2. Students construct various time lines of key events, people, and periods of the historical era they are studying.

• •

Calendars Historians rely on *calendars,* or dating systems, to measure time. Cultures throughout the world have developed different calendars based on important events in their history. Western nations begin their calendar on the year in which Jesus was thought to have been born. The Jewish calendar begins about 3,760 years before the Christian calendar. This is the time when Jewish tradition says the world was created. Muslims date their calendar from the time their first leader, Muhammad, left the city of Makkah for Madinah. This was A.D. 622 in the Christian calendar.

▲ About A.D. 500, a Christian monk, or religious person, developed the Western way of dating events.

The dates in this book are based on the Western calendar. In the Western calendar, the years before the birth of Jesus are known as "B.C.," or "before Christ." The years after are called "A.D.," or *anno Domini.* This phrase comes from the Latin language and means "in the year of the Lord."

Dating Events To date events before the birth of Christ, or "B.C.," historians count backwards from A.D. 1. There is no year "0." The year before A.D. 1 is 1 B.C. (Notice that "A.D." is written before the date, while "B.C." is written following the date.) Therefore, a date in the 100 years before the birth of Christ lies between 100 B.C. and A.D. 1.

To date events after the birth of Christ, or "A.D.," historians count forward, starting at A.D. 1. A date in the first 100 years after the birth of Christ is between A.D. 1 and A.D. 100.

◀ A people called the Minoans made this stone calendar.

Dating Archaeological Finds One of the most important and difficult jobs for archaeologists is dating the artifacts that they find. Artifacts include a variety of objects made by people, such as weapons, tools, or pottery. The earliest artifacts are pieces of hard rock that were chipped into cutting or digging tools or into weapons.

How do archaeologists determine the age of these artifacts? Early scientists correctly assumed that artifacts buried more deeply in the ground are older than those closer to the surface. In most cases, that observation is still true today.

Another way that archaeologists date artifacts is by using trees. Each year, trees form a new growth ring. Scientists count the number of rings in a wooden object, such as a house beam, and compared the pattern with the rings of a tree whose age they knew. In that way, they can identify dates as far back as 3,000 years.

In 1946 an American scientist named Willard Frank Libby discovered that all living things contain a radioactive element called carbon 14. After plants, animals, and humans die, the carbon 14 gradually disappears. By measuring how much carbon 14 a skeleton or the remains of a wooden boat contain today, scientists can estimate how old an object is. This method is called radiocarbon dating.

Radiocarbon dating, however, is only accurate for dating objects that are no more than about 50,000 years old. Another method—thermoluminescence (THUHR • moh • LOO • muh • NEH • suhns) dating—helps scientists to make more precise measurements back to 200,000 years. This method dates an object by measuring the light given off by particles trapped in the soil surrounding the artifact or fossil.

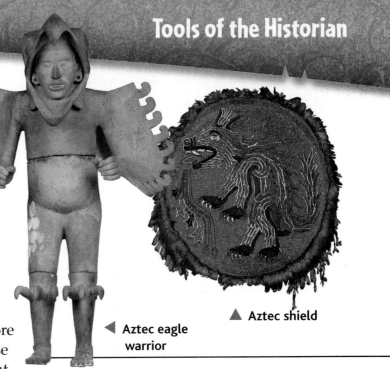

◀ **Aztec eagle warrior**

▲ **Aztec shield**

New methods for analyzing remains—such as blood, hair, and plant tissues left on rocks, tools, and weapons—give archaeologists still more information. Scientists have discovered that blood molecules can survive millions of years. This discovery can tell us how some tools were used and the types of animals that hunters killed. DNA is also providing new data. By analyzing the remains of plants on stone tools, for example, scientists can find out more about early farming.

Although scientists have developed many methods to measure the age of artifacts, what we know about the past will continue to change as new information and new methods of dating are discovered.

Thinking Like a Historian

1. **Identify** What do "B.C." and "A.D." mean? How are they used?

2. **Dating Artifacts** Why is it important to identify the dates of artifacts?

3. **Comparing and Contrasting** As you read, use the Internet to find out the current year in the calendars mentioned in your text. Why are calendars different from culture to culture?

Organizing Time

Historical and Social Sciences Analysis Skills

Chronological and Spatial Thinking

CS1. Students explain how major events are related to one another in time.

CS2. Students construct various time lines of key events, people, and periods of the historical era they are studying.

Periods of History Historians divide history into blocks of time known as *periods,* or *eras.* For example, a period of 10 years is called a *decade.* A period of 100 years is known as a *century.* Centuries are grouped into even longer time periods, which are given names.

The first of these long periods is called *Prehistory.* Prehistory refers to the time before people developed writing, about 5,500 years ago. This is followed by the period known as *Ancient History,* ending c. A.D. 500. (c., or *circa,* means "about"). Historians call the next thousand years the *Middle Ages,* or the medieval

◀ Tools made by prehistoric people

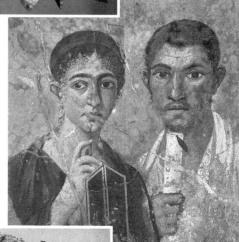

▲ A young couple of ancient Rome

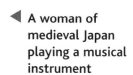

◀ A woman of medieval Japan playing a musical instrument

◀ Educated Europeans of the early modern period discussing new ideas

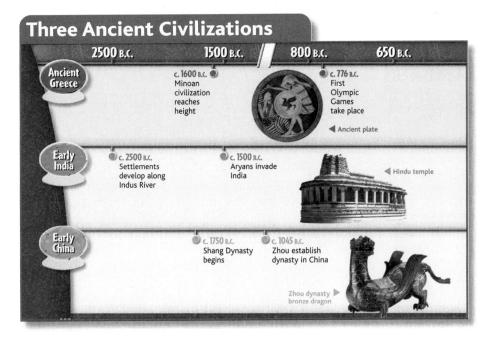

Three Ancient Civilizations

| 2500 B.C. | 1500 B.C. | 800 B.C. | 650 B.C. |

Ancient Greece

c. 1600 B.C.
Minoan civilization reaches height

c. 776 B.C.
First Olympic Games take place

◀ Ancient plate

Early India

c. 2500 B.C.
Settlements develop along Indus River

c. 1500 B.C.
Aryans invade India

Hindu temple ▶

Early China

c. 1750 B.C.
Shang Dynasty begins

c. 1045 B.C.
Zhou establish dynasty in China

Zhou dynasty ▶
bronze dragon

A time line also labels historical events. Each event on the time line appears beside the date when the event took place. Sometimes events and their dates are shown on a single time line. In other cases, two or more time lines are stacked one on top of the other. These are called multilevel time lines. They help you to compare events in different places at certain periods of time. For example, the multilevel time line on this page shows events in the three great ancient civilizations of Greece, India, and China during the period from 2500 B.C. to 650 B.C. The skill lesson "Reading a Time Line" on page 533 will help you learn to work with time lines.

period. After that, from c.1500, *Modern History* begins and continues to the present day. In this book, you will study history from prehistory to the end of the ancient period.

What Is a Time Line? Which came first: the American Civil War or World War II? Did the train come before or after the invention of the airplane? In studying the past, historians focus on *chronology*, or the order of dates in which events happened.

You might be wondering how to make sense of the flow of dates and events. An easy way is to use or make a time line. A *time line* is a diagram that shows the order of events within a period of time.

Most time lines are divided into sections in which the years are evenly spaced. In some cases, however, a spread of time may be too long to show all of the years in even spaces. To save space, a period of time may be omitted from the time line. Where this happens, a slanted or jagged line appears on the time line to show a break in the even spacing of events. For example, the time line above shows a break between 1500 B.C. and 800 B.C.

Thinking Like a Historian

1. **Reading a Time Line** Look over the time line above to get an idea of what a time line shows. What is the title? When does it begin and end? What two features make this time line different from many other time lines? Why are they used?

2. **Understanding a Time Line** Why do you think the dates on the time line are marked with a "c."?

3. **Making a Time Line** Create a time line using the terms B.M.B. (before my birth) and A.M.B. (after my birth). Fill in the time line with five key events that happened before and after you were born. Illustrate the time line with copies of photos from your family album.

Historical and Social Sciences Analysis Skills

Chronological and Spatial Thinking

CS3. Students use a variety of maps and documents to identify physical and cultural features of neighborhoods, cities, states, and countries and to explain the historical migration of people, expansion, and disintegration of empires, and the growth of economic systems.

Geography is the study of the earth and its physical features. In this text, you will discover how geography has shaped the course of events in world history. Sometimes the study of geography is broken down into five themes. *The Five Themes of Geography* are:

- **location** (Where is it?)
- **place** (What is it like?)
- **human/environment interaction** (What is the relationship between people and their surroundings?)
- **movement** (How do people in one area relate to people in other areas?)
- **region** (What common features bring geographical areas together?)

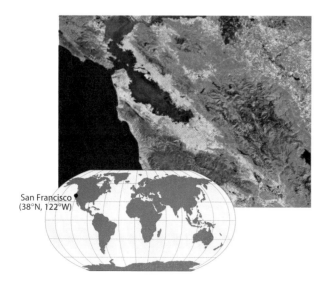

San Francisco
(38°N, 122°W)

Location

"Where is it?" In using geography, historians first look at where a place is located. Every place has an absolute location and a relative location. *Absolute location* refers to the exact spot of a place on the earth's surface. For example, the city of San Francisco, California, is located at one place and one place only. No other place on Earth has exactly the same location.

Relative location tells where a place is, compared with one or more other places. San Francisco is northwest of Los Angeles and southwest of Seattle. Knowing a place's relative location may help a historian understand how it was settled and how its culture developed. For example, people in California have settled in coastal areas and valleys because inland areas have many mountains or deserts. They also have turned to the sea for food and trade.

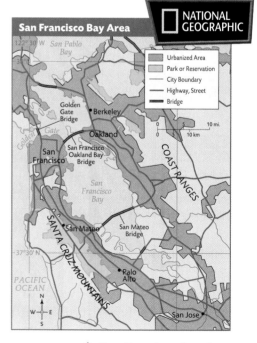

▲ San Francisco Bay Area

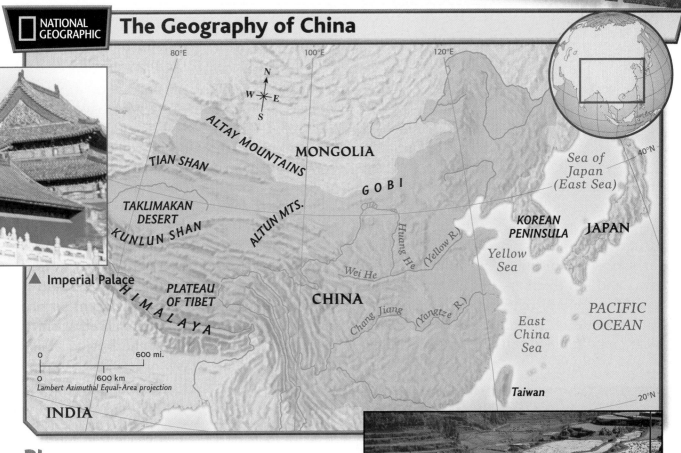

NATIONAL GEOGRAPHIC

The Geography of China

▲ Imperial Palace

Place

"What is it like?" *Place* describes all of the characteristics that give an area its own special quality. These can be physical features, such as mountains, waterways, climate, and plant or animal life. Places can also be described by human characteristics, such as language, religion, and architecture. For example, rivers, deserts, and mountains helped shape the civilization of China. Under rulers known as emperors, the Chinese built grand palaces and temples.

Human/Environment Interaction

"What is the relationship between people and their surroundings?" Landforms, waterways, climate, and natural resources all have helped or hindered human activities.

▲ Growing rice in China

People have responded to their environment, or natural surroundings, in different ways. Sometimes they have adjusted to it. For example, people throughout history have worn light clothing in hot places. At other times, people have changed their environment to meet their needs. They have irrigated, or brought water to dry land, so they could grow crops, or they have built terraces in mountain areas to hold water for growing crops such as rice.

Movement

"How do people in one area affect people in other areas?" Historians answer this question with the theme of *movement*. Throughout history, people, ideas, goods, and information have moved from place to place. Transportation—the movement of people and goods—has allowed people to use products made in places far away. This has increased the exchange of ideas and cultures. Communication—the movement of ideas and information—has allowed people to find out about other parts of the world. Today people receive almost instant communication by radio, television, and computer.

The movement of people to different places is called migration. Why have people migrated throughout history? Some have been forced to move because of wars, famine, or enslavement. Others have chosen to move to seek a better life. During the A.D. 400s, various groups of Germanic peoples invaded the Roman Empire. They were pushed out of their lands by other groups. At the same time, they were drawn to Rome's fertile fields, milder climate, and highly advanced civilization. The Germanic invasions led to the fall of the Roman Empire. The invaders set up kingdoms in Roman territory.

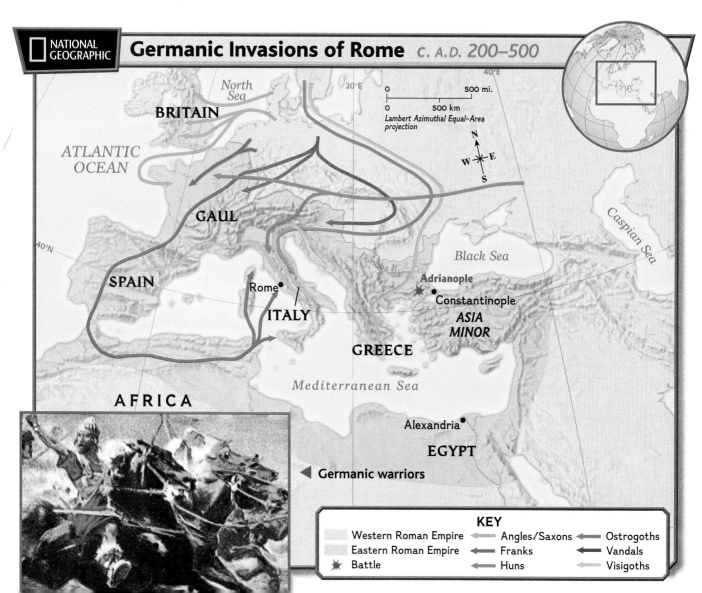

NATIONAL GEOGRAPHIC

Germanic Invasions of Rome *C. A.D.* **200–500**

0 — 500 mi.
0 — 500 km
Lambert Azimuthal Equal-Area projection

North Sea

BRITAIN

ATLANTIC OCEAN

GAUL

SPAIN

Rome

ITALY

AFRICA

Danube R.

Black Sea

Adrianople

Constantinople

ASIA MINOR

GREECE

Mediterranean Sea

Alexandria

EGYPT

Caspian Sea

◀ Germanic warriors

KEY

Western Roman Empire	⬅ Angles/Saxons	⬅ Ostrogoths
Eastern Roman Empire	⬅ Franks	⬅ Vandals
✳ Battle	⬅ Huns	⬅ Visigoths

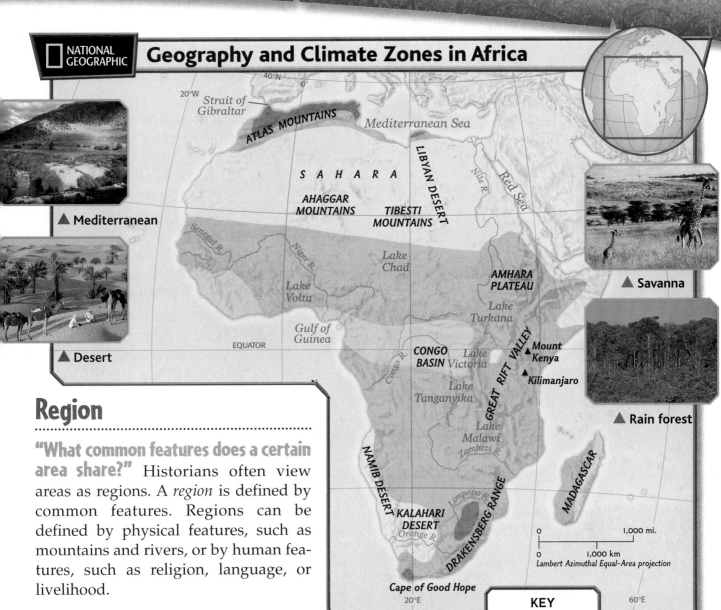

NATIONAL GEOGRAPHIC
Geography and Climate Zones in Africa

▲ Mediterranean

▲ Desert

40°N
20°W
0°
Strait of Gibraltar
ATLAS MOUNTAINS
Mediterranean Sea
SAHARA
LIBYAN DESERT
AHAGGAR MOUNTAINS
TIBESTI MOUNTAINS
Nile R.
Red Sea
Senegal R.
Niger R.
Lake Chad
AMHARA PLATEAU
Lake Volta
Lake Turkana
Gulf of Guinea
EQUATOR
Congo R.
CONGO BASIN
Lake Victoria
Mount Kenya
Kilimanjaro
GREAT RIFT VALLEY
Lake Tanganyika
Lake Malawi
Zambezi R.
NAMIB DESERT
Limpopo R.
MADAGASCAR
DRAKENSBERG RANGE
KALAHARI DESERT
Orange R.
Cape of Good Hope
20°E
60°E

▲ Savanna

▲ Rain forest

0   1,000 mi.
0   1,000 km
Lambert Azimuthal Equal-Area projection

KEY
Desert
Mediterranean
Rain forest
Savanna

Region

"What common features does a certain area share?" Historians often view areas as regions. A *region* is defined by common features. Regions can be defined by physical features, such as mountains and rivers, or by human features, such as religion, language, or livelihood.

Six Essential Elements

Recently geographers have broken down the study of geography into *Six Essential Elements*. These elements are:
- The World in Spatial Terms
- Places and Regions
- Physical Systems
- Human Systems
- Environment and Society
- The Uses of Geography

You will learn about these elements in the Geography Handbook on pages 78–79. Knowing them will help you in your study of history.

Thinking Like a Historian

1. **Identifying** How are absolute location and relative location different?

2. **Analyzing Themes** What characteristics do geographers use to describe a place?

3. **Linking History and Geography** Make a list of the Five Themes of Geography. Under each theme, explain how you think geography has shaped the history of your community.

What Is a Historical Atlas?

Historical and Social Sciences Analysis Skills

Chronological and Spatial Thinking

CS3. Students should use a variety of maps and documents to identify physical and cultural features of neighborhoods, cities, states, and countries and to explain the historical migration of people, expansion and disintegration of empires, and the growth of economic systems.

• •

Historical Maps An *atlas* is a book of maps showing different parts of the world. A *historical atlas* has maps showing different parts of the world at different periods of history. Maps that show political events, such as invasions, battles, and boundary changes, are called *historical maps.* The maps shown below are both examples of historical maps.

Some historical maps show how territories in a certain part of the world changed over time. One map below shows the areas of Europe, Asia, and Africa ruled by Alexander the Great in 323 B.C. The other map shows the same region as it looks today. The maps help you compare historical changes in this region from ancient times to today.

In the larger map, Alexander's empire stretches from the eastern Mediterranean Sea in the west to the Indus River in the east. There are no political borders to show the territorial spread of empires and countries. Instead, other historical details are shown. For example, the different arrows on the larger map represent the movement of Alexander's armies as they conquered new lands. On the smaller map, lines show the modern boundaries of countries in the same region today.

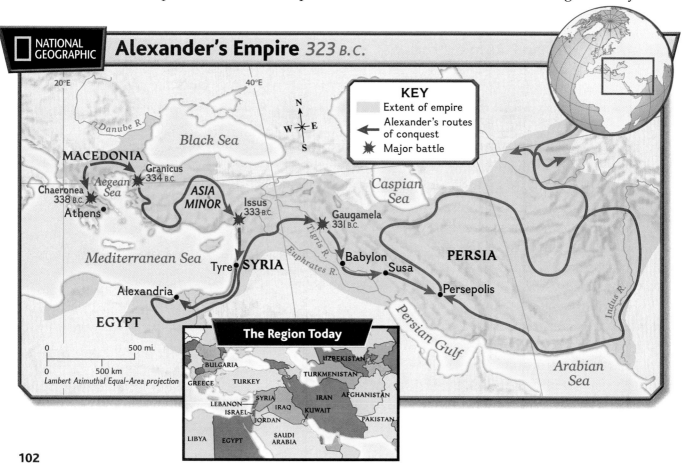

NATIONAL GEOGRAPHIC

Alexander's Empire *323 B.C.*

KEY
- Extent of empire
- ← Alexander's routes of conquest
- ✹ Major battle

MACEDONIA
Granicus 334 B.C.
Chaeronea 338 B.C.
Athens
Aegean Sea
ASIA MINOR
Issus 333 B.C.
Gaugamela 331 B.C.
Danube R.
Black Sea
Caspian Sea
Mediterranean Sea
Tyre • SYRIA
Alexandria
EGYPT
Babylon
Susa
Persepolis
PERSIA
Tigris R.
Euphrates R.
Persian Gulf
Indus R.
Arabian Sea

0 — 500 mi.
0 — 500 km
Lambert Azimuthal Equal-Area projection

The Region Today

BULGARIA
GREECE
TURKEY
LEBANON
ISRAEL
SYRIA
JORDAN
IRAQ
LIBYA
EGYPT
SAUDI ARABIA
KUWAIT
IRAN
UZBEKISTAN
TURKMENISTAN
AFGHANISTAN
PAKISTAN

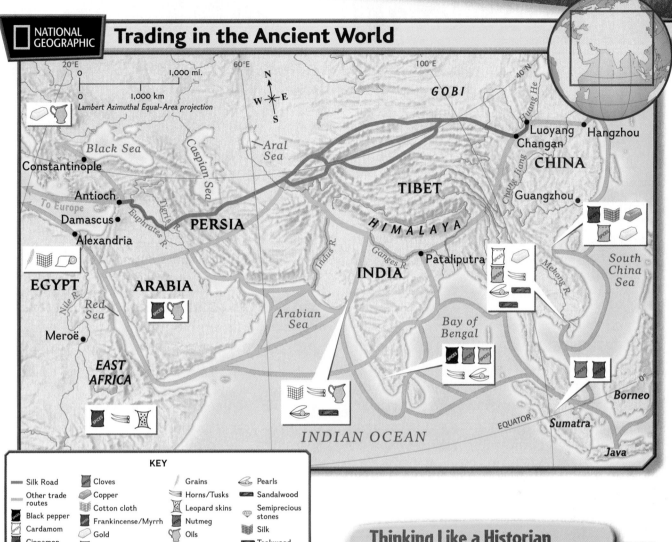

NATIONAL GEOGRAPHIC **Trading in the Ancient World**

KEY

- Silk Road
- Other trade routes
- Black pepper
- Cardamom
- Cinnamon
- Cloves
- Copper
- Cotton cloth
- Frankincense/Myrrh
- Gold
- Ginger
- Grains
- Horns/Tusks
- Leopard skins
- Nutmeg
- Oils
- Papyrus
- Pearls
- Sandalwood
- Semiprecious stones
- Silk
- Teakwood

Historical Routes On some maps, however, lines may show *historical routes.* These are roads, trails, or courses over which people, animals, vehicles, and goods have traveled in different periods of history. Such transportation and communication routes are often colored in order to make the map easier to read. On the map above, the purple line shows the Silk Road, the ancient trading route that linked parts of Asia and Europe.

On maps showing historical routes, the key gives important clues to what information is shown on the maps. This map's key shows different goods traded throughout the ancient world.

Thinking Like a Historian

1. **Comparing Maps** Alexander the Great's empire included many different territories in Europe, Asia, and Africa. In what territory was the city of Persepolis located? What present-day country covers this area today?

2. **Reading a Map Key** Look at the map of trading in the ancient world. What goods came from the southern part of India? How were goods carried from one place to another place in ancient times?

3. **Analyzing Maps** Select any chapter in your textbook. List the titles of the maps found in the particular chapter you have chosen. Beside each map's title, state what kind of symbols are used in each map key and what they represent.

How Does a Historian Work?

▲ Students studying history

Asking Questions About the Past Historians are like detectives. They look for evidence to solve problems about the past. Historians begin by asking questions such as: Why did two particular countries go to war? What effect did their fighting have on peoples' lives? Such questions help historians focus on historical problems. By asking questions, historians can better identify the issues. They also can determine how and why events happened and what the effects of these events were.

Is It Fact or Opinion? Historical sources may contain facts and opinions. A *fact* can be proved, or observed; an *opinion,* on the other hand, is a personal belief or conclusion. We often hear facts and opinions mixed in everyday conversation—in advertising, in political debate, and in historical sources. Although some opinions can be supported by facts, in an argument they do not carry as much weight as facts.

Sources, such as letters, diaries, and speeches express personal views. This means they state what a person thinks about another person or an event. As a result, the

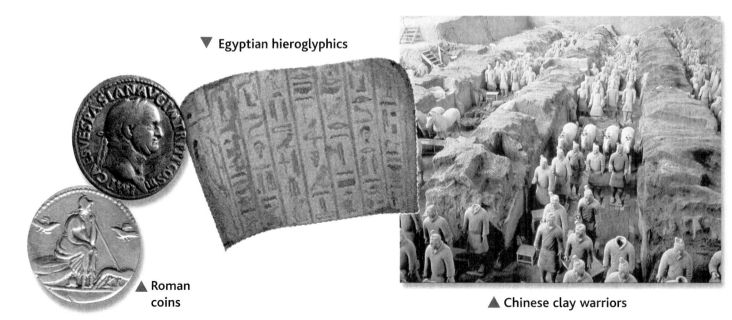

▼ Egyptian hieroglyphics

▲ Roman coins

▲ Chinese clay warriors

▼ Romulus and Remus

▲ The city of Rome at the height of the Roman Empire

historian must be able to separate facts from opinions. In other words, separating known truth about something from what people say about it. This skill is important because it helps the historian decide whether or not the information is accurate and the historical source can be trusted.

Is It Relevant? Historians often must sift through a lot of information to find what they need. As a result, they must determine whether or not each piece of evidence is *relevant*. This means selecting only the data that helps answer their research questions. Relevant information applies directly to the topic or purpose that the historian has chosen. For example, if you are researching family life in ancient Rome, information about marriage and children would be relevant information. A description of Roman government or trade would not be relevant because it does not explain the type of families found in the Roman Empire.

Is It Important? In deciding whether information is relevant, historians also must figure out what information is essential, or important, and what is incidental, or unimportant. The fact that the Egyptian female ruler Hatshepsut was beautiful may or may not have had any effect on Egypt's foreign trade. However, the fact that the Egyptian ruler Tutankhamen came to the throne at 10 years of age more than likely affected his ability to rule Egypt.

Is There Supporting Evidence? Another important task of the historian is to determine whether information in a source is verifiable. This means the historian must check to see if the information can be proved by other evidence already known to be truthful.

Thinking Like a Historian

Fact or Opinion? Suppose you were an historian researching the history of Rome. You discovered this information about the founding of the city. What in this account might be fact? What might be opinion?

Romulus and his twin brother Remus founded Rome around 753 B.C. Quarrels over the kingship of Rome led to the death of Remus. Romulus populated Rome with people fleeing harsh rule everywhere. After a long reign, the proud Romulus vanished in a thunderstorm and became the god Quirinus.

How Does a Historian Work?

Where's the Evidence Found?

Historians generally find evidence in primary sources and secondary sources. *Primary sources* are first-hand pieces of evidence from people who saw or experienced the events described. They include written documents, such as letters, diaries, and official records. They also include spoken interviews, as well as objects such as photos, paintings, clothing, and tools. The skill "Analyzing Primary Source Documents" on page 538 will give you a chance to work with written primary sources.

Secondary sources are often created long *after* the events. Secondary sources are partially based on primary sources. They include biographies, encyclopedias, and history books—even this textbook!

Historians study secondary sources for background information and for a larger view of an event. However, to get new evidence, historians must turn to the first-hand information found only in primary sources.

▲ Scientist studying Dead Sea Scrolls from southwest Asia

How Are Sources Examined?

Historians *analyze*, or examine, primary and secondary sources. First, they determine who the author of a source is and what can be known about the author. Then historians consider *where* and *when* the source was created. Another important question asked by historians is *why* a source was created. In what context, or setting, did it appear? Was it a letter meant to be kept secret? Was it a government document published for all citizens to read? Historians also ask: To what audience was the source addressed? What is known about this audience? By answering these questions, historians gain insights into the people and events behind the source.

◀ Necklace, early India

▲ Head of a shovel, early China

▲ Ruins of Mayan temple in Central America

Can the Sources Be Trusted?

Historians examine sources for *credibility*, or truthfulness. This is because each source reflects a *point of view*, or a general attitude about people and life. The creator of a source has a point of view that selects what events were important and which people were key players. A point of view is the particular focus a person takes when considering a problem or situation.

Being Aware of Bias

Sometimes a writer's point of view is expressed as a *bias*, or an unreasoned judgment about people and events. A bias is a one-sided, unexamined view. A person who is biased has made a judgment about an event, a person, or a group without really considering the many parts of the situation. Biased speakers and writers can be detected in various ways. Their statements use emotional words like *stupid*, *ignorant*, and *impossible*, or *great*, and *wonderful*. They also tend to use words that allow no exceptions, like *always* and *never*.

Finding a Balance

Historians seek to uncover point of view and bias in historical documents and articles. They look for the ideas and facts that the author of a source emphasizes. They also think about what ideas and facts the author might be leaving out.

To make sense of the past, historians must weigh the known evidence and try to figure out what the facts are. Then they need to bring the facts together to answer the questions that interest them. In doing this, they must use their judgment. This means their own viewpoints come into play.

Historians try to be aware of point of view and bias both in their sources and in themselves. Therefore, they check new sources and their own ideas against sources already known to be trustworthy. To get a balanced picture, historians study documents that present other points of view.

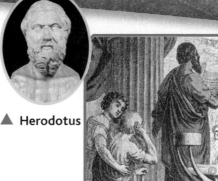

▲ Herodotus

▲ Herodotus reading to a crowd

Thinking Like a Historian

The famous Greek historian Herodotus (hih·RAH·duh·tuhs) wrote *History of the Persian Wars*. This is thought to be the first real history in Western civilization. Herodotus described the conflict between the Greeks and the Persians as one between freedom and dictatorship. Here he tells of the Persian ruler's address to Persian nobles:

"And truly I have pondered upon this, until at last I have found out a way whereby we may at once win glory, and likewise get possession of a land which is as large and as rich as our own . . . while at the same time we obtain satisfaction and revenge . . . My intent is to . . . march an army through Europe against Greece, that thereby I may obtain vengeance from the Athenians from the wrongs committed by them against the Persians and against my father."

—Herodotus,
The Persian Wars, *Book VII*

Understanding Evidence Herodotus's account is considered a primary source about the Persian Wars. Why? Would an account of the Persian Wars written by a modern historian also be considered a primary source? Explain.

Making Sense of the Past

Historical and Social Sciences Analysis Skills

Historical Interpretation

HI1. Students explain the central issues and problems from the past, placing people and events in a matrix of time and place.

HI2. Students understand and distinguish cause, effect, sequence, and correlation in historical events, including the long- and short-term casual relations.

HI3. Students explain the sources of historical continuity and how the combination of ideas and events explains the emergence of new patterns.

● ●

Interpreting History You probably have heard the phrase "The facts do not speak for themselves." This means that bits and pieces of information by themselves do not reveal the truth. Like pieces of a puzzle, they have to be put together by people using their reason.

In the same way, historians must use their knowledge to give historical facts (dates, names, places and events) meaning and put them in an order that people can easily understand. Historians piece together the credible evidence and draw conclusions. They use their own thinking and knowledge of the past to *interpret*, or explain, the meaning of events. Then, they present their findings in a clear, readable, and convincing form.

Providing a Setting Historians look at people and events of history in the matrix, or setting, of time and space. They also connect historical people and events to central issues. Central issues are main ideas, such as war and peace, the rise of scientific inventions, and the forms of governments and societies. Through these links, historians can grasp the whole picture or story.

Historians also sequence events, or place events in the order in which they occurred. Sequencing helps historians organize information. From the pattern of the data, they can determine how events are related to each other. The relationship among these events can help historians identify other important ideas, such as historical importance and cause and effect.

Chinese students taking an exam ▶

◀ **Hindu temple**

The Decline of Rome

Weak Roman Government
• Dishonest government officials provide poor leadership.

Social Problems
• Famine and disease spread throughout the empire.

Declining Economy
• Income and wages fall.
• Wealthy fail to pay taxes.

Reform Fails and Rome Divides in Two
• Government fails to keep order.
• Violence and tension increase.
• Diocletian divides the empire.

Eastern Roman Empire
• Constantinople becomes the new capital.
• The empire survives attacks and prospers.

Western Roman Empire
• Numerous attacks threaten the empire.
• Territory is slowly lost to invaders.

Byzantine Empire
• This empire is created from the Eastern Roman Empire and lasts nearly 1,000 years.

Rome Falls
• The city of Rome falls in A.D. 476.
• The Western Roman Empire is divided into Germanic kingdoms by A.D. 550.

Cause and Effect Historical events are linked by cause and effect. A *cause* is what makes an event happen. The event that happens as a result of the cause is known as an *effect*. Historians look for cause-and-effect links to explain *why* events happen.

Usually, one event is produced by many causes. Similarly, one event often produces several different effects. These cause-and-effect links form what is called a *cause-and-effect chain*. Because many historical events are related, cause-and-effect chains can become very long and include events over a long period of time. The chart above shows such a chain of events.

Change and Continuity Historians look at the differences and similarities of events. History is a story of change. Therefore, historians study how events greatly differ from each other. Some historical changes have occurred quickly. For example, in a few short years during the 330s B.C., Alexander the Great conquered a huge empire that covered parts of Europe, Africa, and Asia. Other changes, such as the spread of Christianity in the Roman Empire, took place more slowly.

While looking at historical changes, historians also search for continuity, or the unbroken patterns in history. They study how traditions and concerns link people across time and place. For example, life in India today is affected by the Hindu religion, which is more than 3,000 years old. Also, passing exams was as important to students in early China as it is to students today.

Thinking Like a Historian

1. **Recognizing Cause and Effect** Study the cause-and-effect chart on this page. What were three major causes of Rome's decline? What were two important effects of Rome's decline upon history?

2. **Applying Cause and Effect** Read an account of a recent event in your community as reported in a local newspaper. Determine at least one cause and effect of that event. Show the cause-and-effect relationship in a chart.

Making Sense of the Past

Historical and Social Sciences Analysis Skills

Historical Interpretation

HI4. Students recognize the role of chance, oversight, and error in history.

HI5. Students recognize that interpretations of history are subject to change as new information is uncovered.

HI6. Students interpret basic indicators of economic performance and conduct cost-benefit analyses of economic and political issues.

▲ Ruins of the walls of Great Zimbabwe

◄ Alexander the Great on his horse

Error and Chance in History History often has been made by chance, oversight, or error. For example, Christopher Columbus believed that his voyage in 1492 had brought him to the East Indies, the islands off the coast of Asia. Today the Caribbean islands are often called the West Indies. Also, the Native Americans whom Columbus met came to be called Indians.

Explorations after Columbus, however, made it clear that Columbus had not reached Asia at all. He had found a part of the globe unknown to Europeans, Asians, and Africans. In the following years, the Spanish explored most of the Caribbean region. In time their voyages led to the rise of the Spanish Empire in the Americas.

Mistakes have not only shaped historical events. They also have influenced peoples' understanding of the past. For example, Portuguese traders in the 1500s were the first Europeans to see the vast stone ruins of Great Zimbabwe in south central Africa. They believed they had found the fabled capital of the Queen of Sheba mentioned in the Bible. Later travelers came to the conclusion that the ruins were the work of Egyptians or Phoenicians. These incorrect views were held

for nearly 400 years. Then, British archaeologists studying the ruins in the early 1900s proved that the ruins were built by a powerful African civilization. The people of this civilization were the ancestors of the Shona, a group that live in the country of Zimbabwe today.

Different Interpretations History is often called an ongoing discussion about the past. Historians discuss what the facts are. They also argue about how to interpret the facts. What causes these differences?

Despite the efforts of the best minds, some facts are ambiguous, or not very clear to interpret. What the facts mean often depends on the historian's judgment. In addition, historians have different values and come to the evidence with different points of view. As a result, historians often arrive at different interpretations of the same event. For example, some historians see Alexander the Great as a skilled leader who brought order to the lands he conquered; others see Alexander as brave, but cruel and reckless. It is, therefore, important to be able to carefully analyze a historian's interpretation.

The discussion among historians also continues because historians find new evidence that leads them to question old interpretations. Sometimes historians take a new look at existing evidence and see things that others have ignored. As they do so, they may correct an earlier historian's mistake or explain events differently.

The questions that historians ask reflect the issues of the times in which they live. As a result, there is never a final, complete version of history that satisfies everyone. There will always be new questions to ask of the past, and historians will always ask these questions while they are writing history.

Economics and History Many historians investigate economies, or the ways societies produce, sell, and buy goods. Statistics, or mathematical data, are scarce for the economies of long ago. However, statistics for modern economies are abundant and provide historians with much information. Economists, or scientists who study economies, have developed economic indicators to measure a modern economy's performance.

Economic indicators are statistics that tell how well an economy is doing and how well the economy is going to do in the future. They include the number of jobless, the rate at which prices rise over periods of time, and the amount of goods and services that are made and sold.

Historians also analyze the costs and benefits of economic and political issues. This analysis requires figuring out the costs of any historical action and comparing it with the benefits of that action.

▲ **Roman soldiers**

Thinking Like a Historian

The Growth of Rome

Rome's armies were victorious wherever they went. They brought Roman ideas and practices to new places. Yet problems were building at home. The use of enslaved labor from conquered lands hurt farmers. Dishonest officials stole money, and the gap between rich and poor grew. Cities became overcrowded and dangerous.

Read the paragraph above about the growth of Rome. Then create a table like the one below. In the left column, write the costs brought by Rome's growth. In the right column, write the benefits that came with this growth.

Costs	Benefits
1	1
2	2
3	3
4	4

Links Across Time

Historical and Social Sciences Analysis Skills

Chronological and Spatial Thinking

CS1. Students explain how major events are related to one another in time.

▲ Fighting today between Palestinians and Israelis

Unit 1 Mesopotamia, Egypt, and Israel

About 3500 B.C., some of the world's earliest civilizations developed in Southwest Asia and North Africa. For centuries, people in these regions have fought over scarce land and water. Religious and ethnic differences also have led to wars.

Today, one of the fiercest and longest conflicts has been between Palestinian Arabs and Israelis. Although many Palestinian Arabs and Israelis support peace efforts, hatred and fears run deep on both sides.

▼ Ancient warriors attack a walled city

India, China, and America

During ancient times, powerful trading empires arose in India, China, and the Americas. These empires united a variety of peoples and spread new ideas and products. In early China, a powerful ruler began the building of the Great Wall to keep out attackers. Today, modern China is building the Three Gorges Dam to provide electric power for its growing cities.

Great Wall of China ▶

Three Gorges Dam ▲

Unit 3 **The Greeks and the Romans**

Ancient Greece and Rome helped lay the foundations of Western civilization. Their peoples admired the deeds of heroes. The ancient Greeks held the first Olympic games about 776 B.C. Today the modern Olympics draw athletes from all over the world.

▼ **Racers in modern Olympics**

▼ **Ancient Greek athletes**

Thinking Like a Historian

As you read *Journey Across Time: Ancient Civilizations*, notice how the past affects the present. When you begin each unit, collect newspaper or magazine articles about a current event from the area you are studying. Then, after completing each unit, write down how you think a past event in that region is related to the current event.

Unit 1

Mesopotamia, Egypt, and Israel

Why It's Important

Each civilization that you will study in this unit made important contributions to history.

- The Mesopotamians developed the world's first law codes.
- Egyptians built the pyramids and invented papyrus—the world's first paper.
- Israelite scripture influenced religions in Europe and Asia.

8000 B.C.   **5000 B.C.**   **2000 B.C.**

First Civilizations
Chapter 1

c. 8000 B.C.
Farming begins in southwest Asia

c. 3200 B.C.
Sumerians in Mesopotamia develop writing

c. 1790 B.C.
Hammurabi introduces code of laws

Hammurabi stands ▶ before a god

Ancient Egypt & Kush
Chapter 2

c. 5000 B.C.
Hunter-gatherers settle Nile River valley

c. 2540 B.C.
Egyptians complete building of Great Pyramid

c. 1500 B.C.
Queen Hatshepsut becomes pharaoh

◀ Pyramids at Giza, Egypt c. 2540 B.C.

Ancient Israelites
Chapter 3

c. 1800 B.C.
Abraham enters Canaan

◀ Abraham leads Israelites to Canaan

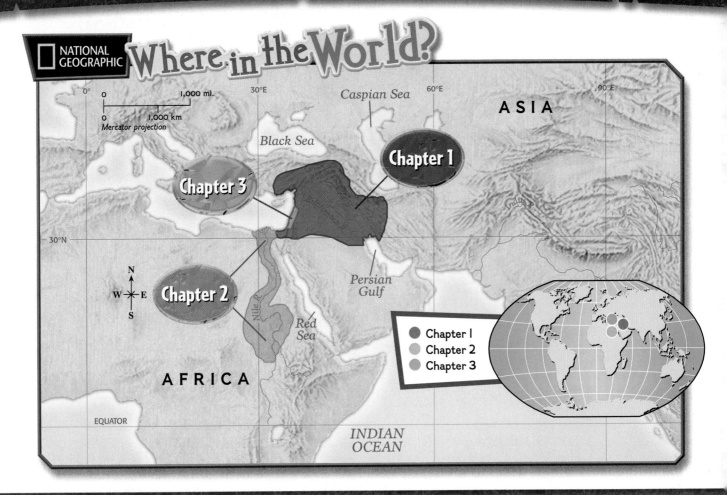

Where in the World?

1,000 mi.
1,000 km
Mercator projection

Caspian Sea

ASIA

Black Sea

Chapter 1

Chapter 3

30°N

N
W — E
S

Chapter 2

Persian
Gulf

Nile R.

Red
Sea

● Chapter 1
● Chapter 2
● Chapter 3

AFRICA

EQUATOR

INDIAN
OCEAN

| 1000 B.C. | 750 B.C. | 500 B.C. | 250 B.C. | A.D. 1 |

c. 744 B.C.
Assyria expands
into Babylon

c. 612 B.C.
Chaldeans capture
Assyrian capital

◄ Hanging gardens of
Babylon c. 600 B.C.

c. 1000 B.C.
Kush breaks
free of Egypt

728 B.C.
Kush
conquers
Egypt

Kushite king Taharqa ►
c. 680 B.C.

c. 1000 B.C.
King David rules Israel

586 B.C.
Chaldeans
capture
Jerusalem

168 B.C. Maccabean revolt

A.D. 70
Romans
destroy temple
in Jerusalem

◄ Solomon's temple,
built c. 950 B.C.

◄ Ancient Jerusalem

115

Unit 1

Places to Locate

Mediterranean Sea

1 Ishtar Gate

See First Civilizations
Chapter 1

2 Sumerian figures

See First Civilizations
Chapter 1

AFRICA

5

3

4

Red
Sea

People to Meet

Ötzi

c. 3300 B.C.
**Iceman found in
the Alps**
Chapter 1, page 129

Hammurabi

Ruled c. 1792–1750 B.C.
Babylonian king
Chapter 1, page 138

Hatshepsut

Ruled c. 1473–1458 B.C.
Egyptian pharaoh
Chapter 2, page 182

ASIA

Caspian Sea

Persian Gulf

3 Egyptian sphinx

See Ancient Egypt and Kush Chapter 2

4 Kushite pyramids

See Ancient Egypt and Kush Chapter 2

5 Western Wall

See Ancient Israelites Chapter 3

①

②

Ramses II

Ruled 1279–1213 B.C.
Egyptian ruler
Chapter 2, page 185

Ruth and Naomi

c. 1100 B.C.
Israelite women
Chapter 3, page 219

King David

Ruled c. 1000–970 B.C.
King of Israel
Chapter 3, page 208

Chapter 1

The First Civilizations

Ruins of a ziggurat in Iraq ▶

Where & When?

3000 B.C.	2000 B.C.	1000 B.C.
c. 3000 B.C. Bronze Age begins	c. 1792 B.C. Hammurabi rules Mesopotamia	612 B.C. Nineveh captured; Assyrian Empire crumbles

The Big Ideas

Section 1 Early Humans

Studying the past helps to understand the present. Scientists who study the past have learned that the earliest humans hunted animals and gathered plants for food. When farming developed, people settled in villages and towns.

Section 2 Mesopotamian Civilization

Religion shapes how culture develops, just as culture shapes how religion develops. In early Mesopotamian civilizations, religion and government were closely linked. Kings created strict laws to govern people.

Section 3 New Empires

Conflict often brings about great change. New empires arose in Mesopotamia around 900 B.C. These civilizations included the Assyrians and the Chaldeans. They used powerful armies and iron weapons to conquer the region.

 View the Chapter 1 video in the Glencoe Video Program.

 **FOLDABLES™ Study Organizer**

Compare and Contrast *Make this foldable to help you compare and contrast the ancient civilizations of Mesopotamia.*

Step 1 *Fold a sheet of paper in half from side to side.*

Fold it so the left edge lies about $\frac{1}{2}$ inch from the right edge.

Step 2 *Turn the paper and fold it into thirds.*

Step 3 *Unfold and cut the top layer only along both folds.*

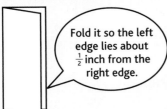 This will make three tabs.

Step 4 *Label as shown.*

The First Civilizations

| Early Humans | Meso-potamia | New Empires |

Reading and Writing
As you read the chapter, write notes under each appropriate tab of your foldable. Keep in mind that you are trying to compare these civilizations.

Reading Skill

1 Learn It!

Before you read, take time to preview the chapter. This will give you a head start on what you are about to learn. Follow the steps below to help you quickly read, or skim, Section 1 on page 123.

2–The **Main Idea** under each main head tells you the main point of what you are about to read.

3–The **Reading Connection** helps you to link what you might already know to what you are about to read.

Early Humans

Main Idea Paleolithic people adapted to their environment and invented many tools to help them survive.

Reading Connection What do you view as the greatest human achievement–sending people to the moon, perhaps, or inventing the computer? Read to learn about the accomplishments of people during the Paleolithic Age.

History is the story of humans . . .

Tools of Discovery

1–Read the main headings in large red type. They show the main topics covered in the section or chapter.

4–Under each main head, read the subheads in blue type. Subheads break down each main topic into smaller topics.

Reading Tip

As you skim, also look at pictures, maps, and charts.

2 Practice It!

Read to Write ⋯⋯
Use each main head, the main ideas, and the subheads in Section 2 of this chapter to create a study outline.

Section 3 New Empires

Skim all of the main heads and main ideas in Section 3 starting on page 142. Then, in small groups, discuss the answers to these questions.

- Which part of this section do you think will be most interesting to you?
- What do you think will be covered in Section 3 that was not covered in Section 2?
- Are there any words in the Main Ideas that you do not know how to pronounce?
- Choose one of the Reading Connection questions to discuss in your group.

Hanging Gardens ▶
of Babylon

3 Apply It!

Skim Section 2 on your own. Write one thing in your notebook that you want to learn by reading this chapter.

Early Humans

History
Social Science Standards

WH6.1 Students describe what is known through archaeological studies of the early physical and cultural development of humankind from the Paleolithic era to the agricultural revolution.

Guide to Reading

Looking Back, Looking Ahead
Today people live in towns and cities of various sizes. Early humans lived by moving from place to place, forming settlements, and exploring different ways to provide for themselves and their families.

Focusing on the Main Ideas
• Paleolithic people adapted to their environment and invented many tools to help them survive.
(page 123)

• In the Neolithic Age, people started farming, building communities, producing goods, and trading.
(page 127)

Locating Places
Jericho (JEHR•ih•KOH)
Çatal Hüyük
 (chah•TAHL hoo•YOOK)

Content Vocabulary
anthropologist
 (AN•thruh•PAH•luh•jihst)
archaeologist
 (AHR•kee•AH•luh•jihst)
artifact (AHR•tih•FAKT)
fossil (FAH•suhl)
nomad (NOH•MAD)
technology (tehk•NAH•luh•jee)
domesticate (duh•MEHS•tih•KAYT)
specialization
 (SPEH•shuh•luh•ZAY•shuhn)

Academic Vocabulary
task
revolution (REH•vuh•LOO•shuhn)

Reading Strategy
Determine Cause and Effect Draw a diagram like the one below. Use it to explain how early humans adapted to their environment.

| Cause: | → | Effect: |
| Cause: | → | Effect: |

NATIONAL GEOGRAPHIC **Where&When?**

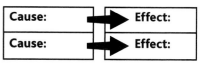

Çatal Hüyük •

• Jericho

| 8000 B.C. | 6000 B.C. | 4000 B.C. | 2000 B.C. |

c. 8000 B.C.
Jericho founded

c. 6700 B.C.
Çatal Hüyük settled

c. 3000 B.C.
Bronze Age begins

WH6.1 Students describe what is known through archaeological studies of the early physical and cultural development of humankind from the Paleolithic era to the agricultural revolution. WH6.1.1 Describe the hunter-gatherer societies, including the development of tools and the use of fire. WH6.1.2 Identify the locations of human communities that populated the major regions of the world and describe how humans adapted to a variety of environments. WH6.2.9 Trace the evolution of language and its written forms.

Early Humans

Main Idea Paleolithic people adapted to their environment and invented many tools to help them survive.

Reading Connection What do you view as the greatest human achievement—sending people to the moon, perhaps, or inventing the computer? Read to learn about the accomplishments of people during the Paleolithic Age.

History is the story of humans in the past. It tells what people did and what happened to them. Historians are people who study and write about the human past. They define history as the period of time that began after people learned to write, about 5,500 years ago. But the story of people really begins in prehistory—the time *before* people developed writing.

Tools of Discovery What we know about the earliest people comes from the things they left behind. Scientists have worked to uncover clues about early human life. **Anthropologists** (AN•thruh•PAH•luh•jihsts) focus on human society. They study how humans developed and how they related to one another. **Archaeologists** (AHR•kee•AH•luh•jihsts) hunt for evidence buried in the ground where settlements might once have been. They dig up and study **artifacts** (AHR•tih•FAKTS)—weapons, tools, and other things made by humans. They also look for **fossils** (FAH•suhls)—traces of plants or animals that have been preserved in rock.

British archaeologists Louis and Mary Leakey and their son Richard are probably the most-famous fossil hunters. Their findings convinced many scientists and anthropologists that the ancestors of human beings first appeared somewhere in East Africa millions of years ago.

▲ Dr. Donald Johanson is shown here in 1982 with the skeletal remains of Lucy, a 3-million-year-old hominid

In the 1930s, Louis and Mary Leakey began digging for fossils in the Olduvai Gorge in Tanzania. Archaeologists know that in certain areas of the world, layers of dirt and rock have been piled up slowly over time by the action of wind and water. If you dig in those places, the deeper you find things, the older they are, because they were buried further back in time. The Olduvai Gorge is very deep, and along its walls are layers of dirt from as far back as 2 million years ago. This made it a very good location to look for fossils.

In the 1940s and 1950s, Louis and Mary found many fossils of hominids. Hominids are creatures that walk on two legs. Human beings are the only type of hominid still alive today. All the others are extinct. Anthropologists think that human beings developed from earlier types of hominids.

In 1959 Mary Leakey discovered the skull of a creature nearly 2 million years old. This showed that hominids lived at least that long ago. In 1974 Donald

Johanson, an American anthropologist from Chicago, made an even more amazing discovery. He unearthed nearly an entire skeleton of a female hominid in Ethiopia. The hominid was nicknamed Lucy and was nearly 3 million years old.

Before Lucy was found, anthropologists thought hominids lived in the open on Africa's plains and used tools to hunt other animals. They thought hominids had begun walking on two legs so they could carry their tools while they hunted. Lucy's remains showed that hominids began walking on two legs long before they used tools.

Scientists' ideas about hominids were changed again in 1992. That year Tim White, an anthropologist from California, uncovered a hominid that was 4.4 million years old. Its teeth and bones showed that hominids had begun walking on two legs while living in Africa's jungles, before they moved out onto Africa's plains.

Based on the work of these and other anthropologists, many scientists today think that the first human beings developed in East Africa. Slowly, over thousands of years, human beings spread out of Africa, probably in search of food and new places to live as their population increased. Gradually, they settled throughout the world.

Who Were the Hunter-Gatherers?

Historians call the prehistoric period of human history the Stone Age. The name comes from the fact that people during this time used stone to make tools and weapons. The earliest part of the period is the Paleolithic or Old Stone Age. *Paleolithic*

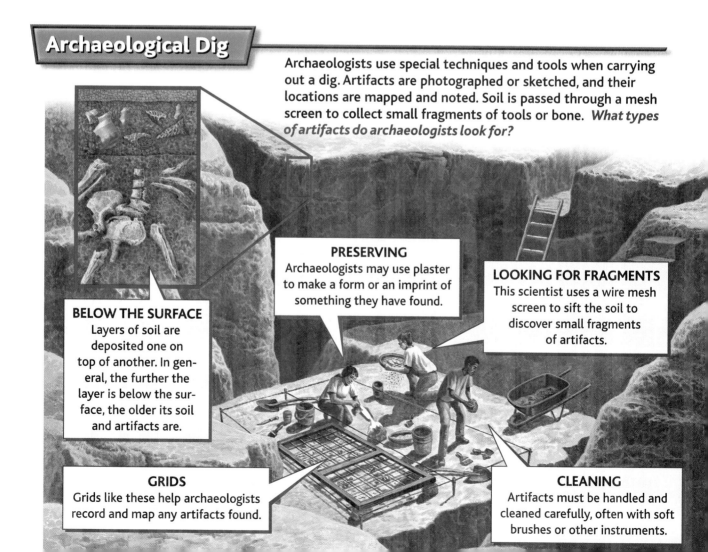

Archaeological Dig

Archaeologists use special techniques and tools when carrying out a dig. Artifacts are photographed or sketched, and their locations are mapped and noted. Soil is passed through a mesh screen to collect small fragments of tools or bone. *What types of artifacts do archaeologists look for?*

BELOW THE SURFACE
Layers of soil are deposited one on top of another. In general, the further the layer is below the surface, the older its soil and artifacts are.

PRESERVING
Archaeologists may use plaster to make a form or an imprint of something they have found.

LOOKING FOR FRAGMENTS
This scientist uses a wire mesh screen to sift the soil to discover small fragments of artifacts.

GRIDS
Grids like these help archaeologists record and map any artifacts found.

CLEANING
Artifacts must be handled and cleaned carefully, often with soft brushes or other instruments.

means "old stone" in the Greek language. Paleolithic times began roughly 2.5 million years ago and lasted until around 8000 B.C.

Try to imagine the world during the Stone Age, long before any roadways, farms, or villages existed. Early humans spent most of their time searching for food. They hunted animals, caught fish, ate insects, and gathered nuts, berries, fruits, grains, and plants.

Because they hunted and gathered food, Paleolithic people were always on the move. They were **nomads** (NOH•MADS), or people who regularly move from place to place without fixed homes. They traveled in bands or groups of 30 or so members because it was safer and made the search for food easier.

Men and women did different **tasks** within the group. Women stayed close to the campsite, which was typically near a stream or other water source. They cared for the children and searched nearby woods and meadows for berries, nuts, and grains.

Men hunted animals—an activity that sometimes took them far from camp. They had to learn the habits of animals and make tools for hunting. At first, they used clubs or drove the animals off cliffs. Over time, Paleolithic people invented spears, traps, and bows and arrows.

Adapting to the Environment The way that Paleolithic people lived depended on where they lived. Those in warm climates needed little clothing or shelter. People in cold climates sought protection from the weather in caves. Over time, Paleolithic people created new kinds of shelter. The most common was probably made of animal hides held up by wooden poles.

Paleolithic people made a life-changing discovery when they learned to tame fire. Fire gave warmth to those gathered around it. It lit the darkness and scared away wild

Primary Source — Paleolithic Cave Paintings

The oldest examples of Paleolithic art are cave paintings found in Spain and France. Most of the paintings are of animals. The paintings show that Paleolithic artists often used several colors and techniques. They sometimes used the uneven surface of the rock to create a three-dimensional effect.

▲ **Painting of bison in Spanish cave**

DBQ Document-Based Question

Why do you think Paleolithic artists painted what they did?

animals. Food cooked over the fire tasted better and was easier to digest. In addition, cooked meat could be kept longer.

Archaeologists believe that early humans started fires by rubbing two pieces of wood together. Paleolithic people later made drill-like wooden tools to start fires.

What Were the Ice Ages? Paleolithic people needed fire in order to survive the Ice Ages. These were long periods of extreme cold. The last Ice Age began about 100,000 B.C. From then until about 8000 B.C., thick ice sheets covered parts of Europe, Asia, and North America.

The Ice Age was a threat to human life. People risked death from the cold and also from hunger. Early humans had to adapt by changing their diet, building sturdier shelters, and using animal furs to make warm clothing. The mastery of fire helped people live in this environment.

Language, Art, and Religion
Another advance during Paleolithic times was the development of spoken language. Language made it far easier for people to work together and to pass on knowledge.

Early people expressed themselves not only in words but in art. They crushed yellow, black, and red rocks to make powders for paint. Then they dabbed this on cave walls, creating scenes of lions, oxen, panthers, and other animals. Historians are not sure why cave paintings were created. They may have had religious meaning or been used to explain people's role in the universe. Early people also might have thought that painting an animal would bring good luck in the hunt.

The Invention of Tools
Paleolithic people were the first to use **technology** (tehk•NAH•luh•jee)—tools and methods that help humans perform tasks. People often used a stone called flint to make tools. By hitting flint with a hard stone, they could make it flake into pieces with very sharp edges. To make hand axes or hunting spears, they tied wooden poles to pieces of flint that were the right shape for the tool.

Over time, early people grew more skilled at making tools. They crafted smaller and sharper tools, such as fishhooks and needles made from animal bones. They used needles to make nets and baskets and to sew animal hides together for clothing.

Reading Check **Contrast** What is the difference between a fossil and an artifact?

NATIONAL GEOGRAPHIC
The Way It Was

Focus on Everyday Life

Tools One of the most important advances of prehistoric people was the creation of stone tools. Tools made hunting, gathering, building shelter, and making clothing much easier.

The first tools were made of stones. Early humans quickly learned that grinding, breaking, and shaping stones to create sharp edges made them more useful.

As technology advanced, people began making specific tools such as food choppers, meat scrapers, and spear points. In time, people learned that hitting a stone in a particular way would produce a flake—a long, sharp chip. Flakes were similar to knives in the way they were used.

Connecting to the Past
1. Why do you think early people chose stones to make their first tools?
2. How were flakes created?

WH6.1.2 Identify the locations of human communities that populated the major regions of the world and describe how humans adapted to a variety of environments.

WH6.1.3 Discuss the climatic changes and human modifications of the physical environment that gave rise to the domestication of plants and animals and new sources of clothing and shelter.

The Agricultural Revolution

Main Idea In the Neolithic Age, people started farming, building communities, producing goods, and trading.

Reading Connection Did you know that, today, more than a third of the world's people work in agriculture? Read to learn how farming began and how it changed the world.

After the last Ice Age ended, people entered the Mesolithic Age. *Mesolithic* means "middle stone" in Greek. At this time, people changed from hunting to herding animals. They began to **domesticate** (duh •MEHS•tih•KAYT), or tame animals for human use. Animals provided meat, milk, and wool. They also carried goods and people and pulled carts. Even so, most Mesolithic people remained nomadic. They moved from place to place in search of grass to feed their herds. They also continued to gather seeds, fruits, and vegetables to eat.

The Mesolithic Age came to an end when people made another important discovery. They realized that they could plant seeds and grow their own food. They may have learned this from the seeds they had stored in dirt pits. Some of the seeds might have sprouted and shown people that if they put seeds in dirt and waited long enough, they could grow plants.

With this new knowledge, people could stay in one place and grow grains and vegetables. Gradually, farming began to replace hunting and gathering for many people. They began to build villages and claim land for their farms. This changed the way people lived and marked the beginning of the Neolithic Age, or New Stone Age, which began about 8000 B.C. and lasted until about 4000 B.C.

Why Was Farming Important?

Historians call the changes in the Neolithic Age the agricultural revolution. The word **revolution** refers to changes that greatly affect many areas of life. Some historians consider the farming revolution the most important event in human history.

Farming did not begin in one region and spread. People in different parts of the world discovered how to grow crops at about the same time. In Asia, people grew wheat, barley, rice, soybeans, and a grain called millet. In Mexico, farmers grew corn, squash, and potatoes. In Africa, they grew millet and a grain called sorghum.

Farming greatly increased the number of calories that could be

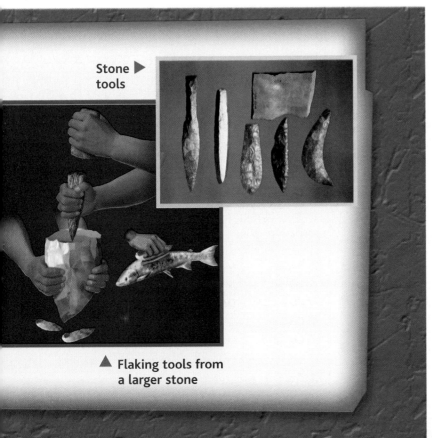

Stone ▶
tools

▲ Flaking tools from a larger stone

127

produced from an area of land. This made it possible to feed more people and led to an increase in the world's population. Farming regions also had a higher population density. People lived closer together and did not have to spread out as much as they used to when they hunted and gathered food.

Farming also changed the kind of food people ate. Instead of a diet rich in meat and vegetables, people now ate a lot of grain—usually in the form of bread. Anthropologists think that people in the early days of farming were not as healthy as hunter-gatherers because they did not have enough variety in their diet.

Farming required people to stay in one place for a long time. This made it easier for diseases to spread and infect many people. Because people stayed in one place, they also tended to pollute their environment. Their water became dirty, and they left garbage near their farms. This too helped the spread of disease.

People had to work harder and for much longer hours when farming. People had to till the soil in order to plant seeds. They had to weed the fields by hand. Then they had to gather the crops by hand when they were ready. There were no machines to make the work quick and easy. People had to walk through their fields, often bent over at the waist, gathering the crops they had grown.

Despite the problems of diet and disease and the hard work people had to do, the farming revolution greatly improved the lives of most people. Fewer people starved to death, and more children lived to adulthood. Settling in one place to farm also led to a much more organized society and made possible the world's first towns and cities.

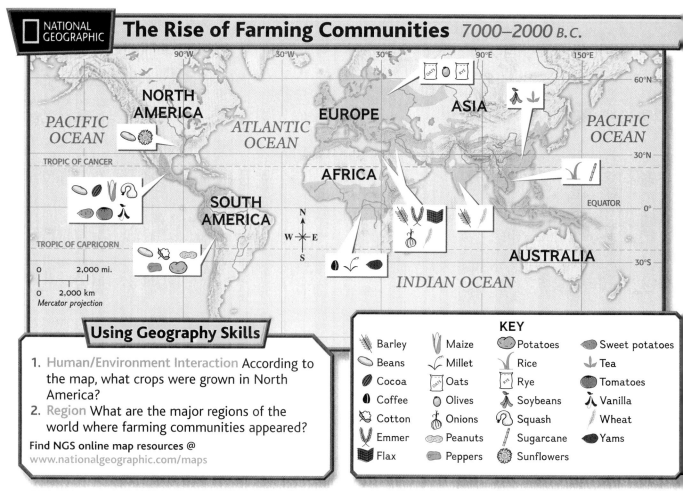

NATIONAL GEOGRAPHIC

The Rise of Farming Communities 7000–2000 B.C.

Using Geography Skills

1. Human/Environment Interaction According to the map, what crops were grown in North America?
2. Region What are the major regions of the world where farming communities appeared?

Find NGS online map resources @
www.nationalgeographic.com/maps

KEY

Barley	Maize	Potatoes	Sweet potatoes
Beans	Millet	Rice	Tea
Cocoa	Oats	Rye	Tomatoes
Coffee	Olives	Soybeans	Vanilla
Cotton	Onions	Squash	Wheat
Emmer	Peanuts	Sugarcane	Yams
Flax	Peppers	Sunflowers	

Biography

WH6.1.2 Identify the locations of human communities that populated the major regions of the world and describe how humans adapted to a variety of environments.

WH6.1.3 Discuss the climatic changes and human modifications of the physical environment that gave rise to the domestication of plants and animals and new sources of clothing and shelter.

ÖTZI THE ICEMAN
c. 3300 B.C.

How do archaeologists and historians know so much about how people lived in the Stone Age? In addition to studying fossils, they have had the chance to study an actual person from the Neolithic Age and his tools. In A.D. 1991 two hikers discovered the frozen body of a man near the border between Austria and Italy. The man was called "Ötzi" after the Ötztal Alps, the mountains where he was found. Scientists studied Ötzi's body, his clothes, and the items found with him and learned that he lived 5,300 years ago, during the Neolithic Age.

Ötzi was dressed warmly because of the cold climate. He was wearing a fur hat and a long grass cloak. Under the cloak was a leather jacket that was well-made but had been repaired several times. To keep his feet warm, he had stuffed grass in the bottom of his leather shoes. Ötzi was carrying a bow and arrows, a copper ax, and a backpack. Experts believe Ötzi was a shepherd who traveled with his herd. He probably returned to his village only twice a year.

▲ Scientists created this reproduction to show what Ötzi may have looked like.

From recent tests, scientists have learned more about the last hours of Ötzi's life. Shortly before he died, Ötzi ate a type of flat bread that is similar to a cracker, an herb or other green plant, and meat. Pollen found in Ötzi's stomach showed that he ate his last meal in the valley, south of where he was found. When Ötzi finished eating, he headed up into the mountains. Eight hours later, he died. Scientists believe that Ötzi's last hours were violent ones. When found, he had a knife clutched in his right hand. Wounds on his right hand suggest that he tried to fight off an attacker. His left shoulder had been deeply pierced by an arrow. Some scientists think Ötzi may have wandered into another tribe's territory. Ötzi is now displayed at the South Tyrol Museum of Archaeology in Bolzano, Italy.

Then and Now

If scientists 5,300 years from now discovered the remains of someone from our time, what might they conclude about our society?

Comparing the Neolithic and Paleolithic Ages

	Paleolithic Age	Neolithic Age

Description of Art and Crafts	Paleolithic people painted cave walls. They usually painted animals.	Neolithic people made pottery and carved objects out of wood. They also built shelters and tombs.
How Humans Obtained Food	People hunted animals and gathered nuts, berries, and grains.	People began to farm in permanent villages. They continued to raise and herd animals.
How Humans Adapted	People learned to make fire, created a language, and made simple tools and shelters.	People built mud-brick houses and places of worship. They specialized in certain jobs and used copper and bronze to create more useful tools.
Work of Women and Men	Women gathered food and cared for children. Men hunted.	Women cared for children and performed household tasks. Men herded, farmed, and protected the village.

Understanding Charts

Humans made great advances from the Paleolithic Age to the Neolithic Age.
1. How did the work of men change from the Paleolithic Age to the Neolithic Age?
2. **Describe** What advances were made in toolmaking between the Paleolithic and Neolithic Ages?

The Growth of Villages People who farmed could settle in one place. Herders remained nomadic and drove their animals wherever they could find grazing land. Farmers, however, had to stay close to their fields to water the plants, keep hungry animals away, and harvest their crops. They began to live in villages, where they built permanent homes.

During the Neolithic Age, villages were started in Europe, India, Egypt, China, and Mexico. Some of the earliest known communities have been found in the Middle East. One of the oldest is **Jericho** (JEHR•ih•KOH) in the West Bank between what are now Israel and Jordan. It dates back to about 8000 B.C.

Another well-known Neolithic community is **Çatal Hüyük** (chah•TAHL hoo•YOOK) in present-day Turkey. Little of the community remains, but it was home to some 6,000 people between about 6700 B.C. and 5700 B.C. These people lived in simple mud-brick houses that were packed tightly together and decorated inside with wall paintings. They used other buildings as places of worship. Along with farming, the people hunted, raised sheep and goats, and ate fish and bird eggs from nearby marshes.

The Benefits of a Settled Life Neolithic people found greater security by living in settled communities. Steady food supplies led to healthy, growing populations. Soon villagers produced a food surplus. That is, they grew more food than they needed. They were able to trade their extra food for other goods made by people in their community or who lived nearby.

The food surplus made it possible for people to practice **specialization** (SPEH•shuh•luh•ZAY•shuhn), or the development of different kinds of jobs. Because not everyone was needed for farming, some people had the time to develop other types of skills. They made pottery from clay to store their grain and other foods. Others used plant fibers to make mats and to weave cloth. This led to a new type of clothing. Early humans had worn only animal skins. Now people could use wool and other fabrics for clothes as well. These craftspeople, like farmers, also took part in trade. They exchanged the things they made for goods they did not have.

In late Neolithic times, people continued to make advances. Toolmakers created better farming tools, such as the sickle for cutting grain. In some places, people began to work with metals. At first they used copper. They heated rocks to melt the copper inside and then poured the melted copper into molds for tools and weapons.

After 4000 B.C., craftspeople in western Asia mixed copper and tin to form a metal called bronze. Bronze was harder and longer lasting than copper. It became widely used between 3000 B.C. and 1200 B.C., the period known as the Bronze Age.

 **Reading Check** **Compare** How did the Paleolithic and Neolithic Ages differ?

History Online

Study Central Need help understanding the lives of early humans? Visit ca.hss.glencoe.com and click on Study Central.

Section 1 Review

Reading Summary

Review the Main Ideas

- Early humans were nomads who moved around to hunt animals and gather food. They built shelters and used fire to survive. In time, they developed language and art.

- During the farming revolution, people began to grow crops and domesticate animals, which allowed them to settle in villages.

What Did You Learn?

1. Who are archaeologists, and what do they study?

2. How did domesticating animals help the Neolithic people?

Critical Thinking

3. **Determine Cause and Effect** Draw a diagram like the one below. List some of the effects that farming had on people's lives. **CA HI2.**

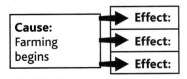

Cause: Farming begins	→	Effect:
	→	Effect:
	→	Effect:

4. **The Big Ideas** How do changes in the Neolithic Age still affect people today? **CA HI2.**

5. **Compare** Compare the technology of the Paleolithic Age with that of the Neolithic Age. **CA CS1.**

6. **Analyze** Why was the ability to make a fire so important? **CA HI2.**

7. **Reading** **Previewing** Create a three-column chart. In the first column, write what you knew about early humans before you read this section. In the second column, write what you learned after reading. In the third, write what you still would like to know. **CA 6RC2.4**

Mesopotamian Civilization

Guide to Reading

 History Social Science Standards

WH6.2 Students analyze the geographic, political, economic, religious, and social structures of the early civilizations of Mesopotamia, Egypt, and Kush.

Looking Back, Looking Ahead

In Section 1, you learned how farming allowed people to settle in one place. Some people settled in an area called Mesopotamia.

Focusing on the Main Ideas

- Civilization in Mesopotamia began in the valleys of the Tigris and Euphrates Rivers. *(page 133)*

- Sumerians invented writing and made other important contributions to later peoples. *(page 136)*

- Sumerian city-states lost power when they were conquered by outsiders. *(page 139)*

Locating Places

Tigris River (TY•gruhs)
Euphrates River (yu•FRAY•teez)
Mesopotamia
    (MEH•suh•puh•TAY•mee•uh)
Sumer (SOO•muhr)
Babylon (BA•buh•luhn)

Meeting People

Sargon (SAHR•GAHN)
Hammurabi (HA•muh•RAH•bee)

Content Vocabulary

civilization
    (SIH•vuh•luh•ZAY•shuhn)
irrigation (IHR•uh•GAY•shuhn)
city-state
artisan (AHR•tuh•zuhn)
cuneiform (kyoo•NEE•uh•FAWRM)
scribe (SKRYB)
empire (EHM•PYR)

Academic Vocabulary

complex (kahm•PLEHKS)
consist (kuhn•SIHST)
code (KOHD)

Reading Strategy

Sequencing Information Use a diagram to show how the first empire in Mesopotamia came about.

| city-states formed | → | | → | |

3000 B.C.	2250 B.C.	1500 B.C.
3000 B.C. City-states arise in Sumer	**c. 2340 B.C.** Sargon conquers Babylon	**c. 1792 B.C.** Hammurabi rules Mesopotamia

Babylon • Uruk

WH6.2.1 Locate and describe the major river systems and discuss the physical settings that supported permanent settlement and early civilizations. WH6.2.2 Trace the development of agricultural techniques that permitted the production of economic surplus and the emergence of cities as centers of culture and power. WH6.2.3 Understand the relationship between religion and the social and political order in Mesopotamia and Egypt.

Mesopotamia's Civilization

Main Idea Civilization in Mesopotamia began in the valleys of the Tigris and Euphrates Rivers.

Reading Connection Do you live in a region that receives plenty of rain or in a region that is dry? Think about how that affects you as you read how the Sumerians' environment affected them.

Over thousands of years, some of the early farming villages developed into civilizations. **Civilizations** (SIH•vuh•luh•ZAY•shuhns) are **complex** societies. They have cities, organized governments, art, religion, class divisions, and a writing system.

Why Were River Valleys Important?

The first civilizations arose in river valleys because good farming conditions made it easy to feed large numbers of people. The rivers also provided fish, freshwater to drink, and made it easy to get from one place to another and to trade. Trade enabled goods and ideas to move from place to place. It was no accident, then, that cities grew up in these valleys and became the centers of civilizations.

As cities took shape, so did the need for organization. Someone had to make plans and decisions about matters of common concern. People formed governments to do just that. Their leaders took charge of food supplies and building projects. They made laws to keep order and assembled armies to defend themselves from enemies.

With fewer worries about meeting their basic needs, people in the river valleys had more time to think about other things. They

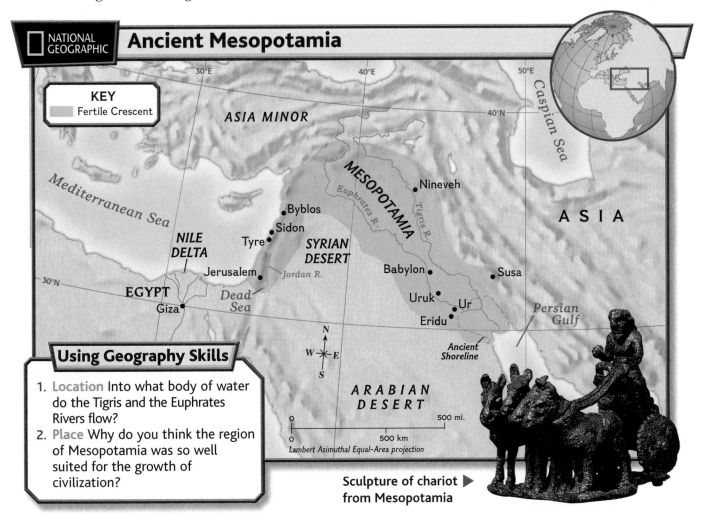

NATIONAL GEOGRAPHIC

Ancient Mesopotamia

KEY
Fertile Crescent

ASIA MINOR

MESOPOTAMIA

Mediterranean Sea

Caspian Sea

Nineveh

Euphrates R.

Tigris R.

ASIA

Byblos
Sidon
Tyre

SYRIAN DESERT

NILE DELTA

Jerusalem

Jordan R.

Babylon

Susa

EGYPT

Dead Sea

Uruk
Ur

Persian Gulf

Giza

Eridu

Ancient Shoreline

ARABIAN DESERT

500 mi.
500 km
Lambert Azimuthal Equal-Area projection

Using Geography Skills

1. **Location** Into what body of water do the Tigris and the Euphrates Rivers flow?
2. **Place** Why do you think the region of Mesopotamia was so well suited for the growth of civilization?

Sculpture of chariot ▶ from Mesopotamia

placed emphasis, or special importance, on religions and the arts. They also invented ways of writing and created calendars to tell time.

Early civilizations shared another feature—they had a class structure. That is, people held different ranks in society depending on what work they did and how much wealth or power they had.

The Rise of Sumer The earliest-known civilization arose in what is now southern Iraq, on a flat plain bounded by the **Tigris River** (TY•gruhs) and the **Euphrates River** (yu•FRAY•teez). Later, the Greeks called this area **Mesopotamia** (MEH•suh•puh•TAY•mee•uh), which means "the land between the rivers." Mesopotamia lay in the eastern part of the Fertile Crescent, a curving strip of land that extends from the Mediterranean Sea to the Persian Gulf.

Mesopotamia had a hot, dry climate. In the spring, the rivers often flooded, leaving behind rich soil for farming. The problem was that the flooding was very unpredictable. It might flood one year, but not the next. Every year, farmers worried about their crops.

Over time, the farmers learned to build dams and channels to control the seasonal floods. They also built walls, waterways, and ditches to bring water to their fields. This way of watering crops is called **irrigation** (IHR•uh•GAY•shuhn). Irrigation allowed the farmers to grow plenty of food and support a large population. By 3000 B.C., many cities had formed in southern Mesopotamia in a region known as **Sumer** (SOO•muhr).

Sumerian Ziggurat

The top of the ziggurat was considered to be a holy place, and the area around the ziggurat contained palaces and royal storehouses. The surrounding walls had only one entrance because the ziggurat also served as the city's treasury. *How did people reach the upper levels of the ziggurat?*

▲ Statues of Sumerians

What Were City-States? Geography helped to isolate Sumerian cities from each other. Beyond the areas of settlement lay mudflats and patches of scorching desert. This terrain made travel and communication difficult. Each Sumerian city and the land around it became a separate **city-state.** Each city-state had its own government and was not part of any larger unit.

Sumerian city-states often went to war with one another. They fought to gain glory and to control more territory. For protection, each city-state surrounded itself with a wall. Because stone and wood were in short supply, the Sumerians used river mud as their main building material. They mixed the mud with crushed reeds, formed bricks, and left them in the sun to dry. The hard waterproof bricks were used for walls, as well as homes, temples, and other buildings.

Gods and Rulers The Sumerians believed in many gods. Each was thought to have power over a natural force or a human activity—flooding, for example, or basket weaving. The Sumerians tried hard to please their gods. They built a grand temple called a ziggurat (ZIH•guh•RAT) to the chief god. The word *ziggurat* means "mountain of god" or "hill of heaven."

With tiers like a giant square wedding cake, the ziggurat dominated the city. At the top was a shrine, or special place of worship that only priests and priestesses could enter. The priests and priestesses were powerful and controlled much of the land. They may even have ruled at one time.

▲ A portion of the Royal Standard of Ur, a decorated box that shows scenes of Sumerian life

◀ These ruins are from the Sumerian city-state of Uruk. *What was a city-state?*

WH6.2.2 Trace the development of agricultural techniques that permitted the production of economic surplus and the emergence of cities as centers of culture and power. **WH6.2.3** Understand the relationship between religion and the social and political order in Mesopotamia and Egypt. **WH6.2.9** Trace the evolution of language and its written forms.

Later, kings ran the government. They led armies and organized building projects. The first kings were probably war heroes. Their position became hereditary, which meant that after a king died, his son took over.

What Was Life Like in Sumer?

While Sumerian kings lived in large palaces, ordinary people lived in small mud-brick houses. Most people in Sumer farmed. Some, however, were **artisans** (AHR•tuh•zuhns), or skilled workers who made metal products, cloth, or pottery. Other people in Sumer worked as merchants or traders. They traveled to other cities and towns and traded tools, wheat, and barley for copper, tin, and timber—things that Sumer did not have.

People in Sumer were divided into three social classes. Generally, a person had to stay in the social class into which he or she was born. Only rarely could someone move up. The upper class included kings, priests, warriors, and government officials. In the middle class were artisans, merchants, farmers, and fishers. These people made up the largest group. The lower class were enslaved people who worked on farms or in the temples.

Enslaved people were forced to serve others. Slaveholders thought of them as property. Some slaves were prisoners of war. Others were criminals. Still others were enslaved because they had to pay off their debts. Debts are money or goods owed to others.

In Sumer, women and men had separate roles. Men headed the households. They also could decide whom their children would marry. Only males could go to school. Women, however, did have some rights. They could buy and sell property and run businesses.

Reading Check **Explain** How did Mesopotamian control of the Tigris and Euphrates Rivers benefit their society?

A Skilled People

Main Idea Sumerians invented writing and made other important contributions to later peoples.

Reading Connection Do you like to read? If so, you owe a debt to the Sumerians, because they were the first to invent writing. Read about this achievement and others.

The Sumerians left a lasting mark on world history. Their ideas and inventions were copied and improved upon by other peoples. As a result, Mesopotamia has been called the "cradle of civilization."

Why Was Writing Important?

The people of Sumer created many things that still affect our lives today. Probably their greatest invention was writing. Writing is important because it helps people keep records and pass on their ideas to others.

People in Sumer developed writing to keep track of business deals and other events. Their writing was called **cuneiform** (kyoo•NEE•uh•FAWRM). It **consisted** of hundreds of wedge-shaped marks cut into damp clay tablets with a sharp-ended reed. Archaeologists have found thousands of these cuneiform tablets, telling us much about Mesopotamian life.

Only a few people—mostly boys from wealthy families—learned how to write. After years of training, they became **scribes** (SKRYBS), or record keepers. Scribes held honored positions in society, often going on to become judges and political leaders.

Sumerian Literature

The Sumerians also produced works of literature. The world's oldest known story comes from Sumer. It is called the *Epic of Gilgamesh* (GIHL•guh•MEHSH). An epic is a long poem that tells the story of a hero. The hero Gilgamesh is a king who travels around the world with a friend and performs great deeds. When his friend dies, Gilgamesh searches for a way to live forever. He learns that this is possible only for the gods. This epic poem is still studied today.

Advances in Science and Math The Mesopotamians' creativity also extended to technology. You read earlier about Sumerian irrigation systems. Sumerians also invented the wagon wheel to help carry people and goods from place to place. Another breakthrough was the plow, which made farming easier. Still another invention was the sailboat, which replaced muscle power with wind power.

Sumerians developed many mathematical ideas. They used geometry to measure fields and put up buildings. They also created a number system based on 60. We have them to thank for our 60-minute hour, 60-second minute, and 360-degree circle.

In addition, Sumerian people watched the skies to learn the best times to plant crops and to hold religious festivals. They recorded the positions of the planets and stars and developed a 12-month calendar based on the cycles of the moon.

✓ **Reading Check** **Identify** How did the use of mathematics benefit the Sumerians?

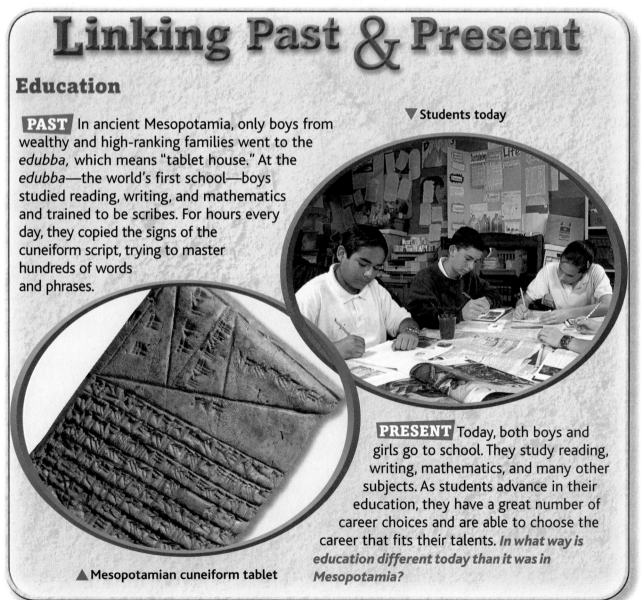

Linking Past & Present

Education

PAST In ancient Mesopotamia, only boys from wealthy and high-ranking families went to the *edubba*, which means "tablet house." At the *edubba*—the world's first school—boys studied reading, writing, and mathematics and trained to be scribes. For hours every day, they copied the signs of the cuneiform script, trying to master hundreds of words and phrases.

▼ **Students today**

PRESENT Today, both boys and girls go to school. They study reading, writing, mathematics, and many other subjects. As students advance in their education, they have a great number of career choices and are able to choose the career that fits their talents. *In what way is education different today than it was in Mesopotamia?*

▲ **Mesopotamian cuneiform tablet**

WH6.2.2 Trace the development of agricultural techniques that permitted the production of economic surplus and the emergence of cities as centers of culture and power.
WH6.2.4 Know the significance of Hammurabi's Code.

Biography

HAMMURABI
Reigned c. 1792–1750 B.C.

▲ Hammurabi

Hammurabi was a young man when he succeeded his father, Sinmuballit, as king of Babylon. When Hammurabi became king, Babylon was already a strong kingdom in Mesopotamia. During his reign, however, Hammurabi transformed Babylon from a small city-state into a large, powerful state. He also united the other city-states of Mesopotamia under one rule.

Hammurabi was directly involved in the ruling of his kingdom. He personally directed projects, such as building city walls, restoring temples, and digging and cleaning irrigation canals. A great deal of planning went into his projects. City streets, for example, were arranged in straight lines and intersected at right angles, much like the way our cities are planned today.

One of Hammurabi's goals was to control the Euphrates River because it provided water for Babylon's farms and trade routes for cargo ships. He also needed to control the river's annual flooding so that villages and crops would not be washed away. Hammurabi did this by issuing laws controlling the use of irrigation ditches. His laws protected the area and helped bring water to the fields. That was one reason he developed a strict law code, or collection of laws: damaged irrigation channels could cause many people to be injured or even killed.

Hammurabi fought for many years against his enemies to control the river. He even used water to defeat them. Sometimes he would dam the river to withhold water needed for drinking and for crops, and then release a sudden damaging flood. Because of Hammurabi's efforts, the center of power in Mesopotamia shifted from the south to Babylon in the north where it remained for the next 1,000 years.

Then and Now

Find a copy of the Code of Hammurabi, either on-line or in a reference book. Notice the kinds of situations and the punishments that are described. How do these compare with current laws and punishments that exist in the United States?

Sargon and Hammurabi

Main Idea Sumerian city-states lost power when they were conquered by outsiders.

Reading Connection Have you heard of the Roman Empire, the Aztec Empire, or the British Empire? The rise and fall of empires is an important part of history. Read on to learn about the first empires in the world.

Over time, conflicts weakened Sumer's city-states. They became vulnerable to attacks by outside groups such as the Akkadians (uh•KAY•dee•uhnz) of northern Mesopotamia.

The king of the Akkadians was named **Sargon** (SAHR•GAHN). In about 2340 B.C., Sargon conquered all of Mesopotamia creating the world's first empire. An **empire** (EHM•PYR) is a group of many different lands under one ruler. Sargon's empire lasted for more than 200 years before falling to invaders.

In the 1800s B.C., a new group of people became powerful in Mesopotamia. They built the city of **Babylon** (BA•buh•luhn) by the Euphrates River. It quickly became a center of trade. Beginning in 1792 B.C., the Babylonian king, **Hammurabi** (HA•muh•RAH•bee), began conquering cities to the north and south and created the Babylonian Empire.

Hammurabi is best known for his law **code,** or collection of laws. (See pages 140 and 141.) The code covered crimes, farming and business activities, and marriage and the family—almost every area of life. Before the law code, rulers could treat others nearly any way they wanted. The code forced all people to follow the law in how they treated others. Hammurabi's code influenced later law codes, including those of Greece and Rome.

Reading Check **Explain** Why was Sargon's empire important?

Study Central Need help understanding the Sumerian civilization? Visit ca.hss.glencoe.com and click on Study Central.

Section 2 Review

Reading Summary

Review the Main Ideas

- In time, farming villages developed into civilizations with governments, art, religion, writing, and social class divisions. The first city-states developed in Mesopotamia.

- Many important ideas and inventions, including writing, the wheel, the plow, and a number system based on 60, were developed in the region of Mesopotamia.

- Several empires, including the Babylonian Empire, took control of Mesopotamia.

What Did You Learn?

1. What is a civilization?

2. What was the Code of Hammurabi?

Critical Thinking

3. **Summarize Information** Draw a chart like the one below. Use it to list the achievements of Mesopotamians that helped improve their civilization's economy. **CA HI6.**

Achievements of Mesopotamian Civilization

4. **Geography Skills** How did the geography of Mesopotamia shape the growth of population and creation of a civilization? **CA CS3.**

5. **The Big Ideas** How did the Sumerian religion affect Sumerian society? **CA HI2.**

6. **Persuasive Writing** Imagine you are living in a city-state in ancient Sumer. Write a letter to a friend describing which Mesopotamian idea or invention you believe will be the most important to humanity. **CA 6WS1.2**

You Decide . . .

WH6.2.4 Know the significance of Hammurabi's Code.

Hammurabi's Laws: Fair or Cruel?

Fair

Around 1750 B.C., King Hammurabi wrote 282 laws to govern the people of Babylon. Historians and scholars agree that these ancient laws were the first to cover almost all aspects of society. However, historians and scholars do not agree whether Hammurabi's laws were fair or cruel.

Those who see the laws as just and fair give the following reasons. They say the laws

- stated what all people needed to know about the rules of their society
- brought order and justice to society
- regulated many different activities, from business contracts to crime.

King Hammurabi wrote an introduction to his list of laws. In that introduction, he says that the laws were written to be fair. His intention was "to bring about the rule of righteousness in the land, to destroy the wicked and evil-doers, so that the strong should not harm the weak. . . ."

Some of the laws reflect that fairness.

- Law 5: If a judge makes an error through his own fault when trying a case, he must pay a fine, be removed from the judge's bench, and never judge another case.
- Law 122: If someone gives something to someone else for safekeeping, the transaction should be witnessed and a contract made between the two parties.
- Law 233: If a contractor builds a house for someone and the walls start to fall, then the builder must use his own money and labor to make the walls secure.

Stone monument showing ▶ Hammurabi (standing) and his code

▲ **Cuneiform tablet with the text of the introduction to the Code of Hammurabi**

Cruel

Some historians and scholars think Hammurabi's laws were cruel and unjust. They say the laws

- called for violent punishments, often death, for nonviolent crimes
- required different punishments for accused persons of different social classes
- allowed no explanation from an accused person.

Some of the laws reflect this cruelty.

- Law 3: If someone falsely accuses someone else of certain crimes, then he shall be put to death.

- Law 22: If someone is caught in the act of robbery, then he shall be put to death.

- Law 195: If a son strikes his father, the son's hands shall be cut off.

- Law 202: If someone strikes a man of higher rank, then he shall be whipped 60 times in public.

You Be the Historian

DBQ **Document-Based Questions**

1. Why do some people think Hammurabi's laws were fair? **CA HR5.**

2. Why do others think the laws were cruel? **CA HR5.**

3. Were the laws fair or cruel? Take the role of a historian. Write a brief essay that explains how you view Hammurabi's laws. Be sure to use facts to support your position. You can compare Hammurabi's laws to our modern laws to support your

Section 3

New Empires

Guide to Reading

History Social Science Standards

WH6.2 Students analyze the geographic, political, economic, religious, and social structures of the early civilizations of Mesopotamia, Egypt, and Kush.

Looking Back, Looking Ahead

In Section 2, you learned about the empires of Sargon and Hammurabi. Later empires—those of the Assyrians and the Chaldeans—used their military power in new ways.

Focusing on the Main Ideas

• Assyria's military power and well-organized government helped it build a vast empire in Mesopotamia by 650 B.C. *(page 143)*

• The Chaldean Empire built important landmarks in Babylon and developed the first calendar with a seven-day week. *(page 145)*

Locating Places

Assyria (uh•SIHR•ee•uh)
Persian Gulf (PUHR•zhuhn)
Nineveh (NIH•nuh•vuh)
Hanging Gardens

Meeting People

Nebuchadnezzar
(NEH•byuh•kuhd•NEH•zuhr)

Content Vocabulary

province (PRAH•vuhns)
caravan (KAR•uh•VAN)
astronomer (uh•STRAH•nuh•muhr)

Academic Vocabulary

core (KOHR)
interval (IHN•tuhr•vuhl)
route (ROWT)

Reading Strategy

Compare and Contrast Complete a Venn diagram like the one below listing the similarities and differences between the Assyrian Empire and the Chaldean Empire.

Assyrians — Chaldeans

NATIONAL GEOGRAPHIC Where & When?

Nineveh
Babylon

900 B.C.

c. 900 B.C.
Assyrians control Mesopotamia

700 B.C.

612 B.C.
Nineveh captured; Assyrian Empire crumbles

500 B.C.

539 B.C.
Persians conquer Chaldeans

The Assyrians

Main Idea Assyria's military power and well-organized government helped it build a vast empire in Mesopotamia by 650 B.C.

Reading Connection Today, many countries have armed forces to protect their interests. Read to discover how the Assyrians built an army strong enough to conquer all of Mesopotamia.

About 1,000 years after Hammurabi, a new empire arose in Mesopotamia. It was founded by a people called the Assyrians (uh•SIHR•ee•uhns), who lived in the north near the Tigris River. **Assyria** (uh•SIHR•ee•uh) had fertile valleys that attracted outside invaders. To defend their land, the Assyrians built a large army. Around 900 B.C., they began taking over the rest of Mesopotamia.

Why Were the Assyrians So Strong? The Assyrian military was well organized. At its **core** were groups of foot soldiers armed with spears and daggers. Other soldiers were experts at using bows and arrows. The army also had chariot riders and soldiers who fought on horseback.

This fearsome and mighty force was the first large army to use iron weapons. For centuries, iron had been used for tools, but it was too soft to serve as a material for weapons. Then a people called the Hittites (HIH•TYTZ), who lived northwest of Assyria, developed a way of making iron stronger. They heated iron ore, hammered it, and rapidly cooled it. The Assyrians learned this technique from the Hittites. They produced iron weapons that were stronger than those made of copper or tin.

The Assyrians at War

When attacking a walled city, the Assyrians used massive war machines. The wheeled battering ram was powered by soldiers. It was covered to protect the soldiers inside, but it had slits so they could shoot arrows out.
What other methods did Assyrian soldiers use to attack cities?

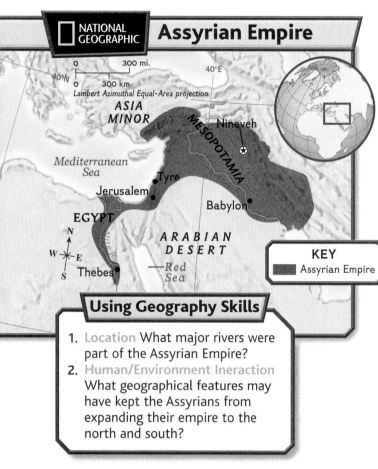

Assyrian Empire

NATIONAL GEOGRAPHIC

0   300 mi.
0   300 km
Lambert Azimuthal Equal-Area projection

40°N   40°E

ASIA MINOR

MESOPOTAMIA

Nineveh

Mediterranean Sea

Tyre

Jerusalem

Babylon

EGYPT

ARABIAN DESERT

Thebes

Red Sea

N W E S

KEY
Assyrian Empire

Using Geography Skills

1. **Location** What major rivers were part of the Assyrian Empire?
2. **Human/Environment Ineraction** What geographical features may have kept the Assyrians from expanding their empire to the north and south?

◄ Assyrian winged bull statues stood as guardians at city gates.

The Assyrians were ferocious warriors. To attack cities, they tunneled under walls or climbed over them on ladders. They loaded tree trunks onto movable platforms and used them as battering rams to knock down city gates. Once a city was captured, the Assyrians set fire to its buildings. They also carried away its people and goods.

Anyone who resisted Assyrian rule was punished. The Assyrians drove people from their lands and moved them into foreign territory. Then they brought in new settlers and forced them to pay heavy taxes.

A Well-Organized Government
Assyrian kings had to be strong to rule their large empire. By about 650 B.C., the empire stretched from the **Persian Gulf** (PUHR•zhuhn) in the east to Egypt's Nile River in the west. The capital was at **Nineveh** (NIH•nuh•vuh) on the Tigris River.

Assyrian kings divided the empire into **provinces** (PRAH•vuhn•suhs), or political districts. They chose officials to govern each province. The job of these officials was to collect taxes and enforce the king's laws.

Assyrian kings built roads to join all parts of their empire. Government soldiers were posted at stations along the way to protect traders from bandits. Messengers on government business used the stations to rest and change horses.

Life in Assyria
The Assyrians lived much like other Mesopotamians. Their writing was based on Babylonian writing, and they worshiped many of the same gods. Their laws were similar, but lawbreakers often faced more brutal and cruel punishments in Assyria.

As builders, the Assyrians showed great skill. They erected large temples and palaces that they filled with wall carvings and statues. The Assyrians also produced and collected literature. One of the world's first libraries was in Nineveh. It held 25,000 tablets of stories and songs to the gods. Modern historians have learned much about ancient civilizations from this library.

✓ **Reading Check** **Explain** Why were the Assyrian soldiers considered brutal and cruel?

The Chaldeans

Main Idea The Chaldean Empire built important landmarks in Babylon and developed the first calendar with a seven-day week.

Reading Connection What landmarks exist in your town or the nearest city? Read to learn some of the special landmarks that made the Chaldean capital of Babylon famous.

Assyria's cruel treatment of people led to many rebellions. About 650 B.C., the Assyrians began fighting each other over who would be their next king. Because the Assyrians were not united, a group of people called the Chaldeans (kahl•DEE•uhns) were able to rebel.

The Chaldean people had moved from the Arabian Peninsula into southern Mesopotamia about 1000 B.C. Their small kingdom was quickly conquered by the Assyrians but the Chaldeans hated their new rulers. With the Assyrians busy fighting each other, King Nabopolassar of the Chaldeans decided the time had come to fight back.

In 627 B.C. Nabopolassar led his people in rebellion against the Assyrians. The Chaldeans joined with the Medes, another people in the region who wanted to break free from the Assyrians. Together the Chaldeans and Medes defeated Assyria's army. In 612 B.C. they captured the Assyrian capital of Nineveh and finally put an end to the hated Assyrian empire.

Nabopolassar and his son, the famous King **Nebuchadnezzar** (NEH•byuh•khud•NEH•zuhr), then went on to build their own empire. By 605 B.C., the Chaldeans had

History Online

Web Activity Visit ca.hss.glencoe.com and click on *Chapter 1—Student Web Activity* to learn more about the first civilizations.

Hanging Gardens

The Hanging Gardens of Babylon were considered one of the Seven Wonders of the Ancient World. A complex irrigation system brought water from the Euphrates River to the top of the gardens. From there, the water flowed down to each of the lower levels of the gardens. *What other sights made Babylon a grand city?*

▲ Ruins of the Hanging Gardens

conquered nearly all of the lands the Assyrians had ruled. They made Babylon the capital of their empire, and because of this, the Chaldean Empire is sometimes called the New Babylonian Empire.

The City of Babylon The Chaldeans rebuilt the city of Babylon as the glorious center of their empire. The city became the world's largest and richest city. It was surrounded by a brick wall so wide that two chariots could pass on the road on top of it. Built into the wall at 100-yard (91.4-m) **intervals** were towers where soldiers kept watch.

Large palaces and temples stood in the city's center. A huge ziggurat reached more than 300 feet (91.4 m) into the sky. Another marvel, visible from any point in Babylon, was an immense staircase of greenery: the **Hanging Gardens** at the king's palace.

These terraced gardens showcased large trees, masses of flowering vines, and other beautiful plants. A pump brought in water from a nearby river. Nebuchadnezzar built the gardens to please his wife, who missed the mountains and plants of her homeland in the northwest.

One Greek historian in the 400s B.C. described the beauty of Babylon. He wrote, "In magnificence, there is no other city that approaches it." Outside the center of Babylon stood houses and marketplaces. There, artisans made pottery, cloth, baskets, and jewelry. They sold their wares to passing **caravans** (KAR•uh•VANZ), or groups of traveling merchants. Because Babylon was located on the major trade **route** between the Persian Gulf and the Mediterranean Sea, it became rich from trade.

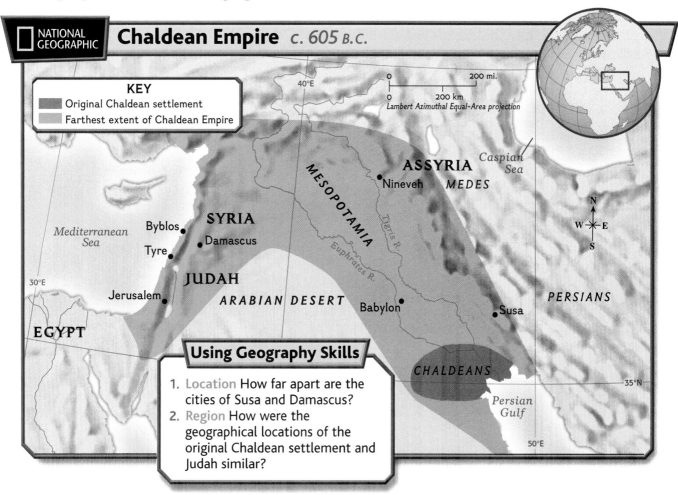

NATIONAL GEOGRAPHIC

Chaldean Empire *c. 605 B.C.*

KEY
- Original Chaldean settlement
- Farthest extent of Chaldean Empire

200 mi.
200 km
Lambert Azimuthal Equal-Area projection

ASSYRIA
- Nineveh
MEDES
Caspian Sea

MESOPOTAMIA

SYRIA
- Byblos
- Damascus
- Tyre

Mediterranean Sea

Tigris R.
Euphrates R.

JUDAH
- Jerusalem
ARABIAN DESERT
- Babylon
- Susa

PERSIANS

EGYPT

CHALDEANS

Persian Gulf

Using Geography Skills

1. **Location** How far apart are the cities of Susa and Damascus?
2. **Region** How were the geographical locations of the original Chaldean settlement and Judah similar?

Babylon was also a center of science. Like earlier people in Mesopotamia, the Chaldeans believed that changes in the sky revealed the plans of the gods. Their **astronomers** (uh•STRAH•nuh•muhrs)—people who study the heavenly bodies—mapped the stars, the planets, and the phases of the moon. The Chaldeans made one of the first sundials and were the first to develop a seven-day week.

Why Did the Empire Fall? A number of weak leaders, along with poor harvests and decreased trade, caused the Chaldeans to lose their power. In 539 B.C. Persians from the northeast captured Babylon and made Mesopotamia part of the new Persian Empire.

▲ **The Ishtar Gate was at the main entrance to ancient Babylon.** *Describe the wall that surrounded Babylon.*

✓ **Reading Check** **Identify** What were the Hanging Gardens of Babylon?

History Online

Study Central Need help understanding the Assyrians and Chaldeans? Visit ca.hss.glencoe.com and click on Study Central.

Section 3 Review

Reading Summary
Review the Main Ideas

- Using cavalry and foot soldiers armed with iron weapons, the Assyrians created a large empire that included all of Mesopotamia and extended into Egypt.

- The Chaldeans built a large empire in Mesopotamia that included Babylon, the largest and richest city in the world at that time.

What Did You Learn?

1. Why was the Assyrian army a powerful fighting force?

2. What were some of the accomplishments of Chaldean astronomers?

Critical Thinking

3. **Summarize Information** Draw a chart like the one below. Use it to describe the city of Babylon and why it became powerful. **CA HI2.**

Babylon Under Chaldeans

4. **Analyze** How did the Assyrians set up a well-organized government? **CA 6RC2.0**

5. **The Big Ideas** Why do you think the Assyrians took conquered peoples from their lands and moved them to other places? **CA CS3.**

6. **Explain** Why did the Chaldeans join with the Medes to fight the Assyrians? **CA HI1.**

7. **Science Link** What different types of knowledge and skills would the Babylonians need to build the Hanging Gardens? **CA 6RC2.3**

8. **Analysis** **Posing Questions** Write four questions about the Chaldeans you would like answered. Use the library and Internet to research and write answers to your questions. **CA HR1.**

Analyzing Primary Sources

WH6.2.9 Trace the evolution of language and its written forms.

Ancient Forms of Communication

▲ Sculpture of chariot from Mesopotamia

Long before the rise of civilization, early people expressed themselves through paintings. People may have used these images to explain the universe. Later, people in Mesopotamia began using writing not only to express their ideas, but also to record important events and tell stories. These include epic stories of heroes, proverbs about how to live properly, and law codes.

Study the painting and the passages that follow, and then answer the questions on page 149.

Reader's Dictionary

old ones: the elders or leaders of the city

Enkidu (ehn•KEE•doo): Gilgamesh's friend and traveling companion

Cave Painting

One of the earliest forms of communication was through art. Beginning around 30,000 B.C., people began to crush rocks to make powder for painting on cave walls. The images they painted include animals, hunting scenes, and people engaged in various activities. These paintings may have had a religious meaning or may have been intended to record events.

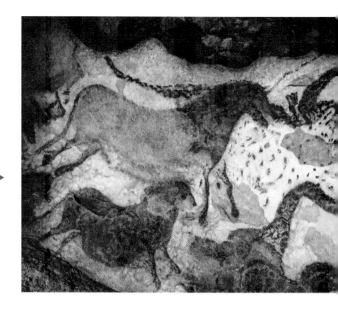

This cave painting is in Lascaux, France. ▶ The cave is filled with images drawn or carved by people during the Paleolithic Age, about 15,000 years ago. The images show animals and people, and tell stories about Paleolithic life.

Advice for Gilgamesh

The Epic of Gilgamesh *is a legend about the travels of Gilgamesh, king of Uruk in Babylonia. It was written about 2000 B.C. In the following passage, Gilgamesh is warned about going on a dangerous adventure alone.*

The **old ones** shaped their mouths and spoke,
  saying to Gilgamesh,
"Do not trust all that strength of yours,
  Gilgamesh.
Make sure your eyes are wide, your blow certain.

The one who walks in front guards his friend;
the one who knows the way safeguards his
  companion.

Let **Enkidu** go before you as you march;
he knows the way of the forest, to the cedars.
He has seen battle, understands warfare.
Enkidu will watch over the friend, make the
  way safe for his companion."

—*Gilgamesh*, John Gardner and John Maier, trans.

The Code of Hammurabi

The following is law seven from the Code of Hammurabi. He ruled Babylon from around 1792 B.C. to 1750 B.C.

7. If any one buy from the son or the slave of another man, without witnesses or a contract, silver or gold, a male or female slave, an ox or a sheep, an ass or anything, or if he take it in charge, he is considered a thief and shall be put to death.

—"Code of Hammurabi," L. W. King, trans.

Stone monument ▶ showing Hammurabi (standing)

DBQ Document-Based Questions

Cave Painting
1. What kind of animals are shown?
2. Why do you think this image was painted?

The Epic of Gilgamesh
3. What do the old ones tell Gilgamesh to do instead of relying on his strength? Why?
4. Why do the old ones think it is a good idea for Enkidu to accompany Gilgamesh?

The Code of Hammurabi
5. What is the punishment for making a deal without a witness or a contract?

6. Do you think the punishment would be the same if there were a witness or a contract? Why?

Read to Write
7. How do you think the author of the *Epic of Gilgamesh* would have used words to express the image of the cave painting?
8. Based on the primary sources, explain what values you think were important to people in ancient Mesopotamia. How do these values compare to ours today? **CA HI2.; HR4.**

Review Content Vocabulary

1. Write a brief paragraph that describes and compares the following terms.

archaeologist   artifact

fossil   anthropologist

Indicate which of the following statements are true. Replace the word in italics to make any false statements true.

___ 2. An *artisan* kept records in cuneiform.

___ 3. Assyrian kings divided their empire into political districts called *provinces*.

___ 4. A *civilization* is a group of many different lands under one ruler.

Review the Main Ideas

Section 1 • Early Humans

5. How did Paleolithic people adapt to their environment?

6. What were the major differences between people who lived in the Paleolithic period and those who lived in the Neolithic period?

Section 2 • Mesopotamian Civilization

7. Where were the first civilizations in Mesopotamia?

8. What kinds of contributions did Sumerians make?

9. How did Sumerian city-states lose power?

Section 3 • New Empires

10. What helped Assyria build an empire in Mesopotamia?

11. What scientific advancement did the Chaldeans make?

Critical Thinking

12. **Explain** Why do you think Mesopotamia is sometimes called the "cradle of civilization"? **CA 6RC2.3**

13. **Analyze** Why was the development of farming called a revolution? **CA HI3.**

14. **Describe** What rights did women have in the city-states of Sumer? **CA 6RC2.0**

15. **Predict** How successful do you think the Assyrian army would have been if it had not learned how to strengthen iron? **CA HI4.**

Geography Skills

Study the map below and answer the following questions.

16. **Location** On what continent was the earliest fossil evidence of humans found? **CA CS3.**

17. **Movement** Based on fossil evidence, where did early humans go first, Europe or Australia? **CA CS3.**

18. **Analyze** Which three continents are not shown on this map? How do you think early humans reached those continents? **CA CS3.**

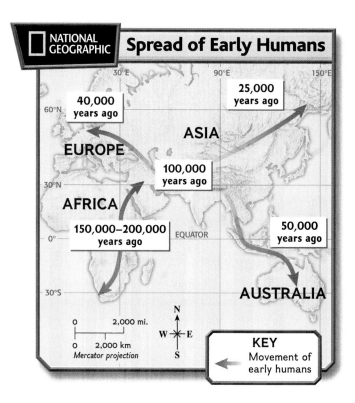

NATIONAL GEOGRAPHIC — **Spread of Early Humans**

40,000 years ago

25,000 years ago

EUROPE

ASIA

100,000 years ago

AFRICA

150,000–200,000 years ago   EQUATOR

50,000 years ago

AUSTRALIA

KEY Movement of early humans

2,000 mi.

2,000 km
Mercator projection

Read to Write

19. **The Big Ideas** Expository Writing Most of what we know about early humans comes from scientific discoveries. Write two to three paragraphs explaining how these scientists help historians gather information about the past. **CA 6WA2.2**

20. Using Your **FOLDABLES** Use your Chapter 1 foldable to create an illustrated time line. Your time line should extend from the date Jericho was founded to the fall of the Chaldean Empire. Create drawings or photocopy maps, artifacts, or architecture to illustrate your time line. **CA 6WS1.3**

Using Academic Vocabulary

21. Use the words listed below as you write a two- to three-paragraph summary of Chapter 1. Make sure that you cover all of the important events and cultures that appear in the chapter. **CA HI1.**

task	code
revolution	core
complex	interval
consist	route

Economics Connection

22. Persuasive Writing Suppose you are a merchant in Çatal Hüyük. A new group of people wants to trade with your village. Write a short speech to persuade your village that there are economic benefits to trading with other people. **CA HI6.**

Linking Past and Present

23. Analyzing Information Imagine you are a nomad who travels from place to place to hunt and gather food. What things would you carry with you to help you survive? Make a list of items and discuss it with your classmates. **CA 6RC2.4**

Reviewing Skills

24. **Reading Skill** Previewing Imagine that a friend has to read Section 3. Write a few paragraphs telling him or her how to preview the section. **CA 6RC2.4**

History Online
Self-Check Quiz To help you prepare for the Chapter Test, visit ca.hss.glencoe.com

25. **Analysis Skill** Researching Many important scientific discoveries, such as Lucy in 1974, changed the way that scientists understand early human history. Use your local library to research the discovery by anthropologist Tim White in 1992. What kind of new information did this discovery provide about early hominids? Write a research paper describing the importance of this discovery. **CA HI5.**

Standards Practice

Select the best answer for each of the following questions.

26 **Which of these was a purpose of the ziggurat in ancient Mesopotamia?**

A weapon storage

B schoolhouse

C office for recording votes

D the city's treasury

27 **The importance of ancient poems such as the *Epic of Gilgamesh* is that they continue to provide people with**

A historically accurate descriptions of events.

B fantastic adventures with great heroes.

C a deeper understanding of future events.

D stories about real, historic people.

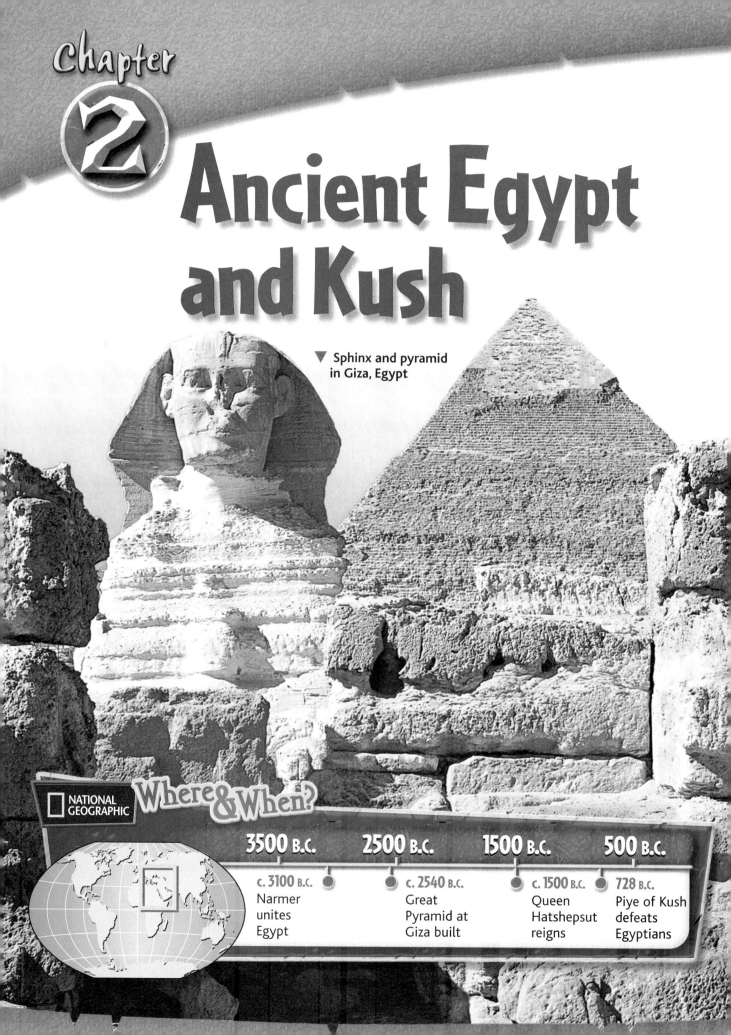

Chapter 2

Ancient Egypt and Kush

▼ Sphinx and pyramid in Giza, Egypt

NATIONAL GEOGRAPHIC **Where&When?**

3500 B.C.	2500 B.C.	1500 B.C.	500 B.C.
c. 3100 B.C. Narmer unites Egypt	**c. 2540 B.C.** Great Pyramid at Giza built	**c. 1500 B.C.** Queen Hatshepsut reigns	**728 B.C.** Piye of Kush defeats Egyptians

The Big Ideas

 The Nile Valley

Physical geography plays a role in how civilizations develop and decline. The fertile land along the great Nile River supported the Egyptian civilization.

 Egypt's Old Kingdom

Religion shapes how culture develops, just as culture shapes how religion develops. During the Old Kingdom period, Egypt built a strong kingdom in which religion was deeply woven into Egyptian culture.

 The Egyptian Empire

All civilizations depend upon leadership for survival. Many changes occurred during Egypt's Middle and New Kingdoms. When strong leaders ruled the country, it expanded into a great empire as arts, literature, and architecture blossomed.

 **The Civilization of Kush**

As different societies interact, they often bring about change in each other. South of Egypt a new civilization arose called Kush. Kushites adopted Egyptian ways and eventually conquered Egypt itself.

 View the Chapter 2 video in the Glencoe Video Program.

 FOLDABLES™
Study Organizer

Summarizing Information *Make this foldable to help you summarize the key events and ideas from ancient Egypt and Kush.*

Step 1 *Stack two sheets of paper so that the front sheet is one inch higher than the back sheet.*

Step 2 *Fold down the top edges of the paper to form four tabs. Align the edges so that all of the layers or tabs are the same distance apart.*

This makes all the tabs the same size.

Step 3 *Crease the paper to hold the tabs in place, then staple them together. Cut the top three thicknesses to create a layered book.*

Staple together along the fold.

Step 4 *Label the booklet as shown and take notes on the inside.*

Reading and Writing *As you read the chapter, take notes under the appropriate tabs. Write main ideas and key terms under the "what" tab.*

Get Ready to Read
Summarizing

Reading Skill

1 Learn It!

Good readers naturally summarize while they read to make sure they understand the text. Summarizing helps you organize information and focus on main ideas. By restating the important facts in a short summary, you can reduce the amount of information to remember.

A summary of a longer selection may be a short sentence or paragraph, which includes the main ideas. When summarizing, be brief and do not include many supporting details. Try to restate the text in a way that makes sense to you and will help you remember. Read the passage in Section 1 labeled **Egypt's Social Classes** on pages 163–164. Then look at the main ideas below from that passage and read the summary.

Summary: Egyptian society was divided into social groups based on wealth and power.

Main Idea: Egypt's upper class was made up of nobles, priests, and other rich Egyptians who worked as the government officials.

Main Idea: Egypt's middle class included traders, merchants, artisans, and makers of goods.

Main Idea: Farmers were the largest group of early Egyptians, while many of Egypt's city dwellers were unskilled laborers.

Reading Tip

As you read and summarize in your own words, try not to change the author's original meanings or ideas.

2 Practice It!

Read about **The Middle Kingdom** on pages 179–180. With a partner, summarize the main points. One person should summarize what he or she read while the other listens. Then the second person should summarize again, adding details that the partner may have left out.

Read to Write ·····

After reading Section 2, write a paragraph that summarizes what you remember about Egyptian leaders, religion, and way of life in the Old Kingdom.

> When you are finished reading, look at the following list to see if you included all the important ideas.
>
> - The Middle Kingdom was a golden age of peace and prosperity in Egypt.
>
> - During the Middle Kingdom, Egypt expanded its territory with new lands.
>
> - During the Middle Kingdom, the arts, literature, and architecture thrived.
>
> - The Hyksos took control of Egypt for 150 years, ending the Middle Kingdom, until Ahmose led an uprising that drove them out.

▲ Tutankhamen's gold mask

3 Apply It!

As you read this chapter, practice summarizing. Stop after each section and write a brief summary.

The Nile Valley

Guide to Reading

History Social Science Standards

WH6.2 Students analyze the geographic, political, economic, religious, and social structures of the early civilizations of Mesopotamia, Egypt, and Kush.

Looking Back, Looking Ahead

In Chapter 1, you learned about early civilizations in Mesopotamia. At about the same time, another civilization was forming near the Nile River. We call this civilization ancient Egypt.

Focusing on the Main Ideas

- The Egyptian civilization began in the fertile Nile River valley, where natural barriers discouraged invasions. *(page 157)*

- The Egyptians depended on the Nile's floods to grow their crops. *(page 159)*

- Around 3100 B.C., Egypt's two major kingdoms, Upper Egypt and Lower Egypt, were combined into one. *(page 161)*

- Egyptian society was divided into social groups based on wealth and power. *(page 163)*

Locating Places
Egypt (EE•jihpt)
Nile River (NYL)
Sahara (suh•HAR•uh)

Content Vocabulary
cataract (KA•tuh•RAKT)
delta (DEHL•tuh)
papyrus (puh•PY•ruhs)
hieroglyphics (HY•ruh•GLIH•fihks)
dynasty (DY•nuh•stee)

Academic Vocabulary
feature (FEE•chuhr)
technology (tehk•NAH•luh•jee)
labor (LAY•buhr)

Reading Strategy
Organizing Information Create a diagram to describe Egyptian irrigation systems.

Irrigation

NATIONAL GEOGRAPHIC Where&When?

Memphis
Nile R.

5000 B.C.

c. 5000 B.C.
Agriculture begins along Nile River

4000 B.C.

c. 4000 B.C.
Egypt is made up of two kingdoms

3000 B.C.

c. 3100 B.C.
Narmer unites Egypt

WH6.2 Students analyze the geographic, political, economic, religious, and social structures of the early civilizations of Mesopotamia, Egypt, and Kush.

WH6.2.1 Locate and describe the major river systems and discuss the physical settings that supported permanent settlement and early civilizations.

Settling the Nile

Main Idea The Egyptian civilization began in the fertile Nile River valley, where natural barriers discouraged invasions.

Reading Connection Did you know that the Nile River is longer than the Amazon, the Mississippi, and every other river in the world? Read on to learn when ancient peoples first moved to its fertile banks.

Between 6000 B.C. and 5000 B.C., hunters and food gatherers moved into the green Nile River valley from less fertile areas of Africa and southwest Asia. They settled down, farmed the land, and created several dozen villages along the riverbanks. These people became the earliest Egyptians.

A Mighty River Although **Egypt** (EE•jihpt) was warm and sunny, the land received little rainfall. For water, the Egyptians had to rely on the **Nile River** (NYL). They drank from it, bathed in it, and used it for farming, cooking, and cleaning. The river provided fish and supported plants and animals. To the Egyptians, the Nile was a precious gift. They praised it in a song: "Hail O Nile, who comes from the earth, who comes to give life to the people of Egypt."

Even today, the Nile inspires awe. It is the world's longest river, flowing north from mountains in the heart of Africa to the Mediterranean Sea. This is a distance of some 4,000 miles (6,437 km). Traveling the length of the Nile would be like going from Georgia to California, and then back again.

The Nile begins as two separate rivers. One river, the Blue Nile, has its source in the mountains of eastern Africa. The other, the White Nile, starts in marshes in central Africa. The two rivers meet and form the Nile just south of Egypt. There, narrow cliffs and boulders in the Nile form wild rapids called **cataracts** (KA•tuh•RAKTS). Because of the cataracts, large ships can use the Nile only for its last 650 miles (1,046 km), where it flows through Egypt.

A Sheltered Land In Egypt, the Nile runs through a narrow, green valley. Look at the map below. You can see that the Nile looks like the long stem of a flower. Shortly before the Nile reaches the Mediterranean Sea, it divides into different branches that look like the flower's blossom. These branches fan out over an area of fertile soil called a **delta** (DEHL•tuh).

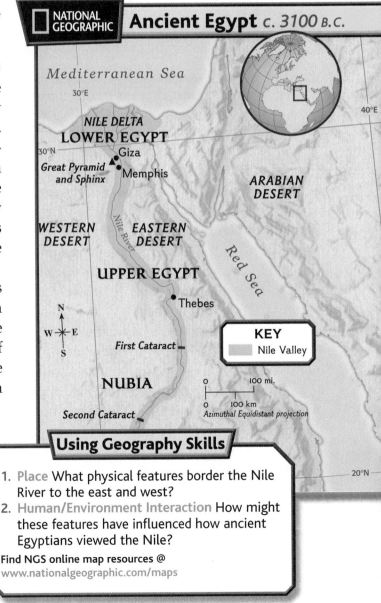

NATIONAL GEOGRAPHIC

Ancient Egypt c. 3100 B.C.

Using Geography Skills

1. Place What physical features border the Nile River to the east and west?
2. Human/Environment Interaction How might these features have influenced how ancient Egyptians viewed the Nile?

Find NGS online map resources @
www.nationalgeographic.com/maps

157

▲ Today, the Nile River valley makes up only about 3 percent of Egypt's land, yet most Egyptians live and work in the area. *How did Egypt's physical setting support settlements and early civilization?*

On both sides of the Nile Valley and its delta, deserts unfold as far as the eye can see. To the west is a vast desert that forms part of the **Sahara** (suh•HAR•uh), the largest desert in the world. To the east, stretching to the Red Sea, is the Eastern Desert. In some places, the change from green land to barren sand is so abrupt that a person can stand with one foot in each.

The ancient Egyptians called the deserts "the Red Land" because of their burning heat. Although these vast expanses could not support farming or human life, they did serve a useful purpose: they kept outside armies away from Egypt's territory.

Other geographic **features** also protected the Egyptians. To the far south, the Nile's dangerous cataracts blocked enemy boats from reaching Egypt. In the north, the delta marshes offered no harbors for invaders approaching from the sea. In this regard, the Egyptians were luckier than the

people of Mesopotamia. In that region, few natural barriers protected the cities. The Mesopotamians constantly had to fight off attackers, but Egypt rarely faced threats. As a result, Egyptian civilization was able to grow and prosper.

Despite their isolation, the Egyptians were not completely closed to the outside world. The Mediterranean Sea bordered Egypt to the north, and the Red Sea lay beyond the desert to the east. These bodies of water gave the Egyptians a way to trade with people outside Egypt.

Within Egypt, people used the Nile for trade and transportation. Winds from the north pushed sailboats south. The flow of the Nile carried them north. Egyptian villages thus had frequent, friendly contact with one another, unlike the hostile relations between the Mesopotamian city-states.

✔ **Reading Check** **Summarize** Describe the physical environment in Egypt.

The River People

Main Idea The Egyptians depended on the Nile's floods to grow their crops.

Reading Connection When you hear about floods, do you picture terrible damage and loss of life? Read on to learn why the Egyptians welcomed, rather than feared, the flooding of the Nile.

In Chapter 1, you learned that the people of Mesopotamia had to tame the floods of the Tigris and Euphrates Rivers in order to farm. They learned to do so, but the unpredictable rivers remained a constant threat.

Regular Flooding Like the Mesopotamians, the Egyptians also had to cope with river floods. However, the Nile floods were much more consistent and gentle than those of the Tigris and the Euphrates. As a result, the Egyptians were able to farm and live securely. They did not worry that sudden, heavy overflows would destroy their homes and crops, or that too little flooding would leave their fields parched.

Every spring, heavy rains from central Africa and melting snows from the highlands of East Africa added to the waters of the Nile as it flowed north. From July to October, the Nile spilled over its banks. When the waters went down, they left behind a layer of dark, fertile silt, or mud. Because of these deposits, the Egyptians called their land *Kemet* (KEH•meht), "the Black Land."

How Did the Egyptians Use the Nile? The Egyptians took advantage of the Nile's floods to become successful farmers. They planted wheat, barley, and flax seeds in the wet, rich soil. Over time, they grew more than enough food to feed themselves and the animals they raised.

One reason for their success was the wise use of irrigation. Egyptian farmers first dug basins, or bowl-shaped holes, in the earth to trap the floodwaters. The farmers then dug canals to carry water from the basins to fields beyond the river's reach. The Egyptians also built dikes, or earthen banks, to strengthen the basin walls.

In time, Egyptian farmers developed other **technology** to help them in their work. For example, they used a shadoof (shuh•DOOF), a bucket attached to a long pole, to lift water from the Nile to the basins. Many Egyptian farmers still use this device today.

 **"Hymn to the Nile"**

This passage is part of a hymn written around 2100 B.C. It shows how important the Nile River was to the people of ancient Egypt.

"You create the grain, you bring forth the barley, assuring perpetuity [survival] to the temples. If you cease your toil and your work, then all that exists is in anguish."

—author unknown, "Hymn to the Nile"

▲ A shadoof

DBQ **Document-Based Question**

How does this hymn show that the ancient Egyptians thought of the Nile as sacred?

Early Egyptians also developed geometry to survey, or measure, land. When floods washed away boundary markers dividing one field from the next, the Egyptians surveyed the fields again to see where one began and the other ended.

Egyptians used **papyrus** (puh•PY•ruhs), a reed plant that grew along the Nile, to make baskets, sandals, and river rafts. Later, they used papyrus for papermaking. They did this by cutting strips from the stalks of the plant. Then they soaked them in water, pounded them flat, dried them, and then joined them together to make paper.

What Were Hieroglyphics? The Egyptians used their papyrus rolls as writing paper. Like the people of Mesopotamia, the Egyptians developed their own system of writing. Originally, it was made up of thousands of picture symbols. Some symbols stood for objects and ideas. To communicate the idea of a boat, for example, a scribe would draw a boat. Later, Egyptians created symbols that stood for sounds, just as the letters of our alphabet do. Combining both picture symbols and sound symbols created a complex writing system that was later called **hieroglyphics** (HY•ruh•GLIH•fihks).

In ancient Egypt, few people could read and write. Some Egyptian men, however, went to special schools located at Egyptian temples to study reading and writing and learn to become scribes. Scribes kept records and worked for the rulers, priests, and traders. Scribes also painstakingly carved hieroglyphics onto stone walls and monuments. For everyday purposes, scribes invented a simpler script and wrote or painted on papyrus.

✓ **Reading Check** **Explain** How did living on the banks of the Nile help farmers?

NATIONAL GEOGRAPHIC

The Way It Was

Focus on Everyday Life

From Farming to Food Harvesting wheat and turning it into bread was vital to the ancient Egyptians. Some people were full-time farmers, but many others were drafted by the government to help during busy seasons.

▲ Tomb painting showing wheat being harvested

The process began as men cut the wheat with wooden sickles and women gathered it into bundles. Animals trampled the wheat to separate the kernels from the husks. The grain was then thrown into the air so the wind would carry away the lightweight seed coverings. Finally, the grain was stored in silos for later use.

▲ Tomb painting showing Egyptian man and woman plowing and planting

WH6.2.2 Trace the development of agricultural techniques that permitted the production of economic surplus and the emergence of cities as centers of culture and power.

WH6.2.6 Describe the role of Egyptian trade in the eastern Mediterranean and Nile valley.

A United Egypt

Main Idea Around 3100 B.C., Egypt's two major kingdoms, Upper Egypt and Lower Egypt, were combined into one.

Reading Connection What types of services does your local government provide? Read on to find out about the government in ancient Egypt.

In Egypt, as in Mesopotamia, skillful farming led to surpluses—extra amounts—of food. This freed some people to work as artisans instead of farmers. They wove cloth, made pottery, carved statues, or shaped copper into weapons and tools.

As more goods became available, Egyptians traded with each other. Before long, Egyptian traders were carrying goods beyond Egypt's borders to Mesopotamia. There they may have picked up ideas about writing and government.

The Rise of Government The advances in farming, crafts, and trade created a need for government in Egypt. Irrigation systems had to be built and maintained, and surplus grain had to be stored and passed out in times of need. In addition, disputes over land ownership had to be settled. Gradually, government emerged to plan and to direct such activities.

The earliest rulers were village chiefs. Over time, a few strong chiefs united groups of villages into small kingdoms. The strongest of these kingdoms eventually overpowered the weaker ones. By 4000 B.C., Egypt was made up of two large kingdoms. In the Nile delta was Lower Egypt. To the south, upriver, lay Upper Egypt. About 3100 B.C., Narmer (NAR•muhr), the king of Upper Egypt, led his armies north and took control of Lower Egypt. The two kingdoms became unified.

◄ Wheat being harvested today

Baking bread in pots ▶

Turning grain into bread was a long process. Women ground the grain into flour, then men pounded it until it became very fine. For the wealthy, seeds, honey, fruit, nuts, and herbs were added to the dough for flavor. Unfortunately, it was almost impossible to keep small stones and sand out of the flour. As a result, many Egyptians developed tooth decay as these particles wore down their tooth enamel.

▲ A replica of an ancient Egyptian bakery

Connecting to the Past

1. How did the government ensure that enough people were available to harvest the wheat?

2. Why do you think seeds, fruit, and other additives were reserved for the wealthy?

Comparing Mesopotamia to Egypt

	Mesopotamia	Egypt
Natural Defenses	Flat mud plains; few natural defenses	Many defenses: Nile delta, Sahara, Eastern Desert, and cataracts
Rivers	Tigris and Euphrates Rivers	Nile River
Floods	Unpredictable, and a constant threat to the people	Dependable and regular; not feared
Economy	Farming and trade	Farming and trade
Government	City-state led by kings and priests; eventually empires formed	Villages led by chiefs, then united into kingdoms; kingdoms later united and ruled by pharaohs
Work of Artisans	Metal products, pottery, cloth	Metal products, pottery, cloth
Advances	• Cuneiform writing • Number system based on 60 • 12-month calendar • Wagon wheel, plow, sailboat	• Hieroglyphic writing • 365-day calendar • Number system based on 10, and fractions • Medicine and first medical books

Understanding Charts

The civilizations of both Mesopotamia and Egypt depended on rivers for fertile lands and irrigation.
1. Which civilization had greater natural defenses? Explain.
2. Compare Use the chart to compare the governments of the two civilizations.

Egypt's Ruling Families

Narmer ruled from Memphis, a city he built on the border between the two kingdoms. Memphis developed into a center of culture and power along the Nile.

To symbolize the kingdom's unity, Narmer wore a double crown. The helmet-like white crown represented Upper Egypt, and the open red crown represented Lower Egypt.

Narmer's united kingdom held together long after his death. Members of his family passed the ruling power from father to son to grandson. Such a line of rulers from one family is called a **dynasty** (DY•nuh•stee). When one dynasty lost control of the kingdom, another took its place.

Over time, ancient Egypt would be ruled by 31 dynasties, which together lasted an estimated 2,800 years. Historians group Egypt's dynasties into three main time periods called kingdoms. The earliest period, the Old Kingdom, was followed by the Middle Kingdom and then the New Kingdom. Each marked a long period of strong leadership and stability.

Reading Check **Explain** How were the kingdoms of Upper and Lower Egypt combined?

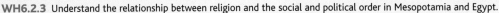

WH6.2 Students analyze the geographic, political, economic, religious, and social structures of the early civilizations of Mesopotamia, Egypt, and Kush.

WH6.2.3 Understand the relationship between religion and the social and political order in Mesopotamia and Egypt.

Early Egyptian Life

Main Idea Egyptian society was divided into social groups based on wealth and power.

Reading Connection Did you play with dolls or balls when you were young? Egyptian children did too. Keep reading for more details about the Egyptians' daily life.

If you made a diagram of the different social groups or classes in ancient Egypt, you would find that they make a pyramid shape. At the top was the king and his family. Beneath that level was a small upper class of priests, army commanders, and nobles. Next came a larger base of skilled middle-class people, such as scribes, traders, and artisans. At the bottom was the largest group—unskilled workers and farmers.

Egypt's Social Classes

Egypt's upper class was made up of nobles, priests, and other wealthy Egyptians who worked as the government officials. They lived in cities and on large estates along the Nile River. They had elegant homes made of wood and mud bricks, with beautiful gardens and pools filled with fish and water lilies. Wealthy families had servants to wait on them and to perform household tasks. The men and women dressed in white linen clothes and wore heavy eye makeup and jewelry.

Egypt's middle class included people who ran businesses or produced goods. They lived in much smaller homes and dressed more simply. Artisans formed an important group within the middle class. They produced linen cloth, jewelry, pottery, and metal goods.

Ancient Egyptian society was ▶ highly structured. At the top was the pharaoh and his family. At the bottom was the group with the least wealth—unskilled workers. *What group was just below the pharaoh in Egyptian society?*

Pharaoh

Priests and nobles

Traders, artisans, shopkeepers, and scribes

Farmers and herders

Unskilled workers

CHAPTER 2 • Ancient Egypt   **163**

Farmers were part of the largest group of early Egyptians. Some rented their land from their ruler, paying him with a large portion of their crops. Most worked the land of wealthy nobles. They lived in villages along the Nile, in one-room huts with roofs made of palm leaves. They had a simple diet of bread, beer, vegetables, and fruit.

Many of Egypt's city dwellers were unskilled workers who did physical **labor.** Some unloaded cargo from boats and carried it to markets. Others made and stacked mud bricks for buildings. Workers lived in crowded city neighborhoods. They had small mud-brick homes with hard-packed dirt floors and a courtyard for the family's animals. On the flat rooftops, families talked, played games, and slept. Women worked on the rooftops, drying fruit, making bread, and weaving cloth.

Family Life In ancient Egypt, the father headed the family. However, Egyptian women had more rights than females in most other early civilizations. In Egypt, women could own and pass on property. They could buy and sell goods, make wills, and obtain divorces. Upper-class women were in charge of temples and could perform religious ceremonies.

Few Egyptians sent their children to school. Mothers taught their daughters to sew, cook, and run a household. Boys learned farming or skilled trades from their fathers. Egyptian children had time for fun, as well. They played with board games, dolls, spinning tops, and stuffed leather balls.

✓ **Reading Check** **Identify** How was Egyptian society organized?

Study Central Need help understanding the rise of Egyptian civilization? Visit ca.hss.glencoe.com and click on Study Central.

Section ❶ Review

Reading Summary

Review the Main Ideas

- The deserts on either side of the Nile Valley, along with the Nile cataracts and delta marshes, protected Egypt from invaders.

- The Egyptians became successful farmers using the Nile River's floods and irrigation.

- About 3100 B.C., Narmer united Lower Egypt and Upper Egypt.

- Egypt's society was divided into upper-class priests and nobles, middle-class artisans and merchants, and lower-class workers and farmers.

What Did You Learn?

1. What is papyrus and how did the Egyptians use it?

2. What rights did women have in ancient Egypt?

Critical Thinking

3. **Cause and Effect** Draw a diagram to show three things that led to the growth of government in ancient Egypt. **CA HI2.**

☐	
☐	→ Growth of Government in Ancient Egypt
☐	

4. **The Big Ideas** How did the geography of the Nile River valley lead to the growth of a civilization there? **CA CS1.**

5. **Draw Conclusions** How do Egyptian hieroglyphics help us learn about their society and culture? **CA HR4.**

6. **Analyze** What was the significance of Narmer's double crown? **CA HI1.**

7. **Reading** Summarizing Using what you have learned in this section, summarize the yearly cycle of the Nile River. Be sure to describe how this cycle affected farmers in ancient Egypt. **CA 6RC2.4**

Section 2

Egypt's Old Kingdom

Guide to Reading

Looking Back, Looking Ahead

In Section 1, you learned that Egyptian dynasties are divided into the Old Kingdom, Middle Kingdom, and New Kingdom. In Section 2, you will learn about the Egyptians' leaders, religion, and way of life in the Old Kingdom.

Focusing on the Main Ideas

- Egypt was ruled by all-powerful pharaohs. *(page 166)*

- The Egyptians believed in many gods and goddesses and in life after death for the pharaohs. *(page 167)*

- The Egyptians of the Old Kingdom built huge stone pyramids as tombs for their pharaohs. *(page 168)*

Locating Places
Giza (GEE•zuh)

Meeting People
King Khufu (KOO•foo)

Content Vocabulary
pharaoh (FEHR•oh)
deity (DEE•uh•tee)
embalming (ihm•BAHM•ihng)
mummy (MUH•mee)
pyramid (PIHR•uh•MIHD)

Academic Vocabulary
period (PIHR•ee•uhd)
welfare (WEHL•FAR)
structure (STRUHK•chuhr)
principle (PRIHN•suh•puhl)

Reading Strategy
Organizing Information Use a graphic organizer like the one below to identify the different beliefs in Egypt's religion.

Egyptian beliefs

History Social Science Standards

WH6.2 Students analyze the geographic, political, economic, religious, and social structures of the early civilizations of Mesopotamia, Egypt, and Kush.

 Where & When?

2600 B.C.	2400 B.C.	2200 B.C.
c. 2600 B.C. Old Kingdom period begins	c. 2540 B.C. Great Pyramid at Giza built	c. 2300 B.C. Old Kingdom declines

Memphis • Giza

Nile R.

Old Kingdom Rulers

Main Idea Egypt was ruled by all-powerful pharaohs.

Reading Connection Would you want your student body president or your sports team captain to have unlimited power? Think what it would be like to have such a leader as you read about the rulers of ancient Egypt.

Around 2600 B.C., the **period** known as the Old Kingdom began in Egypt. The Old Kingdom lasted until about 2300 B.C. During those years, Egypt grew and prospered. The Egyptians built cities, expanded trade, and established a strong government.

The Egyptian kings, or **pharaohs** (FEHR•ohs) as they were called, lived with their families in grand palaces. In fact, the word *pharaoh* originally meant "great house." The pharaoh was an all-powerful ruler who guided Egypt's every activity. His word was law, and it had to be obeyed without question.

Pharaohs appointed many officials to carry out their wishes. These officials saw to it that irrigation canals and grain storehouses were built and repaired. They made sure that crops were planted as the pharaoh directed. They also controlled trade and collected tax payments of grain from farmers.

Why did Egyptians willingly serve the pharaoh? One reason was that they believed the unity of the kingdom depended on a strong leader. Another was that they considered the pharaoh to be the son of Re (RAY), the Egyptian sun god. As a result, his subjects paid him the greatest respect. Whenever he appeared in public, people played music on flutes and cymbals. Bystanders along the road had to bow down and "smell the earth," or touch their heads to the ground.

The Egyptians thought their pharaoh was a god on earth who controlled Egypt's **welfare.** He carried out certain rituals that were thought to benefit the kingdom. For example, he drove a sacred bull around Memphis, the capital city. The Egyptians believed this ceremony would keep the soil rich and ensure good crops. The pharaoh was also the first to cut ripe grain. Egyptians believed this would bring a good harvest.

✓ **Reading Check** **Analyze** Why did the pharaohs hold so much power?

◄ The Great Sphinx, a huge statue with the head of a man (perhaps a pharaoh) and the body of a lion, stands guard outside the tomb of a pharaoh. *What did the word pharaoh mean, and why was it used for Egypt's rulers?*

Egypt's Religion

Main Idea The Egyptians believed in many gods and goddesses and in life after death for the pharaohs.

Reading Connection Have you seen mummies in horror movies? Maybe you've even wrapped yourself in strips of cloth to be a mummy for a costume party. Keep reading to find out how the ancient Egyptians made mummies, and why.

Religion was deeply woven into Egyptian culture. Like the people of Mesopotamia, the ancient Egyptians worshiped many **deities** (DEE•uh•teez), or gods and goddesses. The Egyptians believed these deities controlled the forces of nature and human activities.

The main Egyptian god was the sun god Re. This was probably because of Egypt's hot, sunny climate and the importance of the sun for good harvests. Another major god was Hapi (HAH•pee), who ruled the Nile River. The most important goddess was Isis (EYE•suhs). She represented the loyal wife and mother, and she ruled over the dead with her husband Osiris (oh•SY•ruhs).

Life After Death

Unlike the Mesopotamians, who imagined a gloomy life after death, the Egyptians took a hopeful view. They believed that life in the next world would be even better than life on Earth. Following a long journey, the dead would reach a place of peace and plenty.

One of the most important manuscripts written in ancient Egypt was the *Book of the Dead*. This was a collection of spells and prayers that Egyptians studied to obtain life after death. They believed that the god Osiris would meet newcomers at the entrance to the next world. If they had led good lives and knew the magic spells, Osiris would grant them life after death.

▲ During the embalming process, the pharaoh's body was placed on a special table. The chief embalmer was dressed as Anubis, the god of mummification. *Why did the Egyptians embalm the pharaoh's body?*

For centuries, Egyptians believed that only the pharaohs and a special few people could enjoy the afterlife. They also believed that the pharaoh's spirit needed a body to make the journey to the afterlife. If the pharaoh's body decayed after death, his spirit would be forced to wander forever. It was vital that a pharaoh's spirit reach the next world. There, the pharaoh would continue to care for Egypt.

To protect the pharaoh's body, the Egyptians developed a process called **embalming** (ihm•BAHM•ihng). First, priests removed the body's organs. A special kind of salt was then applied to the body, and it was stored for a number of days to dry. After this, the body was filled with spices and perfumes, then stitched closed. Next, it was cleaned with oils and tightly wrapped with long strips of linen. The wrapped body was known as a **mummy** (MUH•mee). It was put in several wooden coffins, one fitting inside the other. The pharaoh was then ready for burial in a tomb.

Egyptian Medicine

In the course of embalming the dead, the Egyptians learned much about the human body. Egyptian doctors used herbs and drugs to treat many different illnesses. They grew skilled at sewing up cuts and setting broken bones.

Some doctors focused on treating particular parts of the body, becoming the first specialists in medicine. Egyptians also wrote the world's first medical books using scrolls of papyrus.

✓ **Reading Check** **Identify** Who were some of the Egyptians' main gods and goddesses?

The Pyramids

Main Idea The Egyptians of the Old Kingdom built huge stone pyramids as tombs for their pharaohs.

Reading Connection Do you think the Statue of Liberty or the White House will still be standing in 4,000 years? The giant pyramids of Egypt have stood for about that long. Read to find out how and why they were built.

No ordinary tomb would do for a pharaoh of Egypt. Instead, the Egyptians built mountainlike **pyramids** (PIHR•uh•MIHDS) entirely of stone. These gigantic **structures,** the size of several city blocks, protected the bodies of dead pharaohs from floods, wild animals, and grave robbers. The pyramids also held supplies that the pharaoh might need in the spirit world, including clothing, furniture, jewelry, and food.

Egypt's Religion

▼ Osiris

▲ In this painting, the god Osiris (seated at right) watches as other animal-headed gods weigh a dead man's soul and record the results. The scales have balanced, so the dead man may enter the underworld. *What was the Book of the Dead?*

How Was a Pyramid Built? It took thousands of people and years of backbreaking labor to build a pyramid. Most of the work was done by farmers during the Nile floods, when they could not tend their fields. In addition, surveyors, engineers, carpenters, and stonecutters lent their skills.

Each pyramid sat on a square base, with the entrance facing north. To determine true north, the Egyptians studied the heavens and developed **principles** of astronomy. With this knowledge, they invented a 365-day calendar with 12 months grouped into 3 seasons. This calendar became the basis for our modern calendar.

To determine the amount of stone needed for a pyramid, as well as the angles necessary for the walls, the Egyptians made advances in mathematics. They invented a system of written numbers based on 10. They also created fractions, using them with whole numbers to add, subtract, and divide.

After the pyramid site was chosen, workers went wherever they could find stone—sometimes hundreds of miles away. Skilled artisans used copper tools to cut the stone into huge blocks. Other workers tied the blocks to wooden sleds and pulled them to the Nile over a path "paved" with logs. Next, they loaded the stones onto barges that transported them to the building site. There, workers unloaded the blocks and dragged or pushed them up ramps to be set in place.

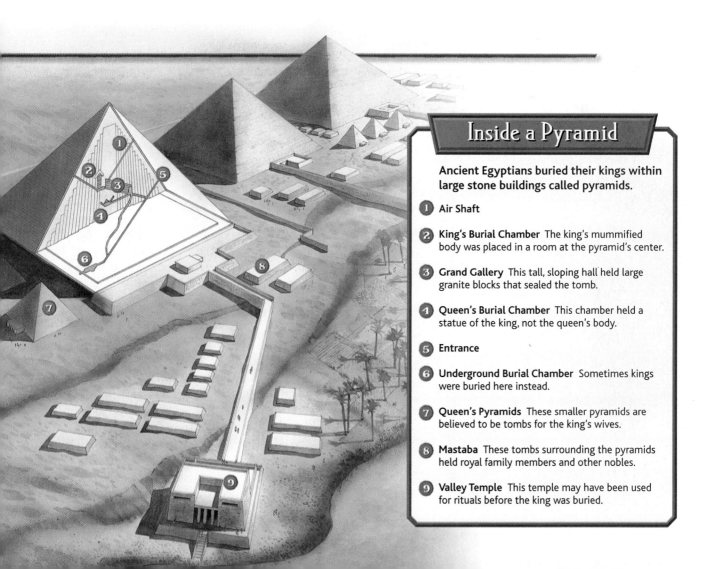

Inside a Pyramid

Ancient Egyptians buried their kings within large stone buildings called pyramids.

1. **Air Shaft**

2. **King's Burial Chamber** The king's mummified body was placed in a room at the pyramid's center.

3. **Grand Gallery** This tall, sloping hall held large granite blocks that sealed the tomb.

4. **Queen's Burial Chamber** This chamber held a statue of the king, not the queen's body.

5. **Entrance**

6. **Underground Burial Chamber** Sometimes kings were buried here instead.

7. **Queen's Pyramids** These smaller pyramids are believed to be tombs for the king's wives.

8. **Mastaba** These tombs surrounding the pyramids held royal family members and other nobles.

9. **Valley Temple** This temple may have been used for rituals before the king was buried.

▲ The pyramid shown above is that of King Khafre, son of Khufu. Although it is smaller than the Great Pyramid, Khafre's pyramid was built on higher ground so as to appear taller. *About how tall is the Great Pyramid?*

The Great Pyramid About 2540 B.C., the Egyptians built the largest and grandest of the pyramids known as the Great Pyramid. It is located about 10 miles from the modern city of Cairo. This pyramid, built for **King Khufu** (KOO•foo), is one of three still standing in **Giza** (GEE•zuh) on the west bank of the Nile. It rises nearly 500 feet (153 m) above the desert, covers an area about the size of nine football fields, and contains more than 2 million stone blocks. Each block weighs an average of 2.5 tons.

The Great Pyramid was the tallest structure in the world for more than 4,000 years. It is equal to the size of a 48-story building and is the largest of about 80 pyramids found in Egypt. The Great Pyramid is truly a marvelous structure because the Egyptians built it without using beasts of burden, special tools, or even the wheel.

✓ **Reading Check** **Explain** What was the purpose of pyramids?

History Online

Study Central Need help with the Old Kingdom in Egypt? Visit ca.hss.glencoe.com and click on Study Central.

Section 2 Review

What Did You Learn?

1. How was stone for a pyramid transported to the building site?

2. What did Egyptians learn from embalming bodies?

Critical Thinking

3. **Organize Information** Draw a diagram like the one below. Fill in details about the pharaohs of the Old Kingdom and their duties. **CA 6RC2.4**

Pharaohs

4. **Math Connection** How did the building of the pyramids lead to advances in science and mathematics? **CA HI2.**

5. **The Big Ideas** How did the Egyptians' religious beliefs compare to those of the Mesopotamians? **CA 6RC2.3**

6. **Persuasive Writing** Suppose you are an Egyptian pharaoh who wants a pyramid built to house your tomb. Write a letter to the farmers and workers in your kingdom explaining why it is their duty to build the pyramid for you. **CA 6WA2.5**

Reading Summary

Review the **Main Ideas**

• The all-powerful rulers of Egypt, called pharaohs, were believed to be related to Egypt's main god.

• The Egyptians believed in many gods and goddesses. They also believed in life after death for the pharaoh, whose body would be mummified before burial.

• The pyramids, built as huge stone tombs for the pharaohs, required many years and thousands of workers to construct.

WORLD LITERATURE

THE EGYPTIAN CINDERELLA

By Shirley Climo

Before You Read

The Scene: This story takes place in ancient Egypt, along the Nile River. It occurs during the time of the Pharaoh Amasis, about 550 B.C.

The Characters: Rhodopis is a Greek girl who is enslaved by an Egyptian man. There are three servant girls who work with her. Amasis is the pharaoh of Egypt.

The Plot: The Pharaoh announces that he will hold court for all of his subjects. The rest of the servant girls get to go, but Rhodopis is left behind.

Vocabulary Preview

snatched: to grab something quickly

bidding: an order

gilded: covered with or containing gold

sash: a band of fabric worn around the waist or over the shoulder

tunic: a knee-length piece of clothing that is usually tied up with a belt

din: a loud, confused mixture of noise

rushes: plants that are found in or near water

Have you ever felt unappreciated or ignored? In this story, a girl who is normally taken for granted learns to overcome the bad way others treat her.

171

As You Read

Many different areas of the world have their own version of the Cinderella story. This tale from ancient Egypt uses the main ideas of the story and combines them with Egyptian history. Many of the characters in this tale were based on real people who lived in Egypt thousands of years ago. How does this version of the story differ from the one you know?

Long ago in the land of Egypt where the green Nile River widens to meet the blue sea, there lived a maiden called Rhodopis. When she was still a small child, Rhodopis had been stolen by pirates. She was snatched from her home in Greece, taken across the sea to Egypt and there sold as a slave.

Like the Egyptian servant girls, Rhodopis went to the water's edge each day to wash clothes or to gather the reeds that grew along the riverbank. But Rhodopis looked different from the Egyptian girls. Their eyes were brown and hers were green. Their hair hung straight to their shoulders, while the breeze blew hers into tangles. Their skin glowed like copper, but her pale skin burned red beneath the sun. That was how she got her name, for Rhodopis meant "rosy-cheeked" in Greek. . . .

Although her master was kind, he was old and liked to doze beneath a fig tree. He seldom heard the servant girls tease Rhodopis. He never saw them ordering her about. . . .

Rhodopis found friends among the animals instead. Birds ate crumbs from her hands. She coaxed a monkey to sit upon her shoulder and charmed a hippopotamus with her songs. It would raise its huge head from the muddy water and prick its small ears to listen.

Sometimes, when her chores were done and the day had cooled, Rhodopis would dance for her animal companions. She twirled so light that her tiny bare feet scarcely touched the ground. One evening her master awakened to see her dance.

"No goddess is more nimble!" he called out. "Such a gift deserves reward." He tugged his chin whiskers, thinking, and then declared, "You shall go barefoot no longer."

Her master ordered a pair of dainty slippers made especially for Rhodopis. The soles were of real leather, and the toes were gilded with rose-red gold. Now when Rhodopis danced, her feet sparkled like fireflies.

The rose-red slippers set Rhodopis more apart than ever. The Egyptian servant girls were jealous, for they wore clumsy sandals woven from papyrus.[1] Out of spite they found new tasks for her to do, keeping Rhodopis so busy that she was too tired to dance at night.

One evening, Kipa, who was chief among the servant girls, announced, "Tomorrow we sail for Memphis to see the Pharaoh. His Majesty is going to hold court for all his subjects."

"There will be musicians and dancing," said another servant girl, eyeing the rose-red slippers.

---

[1]**papyrus:** a plant that grows by the Nile River

"There will be feasting," added a third.

"Poor Rhodopis! You must stay behind," Kipa jeered. "You have linen to wash and grain to grind and the garden to weed."

The next morning, just as Ra[2] the Sun was climbing into the sky, Rhodopis followed the servant girls to the riverbank. . . . Perhaps they will let me come along to see the Pharaoh after all, she thought. But the three servant girls poled their raft around the bend in the river without giving Rhodopis a backward glance.

---

[2]**Ra:** the ancient Egyptian sun god, also known as Re.

Rhodopis sighed, and turned to the basket piled high with dirty clothes. "Wash the linen, weed the garden, grind the grain." She slapped the wooden paddle against the cloth in time to her song.

The hippopotamus, tired of so dull a tune, pushed out of the reeds and splashed into the river.

"Shame!" cried Rhodopis, shaking her paddle. "You splattered mud on my beautiful slippers!"

She polished the shoes on the hem of her tunic until the rosy gold glittered in the sun. Then she carefully put them on the bank behind her.

"Wash the linen, weed the garden . . . " Rhodopis began again, when suddenly a shadow fell on the water. Rhodopis jumped up. A great falcon, the symbol of the god Horus,[3] circled in the sky with wings spread so wide that they blotted out the sun.

"Greetings to you, Proud Horus," Rhodopis murmured. She bowed her head and felt a rush of air on the back of her neck.

When Rhodopis dared to lift her eyes, she saw the falcon soar away. Dangling from his talons was one of her beautiful slippers. "Stop!" she pleaded. "Come back!"

But the bird did not heed her. He flew toward the sun until he was no more than a dark speck against the gold. . . .

After Rhodopis had lost sight of the falcon, the mighty bird followed the course of the Nile to the city of Memphis, to the square where the Pharaoh was

---

[3]**Horus:** the falcon-headed god of ancient Egypt

holding court. There the falcon watched and waited.

The Pharaoh's name was Amasis.[4] On his head he wore the red-and-white crown of the Two Egypts.[5] The double crown was heavy and pinched his ears. He preferred driving his chariot fast as the wind to sitting on the throne. Amasis yawned.

At that very moment, the falcon dropped the rose-red slipper into his lap.

The slipper was so bright that Amasis thought it was a scrap of the sun. Then he saw the falcon wheeling overhead.

"The god Horus sends me a sign!" exclaimed the Pharaoh. He picked up the rose-red slipper. "Every maiden in Egypt must try this shoe! She whose foot it fits shall be my queen. That is the will of the gods."

Amasis dismissed the court, called for his chariot, and began his search at once. . . .

The Pharaoh journeyed to distant cities, he tracked the desert where pyramids tower over the sand, and he climbed the steep cliffs where falcons nest. The rose-red slipper was always in his hand. Wherever he went, women and girls, rich or poor, flocked to try on this slipper. But none could fit into so small a shoe.

The longer Amasis searched, the more determined he became to marry the maiden who had lost the tiny slipper. He

summoned his royal barge and vowed to visit every landing along the Nile. The barge was hung with sails of silk. Trumpets blared and oarsmen rowed to the beat of gongs. The din was so dreadful that when the barge rounded the bed in the river, Rhodopis fled in alarm. But the servant girls ran to the water's edge. . . .

Amasis held up the rose-red slipper. "Whoever can wear this shoe shall be my queen."

The servant girls knew that shoe, and knew its owner, too. Yet they clapped their hands over their mouths and said nothing. If one of them could wear it . . .

First Kipa, then the others, tried to put on the slipper. Each cramped her foot and curled her toes and squeezed until tears ran down her cheeks. Still her heel hung over.

---

[4]**Amasis:** pharaoh of Egypt from 570–526 B.C.
[5]**red-and-white crown of the Two Egypts:** a crown worn to symbolize Egypt's unity

"Enough!" said Amasis wearily. He would have set sail again had he not chanced to see Rhodopis peering through the rushes.

"Come!" he commanded. "You must try this rose-red slipper."

The servant girls gawked openmouthed as the Pharaoh kneeled before Rhodopis. He slipped the tiny shoe on her foot with ease. Then Rhodopis pulled its mate from the folds of her tunic.

"Behold!" cried Amasis. "In all this land there is none so fit to be queen!"

"But Rhodopis is a slave!" protested one of the servant girls.

Kipa sniffed. "She is not even Egyptian."

"She is the most Egyptian of all," the Pharaoh declared. "For her eyes are as green as the Nile, her hair as feathery as papyrus, and her skin the pink of a lotus flower."

The Pharaoh led Rhodopis to the royal barge, and with every step, her rose-red slippers winked and sparkled in the sun.

Responding to the Literature

1. What does Rhodopis receive as a gift from her master?

2. Which god does Amasis think is sending him a sign?

3. **Drawing Conclusions** In what ways does the fact that Rhodopis is actually a Greek affect the story? Why do you think this is so? **CA 6RL3.2**

4. **Analyze** How does the author use the setting to advance the action of the story? **CA 6RL3.3**

5. **Read to Write** Pretend that you are Rhodopis. What might you have done if it had been your slipper that was taken? Write two to three paragraphs explaining what you would have done to get the slipper back. **CA 6WS1.2**

Reading on Your Own...

Are you interested in the story of early humans, the exciting world
of ancient Egypt, or the history of the Israelites?
If so, check out these other great books.

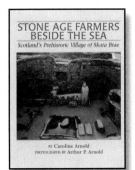

Nonfiction

Stone Age Farmers Beside the Sea by Caroline Arnold introduces the prehistoric village of Skara Brae in northern Scotland. This book describes the daily lives and experiences of people who lived over five thousand years ago. **The content of this book is related to** *History–Social Science Standard WH6.1.*

Fiction

Boy of the Painted Cave by Justin F. Denzel tells the story of a young cave boy named Tao. Tao wants to be a cave painter but it is forbidden by his clan. The book tells of his struggle against those around him. **The content of this book is related to** *History–Social Science Standard WH6.1.*

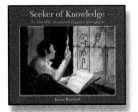

Biography

Seeker of Knowledge by James Rumford describes the life and events of Jean-François Champollion, the man who first deciphered Egyptian hieroglyphs. The book explains how Jean-François was able to learn to read the hieroglyphs. **The content of this book is related to** *History–Social Science Standard WH6.2.*

Biography

Herod the Great by Robert Green tells the story of the life and reign of King Herod. The book describes the major successes and failures of the king of Judaea. **The content of this book is related to** *History–Social Science Standard WH6.3.*

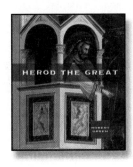

Section 3

The Egyptian Empire

Guide to Reading

History Social Science Standards

WH6.2 Students analyze the geographic, political, economic, religious, and social structures of the early civilizations of Mesopotamia, Egypt, and Kush.

Looking Back, Looking Ahead

During the Old Kingdom, Egyptians established their civilization. During the Middle Kingdom and the New Kingdom, Egypt's powerful pharaohs expanded the empire by conquering other lands.

Focusing on the Main Ideas

- The Middle Kingdom was a golden age of peace, prosperity, and advances in the arts and architecture. *(page 179)*

- During the New Kingdom, Egypt acquired new territory and reached the height of its power. *(page 180)*

- Akhenaton tried to change Egypt's religion, while Tutankhamen is famous for the treasures buried with him in his tomb. *(page 183)*

- Under Ramses II, Egypt regained territory and built great temples, but the empire fell by 1150 B.C. *(page 184)*

Locating Places

Thebes (THEEBZ)

Meeting People

Ahmose (AHM•OHS)
Hatshepsut (hat•SHEHP•soot)
Thutmose III (thoot•MOH•suh)
Akhenaton (AHK•NAH•tuhn)
Tutankhamen
    (TOO•TANG•KAH•muhn)
Ramses II (RAM•SEEZ)

Content Vocabulary

tribute (TRIH•byoot)

Academic Vocabulary

restore (rih•STOHR)
maintain (mayn•TAYN)
construct (kuhn•STRUHKT)

Reading Strategy

Categorizing Information Create a diagram to show the major accomplishments of Ramses II.

Ramses

NATIONAL GEOGRAPHIC Where & When?

Memphis
Thebes
Nile R.

2400 B.C.	1600 B.C.	800 B.C.
c. 2050 B.C. Middle Kingdom begins	c. 1500 B.C. Queen Hatshepsut reigns	c. 1279 B.C. Ramses II takes the throne

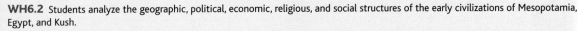

WH6.2 Students analyze the geographic, political, economic, religious, and social structures of the early civilizations of Mesopotamia, Egypt, and Kush.

WH6.2.5 Discuss the main features of Egyptian art and architecture.

The Middle Kingdom

Main Idea The Middle Kingdom was a golden age of peace, prosperity, and advances in the arts and architecture.

Reading Connection Have you heard older people talk about enjoying their "golden years"? Countries can also experience such happy, productive times. In the following paragraphs, you'll learn why the Middle Kingdom was a golden age for Egypt.

About 2300 B.C., the pharaohs lost control of Egypt as nobles battled one another for power. Almost 200 years of confusion followed. Finally, a new dynasty of pharaohs came to power. They moved their capital south from Memphis to a city called **Thebes** (THEEBZ). There they **restored** order and stability, ushering in a new period called the Middle Kingdom.

The Middle Kingdom lasted from about 2050 B.C. to 1670 B.C. During this interval, Egyptians enjoyed a golden age of stability, prosperity, and achievement.

The Drive for More Land
During the Middle Kingdom, Egypt took control of new lands. Soldiers captured Nubia to the south and attacked what is now Syria. The conquered peoples sent **tribute** (TRIH•byoot), or forced payments, to the Egyptian pharaoh, enriching the kingdom.

Within Egypt, the pharaohs added more waterways and dams. They increased the amount of land being farmed and built a canal between the Nile River and the Red Sea.

History Online

Web Activity Visit ca.hss.glencoe.com and click on *Chapter 2—Student Web Activity* to learn more about ancient Egypt.

▲ This artwork with gold inlay from the Middle Kingdom period shows a funeral boat. *How did architecture change during the Middle Kingdom?*

The Arts Blossom
During the Middle Kingdom, arts, literature, and architecture thrived. Painters covered the walls of tombs and temples with colorful scenes of the deities and daily life. Sculptors created large wall carvings and statues of the pharaohs, showing them as ordinary people rather than godlike figures. Poets wrote love songs and tributes to the pharaohs.

A new form of architecture was also created. Instead of building pyramids, pharaohs had their tombs cut into cliffs west of the Nile River. This area became known as the Valley of the Kings.

Who Were the Hyksos?
The Middle Kingdom came to an end in 1670 B.C. Nobles were again plotting to take power from the pharaohs. This time, however, Egypt also faced a serious threat from outside. A people known as the Hyksos (HIHK•SAHS), from western Asia, attacked Egypt.

WH6.2 Students analyze the geographic, political, economic, religious, and social structures of the early civilizations of Mesopotamia, Egypt, and Kush. WH6.2.6 Describe the role of Egyptian trade in the eastern Mediterranean and Nile valley. WH6.2.7 Understand the significance of Queen Hatshepsut and Ramses the Great.

The Hyksos were mighty warriors. They crossed the desert in horse-drawn chariots and used weapons made of bronze and iron. Egyptians had always fought on foot with copper and stone weapons. They were no match for the invaders.

The Hyksos ruled Egypt for about 150 years. Then, around 1550 B.C., an Egyptian prince named **Ahmose** (AHM•OHS) led an uprising that drove the Hyksos out of Egypt.

✓ Reading Check **Explain** What advances in art were made during the Middle Kingdom?

The New Kingdom

Main Idea During the New Kingdom, Egypt acquired new territory and reached the height of its power.

Reading Connection Do you know the names of any women who hold political office? In ancient civilizations, women rarely held positions of power. Read to learn how a woman became ruler of Egypt.

Ahmose's reign in Egypt began a period known as the New Kingdom. During this time, from about 1550 B.C. to 1080 B.C., Egypt became even richer and more powerful.

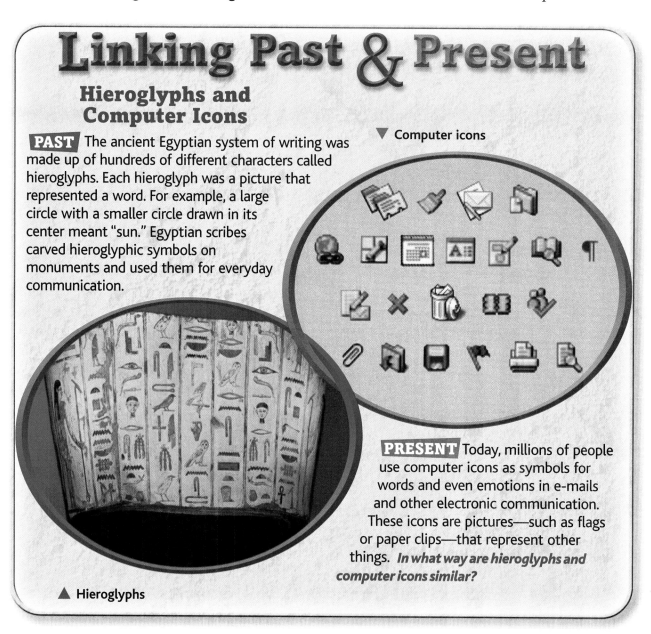

Linking Past & Present

Hieroglyphs and Computer Icons

PAST The ancient Egyptian system of writing was made up of hundreds of different characters called hieroglyphs. Each hieroglyph was a picture that represented a word. For example, a large circle with a smaller circle drawn in its center meant "sun." Egyptian scribes carved hieroglyphic symbols on monuments and used them for everyday communication.

▼ **Computer icons**

PRESENT Today, millions of people use computer icons as symbols for words and even emotions in e-mails and other electronic communication. These icons are pictures—such as flags or paper clips—that represent other things. *In what way are hieroglyphs and computer icons similar?*

▲ **Hieroglyphs**

A Woman Ruler About 1473 B.C., a queen named **Hatshepsut** (hat•SHEHP•soot) came to power in Egypt. She ruled first with her husband and then, after his death, on behalf of her young nephew. Finally she made herself pharaoh. Hatshepsut became one of the few women to rule Egypt.

Hatshepsut was more interested in trade than conquest. During her reign, Egyptian traders sailed across the eastern Mediterranean and south along the east coast of Africa. One product Egyptians wanted to find was wood. The Nile Valley had few trees, and the Egyptians needed wood for boats and for wood cabinets that the upper class liked to have in their homes.

The search for wood took Egyptian traders to the east coast of the Mediterranean Sea where the country of Lebanon is located today. The area had many trees, and the people in the region, called the Phoenicians, were famous for their crafts. They made beautiful wooden furniture and were among the first people to learn how to make glass.

The Egyptians traded wheat as well as paper, gold, copper, and tools for Phoenician wood and furniture. The Phoenicians then traded Egyptian goods to other people. In this way, Egyptian food and goods spread across the Middle East. Egypt's trade in the eastern Mediterranean helped make the kingdom wealthier.

Expanding the Empire When Hatshepsut died, her nephew, **Thutmose III** (thoot•MOH•suh), became pharaoh. Thutmose's armies expanded Egypt's borders north to the Euphrates River in Mesopotamia. His troops also moved south and regained control of Nubia, which had broken free from Egypt earlier.

Thutmose's empire grew rich from trade and tribute. In addition to claiming gold, copper, ivory, and other valuable goods

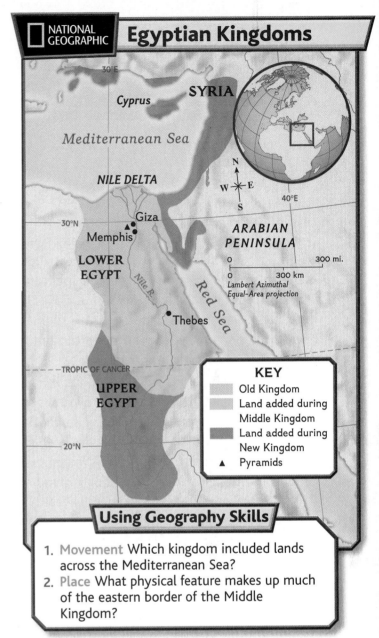

NATIONAL GEOGRAPHIC — **Egyptian Kingdoms**

SYRIA
Cyprus
Mediterranean Sea
NILE DELTA
Giza
Memphis
LOWER EGYPT
Nile R.
Thebes
ARABIAN PENINSULA
Red Sea
TROPIC OF CANCER
UPPER EGYPT
30°E
30°N
40°E
20°N

0   300 mi.
0   300 km
Lambert Azimuthal Equal-Area projection

KEY
- Old Kingdom
- Land added during Middle Kingdom
- Land added during New Kingdom
- ▲ Pyramids

Using Geography Skills

1. **Movement** Which kingdom included lands across the Mediterranean Sea?
2. **Place** What physical feature makes up much of the eastern border of the Middle Kingdom?

from conquered peoples, Egypt enslaved many prisoners of war. These unfortunate captives were put to work rebuilding Thebes. They filled the city with beautiful palaces, temples, and monuments.

Slavery had not been widespread in Egypt before. During the New Kingdom, however, it became common. Enslaved people did have some rights. They could own land, marry, and eventually be granted their freedom.

✓ Reading Check **Summarize** Describe Egyptian trade during the rule of Hatshepsut.

WH6.2.7 Understand the significance of Queen Hatshepsut and Ramses the Great.

HATSHEPSUT
Reigned 1473–1458 B.C.

Hatshepsut ▶

Hatshepsut was the daughter of King Thutmose I and Queen Aahmes. Even as a young princess, she was confident, describing herself as "exceedingly good to look upon . . . a beautiful maiden" who was "serene [peaceful] of nature." During her marriage to King Thutmose II, Hatshepsut influenced her husband's decisions and hoped to someday have more power. She saw an opportunity when Thutmose died and declared herself pharaoh.

Because the position of pharaoh was usually passed from father to son, Hatshepsut had to prove that she was a good leader. She often wore men's clothing to convince the people that she could handle what had always been a man's job. Unlike other pharaohs, Hatshepsut avoided military conquests. She focused her attention instead on expanding Egypt's economy. She restored Egypt's wealth through trade with Africa, Asia, and throughout the eastern Mediterranean. Returning home from trading expeditions, cargo ships were loaded with wood, ebony, furniture, ivory, incense, and myrrh. During her reign, Hatshepsut also rebuilt many of Egypt's great temples, including the temple at Karnak. In her temple at Deir el Bahri, the reliefs on the walls recorded the major events of Hatshepsut's reign.

"A dictator excellent of plans"
–Egyptian scribe quoted in *Barbarian Tides*

▲ Hatshepsut's temple at Deir el-Bahri

Then and Now

Make a list of Hatshepsut's strengths as a leader. Then choose a present-day female leader and list her leadership strengths. Write a paragraph comparing their similarities and differences.

Legacies of Two Pharaohs

Main Idea Akhenaton tried to change Egypt's religion, while Tutankhamen is famous for the treasures buried with him in his tomb.

Reading Connection If you ask people to name an Egyptian pharaoh, the answer you're likely to get is "King Tut." Read on to find out more about him and his predecessor.

About 1370 B.C., Amenhotep IV (AH•muhn•HOH•TEHP) came to the throne. With the help of his wife, Nefertiti (NEHF•uhr•TEET•ee), Amenhotep tried to lead Egypt in a new direction.

A Religious Reformer Amenhotep realized that Egypt's priests were gaining power at the expense of the pharaohs. In an attempt to **maintain** his own power, Amenhotep introduced a new religion that swept away the old gods and goddesses. Instead, only one god, called Aton (AH•tuhn), was to be worshiped.

When Egypt's priests resisted these changes, Amenhotep removed many from their positions, seized their lands, and closed temples. He then changed his name to **Akhenaton** (AHK•NAH•tuhn), which means "Spirit of Aton." He began ruling Egypt from a new city far from Thebes.

To most Egyptians, Akhenaton's attacks on the gods seemed to be an attack on Egypt itself. They refused to accept Aton as the only god.

Meanwhile, Akhenaton became so devoted to his new religion that he neglected his duties as pharaoh. The administrators he appointed were not as experienced as the priests they replaced, and Akhenaton took no action when the Hittites, enemies from what is now Turkey, attacked Egypt. As a result, Egypt lost most of its lands in western Asia, greatly shrinking the empire.

NATIONAL GEOGRAPHIC The Way It Was

Focus on Everyday Life

Cats in Ancient Egypt In ancient Egypt, cats were loved and even worshiped. Egyptians valued the ability of wild cats to protect villages' grain supplies from mice and rats. Over several hundred years, cats became tame, and their role developed from valued hunter to adored family pet to goddess.

In ancient Egyptian tombs, archaeologists have found many wall paintings, carvings, and statues of cats. Often the statues were adorned with beautiful jewelry, such as silver or gold earrings, nose rings, and collars. When an Egyptian family's cat died, its owners shaved their eyebrows to show their grief and had the cat's body mummified.

Egyptians worshiped cats because they associated them with the goddess Bastet. She represented motherhood, grace, and beauty, and often appears in paintings and statues as a woman with the head of a cat.

▲ Egyptian goddess depicted as a cat

Connecting to the Past
1. Why did ancient Egyptians first value cats?
2. With what goddess did the ancient Egyptians associate cats?

◀ Tutankhamen's gold mask

The Boy King

When Akhenaton died, his son-in-law inherited the throne. The new pharaoh, **Tutankhamen** (TOO•TANG•KAH•muhn), was a boy about 10 years old. He relied on help from palace officials and priests, who convinced him to restore the old religion. After ruling for only nine years, Tutankhamen died unexpectedly. He may have suffered a fall or been murdered; no one is sure.

What *is* certain is that "King Tut," as he is nicknamed, played only a small role in Egypt's history. Why, then, is he the most famous of all pharaohs? The boy king captured people's imaginations after a British archaeologist, Howard Carter, found his tomb in A.D. 1922.

The tomb contained the king's mummy and incredible treasures, including a brilliant gold mask of the young pharaoh's face. Carter's find was a thrilling discovery, because most royal tombs in Egypt were looted by robbers long ago.

✓ **Reading Check** **Evaluate** Why was the discovery of Tutankhamen's tomb so important?

The End of the New Kingdom

Main Idea Under Ramses II, Egypt regained territory and built great temples, but the empire fell by 1150 B.C.

Reading Connection Egypt remained mighty for thousands of years, but it finally fell to outsiders. Read to learn about Egypt's last great pharaoh and the empire's decline.

During the 1200s B.C., pharaohs worked to make Egypt great again. The most effective of these pharaohs was **Ramses II** (RAM•SEEZ). He reigned for a remarkable 66 years, from 1279 B.C. to 1213 B.C. During this time, Egyptian armies regained lands in western Asia and rebuilt the empire. Ramses also launched an ambitious building program, **constructing** several major new temples.

▲ Temple of Karnak

Biography

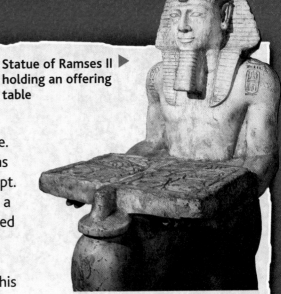

Statue of Ramses II ▶ holding an offering table

RAMSES II
Reigned 1279–1213 B.C.

Ramses II began his military training at a very young age. Ramses' father, Seti I, allowed his 10-year-old son to serve as a captain in his army. Seti also made his son co-ruler of Egypt. By the time Ramses was crowned pharaoh of Egypt, he was a great warrior and an experienced leader. Nine kings who ruled after Ramses II named themselves in his honor. Many centuries later, archaeologists nicknamed the pharaoh "Ramses the Great" because of his fame on the battlefield, his construction and restoration of buildings and monuments, and his popularity among the Egyptian people. His subjects fondly called him "Sese," an abbreviation of Ramses.

Ramses continued in his father's footsteps by trying to restore Egyptian power in Asia. Like many New Kingdom pharaohs, Ramses did this through warfare. He secured Egypt's control of the nearby region of Canaan, an area where the ancient Israelites later lived. In the early years of his reign, Ramses defeated forces in southern Syria and continuously battled Egypt's longtime enemy, the Hittites. Details about one costly battle with the Hittites were carved on temple walls, showing the Egyptians succeeding against great odds.

"They all came bowing down to him, to his palace of life and satisfaction."

–hieroglyphic translation by James B. Pritchard, *Ancient Near Eastern Texts*

During his 66-year reign, Ramses II undertook a large-scale building program. He could afford such an expensive plan because Egypt was very prosperous during his reign. He restored the damaged Sphinx, completed the Temple of Karnak, and built himself a city with four temples as well as beautiful gardens and orchards. He is famous for the temple built at Abu Simbel. It was carved out of a solid rock cliff and featured four huge statues of Ramses II, two on each side of the doorway.

▲ Coffin of Ramses II

Then and Now

Use the Internet and your local library to learn about Mount Rushmore, a monument in South Dakota. Describe Mount Rushmore, and then compare it to the temple of Ramses at Abu Simbel.

Why Were Temples Built? Under Ramses II and other New Kingdom rulers, scores of new temples rose throughout Egypt. Many were built by enslaved people captured in war. The most magnificent was Karnak at Thebes. Its huge columned hall decorated with colorful paintings still impresses visitors today.

Unlike modern churches, temples, and mosques, Egyptian temples did not hold regular religious services. Instead, most Egyptians prayed at home. They considered the temples as houses for the gods and goddesses. Priests and priestesses, however, performed daily temple rituals, washing statues of the deities and bringing them food.

The temples also served as banks. Egyptians used them to store valuable items, such as gold jewelry, sweet-smelling oils, and finely woven cloth.

Egypt's Decline and Fall After Ramses II, Egypt's power began to fade. Later pharaohs had trouble keeping neighboring countries under Egyptian control. Groups from the eastern Mediterranean attacked Egypt by sea, using strong iron weapons. The Egyptians had similar arms, but they paid dearly for them because Egypt lacked iron ore.

By 1150 B.C., the Egyptians had lost their empire and controlled only the Nile delta. Beginning in the 900s B.C., Egypt came under the rule of one outside group after another. The first conquerors were the Libyans from the west. Then, about 750 B.C., the people of Kush, a land to the south, began to conquer Egypt. Finally, in 670 B.C., Egypt was taken over by the Assyrians, a powerful society from the north.

✓ **Reading Check** **Analyze** Why did Egyptian rulers lose control of their empire?

Study Central Need help with the reigns of Hatshepsut and Ramses the Great? Visit ca.hss.glencoe.com and click on Study Central.

Section 3 Review

Reading Summary

Review the **Main Ideas**

- During the Middle Kingdom, Egypt expanded its borders, and the arts flourished.

- Under New Kingdom rulers, Egypt built a strong empire and expanded trade.

- Akhenaton failed in his attempt to create a new religion. Tutankhamen ruled briefly but gained fame because of treasures found buried with him.

- Ramses II was Egypt's last great pharaoh. In the 900s B.C., Egypt lost power to outside invaders.

What Did You Learn?

1. What improvements did the Middle Kingdom rulers make?

2. What purposes did temples serve in Egypt?

Critical Thinking

3. **Organizing Information** Create a chart like the one below. Fill in details about Egypt's Middle Kingdom and Egypt's New Kingdom. **CA 6RC2.4**

Middle Kingdom	New Kingdom

4. **Evaluate** Why was the reign of Hatshepsut considered unusual? **CA 6RC2.6**

5. **The Big Ideas** How did Akhenaton upset the traditional order in Egypt? **CA HI2.**

6. **Compare and Contrast** Describe the similarities and differences between the rule of Hatshepsut and Ramses II. **CA 6WS1.3**

7. **Expository Writing** Which Egyptian ruler do you think had the greatest effect upon Egyptian history? Write a short essay to explain your answer. **CA 6WA2.2**

The Civilization of Kush

Guide to Reading

Looking Back, Looking Ahead

In Sections 1, 2, and 3, you learned about the rise and fall of civilizations in ancient Egypt. Another civilization in early Africa was Kush. It was located near Egypt and was very similar.

Focusing on the Main Ideas

- To the south of Egypt, the Nubians settled in farming villages and became strong warriors. *(page 188)*

- The people of Kush devoted themselves to ironworking and grew wealthy from trade. *(page 189)*

Locating Places

Nubia (NOO•bee•uh)
Kush (KUHSH)
Kerma (KAR•muh)
Napata (NA•puh•tuh)
Meroë (MEHR•oh•ee)

Meeting People

Kashta (KAHSH•tuh)
Piye (PY)

Content Vocabulary

savanna (suh•VA•nuh)

Academic Vocabulary

collapse (kuh•LAPS)
decline (dih•KLYN)

Reading Strategy

Compare and Contrast Use a Venn diagram like the one below to show the similarities and differences between Napata and Meroë.

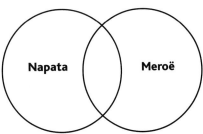

Napata   Meroë

History Social Science Standards

WH6.2 Students analyze the geographic, political, economic, religious, and social structures of the early civilizations of Mesopotamia, Egypt, and Kush.

NATIONAL GEOGRAPHIC Where&When?

800 B.C.	700 B.C.	600 B.C.	500 B.C.

c. 750 B.C.
Kashta of Kush conquers part of Egypt

728 B.C.
Piye of Kush defeats Egyptians

c. 540 B.C.
Kush moves capital to Meroë

Nile R.

Napata
• Meroë

WH6.2.8 Identify the location of the Kush civilization and describe its political, commercial, and cultural relations with Egypt.
WH6.2.9 Trace the evolution of language and its written forms.

Nubia

Main Idea To the south of Egypt, the Nubians settled in farming villages and became strong warriors.

Reading Connection Are you on good terms with your neighbors? It's not always easy—for individuals or countries. Read on to find out about the Egyptians' neighbors to the south and the ways the two civilizations mixed.

The Egyptians were not alone in settling along the Nile River. Farther south, in present-day Sudan, another strong civilization arose. This was in a region called **Nubia** (NOO•bee•uh), later known as **Kush** (KUHSH).

Historians do not know exactly when people arrived in Nubia. Evidence suggests that cattle herders arrived in about 2000 B.C. They grazed their herds on the **savannas** (suh•VA•nuhs), or grassy plains, that stretch across Africa south of the Sahara. Later, people settled in farming villages in Nubia. They grew crops, but they were also excellent hunters, skilled at using the bow and arrow. Soon the Nubians began forming armies known for their fighting skills.

The Kingdom of Kerma The more powerful Nubian villages gradually took over the weaker ones and created the kingdom of **Kerma** (KAR•muh). Kerma developed close ties with Egypt to the north. The Egyptians were happy to trade for Kerma's cattle, gold, ivory, and enslaved people. They also admired Nubian skills in warfare and hired Nubian warriors to fight in their armies.

Kerma became a wealthy kingdom. Its artisans made fine pottery, jewelry, and metal goods. Like Egyptian pharaohs, the kings of Kerma were buried in tombs that held precious stones, gold, jewelry, and pottery. These items were as splendid as those found in Egypt during the same period.

▲ In this wall painting, four Nubian princes offer rings and gold to an Egyptian ruler.
What kingdom was formed when more powerful Nubian villages took over weaker ones?

Why Did Egypt Invade Nubia? As you learned earlier, the Egyptian pharaoh Thutmose III sent his armies into Nubia in the 1400s B.C. After a 50-year war, the kingdom of Kerma **collapsed**, and the Egyptians took control of much of Nubia. They ruled the Nubians for the next 700 years.

During this time, the people of Nubia adopted many Egyptian ways. They began to worship Egyptian gods and goddesses along with their own. They learned how to work copper and bronze and changed Egyptian hieroglyphs to fit their own language. As people and goods continued to pass between Nubia and Egypt, the two cultures mixed.

Reading Check **Identify** Where was Kush located in relation to Egypt?

The Rise of Kush

Main Idea The people of Kush devoted themselves to ironworking and grew wealthy from trade.

Reading Connection Do you and your friends ever trade video games or CDs? Trading may be a casual activity for you, but it was essential to ancient peoples. Read to find how Kush took advantage of its location along an important trade route.

As Egypt **declined** at the end of the New Kingdom, Nubians saw their chance to break away. By 850 B.C., a Nubian group had formed the independent kingdom of Kush. For the next few centuries, powerful Kushite kings ruled from the city of **Napata** (NA•puh•tuh).

Napata was in a favorable location. It stood along the upper Nile where trade caravans crossed the river. Caravans soon carried gold, ivory, valuable woods, and other goods from Kush to Egypt.

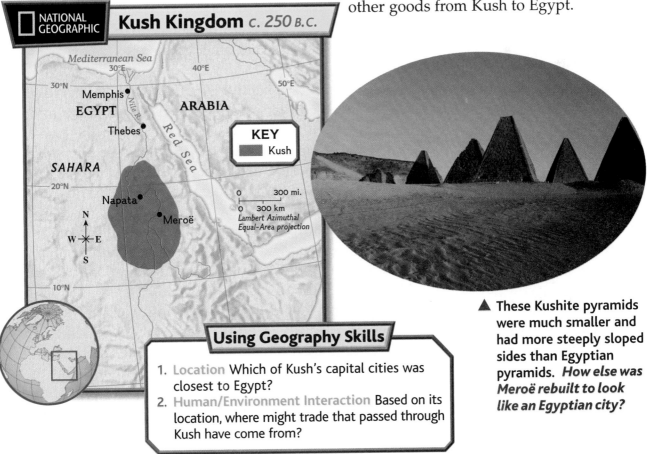

NATIONAL GEOGRAPHIC

Kush Kingdom C. 250 B.C.

KEY
Kush

Mediterranean Sea
30°E   40°E
30°N   50°E
Memphis
EGYPT   ARABIA
Thebes
Red Sea
Nile R.
SAHARA
20°N
Napata
Meroë
0   300 mi.
0   300 km
Lambert Azimuthal
Equal-Area projection
N W E S
10°N

▲ These Kushite pyramids were much smaller and had more steeply sloped sides than Egyptian pyramids. *How else was Meroë rebuilt to look like an Egyptian city?*

Using Geography Skills

1. Location Which of Kush's capital cities was closest to Egypt?
2. Human/Environment Interaction Based on its location, where might trade that passed through Kush have come from?

Selecting a New King

When their king died, the Kushites asked the god Amon-Re to appoint a new leader. "[The Kushite officials said] 'We have come to you, O Amon-Re . . . that you might give to us a lord. . . . That beneficent office [helpful task] is in your hands—may you give it to your son whom you love!'

Then they offered the king's brothers before this god, but he did not take one of them. For a second time there was offered the king's brother . . . Aspalta . . .

[Amon-Re said] 'He is your king.'"

▲ Lion statue in honor of King Aspalta

—author unknown, c. 600 B.C., "The Selection of Aspalta as King of Kush"

DBQ Document-Based Question

Do you think Aspalta was qualified to be king? Why or why not?

In time, Kush became rich enough and strong enough to take control of Egypt. About 750 B.C., a Kushite king named **Kashta** (KAHSH•tuh) headed north with a powerful army. His soldiers began the conquest of Egypt that his son **Piye** (PY) completed in 728 B.C. Piye founded the Twenty-fifth Dynasty that ruled both Egypt and Kush from Napata.

The kings of Kush greatly admired Egyptian culture. In Napata they built white sandstone temples and monuments similar to those of the Egyptians. The Kushites also built small pyramids in which to bury their kings. The ruins of these pyramids can still be seen today.

The Importance of Iron Kush's rule in Egypt did not last long. During the 600s B.C., the Assyrians invaded Egypt. Armed with iron weapons, they drove the Kushites back to their homeland in the south.

Despite their losses, the Kushites gained something from the Assyrians—the secret of making iron. The Kushites became the first Africans to devote themselves to iron-working. Soon, farmers in Kush were using iron for their hoes and plows instead of copper or stone. With these superior tools, they were able to grow large amounts of grain and other crops.

Kush's warriors also began using iron spears and swords, increasing their military power. Meanwhile, traders from Kush transported iron products and enslaved people as far away as Arabia, India, and China. In return, they brought back cotton, textiles, and other goods.

A New Capital About 540 B.C., Kush's rulers left Napata and moved farther south to be out of the Assyrians' reach. In the city of **Meroë** (MEHR•oh•ee), they set up a royal court. Like Napata, the new capital had access to the Nile River for trade and transportation. The rocky desert east of Meroë, however, contained rich deposits of iron ore. As a result, Meroë became not only a trading city but also a center for making iron.

With their growing wealth, Kush's kings rebuilt Meroë to look like an Egyptian city. Small pyramids stood in the royal graveyard. A huge temple sat at the end of a grand avenue lined with sculptures of rams. Sandstone palaces and red-brick houses had walls decorated with paintings or blue and yellow tiles.

Building a Profitable Trade Meroë became the core, or center of a huge trading network that stretched north to Egypt's border and south into central Africa. Kush's traders received leopard skins and valuable woods from the interior of Africa. They traded these goods, along with enslaved workers and iron products, to people throughout the Mediterranean and the Indian Ocean area.

Kush remained a great trading power for some 600 years. By the A.D. 200s, though, the kingdom began to weaken. As Kush declined, another kingdom rose to take its place. The kingdom is called Axum and was located in what is today the country of Ethiopia. Around A.D. 350, the armies of Axum burned Meroë to the ground. You will read more about the kingdom of Axum when you study Africa.

✓ **Reading Check** **Explain** How did Kush become a wealthy kingdom?

Kushite King

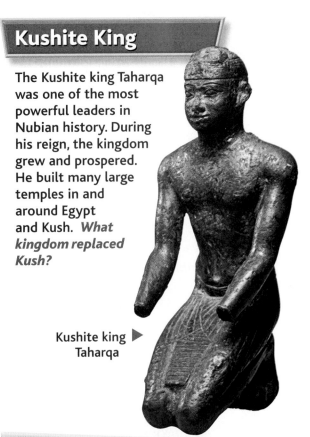

The Kushite king Taharqa was one of the most powerful leaders in Nubian history. During his reign, the kingdom grew and prospered. He built many large temples in and around Egypt and Kush. *What kingdom replaced Kush?*

Kushite king ▶
Taharqa

History **O**nline

Study Central Need help with the kingdom of Kush? Visit ca.hss.glencoe.com and click on Study Central.

Section 4 Review

Reading Summary

Review the Main Ideas

- In the Nile Valley to the south of Egypt, the Nubians founded the kingdom of Kerma and traded with the Egyptians.

- The Kushites set up a capital at Meroë that became a center for ironmaking and the base of a huge trading network.

What Did You Learn?

1. Who were the Nubians?

2. What were the Kushites' most important economic activities?

Critical Thinking

3. **Sequencing** Draw a diagram to show events that led up to the Kushite conquest of Egypt. **CA 6RC2.4**

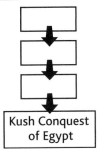

Kush Conquest of Egypt

4. **Geography Skills** Why was Napata's location beneficial? **CA CS3.**

5. **The Big Ideas** How did Egypt's culture affect Kush? **CA 6RC2.0**

6. **Compare** How were Kush and Egypt similar? **CA 6RC2.2**

7. **Analysis** **Posing Questions** If you wanted to learn more about Kush, what questions would you ask? Write three questions and exchange them with a class-mate. Research each other's questions and write a summary of your findings. **CA HR1.**

Analyzing Primary Sources

WH6.2.7 Understand the significance of Queen Hatshepsut and Ramses the Great. **WH6.2.8** Identify the location of the Kush civilization and describe its political, commercial, and cultural relations with Egypt.

The Mighty Pharaohs

In Egypt and Kush, rulers were greatly respected. The Egyptians believed that their pharaohs were the sons of the sun god, Re. Because of these beliefs, the pharaoh had enormous power. His word had to be followed without question.

Read the passages and study the image that follows. Then answer the questions on page 193.

Tutankhamen's gold mask ▶

Reader's Dictionary

Re (RAY): god of sun

begat (bih•GAT): fathered

spake: spoke

Osiris (oh•SY•ruhs): a god, king of the Afterworld

stele (STEE•lee): a vertical, engraved stone slab

remnant (REHM•nuhnt): remainder

Amon (A•muhn): god of Thebes; important Egyptian god

Ramses II Rebuilds

Ramses II, one of the great pharaohs of Egypt, ruled from 1279–1213 B.C. Ramses II undertook a large-scale building project. The following passage comes from an inscription describing his order to finish building his father's tomb.

"I came forth from **Re,** although ye say, from [Seti I], who brought me up. . . . When my father appeared to the public, . . . [h]e said concerning me: 'Crown him as king, that I may see his beauty while I live with him.' . . . My mighty deeds for my father as a child, I will now complete, being Lord of the Two Lands; I will construct them in the proper way . . . I will lay the walls in the temple of him that **begat** me. . . . I will cover its house, I will erect its columns, I will set stones in the places of the lower foundation, making monument upon monuments." . . .

Then **spake** the royal companions, and they answered the Good God: "Thou art Re, thy body is his body. There has been no ruler like thee, (for) thou art unique, like the son of **Osiris,** thou hast achieved the like of his designs."

—Anonymous, "Ramses II Finds the Necropolis Buildings in Ruins"

A Kushite Warrior-King

Around 728 B.C., the Kushite king Piye finished his conquest of Egypt. He was angry to discover that some of the enemy had not been destroyed. The following description appears on Piye's victory **stele.**

Then his majesty was enraged thereat like a panther (saying): "Have they allowed a **remnant** of the army of the Northland to remain? . . . Not causing their death, in order to destroy the last of them? I swear: as Re loves me! As my father **Amon** favors me! I will myself go northward, that I may destroy that which he has done, that I may make him turn back from fighting, forever."

—Anonymous, "The Nubian Invasion"

A Sphinx of Kush

The people of Kush adopted many Egyptian ways, especially while they ruled Egypt. This granite sphinx is of the daughter of King Piye from about 660 B.C. Egyptians believed that sphinx statues had magical powers to guard tombs and temples.

▼ This sphinx has the face of King Piye's daughter. It guards a sacred offering vessel. The vessel was filled with gifts to the god Amon. These offerings were protected by the sphinx, which held the vessel in its hands so no one could steal it.

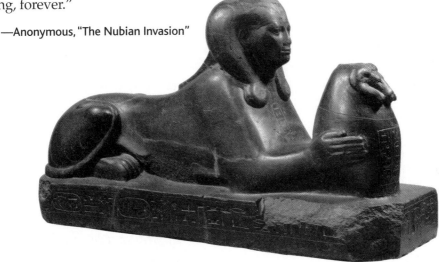

DBQ Document-Based Questions

Ramses II Rebuilds

1. Who does Ramses say is his father?
2. Why does Ramses want to finish Seti's tomb?
3. Ramses's royal companions say that he is Re, the sun god. Why do you think they say this?

A Kushite Warrior-King

4. Why is Piye so angry?
5. According to Piye, what is his relationship with the Egyptian gods Re and Amon? Why is this relationship important?

A Sphinx of Kush

6. The Egyptians were known for creating sphinxes, yet this sphinx was made for a daughter of a king of Kush. Why do you think this is so?
7. Compare this sphinx to the images of the Great Sphinx on pages 152 and 166. How are they alike? How are they different?

Read to Write

8. Reread the two passages, as well as the information about the sphinx. What do these primary sources tell you about the role of religion in the lives of Egyptian rulers? How do they demonstrate the power of pharaohs?
   CA HR3.

Review Content Vocabulary

Match the definitions in the second column to the terms in the first column. Write the letter of each definition.

___ 1. savanna   a. area of fertile soil at the end of a river

___ 2. tribute   b. reed plant used to make baskets, rafts, and paper

___ 3. cataract   c. grassy plain

___ 4. delta   d. rapids

___ 5. hieroglyphics   e. Egyptian writing system

___ 6. pharaoh   f. forced payments

___ 7. papyrus   g. title for Egyptian leaders

Review the Main Ideas

Section 1 • The Nile Valley

8. What natural barriers protected Egypt from invasion?

9. What two areas of Egypt were united around 3100 B.C.?

Section 2 • Egypt's Old Kingdom

10. What were the Egyptians' religious beliefs?

11. Where did Egyptians of the Old Kingdom bury their pharaohs?

Section 3 • The Egyptian Empire

12. During what period did Egypt reach the height of its power?

13. Why are Akhenaton and Tutankhamen well-known?

Section 4 • The Civilization of Kush

14. Where did the Nubians live?

15. What made the Kushites wealthy?

Critical Thinking

16. **Describe** Identify the four social groups in ancient Egypt, and explain who belonged to each group. **CA 6RC2.4**

17. **Synthesize** How do you think religious leaders reacted to Akhenaton's changes? **CA HI2.**

18. **Analyze** Do you agree that Egyptian civilization can be called "the Gift of the Nile"? Explain. **CA HR2.**

19. **Compare** In what ways did Meroë look like an Egyptian city? **CA 6RC2.2**

Geography Skills

Study the map below and answer the following questions.

20. **Location** The Nile River delta empties into what body of water? **CA CS3.**

21. **Movement** Why would ancient Egyptians find it easier to travel north and south than to travel east and west? **CA CS3.**

22. **Human/Environment Interaction** Why is Egyptian farming along the Nile? **CA CS3.**

NATIONAL GEOGRAPHIC **Ancient Egypt**

Read to Write

23. The Big Ideas Expository Writing Imagine that you are an Egyptian pharaoh. How would you make sure that your empire is stable and strong? Use real-life pharaohs to help you determine what kinds of things you would do. Write an essay describing your policies and what you hope to achieve through them. **CA 6WS1.2**

24. Using Your FOLDABLES Use your foldable to write a description of one of the civilizations in this chapter. Include such things as religious life, family life, and contributions. When you are finished, discuss similarities and differences among the civilizations with a classmate. **CA 6WS1.3**

Using Academic Vocabulary

Use the terms below to fill in the blanks in the following sentences.

- **a.** feature
- **b.** technology
- **c.** labor
- **d.** welfare
- **e.** structure
- **f.** principle
- **g.** restore
- **h.** construct

25. An important ____ of Egyptian pyramids is the shape.

26. The shadoof is an example of Egyptian ____.

27. A pyramid is a large ____ made of stone blocks.

28. Pharaohs were in charge of providing for the ____ of their people.

29. Egyptian pharaohs used farmers to help ____ their pyramids.

Reviewing Skills

30. Reading Skill Summarizing Using information from the text, create a short story about Hatshepsut. Use this writing exercise to summarize life in ancient Egypt during her reign. The story should compare Hatshepsut to other Egyptian rulers and explain the differences in her policies. The events of the story should also show the different social classes in Egypt and explain the problems Hatshepsut faced as a woman pharaoh. **CA 6WA2.1**

History Online

Self-Check Quiz To help prepare for the Chapter Test, visit ca.hss.glencoe.com

31. Analysis Skill Building a Time Line Take a look back through the chapter. As you go, make a list of each important leader in ancient Egypt. Create a time line of these leaders, placing them in chronological order. For each entry, include a short summary of their reign. Describe their significant accomplishments or mistakes, and how these actions affected Egypt. **CA CS2.**

Standards Practice

Use the map below to answer the following question.

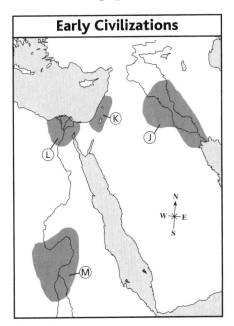

Early Civilizations

32 Which area on the map was the home of the Kushite kingdom?

- **A** J
- **B** K
- **C** L
- **D** M

Chapter 3

The Ancient Israelites

The wall surrounding the ▼
old city of Jerusalem

NATIONAL GEOGRAPHIC **Where&When?**

2000 B.C.	1300 B.C.	600 B.C.	A.D. 100
c. 1800 B.C. Israelites settle in Canaan	c. 1290 B.C. Moses leads Israelites from Egypt	722 B.C. Assyrians conquer Israel	A.D. 66 Jews revolt against Romans

The Big Ideas

History Online

Chapter Overview Visit ca.hss.glencoe.com for a preview of Chapter 3.

Section 1
The First Israelites

Religion shapes how culture develops, just as culture shapes how religion develops. Abraham founded the 12 tribes of Israel in the land of Canaan. The Israelites believed in one God who gave commandments telling people how to live good lives.

Section 2
The Kingdom of Israel

All civilizations depend upon leadership for survival. Under David and Solomon, the people of Israel built a powerful kingdom with a new capital in Jerusalem.

Section 3
The Growth of Judaism

Religion shapes how culture develops, just as culture shapes how religion develops. The Jews continued to keep their religion even though other people ruled them. They settled in many places in Asia and Europe.

View the Chapter 3 video in the Glencoe Video Program.

FOLDABLES™
Study Organizer

Summarizing Information *Make this foldable and use it to organize note cards with information about the Israelites.*

Step 1 *Fold a horizontal sheet of paper (11"x17") into thirds.*

Step 2 *Fold the bottom edge up two inches and crease well. Glue the outer edges of the tab to create three pockets.*

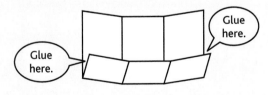

Glue here.

Glue here.

Step 3 *Label the pockets as shown. Use these pockets to hold notes taken on index cards or quarter sheets of paper.*

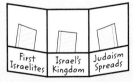

First Israelites Israel's Kingdom Judaism Spreads

Reading and Writing
As you read the chapter, summarize key facts on note cards or on quarter sheets of paper about Israel and the growth and spread of Judaism. Organize your notes by placing them in your pocket foldable inside the appropriate pockets.

197

Making Connections

1 Learn It!

Make connections between what you read and what you already know. Connections can be based on personal experiences (text-to-self), what you have read before (text-to-text), or events in other places (text-to-world).

As you read, ask connecting questions. Are you reminded of a personal experience? Have you read about the topic before? Did you think of a person, place, or event in another time? Read the excerpt below, and make connections to your own knowledge and experience.

Text-to-self:
Do you remember learning the alphabet? Have you tried to learn the alphabet in another language?

Text-to-text:
What did you read about cuneiform and hiero-glyphics in the earlier chapters?

Through trade, the Phoenicians spread ideas and goods. One of their most important ideas was an alphabet, or a group of letters that stood for sounds. The letters could be used to spell out the words in their language.

The alphabet made writing simpler and helped people keep records. The Phoenicians brought the idea of an alphabet to the Greeks, who passed it on to the Romans. Most Western alphabets are based on the Roman alphabet.

— from page 205

Reading Tip

Make connections with memorable times in your life. The better the connection, the more likely you will remember.

Text-to-world:
How do people share ideas? What other alphabets exist besides Western alphabets?

2 Practice It!

Read the following paragraphs with a partner. Each of you should then list the connections you made to the reading. Compare your lists and discuss your answers. What things in your lives relate to the story of David and Goliath?

Read to Write

Choose a connection you made that was different than your partner's. Write a detailed paragraph explaining why you made it.

> David's fame as a warrior spread. The Bible shows his fame by telling this story. Just before a battle against the Philistines, a giant Philistine named Goliath called out in a loud voice. He dared any Israelite to fight him one-on-one. David stepped forward with his shepherd's staff, a slingshot, and five smooth stones.
>
> "Am I a dog that you come against me with a staff?" Goliath roared. He rushed forward with a heavy spear, but David was too quick for him. He hurled one stone straight at the giant's forehead, and Goliath dropped dead on the spot.
>
> — *from page 209*

▲ David versus Goliath

3 Apply It!

As you read this chapter, choose five words or phrases that make a connection to something you already know.

The First Israelites

Guide to Reading

History Social Science Standards

WH6.3 Students analyze the geographic, political, economic, religious, and social structures of the Ancient Hebrews.

Looking Back, Looking Ahead

You have read how the Egyptians built a great civilization. At about the same time, another nation was forming. The Egyptians called the people of this nation *habiru,* or foreigners. The people called themselves Israelites or the Children of Israel.

Focusing on the Main Ideas

• The Israelites believed in one God who set down moral laws for his people. They recorded their history in the Bible. *(page 201)*

• The Israelites had to fight the Canaanites to return to their promised land. *(page 204)*

Meeting People

Abraham

Jacob

Moses

Deborah

Phoenician (fih•NEE•shuhn)

Locating Places

Canaan (KAY•nuhn)

Mount Sinai (SY•NY)

Content Vocabulary

monotheism (MAH•nuh•thee•IH•zuhm)

tribe

Torah (TOHR•UH)

covenant (KUHV•nuhnt)

alphabet

Academic Vocabulary

focus (FOH•kuhs)

occupy (AH•kyuh•PY)

create (kree•AYT)

Reading Strategy

Sequencing Information Create a sequence chart to help trace the movement of the Israelites.

☐ → ☐ → ☐

NATIONAL GEOGRAPHIC Where & When?

1400 B.C.

c. 1290 B.C. Moses leads Israelites from Egypt

1200 B.C.

c. 1125 B.C. Deborah defeats Canaanites

1000 B.C.

c. 1000 B.C. Israelites settle in Canaan

Jerusalem

Memphis

WH6.3.1 Describe the origins and significance of Judaism as the first monotheistic religion based on the concept of one God who sets down moral laws for humanity. WH6.3.2 Identify the sources of the ethical teachings and central beliefs of Judaism (the Hebrew Bible, the Commentaries): belief in God, observance of law, practice of the concepts of righteousness and justice, and importance of study; and describe how the ideas of the Hebrew traditions are reflected in the moral and ethical traditions of Western civilization. WH6.3.3 Explain the significance of Abraham, Moses, Naomi, Ruth, David, and Yohanan ben Zaccai in the development of the Jewish religion. WH6.3.4 Discuss the locations of the settlements and movements of Hebrew peoples, including the Exodus and their movement to and from Egypt, and outline the significance of the Exodus to the Jewish and other people.

The Early Israelites

Main Idea The Israelites believed in one God who set down moral laws for his people. They recorded their history in the Bible.

Reading Connection Where do your ideas about right and wrong come from? Read on to find out how the Israelites developed their ideas about right and wrong.

About 1200 B.C., great changes took place around the Mediterranean Sea. Empires fell and new people entered the region. Many set up small kingdoms. Around 1000 B.C., a people called Israelites (IHZ•ruh•LYTS) built a kingdom in **Canaan** (KAY•nuhn). Canaan was a region along the Mediterranean Sea in southwest Asia.

Who Were the Israelites? Although the Israelite population was small, the religion they practiced would one day affect much of the world. Most people at this time worshiped many gods and goddesses. The Israelite religion **focused** on only one God. The belief in one god is called **monotheism** (MAH•nuh•thee•IH•zuhm).

The Israelite faith became the religion known today as Judaism (JOO•dee•IH•zuhm). The followers of Judaism were eventually known as Jews. Judaism influenced Christianity and Islam, and also helped shape the beliefs and practices of societies in Europe and America.

The Israelites spoke a language called Hebrew. They wrote down their history and many of their religious beliefs in what later became the Hebrew Bible. Through this book, Jewish values and religion later influenced religious beliefs in Europe.

The earliest Israelites were herders and traders. According to the Bible, they came from Mesopotamia and settled in Canaan.

Today, Lebanon, Israel, and Jordan **occupy** the land that was once Canaan.

The Israelites believed they were descended from a man named **Abraham.** In the Bible, it says that God told Abraham and his followers to leave Mesopotamia and go to Canaan. There, they were to worship the one true God. In return, God promised that the land of Canaan would belong to Abraham and his descendants. According to the Bible, this is the reason that the Israelites settled in Canaan.

Abraham had a grandson named **Jacob.** Jacob was also called Israel, which means "one who struggles with God." Later this name was given to Jacob's descendants.

According to the Bible, Jacob raised 12 sons in Canaan. His family was divided into **tribes,** or separate family groups. These groups later became known as the 12 tribes of Israel. The Israelites resided in Canaan for about 100 years. Then a long drought began. Crops withered and livestock died. To survive, the Israelites went to Egypt.

▲ This photograph of modern-day Israel shows the landscape Abraham led the Israelites through. *Why did the Israelites eventually leave Canaan?*

Moses and the Ten Commandments

▲ Jews celebrating Passover today

▲ In this painting, Moses watches as the Red Sea closes in on the Egyptian soldiers who were pursuing the Israelites. *What is the Israelites' escape from Egypt called?*

From Slavery to Freedom Life was not good in Egypt. The Egyptian pharaoh enslaved the Israelites. To prevent a rebellion he ordered all baby boys born to Israelites thrown into the Nile River.

The Bible says that one desperate mother put her baby in a basket and hid it on the riverbank. The pharaoh's daughter found the baby and named him **Moses.**

Around 1290 B.C., while tending sheep in the wilderness outside Egypt, Moses saw a burning bush and heard a voice. He believed that God was telling him to lead the Israelites out of Egypt to freedom.

To get the pharaoh to let the Israelites go, the Bible says that God sent 10 plagues to trouble Egypt. The last plague God sent killed all first-born children, except for those of Israelites who marked their doorway with lamb's blood. This plague convinced the pharaoh to let the Israelites

leave. Jews today celebrate a holiday called Passover to remember this event.

As Israelites headed east out of Egypt, the pharaoh changed his mind and sent his army after the Israelites. According to the Bible, God parted the Red Sea to let his people pass. When the Egyptians followed, the water flowed back and drowned the soldiers. The Israelite escape from Egypt is known as the Exodus.

What Are the Ten Commandments? On their way back to Canaan, the Israelites had to travel through the Sinai desert. The Bible says that during this journey, Moses went to the top of **Mount Sinai** (SY•NY). There, he received laws from God. These laws were known as the **Torah** (TOHR•uh). They later became the first part of the Hebrew Bible. The Torah described a **covenant** (KUHV•nuhnt), or agreement, with God. In the agreement, God promised to return the Israelites to Canaan if they followed his laws.

▲ **The Ark of the Covenant was a box, which, according to Jewish beliefs, held the Ten Commandments.**
How did the Ten Commandments help shape the basic moral laws of many European nations?

The Ten Commandments

According to the Bible, Moses received the Ten Commandments and other laws from God on Mount Sinai. Moses and the Israelites promised to follow these laws.

1. Do not worship any god except me.
2. Do not . . . bow down and worship idols.
3. Do not misuse my name.
4. Remember that the Sabbath Day belongs to me.
5. Respect your father and your mother.
6. Do not murder.
7. Be faithful in marriage.
8. Do not steal.
9. Do not tell lies about others.
10. Do not want anything that belongs to someone else.

—Exodus 20:3-17

◀ **Moses with the Ten Commandments**

▲ **Mount Sinai**

The Torah explained what God considered to be right and wrong. The most important part of the Torah is the Ten Commandments. They are summarized in the box to the right. The Ten Commandments told the Israelites to be loyal only to God, whose name was never to be misused. They must never worship any other gods or images. The belief that there should be only one god became the foundation for both Christianity and Islam.

The Ten Commandments helped shape the basic moral laws of many nations. The Ten Commandments told people not to steal, murder, or tell lies about others. They told people to avoid jealousy and to honor their parents. The Ten Commandments also helped develop a belief that laws should apply to everyone equally.

Reading Check **Identify** What is the Israelite belief in one god called?

DBQ Document-Based Questions

1. How many of the commandments tell people how to interact with other people?
2. How many tell them how to worship and show respect for God?

WH6.3.3 Explain the significance of Abraham, Moses, Naomi, Ruth, David, and Yohanan ben Zaccai in the development of the Jewish religion. **WH6.3.4** Discuss the locations of the settlements and movements of Hebrew peoples, including the Exodus and their movement to and from Egypt, and outline the significance of the Exodus to the Jewish and other people.

The Promised Land

Main Idea The Israelites had to fight the Canaanites to return to their promised land.

Reading Connection What qualities do you think a good leader should have? Read on to find out about the leaders of the Israelites.

It probably took the Israelites about 40 years to reach Canaan. Moses never lived to see the Promised Land. After Moses died, a leader named Joshua took over and brought the Israelites into Canaan. When they arrived, however, they found other people living there. Most were Canaanites (KAY•nuh•NYTS). The Israelites believed it was God's will that they conquer the Canaanites, so Joshua led them into battle.

The story of the war is told in the Bible. Joshua led the Israelites to the city of Jericho and told them to march around the city's walls. For six days, they marched while seven priests blew their trumpets. On the seventh day, the trumpets sounded one last time, and Joshua told the Israelites to raise a great shout. According to the story, the walls of Jericho crumbled, and the Israelites overran the city.

Joshua led the Israelites in three more wars. The land they seized was divided among the 12 tribes.

Who Were the Fighting Judges?
After Joshua died, the Israelites looked to judges for leadership. A judge was usually a military leader. Generally, he or she commanded 1 or 2 tribes, but seldom all 12. The Bible tells about Barak, Gideon, Samuel, Eli, Samson, and others, including a woman judge. Her name was **Deborah.**

Deborah told Barak to attack the army of the Canaanite king Jabin. She went along to the battlefield as an adviser. With Deborah's help, Barak and 10,000 Israelites destroyed King Jabin and his army in about 1125 B.C.

Over time, the Israelites won control of the hilly region in central Canaan. The Canaanites kept the flat, coastal areas. To protect themselves, the Israelites built walled towns. They also **created** an alphabet and a calendar based on Canaanite ideas.

The Phoenician Alphabet
One group of Canaanites, the **Phoenicians** (fih•NEE•shuhns), lived in cities along the Mediterranean Sea. The Phoenicians were skilled sailors and traders.

▲ According to the Bible story, the walls of Jericho came down as the trumpets of the Israelites sounded. *Who led the Israelites in their return to Canaan?*

▲ The town of Jericho today

Their ships carried goods across the Mediterranean to Greece, Spain, and even western Africa.

Through trade, the Phoenicians spread ideas and goods. One of their most important ideas was an **alphabet,** or a group of letters that stood for sounds. The letters could be used to spell out the words in their language.

The alphabet made writing simpler and helped people keep records. The Phoenicians brought the idea of an alphabet to the Greeks, who passed it on to the Romans. Most Western alphabets are based on the Roman alphabet.

✓ Reading Check **Identify** Who led the Israelites into Canaan, and what city did they conquer under his leadership?

Alphabets

Modern Characters	Ancient Phoenician	Ancient Hebrew	Ancient Greek	Early Roman
A	⟨ ⟨	⟨	⟨ ⟨ ⟨	⟨ ⟨ ⟨
B	⟨ ⟨	⟨ ⟨	⟨ ⟨	B B
G	⟨ ⟨	⟨ ⟨	⟨ ⟨ ⟨	C C
D	⟨ ⟨	⟨ ⟨	⟨ ⟨ ⟨	D D
E	⟨	⟨	⟨ ⟨ ⟨	E
F	⟨	⟨	⟨ ⟨ ⟨	F
Z	Z		I	Z
TH	⟨		⊙	
I	⟨ ⟨	⟨	⟨ ⟨	I

▲ Many ancient alphabets used similar symbols to represent letters. *Which modern letter most closely resembles its Phoenician character?*

History Online

Study Central Need help with understanding the history of the Israelites? Visit ca.hss.glencoe.com and click on Study Central.

Section ❶ Review

Reading Summary

Review the (Main Ideas)

- Led by Abraham, the Israelites settled in Canaan. They later moved to Egypt and were enslaved, but then escaped. The Israelites used the Ten Commandments as rules to live by.

- Joshua and the judges, including Deborah, won back territory in central Canaan for the Israelites.

What Did You Learn?

1. Why was the religion of Israel unique in the ancient world?

2. What is the Torah, and how did the Israelites obtain it?

Critical Thinking

3. **Summarizing Information** Use a web diagram like the one below to list Jewish ideas that are important in our society. **CA 6RC2.4**

4. **Analyze** What was the importance of the Phoenician alphabet? **CA HI2.**

5. **Summarize** What problems did the Israelites face when they returned to Canaan? **CA 6RC2.0**

6. **The Big Ideas** How do the Ten Commandments influence today's society? **CA HI2.**

7. **Reading** **Making Connections** When the Israelites reached Canaan, they had to fight to settle there. Is there anywhere today where people fight over who owns the land? Using magazines and the Internet, prepare a report about one such place today. **CA 6WA2.3**

Section 2

The Kingdom of Israel

History Social Science Standards

WH6.3 Students analyze the geographic, political, economic, religious, and social structures of the Ancient Hebrews.

Guide to Reading

Looking Back, Looking Ahead

In Section 1, you read about the constant fighting between the Israelites and the Canaanites. The tribes of Israel longed for peace. Many thought the way to peace was to unite as one nation.

Focusing on the Main Ideas

- The Israelites chose a king to unite them against their enemies. *(page 207)*

- King David built an Israelite empire and made Jerusalem his capital city. *(page 209)*

- The Israelites were conquered and forced to leave Israel and Judah. *(page 210)*

Meeting People
Philistine (FIH•luh•STEEN)
Saul (SAWL)
David
Solomon (SAHL•uh•muhn)
Nebuchadnezzar (NEH•byuh•kuhd•NEH•zuhr)

Locating Places
Jerusalem (juh•ROO•suh•luhm)
Judah (JOO•duh)

Content Vocabulary
prophet (PRAH•fuht)
empire (EHM•PYR)
tribute (TRIH•byoot)
proverb (PRAH•VUHRB)

Academic Vocabulary
instruct (ihn•STRUHKT)
symbol (SIHM•buhl)

Reading Strategy
Categorizing Information Complete a chart like the one below identifying characteristics of Israel and Judah.

	Israel	Judah
Location		
Capital City		
Date Conquered		
Conquered By		

NATIONAL GEOGRAPHIC Where & When?

Samaria • Babylon •
• Jerusalem

1000 B.C.	750 B.C.	500 B.C.
c. 1000 B.C. David becomes king	**722 B.C.** Assyrians conquer Israel	**597 B.C.** Nebuchadnezzar captures Jerusalem

The Israelites Choose a King

Main Idea **The Israelites chose a king to unite them against their enemies.**

Reading Connection What does "united we stand, divided we fall" mean to you? Read on to find out what it meant to the 12 tribes of Israel.

Around 1000 B.C., the strongest people living in Canaan were not the Israelites, but the **Philistines** (FIH•luh•STEENS). The Philistines had strong cities, and they knew how to make iron tools and weapons. Fearing the power of the Philistines, many Israelites copied their ways and worshiped their gods.

The 12 tribes often quarreled. If they were going to save their religion and way of life, they would have to learn how to work together. They needed a king to unite them against the Philistines.

History Online

Web Activity Visit ca.hss.glencoe.com and click on *Chapter 3—Student Web Activity* to learn more about the ancient Israelites.

The Rule of King Saul In 1020 B.C. the Israelites asked Samuel to choose a king. Samuel was a judge and a **prophet** (PRAH•fuht). A prophet is a person who claims to be **instructed** by God to share God's words. Samuel warned that a king would tax the Israelites and make them slaves. The Israelites still demanded a king, so they chose a warrior-farmer named **Saul** (SAWL).

Samuel anointed Saul as king. In other words, he blessed him with oil to show that God had chosen him. Saul was tall and handsome and had won many battles.

Saul defeated the Israelites' enemies in battle after battle. However, according to the Bible, the king displeased God by disobeying some of his commands. God then chose another king and instructed Samuel to anoint him in secret. The new king was a young shepherd named **David.**

✓ Reading Check **Explain** Why did the Israelites want a king?

▼ According to the Bible, David had to be called in from the fields where he was tending his sheep when Samuel arrived to anoint him. *Why did God have Samuel anoint David?*

Biography

DAVID
Reigned c. 1000–970 B.C.

The story of David's life is told in several books of the Old Testament, including Samuel I and II and Psalms. During his youth, David worked as an aide in King Saul's court. While at court, he formed a close friendship with the king's son, Jonathan. David fought courageously against the Philistines as a soldier in Saul's army. He also killed the Philistine giant, Goliath, with only a slingshot and stones. The first book of Samuel tells how David's harp playing pleased King Saul. But the king grew jealous of David's growing popularity as a brave soldier. He decided to have David killed.

To save his own life, David fled into the desert. During this time, David led a group of other people who were hiding from the king. David and his band protected people from raiders and returned possessions that had been stolen. By the time David returned to Jerusalem, he was well-known throughout the land.

After the death of King Saul, David became the second king of Israel. David successfully united all the tribes of Israel. He then conquered Jerusalem and made it the kingdom's capital. During his reign, David built Israel into an empire and dominated neighboring kingdoms.

David was not only a brave warrior and successful leader, he was also a talented poet. Many of the hymns in the Old Testament's book of Psalms have been credited to David, including Psalm 23, which begins "The Lord is my shepherd, I shall not want; he makes me lie down in green pastures. He leads me beside still waters; he restores my soul. He leads me in paths of righteousness for his name's sake."

▲ King David

"The sweet psalmist of Israel"
–David, 2 Samuel 23:1

Then and Now

In David's time, kings were expected to excel in battle. Use your research skills to find at least three U.S. presidents who built their reputations in the military.

David and Solomon

Main Idea King David built an Israelite empire and made Jerusalem his capital city.

Reading Connection What person do you think was most important in the history of the United States? Read to learn why King David is so important to the history of the Jewish people.

David's fame as a warrior spread. The Bible shows his fame by telling this story. Just before a battle against the Philistines, a giant Philistine named Goliath called out in a loud voice. He dared any Israelite to fight him one-on-one. David stepped forward with his shepherd's staff, a slingshot, and five smooth stones.

"Am I a dog that you come against me with a staff?" Goliath roared. He rushed forward with a heavy spear, but David was too quick for him. He hurled one stone straight at the giant's forehead, and Goliath dropped dead on the spot.

Saul put David in charge of the army. As his victories grew, Israelite women sang his praises. "Saul has slain his thousands, and David his ten thousands." Saul grew envious and plotted to kill David.

David hid out in enemy territory until Saul and his three sons were killed in battle. The bitter rivalry was over. David was able to take the throne in about 1000 B.C.

Once in power, David drove the Philistines from the area. He conquered other neighboring nations and created an **empire** (EHM•PYR). An empire is a nation that rules several other nations. Conquered peoples in the area had to pay David and the Israelites **tribute** (TRIH•byoot). Tribute is money or slaves given to a stronger ruler.

David made the Israelites pay heavy taxes. He needed money to expand his new capital of **Jerusalem** (juh•ROO•suh•luhm). He wanted a fine temple there so that

Primary Source

Proverbs

Solomon's proverbs are recorded in the Bible. Read these three, then answer the question.

"What you gain by doing evil won't help you at all, but being good can save you from death.

———

At harvest season it's smart to work hard, but [unwise] to sleep.

———

You will be safe, if you always do right, but you will get caught, if you are dishonest."

—Proverbs 10: 2, 5, 9

▲ King Solomon

DBQ **Document-Based Question**

How would the third proverb above convince people to tell the truth?

sacred religious objects cherished by the Israelites would finally have a permanent home. David died before he built the temple, but for centuries, the Israelites remembered him as their greatest king.

The Rule of King Solomon When David died, his son **Solomon** (SAHL•uh•muhn) became king. It was Solomon who built a splendid stone temple in Jerusalem. It became the **symbol** and center of the Jewish religion.

In the Bible, Solomon was known for his wise sayings, or **proverbs** (PRAH•VUHRBS), but many Israelites hated his rule. Solomon taxed the people to pay for his great buildings.

WH6.3.2 Identify the sources of the ethical teachings and central beliefs of Judaism (the Hebrew Bible, the Commentaries): belief in God, observance of law, practice of the concepts of righteousness and justice, and importance of study; and describe how the ideas of the Hebrew traditions are reflected in the moral and ethical traditions of Western civilization. WH6.3.4 Discuss the locations of the settlements and movements of Hebrew peoples, including the Exodus and their movement to and from Egypt, and outline the significance of the Exodus to the Jewish and other people.

The Israelites in the north were especially unhappy with Solomon. To get more money, Solomon had made many of their young men work in the mines of a neighboring country.

When Solomon died, the northerners rebelled and fighting broke out. Ten of the 12 tribes set up their own nation in the north. It was called the kingdom of Israel, and its capital was Samaria. In the south, the other two tribes founded the smaller kingdom of **Judah** (JOO•duh). Its capital was Jerusalem, and its people were called Jews.

✓ **Reading Check** **Explain** What did King David accomplish for Israel?

A Troubled Time

Main Idea The Israelites were conquered and forced to leave Israel and Judah.

Reading Connection Have you ever moved and left a home you loved? Read to find out why many Israelites were forced to leave their home.

While the Israelites were dividing their kingdom, the Assyrians and Chaldeans (kal•DEE•uhns) were building empires in southwest Asia. These peoples wanted to control the trade routes that ran through the Israelite kingdoms. Small and weak, the kingdoms of Israel and Judah felt threatened by their powerful neighbors.

▼ The temple built by Solomon is thought to have been about 180 feet long. It contained large quantities of imported cedar wood and fine stone. *Why did the Israelites become unhappy with Solomon?*

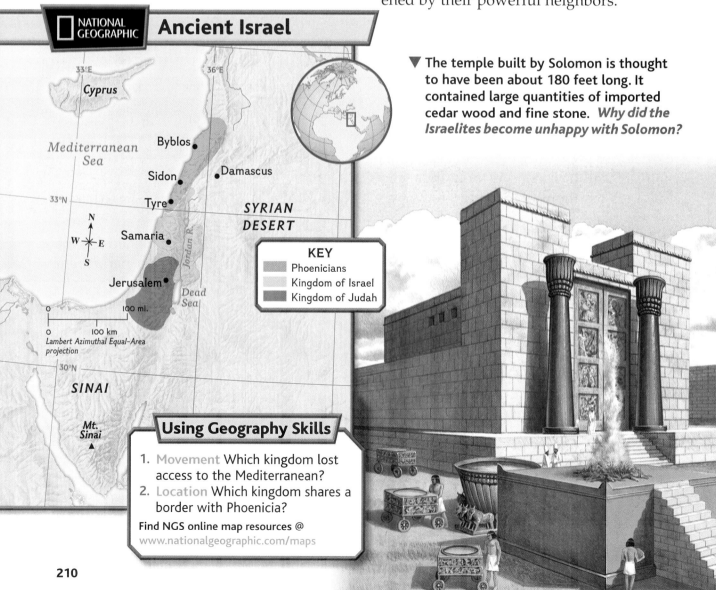

NATIONAL GEOGRAPHIC Ancient Israel

Cyprus

Mediterranean Sea

Byblos

Sidon •Damascus

Tyre

SYRIAN DESERT

Samaria

Jerusalem

Dead Sea

Jordan R.

0   100 mi.

0   100 km
Lambert Azimuthal Equal-Area projection

KEY
- Phoenicians
- Kingdom of Israel
- Kingdom of Judah

SINAI

Mt. Sinai ▲

Using Geography Skills

1. **Movement** Which kingdom lost access to the Mediterranean?
2. **Location** Which kingdom shares a border with Phoenicia?

Find NGS online map resources @ www.nationalgeographic.com/maps

Major Hebrew Prophets

Name	Time Period	Teachings
Elijah	874–840 B.C.	Only God should be worshiped—not idols or false gods.
Amos	780–740 B.C.	The kingdom of King David will be restored and will prosper.
Hosea	750–722 B.C.	God is loving and forgiving.
Isaiah	738–700 B.C.	God wants us to help others and promote justice.
Micah	735–700 B.C.	Both rich and poor have to do what is right and follow God.
Jeremiah	626–586 B.C.	God is just and kind—he rewards as well as punishes.
Ezekiel	597–571 B.C.	Someone who has done wrong can choose to change.

Understanding Charts

The Israelites believed that God shared his word with them through a series of prophets.

1. Which prophet taught that both the rich and the poor needed to obey God's word?
2. Compare What do the teachings of Isaiah, Micah, and Ezekiel have in common?

Who Were the Prophets? During this troubled time, many Israelites forgot their religion. The rich mistreated the poor, and government officials stole money.

The prophets wanted to bring Israelites back to God's laws. Their special message was that being faithful meant more than going to a temple to worship. It meant working for a just society. The prophet Amos said that justice should "roll down like waters and righteousness as a mighty stream." The goal of a just society became an important part of Christianity and Islam.

What Caused the Fall of Israel? The warlike Assyrians were feared everywhere in the region. When they conquered a nation, the Assyrians destroyed its main buildings and scattered the population. Assyrians then settled in the territory.

In 722 B.C. the Assyrians conquered Israel and scattered the 10 tribes across their empire. Over time, the Israelites who were forced to move lost their religion and way of life. They are often called the "lost tribes of Israel."

The Assyrians settled the area around Samaria and became known as Samaritans. The Assyrian settlers were afraid that Israel's God might punish them for taking the Israelites' land, so they offered sacrifices to Israel's God. They also read the Torah and followed the Israelites' religious laws. After many years, the Samaritans worshiped only the God of Israel.

The people of Judah looked down on the Samaritans. They believed that God accepted only the sacrifices from the temple at Jerusalem. They did not believe that other people were God's people too.

Why Did Judah Fall?
Now, only the small kingdom of Judah was left of the once proud empire of David. It did not last long, because the Egyptians conquered it about 620 B.C. The Jews were able to keep their king but paid tribute to Egypt.

However, Egyptian rule was cut short when the Chaldeans conquered Egypt in 605 B.C. The Chaldeans became the new rulers of Judah. At first, the Chaldeans treated the Israelites like the Egyptians had before. They allowed the Jews to keep their king as long as they paid tribute.

Several years later, the Jews united with the Egyptians to rebel against the Chaldeans. Judah held out against the Chaldean invasion until 597 B.C. That year, King Nebuchadnezzar (NEH•byuh•kuhd•NEH•zuhr) of the Chaldeans captured Jerusalem. He punished the Jews severely. He made 10,000 Jews leave the city and live in Babylon, the Chaldean capital. Then he appointed a new Jewish king.

Soon the new king of Judah was planning a revolt against the Chaldeans. A prophet named Jeremiah warned the king that another revolt was dangerous, but the king did not listen. In 586 B.C. he revolted. This time, the Chaldean ruler crushed Jerusalem. He destroyed the temple, captured the king, and took him and thousands of Jews to Babylon. In Jewish history, this time became known as the Babylonian Captivity.

✓ **Reading Check** **Explain** Why did the Assyrians and Chaldeans want to control the land belonging to the Israelites?

History Online

Study Central Need help understanding the reigns of David and Solomon? Visit ca.hss.glencoe.com and click on Study Central.

Section 2 Review

Reading Summary
Review the Main Ideas

- Saul was the first king of the Israelites. He united the 12 tribes into one kingdom.

- King David built an Israelite empire and made Jerusalem his capital. Solomon built a great temple at Jerusalem, but after he died, the Israelites split into two kingdoms—Israel and Judah.

- The Assyrians and then the Chaldeans conquered Israel and Judah, and forced many Israelites to leave their homeland.

What Did You Learn?

1. Why was David anointed king while Saul was still in charge of the Israelites?

2. Who were the prophets, and why were they important to the Israelites?

Critical Thinking

3. **The Big Ideas** Draw a chart like the one below. Use it to compare the accomplishments of King David and King Solomon. **CA 6RC2.4**

King David	King Solomon

4. **Summarize** What happened to the Israelites after the death of Solomon? **CA HI2.**

5. **Describe** Who were the Samaritans, and what did the people of Judah think of them? **CA HR5.**

6. **Infer** Why do you think the Assyrians and Chaldeans moved Jews away from Israel and Judah? **CA CS3.**

7. **Analysis** **Understanding the Past** Create a summary of the major events and important people in this section. Use this summary to help you understand the history of the Israelites. **CA HI1.**

Section 3

The Growth of Judaism

Guide to Reading

Looking Back, Looking Ahead

In Section 2, you learned that the Chaldeans forced thousands of Jews to go to Babylon. Life in Babylon was very difficult. Many of Judah's people looked to their religion for hope and strength.

Focusing on the Main Ideas

- The Jews continued their religion during their exile in Babylon. *(page 214)*

- Jews spread their beliefs to the Greek world and regained control of Judah. *(page 215)*

- Religion shaped the Jewish way of life. *(page 217)*

- Under Roman rule, the Jews were divided and rebellious. In response, the Romans destroyed the temple and exiled the Jews. *(page 220)*

Locating Places

Babylon (BA•buh•luhn)

Meeting People

Judas Maccabeus
    (JOO•duhs   MAK•uh•BEE•uhs)
Herod (HEHR•uhd)
Zealot (ZEH•luht)
Johanan ben Zakkai
    (YOH•kah•nahn behn zah•KY)

Content Vocabulary

exile (EHG•ZYL)
Sabbath (SA•buhth)
synagogue (SIH•nuh•GAHG)
Diaspora (dy•AS•pruh)
messiah (muh•SY•uh)
rabbi (RA•BY)

Academic Vocabulary

series (SIHR•eez)
version (VUHR•zhuhn)
trace (TRAYS)

Reading Strategy

Summarizing Information Use a diagram to describe the Maccabees.

Maccabees

History Social Science Standards

WH6.3 Students analyze the geographic, political, economic, religious, and social structures of the Ancient Hebrews.

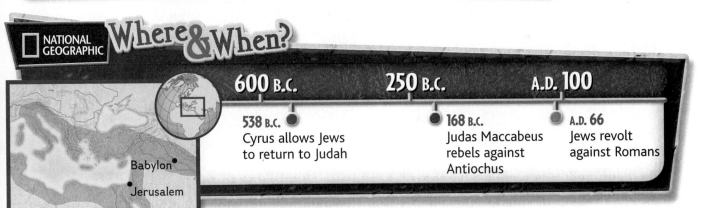

NATIONAL GEOGRAPHIC Where & When?

600 B.C.   250 B.C.   A.D. 100

538 B.C. Cyrus allows Jews to return to Judah

168 B.C. Judas Maccabeus rebels against Antiochus

A.D. 66 Jews revolt against Romans

Babylon
Jerusalem

WH6.3.2 Identify the sources of the ethical teachings and central beliefs of Judaism (the Hebrew Bible, the Commentaries): belief in God, observance of law, practice of the concepts of righteousness and justice, and importance of study; and describe how the ideas of the Hebrew traditions are reflected in the moral and ethical traditions of Western civilization.

Exile and Return

Main Idea The Jews continued their religion during their exile in Babylon.

Reading Connection Have you ever learned something important by experiencing a hardship? Read on to find out what lessons the Jews learned from hard times.

The Jews called their time in Babylon an **exile** (EHG•zyl). This means they were forced to live in a foreign land. During their exile, the Israelite religion became what we call Judaism.

While in **Babylon** (BA•buh•luhn), small groups of Jews met on the **Sabbath** (SA•buhth). This was their weekly day of worship and rest. Today, the Jewish Sabbath is Saturday. These weekly meetings took place at **synagogues** (SIH•nuh•GAHGS), or Jewish houses of worship. The synagogue meetings gave the people hope.

Why Did Jews Return to Judah?

During the 500s B.C., a group of people called Persians swept across southwest Asia. The Persians defeated the Chaldeans and took over Babylon. In 538 B.C. the Persian king Cyrus permitted Jews to return to Judah.

Some Jews stayed in Babylon, but many went home. They rebuilt Jerusalem and the temple. Cyrus appointed officials to rule the country and collected taxes from the people. Because Persians controlled their government, the Jews looked to their religion for leadership.

The leaders of the Jews became the temple priests and scribes. Many scribes became religious scholars. Under a scribe named Ezra, the Jews wrote the five books of the Torah on pieces of parchment. They sewed the pieces together to make long scrolls. The Torah and writings that were added later made up the Hebrew Bible.

◀ Torah scrolls are carried in decorated cases such as this one from the main synagogue in Jerusalem. *What larger text is made up of the Torah and other important writings?*

▼ Torah scrolls

▲ A rabbi reads from the Torah.

What Is in the Hebrew Bible? The Hebrew Bible is really a **series** of books collected together. It includes the five books of the Torah and 34 other books. These books describe events in Jewish history. The Jews believed that God had a special role for them in history.

For example, Genesis, the first book of the Torah, tells how God created the earth in six days and rested on the seventh day. He also created the first man and woman, Adam and Eve. Genesis also tells how God punished the world for its bad behavior. In Genesis, God tells Noah to build an ark, or large boat. Noah, his family, and two of every animal on Earth boarded the ark. Then a great flood covered the land, and only those on the ark escaped drowning. After the flood, God promised to never again destroy the world with a flood.

Genesis also explains why the world has many languages. It tells how the people in the city of Babel tried to build a tower to heaven. God disapproved and made the people speak in different languages, then scattered them across the earth.

The Jews Look to the Future Parts of the Bible described God's plan for a peaceful future. The book of Daniel addressed this issue. Daniel lived in Babylon and was a trusted adviser of the king. However, he refused to worship Babylonian gods. The Chaldeans threw Daniel into a lion's den, but God protected Daniel from the lions. The story was meant to remind Jews that God would rescue them.

The Jews believed that evil and suffering would eventually be replaced by goodness. Christians and Muslims share this idea of good triumphing over evil.

Reading Check **Identify** Who allowed the Jews to return to Judah?

The Jews and the Greeks

Main Idea Jews spread their beliefs to the Greek world and regained control of Judah.

Reading Connection How do you show loyalty to friends and family? Read to learn how Jews showed loyalty to their religion and country.

In 334 B.C. a Greek king named Alexander the Great began taking over kingdoms around the Mediterranean. In 331 B.C. his armies defeated the Persians, so Judah came under his control. Alexander allowed the Jews to stay in Judah. However, Alexander, who loved all things Greek, introduced the Greek language and Greek ways to Judah.

What Was the Diaspora? At the time, Jews were also living in other parts of Alexander's empire. Many still lived in Babylon. Some lived in Egypt and other lands around the Mediterranean Sea. The Jews outside of Judah became known as the

▲ According to the Bible, Daniel is thrown into a lion's den for refusing to worship the Babylonian gods. God, however, kept Daniel safe from the lions. *What lesson did this story present to the Jews?*

Diaspora (dy•AS•pruh). *Diaspora* is a Greek word that means "scattered."

Many Jews of the Diaspora learned the Greek language and Greek ways but remained loyal to Judaism. A group of them copied the Hebrew Bible into Greek. This Greek **version** helped people who were not Jews to read and understand the Hebrew Bible. As a result, Jewish ideas spread throughout the Mediterranean world.

Who Were the Maccabees?

In 168 B.C. a Greek ruler named Antiochus (an•TY•uh kuhs) controlled Judah. He decided to make the Jews of Judah worship Greek gods and goddesses. A priest named **Judas Maccabeus** (JOO•duhs   MAK•uh•BEE•uhs) and his followers rebelled. They fled to the hills and formed an army known as the Maccabees.

After many battles, the Maccabees drove the Greeks out of Judah. They destroyed all **traces** of Greek gods and goddesses in their temple and made it a temple for worshiping the God of Israel. Each year Jews recall the cleansing of the temple when they celebrate Hanukkah (HAH•nuh•kuh).

Priests from Judas Maccabeus's family became the new rulers of Judah. Under their leadership, Judah took over land that had been part of the kingdom of Israel.

✓ **Reading Check** **Analyze** How did Alexander the Great affect the Israelites?

Major Jewish Holidays

Name	Time of Year	Length	Reason for the Holiday	Customs
Passover	April	8 days (7 in Israel)	to celebrate God's passing over of the Jews during the final plague in Egypt that enabled the Jews to return to the Promised Land	limited work; some fasts; sell certain foods that cannot be eaten or owned during the holiday; perform rituals
Rosh Hoshana	September or October	2 days	to celebrate the Jewish New Year	plan changes for the new year; no work; synagogue services; a shofar (horn) is blown in synagogues
Yom Kippur	September or October	25 hours	to make amends for sins of the past year	no work; synagogue services; pray; fast; apologize for wrongs during the past year
Hanukkah	December	8 days	to celebrate the Maccabees' victory and reclaiming of the temple in Jerusalem	light candles each night; eat fried foods; play a game called dreidel; give gifts

◀ A menorah is an eight-branched candle stand used by Jews to celebrate Hanukkah.

WH6.3.2 Identify the sources of the ethical teachings and central beliefs of Judaism (the Hebrew Bible, the Commentaries): belief in God, observance of law, practice of the concepts of righteousness and justice, and importance of study; and describe how the ideas of the Hebrew traditions are reflected in the moral and ethical traditions of Western civilization.

The Jewish Way of Life

Main Idea Religion shaped the Jewish way of life.

Reading Connection What types of things influence the way you live? Read to find out how religion influenced Jewish life.

Jewish law set out many rules for Jews to follow that affected their daily life. These laws influenced their education, the foods they ate, and even the clothes they wore. The laws emphasized self-control and reminded Jews of their religion. This became important when they no longer had their own land and king.

Jewish Clothing Jewish law forbade mixing some fabrics. So women used flax or wool to make cloth but did not combine the two.

Jewish men wore tunics made of linen next to their skin. Some men layered another tunic on top of the first. In cold weather, they added wool or sheepskin cloaks. On their heads, they wore caps or turbans. On their feet, they wore sandals.

Women draped themselves in long, simple dresses. They covered their heads with shawls. Only wealthy women could afford leather shoes. They also wore makeup and jewelry.

Linking Past & Present

Head Coverings

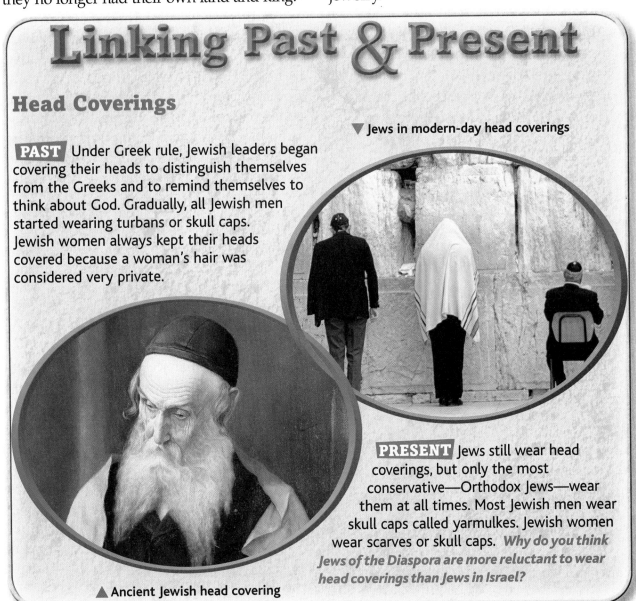

PAST Under Greek rule, Jewish leaders began covering their heads to distinguish themselves from the Greeks and to remind themselves to think about God. Gradually, all Jewish men started wearing turbans or skull caps. Jewish women always kept their heads covered because a woman's hair was considered very private.

▼ **Jews in modern-day head coverings**

PRESENT Jews still wear head coverings, but only the most conservative—Orthodox Jews—wear them at all times. Most Jewish men wear skull caps called yarmulkes. Jewish women wear scarves or skull caps. *Why do you think Jews of the Diaspora are more reluctant to wear head coverings than Jews in Israel?*

▲ **Ancient Jewish head covering**

Young People In...

Education in Ancient Israel and Judah

Early Israelites placed a high value on education. Rabbis—Jewish religious teachers—taught their followers, "If you have knowledge, you have everything." Unfortunately, only boys were allowed to go to school.

Fathers taught their young sons the commandments. They also taught them about the meanings of Jewish traditions and holy feasts. At age five, boys went to a school that was connected with the synagogue. There, the hazan, or minister of the synagogue, taught them the Torah. Everything the students learned—from the alphabet to Jewish history—they learned from the Torah.

Jewish laws decided the stages of students' education. Different subjects were introduced at the ages of 5, 10, and 13. Most Jewish boys finished their education at age 13. At that age, boys became adults.

▲ Children studying the Torah today

Connecting to the Past

1. Why was education important to the ancient Israelites?

2. What was a father's role in his son's education?

Family Life The Jews placed great importance on family. Sons were especially valued because they carried on the family name. Upon a father's death, the son became head of the family.

Education was also important. Jewish children's first teachers were their mothers. When sons grew old enough, fathers taught them how to earn an income and to worship God. Later, elders took over the religious education of boys and taught them the Torah. Because reading the Torah was central to Jewish life, religious teachers became important community leaders.

Mothers educated their daughters at home. The girls learned to be good wives, mothers, and housekeepers. This included learning Jewish laws about food and clothing. They also learned about the courageous women of ancient Israel. One of these women was named Ruth. Her biography appears on the next page. Her courage and devotion to her family provided an example for Jewish girls to follow.

The Jewish Diet Under Jewish law, Jews could eat only certain animals. For example, they could eat beef and lamb but not pork. They could eat scaly fish, like salmon, but not smooth-skinned fish, like eels. Laws about food were known as kashrut, which means "that which is proper."

Today, food that is prepared according to Jewish dietary laws is called kosher. Animals used for kosher meat must be killed in a special way. The meat must be inspected, salted, and soaked. To be kosher, Jews must not cook or eat milk products with meat.

In ancient times, everyday meals were made up of fish, fruit, vegetables, and barley bread. Beverages included mainly milk, water, wine, and beer.

✓ **Reading Check** **Analyze** Why were sons especially valued in Jewish society?

Biography

RUTH AND NAOMI

To show the importance of family love and devotion, Jewish girls learned about the relationship between Ruth and Naomi. The Book of Ruth in the Hebrew Bible tells about Ruth's life and of her dedication to her mother-in-law, Naomi. Years before, there was so little food in Bethlehem that Naomi, her husband, and their two sons moved to the kingdom of Moab. There, one of their sons met Ruth and married her. Tragically, Naomi's husband and both of her sons died. Naomi wanted to return to Bethlehem, but she urged Ruth to stay in Moab with her parents and friends. Ruth refused to leave Naomi by herself. She insisted on traveling with her to Bethlehem. Ruth said to Naomi, "Wherever you go, I will go; wherever you lodge; I will lodge; your people shall be my people, and your God my God."

▲ Naomi and Ruth

Naomi and Ruth arrived in Bethlehem at the beginning of the barley harvest. Because Ruth was from Moab, she was considered an outsider by the Israelites. Furthermore, because Ruth was a widow and did not have children, she did not have any property rights. To survive in Bethlehem, she had to rely upon her mother-in-law's advice and the kindness of a wealthy landowner named Boaz.

During the harvest, Ruth worked in Boaz's fields, gathering grain left behind on the ground by the reapers. It was hard work that began at dawn and ended at dusk, but Ruth never complained. She soon earned the respect and admiration of her new people. In time, Ruth married Boaz. They had a son named Obed. In the Hebrew Bible, at the end of the Book of Ruth, Obed is named as the grandfather of David, the future king of Israel.

Then and Now

To survive in Bethlehem, Ruth had to rely on Naomi and Boaz. If a present-day woman moved to a new city, what resources would she use to help her find work, shelter, and other necessities?

WH6.3.2 Identify the sources of the ethical teachings and central beliefs of Judaism (the Hebrew Bible, the Commentaries): belief in God, observance of law, practice of the concepts of righteousness and justice, and importance of study; and describe how the ideas of the Hebrew traditions are reflected in the moral and ethical traditions of Western civilization. **WH6.3.3** Explain the significance of Abraham, Moses, Naomi, Ruth, David, and Yohanan ben Zaccai in the development of the Jewish religion. **WH6.3.5** Discuss how Judaism survived and developed despite the continuing dispersion of much of the Jewish population from Jerusalem and the rest of Israel after the destruction of the second Temple in A.D. 70.

The Jews and the Romans

Main Idea Under Roman rule, the Jews were divided and rebellious. In response, the Romans destroyed the temple and exiled the Jews.

Reading Connection Do you consider freedom worth fighting for? Read to find out what happened to the Jews after they fought for their freedom.

In 63 B.C. a people known as the Romans conquered Judah. Led by powerful generals, the Romans were intent on expanding their empire. The Roman capital was far to the west in what is today the country of Italy. When the Romans conquered Judah, they renamed it Judaea (joo•DEE•uh). At first, the Romans allowed Jewish rulers to run Judaea.

NATIONAL GEOGRAPHIC

HISTORY MAKERS

Dead Sea Scrolls

In A.D. 1947 shepherd boys in the Judaean desert near the Dead Sea found the first of the Dead Sea Scrolls in a cave. The Dead Sea Scrolls are ancient scrolls of leather, papyrus, and copper written between 200 B.C. and A.D. 68. The documents include the oldest complete copy of the book of Isaiah and pieces of many other books of the Hebrew Bible. Most scholars believe that the scrolls were part of a library that belonged to an early Jewish community.

The Rule of King Herod The most famous ruler of Judaea during this time was King **Herod** (HEHR•uhd). He was known for his cruelty and the additions he made to the Jewish temple in Jerusalem. He made the temple one of the most awe-inspiring buildings in the Roman world. Today he is best known as the king who ruled Judaea when Jesus was born.

Shortly after Herod died, the Romans replaced the Jewish king with Roman officials. The Jews were eager to regain control, but because they had splintered into different groups, they did not have as much power.

One group of Jews was known as the Pharisees (FAR•uh•seez). They taught the Torah and that people should strictly obey its teachings. They also taught how to apply the Torah's laws to daily life. In doing so, they helped make Judaism a religion of the home and family. The Pharisees also taught in synagogues and were supported by the common people.

One of the main teachings that set the Pharisees apart from other groups was their support of the oral traditions. These were teachings of Jewish leaders and interpretations of Jewish writings that had been passed down over time by word of mouth. The Pharisees believed the oral traditions were very important in helping people obey the commandments.

The Sadducees (SA•juh•seez) also accepted the Torah. However, they were more concerned about how it applied to the priests in the Temple. This was because many of them were priests and scribes. They did not agree with many of the Pharisees' teachings. For example, they did not hold to the oral traditions. Instead, they emphasized the law and commandments.

▲ Today Jews come to the Western Wall, also known as the Wailing Wall, to pray. *What structure is the Western Wall the remains of?*

A third group was called Essenes (ih•SEENZ). They were priests who broke away from the Temple in Jerusalem. Many Essenes lived together in the desert. They spent their lives praying and waiting for God to deliver the Jews from the Romans. Like the Sadducees, they followed the written law strictly.

In A.D. 1947 ancient scrolls were found in the desert near the Dead Sea. They became known as the Dead Sea Scrolls, and were probably written by Essenes. The scrolls have helped historians understand more about Judaism during Roman times.

Jewish Revolts During the A.D. 60s, Jewish hatred of Roman rule was at its peak. Many Jews were waiting for a **messiah** (muh•SY•uh), or deliverer sent by God. Other Jews known as **Zealots** (ZEH•luhts) wanted to fight the Romans for their freedom.

In A.D. 66 the Zealots revolted against the Romans and drove them out of Jerusalem. Four years later, the Romans retook Jerusalem. They killed thousands of Jews and forced many others to leave. The Romans also destroyed the temple in Jerusalem. The Western Wall is all that remains of it today.

This was a very difficult time for the Jews, but they were able to keep the city of Jerusalem. For a number of years they were able to prosper despite not being able to govern their own lands.

Eventually some Jews decided they were willing to fight for freedom again. In

A.D. 132 a military leader named Simon Bar Kochba led the Jews successfully in battle against the Romans. However, the Romans had a better military, and they were able to regroup. Three years later, they crushed the revolt. Bar Kochba and many Jewish leaders were killed during the fighting.

This time, the Romans forbade Jews to live in or even visit Jerusalem. The city was destroyed, as were Bethlehem and Jericho. The Romans began calling the region of Judah by the name of Palestine. This name refers to the Philistines, whom the Israelites had conquered hundreds of years before.

Jewish Teachers Despite losing their land, the Jews managed to survive. They no longer had priests. Instead, leaders called **rabbis** (RA•BYZ) became important. The primary role of the rabbis was to teach from the Torah to interpret its meanings, and to provide guidance to the people in their care.

One of the most famous rabbis was **Johanan ben Zakkai** (YOH•kah•nahn behn zah•KY). Zakkai was a Pharisee who had an important political influence during the Roman rule of Judaea. Although the Romans sacked Jerusalem in A.D. 70 because of the Jewish revolt, Zakkai convinced the Romans not to destroy the Jewish city of Jamnia. Instead, they allowed him to settle there and found a school to continue teaching the Jews.

Zakkai helped Judaism survive the destruction and loss of the temple. He placed great emphasis on the study of the Torah. He also emphasized acts of loving kindness. As a result of his efforts, Zakkai's school became a center of Torah studies for hundreds of years. Other rabbis founded

Primary Source

The Talmud

One of the Ten Commandments tells Jews to keep the Sabbath holy. Part of the Talmud declares that most types of work and business are not allowed on the Sabbath, or Jewish day of worship. This passage identifies the only times it is okay to break those rules.

> "One is permitted to remove debris on the Sabbath in order to save a life or to act for the benefit of the community; and we may assemble in the synagogue on the Sabbath to conduct public business [i.e., matters of community concern]."

—*The Talmud for Today*,
Rabbi Alexander Feinsilver,
trans. and ed.

▼ Jews reading the Talmud today

DBQ Document-Based Question

Why do you think these exceptions were made for the benefit of the community?

Torah schools in places as far away as Babylon and Egypt.

The rabbis wanted to save and pass on teachings about the Torah. They did this by combining their teachings into books called commentaries. The Talmud is the most important book of commentaries. It deals with almost every aspect of daily life. For example, the Talmud discusses agricultural activities, feasts, prayer, marriages, and rules for copying sacred texts. To this day, the Talmud remains an important record of Jewish law.

For 2,000 years, most Jews lived outside of Palestine. They often faced hatred and persecution. In A.D. 1948 Palestine was divided, and a new Jewish nation called Israel was created.

✔ Reading Check **Explain** How did the Roman conquest affect the Jews?

◀ **Restoration of the Dead Sea Scrolls**

▼ **The Dead Sea Scrolls were damaged and had to be put together piece by piece.**

History Online

Study Central Need help understanding Judaism? Visit ca.hss.glencoe.com and click on Study Central.

Section 3 Review

Reading Summary

Review the Main Ideas

- During their exile in Babylon, the Jews developed their religion, which is based upon the stories in the Hebrew Bible.

- Jews spread their ideas to the Greek world. About 168 B.C., they fought the Greeks for control of Judah.

- Religious laws concerning food and clothing affected everyday Jewish life.

- In 63 B.C. Judah was taken over by the Roman Empire.

What Did You Learn?

1. What was the Diaspora?

2. What was education like within a Jewish family?

Critical Thinking

3. **Organizing Information** Draw a table to describe the differences between these three Jewish groups. **CA 6RC2.2**

Pharisees	Sadducees	Essenes

4. **Summarize** How did the Jews practice their religion during the exile in Babylon? **CA 6RC2.0**

5. **Identify** Who were the Zealots, and why were they important? **CA 6RC2.3**

6. **The Big Ideas** Do you think that Jewish beliefs and values would have spread so widely if Israel and Judah had not been conquered by other peoples? Explain. **CA HI2.**

7. **Persuasive Writing** Imagine you are living in Judaea during the Roman conquest. Write a letter to a friend describing what you think about the Romans and what actions you would like to see taken to make Judaea free again. **CA 6WS1.1; 6WA2.5**

Analyzing Primary Sources

Words to Live By

The ancient Israelites believed that they were a chosen people who had a special relationship with God. Through this relationship, they believed that God had given them specific instructions on how to live and act. These instructions were included in the Hebrew Bible.

Read the following passages on pages 224 and 225, and answer the questions that follow.

▲ **Torah scrolls**

Reader's Dictionary

ark: a ship

covenant (KUHV•nuhnt): in the Bible, the solemn promises God made to humans

bow: a rainbow

haughty (HAH•tee): too proud

abomination (uh•BAH•muh•NAY•shuhn): something hateful

humility (hyoo•MIH•luh•tee): modesty

Noah and the Ark

According to the Bible, at the time of Noah, people throughout the earth had become wicked. God sent a flood to destroy them, but saved Noah and his family.

And God said to Noah, "I have determined to make an end of all flesh, for the earth is filled with violence through them. Behold, I will destroy them with the earth. Make yourself an **ark**. . . .

For behold, I will bring a flood of waters upon the earth to destroy all flesh in which is the breath of life under heaven. Everything that is on the earth shall die. . . . and you shall come into the ark, you, your sons, your wife, and your sons' wives with you.

And of every living thing of all flesh, you shall bring two of every sort into the ark. . . .

Noah entered the ark with his family and the animals. It then rained for 40 days and nights. Then God commanded them to leave the ark.

Then God said to Noah and to his sons with him, "Behold I establish my **covenant** with you . . . that never again shall all flesh be cut off by the waters of the flood, and never again shall there be a flood to destroy the earth." And God said, "This is the sign of the covenant that I make between me and you. . . . I have set my **bow** in the cloud, and it shall be a sign of the covenant between me and the earth."

—Genesis 6:13, 14, 17, 18, 19;
Genesis 9:8, 9, 11, 12, 13

Proverbs

Proverbs are short sayings that share a truth or observation in a way that is easy to remember. The Book of Proverbs in the Bible contains a collection of parables and sayings, some about everyday life and some more spiritual in nature.

Pride goes before destruction,
and a **haughty** spirit before a fall.

—Proverbs 16:18

Whoever gives thought to the word will
   discover good,
and blessed is he who trusts in the LORD.

—Proverbs 16:20

He who justifies the wicked and he who
   condemns the righteous
are both alike an **abomination** to the LORD.

—Proverbs 17:15

The reward for **humility** and fear of the LORD
   is riches and honor and life.

—Proverbs 22:4

A picture of the Ark of the Covenant ▶

Singing the Praises of God

The Book of Psalms of the Bible contains sacred songs or hymns that were sung in worship in the temple. They tell about the Israelites' relationship with God. Following is a psalm that was attributed to David, the second king of Israel.

Hear my cry, O God,
   listen to my prayer;
from the end of the earth I call to you
   when my heart is faint.
Lead me to the rock
   that is higher than I,
for you have been my refuge,
   a strong tower against the enemy.

—Psalm 61:1–3

DBQ Document-Based Questions

Noah and the Ark

1. Why do you think God chose to make a covenant with Noah?
2. Why did God tell Noah to bring two of every living thing, male and female, into the ark?
3. What was the sign God gave that he would not cover the earth with a flood again?

Proverbs

4. Rewrite in your own words what you think each of the proverbs means.

Singing the Praises of God

5. What does it mean to say that God has a strong tower against the enemy?
6. Think about what the rock and tower represent. What do these images tell you about how the writer views God?

Read to Write

7. Reread the passages. Do you think that Noah would agree with the psalm and the proverbs? Explain. What do all of these passages tell you about the relationship the ancient Israelites believed they had with God? **CA HR5.**

Review Content Vocabulary

Match the definitions in the second column to the terms in the first column.

1. tribe
2. prophet
3. synagogue
4. Sabbath
5. messiah
6. monotheism
7. covenant
8. exile

a. claims to be inspired by God
b. Jewish house of worship
c. family group
d. holy day of worship and rest
e. forced absence
f. belief in one god
g. deliverer sent by God
h. agreement

Review the Main Ideas

Section 1 • The First Israelites

9. Where did the Israelites record their history and religious beliefs?
10. Why did the Israelites fight the Canaanites?

Section 2 • The Kingdom of Israel

11. Why did the Israelites choose a king?
12. Where did David build his capital city?
13. What happened when the Israelites were conquered?

Section 3 • The Growth of Judaism

14. To where were the Jews exiled?
15. How did Jewish ideas spread throughout the Mediterranean world?
16. How did religion influence Jewish life?
17. How did Romans respond to Jewish rebellions?

Critical Thinking

18. **Contrast** How was the Jewish religion different from religions of other ancient cultures? **CA 6RC2.2**

19. **Analyze** Why do you think the Israelites felt so strongly about a Promised Land? **CA 6RC2.0**
20. **Compare and Contrast** How were Saul and David similar, and how were they different? **CA HI2.**
21. **Explain** How did the Jewish religion survive during the exile of the Jews? **CA HI1.**
22. **Describe** What is celebrated on the Jewish holiday Hanukkah? **CA 6RC2.0**

Geography Skills

Study the map below and answer the following questions.

23. **Location** Which kingdom—Israel or Judah—had an advantage when it came to trade? Why? **CA CS3.**
24. **Identify** About how far is Jerusalem from Damascus? **CA CS3.**
25. **Analyze** Which kingdom had the most access to the Mediterranean? **CA CS3.**

NATIONAL GEOGRAPHIC **Israelite Kingdoms**

Byblos
Mediterranean Sea
Sidon
Damascus
SYRIAN DESERT
Tyre
Samaria
Jordan R.
Jerusalem
Dead Sea
0   100 mi.
0   100 km
Lambert Azimuthal Equal-Area projection

KEY
Phoenicians
Kingdom of Israel
Kingdom of Judah

Read to Write

26. **The Big Ideas** **Understanding Perspective** Write a letter to a friend describing the things Solomon is doing as leader. Mention which of these things the people like and which they do not like. Also discuss whether Solomon's policies were successful in helping the kingdom. **CA 6WS1.1** **CA HR5.**

27. **Summarize** Choose three events in this chapter that you think were the most important to the history of the Israelites. Write a headline that might have appeared in a newspaper of that time. **CA HI1.**

28. **Using Your FOLDABLES** Use the information you wrote in your three-pocket foldable to create a fill-in-the-blank quiz for a classmate. Write a paragraph about one of the sections, leaving blanks for your classmate to fill in. **CA HR1.**

Using Academic Vocabulary

29. Match the words from column A with the correct word or phrase in column B.

A	B
trace	sign
focus	take control of
instruct	build
symbol	main interest
occupy	small amount
create	teach

Linking Past and Present

30. **Making Comparisons** Trace the route of one of the journeys of the Israelites on a map of ancient times. Then trace the route again on a map showing that region as it is today. Identify the current nations and landmarks in that region. **CA CS3.**

Building Citizenship

31. **Making Connections** How are the Ten Commandments reflected in the laws of our own society today? Write an essay explaining the connection between the Israelites "rule of law" and laws in the United States. **CA 6RC2.3**

Reviewing Skills

32. **Reading Skill** **Making Connections** The discovery of the Dead Sea Scrolls in 1947 helped scientists to learn about early Jewish people. Research other important discoveries that helped us to understand people and events from long ago. Write a report describing how these discoveries were made and what impact they had. **CA 6WA2.3** **CA HI5.**

33. **Analysis Skill** **Understanding Time and Place** Create a detailed story about the ancient Israelites. Be sure to describe each important event along the way, including details of where and when they traveled and reasons for their departure. **CA HI1.**

Standards Practice

Read the passage below and answer the following question.

"What you gain by doing evil won't help you at all, but being good can save you from death."

34. **This proverb by Solomon reflects what important Jewish teaching?**

   A Working hard is all that matters.

   B Doing what is right and good is the best solution.

   C As long as you are happy, it doesn't matter if you are good or evil.

   D Treat others as you would like to be treated.

Making Comparisons

Compare the peoples that you have read about by reviewing the information below. Can you see how these groups helped to build the world we live in today?

Where in the World?

● Chapter 1
● Chapter 2
● Chapter 3

	First Civilizations Chapter 1	Ancient Egypt Chapter 2	Ancient Israelites Chapter 3
Where did these groups develop?	• Between the Tigris and Euphrates Rivers	• Along the banks of the Nile River	• In an area called Canaan
Who are some important people?	• Sargon, c. 2340–2279 B.C. • Hammurabi, c. 1792–1750 B.C. • Nebuchadnezzar, c. 605–562 B.C.	• King Khufu, c. 2540 B.C. • Hatshepsut, c. 1470 B.C. • Ramses II, c. 1279–1213 B.C. • Kashta, c. 750 B.C.	• Abraham, c. 1800 B.C. • Moses, c. 1250 B.C. • David, c. 1000–970 B.C. • The Maccabees, 168 B.C.
Where did most of the people live?	• Most people lived on farms near walled cities • The center of the city was the ziggurat	• Some people lived in large cities • Most people lived in villages along the Nile	• Most people lived in small villages or near the city of Jerusalem

	First Civilizations Chapter 1	**Ancient Egypt** Chapter 2	**Ancient Israelites** Chapter 3
What were these people's beliefs?	• Worshiped many different gods • The gods appointed the rulers	• Worshiped gods and goddesses • Believed in life after death	• Worshiped one God • Used the Bible as a record of their history
What was their government like?	• Early Mesopotamians were ruled by priests • Later, kings ruled the people; they believed kings had divine approval	• King was a ruler-priest and believed to be a god • Pharaoh owned all land in Egypt	• Early Israelites were led by prophets • Later, they were led by judges, then kings
What was their language and writing like?	• Early: cuneiform, or wedge-shaped characters • Later: a Semitic language	• Hieroglyphics: images that stood for ideas	• Adapted Phoenician characters to form letters and words
What contributions did they make?	• Developed writing • Created system of mathematics • Studied systems of time and created calendars • Introduced iron weapons	• Built machines to move water to crops • Developed a calendar • Built large temples and pyramids	• Developed ideas of legal system • Passed on ideas of justice, fairness, and compassion in society and government
How do these contributions affect me? *Can you add any?*	• Similar measurements are still used in building today • Our system of time is based on seconds, minutes, and hours	• Pyramids and other structures still amaze people today	• Many religions today are based on ideas similar to those of the early Israelites

229

Unit

India, China, and the Americas

Why It's Important

- India developed a system of numerals and advanced mathematics.
- The Chinese invention of paper changed how people record information.
- The Maya developed a complex civilization in the Americas.

c. 15,000 B.C.	3000 B.C.	2500 B.C.	2000 B.C.

Early India
Chapter 4

c. 3000 B.C.
India's first civilization begins

c. 2300 B.C.
Harappans begin to trade with Mesopotamians

◄ Hara pries c. 20

Early China
Chapter 5

c. 3000 B.C.
Neolithic pottery is produced in China

Early ► Chinese pottery c. 3000 B.C.

c. 2000 B.C.
Xia dynasty founded

Ancient Americas
Chapter 6

c. 15,000 B.C.
First humans cross land bridge into North America

◄ Early humans hunting a woolly mammoth c. 10,000 B.C.

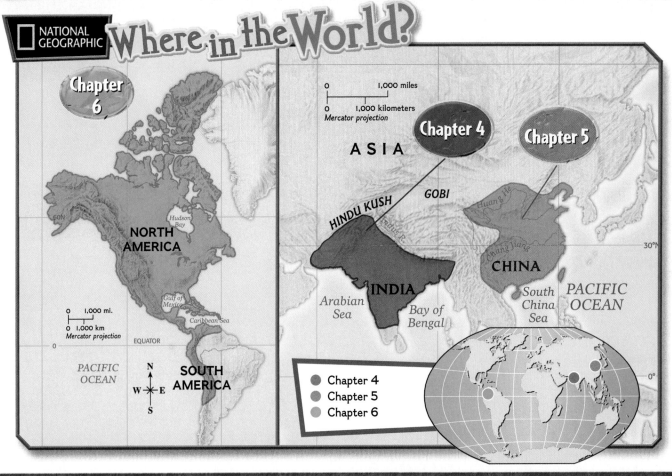

NATIONAL GEOGRAPHIC — Where in the World?

Chapter 6

Chapter 4

Chapter 5

ASIA

GOBI

HINDU KUSH

Huang He

Shang Jiang

30°N

NORTH AMERICA

Hudson Bay

60N

INDIA

CHINA

Arabian Sea

Bay of Bengal

South China Sea

PACIFIC OCEAN

Gulf of Mexico

Caribbean Sea

1,000 mi.
1,000 km
Mercator projection

EQUATOR

PACIFIC OCEAN

SOUTH AMERICA

N
W—E
S

1,000 miles
1,000 kilometers
Mercator projection

● Chapter 4
● Chapter 5
● Chapter 6

0°

1500 B.C.	1000 B.C.	500 B.C.	A.D. 1	A.D. 500

1500 B.C.
...yans enter
...dia

563 B.C.
The Buddha is
born in Nepal

321 B.C.
Mauryan
dynasty
founded

A.D. 320
Gupta empire
founded

◄ Buddhist
shrine in
India
c. 200 B.C.

c. 1750 B.C.
Shang
dynasty
begins

551 B.C.
Confucius is born

200 B.C.
Silk Road established

◄ Bronze vessel
from the
Shang dynasty

c. 1200 B.C.
Olmec
Empire begins

c. A.D. 500
Height of Mayan
power in
Mesoamerica

Mayan figure ►

Places to Locate

1 Hindu god Siva

See Early India
Chapter 4

2 Buddhist temple

See Early India
Chapter 4

NORTH AMERICA

5 **4**

SOUTH AMERICA

People to Meet

Siddhartha Gautama

c. 563–483 B.C.
Founder of Buddhism
Chapter 4, page 251

Confucius

551–479 B.C.
Chinese philosopher
Chapter 5, page 289

Chandragupta Maurya

Ruled 321–298 B.C.
Founder and king of Mauryan empire
Chapter 4, page 261

EUROPE

ASIA

Indian
Ocean

3 Terra-cotta soldiers

See Early China
Chapter 5

4 Mayan god

See Ancient Americas
Chapter 6

5 Tikal

See Ancient Americas
Chapter 6

Asoka

Ruled c. 273–232 B.C.
Philosopher-king of India
Chapter 4, page 263

**Qin
Shihuangdi**

c. 259–210 B.C.
**Built the first Great
Wall of China**
Chapter 5, page 297

**Jasaw Chan
K'awiil I**

Ruled A.D. 682–734
Mayan king
Chapter 6, page 319

Early India

The Hindu temple of Devi Jagadambi in Khajuraho, India ▼

NATIONAL GEOGRAPHIC — Where & When?

2500 B.C.	1500 B.C.	500 B.C.	A.D. 500
c. 3000 B.C. India's first civilization begins	c. 1500 B.C. The Aryans invade India	563 B.C. The Buddha is born	A.D. 320 The Gupta empire begins

Chapter Overview Visit ca.hss.glencoe.com for a preview of Chapter 4.

The Big Ideas

India's First Civilizations

People's social status affects how they live. The earliest Indian civilization developed on the Indus River. Later, the Aryans arrived in northern India. They created a new social system that determined how people lived.

Hinduism and Buddhism

Religion shapes how culture develops, just as culture shapes how religion develops. India's two main religions were Hinduism and Buddhism. These two religions affected every aspect of people's lives.

India's First Empires

Civilizations are strengthened by a variety of advances. Early India had two great empires: the Maurya and the Gupta. Both empires made advances in the arts, sciences, and math.

 View the Chapter 4 video in the Glencoe Video Program.

FOLDABLES™
Study Organizer

Identifying *Make this foldable to help you identify and learn key terms.*

Step 1 *Stack four sheets of paper, one on top of the other. On the top sheet of paper, draw a large circle.*

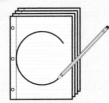

Step 2 *With the papers still stacked, cut out all four circles at the same time.*

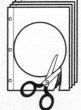

Reading and Writing
As you read the chapter, write the terms from Building Your Vocabulary in your foldable. Write a definition for each term. Then turn your foldable over (upside down) to write a short sentence using each term.

Step 3 *Staple the paper circles together at one point around the edge.*

Staple here.

This makes a circular booklet.

Step 4 *Label the front circle as shown and take notes on the pages that open to the right.*

Chapter 4 Key Terms

Questioning

1 Learn It!

One way to make sure you understand what you are reading is to ask questions of the text. Learn to ask good questions by using question starters such as *who, what, when, where, why,* and *how.* Think deeply about the main ideas, and ask questions such as "What would have happened if . . . ?"

An easy way to practice asking questions during reading is to turn the headings into questions. A heading that reads "China Reunites" can be turned into "How did China reunite?" The author has done this for you in some places in this chapter. When you turn the heading into a question, you can expect that it will be answered in the passage. Read the following passage from Section 2.

> **Hinduism** (HIHN • doo • IH • zuhm) is one of the oldest religions in the world, and today it is the third largest. It began with the religion of the Aryans, who arrived in India about 1500 B.C. The Aryans believed in many gods and goddesses who controlled the forces of nature. We know about Aryan religion from their ancient hymns and poetry, especially their epics, or long poems.
>
> — *from page 247*

Reading Tip

Make studying like a game. Create questions and then read to find answers to your own questions.

Here are some questions you might ask about this paragraph:
- What is the oldest religion in the world?
- What is the largest religion in the world today?
- Who were the Aryans, and why did they come to India?

2 Practice It!

Read the following paragraph. Then answer these questions with a partner: **Who built India's first empire? What assistance was provided by Alexander the Great?**

India's first empire was founded by Chandragupta Maurya (CHUHN • druh • GUP • tuh MAH • oor • yuh). Chandragupta was an Indian prince who conquered a large area in the Ganges River valley soon after Alexander invaded western India. Alexander's invasion weakened many of India's kingdoms. After Alexander left, Chandragupta seized the opportunity to conquer and unite almost all of northern India.

—*from page 260*

Read to Write

Write a *What If?* paragraph based on what you read in this chapter. For example, *what if* Alexander had not left India, or *what if* Hinduism were influenced by other religions of the time? Your paragraph should answer your *What If?* questions.

Ganesha ▶

3 Apply It!

As you read the chapter, look for answers to section headings that are in the form of questions.

Section 1

India's First Civilizations

Guide to Reading

Looking Back, Looking Ahead
In India, just as in Egypt and Mesopotamia, the first civilizations developed in fertile river valleys.

Focusing on the Main Ideas
- Climate and geography influenced the rise of India's first civilization. *(page 239)*
- The Aryans introduced new ideas and technology to India. *(page 242)*
- The Aryans created a caste system that separated Indians into groups. *(page 243)*

Locating Places
Himalaya (HIH•muh•LAY•uh)
Ganges River (GAN•JEEZ)
Indus River (IHN•duhs)
Deccan Plateau (DEH•kuhn pla•TOH)
Harappa (huh•RA•puh)
Mohenjo-Daro (moh•HEHN•joh   DAHR•oh)

Meeting People
Aryans (AR•ee•uhnz)
Brahmans (BRAH•muhns)

Content Vocabulary
subcontinent (SUHB•KAHN•tuhn•uhnt)
monsoon (mahn•SOON)
Sanskrit (SAN•SKRIHT)
raja (RAH•juh)
caste (KAST)
guru (GUR•oo)

Academic Vocabulary
similar (SIH•muh•luhr)
individual (IHN•duh•VIHJ•wuhl)

Reading Strategy
Organizing Information Complete a diagram like the one below showing how the Aryans changed India.

Major Ways Aryans Changed India			
↓	↓	↓	↓

History Social Science Standards

WH6.5 Students analyze the geographic, political, economic, religious, and social structures of the early civilizations of India.

NATIONAL GEOGRAPHIC

Where & When?

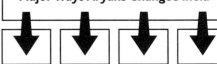

Khyber Pass • Harappa
Ganges R.

3000 B.C.

c. 3000 B.C.
India's first civilization begins

2000 B.C.

c. 1500 B.C.
Aryans arrive in India

1000 B.C.

c. 1000 B.C.
Aryans control northern India

WH6.5 Students analyze the geographic, political, economic, religious, and social structures of the early civilizations of India.
WH6.5.1 Locate and describe the major river system and discuss the physical setting that supported the rise of this civilization.

The Land of India

Main Idea Climate and geography influenced the rise of India's first civilization.

Reading Connection Do you have tornadoes or hurricanes where you live? Read to find out how geography and weather affected India's first civilization.

Look at the map below. India looks like a diamond hanging from the bottom of Asia. India is a **subcontinent** (SUHB•KAHN•tuhn•uhnt) because even though it is part of Asia, huge mountains separate it from the rest of Asia. These mountains are the **Himalaya** (HIH•muh•LAY•uh), the highest mountains in the world.

Today, six nations make up the Indian subcontinent: India; Pakistan in the northwest; Nepal; Bhutan; Bangladesh in the northeast; and Sri Lanka, an island to the southeast.

India has two very fertile river valleys. Both are fed by the mountains in the north. When the snow in the Himalaya melts, water flows into the **Ganges River** (GAN•JEEZ) and the **Indus River** (IHN•duhs). If the water is controlled, the land near these rivers can be used for farming.

The Ganges River runs south of the Himalaya and flows into the Indian Ocean. The Indus River empties into the Arabian Sea. South of the river valleys is the dry and hilly **Deccan Plateau** (DEH•kuhn pla•TOH). The east and west coasts of India are lush, fertile plains.

Monsoons (mahn•SOONZ) are an important part of the Indian climate. A monsoon is a strong wind that blows one direction in winter and the opposite direction in summer. The winter monsoon brings the cold, dry air of the mountains. The summer monsoon brings warm, wet air from the Arabian Sea, which produces drenching rains.

When the monsoon rains begin, many farmers celebrate. If the rains come on time and the rainy season lasts long enough, the crop will be good. If the rains are delayed, a drought will occur. This extended period

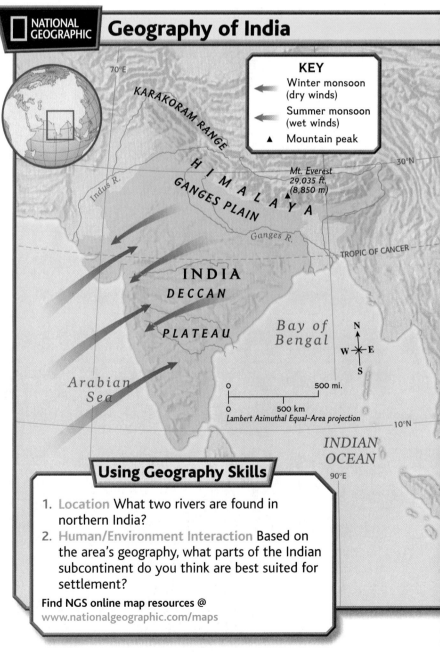

NATIONAL GEOGRAPHIC **Geography of India**

KEY
← Winter monsoon (dry winds)
← Summer monsoon (wet winds)
▲ Mountain peak

KARAKORAM RANGE

70°E

HIMALAYA

GANGES PLAIN

Indus R.

Mt. Everest 29,035 ft. (8,850 m)

30°N

Ganges R.

TROPIC OF CANCER

INDIA

DECCAN

PLATEAU

Bay of Bengal

N
W—E
S

Arabian Sea

0   500 mi.
0   500 km
Lambert Azimuthal Equal-Area projection

10°N

INDIAN OCEAN

90°E

Using Geography Skills

1. Location What two rivers are found in northern India?
2. Human/Environment Interaction Based on the area's geography, what parts of the Indian subcontinent do you think are best suited for settlement?

Find NGS online map resources @
www.nationalgeographic.com/maps

without rain can be disastrous for farmers. Few crops will be harvested, and many people will starve.

India's First Civilization

In earlier chapters, you learned about civilizations that began in river valleys. Indian civilization also began in a river valley.

India's first civilization grew up near the Indus River. When the summer monsoon began, the river rose higher and higher. When the river flooded nearby land, it left behind silt, a rich, fertile soil.

Farmers used the rich soil to grow crops to feed their families. Because people had a plentiful supply of food, they could spend time doing other things, such as making tools or building houses. As people began to trade their extra food and goods with other people, their wealth grew. This allowed them to build larger and larger cities.

India's first civilization in the Indus River valley began about 3000 B.C. and lasted until 1500 B.C. This region is today part of Pakistan. More than a thousand villages and towns were part of this civilization, which stretched from the Himalaya to the Arabian Sea. We know about these people from studying the ruins of two major cities, **Harappa** (huh•RA•puh) and **Mohenjo-Daro** (moh•HEHN•joh DAHR•oh). Archaeologists call this civilization the Harappan or Indus civilization.

Harappa and Mohenjo-Daro

Harappa and Mohenjo-Daro were large cities for their time. The well-planned cities had as many as 35,000 people. A fortress was built on a brick platform to keep guard over the residents. There were wide main streets and smaller side streets. A wall surrounded each neighborhood, and narrow lanes separated the houses.

Early Indian Civilization

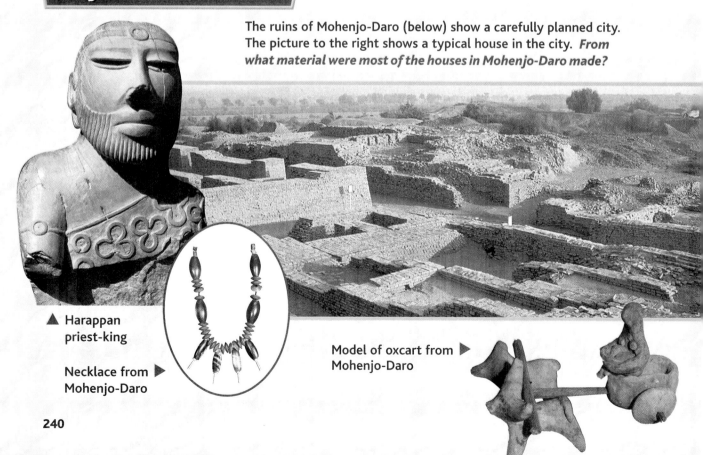

The ruins of Mohenjo-Daro (below) show a carefully planned city. The picture to the right shows a typical house in the city. *From what material were most of the houses in Mohenjo-Daro made?*

▲ Harappan priest-king

Necklace from ▶ Mohenjo-Daro

Model of oxcart from ▶ Mohenjo-Daro

Most houses had flat roofs and were constructed with mud bricks that were baked in ovens. Some houses were larger than others, but they all had a **similar** layout. There was a courtyard in the middle and smaller rooms around it.

These ancient city dwellers had some surprising conveniences. Wells supplied water, and residents even had indoor bathrooms. Wastewater flowed to drains under the streets, running through pipes to pits outside the city walls. Houses also had garbage chutes connected to a bin in the street. In addition, residents built large granaries to store food for the entire city.

Harappan Society The Harappans used a special script to write on seals and stamps. However, historians have not agreed on how to decipher these markings. Because the Harappans did not leave other historical records, we do not know much about their society or government. From the ruins, though, we can tell that the royal palace and the temple were both enclosed in the fortress. This reveals that religion and politics were closely connected.

Most Harappans were farmers. They grew rice, wheat, barley, peas, and cotton. City dwellers made copper and bronze tools, clay pottery, and cotton cloth, as well as jewelry from gold, shells, and ivory. Archaeologists have also found many toys among the ruins, such as small monkeys that could be made to climb up a string.

It is likely that the Harappans began trading with the Mesopotamians about 2300 B.C. Some Harappan sailors followed the coastline and crossed the Arabian Sea, and others traveled the difficult overland route through the mountains.

✓ **Reading Check** **Explain** How did India's geography help early civilizations?

Roofs were used to dry crops in the sun. The dried crops were then placed in cool storage rooms in the house.

Outer walls of buildings had no windows. This helped prevent the hot summer sun from heating the insides of the house.

Bathrooms had an advanced drainage system. Drains started from houses and joined the main sewer, which carried the water out of town.

Almost every building had its own well. Cool water was pulled up when needed.

WH6.5.2 Discuss the significance of the Aryan invasions.

WH6.5.7 Discuss important aesthetic and intellectual traditions (e.g., Sanskrit literature, including the *Bhagavad Gita;* medicine; metallurgy; and mathematics, including Hindu-Arabic numerals and the zero).

The Aryans

Main Idea) **The Aryans introduced new ideas and technology to India.**

Reading Connection What would your life be like without cars or computers? Read to find out how new ideas and technology affected the Indians.

The Harappan civilization collapsed about 1500 B.C. Historians think that several earthquakes and floods damaged the cities. Then the Indus River changed its course, killing many people and forcing others to flee the area. In the years that followed, a group of people called the **Aryans** (AR•ee•uhnz) began settling in the region. Soon a new civilization emerged.

Who Were the Aryans? The Aryans came from central Asia where they raised and herded animals. The Aryans were not a race or ethnic group. They were part of a larger group of people historians refer to as the Indo-Europeans. The Indo-Europeans all spoke similar languages. Some migrated south to India and Iran. Others went west to Europe.

Cattle were a prized possession among the Aryans because they provided meat, milk, and butter. Cattle were so important that they were even used as money. **Individual** wealth was measured by the number of cattle a person owned.

The Aryans were good warriors. They were expert horse riders and hunters. They had metal-tipped spears and wooden chariots, which the Aryans sometimes used to invade nearby villages for food.

About 2000 B.C., the Aryans began leaving their home territory. They moved in waves, and some groups crossed through the mountain passes in the Himalaya. They entered the Indus River valley around 1500 B.C.

Around 1000 B.C., the Aryans had begun expanding across the Punjab and Ganges Plains and south into the Deccan Plateau. Their civilization spread to all of India except the southern tip.

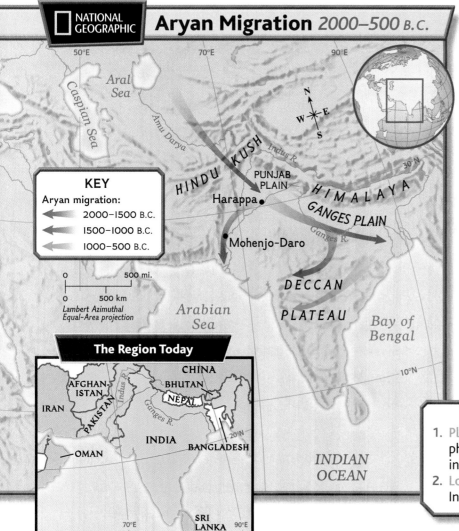

NATIONAL GEOGRAPHIC

Aryan Migration *2000–500 B.C.*

KEY
Aryan migration:
2000–1500 B.C.
1500–1000 B.C.
1000–500 B.C.

0   500 mi.
0   500 km
Lambert Azimuthal
Equal-Area projection

The Region Today

Aral Sea
Caspian Sea
Amu Darya
HINDU KUSH
Indus R.
PUNJAB PLAIN
Harappa
HIMALAYA
GANGES PLAIN
Ganges R.
Mohenjo-Daro
DECCAN PLATEAU
Arabian Sea
Bay of Bengal
INDIAN OCEAN

AFGHAN-ISTAN
IRAN
PAKISTAN
CHINA
BHUTAN
NEPAL
INDIA
BANGLADESH
OMAN
SRI LANKA

Using Geography Skills

1. Place After crossing the mountains, what physical feature did the Aryans follow into India?
2. Location Into what area of southern India did the Aryans travel?

The Aryans Bring Change When the Aryans arrived in India, they no longer lived as nomads. They became farmers but continued to raise cattle. Eventually, the Aryans would declare that cattle were sacred and forbid them to be used as food.

Because Aryans were skilled ironworkers, they improved farming in India. They invented an iron plow to help clear India's many jungles and constructed canals to irrigate. They slowly turned the Ganges River valley into good farmland.

India's varied climate supported many types of crops. In the north, farmers grew grains such as wheat, barley, and millet. Rice was grown in the river valleys. In the south, there was a mix of crops, including spices such as pepper, ginger, and cinnamon.

The Aryans also brought a new language to India. As nomads, they had no written language, but in India they developed a written language called **Sanskrit** (SAN•SKRIHT). Now the songs, stories, poems, and prayers that Aryans had known for many centuries could be written down.

The Aryans were organized into tribes. Each tribe was led by a **raja** (RAH•juh), or prince. The rajas ran their own small kingdoms, which often fought among themselves. Rajas fought over cattle and treasure and over women kidnapped from other states. These small rival kingdoms existed in India for about a thousand years, from 1500 B.C. to 400 B.C.

Reading Check **Analyze** How did the arrival of the Aryans change India?

Web Activity Visit ca.hss.glencoe.com and click on *Chapter 4—Student Web Activity* to learn more about India.

Society in Ancient India

Main Idea **The Aryans created a caste system that separates Indians into groups.**

Reading Connection Have you ever wondered why some people seem to be treated differently than other people? As you read, try to find out why this idea was accepted in India.

One of the results of the Aryan arrival in India was the development of a caste system. A **caste** (KAST) is a social group that someone is born into and cannot leave.

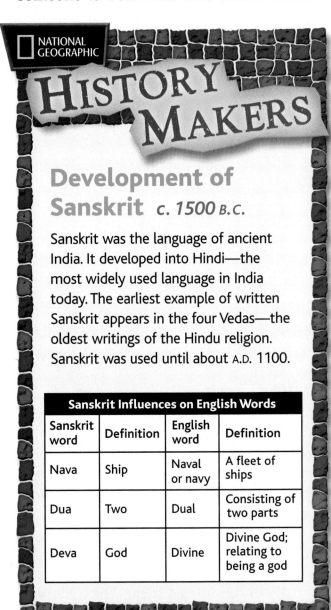

NATIONAL GEOGRAPHIC

HISTORY MAKERS

Development of Sanskrit c. 1500 B.C.

Sanskrit was the language of ancient India. It developed into Hindi—the most widely used language in India today. The earliest example of written Sanskrit appears in the four Vedas—the oldest writings of the Hindu religion. Sanskrit was used until about A.D. 1100.

Sanskrit Influences on English Words			
Sanskrit word	Definition	English word	Definition
Nava	Ship	Naval or navy	A fleet of ships
Dua	Two	Dual	Consisting of two parts
Deva	God	Divine	Divine God; relating to being a god

◀ A Brahman

Today, Untouchables refer to ▶
themselves as *Dalit*, which
means "oppressed." *Why did
the Aryans create the caste
system?*

Early India's Social System

Brahmans Priests

Kshatriyas Warriors, rulers

Vaisyas Common people

Sudras Unskilled laborers,
servants

Pariahs Untouchables

A caste dictates what job you will have, whom you can marry, and with whom you can socialize. In India, no one uses the word caste, which is the word Portuguese merchants used to describe India's social groups. Indians call these groups *jati*. Thousands of *jati* exist in India.

Why was this system created? No one is sure, but ideas about skin color were probably part of it. The Aryans were a light-skinned people. They thought they were better than the dark-skinned people they encountered in India. This idea was wrong, but the Aryans believed it.

Another reason the Aryans might have created the caste system was because the people they had encountered in India greatly outnumbered them. The caste system kept groups separate and set the rules for everyone's behavior. This helped the Aryans maintain control.

Social Levels of the Caste System The thousands of different castes, or *jati*, in India were grouped together into four classes called *varnas*. The top two *varnas* were **Brahmans** (BRAH•muhns) and Kshatriyas (KSHA•tree•uhs). Brahmans were the priests—the only people who could perform religious ceremonies. The Kshatriyas were warriors who ran the government and army.

Next were the Vaisyas (VYSH•yuhs), or commoners. Vaisyas were usually farmers and merchants. Below the Vaisyas came the Sudras (SOO•druhs). Sudras were not Aryans. Sudras were manual laborers and servants and had few rights. Most Indians belonged to the Sudra *varna*.

There was one group that did not belong to any *varna*. Its members were called Pariahs, or the Untouchables. They performed work other Indians thought was too dirty, such as collecting trash, skinning animals, or handling dead bodies.

Life for an Untouchable was very hard. Most Indians believed that being near an

Untouchable was harmful, so they forced them to live apart from others. When Untouchables traveled, they had to tap two sticks together so that everyone would hear them coming and have time to move away.

The Role of Men and Women In ancient India, the family was the center of life. Grandparents, parents, and children all lived together in an extended family. The oldest man in the family was in charge.

Men had many more rights than women. Unless there were no sons in a family, only a man could inherit property. Only men could go to school or become priests.

In families at the top of society, a boy had a **guru** (GUR•oo), or teacher, until he went to the city for more education. Young men from these families could marry only after finishing 12 years of schooling.

In India, parents arranged marriages for their children. Even today, parents arrange 90 percent of marriages in India. Boys and girls often married in their teens. Divorce was not allowed, but if a couple could not have children, the husband could marry a second wife.

One custom shows how the lives of Indian men were considered to be more important than the lives of Indian women. In India, people were cremated or burned when they died. When a man from a prominent family died, his wife was expected to leap into the flames. This practice was called suttee (suh•TEE). If the wife resisted and did not kill herself, it was a great shame. Everyone would avoid the woman from then on.

☑ **Reading Check** **Identify** What were the five major groups in Indian society?

History Online

Study Central Need help understanding Aryan society? Visit ca.hss.glencoe.com and click on Study Central.

Section ❶ Review

Reading Summary

Review the **Main Ideas**

- India's first civilization, including the cities of Harappa and Mohenjo-Daro, developed in the fertile Indus River valley.

- The Aryans, a group of nomadic herders, arrived in northern India about 1500 B.C. They brought the iron plow and the Sanskrit language to India.

- India's caste system divided people into rigid social and economic classes. Ancient Indian society favored men over women.

What Did You Learn?

1. Describe the cities of Harappa and Mohenjo-Daro.

2. Why are monsoons important to Indian farmers?

Critical Thinking

3. **Cause and Effect** Why did the Harappan civilization collapse? **CA 6RC2.7**

4. **Cause and Effect** Draw a diagram to show how the Aryans changed the lifestyle of the Indians. **CA 6RC2.4**

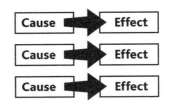

Cause	→	Effect
Cause	→	Effect
Cause	→	Effect

5. **The Big Ideas** In what ways did the caste system affect the people who lived in India? **CA 6RC2.3**

6. **Explain** How did the Aryans control people in India? **CA CS3.**

7. **Persuasive Writing** Write a description of Harappa or Mohenjo-Daro that could have been used to attract people to the city. **CA 6WA2.5**

8. **Reading** **Questioning** Create a list of questions about India's geography that will help you understand how it shaped Indian civilization. **CA HR1.**

Section 2

Hinduism and Buddhism

Guide to Reading

Looking Back, Looking Ahead

Much of Indian civilization is based on Aryan ideas and culture, which you learned about in the last section. One of the most important and long-lasting contributions of the Aryans is the main religion of India, Hinduism.

Focusing on the Main Ideas

- Hinduism grew out of the ancient beliefs of the Aryans. *(page 247)*

- A new religion, Buddhism, appealed to many people in India and other parts of Asia. *(page 249)*

Locating Places
Nepal (nuh•PAWL)
Tibet (tuh•BEHT)

Meeting People
Siddhartha Gautama (sih•DAHR• tuh   GOW•tuh•muh)
Dalai Lama (DAH•LY   LAH•muh)

Content Vocabulary
Hinduism (HIHN•doo•IH•zuhm)
Brahman (BRAH•muhn)
reincarnation (REE•ihn•kahr•NAY•shuhn)
dharma (DAHR•muh)
karma (KAHR•muh)
Buddhism (BOO•DIH•zuhm)
nirvana (nihr•VAH•nuh)
theocracy (thee•AH•kruh•see)

Academic Vocabulary
affect (uh•FEHKT)
require (rih•KWYR)
area (AR•ee•uh)
aware (uh•WAR)

Reading Strategy
Summarizing Information Create a web diagram like the one below. In the ovals, identify major beliefs of Hinduism.

Hinduism

History Social Science Standards

WH6.5 Students analyze the geographic, political, economic, religious, and social structures of the early civilizations of India.

NATIONAL GEOGRAPHIC Where & When?

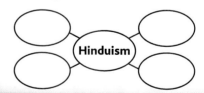

NEPAL
Ganges R.
SRI LANKA

1500 B.C.	800 B.C.	100 B.C.
c. 1500 B.C. Aryans bring early Hindu ideas to India	c. 563 B.C. The Buddha is born in Nepal	c. 200 B.C. Theravada Buddhism spreads to Sri Lanka

Hinduism

Main Idea Hinduism grew out of the ancient beliefs of the Aryans.

Reading Connection Have you ever wondered why most people try to behave properly or do good deeds? As you read this section, find out how a Hindu would answer this question.

Hinduism (HIHN•doo•IH•zuhm) is one of the oldest religions in the world, and today it is the third largest. It began with the religion of the Aryans, who arrived in India about 1500 B.C. The Aryans believed in many gods and goddesses who controlled the forces of nature. We know about Aryan religion from their ancient hymns and poetry, especially their epics, or long poems.

For centuries, the priests, or Brahmans, recited these works, and much later they were written down in Sanskrit. Over the centuries, Aryan religion changed. It borrowed some religious ideas from the people the Aryans conquered in India. This mix of beliefs eventually became Hinduism.

Early Hinduism Hinduism grew out of the religious customs of many people over thousands of years. This might explain why Hinduism has thousands of gods and goddesses. Hindus tend to think of all gods and goddesses as different parts of one universal spirit. This universal spirit is called **Brahman** (BRAH•muhn). In its earliest forms, the worship of this spirit is sometimes called Brahmanism.

The search for a universal spirit is described in the ancient religious writings known as the Upanishads (oo•PAH•nih•SHADZ). Those writings say that every living being has a soul that wants to be reunited with Brahman and that this happens when a person dies.

The Upanishads describe how a person unites with Brahman: A soul that becomes one with Brahman is like a lump of salt thrown into water. The lump of salt is gone, but the water tastes salty. The salt has become part of the water.

◀ Hindu temple

▲ **Hindus meet to discuss holy writings.**
What ancient religious writings describe the search for a universal spirit?

247

Major Hindu Gods and Goddesses

Name	Realm
Brahma	creator of the world
Vishnu	preserver of the world
Siva	destroyer of the world
Ganesha	lord of existing beings; remover of obstacles
Krishna	teacher of the world
Lakshmi	goddess of light, beauty, good fortune, and wealth
Saraswati	goddess of knowledge, music, and creative arts
Parvati	universal mother
Surya	god of the sun

Ganesha ▶

◀ Siva

Understanding Charts

Brahma, Vishnu, and Siva are considered to be the three main Hindu gods.
1. Which god is known as the "teacher of the world"?
2. Conclude Why does Hinduism have so many gods?

What Is Karma? Hindus believe that a soul is not joined to the Brahman immediately after a person dies. Instead, a person must pass through many lives to be united with Brahman. On its journey, a soul might be reborn into a higher caste. If an individual lived a bad life, he or she might be reborn into a lower caste.

This idea of passing through many lives to reach the Brahman is called **reincarnation** (REE•ihn•kahr•NAY•shuhn). It is very important in Hinduism and it influences how Hindus live their daily lives. It even **affects** how they treat animals because they consider all life sacred.

To earn the reward of a better life in their next life, Hindus believe they must perform their duty. **Dharma** (DAHR•muh) is the divine law. It **requires** people to perform the duties of their caste. A farmer has different duties than a priest and men have different duties than women.

The consequences of how a person lives are known as **karma** (KAHR•muh). Hindus believe that if they do their duty and live a good life, they will have good karma. This good karma moves them closer to the Brahman in their next life.

How did the belief in reincarnation affect Indians? For one thing, it made them more accepting of the caste system. People believed they had to be happy with their role in life and do the work of their caste.

A dedicated Hindu believes that the people in a higher caste are superior and that they are supposed to be on top. The belief in reincarnation gave hope to everyone, even servants. If servants did their duty, they might be reborn into a higher caste in their next life.

✓ Reading Check **Explain** How did the beliefs of the Aryans influence Hinduism?

Buddhism

Main Idea A new religion, Buddhism, appealed to many people in India and other parts of Asia.

Reading Connection What do you think makes a person free and happy? Find out how the Buddha answered this important question as you read this section.

By 600 B.C., many Indians began to question Hindu ideas. The Brahman priests seemed to focus only on their temple ceremonies and not on the needs of the people. Ordinary Hindus wanted a simpler, more spiritual religion. Many would find what they needed in **Buddhism** (BOO•DIH• zuhm), a new religion founded by **Siddhartha Gautama** (sih•DAHR•tuh GOW•tuh•muh).

Who Is the Buddha?
Prince Siddhartha Gautama was born around 563 B.C. in a small kingdom near the Himalaya. Today, this **area** is in southern **Nepal** (nuh•PAWL).

Siddhartha seemed to have it all. He was wealthy and handsome, happily married, and had a fine new son. Then one day he decided to explore the kingdom beyond the palace walls. As he traveled, he became very upset. He saw beggars, people who were ill, and people broken down by age with no home and nowhere to go. For the first time, he was truly **aware** of suffering.

Then and there, Siddhartha decided to seek an answer to this great riddle: Why did people suffer and how could their suffering be cured? He left his family and riches and began his search. At first he lived like a hermit, fasting and sleeping on the hard ground. Siddhartha nearly starved, but he still had no answer to his questions.

Then he decided to meditate for as long as it took to get the answer. Legend tells us that Siddhartha sat under a tree to meditate, and after 49 days, he finally understood. It was as if he had seen a great light.

▲ This shrine in northern India marks the location where it is believed the Buddha delivered his first sermon. *With what groups of Indians did the Buddha's message become popular?*

Siddhartha spent the rest of his life wandering the countryside and telling people what he had discovered. His lessons about life and the nature of suffering became known as Buddhism. To his followers, he became known as the Buddha, or "Enlightened One."

What Is Buddhism?
To understand the Buddha's ideas, one first has to see the world as he did. Like any good Hindu, Siddhartha did not think that the normal, everyday world was real. Trees, houses, animals, the sky, and the oceans were just illusions. So were poverty, sickness, pain, and sorrow.

Siddhartha believed that the only way to find the truth about the world was to give up all desires. By giving up the desire for fame, the desire for money, and the desire for all worldly things, pain and sorrow would vanish.

If a person gave up all desires, he or she would reach **nirvana** (nihr•VAH•nuh). Nirvana is not a place but a state of wisdom. The word *nirvana* came from the Sanskrit word for blowing out a candle flame.

Morality in the Eightfold Path

This passage describes the way a person should act according to the Eightfold Path.

▲ The Buddha

"He avoids the killing of living beings. . . . He avoids stealing, and abstains from [avoids] taking what is not given to him. Only what is given to him he takes, waiting till it is given; and he lives with a heart honest and pure. . . . He avoids lying. . . . He speaks the truth, is devoted to the truth, reliable, worthy of confidence, no deceiver of men."

—*The Word of the Buddha*, Nyanatiloka, trans.

DBQ Document-Based Question

According to the passage, what is the correct way to accept something?

The heart of the Buddha's teachings is contained in the Four Noble Truths. The Four Noble Truths are:

1. *Life is full of suffering.*
2. *People suffer because they desire worldly things and self-satisfaction.*
3. *The way to end suffering is to stop desiring things.*
4. *The only way to stop desiring things is to follow the Eightfold Path.*

The Buddha's fourth truth says people should follow eight steps to eliminate suffering. These eight steps, known as the Buddha's Eightfold Path, are:

1. *Know and understand the Four Noble Truths.*
2. *Give up worldly things and don't harm others.*
3. *Tell the truth, don't gossip, and don't speak badly of others.*
4. *Don't commit evil acts, like killing, stealing, or living an unclean life.*
5. *Do rewarding work.*
6. *Work for good and oppose evil.*
7. *Make sure your mind keeps your senses under control.*
8. *Practice meditation as a way of understanding reality.*

One reason the principles of Buddhism became popular was that the Buddha did not accept the caste system. A person's place in life depended on the person, he thought. The Buddha did believe in reincarnation, but with a difference. If people wanted to stop being reborn into new lives, the Buddha said, they would only have to follow his Eightfold Path.

Many people liked the Buddha's message, especially Untouchables and low-caste Indians. For the first time, these groups heard that they, too, could reach enlightenment.

Buddhism in Southeast Asia For more than 40 years, the Buddha preached his ideas. Disciples gathered around him, and after his death, they spread his message all over Asia.

As more and more people practiced Buddhism, disagreements arose about the Buddha's ideas. Finally, Buddhists split into two groups. The first was Theravada Buddhism. *Theravada* means "teachings of the elders." It sees the Buddha as a great teacher, not a god.

Buddhist teachers and merchants spread the ideas of Theravada to the south and to the east. It was adopted in Ceylon in the 200s B.C. Ceylon, an island located near the southern tip of India, is now called Sri Lanka.

Biography

THE BUDDHA
c. 563–483 B.C.

The Buddha ▶

Siddhartha Gautama—the thinker and teacher who would later be called the Buddha—was born in what is now Nepal. According to legend, his mother had a dream shortly before his birth that was interpreted to mean that her son would become a great leader.

The Gautama family belonged to the warrior caste. Siddhartha's father, Suddhodana, ruled a group called the Shakyas. His mother, Maya, died shortly after his birth.

Siddhartha was very intelligent. According to legend, the young man knew 64 languages and mastered all his studies without needing instruction.

At age 29, Siddhartha realized that he wanted to search for truth, enlightenment, and a way to rise above suffering. He left his wife, Yasodhara, and son, Rahula, to study with priests.

At age 35, Siddhartha is said to have reached full enlightenment while sitting beneath a tree. The Buddha began traveling to teach others about his discoveries and about the nature of life and suffering.

> **"Our life is shaped by our mind; we become what we think."**
> –The Buddha

◀ **Sculpture of the Buddha sitting on a cobra**

Then and Now

What types of present-day occupations often involve traveling to teach others? Why is this type of teaching easier today than in ancient times?

Theravada Buddhism also became popular in Myanmar, Thailand, Cambodia, and Laos.

Mahayana Buddhism

The second kind of Buddhism is called Mahayana Buddhism. It teaches that the Buddha is a god who came to save people. Mahayana Buddhists

▲ **A Tibetan monk today**

believe that following the Eightfold Path is too hard for most people in this world. They believe that by worshiping the Buddha instead, people will go to a heaven after they die. There, they can follow the Eightfold Path and reach nirvana.

Mahayana Buddhists also have special affection for the bodhisattvas (BOH•dih•SUHT•vuhz). Bodhisattvas are the enlightened people who postpone going to heaven. Instead, bodhisattvas have decided to stay on Earth to help others and do good deeds.

Mahayana Buddhism spread northward into China and from there to Korea and Japan. A special kind of Mahayana Buddhism developed in central Asia in the country of **Tibet** (tuh•BEHT). There it mixed with Tibet's traditional religion and with Hinduism.

In Tibet, the Buddhist leaders, called lamas, also led the government. When religious leaders head a government, it is called a **theocracy** (thee•AH•kruh•see). The **Dalai Lama** (DAH•ly LAH•muh) was the lama who headed the government, and the Panchen Lama was the lama who led the religion. Both were considered reincarnations of the Buddha.

Today, many Buddhists live in countries like Thailand, Cambodia, and Sri Lanka, but few live in India where the Buddha first preached.

What Is Jainism? While Buddhism did not last in India, another religion that challenged Hindu beliefs has survived. This religion is called Jainism. Followers of Jainism believe that there were 24 saints who taught Jainism to the world. The last and greatest was named Mahavira.

Mahavira lived at about the same time as the Buddha. Like the Buddha, Mahavira was also born in northern India to a noble family. He, too, gave up his wealthy lifestyle and traveled throughout the country. After many years he became enlightened and began to teach Jainism.

Jainism rejected the caste system of Hinduism. Mahavira's followers stress the idea of ahimsa, or nonviolence to all living things. Because all life is sacred, the Jains, as Mahavira's followers came to be called, tried to avoid harming any other living creature. They would even use brooms to sweep aside insects so that they would not step on them. Jains refused to farm for fear of plowing under worms and other things living in the earth.

Jains believe in living a very strict life. By living this way and practicing ahimsa, Jains hope to achieve nirvana. They also practice tolerance toward all other religions and ideas.

Ahimsa's Impact Today The concept of ahimsa has had an important influence in modern times. Mohandas Gandhi, an Indian political and spiritual leader in the 1900s, used ahimsa very effectively. India had been under British control since the middle of the 1700s. Gandhi and his followers led peaceful protests to gain British attention. He practiced passive nonviolent resistance by peacefully disobeying the law. By using nonviolence, he hoped to shame the British into discussing the situation in

India. His efforts eventually helped India gain its independence.

Occasionally political leaders in the United States have adopted Gandhi's belief in ahimsa and used nonviolent protest to bring about change. Perhaps the most famous example of this was Martin Luther King, Jr., who led civil rights protests in the 1950s and 1960s. During this period in U.S. history, many African Americans did not have the same opportunities as other people. There were also laws in parts of the United States that kept African Americans and white Americans segregated, or separate, from each other.

Martin Luther King, Jr., learned and followed many concepts taught by Gandhi. King believed that living by the principles of ahimsa and practicing passive resistance would be more effective than violence in gaining rights for African Americans. Like

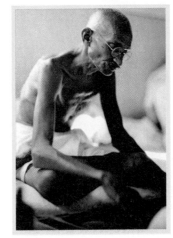

Gandhi (left) and Martin Luther King, Jr., (below) both believed in nonviolent protest.

Gandhi, King was able to bring about great change in his country.

Reading Check **Describe** How did Buddhism spread throughout Asia?

History Online

Study Central Need help understanding Hinduism, Buddhism, and Jainism? Visit ca.hss.glencoe.com and click on Study Central.

Section 2 Review

Reading Summary

Review the Main Ideas

- Hinduism is an old religion with many gods. Hindus believe in reincarnation and that a person's place in life is determined by his or her karma.

- In the 500s B.C., Siddhartha Gautama founded the religion of Buddhism in northern India. According to Buddhism, a person who follows the Four Noble Truths and the Eightfold Path can achieve nirvana.

What Did You Learn?

1. What are the Upanishads?

2. What is reincarnation?

Critical Thinking

3. **Compare and Contrast** Draw a chart like the one below. Then add details to compare the two main branches of Buddhism. **CA 6RC2.4**

Branches of Buddhism	
Theravada Buddhism	Mahayana Buddhism

4. **Analyze** How has ahimsa influenced people today? **CA HI2.**

5. **Explain** What is the importance of the Four Noble Truths and the Eightfold Path? **CA HR4.**

6. **The Big Ideas** How did the belief in reincarnation strengthen the caste system and provide hope for the lower classes? **CA HI3.**

7. **Narrative Writing** Write a short story describing Siddhartha Gautama's journey to enlightenment. **CA 6WA2.1**

The Tiger, the Brahman, and the Jackal

Selected and edited by Joseph Jacobs

Before You Read

The Scene: The story takes place in India, near a jungle.

The Characters: A Brahman man walking through a jungle comes across a tiger who is caught in a cage. Later on, the Brahman meets a friendly jackal who tries to help him.

The Plot: A fearsome tiger is trapped in a cage. As a friendly Brahman walks by, the tiger asks him for help.

Vocabulary Preview

contrary: exactly opposite

dexterously: expertly done

fodder: dry food for animals

pious: religious

refuse: garbage or trash

vain: having no success

wretched: very miserable or unhappy

Have you ever tried to do something good for someone but it ended up hurting you? In this story, a friendly man tries to help a trapped tiger, only to be threatened afterward.

As You Read

Throughout India, tales of right and wrong are told even today.
Much like Aesop's fables, many of these tales have animals as
main characters. A collection of Indian stories called the Jatakas
contains many of this type of stories. What kinds of lessons
about right and wrong can this story teach us?

Once upon a time, a tiger was caught in a trap. He tried in vain to get out through the bars, and rolled and bit with rage and grief when he failed.

By chance a poor Brahman came by. "Let me out of this cage, oh pious one!" cried the tiger.

"Nay,[1] my friend," replied the Brahman mildly, "you would probably eat me if I did."

"Not at all!" swore the tiger with many oaths; "on the contrary, I should be for ever grateful, and serve you as a slave!"

Now when the tiger sobbed and sighed and wept and swore, the pious Brahman's heart softened, and at last he consented to open the door of the cage. Out popped the tiger, and, seizing the poor man, cried, "What a fool you are! What is to prevent my eating you now, for after being cooped up so long I am just terribly hungry!"

In vain the Brahman pleaded for his life; the most he could gain was a promise to abide by[2] the decision of the first three things he chose to question as to the justice of the tiger's action.

So the Brahman first asked a *pipal*[3] tree what it thought of the matter, but the *pipal* tree replied coldly, "What have you to complain about? Don't I give shade and shelter to every one who passes by, and don't they in return tear down my branches to feed their cattle? Don't whimper—be a man!"

Then the Brahman, sad at heart, went further afield till he saw a buffalo[4] turning a well-wheel; but he fared no better from it, for it answered, "You are a fool to expect gratitude! Look at me! Whilst I

---

[1]**nay:** no
[2]**abide by:** to accept
[3]**pipal:** a large fig tree; sacred to Buddhists
[4]**buffalo:** water buffalo

255

gave milk they fed me on cotton-seed and oil-cake, but now I am dry they yoke[5] me here, and give me refuse as fodder!" . . .

On this the Brahman turned back sorrowfully, and on the way he met a jackal, who called out, "Why, what's the matter, Mr. Brahman? You look as miserable as a fish out of water!"

The Brahman told him all that had occurred. "How very confusing!" said the jackal, when the recital was ended; "would you mind telling me over again, for everything has got so mixed up?"

The Brahman told it all over again, but the jackal shook his head in a distracted sort of way, and still could not understand.

"It's very odd," said he, sadly, "but it all seems to go in at one ear and out at the other! I will go to the place where it all happened, and then perhaps I shall be able to give a judgment."

So they returned to the cage, by which the tiger was waiting for the Brahman, and sharpening his teeth and claws.

"You've been away a long time!" growled the savage beast, "but now let us begin our dinner."

"*Our* dinner!" thought the wretched Brahman, as his knees knocked together with fright; "what a remarkably delicate way of putting it!"

"Give me five minutes, my lord!" he pleaded, "in order that I may explain matters to the jackal here, who is somewhat slow in his wits."

The tiger consented, and the Brahman began the whole story over again, not missing a single detail, and spinning as long a yarn as possible.

"Oh, my poor brain! oh, my poor brain!" cried the jackal, wringing its paws. "Let me see! how did it all begin? You were in the cage, and the tiger came walking by—"

"Pooh!" interrupted the tiger, "what a fool you are! *I* was in the cage."

"Of course!" cried the jackal, pretending to tremble with fright; "yes! I was in the cage—no I wasn't—dear! dear! where are my wits? Let me see—the tiger was in the Brahman, and the cage came walking by—no, that's not it, either! Well, don't mind me, but begin your dinner, for I shall never understand!"

---

[5]**yoke:** a wooden bar that is placed on an animal's back and attached to a plow

"Yes, you shall!" returned the tiger, in a rage at the jackal's stupidity; "I'll *make* you understand! Look here—I am the tiger—" . . .

"And that is the Brahman—" . . .

"And that is the cage—" . . .

"And I was in the cage—do you understand?"

"Yes—no—Please, my lord—"

"Well?" cried the tiger impatiently.

"Please, my lord!—how did you get in?"

"How!—why in the usual way, of course!"

"Oh, dear me!—my head is beginning to whirl again! Please don't be angry, my lord, but what is the usual way?"

At this the tiger lost patience, and, jumping into the cage, cried, "This way! Now do you understand how it was?"

"Perfectly!" grinned the jackal, as he dexterously shut the door, "and if you will permit me to say so, I think matters will remain as they were!"

Responding to the Literature

1. Which three things did the Brahman ask to help him?

2. Why did the Brahman repeat his story to the jackal?

3. **Drawing Conclusions** This story is told from the perspective of someone who is not directly involved in the events of the story. This is known as third-person narration. How would the story be different if it were told from the point of view of one of the characters, also known as a first-person narration? Rewrite the story from that character's perspective.  CA 6RL3.5; 6WA2.1

4. **Analyze** Authors use different tools, called literary devices, when they write a story. One such device is known as personification. It assigns human emotions and actions to nonhuman things. Write a two- to three-paragraph essay explaining which characters have been personified. How does this literary device help the story? Why do you think the author uses it? CA 6RL3.7

5. **Read to Write** What do you think is the lesson to be learned from this story? Write an essay using examples from the text to support your opinion. CA 6WA2.4

Reading on Your Own...

From the California Reading List

Do you want to learn more about the history of civilizations in India, China, and America? If so, check out these other great books.

Folklore

Once a Mouse ... by Marcia Brown tells the tale of a hermit who befriends a small, frightened mouse. The story tells how the hermit's magic makes the mouse change shapes. *The content of this book is related to History–Social Science Standard WH6.5.*

Biography

Confucius: The Golden Rule by Russell Freedman, a Newbery Award winner, describes the life and times of the great Chinese philosopher Confucius. The book uses stories, legends, and works written by Confucius's students to explain his impact on life in China. *The content of this book is related to History–Social Science Standard WH6.6.*

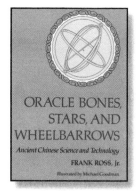

Nonfiction

Oracle Bones, Stars, and Wheelbarrows: Ancient Chinese Science and Technology by Frank Ross, Jr., introduces the reader to the inventions and advancements made by the Chinese people. *The content of this book is related to History–Social Science Standard WH6.6.*

Folklore

Warriors, Gods, and Spirits from Central and South American Mythology by Douglas Gifford discusses the many myths, tales, and important people in Central and South America. The book is filled with colorful drawings and exciting stories of early Native Americans. *The content of this book is related to History–Social Science Standard WH7.7.*

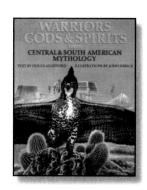

India's First Empires

Guide to Reading

Looking Back, Looking Ahead
In the last section, you learned about Hinduism and Buddhism. Both religions developed when India was a land of small kingdoms. These rival kingdoms would be forced to unite, however, when foreigners invaded.

Focusing on the Main Ideas
- The Mauryan dynasty built India's first great empire.
  (page 260)

- The Gupta empire reunited much of northern India and became wealthy through trade.
  (page 264)

- The Mauryan and Gupta empires made important contributions in literature, mathematics, and science.
  (page 265)

Locating Places
Pataliputra
(PAH•tuh•lih•POO•truh)

Meeting People
Chandragupta Maurya (CHUHN• druh•GUP•tuh   MAH•oor•yuh)
Asoka (uh•SOH•kuh)
Kalidasa (KAH•lih•DAH•suh)

Content Vocabulary
dynasty (DY•nuh•stee)
stupa (STOO•puh)
pilgrim (PIHL•gruhm)

Academic Vocabulary
dominate (DAH•muh•NAYT)
concept (KAHN•SEHPT)

Reading Strategy
Categorizing Information Create a chart, identifying the important dates, capital, and government of the Mauryan empire.

	Mauryan Empire
Dates	
Capital City	
Government	

History Social Science Standards
WH6.5 Students analyze the geographic, political, economic, religious, and social structures of the early civilizations of India.

NATIONAL GEOGRAPHIC Where&When?

Pataliputra•

350 B.C.		A.D. 1		A.D. 350

321 B.C. Chandragupta Maurya founds Mauryan dynasty

232 B.C. Mauryan ruler Asoka dies

A.D. 320 Gupta empire begins

The Mauryan Dynasty

Main Idea The Mauryan dynasty built India's first great empire.

Reading Connection Do you think political leaders should promote religion? How might religion help a king hold his country together? Read to learn why one Indian emperor decided to support Buddhism.

India's princes fought over their small kingdoms for centuries. Then two big invasions taught the Indians a lesson. First, the Persians invaded the Indus Valley in the 500s B.C. and made it part of the great Persian Empire. Then, Alexander the Great, a Greek general you will read about in Chapter 8, invaded India in 327 B.C.

Although Alexander's troops conquered northern India, he did not stay long. His soldiers were homesick and tired and threatened to rebel unless he turned back. The invasion did have one important effect, however. It led to the first great Indian empire.

Who Built India's First Empire?

India's first empire was founded by **Chandragupta Maurya** (CHUHN•druh•GUP•tuh MAH•oor•yuh). Chandragupta was an Indian prince who conquered a large area in the Ganges River valley soon after Alexander invaded western India. Alexander's invasion weakened many of India's kingdoms. After Alexander left, Chandragupta seized the opportunity to conquer and unite almost all of northern India.

He founded the Mauryan dynasty in 321 B.C. A **dynasty** (DY•nuh•stee) is a series of rulers from the same family. To run his empire, Chandragupta set up a centralized government. In a centralized government, rulers run everything from a capital city. To maintain control from his capital of **Pataliputra** (PAH•tuh•lih•POO•truh), Chandragupta had to have a strong army. He also needed a good spy system to make sure no one was planning to rebel. Communications were also important, so he set up a postal system.

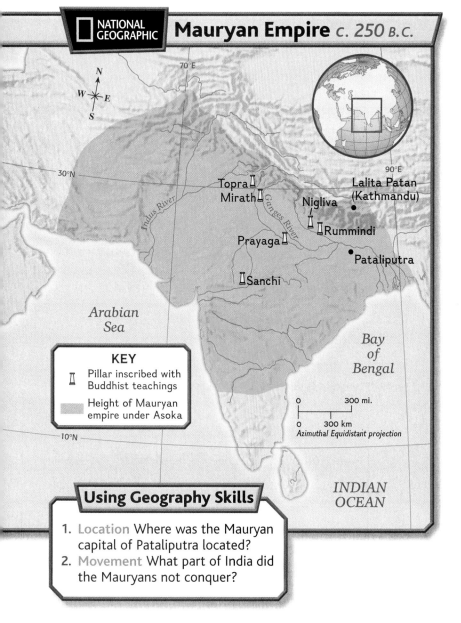

NATIONAL GEOGRAPHIC

Mauryan Empire c. 250 B.C.

Topra
Mirath
Nigliva
Lalita Patan (Kathmandu)
Rummindi
Prayaga
Pataliputra
Sanchi

Indus River
Ganges River

Arabian Sea

Bay of Bengal

INDIAN OCEAN

70°E
90°E
30°N
10°N

0   300 mi.
0   300 km
Azimuthal Equidistant projection

KEY

⌶ Pillar inscribed with Buddhist teachings

Height of Mauryan empire under Asoka

Using Geography Skills

1. **Location** Where was the Mauryan capital of Pataliputra located?
2. **Movement** What part of India did the Mauryans not conquer?

Biography

WH6.5.6 Describe the growth of the Maurya empire and the political and moral achievements of the emperor Asoka.

CHANDRAGUPTA MAURYA
Ruled 321–298 B.C.

Chandragupta Maurya may have come from humble birth, but he was a powerful ruler. Part of his great success was the result of knowing how to take advantage of a good opportunity. Alexander the Great's conquests in northwest India had left the region there, called Punjab, weak. The Indians were not happy about foreign rulers. Beginning in 317 B.C., Chandragupta began attacking the Greek overlords. He was successful and quickly organized a powerful army. Greek rulers left the region rather than prolong the fight.

Later, in 305 B.C., the Greek ruler Seleucus tried to retake Greek territory in India. Chandragupta raised a powerful army with more than 9,000 war elephants. It did not take Seleucus long to rethink engaging in battle. Instead, he formed an alliance with the Indian ruler. Instead of losing territory in war, Chandragupta forced Seleucus to give up lands through a treaty.

After conquering most of India, Chandragupta went about establishing the governmental system. He used local rulers and had a council of governors to help him. Because of the size of the empire, many supervisors were required on the local level. However, Chandragupta maintained authority over most matters. He also developed an extensive spy network to keep him notified of happenings in his capital city and within the army. Having conquered the region himself, he did not want someone else to come along and overthrow him.

Late in his life, Chandragupta is said to have converted to Jainism. Having spent much of his efforts in battle or ruling the country, he decided to turn to a simpler way of living. Despite this, his grandson, Asoka, also became a powerful military leader for a time.

▲ Chandragupta Maurya

Then and Now

Chandragupta used a powerful military to keep the peace. Do you think that a large military is necessary in today's world? Explain and provide examples to support your answer.

▲ This stupa from central India is one of the best-preserved shrines from the 200s B.C. *What other type of structure did Indians create to honor the Buddha?*

The Buddha ▶

Emperor Asoka's Reign Chandragupta founded the Mauryan dynasty, but many historians think the empire's greatest king was **Asoka** (uh•SOH•kuh). Asoka ruled from about 273 B.C. to 232 B.C.

Asoka was an unusual ruler. Like many kings, he was a strong military leader, but he came to hate bloodshed. After one bloody fight, he walked over the battlefield. When he saw the dead and wounded, he was horrified. He later made a vow to dedicate his life to peace and follow the teachings of the Buddha.

Asoka focused on the welfare of others. He created hospitals for people and for animals, too. He built new roads so it was easier to trade and put shelters and shade trees along the roads where travelers could rest.

Asoka sent many Buddhist teachers throughout India and the rest of Asia. They carried the religion to new believers. In India, laborers carved the Buddha's teachings on stone pillars for people to read. Asoka also had laborers build thousands of **stupas** (STOO•puhs). Stupas are Buddhist shrines that have the shape of a dome or mound.

Although he was a Buddhist, Asoka allowed his Hindu subjects to practice their religion. His tolerance was unusual for the time.

With a good road system and a strong ruler, the empire prospered. India became the center of a huge trade network that stretched to the Mediterranean Sea.

The Fall of the Mauryan Empire Asoka died in 232 B.C. Unfortunately, the kings who followed him were not very good leaders, and the empire grew weak.

These kings made bad decisions that turned the people against them. They forced merchants to pay heavy taxes and seized peasants' crops for themselves. Things were so bad that in 183 B.C., the last Mauryan ruler was killed by one of his own generals.

☑ **Reading Check** **Summarize** Why was Asoka an important ruler?

Biography

WH6.5.6 Describe the growth of the Maurya empire and the political and moral achievements of the emperor Asoka.

EMPEROR ASOKA
Reigned c. 273–232 B.C.

▼ Asoka

In the early years of his reign, Asoka was a powerful military ruler. He used his armies to conquer and unify almost all of India under one leader. After watching a very bloody battle that left many people dead, however, he decided to stop fighting and follow Buddhism.

Emperor Asoka vowed to relieve suffering wherever he found it. He discovered that Buddhism reflected his new beliefs, so he became a Buddhist.

Emperor Asoka had a strong, energetic personality. He began preaching Buddhist ideas that people should be honest, truthful, and nonviolent. He preached that people should live with compassion toward all humans and animals. Asoka taught by example and tried to live his life with "little sin and many good deeds." He ordered his government officials to adopt those virtues for their own lives. He helped spread the concepts of Buddhism and ahimsa, or nonviolence, throughout his empire and abroad. At the same time, Asoka practiced tolerance toward other religions.

Emperor Asoka regularly visited people in the rural areas of his kingdom and found practical ways to improve their lives. He founded hospitals and supplied medicine. He ordered wells to be dug and trees to be planted along the roads. He also ordered his officials to keep him informed of the needs of the people in his empire.

◄ Carving from top of pillar created under Asoka

Then and Now

Asoka combined religion and government. Do you think that the two should be combined or kept separate? Explain, providing examples to support your answer.

The Gupta Empire

Main Idea The Gupta empire reunited much of northern India and became wealthy through trade.

Reading Connection What types of products does the United States trade with other countries? Read to learn how the Gupta empire built its wealth on trade.

For 500 years, India had no strong ruler. Once again, small kingdoms fought with one another and made life miserable for their subjects. Then, in A.D. 320, one prince in the Ganges River valley grew more powerful than the others. Like an earlier ruler, his name was Chandragupta. This Chandragupta chose to rule from the old capital of the Mauryan empire—Pataliputra.

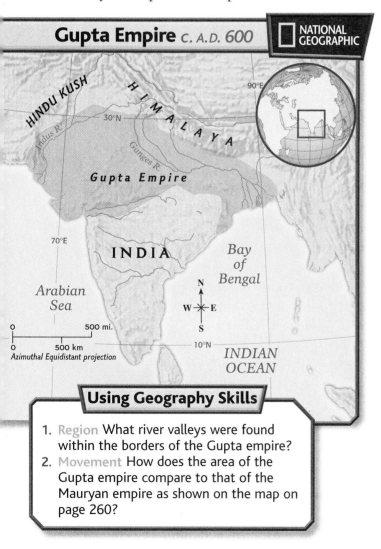

Gupta Empire c. A.D. 600

NATIONAL GEOGRAPHIC

Using Geography Skills

1. **Region** What river valleys were found within the borders of the Gupta empire?
2. **Movement** How does the area of the Gupta empire compare to that of the Mauryan empire as shown on the map on page 260?

Chandragupta founded the Gupta dynasty. When he died, his son, Samudragupta, took over the throne and expanded the Gupta empire in northern India. Soon, the new kingdom **dominated** almost all of northern India. The Guptas ruled for about 200 years. Gupta rulers had one advantage over the earlier Mauryan kings. The empire was smaller and that made it easier to manage.

The Gupta empire grew wealthy from trade. Salt, cloth, and iron were common goods traded in India. Indian merchants also traded with China and with kingdoms in southeast Asia and the Mediterranean. The Gupta rulers controlled much of the trade and became very wealthy. They owned silver and gold mines and large estates.

Trade created jobs for people in India and made many people and cities prosperous. Cities grew up along the trade routes, and many people traveled. Some people, called **pilgrims** (PIHL•gruhms), often used the trade routes to travel to a religious shrine or site. Just as cities today make money from tourism, Indian cities that were famous for their temples became wealthy from donations given by visiting pilgrims.

Asoka had converted to Buddhism, but the Guptas were Hindus like many of their subjects. They made Hinduism the official religion and gave money to support Hindu scholars and Hindu shrines. The shrines they built to Hindu gods and goddesses inspired Hindus. They often had brightly painted sculptures of images from the Upanishads and other sacred writings.

During the Gupta empire, art and science also began to develop. Earlier, you learned that Greece had a golden age of art and learning. India also had a golden age of art and learning during the Gupta empire.

Reading Check **Explain** How did the Gupta empire become wealthy?

WH6.5.7 Discuss important aesthetic and intellectual traditions (e.g., Sanskrit literature, including the *Bhagavad Gita*; medicine; metallurgy; and mathematics, including Hindu-Arabic numerals and the zero).

Indian Literature and Science

Main Idea The Mauryan and Gupta empires made important contributions in literature, mathematics, and science.

Reading Connection What do you think modern movies, books, and television reveal about our values? As you read, try to see if Indian poetry tells a story about values during the Gupta period.

Artists, builders, scientists, and writers produced many works while the Mauryan and Gupta kings ruled.

India's Most Famous Poems
The Vedas of India are ancient hymns and prayers for religious ceremonies. No one is certain how old they are because for a long time they were only recited, not written down. Once Aryan people came to India and developed Sanskrit, then the Vedas could be recorded.

Later, other kinds of literature were also written down in Sanskrit. Two epics are very famous in India, and Indians today still love to read them. The first is the *Mahabharata* (muh•HAH•BAH•ruh•tuh), and the second is the *Ramayana* (rah•mah•YAH•nah). Both of these long poems tell about brave warriors and their heroic deeds.

The *Mahabharata* is the longest poem in any written language—about 88,000 verses. Historians think several different authors wrote it and that it was written down around 100 B.C. It describes a great war for control of an Indian kingdom about 1,000 years earlier.

The best-known section is the Bhagavad Gita (BAH•guh•VAHD GEE•tuh), or "Song of the Lord." In it, the god Krishna accompanies the prince Arjuna to a great battle. Krishna preaches a sermon to Arjuna. He tells him that it is noble to do one's duty even when it is difficult and painful.

Primary Source

The Bhagavad Gita

In the Bhagavad Gita, Arjuna prepares to go into battle. He asks the god Krishna questions about war and death. The following passage is part of Krishna's answer.

"Thou grievest where no grief should be! . . .

. . . .

All, that doth live, lives always! . . .

. . . .

The soul that with a strong and constant calm
Takes sorrow and takes joy indifferently,
Lives in the life undying!

—*Bhagavadgita*, Sir Edwin Arnold, trans.

▼ **Painting titled *Krishna and Maidens***

DBQ Document-Based Question

What does Krishna believe about life after death?

HISTORY MAKERS

The Invention of Zero c. A.D. 500

Early humans understood the idea of nothing, but they did not have a symbol to represent that idea. During the Gupta dynasty, Indian mathematicians invented the symbol "0" and connected it with the idea of nothing. The Indians' invention of zero had a great impact on the study of mathematics and science—then and now. Without the concept of zero, modern technology, such as computers, would not be possible.

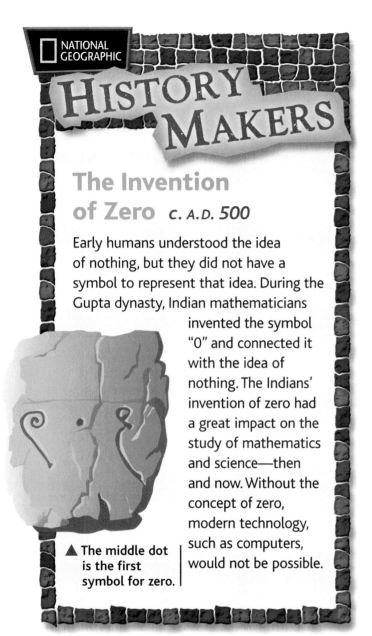

▲ The middle dot is the first symbol for zero.

The teachings in the *Mahabharata,* especially the Bhagavad Gita, contain many of the central beliefs in Hinduism. They provide important religious and moral lessons. Like adventure movies of today, the *Mahabharata* tells thrilling stories about great heroes. For this reason, it has had a great impact on Hinduism. Through the ages, many books have been written on it. It continues to influence Indian philosophy in modern times.

An important writer from the Gupta period is **Kalidasa** (KAH•lih•DAH•suh). He wrote plays, poems, love stories, and comedies. One popular poem, *The Cloud Messenger,* contains beautiful descriptions of northern India's mountains, forests, and rivers.

Music, Art, and Architecture Music played an important part of the religious and social lives of people in India. Many of the early poems like the Bhagavad Gita were probably sung in group settings. At annual festivals people danced, sang, and ate good food. They also used music in their plays. Musical instruments included tambourines, flutes, drums, and lutes.

Much of early Indian art was made of materials that have not survived. What exists today is mostly religious art made in stone. There are many sculptures of the Buddha, for example. These statues teach different Buddhist messages based on the figure's pose. Buddhist temples also used carvings of local scenes of the community.

Hindu architecture typically had carvings of people in different poses that represented different aspects of eternity. They also created images of gods with many hands to show that they had many abilities.

Indian Math and Science Indian mathematicians, especially in the Gupta period, made important contributions. Aryabhata (AHR•yuh•BUHT•uh) was the leading mathematician of the Gupta empire. He was one of the first scientists known to have used algebra. Indian mathematicians developed the idea of zero and a symbol to represent it. They also explained the **concept** of infinity—something without an end.

Gupta mathematicians created the symbols for the numbers 1 to 9 that we use today. These number symbols, or numerals, were adopted by Arab traders in the A.D. 700s. European traders borrowed them from the Arabs. Use of these numbers spread through Europe in the A.D. 1200s, replacing Roman numerals. Today, this system of number symbols is known as the Hindu-Arabic numerical system.

Early Indians also invented mathematical algorithms. An algorithm (AHL•gohr•ih•thuhm) is a series of steps that solve a problem. If you follow the steps, you get the right answer. Computer programmers today often use algorithms to tell computers what to do.

Ancient Indians made important contributions in other scientific fields, especially astronomy. They followed and mapped movements of planets and stars. They understood that the Earth was round and revolved around the sun. They also seem to have understood gravity.

Particularly under the Gupta, Indian scientists made advances in metallurgy, or metal technology. In addition to iron tools and weapons, they made steel tools. An iron pillar in Delhi dating from around 400 A.D. was so well made that it has hardly rusted. The Gupta also made sophisticated gold coins and metal mirrors.

In the field of medicine, Gupta doctors were advanced for their time. They could set broken bones and perform operations. They also invented many medical tools.

An Indian doctor named Shushruta (shoosh•ROO•tah) carried out an early form of plastic surgery. He worked to restore damaged noses. Indian doctors used herbs in treating illnesses. They also believed it was important to remove the causes of a disease and not just cure the disease itself.

Reading Check **Summarize** In what areas of science did ancient Indians make advances?

History Online

Study Central Need help understanding the advances of the Mauryan and Gupta empires? Visit ca.hss.glencoe.com and click on Study Central.

Section 3 Review

Reading Summary

Review the Main Ideas

- The Mauryan empire, under leaders such as Chandragupta Maurya and Asoka, united most of India for over a hundred years.

- The Gupta dynasty reunited northern India and grew wealthy from trade.

- During the Mauryan and Gupta empires, the arts and sciences flourished in India. Several great works of literature, including the *Mahabharata* and the *Ramayana*, came from this period.

What Did You Learn?

1. Describe trade during the Gupta empire.

2. What is the message of the Bhagavad Gita?

Critical Thinking

3. **Organizing Information** Draw a diagram to show the contributions of Indian mathematicians during the Mauryan and Gupta empires. **CA 6RC2.3**

```
        ◯           ◯
          ╲       ╱
       ⟨ Contributions ⟩
          ╱       ╲
        ◯           ◯
```

4. **Analyze** How did Asoka's actions as king show his Buddhist beliefs? **CA HI2.**

5. **The Big Ideas** Create a time line showing the advances in art, science, and math in India. Include information telling why these advances were important. **CA 6WS1.3**

6. **Math Connection** Why would the development of a number system be important in a civilization that depended on trade? **CA HI2.**

7. **Analysis** Many historians say that Asoka was the greatest ruler of the Mauryan dynasty. Reread the section and decide if you agree. Write 3 to 4 paragraphs supporting your opinion. **CA HR5.**

Analyzing Primary Sources

WH6.5.5 Know the life and moral teachings of the Buddha and how Buddhism spread in India, Ceylon, and Central Asia. **WH6.5.7** Discuss important aesthetic and intellectual traditions (e.g., Sanskrit literature, including the *Bhagavad Gita;* medicine; metallurgy; and mathematics, including Hindu-Arabic numerals and the zero).

India's Early Religions

Ancient India's two main religions, Hinduism and Buddhism, used symbols to convey ideas. These symbols represented something deeper and more profound than the simple image. While the two religions shared this common form, they were quite different.

Read the passages on pages 268 and 269, and answer the questions that follow.

Siva ▶

Reader's Dictionary

kinsmen (KIHNZ•mehn): relatives

sandalwood (SAN•duhl•WOOD): a tree with a sweet odor

rosebay (ROHZ•BAY): an herb

jasmine (JAZ•muhn): a sweet-smelling flower

Krishna's Wise Words

In the Hindu religion, the god Krishna is the teacher of the world. In this excerpt from the Hindu epic the Bhagavad Gita, Krishna explains some Hindu beliefs.

19. If any man thinks he slays, and if another thinks he is slain, neither knows the ways of truth. The Eternal in man cannot kill: the Eternal in man cannot die.

20. He is never born, and he never dies. He is in Eternity: he is for evermore. Never-born and eternal, beyond times gone or to come, he does not die when the body dies.

21. When a man knows him as never-born, everlasting, never-changing, beyond all destruction, how can that man kill a man, or cause another to kill?

22. As a man leaves an old garment and puts on one that is new, the Spirit leaves his mortal body and then puts on one that is new.

23. Weapons cannot hurt the Spirit and fire can never burn him. Untouched is he by drenching waters, untouched is he by parching winds.

—*The Bhagavad Gita*, Juan Mascaró, trans.

A Buddhist Story

The Buddha believed it was important for people to follow the Eightfold Path. In the following passages, the Buddha explains a few of his beliefs.

Treasure

A woman buries a treasure in a deep pit, thinking: "It will be useful in time of need, or if the king is displeased with me, or if I am robbed or fall into debt, or if food is scarce, or bad luck befalls me."

But all this treasure may not profit the owner at all, for she may forget where she has hidden it, or goblins may steal it, or her enemies or even her **kinsmen** may take it when she is careless.

But by charity, goodness, restraint, and self-control man and woman alike can store up a well-hidden treasure—a treasure which cannot be given to others and which robbers cannot steal. A wise person should do good—that is the treasure which will not leave one.

Virtue

The perfume of **sandalwood,**
Rosebay or **jasmine**
Cannot travel against the wind,

But the fragrance of virtue
Travels even against the wind,
As far as the ends of the world.

Like garlands woven from a heap of flowers,
Fashion from your life as many good deeds.

—*Teachings of the Buddha*, edited by Jack Kornfield

The Buddha ▶

DBQ Document-Based Questions

Krishna's Wise Words

1. What does Krishna mean when he says that the Spirit leaves the mortal body and puts on another like a change of clothes?

2. Why is the Spirit not affected by weapons or the elements?

A Buddhist Story

3. How do you think the Buddha feels about money or other kinds of material wealth?

4. How can you build up a treasure that will never leave you?

Read to Write

5. Imagine that you have no knowledge of the Hindu and Buddhist religions. After reading the two primary sources above, how would you describe the religious ideas that are important in each religion? Write an essay that describes the similarities between the two religions based on these two passages.
   CA HI2. **CA** 6WA2.2

Review Content Vocabulary

1. Write a paragraph about the basic beliefs of Buddhism using the following words.

reincarnation   karma   dharma

Write the vocabulary word that best completes each sentence.

a. stupa   d. pilgrim

b. caste   e. theocracy

c. raja   f. dynasty

2. Each Aryan tribe was led by a ___.

3. In a ___, government is led by religious leaders.

4. A ___ is a line of rulers who belong to the same family.

5. A ___ travels to religious places.

Review the Main Ideas

Section 1 • India's First Civilizations

6. What new technology did the Aryans introduce to India?

7. What was the purpose of the caste system?

Section 2 • Hinduism and Buddhism

8. What is the link between the Aryans and Hinduism?

9. Describe the differences between Hinduism and Buddhism.

Section 3 • India's First Empires

10. Which dynasty built India's first great empire?

11. What poem expresses many of Hinduism's central beliefs?

Critical Thinking

12. **Compare** How do you think the Eightfold Path is similar to the Ten Commandments of Judaism? **CA 6RC2.2**

13. **Analyze** How does the *Mahabharata* reflect the ideals of ancient India? **CA 6RC2.7**

14. **Explain** How did the monsoons affect the development of India's first civilizations? **CA CS3.**

15. **Predict** What do you think might have happened if Asoka had approved of the slaughter on the battlefield during his wars of conquest? **CA HI2.**

Geography Skills

Study the map below and answer the following questions.

16. **Human/Environment Interaction** Why did Harappa and Mohenjo-Daro develop so near the Indus River? **CA CS3.**

17. **Place** The winter monsoon winds come from the northeast. What makes the winds from that monsoon cold? **CA CS3.**

18. **Location** Name at least two natural features that protected Harappa and Mohenjo-Daro from invaders. **CA CS3.**

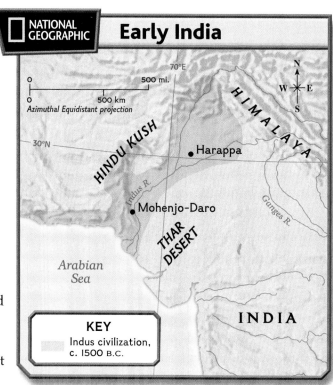

NATIONAL GEOGRAPHIC

Early India

70°E

0 ____ 500 mi.

0 ____ 500 km

Azimuthal Equidistant projection

N W E S

HINDU KUSH

HIMALAYA

30°N

● Harappa

Indus R.

● Mohenjo-Daro

Ganges R.

THAR DESERT

Arabian Sea

I N D I A

KEY

Indus civilization, c. 1500 B.C.

Read to Write

19. **The Big Ideas** **Persuasive Writing** Literature written during the Mauryan empire played an important role in Indian beliefs. Write a paragraph in which you agree or disagree with this statement. **CA 6WA2.5**

20. **Using Your FOLDABLES** Use the information you recorded in your foldable to create a fill-in-the-blank quiz for a classmate. Write a paragraph about one of the sections, leaving blanks for your classmates to fill in. Also write an answer key. **CA 6RC2.4**

Using Academic Vocabulary

21. Using information from technology, write a sentence in the past tense for each of the words below.

affect	aware
require	dominate

Building Citizenship

22. **Analyzing Information** Dharma is the Hindu idea of duty. Is it important for people in a society to do their duty? Make a list of duties Americans have today. Then write a paragraph explaining why those duties are important. **CA HI2.**

23. **Persuasive Writing** Under Emperor Asoka religion and government were combined. Write an essay in which you describe what you think the relationship between government and religion should be. **CA 6WA2.5**

Linking Past and Present

24. **Learning From Writing** After the Aryans arrived in India, they developed a written language called Sanskrit. With this form of writing, the stories, songs, and poems of early India could be recorded. Search your local library for a book of modern poetry. Read some of the poems. How does the book's author introduce the poems? Write an essay describing what the poems tell us about today's society. **CA 6RC2.1**

History Online
Self-Check Quiz To help you prepare for the Chapter Test, visit ca.hss.glencoe.com

Reviewing Skills

25. **Reading Skill** **Questioning** Select a part of the chapter that is interesting and write a series of questions about it that you would like answered. Conduct research and write down answers to the questions you posed. **CA HR1.**

26. **Analysis Skill** **Fact and Opinion** Reread the list of the Four Noble Truths on page 250. Do you agree with these Truths? Why or why not? Write an essay defending your position. **CA HR2.**

Standards Practice

Select the best answer for each of the following questions.

27 **When the Indus River flooded nearby land, it**

A forced early settlers to become nomads.

B left behind rich, fertile soil perfect for farming.

C destroyed the first Indian civilization, Harappa.

D ruined crops and the people starved.

28 **According to Siddhartha, the only way to find the truth about the world was to**

A give up all desires.

B live like a hermit.

C meditate for 49 days.

D fast until you are nearly starved.

Chapter 5

Early China

The first Great Wall of China was built more than 2,000 years ago to keep out invaders. The current wall, which is about 4,000 miles long, was built about 500 years ago. ▼

1800 B.C.	1150 B.C.	500 B.C.	A.D. 150
c. 1750 B.C. Shang dynasty begins	1045 B.C. Wu Wang creates Zhou dynasty	551 B.C. Confucius is born	c. A.D. 100 Silk Road completed

The Big Ideas

Section 1 China's First Civilizations

Physical geography plays a role in how civilizations develop and decline. Chinese civilization was shaped by geography such as mountains and large rivers. Long-lasting dynasties gained power through strong armies.

Section 2 Life in Ancient China

People's social status affects how they live. Early Chinese society had three main social classes: aristocrats, farmers, and merchants. During periods of unrest, ideas such as Confucianism and Daoism developed.

Section 3 The Qin and Han Dynasties

Systems of order, such as law and government, contribute to stable societies. Both the Qin and Han dynasties created strong central governments. New inventions developed during the Han dynasty helped to improve the lives of Chinese people.

 View the Chapter 5 video in the Glencoe Video Program.

Organizing Information *Make this foldable to help you organize information about the important people in the early history of China.*

Step 1 *Fold a sheet of paper in half from side to side.*

Fold it so the left edge lies about $\frac{1}{2}$ inch from the right edge.

Step 2 *Turn the paper and fold it into thirds.*

Step 3 *Unfold and cut the top layer only along both folds.*

This will make three tabs.

Step 4 *Turn the paper and label it as shown.*

Reading and Writing
As you read the chapter, list important people and what they did or taught during these periods in Chinese history.

Get Ready to Read

Monitoring

Reading Skill

1 Learn It!

You can use a variety of techniques to improve your reading. Look at the examples below. Monitoring is a way of discovering your reading strengths and weaknesses. Different people read differently. Some read and understand quickly, while others need to read the same material several times. Successful readers constantly monitor themselves during reading to make sure that the text makes sense.

Did you remember the definition of a *pictograph*? Reread the definition in the text or look in the glossary.

Sometimes reading ahead will help you understand the meaning. This text explains an *ideograph* more clearly by using an example and further defining the term.

Ideographs (IH • dee • uh • GRAFS) are another kind of character used in Chinese writing. They join two or more pictographs to represent an idea. For example, the ideograph for "east" relates to the idea of the sun rising in the east. It is a combination of pictographs that show the sun coming up behind trees.

— *from page 280*

Reading Tip

When you study, read more slowly. When you read for pleasure, you can read more quickly.

- Does the text make sense? If not, try to identify and reread what you do not understand.
- Use any related graphs, charts, illustrations, or photographs on the page to help you find the meaning of the text.
- Is it helpful to think about what you already know about Chinese writing, based on what you may have previously read, seen, or experienced?

2 Practice It!

The paragraph below appears in Section 2 on page 291. Read the passage and answer the questions that follow. Discuss your answers with other students to see how they monitor their reading.

> "Higher good is like water:
> the good in water benefits all,
> and does so without
>   contention.
> It rests where people dislike
>   to be,
> so it is close to the Way.
> Where it dwells becomes
>   good ground;
> profound is the good in its
>   heart,
> Benevolent the good it
>   bestows."
>
> —Laozi, *Tao Te Ching*

- What questions do you still have after reading?
- Do you understand all the words in the passage?
- Did you read the passage differently than you would have read a short story or a newspaper article? How do you read various types of text differently?
- Did you have to stop reading often? Is the reading the appropriate level for you?

Read to Write ⋯⋯⋯

As you reread a section from this chapter, monitor yourself to see how well you understand it. Then describe in a short paragraph what kind of strategies are most helpful to you before, during, and after you read.

▲ Laozi

3 Apply It!

As you read the chapter, identify one paragraph in each section that is difficult to understand. Discuss each paragraph with a partner to improve your understanding.

China's First Civilizations

Guide to Reading

History Social Science Standards

WH6.6 Students analyze the geographic, political, economic, religious, and social structures of the early civilizations of China.

Looking Back, Looking Ahead

In earlier chapters, you learned that many civilizations developed in river valleys. China's civilization also began in a river valley, but mountains and deserts affected its development.

Focusing on the Main Ideas

• Rivers, mountains, and deserts helped shape China's civilization. **(page 277)**

• Rulers known as the Shang became powerful because they controlled land and had strong armies. **(page 278)**

• Chinese rulers claimed that the Mandate of Heaven gave them the right to rule. **(page 281)**

Locating Places
Huang He (HWAHNG HUH)
Chang Jiang (CHAHNG JYAHNG)
Anyang (AHN•YAHNG)

Meeting People
Wu Wang (WOO WAHNG)

Content Vocabulary
dynasty (DY•nuh•stee)
aristocrat (uh•RIHS•tuh•KRAT)
pictograph (PIHK•tuh•GRAF)
ideograph (IH•dee•uh•GRAF)
bureaucracy (byu•RAH•kruh•see)
mandate (MAN•DAYT)
Dao (DOW)

Academic Vocabulary
recover (rih•KUH•vuhr)
interpret (ihn•TUHR•pruht)
link
item

Reading Strategy
Summarizing Information Complete a chart like the one below describing the characteristics of the Shang and Zhou dynasties.

	Shang	Zhou
Dates		
Leadership		
Accomplishments		

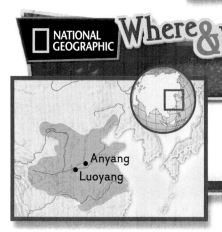

NATIONAL GEOGRAPHIC **Where & When?**

Anyang
Luoyang

1750 B.C.

c. 1750 B.C.
Shang dynasty begins

975 B.C.

1045 B.C.
Wu Wang creates Zhou dynasty

200 B.C.

221 B.C.
Qin dynasty begins

China's Geography

Main Idea Rivers, mountains, and deserts helped shape China's civilization.

Reading Connection Why do you think so many cities and towns were built beside rivers? Read to learn why rivers were important to the development of China.

The **Huang He** (HWAHNG HUH), or Yellow River, flows across China for more than 2,900 miles (4,666 km). It gets its name from the rich yellow soil it carries from Mongolia to the Pacific Ocean. Like rivers in early Mesopotamia and Egypt, China's Huang He regularly flooded the land. These floods destroyed homes and drowned many people. As a result, the Chinese called the Huang He "China's sorrow."

The river, however, also brought a gift. The Huang He is the muddiest river in the world. When the river floods, it leaves behind rich silt in the Huang He valley, nearly 57 pounds for every cubic yard of topsoil. By comparison, the Nile River in Egypt only leaves 2 pounds of silt per cubic yard. The soil is so rich that farmers can grow large amounts of food on very small farms.

China also has another great river, called the **Chang Jiang** (CHAHNG JYAHNG), or the Yangtze River. The Chang Jiang flows for about 3,400 miles (5,471 km) east across central China where it empties into the Yellow Sea. Like the Huang He valley, the Chang Jiang valley also has rich soil for farming.

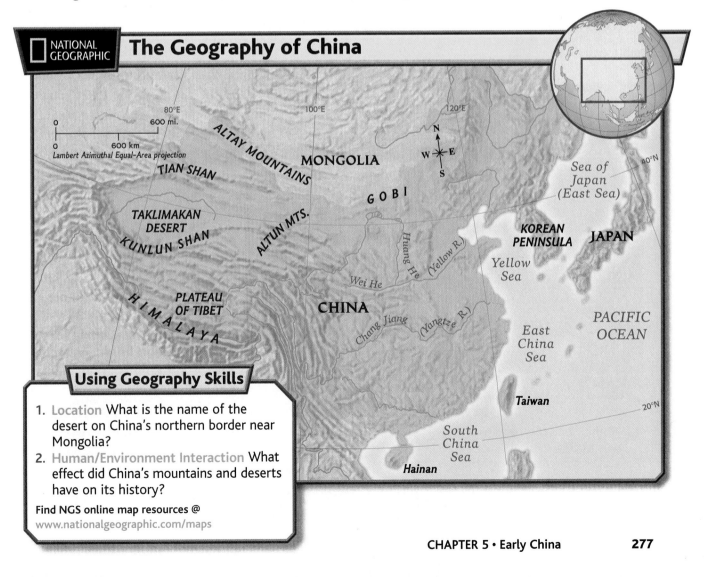

NATIONAL GEOGRAPHIC
The Geography of China

Using Geography Skills

1. **Location** What is the name of the desert on China's northern border near Mongolia?
2. **Human/Environment Interaction** What effect did China's mountains and deserts have on its history?

Find NGS online map resources @
www.nationalgeographic.com/maps

Even though China has rich soil along its rivers, only a little more than one-tenth of its land can be farmed. That is because mountains and deserts cover most of the land. The towering Himalaya close off China to the southwest. The Kunlun Shan and Tian Shan are mountain ranges on China's western border. The Gobi, a vast, cold, rocky desert, spreads east from the mountains. These mountains and deserts shaped much of Chinese history. They were like a wall around the Chinese, separating them from most other peoples.

Over time, the Chinese people united to form one kingdom. They called their homeland "the Middle Kingdom." To them, it was the world's center and its leading civilization. The Chinese developed a way of life that lasted into modern times.

✓ Reading Check **Identify** Name two rivers important to early Chinese civilizations.

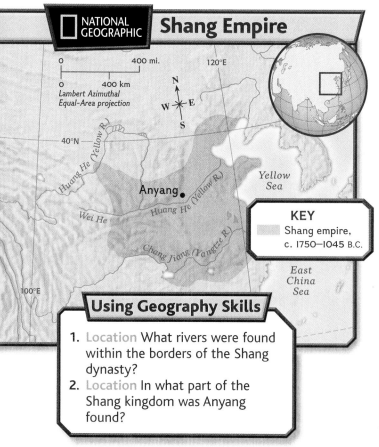

Shang Empire

NATIONAL GEOGRAPHIC

KEY
Shang empire, c. 1750–1045 B.C.

Using Geography Skills

1. Location What rivers were found within the borders of the Shang dynasty?
2. Location In what part of the Shang kingdom was Anyang found?

The Shang Dynasty

Main Idea Rulers known as the Shang became powerful because they controlled land and had strong armies.

Reading Connection Who are the leaders in your community? What gives them their power? Read to learn why some people in early China had more power than others.

Little is known about how Chinese civilization began. Archaeologists, however, have found pottery in the Huang He valley dating back thousands of years. These artifacts show that the Huang He valley was the first center of Chinese civilization. Archaeologists think that people stayed in the valley and farmed the land because of rich soil. As their numbers expanded, they began building towns, and soon after, the first Chinese civilization began.

China's first rulers were probably part of the Xia (SYAH) dynasty. A **dynasty** (DY•nuh•stee) is a line of rulers who belong to the same family. Little is known about the Xia. We know more about the next dynasty, the Shang. The Shang kings ruled from about 1750 B.C. to 1045 B.C.

Who Were the Shang? Archaeologists have found huge walls, royal palaces, and royal tombs from the time of the Shang. These remains show that the Shang may have built the first Chinese cities. One of these cities was **Anyang** (AHN•YAHNG) in northern China. Anyang was China's first capital. From there, the Shang kings ruled the early Chinese people.

The people of the Shang dynasty were divided into groups. The most powerful group was the king and his family. The first Shang king ruled over a small area in northern China. His armies used chariots and bronze weapons to take over nearby areas.

In time, the Shang kings ruled over most of the Huang He valley.

Later, Shang kings chose warlords to govern the kingdom's territories. Warlords are military leaders who command their own armies. However, the king controlled even larger armies who defended the kingdom's borders. The king's armies helped him stay in power.

Under the king, the warlords and other royal officials made up the upper class. They were **aristocrats** (uh•RIHS•tuh•KRATS), nobles whose wealth came from the land they owned. Aristocrats passed their land and their power from one generation to the next.

In Shang China, a few people were traders and artisans. Most Chinese, however, were farmers. They worked the land that belonged to the aristocrats. They grew grains, such as millet, wheat, and rice, and raised cattle, sheep, and chickens. A small number of enslaved people captured in war also lived in Shang China.

Spirits and Ancestors People in Shang China worshiped gods and spirits. Spirits were believed to live in mountains, rivers, and seas. The people believed that they had to keep the gods and spirits happy by making offerings of food and other goods. They believed that the gods and spirits would be angry if they were not treated well. Angry gods and spirits might cause farmers to have a poor harvest or armies to lose a battle.

People also honored their ancestors, or departed family members. Offerings were made in the hope that ancestors would help in times of need and bring good luck. To this day, many Chinese still remember their ancestors by going to temples and burning small paper copies of food and clothing. These copies represent things that their departed relatives need in the afterlife.

The Way It Was

Focus on Everyday Life

The Role of Women

Zheng Zhenxiang was China's first female archaeologist. In 1976 she found the tomb of Fu Hao, China's first female general. In the tomb were more than 2,000 artifacts from the Shang dynasty, including weapons, bronze vessels, jade objects, and bones with Chinese characters carved on them.

▲ Bronze vessel

Fu Hao, the wife of King Wu Ding, was given a royal burial. She was famous for her strength, martial arts skills, and military strategies. She often helped her husband defeat their enemies on the battlefield. Fu Hao was the first female in China's history to receive the highest military rank.

Her tomb and its artifacts reveal the grand civilization of China's Shang dynasty. During this period, the Chinese developed writing, a calendar, and musical instruments.

Jade sculpture of a ▲ seated human figure

Connecting to the Past

1. What was Fu Hao famous for during her life?

2. Describe what the artifacts found in Fu Hao's tomb might reveal about life during that time.

Telling the Future Shang kings believed that they received power and wisdom from the gods, the spirits, and their ancestors. Shang religion and government were closely linked, just as they were in ancient Mesopotamia and Egypt. An important duty of Shang kings was to contact the gods, the spirits, and ancestors before making important decisions.

The kings asked for the gods' help by using oracle (AWR•uh•kuhl) bones. They had priests scratch questions on the bones, such as "Will I win the battle?" and "Will I **recover** from my illness?" Then the priests placed hot metal rods inside the bones, causing them to crack. They believed that the pattern of the cracks formed answers from the gods. The priests **interpreted** the answers and wrote them down for the kings. In this way, kings could make decisions that they believed were guided by the gods and their ancestors. Scratches on oracle bones are the earliest known examples of Chinese writing.

The Chinese Language

The scratches on oracle bones show how today's Chinese writing began. However, the modern Chinese language is much more complex.

Like many other ancient languages, early Chinese writing used pictographs and ideographs. **Pictographs** (PIHK•tuh•GRAFS) are characters that stand for objects. For example, the Chinese characters for a mountain, the sun, and the moon are pictographs. **Ideographs** (IH•dee•uh•GRAFS) are another kind of character used in Chinese writing. They join two or more pictographs to represent an idea. For example, the ideograph for "east" relates to the idea of the sun rising in the east. It is a combination of pictographs that show the sun coming up behind trees.

Unlike Chinese, English and many other languages have writing systems based on an alphabet. An alphabet uses characters that stand for sounds. The Chinese use some characters to stand for sounds, but most characters still represent whole words.

NATIONAL GEOGRAPHIC

HISTORY MAKERS

Chinese Writing

The Chinese writing system was created nearly 3,500 years ago during the Shang dynasty. The earliest examples of Chinese writing have been found on animal bones. The carvings on these bones show that Chinese writing has always used symbols to represent words. Some of the carvings are pictures. For example, the verb *to go* was represented by a picture of a foot. The characters were carved in vertical columns and read from top to bottom, like modern Chinese writing. The writing on the bones recorded the Shang kings' questions about a wide range of topics—from the weather to good fortune. Chinese writing has changed in many ways, but it still reflects its ancient roots in pictures and symbols.

▲ Oracle bone

Shang Artists The people in Shang China developed many skills. Farmers produced silk, which weavers used to make colorful clothes. Artisans made vases and dishes from fine white clay. They also carved statues from ivory and a green stone called jade.

The Shang are best known for their works of bronze. To make bronze objects, artisans made clay molds in several sections. Next, they carved detailed designs into the clay. Then, they fit the pieces of the mold tightly together and poured in melted bronze. When the bronze cooled, the mold was removed. A beautifully decorated work of art remained.

Shang bronze objects included sculptures, vases, drinking cups, and containers called urns. The Shang used bronze urns to prepare and serve food for rituals honoring ancestors.

✔ **Reading Check** **Explain** What was the role of Shang warlords?

The Zhou Dynasty

Main Idea Chinese rulers claimed that the Mandate of Heaven gave them the right to rule.

Reading Connection Who gives you permission to do the things you do? Your mother? Your teacher? Read to find out how the rulers of the Zhou dynasty turned to the heavens for permission to rule.

During the rule of the Shang, a great gap existed between the rich and the poor. Shang kings lived in luxury and began to treat people cruelly. As a result, they lost the support of the people in their kingdom. In 1045 B.C. an aristocrat named **Wu Wang** (WOO WAHNG) led a rebellion against the Shang. After defeating the Shang, Wu began a new dynasty called the Zhou (JOH).

The Zhou Government The Zhou dynasty ruled for more than 800 years—longer than any other dynasty in Chinese history.

Zhou kings ruled much like Shang rulers. The Zhou king was at the head of the government. Under him was a large **bureaucracy** (byu•RAH•kruh•see). A bureaucracy is made up of appointed officials who are responsible for different areas of government. Like the Shang rulers, the Zhou king was in charge of defending the kingdom.

◄ Buffalo-shaped bronze vessel from the Shang dynasty

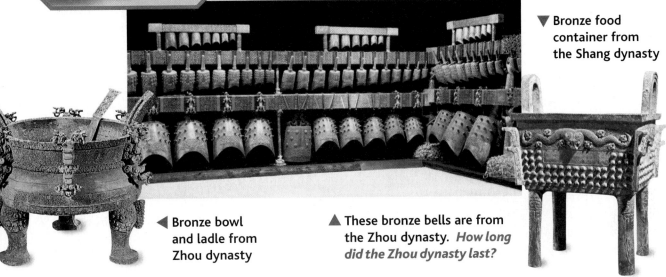

▼ Bronze food container from the Shang dynasty

◄ Bronze bowl and ladle from Zhou dynasty

▲ These bronze bells are from the Zhou dynasty. *How long did the Zhou dynasty last?*

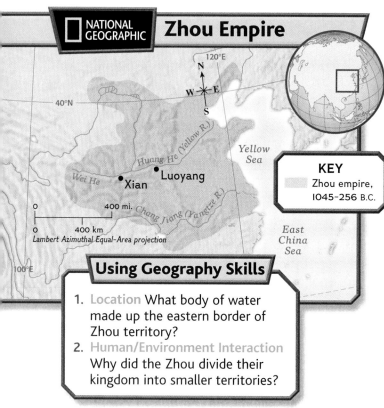

NATIONAL GEOGRAPHIC
Zhou Empire

KEY
Zhou empire,
1045–256 B.C.

Using Geography Skills

1. **Location** What body of water made up the eastern border of Zhou territory?
2. **Human/Environment Interaction** Why did the Zhou divide their kingdom into smaller territories?

The Zhou kings copied the Shang system of dividing the kingdom into smaller territories. The kings put aristocrats they trusted in charge of each territory. The positions the aristocrats held were hereditary. That meant that when an aristocrat died, his son or another relative would take over as ruler of the territory.

The Chinese considered the king their **link** between heaven and earth. His chief duty was to carry out religious rituals. The Chinese believed these rituals strengthened the link between them and the gods. This belief paved the way for a new idea that the Zhou kings introduced to government. They claimed that kings ruled China because they had the Mandate of Heaven.

What Was the Mandate of Heaven?

According to Zhou rulers, a heavenly law gave the Zhou king the power to rule. This **mandate** (MAN•DAYT), or formal order, was called the Mandate of Heaven. Based on the mandate, the king was chosen by heavenly

order because of his talent and virtue. Therefore, he would rule the people with goodness and wisdom.

The Mandate of Heaven worked in two ways. First, the people expected the king to rule according to the proper "Way," called the **Dao** (DOW). His duty was to keep the gods happy. A natural disaster or a bad harvest was a sign that he had failed in his duty. People then had the right to overthrow and replace the king.

The Mandate of Heaven also worked another way. It gave the people, as well as the king, important rights. For example, people had the right to overthrow a dishonest or evil ruler. It also made clear that the king was not a god himself. Of course, each new dynasty claimed it had the Mandate of Heaven. The only way people could question the claim was by overthrowing the dynasty.

New Tools and Trade For thousands of years, Chinese farmers depended on rain to water their crops. During the Zhou dynasty, the Chinese developed irrigation and flood-control systems. As a result, farmers could grow more crops than ever before.

Improvements in farming tools also helped farmers produce more crops. By 550 B.C., the Chinese were using iron plows. These sturdy plows broke up land that had been too hard to farm with wooden plows. As a result, the Chinese could plow more and produce more crops. Because more food could support more people, the population increased. During the late Zhou dynasty, China's population had expanded to about 50 million people.

History **O**nline

Web Activity Visit ca.hss.glencoe.com and click on *Chapter 5—Student Web Activity* to learn more about ancient China.

Trade and manufacturing grew along with farming. An important trade **item** during the Zhou dynasty was silk. Pieces of Chinese silk have been found throughout central Asia and as far away as Greece. This suggests that the Chinese traded far and wide.

◀ This statue of a winged dragon is from the Zhou dynasty. *From what metal did the Chinese make plows and weapons during the Zhou dynasty?*

The Zhou Empire Falls Over time, the local rulers of the Zhou territories became powerful. They stopped obeying the Zhou kings and set up their own states. In 403 B.C. fighting broke out. For almost 200 years, the states battled each other. Historians call this time the "Period of the Warring States."

Instead of nobles driving chariots, the warring states used large armies of foot soldiers. To get enough soldiers, they issued laws forcing peasants to serve in the army.

The armies fought with swords, spears, and crossbows. A crossbow uses a crank to pull the string and shoots arrows with great force.

As the fighting went on, the Chinese invented the saddle and stirrup. These let soldiers ride horses and use spears and crossbows while riding. In 221 B.C. the ruler of Qin (CHIHN), one of the warring states, used a large cavalry force to defeat the other states and set up a new dynasty.

 **Reading Check** **Identify** How did Zhou kings defend their right to rule?

History Online

Study Central Need help learning about China's first civilizations? Visit ca.hss.glencoe.com and click on Study Central.

Section 1 Review

Reading Summary

Review the Main Ideas

- China's first civilizations formed in river valleys. The Chinese were isolated from other people by mountains and deserts.
- The rulers of the Shang dynasty controlled the area around the Huang He valley.
- The Zhou dynasty replaced the Shang and claimed to rule with the Mandate of Heaven. During the Zhou dynasty, farming methods improved and trade increased.

What Did You Learn?

1. What is a dynasty?

2. What were oracle bones, and how were they used?

Critical Thinking

3. **The Big Ideas** How did early Chinese farmers use their natural environment to help themselves? **CA CS3.**

4. **Summarizing Information** Draw a diagram like the one below. Add details that describe the members of Shang society. **CA 6RC2.4**

Shang Society

5. **Evaluate** What were some important technological changes during the Zhou dynasty, and how did they lead to a larger population? **CA HI3.**

6. **Explain** How did ancient Chinese kings maintain control of their dynasties? **CA 6RC2.0**

7. **Reading** **Monitoring** The Mandate of Heaven is discussed on page 282. In writing, describe what words and definitions helped you to understand what this term meant. Then write a definition in your own words. **CA 6RW1.4**

Life in Ancient China

Guide to Reading

History Social Science Standards

WH6.6 Students analyze the geographic, political, economic, religious, and social structures of the early civilizations of China.

Looking Back, Looking Ahead

In Section 1, you learned about the Chinese government under the Zhou dynasty. This section describes what life was like during the Zhou dynasty.

Focusing on the Main Ideas

- Chinese society had three main social classes: landowning aristocrats, farmers, and merchants. *(page 285)*

- Three Chinese philosophies—Confucianism, Daoism, and Legalism—grew out of a need for order. *(page 287)*

Meeting People

Confucius (kuhn•FYOO•shuhs)
Laozi (LOWD•ZOO)
Hanfeizi (HAN•fay•DZOO)

Content Vocabulary

social class
filial piety
(FIH•lee•uhl PY•uh•tee)
Confucianism
(kuhn•FYOO•shuh•NIH•zuhm)
Daoism (DOW•IH•zuhm)
Legalism (LEE•guh•LIH•zuhm)

Academic Vocabulary

convince (kuhn•VIHNS)
promote (pruh•MOHT)

Reading Strategy

Organizing Information Create a pyramid diagram like the one below showing the social classes in ancient China from most powerful (top) to least powerful (bottom).

NATIONAL GEOGRAPHIC **Who & When?**

600 B.C.

● **551 B.C.** Confucius is born

400 B.C.

○ **c. 300 B.C.** Laozi's ideas of Daoism become popular

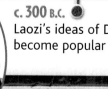

200 B.C.

● **c. 200 B.C.** Hanfeizi develops Legalism

Life in Ancient China

Main Idea Chinese society had three main social classes: landowning aristocrats, farmers, and merchants.

Reading Connection Have you heard the terms *high society* and *working class*? They describe social classes in America. Read on to find out about social classes in early China.

A **social class** includes individuals who share a similar position in society. Early Chinese society had three main social classes:

- landowning aristocrats
- peasant farmers
- merchants

Classes in Chinese Society China's aristocratic families owned large estates in early China. They lived in large houses with tile roofs, courtyards, and gardens. Fine furniture and silk hangings filled their rooms, and their houses were surrounded by walls to keep out bandits.

The aristocratic families did not own large estates for long. Each aristocrat divided his land among his sons. As a result, sons and grandsons owned much less property than their fathers and grandfathers had owned.

Aristocrats relied on farmers to grow the crops that made them rich. About nine out of ten Chinese were farmers. They lived in simple houses inside village walls. The aristocrats owned the fields outside the village walls. In these fields, farmers in northern China grew wheat and a grain called millet. In the south, where the climate was warmer and wetter, they were able to grow rice.

Chinese Village

Chinese farmers lived in small villages made up of several families. They farmed fields outside the village walls.
How did farmers pay for the use of the land they farmed?

Since horses were more valuable as war animals, farmers used oxen and water buffalo to pull plows and carts.

Villagers built walls that surrounded and protected the town.

Foot-pedaled hammers were used to remove grain and rice from their stalks.

Peasants planted and cultivated rice plants in large flooded fields.

To pay for the use of the land, the farmers gave part of their crop to the landowners.

Most farmers also owned a small piece of land where they grew food for their family. A typical family ate fish, turnips, beans, wheat or rice, and millet. The farmers had to pay taxes and work one month each year building roads and helping on other big government projects. In wartime, the farmers also served as soldiers.

In Chinese society, farmers ranked above merchants. The merchant social class included shopkeepers, traders, and bankers. The merchants lived in towns and provided goods and services to the landowners.

Many merchants became quite rich, but landowners and farmers still looked down on them. Chinese leaders believed that government officials should not be concerned with money. As a result, merchants were not allowed to have government jobs.

What Was Life Like in a Chinese Family?

The family was the basic building block of Chinese society. Because farming in ancient China required many workers, people had big families to help them produce more and become wealthier. Even the young children of a family worked in the fields. Older sons raised their own crops and provided food for their parents. Chinese families also took care of people in need—the aged, the young, and the sick.

Chinese families practiced **filial piety** (FIH•lee•uhl PY•uh•tee). This meant that children had to respect their parents and older relatives. Family members placed the needs and desires of the head of the family before their own. The head of the family was the oldest male, usually the father. However, a son could take on this role, and then even his mother had to obey him.

NATIONAL GEOGRAPHIC **The Way It Was**

Focus on Everyday Life

Chinese Farming Farmers in ancient China had to find ways to grow enough food to feed their large population. It was often difficult because of the dry, mountainous land.

Over centuries, farmers learned to cut terraces—flat areas, like a series of deep steps—into the mountain slopes. Terraces made more land available for farming and kept the soil from eroding, or wearing away. Early farmers also used the terraces as a way to irrigate their crops. As rain fell, it flowed down from one terrace to the

▲ Terrace farming in China

Men and women had very different roles in early China. Men were respected because they grew the crops. They went to school, ran the government, and fought wars. The Chinese considered these jobs more important than the work that women did.

Chinese women could not hold government posts. However, women in the royal court could influence government decisions. Wives of rulers or women in the royal family often **convinced** men in power to see things their way. Although their role was limited, women also had an important influence in the home. Most women raised children and saw to their education. Many women also managed the family finances.

☑ **Reading Check** **Explain** Why did the amount of land owned by each aristocrat decrease over time?

Chinese Thinkers

Main Idea Three Chinese philosophies—Confucianism, Daoism, and Legalism—grew out of a need for order.

Reading Connection If people around you were arguing and fighting, what would you do? Read to learn about early Chinese ideas for restoring order.

As the Zhou kingdom weakened in the 500s B.C., violence became common. During the Period of the Warring States, rulers sent armies to destroy enemy states. Whole villages of men, women, and children were beheaded. Many Chinese began looking for ways to restore order to society.

Between 500 B.C. and 200 B.C., Chinese thinkers developed three major theories about how to create a peaceful society. These theories are called Confucianism, Daoism, and Legalism.

next, watering the crops. This method of farming, called terrace farming, is still used in China today.

Farmers in ancient China were the first to use insects to protect their crops from damage by other insects. As early as A.D. 304, Chinese farmers used ants to prevent other insects from damaging their citrus fruit trees. They also used frogs and birds for pest control.

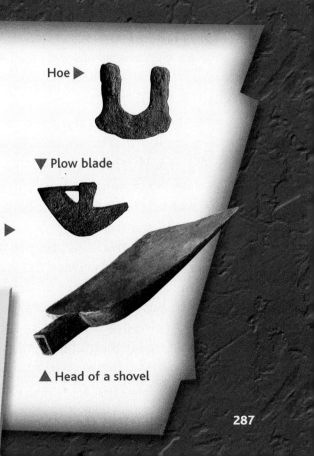

Hoe ▶

▼ Plow blade

The ancient Chinese used bronze and ▶
iron tools like these to farm their
land and harvest crops.

▲ Head of a shovel

Connecting to the Past
1. How did farmers in ancient China increase the amount of productive farmland?
2. What three farming methods helped farmers in ancient China grow more food?

Chinese Numbering System

Chinese Number	English Number	Chinese Number	English Number
零	0	七	7
一	1	八	8
二	2	九	9
三	3	十	10
四	4	百	100
五	5	千	1,000
六	6	万	10,000

Examples:

二十	(2 × 10)
二百	(2 × 100)
三千	(3 × 1,000)
四百五十六	[(4 × 100) + (5 × 10) + (6)]

Understanding Charts

The Chinese system of numbering is based on units of 10. It uses characters to represent 0 through 9 and the powers of 10 (10, 100, 1,000, and so forth).

1. How would you write the number 328 using the Chinese numbering system?
2. **Analyze** What is the English number for 六百四十一 ?

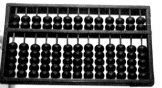

◄ Abacuses were used by the Chinese to solve math problems. These ancient calculators held stones on wooden pegs. The stones would be moved up and down to add, subtract, multiply, and divide.

wives owed their husbands obedience. Above all, rulers had to set good examples. If a king ruled for the common good, his subjects would respect him and society would prosper.

Confucius believed that if each person did his or her duty, society as a whole would do well. He also urged people to be good and to seek knowledge:

> **There are those who act without knowing; I will have none of this. To hear a lot, choose the good, and follow it, to see a lot and learn to recognize it: this is next to knowledge.**
>
> —Confucius, *Analects*

To Confucius, the best way to behave was similar to an idea known as the Golden Rule: "Do unto others as you would have others do unto you." Confucius urged people to "measure the feelings of others by one's own," for "within the four seas all men are brothers."

Confucius traveled through China trying to persuade government leaders to follow his ideas. **Confucianism** (kuhn•FYOO•shuh•NIH•zuhm) taught that all men with a talent for governing should take part in government. Of course, this idea was not popular with aristocrats, and few leaders listened.

Over time, Confucius won many followers who honored him as a great teacher. They wrote down his sayings and carried his message. After Confucius died in 479 B.C., his sayings spread throughout China.

Who Was Confucius?

Confucius (kuhn•FYOO•shuhs) was ancient China's first great thinker and teacher. He wanted to end the problems in China and bring peace to society.

Confucius believed that people needed to have a sense of duty. Duty meant that a person must put the needs of family and community before his or her own needs. Each person owed a duty to another person. Parents owed their children love, and children owed their parents honor. Husbands owed their wives support, and

Biography

CONFUCIUS
551–479 B.C.

Historians believe that the great thinker and teacher Confucius was born in the small state of Lu and named Kong Qui. His parents were poor, although his family had probably been wealthy at one time. One record says that Confucius was only three years old when his father died. His mother may have also died when he was young, because another record describes Confucius as an orphan.

Even as a teenager, Confucius was a talented scholar with strong, fixed beliefs. He devoted himself to learning and mastered literature, history, music, and arithmetic. He served as an apprentice to a bookkeeper and a stable manager but really wanted to obtain a government position. When he was 19, Confucius married and soon had a son and a daughter.

Confucius lived in a time when many people no longer held to traditional values and the government was struggling. Because he was concerned about these problems, Confucius took a government job to help improve society. He taught that the most important thing was for people to do their duty. In addition, he taught that people should honor their promises to others, use education to improve themselves, avoid extreme actions or feelings, and avoid bad people. Confucius also wanted everyone to return to the beliefs and rituals of their ancestors.

Government officials in Lu were not interested in his ideas, so at age 30 Confucius left politics and began a teaching career. He devoted the rest of his life to improving society through learning and teaching. Confucius did not write down any of his ideas, but his followers put together a book of his sayings called the *Lun Yü* (Analects).

Confucius ▶

"What you do not want done to yourself, do not do to others."
–Confucius

Then and Now

Give an example of how the above quotation from Confucius might help society today.

Chinese Philosophers

	Confucianism	Daoism	Legalism
Founder	Confucius 	Laozi 	Hanfeizi 
Main Ideas	People should put the needs of their family and community first.	People should give up worldly desires in favor of nature and the Dao.	Society needs a system of harsh laws and strict punishment.
Influence on Modern Life	Many Chinese today accept his idea of duty to family. His ideas helped open up government jobs to people with talent.	Daoism teaches the importance of nature and encourages people to treat nature with respect and reverence.	Legalists developed laws that became an important part of Chinese history.

Understanding Charts

Three philosophies developed in early China.
1. Which philosophy encourages followers to concentrate on duty and humanity?
2. Conclude Which of these philosophies do you think would be most popular in the world today? Explain.

▲ Some legends state that Laozi rode his water buffalo westward into a great desert and disappeared after writing *Dao De Jing*. **When did the ideas of Daoism become popular?**

What Is Daoism? Daoism (DOW•IH•zuhm) is another Chinese philosophy that **promotes** a peaceful society. Daoism (also called Taoism) is based on the teachings of **Laozi** (LOWD•ZOO). Laozi, or the Old Master, lived around the same time as Confucius. Scholars do not know if Laozi was a real person. However, the ideas credited to him became popular between 500 B.C. and 300 B.C.

The ideas of Daoism are written in *Dao De Jing* (The Way of the Dao). Like Confucianism, Daoism tells people how to behave. Daoists believed that people should give up worldly desires. They should turn to nature and the Dao—the force that guides all things. To show how to follow the Dao, Daoists used examples from nature:

> 66 Higher good is like water:
> the good in water benefits all,
> and does so without contention.
> It rests where people dislike to be,
> so it is close to the Way.
> Where it dwells becomes
> good ground;
> profound is the good in its heart,
> Benevolent the good it bestows. 99

—Laozi, *Tao Te Ching*

In some ways, Daoism is the opposite of Confucianism. Confucius taught that people should work hard to improve the world. Daoism told people to give up their concerns about the world. It said they should seek inner peace and live in harmony with nature. Many Chinese followed both Confucianism and Daoism.

What Is Legalism? A third group of thinkers disagreed with the idea that honorable men in government could bring peace to society. Instead, they argued for a system of laws. People called their thinking **Legalism** (LEE•guh•LIH•zuhm), or the "School of Law."

A scholar named **Hanfeizi** (HAN•fay•DZOO) developed the teachings of Legalism during the 200s B.C. Unlike Confucius or Laozi, Hanfeizi taught that humans were naturally evil. He believed that the government needed to issue harsh laws and stiff punishments to force them to do their duty. His followers believed that a strong ruler was needed to maintain order in society.

Many aristocrats liked Legalism because it favored force and power, and did not require rulers to show kindness or understanding. Its ideas led to cruel laws and punishments for Chinese farmers.

✓ **Reading Check** **Explain** Why did Hanfeizi believe that people needed laws and punishments?

History Online

Study Central Need help understanding Chinese philosophies? Visit ca.hss.glencoe.com and click on Study Central.

Section 2 Review

Reading Summary

Review the Main Ideas

- Early Chinese society had three main social classes: aristocrats, farmers, and merchants. The family was the basis of Chinese society.

- During a time of disorder, three new philosophies developed in China: Confucianism, Daoism, and Legalism.

What Did You Learn?

1. Describe the concept of filial piety.

2. Why did many aristocrats favor the philosophy of Legalism?

Critical Thinking

3. **Compare** Draw a table to compare the three main classes of ancient Chinese society. CA 6WS1.3

Chinese Society		
Aristocrats	Farmers	Merchants

4. **The Big Ideas** Imagine that you are a farmer in early China. Write an essay describing how your social class affects your life. CA 6WS1.2

5. **Writing Questions** Suppose you could interview Confucius about duty. Write five questions you might ask him about the subject. CA HR1.

6. **Expository Writing** Do you think Chinese philosophies could benefit our society today? Write an essay explaining your answer. CA 6WA2.2

You Decide . . .

WH6.6.3 Know about the life of Confucius and the fundamental teachings of Confucianism and Taoism.
WH6.6.4 Identify the political and cultural problems prevalent in the time of Confucius and how he sought to solve them.

Confucius: Solution to China's Problems?

Yes

Beginning in the 500s B.C., Chinese society descended into chaos. Many different thinkers had ideas for fixing China's problems. One of them was Confucius. Were the ideas of Confucius the answer to China's problems?

Confucius believed the best way to restore order to Chinese society was for the ruling classes to return to the moral values of earlier times. When rulers behave in moral ways, he explained, they become models for the rest of society. Rulers cannot just speak about virtues. They need to act virtuously in their lives. Specifically rulers should adopt the following values.

- Rulers should act with love and kindness toward other people, as expressed in the Golden Rule.
- Rulers should follow proper rituals and behave properly when dealing with the people. They should never be arrogant or violent.
- Rulers should love learning and respect ancient wisdom.
- Rulers should be wise and virtuous so that the people will have good examples to follow.

Here is some advice Confucius gave to rulers:

"If you, sir, want goodness, the people will be good. The virtue of the noble person is like the wind, and the virtue of small people is like grass. When the wind blows over the grass, the grass must bend."

"Lead them by means of regulations and keep order among them through punishments, and the people will evade them and lack any sense of shame [or self-respect]. Lead them through moral force and keep order among them through rites, and they will have a sense of shame and will also correct themselves."

—as quoted in *Chinese Religions*

▲ **Statue of Confucius**

Still others believed the best way to restore order was to pass strong laws and make people obey them, by force if necessary. These ideas, known as Legalism, were based on the writings of Hanfeizi. Forget the ideas of the past, said Hanfeizi, because times were different then. A ruler must be firm and pitiless. He must trust no one and punish anyone who disobeys or performs poorly. Emperor Qin Shihuangdi believed in Legalism. He governed ruthlessly saying "People are submissive to power, and few of them can be influenced by doctrines of righteousness."

No

Not everyone agreed with the ideas of Confucius. Followers of Daoism believed that society was having problems because people had stopped living in harmony with nature. The only true model, they argued, was the natural order, not rulers of human society. A Daoist wise man explained:

"I do nothing, and the people are transformed by themselves.

I value tranquility, and the people become correct by themselves.

I take no action, and the people become prosperous by themselves.

I have no desires, and the people of themselves become like uncarved wood."

—as quoted in *Chinese Religions*

You Be the Historian

DBQ Document-Based Questions

1. Do you think a Chinese peasant would have supported Confucius's ideas of law and order? Would an aristocrat have felt the same way? Explain. **CA HR5.**

2. Do you think it is possible to govern a society by following nature's models? Why or why not? **CA 6RC2.0**

3. Do you think that the ideas put forth by Confucius would work well in today's society? Write an essay defending your position. Make sure to use information from the text and examples from today to support your decision. **CA 6WA2.5**

Guide to Reading

History Social Science Standards

WH6.6 Students analyze the geographic, political, economic, religious, and social structures of the early civilizations of China.

Looking Back, Looking Ahead

Each of China's early dynasties was led by rulers who were very different. In this section, you will see how the Qin and Han dynasties differed because of their rulers.

Focusing on the Main Ideas

- Qin Shihuangdi used harsh methods to unify and defend China. *(page 295)*

- Developments during the Han dynasty improved life for all Chinese. *(page 298)*

- The Silk Road carried Chinese goods as far as Greece and Rome. *(page 300)*

- Unrest in China helped Buddhism to spread. *(page 303)*

Locating Places

Guangzhou (GWAHNG•JOH)
Silk Road
Luoyang (loo•WOH•YAHNG)

Meeting People

Qin Shihuangdi (CHIHN SHEE•hwahng•dee)
Liu Bang (lee•OO BAHNG)
Han Wudi (HAHN WOO•DEE)

Content Vocabulary

acupuncture (A•kyuh•PUHNGK•chuhr)

Academic Vocabulary

currency (KUHR•uhn•SEE)
civil (SIH•vuhl)
found
secure (sih•KYUR)

Reading Strategy

Determining Cause and Effect
Complete a diagram like the one below showing the effect of new inventions on Chinese society.

Invention		Effect
	$\longrightarrow$	
	$\longrightarrow$	

NATIONAL GEOGRAPHIC Where & When?

- Changan

200 B.C.

202 B.C.
Liu Bang founds Han dynasty

A.D. 1

c. A.D. 100
Silk Road established

A.D. 190
Rebel armies attack Han capital

A.D. 200

WH6.6.5 List the policies and achievements of the emperor Shi Huangdi in unifying northern China under the Qin Dynasty.

Emperor Qin Shihuangdi

Main Idea Qin Shihuangdi used harsh methods to unify and defend China.

Reading Connection Imagine your city or state without any roads. How would people get from one place to another? Read to find out how a Chinese ruler used roads and canals to unite China.

You have read about the problems in China from about 400 B.C. to 200 B.C. The rulers of powerful local states fought one another and ignored the Zhou kings. One of these states was called Qin. Its ruler took over neighboring states one by one. In 221 B.C. the Qin ruler declared himself **Qin Shihuangdi** (CHIHN SHEE•hwahng•dee),

which means "the First Qin Emperor." The Qin ruler made changes in China's government that would last for 2,000 years.

A Powerful Ruler Qin based his rule on the ideas of Legalism. He had everyone who opposed him punished or killed. Books opposing his views were publicly burned. Qin made the central government stronger than ever before. He appointed government officials, called censors, to make sure government officials did their jobs.

Second in power to the central government were provinces and counties. Under Zhou kings, officials who ran these areas passed on their posts to sons or relatives. Under Qin, only he could fill these posts.

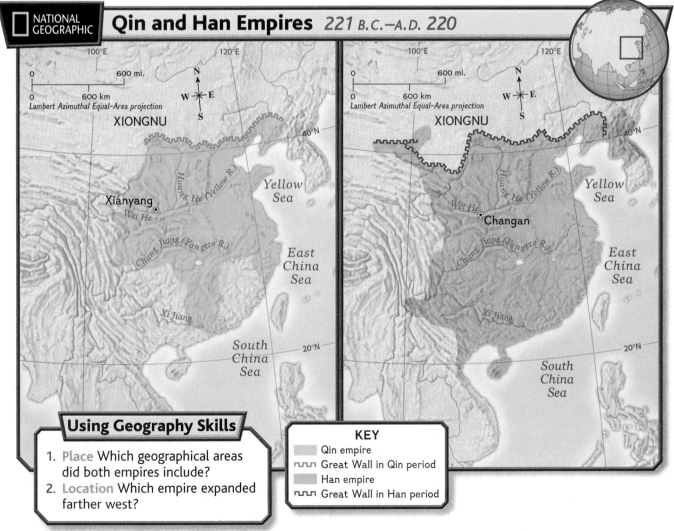

NATIONAL GEOGRAPHIC

Qin and Han Empires 221 B.C.–A.D. 220

Using Geography Skills

1. **Place** Which geographical areas did both empires include?
2. **Location** Which empire expanded farther west?

KEY
- Qin empire
- ᴧᴧᴧ Great Wall in Qin period
- Han empire
- ᴧᴧᴧ Great Wall in Han period

Qin Shihuangdi unified China. He created one **currency,** or type of money, to be used throughout the empire. He also ordered the construction of roads and a huge canal. The canal connected the Chang Jiang in central China to what is today the city of **Guangzhou** (GWAHNG•JOH) in southern China. He used the canal to ship supplies to his troops in far-off territories.

The Great Wall Northern China was bordered by the vast Gobi. Nomads, people who move from place to place with herds of animals, lived in the Gobi. The Chinese knew them as the Xiongnu (SYEHN•NOO). The Xiongnu were masters at fighting on horseback. They often attacked Chinese farms and villages. Several Chinese rulers in the north built walls to keep out the Xiongnu.

Qin Shihuangdi forced farmers to leave their fields and work on connecting and strengthening the walls. The result was the Great Wall of China, built with stone, sand, and piled rubble. However, Qin did not build the wall that we know today. It was built 1,500 years later.

Why Did People Rebel? Many Chinese viewed Qin Shihuangdi as a cruel leader. Aristocrats were angry because he reduced their power. Scholars hated him for burning their writings. Farmers hated him for forcing them to build roads and the Great Wall. Four years after the emperor died in 210 B.C., the people overthrew his dynasty. **Civil** war followed, and a new dynasty soon arose.

✓ Reading Check **Explain** Why did Qin face little opposition during most of his reign?

◀ This artwork shows the Great Wall many years after the reign of Qin Shihuangdi. Most of the wall built by Qin was made of stone and rubble, and was located north of the Great Wall we see today. Little remains of Qin's wall. *Who was the wall meant to keep out?*

Biography

QIN SHIHUANGDI
c. 259–210 B.C.

At the age 13, Ying Zheng became the leader of the Chinese state of Qin. The state was already very powerful because of Zheng's father, the previous ruler. Its government and military were well organized. With the help of his generals, young Zheng defeated Qin's six rival states. By 221 B.C., he had united all of the Chinese states under his rule. To mark a new beginning for China and to show his supremacy, Zheng gave himself the title Qin Shihuangdi—"The First Qin Emperor."

Qin Shihuangdi energetically went to work organizing his country. He divided the land into 36 districts, each with its own governor and a representative who reported directly to him. He made laws and taxes uniform throughout the country. He also standardized weights and measurements. Throughout China, the emperor had his achievements inscribed on stone tablets.

▲ Qin Shihuangdi

"I have brought order to the mass of beings."
–Qin Shihuangdi

Qin Shihuangdi did strengthen and organize China, but many people disliked him because of his harsh laws and punishments. Many people also disliked how he spent lavish amounts of money to build palaces and a gigantic tomb for himself. He had an entire lifelike army—over 6,000 soldiers and horses—built of clay and placed in the tomb.

▲ Part of the terra-cotta army found in Qin Shihuangdi's tomb

Then and Now

Why do you think modern historians disagree in their evaluation of Qin Shihuangdi's leadership?

The Han Dynasty

Main Idea Developments during the Han dynasty improved life for all Chinese.

Reading Connection How much time do you spend studying for tests? Find out why some Chinese people spent years studying for one special test.

In 202 B.C. **Liu Bang** (lee•OO BAHNG) **founded** the Han dynasty. Liu Bang was a peasant who became a military leader and defeated his rivals. He declared himself Han Gaozu—"Exalted Emperor of Han." Although Han Gaozu threw out the harsh policies of the Qin dynasty, he continued to use censors and also divided the empire into provinces and counties.

What Was the Civil Service? The Han dynasty reached its peak under the leadership of **Han Wudi** (HAHN WOO•DEE), which means "Martial Emperor of Han." He ruled from 141 B.C. to 87 B.C. Because

▲ This painting shows students taking a civil service examination. *Why did the civil service system favor rich job seekers?*

Wudi wanted talented people to fill government posts, job seekers had to take long, difficult tests to qualify for the bureaucracy. Those with the highest scores got the jobs.

In time, Wudi's tests became the civil service examinations. This system for choosing Chinese officials was used for 2,000 years. The system was supposed to allow anyone with the right skills to get a government job. However, it actually favored the rich. Only wealthy families could afford to educate their sons for the difficult exams.

Students preparing for these tests learned law and history. More importantly they studied the teachings of Confucius, which had become the official teachings throughout the empire. Students began to memorize the works of Confucius at age seven. After many years of schooling, the students took their civil service examinations. Only one in five passed. Those who failed taught school, took jobs as assistants to officials, or were supported by their families.

The Chinese Empire Grows A large bureaucracy was needed to rule the rapidly growing empire. The population had grown from about 20 million under Han Gaozu to more than 60 million under Han Wudi. This happened in part because Chinese agriculture continued to thrive.

Over time, however, problems began to develop. When farmers died, their land was divided among their sons. When their sons died, their land was again divided among their sons. Gradually, over several generations, the amount of land a family had to farm became smaller and smaller. By the middle of the Han dynasty, the average farmer owned only about one acre of land.

With so little land, farm families could not raise enough to live. As a result, many sold their land to aristocrats and became

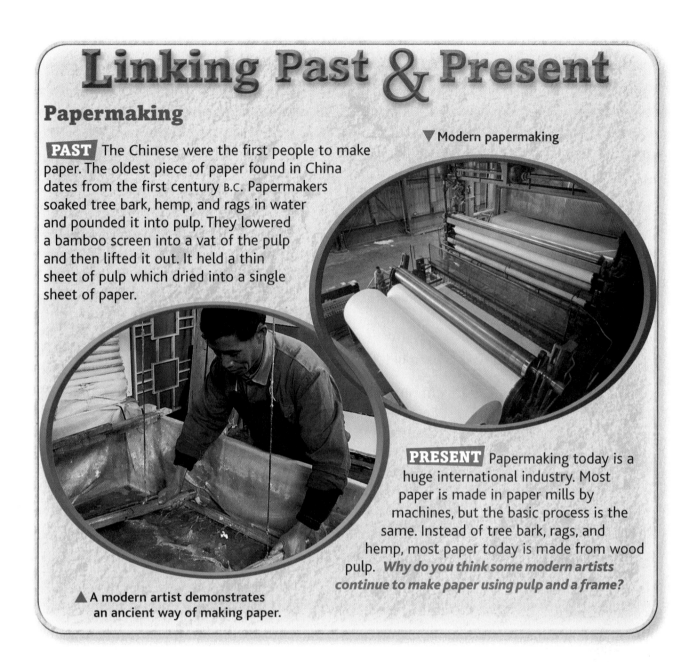

Linking Past & Present

Papermaking

PAST The Chinese were the first people to make paper. The oldest piece of paper found in China dates from the first century B.C. Papermakers soaked tree bark, hemp, and rags in water and pounded it into pulp. They lowered a bamboo screen into a vat of the pulp and then lifted it out. It held a thin sheet of pulp which dried into a single sheet of paper.

▼ Modern papermaking

PRESENT Papermaking today is a huge international industry. Most paper is made in paper mills by machines, but the basic process is the same. Instead of tree bark, rags, and hemp, most paper today is made from wood pulp. *Why do you think some modern artists continue to make paper using pulp and a frame?*

▲ A modern artist demonstrates an ancient way of making paper.

tenant farmers. Tenant farmers work on land that is owned by someone else and pay their rent with crops. Eventually, aristocrats owned thousands of acres and became very wealthy, but the peasants remained trapped in poverty.

China's empire grew in size as well as in population. Han armies added lands to the south and pushed Chinese borders westward. The Han dynasty also made the country more **secure.** After Wudi's armies drove back the Xiongnu—the nomads to the north—China remained at peace for almost 150 years.

During this period of peace, new forms of Chinese literature and art appeared. In literature, the Chinese emphasized the recording of history. Scholars and historians wrote new histories of current events and made copies of old literature.

During the Han dynasty, the focus of art also changed. In earlier periods, artists mostly created religious works for the kings and nobles. Under the Han rulers, many

WH6.6.7 Cite the significance of the trans-Eurasian "silk roads" in the period of the Han Dynasty and Roman Empire and their locations.

beautiful works of art were created for minor families. For example, some wall carvings in the tombs of such families feature scenes of everyday life and historical events. They also include highly decorated products made of the best quality silk.

Although the idea of filial piety had existed in the Zhou dynasty, it became very strong during the Han dynasty as the ideas of Confucius spread and became popular. The stability of the government also helped to strengthen family ties. Although the new scholar class had great influence over the government, the social classes in Chinese society remained the same, and daily life was very similar to what it had been before.

An Era of Inventions New inventions during the Han dynasty helped Chinese workers produce more goods and manufacture more products than ever. Millers used newly invented waterwheels to grind more grain, and miners used new iron drill bits to mine more salt. Ironworkers invented steel. Paper, another Han invention, was used by officials to keep government records.

Chinese medicine also improved under the Han. Doctors discovered that certain foods prevented disease. They used herbs to cure illnesses and eased pain by sticking thin needles into patients' skin. This treatment is known as **acupuncture** (A•kyuh• PUHNGK•chuhr).

The Chinese also invented the rudder and a new way to move the sails of ships. These changes allowed ships to sail into the wind for the first time. Chinese merchant ships could now travel to the islands of Southeast Asia and into the Indian Ocean. As a result, China established trade connections with people who lived as far away as India and the Mediterranean Sea.

✔ Reading Check **Identify** Which inventions helped Chinese society during the Han dynasty?

The Silk Road

Main Idea The Silk Road carried Chinese goods as far as Greece and Rome.

Reading Connection Many of the things we buy today are made in China. How do these goods get to the United States? Read to learn how goods made in China long ago made it all the way to Europe.

Chinese merchants made a lot of money by shipping expensive goods to other countries. Silk was the most valuable trade product. Some of it went by ship to Southeast Asia. However, most went overland on the **Silk Road.**

What Was the Silk Road? Merchants from China began traveling far westward when the emperor Han Wudi sent out a general named Zhang Qian (JAHNG CHYEHN) to explore areas west of China. Zhang had been sent on a mission to find allies for China against its enemies, especially the Xiongnu to the north.

After a journey of about 13 years, Zhang returned to China having failed to find allies for China. However, Zhang had discovered a kingdom far to the west, perhaps in modern-day Kazakhstan, where there were horses of exceptional strength and size.

Emperor Wudi was delighted to hear this because the cavalry of his enemies, the Xiongnu, gave them a great advantage over his army, which was mostly infantry. The emperor encouraged trade to get these horses so that his cavalry could defeat the Xiongnu. The result was the Silk Road, a large network of trade routes stretching 4,000 miles (6,436 km) from western China to southwest Asia. By the A.D. 100s, the various portions of the route were completed.

Merchants used camels to carry their goods across deserts and mountains to central Asia. From there Arabs carried the goods

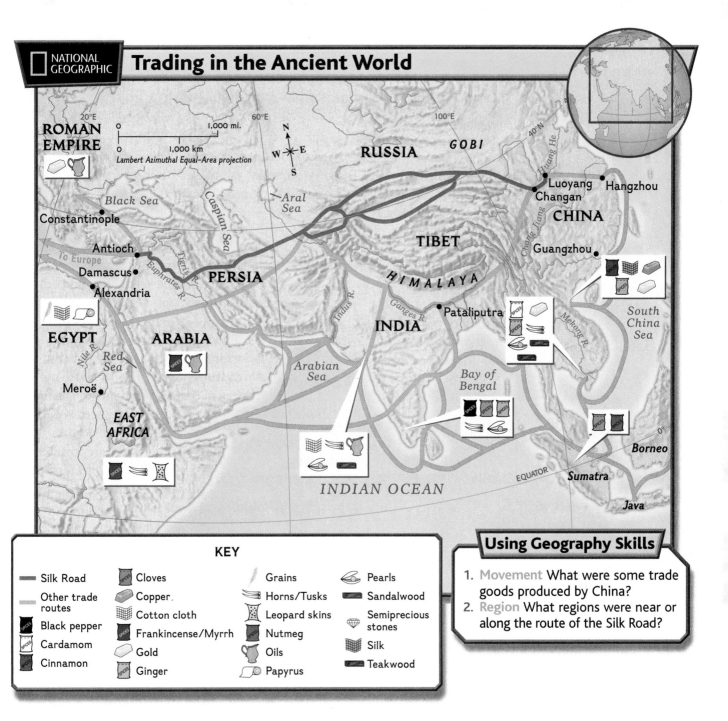

NATIONAL GEOGRAPHIC

Trading in the Ancient World

ROMAN EMPIRE

RUSSIA

GOBI

Black Sea

Constantinople

Antioch

Damascus

Alexandria

PERSIA

EGYPT

ARABIA

Meroë

EAST AFRICA

Red Sea

Arabian Sea

INDIA

Pataliputra

TIBET

HIMALAYA

Ganges R.

Indus R.

Luoyang
Changan
Hangzhou

CHINA

Guangzhou

South China Sea

Bay of Bengal

Mekong R.

Borneo

Sumatra

EQUATOR

Java

INDIAN OCEAN

1,000 mi.
1,000 km
Lambert Azimuthal Equal-Area projection

KEY

- **Silk Road**
- **Other trade routes**
- Black pepper
- Cardamom
- Cinnamon
- Cloves
- Copper
- Cotton cloth
- Frankincense/Myrrh
- Gold
- Ginger
- Grains
- Horns/Tusks
- Leopard skins
- Nutmeg
- Oils
- Papyrus
- Pearls
- Sandalwood
- Semiprecious stones
- Silk
- Teakwood

Using Geography Skills

1. **Movement** What were some trade goods produced by China?
2. **Region** What regions were near or along the route of the Silk Road?

to the Mediterranean Sea. The trip over the Silk Road was extremely difficult, dangerous, and quite expensive.

The Silk Road was broken up into smaller segments, each traveled by different merchants. This was because the terrain was so difficult and changed so much over the course of the Silk Road. There were high, snowy mountains; vast deserts; and long regions of rocky land, as well as rivers and long plains to cross. It would have been extremely difficult for the same animals and

carts to survive the entire journey. Most merchants traveled part of the journey and then sold their goods to someone else who traveled another portion of the journey. Goods passed from one person to another until they went from China all the way to kingdoms along the Mediterranean Sea.

Merchants had to pay taxes to many kingdoms as they moved the goods east and west. Each person who bought goods then charged higher prices to the next person. For this reason, they carried mostly

CHAPTER 5 • Early China   **301**

Four Chinese Dynasties

	SHANG	ZHOU	QIN	HAN
When	1750–1045 B.C.	1045–256 B.C.	221–206 B.C.	202 B.C.–A.D. 220
Important Leaders	Numerous kings with large armies and control over the land; ruled from capital city of Anyang	Wu	Qin Shihuangdi	Liu Bang
Main Ideas and Accomplishments	Developed social classes that included farmers, merchants, aristocrats, and royal family	Longest-lasting dynasty in Chinese history; established Mandate of Heaven	Strengthened central government; created single monetary system	Population and landmass grew under Han; opened China to trade and commerce by building Silk Road
Influences on Chinese Culture	Influenced Chinese religion and culture; created Chinese written language	Developed irrigation and flood-control systems to help farmers grow more crops	Introduced use of censors to check on government officials; Qin built the first Great Wall to keep out invaders	Created government's civil service examination; major inventions: steel, paper, acupuncture, advanced sea travel

Understanding Charts

The four dynasties of early China were separated by brief periods of unrest.
1. Under which dynasty was a single monetary system put in place?
2. Evaluate Which dynasty do you think contributed the most to Chinese culture? Why?

high-priced goods such as silk, spices, tea, and porcelain. In return, they earned great wealth.

The Impact of the Silk Road General Zhang also told the emperor of a mighty empire to the west with large cities full of people "who cut their hair short, wear embroidered clothes, and ride in very small chariots." Zhang was describing the Roman Empire.

The trade begun by the Silk Road brought China into contact with many other civilizations. Some merchants traveled by sea. This sea trade linked the Chinese to civilizations in Southeast Asia, southern India, and Egypt. Both the sea and land trade routes led to an exchange of many different goods and ideas.

Over the years merchants traded many items in addition to silk. These included fruit, vegetables, flowers, grains, and other products. For example, China sent peaches and pears to India, while India sent cotton and spinach to China. In time, Chinese technological advances, such as paper, would also travel to other countries along the Silk Road.

Reading Check **Conclude** Why did merchants carry mostly expensive goods on the Silk Road?

Major Changes in China

Main Idea Unrest in China helped Buddhism to spread.

Reading Connection What do you do when you feel frightened or unsafe? Read to find out how those feelings triggered the spread of Buddhism from India to China.

As you read in Chapter 4, Buddhism began in India, but it soon spread to other countries as well. Merchants and teachers from India brought Buddhism to China during the A.D. 100s. At first, only a few merchants and scholars were interested in the new religion. In time, however, Buddhism became very popular. This was due in part to the collapse of the Han dynasty.

The Han emperors after Wudi were weak and foolish. As a result, the central government lost respect and power. At the same time, as you read earlier, the aristocrats began grabbing more land and wealth. Dishonest officials and greedy aristocrats caused unrest among the farmers.

Wars, rebellions, and plots against the emperor put an end to the Han dynasty. In A.D. 190 a rebel army attacked the Han capital, **Luoyang** (loo•WOH•YAHNG). By A.D. 220, China had plunged into civil war. To make the situation worse, the northern nomads invaded the country.

The collapse of the government and the beginning of the civil war frightened many Chinese. They felt unsafe. Buddhist ideas helped people cope with their stress and fears. Even the followers of other religions found Buddhism attractive. Followers of Confucius and Daoists admired Buddhist concepts. By the 400s, Buddhism had become popular in China.

✓ **Reading Check** **Identify** What groups in China were the first to adopt Buddhism?

Study Central Need help understanding the influence of Silk Road? Visit ca.hss.glencoe.com and click on Study Central.

Section 3 Review

Reading Summary

Review the Main Ideas

- The short-lived Qin dynasty helped to unify China.
- During the Han dynasty, people began taking tests for government jobs. New inventions, such as the waterwheel and paper, were created.
- The Silk Road was an important trade route that linked China to the West.
- As the Han dynasty lost power, many Chinese became followers of Buddhism.

What Did You Learn?

1. Why did Qin Shihuangdi have the Great Wall built?

2. What was the purpose of the civil service examinations?

Critical Thinking

3. **Geography Skills** What geographic features made using the Silk Road difficult? **CA CS3.**

4. **Cause and Effect** Draw a diagram to show the causes of the Han dynasty's fall. **CA 6WS1.3**

5. **The Big Ideas** How did Qin Shihuangdi make China's society more stable? **CA HR3.**

6. **Expository Writing** Pretend you are Zhang Qian and have visited modern-day America. Write a letter to the emperor describing the United States. **CA 6WS1.0**

7. **Analysis** **Economic Analysis** Merchants on the Silk Road had to pay high taxes and pay for protection. Explain why they used the Silk Road if the costs were so high. How did they overcome the high costs? **CA HI6.**

Analyzing Primary Sources

Chinese Ideas About Leadership

WH6.6.3 Know about the life of Confucius and the fundamental teachings of Confucianism and Daoism.

In ancient China, emperors and local rulers wielded enormous power. As you have learned, the Chinese had many different ideas about leadership. For some, leadership was about power and fame. For others, a strong leader needed to be wise and of good character.

Read the following passages on pages 304 and 305, and study the picture and caption below.

▲ Chinese emperor Liu Bang

Reader's Dictionary

magnificence (mag•NIH•fuh•suhns): wonderful appearance

excessive (ihk•SEH•sihv): extreme

courteous (KUHR•tee•uhs): polite

Traveling Companions

This set of bronze figures comes from the tomb of a Chinese official buried in the A.D. 100s. The entire procession included 17 soldiers, 28 attendants, 39 horses, and 14 carriages.

Han Gaozu's Palace

The Chinese historian Sima Qian lived during the Han Dynasty. Qian recorded the following conversation between Gaozu, the first Han ruler, and Gaozu's chief minister, to illustrate why the emperor built large palaces.

Chief Minister Xiao was in charge of the construction of the Eternal Palace. . . . When Gaozu arrived and saw the **magnificence** of the buildings, he was outraged. "Warfare has kept the empire in turmoil for years, and victory is not yet assured. What is the idea of building palaces on such an **excessive** scale?"

"It is precisely because the fate of the empire is not yet settled," Xiao He responded, "that we need to build palaces and halls like these. The true Son of Heaven treats the four quarters as his family estate. If he does not dwell in magnificent quarters, he will have no way to display his authority, nor will he establish the foundation for his heirs to build on."

On hearing this, Gauzo's anger turned into delight.

—Patricia Buckley Ebrey, *The Cambridge Illustrated History of China*

Confucius on Leadership

Confucius believed that leaders had to be good people to govern well.

"If you showed a sincere desire to be good, your people would likewise be good. The virtue of the prince is like the wind; the virtue of the people is like grass. It is the nature of grass to bend when the wind blows upon it."

—Confucius, as quoted in *Simple Confucianism*

"If leaders are **courteous,** their people will not dare to be disrespectful. If leaders are just, people will not dare to be [ungovernable]. If leaders are trustworthy, people will not dare to be dishonest."

—Confucius, *Analeets*

Laozi's Ideal Leader

The Daoist philosopher Laozi also believed that a leader had specific qualities.

The best of all rulers is but a shadowy presence
   to his subjects.

. . . .

Hesitant, he does not utter words lightly.
When his task is accomplished and his work
   done
The people all say, "It happened to us naturally."

—Lao Tzu, *Tao Te Ching*, D.C. Lau, trans.

DBQ Document-Based Questions

Traveling Companions

1. How important do you think an official who traveled with such a procession was? Explain.

Han Gaozu's Palace

2. Why did Gaozu at first object to the building of the palaces? Do you agree with Xiao He's reasons for building the palace? Explain.

Confucius on Leadership and Religion

3. Rewrite Confucius's sayings in your own words.

Laozi's Ideal Leader

4. What kind of leader is Laozi's ideal leader?

Read to Write

5. Imagine that you have been appointed a regional governor during the Han dynasty. Write a letter to your local officials explaining your ideas of how a leader should act. Base your arguments on these sources. Explain why you disagree with some sources and agree with others. **CA HR4.** **CA 6WA2.5**

Review Content Vocabulary

Match the words with the definitions below.

___ 1. dynasty
___ 2. aristocrat
___ 3. bureaucracy
___ 4. mandate
___ 5. social class
___ 6. filial piety
___ 7. acupuncture
___ 8. Daoism
___ 9. Confucianism

   a. right to command
   b. line of rulers in the same family
   c. upper class whose wealth is based on land
   d. The ideas of ___ included a duty to participate in government.
   e. appointed government officials
   f. head of family honored by other members
   g. treatment using thin needles
   h. people with a similar position in society
   i. The teachings of Laozi are the basis of ___.

Review the Main Ideas

Section 1 • China's First Civilizations
10. What geographical features shaped China's civilizations?
11. Why did the Shang rulers become powerful?
12. Under which empire did the Mandate of Heaven begin?

Section 2 • Life in Ancient China
13. What were the three main classes in Chinese society?
14. Identify three Chinese philosophies and the reason they emerged.

Section 3 • The Qin and Han Dynasties
15. What methods did Qin Shihuangdi use to defend China?

16. How did developments during the Han dynasty affect the Chinese people?
17. What was the purpose of the Silk Road?
18. What event helped to spread Buddhism?

Critical Thinking

19. **Contrast** How is the ancient Chinese writing system different from cuneiform and hieroglyphic writing? **CA 6RC2.2**
20. **Describe** How did Shang artisans create bronze urns? **CA 6RC2.0**
21. **Analyze** How is Daoism the opposite of Confucianism in some ways? **CA 6RC2.3**

Geography Skills

Study the map below and answer the following questions.
22. **Human/Environment Interaction** Which dynasty controlled more land? **CA CS3.**
23. **Location** In what direction did the Qin dynasty expand farther? **CA CS3.**
24. **Analyze** How do you think the East China Sea affected expansion? **CA CS3.**

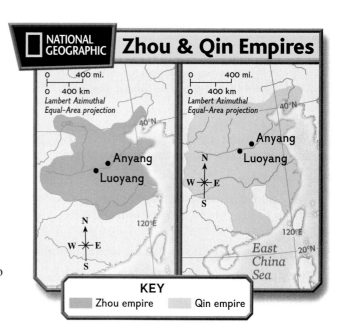

NATIONAL GEOGRAPHIC **Zhou & Qin Empires**

KEY
Zhou empire   Qin empire

Read to Write

25. **The Big Ideas** **Narrative Writing** Write a short story describing life in China during the Han dynasty. Describe how new policies and leaders changed the way people lived. **CA 6WA2.1**

26. **Using Your** **FOLDABLES** Choose one person that you included in your foldable. Write a list of 10 questions that you would ask that person in an interview. Exchange lists with a partner and play the role of the person being interviewed. **CA HR1.**

Using Academic Vocabulary

27. Separate the words below into three categories: Verbs, Nouns, and Adjectives. Keep in mind that some of the words can be placed in more than one column.

recover	promote
interpret	currency
link	civil
item	found
convince	secure

Linking Past and Present

28. **Comparing** The Chinese built the Great Wall to protect themselves. Research ways that countries today protect themselves from enemies. What is similar and different about today's defenses? **CA 6WA2.3**

Building Citizenship

29. **Plan a Debate** With your class, plan and participate in a three-way debate. Divide into three teams. One team will represent the Legalists, one will represent followers of Confucius, and one will represent Daoists. Begin the debate by asking the question "Which philosophy is best for a democratic society?" **CA 6WA2.5**

Reviewing Skills

30. **Analysis Skill** **Using Time Lines** Review the material from this chapter. Create a time line of the dynasties in early China. Under each time line entry, list the important leaders and achievements. **CA CS2.**

History Online
Self-Check Quiz To help prepare for the Chapter Test, visit ca.hss.glencoe.com

31. **Reading Skill** **Monitoring** Read the paragraph below. Make a list of the words to help you understand *Legalism.* **CA 6RW1.4**

[Hanfeizi] believed that the government needed to issue harsh laws and stiff punishments to force [people] to do their duty. His followers believed that a strong ruler was needed to maintain order in society.

Many aristocrats liked Legalism because it favored force and power, and did not require rulers to show kindness or understanding. Its ideas lead to cruel laws and punishments for Chinese farmers.

—from page 291

Standards Practice

Select the best answer for each of the following questions.

32 **A follower of Confucianism would**

   A give up all concerns about the world.

   B live in harmony with nature.

   C agree that humans are naturally evil.

   D put the needs of family and community first.

33 **In order to strengthen the Han government, Han Wudi used _____ to select the most talented people for government jobs.**

   A civil service exams

   B physical labor

   C private schools

   D wealthy families

The Ancient Americas

▼ The ancient Mayan
city of Chichén Itzá

NATIONAL GEOGRAPHIC Where&When?

1100 B.C.		400 B.C.		A.D. 300		A.D. 1000
	c. 1200 B.C. Olmec build an empire		c. A.D. 100 Moche civiliza- tion begins		c. A.D. 500 Mayan civiliza- tion reaches its peak	c. A.D. 950 Mayan cities abandoned

Chapter Overview
Visit ca.hss.glencoe.com for
a preview of Chapter 6.

The Big Ideas

1 The First Americans

Physical geography plays a role in how civilizations develop and decline. The first people in the Americas arrived thousands of years ago. Farming led to the growth of civilizations in what is now Mexico, Central America, and Peru.

2 The Mayan People

Civilizations are strengthened by a variety of advances. The Maya built a complex culture in Mesoamerica with great temples and made advances in science and writing.

View the Chapter 6 video in the Glencoe Video Program.

Compare-Contrast *Make this foldable to help you compare and contrast what you learn about the ancient Americas.*

Step 1 *Fold a sheet of paper in half from side to side.*

Step 2 *Turn the paper and fold it into thirds.*

Step 3 *Unfold and cut only the top layer along both folds.*

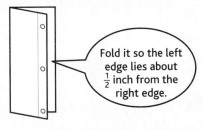

Fold it so the left edge lies about $\frac{1}{2}$ inch from the right edge.

This will make three tabs.

Step 4 *Label as shown.*

Olmec   Both   Maya

Reading and Writing
As you read the sections on the ancient Americas, record important concepts and events under the appropriate tabs. Then record ideas similar to both under the middle tab.

Get Ready to Read

Taking Notes

1 Learn It!

When you do research for a report or study for a test, it helps to write down information so that you can refer to it later. By taking notes, you can:

- phrase the information in your own words
- learn to restate ideas in short, memorable phrases
- stay focused on main ideas and only the most important supporting details.

> **B**
>
> **A**
>
> As the ice froze and the seas fell, an area of dry land was exposed between Asia and Alaska. Scientists call this land bridge Beringia (buh • RIHN • jee • uh), after Vitus Bering, a famous European explorer. They think that people in Asia followed the animals they were hunting across this land bridge into the Americas. By testing the age of bones and tools at ancient campsites, scientists estimate that the first people arrived between 15,000 and 40,000 years ago.
>
> —*from page 313*
>
> **C**

These notes were recorded for the paragraph above.

A. Asians followed animals across Beringia to the Americas

B. Beringia—named after European explorer Vitus Bering

C. People came to Americas about 15,000 to 40,000 years ago

Reading Tip

Read first and take notes afterwards. You are likely to take down too much information if you take notes as you read.

2 Practice It!

Using a two-column chart can make note-taking easier. Write main ideas in the left column. In the right column, write at least two supporting details for each main idea. Read the text from this chapter under the heading **Mayan Culture** on pages 320–321. Then take notes using a two-column chart, such as the one below.

Read to Write ⋯⋯

Choose an important person or place from the chapter. Then do research using at least three sources and take notes using the two-column method. Use your notes to write a brief paragraph summarizing your topic.

Main Idea	Supporting Details
Life in Mayan Cities	1. 2. 3. 4. 5.
Mayan Science and Writing	1. 2. 3. 4. 5.
What Happened to the Maya?	1. 2. 3. 4. 5.

▲ Mayan ballplayer

3 Apply It!

As you read one of the sections, make a chart with important dates, names, places, and events as main ideas. Under each main idea, list at least two details from your reading.

311

The First American

Guide to Reading

Looking Back, Looking Ahead

While civilization flourished in Mesopotamia, India, and China, thousands of miles away in the Americas, new civilizations began to develop.

Focusing on the Main Ideas

- People came to the Americas during the Ice Age, and about 10,000 years ago, farming began in Mesoamerica. (page 313)

- The first civilizations in America were based on farming and trade. (page 315)

Locating Places

Mesoamerica
(MEH•zoh•uh•MEHR•ih•kuh)

Teotihuacán
(TAY•oh•TEE•wuh•KAHN)

Meeting People

Olmec (OHL•mehk)

Maya (MY•uh)

Moche (MOH•cheh)

Content Vocabulary

glacier (GLAY•shuhr)

Academic Vocabulary

expose (ihk•SPOHZ)
estimate (EHS•tuh•MAYT)

Reading Strategy

Summarizing Information Create a chart to show the characteristics of the Olmec and Moche.

	Olmec	Moche
Location		
Dates		
Lifestyle		

History Social Science Standards

WH7.7 Students compare and contrast the geographic, political, economic, religious, and social structures of the Meso-American and Andean civilizations.

NATIONAL GEOGRAPHIC Where & When?

Teotihuacán•

1500 B.C. / **A.D. 1** **A.D. 500**

c. 1200 B.C.
Olmec build an empire

c. A.D. 100
Moche civilization begins

c. A.D. 400
Teotihuacán prospers

WH7.7 Students compare and contrast the geographic, political, economic, religious, and social structures of the Meso-American and Andean civilizations.

Farming in Mesoamerica

Main Idea People came to the Americas during the Ice Age, and about 10,000 years ago, farming began in Mesoamerica.

Reading Connection What would our lives be like if people never learned to farm? Read to learn how farming made civilization possible in Mesoamerica.

We know people came to America a long time ago, but how did they get here? Today, America is not connected by land to the rest of the world, but in the past it was. Scientists have studied the earth's geography during the Ice Age—a period when temperatures dropped sharply. At that time, much of the earth's water froze into huge sheets of ice, or **glaciers** (GLAY•shuhrz).

As the ice froze and the seas fell, an area of dry land was **exposed** between Asia and Alaska. Scientists call this land bridge Beringia (buh•RIHN•jee•uh), after Vitus Bering, a famous European explorer. They think that people in Asia followed the animals they were hunting across this land bridge into the Americas. By testing the age of bones and tools at ancient campsites, scientists **estimate** that the first people arrived between 15,000 and 40,000 years ago.

When the Ice Age ended about 10,000 years ago, the glaciers melted and released water back into the seas. The land bridge to America disappeared beneath the waves.

Hunting and Gathering Hunters in the Americas were constantly on the move in search of food. They fished and gathered nuts, fruits, or roots. They also hunted massive prey, such as the woolly mammoth, antelope, caribou, and bison.

It took several hunters to kill a woolly mammoth, which could weigh as much as 9 tons. These big animals provided meat, hides for clothing, and bones for tools.

As the Ice Age ended, some animals became extinct, or disappeared from the earth. Other animals found ways to survive

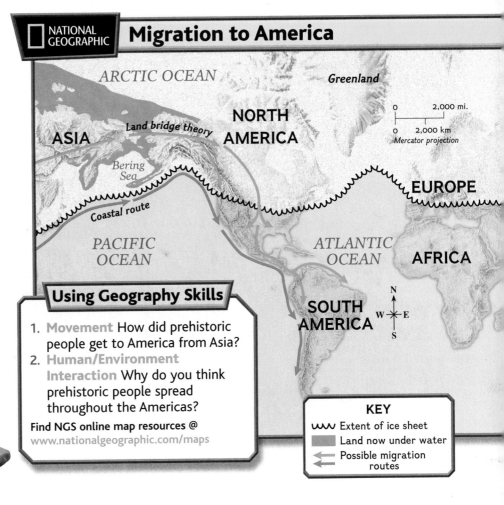

NATIONAL GEOGRAPHIC

Migration to America

Using Geography Skills

1. **Movement** How did prehistoric people get to America from Asia?
2. **Human/Environment Interaction** Why do you think prehistoric people spread throughout the Americas?

Find NGS online map resources @ www.nationalgeographic.com/maps

KEY
∿∿∿ Extent of ice sheet
█ Land now under water
← Possible migration routes

◄ Stone arrowhead

the change in environment. The warm weather, however, opened new opportunities to early Americans.

The Agricultural Revolution in America

The first Americans were hunter-gatherers, but as the Ice Age ended and the climate warmed, people in America made an amazing discovery. They learned that seeds could be planted and they would grow into crops that people could eat.

Farming began in **Mesoamerica** (MEH•zoh•uh•MEHR•ih•kuh) 9,000 to 10,000 years ago. *Meso* comes from the Greek word for "middle." This region includes lands stretching from the Valley of Mexico to Costa Rica in Central America.

The region's geography was ideal for farming. Much of the area had a rich, volcanic soil and a mild climate. Rains fell in the spring, helping seeds to sprout. They decreased in the summer, allowing crops to ripen for harvest. Then, in the autumn, the rains returned, soaking the soil for the next year's crop.

The first crops grown in the Americas included pumpkins, peppers, squash, gourds, and beans. It took longer to develop corn, which grew as a wild grass. Early plants produced a single, one-inch cob. By about 2000 B.C., early Americans had learned the technique of crossing corn with other grasses to get bigger cobs and more cobs per plant. This increased the food supply and allowed Mesoamerican populations to grow. Corn, also known as maize, became the most important food in the Americas.

✓ **Reading Check** **Summarize** How did the agricultural revolution begin in America?

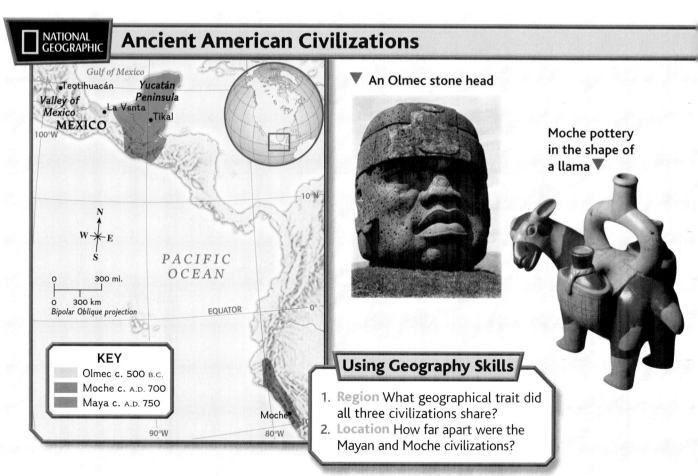

NATIONAL GEOGRAPHIC

Ancient American Civilizations

Gulf of Mexico
•Teotihuacán
Valley of Mexico
Yucatán Peninsula
•La Venta
MEXICO
100°W
•Tikal

10°N

N
W—E
S

PACIFIC OCEAN

0   300 mi.
0   300 km
Bipolar Oblique projection

EQUATOR   0°

KEY
Olmec c. 500 B.C.
Moche c. A.D. 700
Maya c. A.D. 750

Moche•

90°W   80°W

▼ An Olmec stone head

Moche pottery in the shape of a llama ▼

Using Geography Skills

1. Region What geographical trait did all three civilizations share?
2. Location How far apart were the Mayan and Moche civilizations?

Early American Civilizations

Main Idea The first civilizations in America were based on farming and trade.

Reading Connection Have you ever traded something with your friend for something you wanted? Read to find out how early American civilizations traded goods to get what they needed.

Growing corn and other crops allowed Mesoamericans to form more complex societies. Starting around 1500 B.C., the first American civilizations appeared.

Who Were the Olmec?

Near present-day Vera Cruz, Mexico, a people called the **Olmec** (OHL•mehk) built a far-reaching trading empire. It started around 1200 B.C. and lasted about 800 years.

The Olmec enjoyed rich farming resources. For example, they received abundant rainfall and crops grew well. Instead of building irrigation systems, they built drainage systems to divert water to protect their crops.

The Olmec lacked important raw materials. They traded salt and beans with inland peoples to get jade for jewelry and obsidian, or volcanic glass, to make sharp-edged knives. They used other trade goods such as hematite, a shiny volcanic stone, to make polished mirrors and basalt to carve gigantic stone heads.

The Olmec used the region's many rivers as highways for trade, but eventually, the inland peoples seized control of the trade. One of these groups built the first planned city in the Americas. It became known as **Teotihuacán** (TAY•oh•TEE•wuh•KAHN), or "Place of the Gods." The city reached its height around A.D. 400. It had a population of between 120,000 to 200,000 people.

▲ The Pyramid of the Sun is located in the Mesoamerican city of Teotihuacán. At over 200 feet tall, this pyramid is the tallest in present-day Mexico.

▼ This pyramid was in the Mayan city of Tikal, which was located in present-day Guatemala. *What caused the downfall of the Mayan civilization?*

Who Were the Maya? As Teotihuacán's power spread, a people called the **Maya** (MY•uh) built a civilization in the steamy rain forests of the Yucatán Peninsula (YOO•kuh•TAN). They, too, traded throughout Mesoamerica. The Maya used their central location to reach into what is now southern Mexico and Central America. Mayan traders in seagoing canoes paddled along the coast, perhaps reaching as far as the present-day United States. You will read about the Maya in Section 2.

The Moche South of Mesoamerica, a civilization developed on the west coast of South America. The **Moche** (MOH•cheh) people lived in the dry coastal desert where Peru is today.

The Moche civilization lasted from about A.D. 100 to A.D. 700. They dug canals that carried water from rivers in the Andes to their desert homeland. Because of this irrigation, the Moche suffered no shortage of food. They ate corn, squash, beans, and peanuts. They also hunted llamas and guinea pigs and fished in the Pacific Ocean. Llamas also served as pack animals and provided wool for weaving.

This surplus of food freed the Moche to do other things. Moche engineers built huge pyramids, and Moche traders exchanged goods with people as far away as the Amazon River valley. These goods included pottery, cloth, and jewelry.

For all their achievements, the Moche never expanded much beyond their homeland. They were eventually replaced by a civilization called the Inca.

✓ **Reading Check** **Describe** What was America's first civilization? Where did it develop?

History Online

Study Central Need help understanding the rise of civilization in the Americas? Visit ca.hss.glencoe.com **and click on Study Central.**

Section 1 Review

Reading Summary

Review the Main Ideas

- The first Americans were most likely hunter-gatherers who came from Asia across a land bridge. The first civilization appeared in Mesoamerica when people learned to farm.

- A number of civilizations developed in the Americas, including the Olmec and Maya in Central America and Mexico, and the Moche in South America. All were dependent on farming.

What Did You Learn?

1. Why was Mesoamerica's geography ideal for farming?

2. How did the first Americans develop corn?

Critical Thinking

3. **Summarizing Information** Draw a chart like the one below. Add details about the early peoples of Mesoamerica and South America. **CA 6RC2.4**

Mesoamerica
South America

4. **Summarize** How did the first people come to the Americas, and how did they live once they were here? **CA 6RC2.0**

5. **The Big Ideas** How did geography shape Moche civilization? **CA CS3.**

6. **Expository Writing** Write a short essay comparing the civilizations that developed in Mesoamerica and South America. **CA 6WS1.3**

7. **Reading** Taking Notes Review Section 1 and take notes. Create an outline of the section from your notes. Use this outline to review the section. **CA 6RC2.4**

The Mayan People

Guide to Reading

Looking Back, Looking Ahead

In Section 1, you read about the rise of the Maya. They had to use whatever natural resources the land had to offer in order to survive and prosper. As a result, they developed a culture suited to where they lived.

Focusing on the Main Ideas

• The Maya created a civilization of city-states and thrived in Mesoamerica's rain forest. *(page 318)*

• The Maya developed a society of city-states and a culture based on their religion. *(page 320)*

Locating Places
Petén (peh•TEHN)

Meeting People
Jasaw Chan K'awiil I (KAH•WEEL)

Content Vocabulary
sinkhole (SIHNGK•HOHL)
alliance (uh•LY•uhns)

Academic Vocabulary
access (AK•SEHS)
predict (prih•DIHKT)

Reading Strategy
Organizing Information Use a web diagram like the one below to record Mayan achievements.

Mayan Achievements

History Social Science Standards

WH7.7 Students compare and contrast the geographic, political, economic, religious, and social structures of the Meso-American and Andean civilizations.

NATIONAL GEOGRAPHIC Where&When?

Tikal

A.D. 400	A.D. 700	A.D. 1000
c. A.D. 500 Mayan civilization reaches its peak	c. A.D. 682 Jasaw Chan K'awiil I begins to rule Tikal	c. A.D. 950 Mayan cities abandoned

The Mayan People

Main Idea The Maya created a civilization of city-states and thrived in Mesoamerica's rain forest.

Reading Connection What would it be like to live in a jungle? Read to learn how the Maya adapted to life in the jungles of Mesoamerica.

In A.D. 1839 an American lawyer named John Lloyd Stevens and an English artist named Frederick Catherwood slashed their way into the tangled Yucatán rain forest. There they found the vine-covered ruins of an ancient city.

Stevens and Catherwood learned that the people who had built the city were called the Maya. The Maya are the ancestors of millions of Native Americans who still live in present-day Mexico, Guatemala, Honduras, El Salvador, and Belize.

At first glance, it looked like the Maya had settled in one of the worst spots on Earth. They picked the **Petén** (peh•TEHN), the Mayan word for "flat region." Located in present-day Guatemala, the Petén's dense forests nearly blocked out the sun.

The Maya saw what others missed. Swamps and sinkholes gave them **access** to a year-round source of water. The **sinkholes** (SIHNGK•HOHLZ)—areas where the earth has collapsed—connected the Maya with a huge system of underground rivers and streams.

Even with a ready water supply, only an organized culture could have succeeded in building cities and fields in the Petén. The effort required cooperation among many people, which could only be accomplished by having an organized government.

The Maya set up city-states. In each city-state, kings such as **Jasaw Chan K'awiil I** (KAH•WEEL) of the city-state of Tikal supplied the leadership. They led the armies and organized great building projects. Leadership passed from one king to the next, and the city-states often fought with each other.

✓ **Reading Check** **Identify** What was the main advantage of living in a tropical rain forest?

The City of Tikal

1. Temple of the Masks (Temple II)
2. North Acropolis
3. Temple of the Giant Jaguar (Temple I)
4. Stelae
5. Great Plaza
6. Ball Court

▼ The city of Tikal was one of the largest and oldest Mayan cities. Huge temples and monuments were spread throughout the city. The area which you see here was the main religious center of the city. *What Mayan leader built Tikal?*

Biography

WH7.7.2 Study the roles of people in each society, including class structures, family life, warfare, religious beliefs and practices, and slavery.
WH7.7.4 Describe the artistic and oral traditions and architecture in the three civilizations.

JASAW CHAN K'AWIIL I

Ruled A.D. 682–734

When Jasaw Chan K'awiil I began his rule in A.D. 682, the Mayan city-state of Tikal was weak and struggling. Its temples and other buildings were falling into disrepair, and the people were dominated by their great rival city, Calakmul.

Things began to improve in A.D. 695 when Jasaw defeated the armies of Calakmul in battle. Jasaw held a celebration a month later to honor the gods and himself. Tikal began to prosper again, and Jasaw spent the next 40 years rebuilding and strengthening his city-state.

Although Jasaw had been victorious, he spent only part of his time expanding his control over the region. Instead, most of his efforts went toward helping his people and restarting building projects in Tikal.

Jasaw's efforts teach us a great deal about Mayan art, architecture, and customs. For example, he built the famous pyramid in Tikal. The huge structure was 154 feet (47 m) in height, and served as both a temple and as Jasaw's tomb. In the room at the top of the structure, carvings depicted Jasaw's victories and mythological scenes. Jasaw wears clothing similar to the ancient leaders of Tikal to show that he was as great as they were. Other images were carved on bones and on other buildings. They show events from Mayan mythology and history praising Tikal's rulers.

One piece of art was of great importance: the effigy, or image of the god that armies carried into battle. This god was supposed to be the special god of that city. When Jasaw defeated Calakmul, he captured the image of their city's god. The people of Tikal thought this meant that the god of Tikal was more powerful than the others. Jasaw ordered the story of this great accomplishment to be carved on his pyramid so everyone would remember what he had done.

Jasaw began to rebuild Tikal during his reign, but most of the great building projects and military expansion of the city occurred under the reign of his son.

▲ **This Mayan monument depicts Jasaw Chan K'awiil I.**

Then and Now

The Maya emphasized religion and the accomplishments of their rulers in their art and architecture. What do people use as subjects for art today? Why?

319

NATIONAL GEOGRAPHIC

The Way It Was

Sports & Contests

Mayan Ball Game Mayan cities had many ball courts. In a Mayan ball game, teams of two or three players tried to drive a hard rubber ball through a decorated stone ring. Players wore helmets, gloves, and knee and hip guards made of animal hide to protect themselves against the hard rubber balls. They were not allowed to use their hands or feet to throw or bat the ball. They had to use their hips to drive the ball through the stone rings.

Scholars think that a Mayan ball game was more than a sport or contest. It had a religious and symbolic meaning— as well as deadly results. Crowds rewarded the winners as heroes and gave them gifts. However, the losing team was sacrificed to the gods in a ceremony after the game.

▲ Mayan ballplayer

Connecting to the Past

1. How did a player score in a Mayan ball game?
2. Why was losing especially painful for a team?

Mayan Culture

Main Idea The Maya developed a society of city-states and a culture based on their religion.

Reading Connection Did you ever wonder why people need calendars? Read to learn how the Maya developed calendars and math to help them farm.

The rulers of Mayan city-states said they were descended from the sun. They claimed to rule as god-kings and expected people to build huge monuments to honor them. A good example of this is the pyramid built for Jasaw Chan K'awiil I at Tikal.

Life in Mayan Cities As god-kings, Mayan rulers taught their subjects how to please the gods. One way was human sacrifice. When the Maya marched into battle, they wanted captives more than they wanted land. During times of drought, Mayan priests sacrificed captives to Chac, the god of rain and sunlight. The Maya typically only sacrificed captives from the top of a conquered society. Most captives were kept enslaved and put to work.

The Maya believed that the gods controlled everything. As a result, religion was at the core of Mayan life. A huge pyramid with a temple at the top towered over every city. Priests, who claimed to know what the gods wanted, set up a strict class system in which everyone had a place.

Royal Mayan women played an important role in their society. They often married into royal families in other Mayan city-states. This helped form **alliances** (uh•LY•uhns•uhs).

History Online

Web Activity Visit ca.hss.glencoe.com and click on *Chapter 6—Student Web Activity* to learn more about the Americas.

Alliances are political agreements between people or states to work together. In some city-states, such as Calakmul, women occasionally served as all-powerful queens.

Mayan Science and Writing Both queens and kings turned to Mayan priests for advice. The priests thought gods revealed their plans through movements of the sun, moon, and stars, so they studied the sky closely.

The Maya also needed to know when to plant their crops. By watching the sky, the priests learned about astronomy and developed a 365-day calendar. They used it to **predict** eclipses and to schedule religious festivals, plantings, and harvests. To chart the passage of time, the Maya also developed a system of mathematics.

The Maya also invented a written language. Like the Egyptians, the Maya used a type of hieroglyphics. Symbols represented sounds, words, or ideas. Only nobles could read them, however. After the Mayan civilization collapsed, nobody could read Mayan hieroglyphics. Only recently have scholars learned how to read them.

What Happened to the Maya? The Mayan civilization reached its peak in the A.D. 500s. Over the next 300 years, the different Mayan city-states began to collapse. No one is sure why this happened. Some experts say overpopulation drained the cities of food and resources. Others blame a long drought, or period without rain. Still others say that in city after city the poor people rebelled against their rich rulers. Whatever the reason, the Maya began abandoning their cities, and by the A.D. 900s, the cities lay deserted.

 **Reading Check** **Explain** How did the Maya treat enslaved people?

History Online
Study Central Need help understanding the rise of civilization in America? Visit ca.hss.glencoe.com and click on Study Central.

Section 2 Review

What Did You Learn?

1. In what country were Mayan ruins first found?

2. What was the relationship between government and religion in Mayan society?

Critical Thinking

3. **Organizing Information** Draw a diagram like the one below describing the geography of the region in which the Maya lived. **CA 6RC2.4**

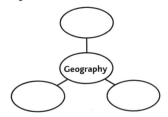

4. **The Big Ideas** How did astronomy and mathematics help Mayan society? **CA HI2.**

5. **Writing a Journal** Imagine you are an archaeologist who has found lost Mayan ruins. Write a journal entry describing your discovery. **CA 6WS1.1**

6. **Analyze** Why do you think only nobles could read the Mayan language?

7. **Analysis** **Understanding Beliefs** Write an essay explaining how the Maya tried to please their gods. What did the Maya hope to receive in return? **CA HI2.**

Reading Summary

Review the Main Ideas

- In the rain forests of Central America, the Maya developed a civilization. They used natural resources, such as sinkholes, and established governments based on city-states.

- The Mayan city-states developed a culture based on their religious beliefs. They made advances in mathematics and science, including a sophisticated calendar.

Analyzing Primary Sources

WH7.7.2 Study the roles of people in each society, including class structures, family life, warfare, religious beliefs and practices, and slavery.

Life From Death

Both the Maya and the people of Teotihuacán believed in a life after death. Both groups of people also decorated their temples and tombs with important images that they wanted future generations of their people to see.

Study the images on pages 322 and 323, and answer the questions that follow.

▲ Statue of Mayan god

Reader's Dictionary

guans (GWAHNZ): large birds that resemble turkeys

The Rain God's Heaven

The people of Teotihuacán believed that people went to heaven after they died. The following song explains some of these beliefs.

. . . . . .

Thus they said:
"When we die,
truly we die not,
because we will live, we will rise,
we will continue living, we will awaken.
This will make us happy."
Thus the dead one was directed,
when he died:
"Awaken, already the sky is rosy,
already sing the flame-colored **guans**,
the fire-colored swallows,
already the butterflies fly."

. . . .

—Michael D. Coe and Rex Koontz,
Mexico: From the Olmecs to the Aztecs

▲ This wall painting in Teotihuacán shows the heaven of the rain god Tlaloc.

Welcoming a New King

This Mayan painting comes from a Mayan tomb. It shows a procession of musicians playing various instruments and people celebrating the choosing of the heir to the throne.

Mayan Warfare

This image of Mayan warriors in a battle comes from the same tomb that has the painting of the procession. The man wearing the jaguar suit standing over the fallen enemy is the king.

DBQ Document-Based Questions

The Rain God's Heaven

1. What does the song tell you about the beliefs of the people of Teotihuacán.

2. What does the image show you about the place people go to after they die?

Welcoming a New King

3. What kinds of instruments do you think the musicians are playing?

4. Why do you think someone would place this image in a tomb?

Mayan Warfare

5. What kinds of weapons do the warriors have?

6. How can you tell who the winner is?

Read to Write

7. Compare the images from Teotihuacán and the Mayan tombs. How are they different? What is the goal of the images on the Mayan tombs compared to the Teotihuacán image? Why do you think the Mayan rulers preferred such images? **CA** HR4.; HR5.

Review Content Vocabulary

Match the definitions in the second column to the terms in the first column. Then write a sentence for each of the words. Use information from the text to help you properly use the words.

1. glacier
2. sinkhole
3. alliance

a. areas of collapsed earth
b. an agreement between people or groups
c. large sheets of ice

Review the Main Ideas

Section 1 • The First Americans

4. When did the first people arrive in the Americas? On which continent did they live originally?

5. How did farming lead to the rise and development of civilizations in present-day Mexico, Central America, and Peru?

6. What were some of the goods traded by the Olmec people?

Section 2 • The Mayan People

7. Where did the Maya build their civilization?

8. How did the Maya honor their kings?

9. What role did royal Mayan women play in society?

Critical Thinking

10. **Analyze** How did the Mayan people make use of the geography of their region? **CA CS3.**

11. **Predict** How might ancient America have been different if the Ice Age had not ended when it did? **CA HI2.**

12. **Explain** What were some of the possible outcomes of playing the Mayan ball game? **CA 6RC2.0**

13. **Describe** What was the role of Mayan priests in government? How did these priests use the stars and sky? **CA 6RC2.3**

Geography Skills

Study the map below and answer the following questions.

14. **Place** Look at a map of modern-day Central America. What countries occupy the former area of the Maya? **CA CS3.**

15. **Location** About how far is Teotihuacán from the Olmec civilization? **CA CS3.**

16. **Movement** Which civilization do you think would be better suited for trade? Why? **CA CS3.**

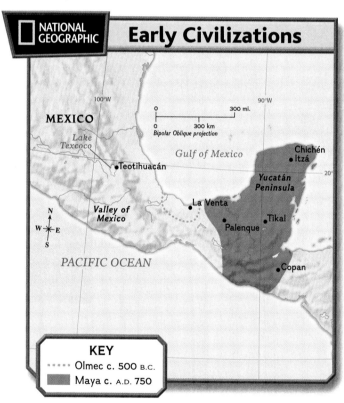

NATIONAL GEOGRAPHIC

Early Civilizations

MEXICO
Lake Texcoco
Teotihuacán
Gulf of Mexico
Chichén Itzá
Yucatán Peninsula
La Venta
Valley of Mexico
Tikal
Palenque
PACIFIC OCEAN
Copan

300 mi.
300 km
Bipolar Oblique projection
100°W
90°W
20°

KEY
Olmec c. 500 B.C.
Maya c. A.D. 750

Read to Write

17. **The Big Ideas** Persuasive Writing Historians are not sure why the Mayan civilization declined. Select one of the theories described on page 321 and do research to find support for that theory. Write an essay persuading others that your theory is correct. **CA 6WA2.5**

18. **Using Your FOLDABLES** Create an outline map of Mesoamerica on poster board. It should be big enough for the entire class to work together. Label each country and the location of each civilization using information from the chapter. Then use your foldables to write facts about each civilization on the map. **CA 6RC2.4** **CA CS3.**

Using Academic Vocabulary

Match each word below with the definition that best fits it.

___19. expose

___20. estimate

___21. access

___22. predict

      a. to guess about what might happen in the future

      b. to uncover something or put it on display

      c. to judge the approximate size or quantity of something

      d. the ability to make use of something

Linking Past and Present

23. **Making Connections** The people of ancient American civilizations built many different types of monuments to honor their gods and their leaders. What kind of monuments do we use in the United States today? Who do we honor with these monuments? How are these monuments similar to those of the ancient Americans? How are they different? Write a short essay explaining the role of monuments in our world today. **CA 6RC2.2**

Reviewing Skills

24. **Reading Skill** **Taking Notes** Use your local library to find a book with information on the history of the Moche people. Read the information, taking notes as you go. Use these notes to write a summary of the Moche civilization and its important events and people. **CA 6WA2.3**

History Online

Self-Check Quiz To help you prepare for the Chapter Test, visit ca.hss.glencoe.com

25. **Analysis Skill** **Understanding Chance** The discovery of an ancient Mayan city in the Yucatán rain forest led to new information and understanding of the Maya. Use your local library and the Internet to research the impact of the discovery. What new things did the world learn about the Maya? How did the chance discovery change the way historians view ancient American civilizations? Write a newspaper article that explains the significance of this discovery. **CA HI4.; HI5.**

Standards Practice

Use the map below to answer the following question.

26 **Which area of the map is known as Mesoamerica?**

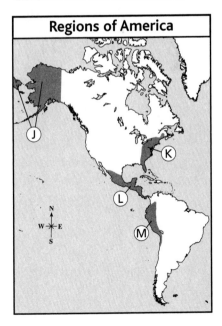

Regions of America

A J

B K

C L

D M

Making Comparisons

Compare the civilizations that you have read about by reviewing the information below. Can you see how the people of these civilizations helped to build the world we live in today?

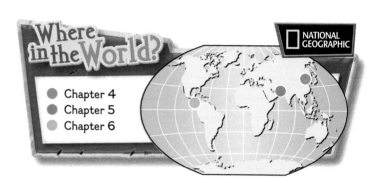

Where in the World?

- Chapter 4
- Chapter 5
- Chapter 6

NATIONAL GEOGRAPHIC

	Early India Chapter 4	**Early China** Chapter 5	**Ancient Americas** Chapter 6
Where did these civilizations develop?	• In the Indus River valley	• In the Huang He valley	• Central America • South America
Who were some important people in these civilizations?	• Siddhartha Gautama, c. 563–483 B.C. • Chandragupta Maurya, ruled c. 321–298 B.C. • Asoka, ruled c. 273–232 B.C.	• Wu Wang, ruled c. 1045–1043 B.C. • Confucius, 551–479 B.C. • Qin Shihuangdi, ruled 221–210 B.C. • Liu Bang, ruled 202–195 B.C.	• Jasaw Chan K'awiil I A.D. 682–734
Where did most of the people live?	• Many lived in farming villages and towns near major rivers • Some lived in very large cities	• Landowning aristocrats lived in large houses with gardens and courtyards • Most people were farmers living in simple houses in villages or cities	• Hunter-gatherers • Farming villages • City-states (Teotihuacán and Tikal)

	Early India Chapter 4	Early China Chapter 5	Ancient Americas Chapter 6
What were these people's beliefs?	• Hinduism: complex religion with many gods representing an eternal spirit • Buddhism: enlightenment available to anyone	• Confucianism: duty directs your life • Daoism: people should try to be in harmony with nature • Legalism: people need harsh laws to be good • Worship of ancestors	• Belief in gods who controlled everything • Practiced human sacrifice
What was their government like?	• The warrior class ran the government, usually ruled by a king	• A king or emperor ruled the country • Aristocrats ran the provinces	• Powerful kings ruled city-states (Maya)
What was their language and writing like?	• Sanskrit: used characters to form letters and words	• Chinese: symbols that represent objects were combined to represent ideas	• Mayan language written in hieroglyphics
What contributions did they make?	• Made advances in medicine, mathematics, science, and literature • Developed two major religions	• Invented paper and gunpowder • Cultivated silk	• Developed trade networks and methods of farming and building
How do these contributions affect me? *Can you add any?*	• "0" is now a part of our number system • Many people still practice Buddhism and Hinduism	• The papermaking process allows us to create books, newspapers, and other paper products • Gunpowder and silk are still in use	• Developed crops, such as corn, beans, and squash, that we still use today

Unit 3

The Greeks and Romans

Why It's Important

Each civilization that you will study in this unit made important contributions to history.

- The Greeks developed the idea of citizenship and created the first democratic governments.
- The Romans introduced the idea of the rule of law.
- Christians introduced religious beliefs that many still follow today.

1500 B.C.		750 B.C.	550 B.C.	350 B.C.

Ancient Greece
Chapters 7 & 8

- **c. 1400 B.C.** Mycenaeans replace Minoans as major power in Mediterranean
- **750 B.C.** Greek colonies established in Europe and Africa
- **594 B.C.** Solon takes power in Athens
- **c. 330 B.C.** Aristotle develops theories about government

Ancient Rome
Chapters 9 & 10

- **650 B.C.** Etruscans rule Rome
- **509 B.C.** Rome becomes a republic
- **312 B.C.** Romans build the Appian

◄ Etruscan mural

◄ Roman so

The Rise of Christianity
Chapter 11

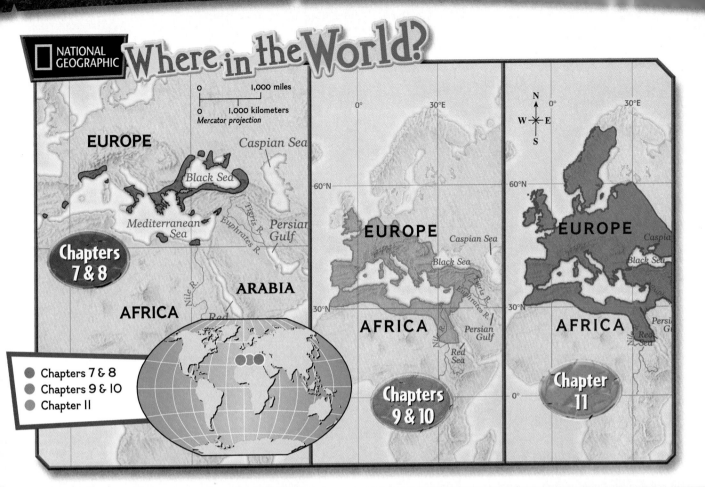

EUROPE

Caspian Sea

Black Sea

Mediterranean Sea

Tigris R.

Euphrates R.

Persian Gulf

Chapters 7 & 8

ARABIA

AFRICA

Nile R.

Red Sea

0 1,000 miles
0 1,000 kilometers
Mercator projection

0° 30°E

60°N

EUROPE

Caspian Sea

Black Sea

30°N

AFRICA

Tigris R.

Euphrates R.

Persian Gulf

Red Sea

Chapters 9 & 10

N
W E
S

0° 30°E

60°N

EUROPE

Caspia

Black Sea

30°N

AFRICA

Persi G

Red Sea

0°

Chapter 11

- ● Chapters 7 & 8
- ● Chapters 9 & 10
- ● Chapter 11

150 B.C.   A.D. 50   A.D. 250   A.D. 450   A.D. 650

c. 100 B.C.
City of Alexandria is the largest in the Mediterranean

◀ The Lighthouse of Alexandria
c. 290 B.C.

146 B.C.
Rome destroys Carthage

44 B.C.
Julius Caesar is killed

A.D. 180
Pax Romana ends

A.D. 312
Constantine comes to power

Emperor Constantine ▶

A.D. 30
Jesus preaches in Galilee and Judaea

C. A.D. 100
Churches founded throughout Roman world

C. A.D. 600
Bishop of Rome takes title of pope

◀ Orthodox Church incense burner c. A.D. 1100

Unit 3 Places to Locate

EUROPE

1 Greek Parthenon

See Ancient Greece
Chapters 7 & 8

2 Alexandria Lighthouse

See Ancient Greece
Chapter 8

3

4

1

Mediterranean

AFRICA

People to Meet

Homer

c. 750 B.C.
Greek poet, wrote *Iliad*
and *Odyssey*
Chapter 8, page 381

Pericles

c. 495–429 B.C.
Athenian general and
leading statesman
Chapter 7, page 361

**Alexander
the Great**

c. 356–323 B.C.
Macedonian
general and king
Chapter 8, page 401

Augustus

63 B.C.–A.D. 14
Roman emperor
Chapter 9, page 44

NATIONAL GEOGRAPHIC

ASIA

MIDDLE EAST

3 Roman aqueduct

See Ancient Rome
Chapters 9 & 10

4 Roman Pantheon

See Ancient Rome
Chapter 10

5 Mount of the Beatitudes

See Rise of Christianity
Chapter 11

Jesus

c. 6 B.C.–A.D. 33
Crucifixion led to rise of
Christianity
Chapter 11, page 504

Paul

c. A.D. 10–65
Christian thinker
Chapter 11, page 507

Constantine

c. A.D. 280–337
Roman emperor
Chapter 10, page 478

Theodora

c. A.D. 500–548
Byzantine empress
Chapter 10, page 488

Chapter 7

The Ancient Greeks

The Parthenon rises above the city of Athens. The people of ancient Greece built this temple to celebrate their goddess Athena. ▶

NATIONAL GEOGRAPHIC Where&When?

700 B.C.	600 B.C.	500 B.C.	400 B.C.
c. 750 B.C. Greece's Dark Age comes to an end	c. 650 B.C. Tyrants over-throw nobles in city-states	480 B.C. Xerxes invades Greece	431 B.C. Peloponnesian War begins

History Online
Chapter Overview Visit
ca.hss.glencoe.com for a
preview of Chapter 7.

The Big Ideas

Section 1 The Early Greeks

Physical geography plays a role in how civilizations develop and decline.
Greece's mountains, climate, and surrounding seas played a large
role in its history. The earliest civilizations in Greece were the
Minoans and the Mycenaeans.

Section 2 Sparta and Athens

**Systems of order, such as law and government, contribute to stable
societies.** Athens and Sparta, the two major city-states in ancient
Greece, developed different governments that emphasized opposite
aspects of society. Sparta focused on its military, while Athens
focused on trade, culture, and democracy.

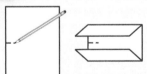

Section 3 Persia Attacks the Greeks

Conflict often brings about great changes. The Persian Empire gained
control of most of southwest Asia. However, when the Persians
tried to conquer the Greeks, Athens and Sparta united to defeat them.

Section 4 The Age of Pericles

Civilizations with strong economies prosper and grow. Under the
leadership of Pericles, Athens became a powerful city-state with a
strong economy and blossoming culture.

 View the Chapter 7 video in the Glencoe Video Program.

FOLDABLES™
Study Organizer

Summarizing Information *Make this foldable to help you organize and
summarize information about the ancient Greeks.*

Step 1 *Mark the
midpoint of a side edge
of one sheet of paper.
Then fold the outside
edges in to touch the
midpoint.*

Step 2 *Fold
the paper in
half again
from side to
side.*

Reading and Writing
*As you read the chapter,
write information under
each appropriate tab. Be
sure to summarize the
information you find by
writing only main ideas
and supporting details.*

Step 3 *Open the
paper and cut along
the inside fold lines
to form four tabs.*

Cut along the
fold lines on
both sides.

Step 4 *Label
as shown.*

The
Early
Greeks | Sparta
and
Athens

Persia
Attacks
the
Greeks | The
Age of
Pericles

Get Ready to Read

Comparing and Contrasting

1 Learn It!

Good readers compare and contrast information as they read. This means they look for similarities and differences. Comparing the ways in which people, places, or ideas are the same or different helps you understand how each is unique. Look for signal words in the text. Some comparison signal words are *same, at the same time, like,* and *still.* Contrast signal words include *some, others, different, however, rather, yet, but,* and *or.* Read the passage about Persian religion and then look at the questions that follow.

1) Persian religion is being compared to Jewish religion.

2) The similarities are high-lighted in blue and the con-trasts in red.

3) *Like* signals a comparison, and *however* signals contrast.

> Like the Jews, Zoroaster believed in one god. He viewed this supreme being as the creator of all things and a force of goodness. However, Zoroaster recognized evil in the world, too. He taught that humans had the freedom to choose between right and wrong, and that goodness would triumph in the end.
>
> — *from page 353*

Reading Tip

Look for the compare and contrast signal words when you take tests.

As you compare and contrast, ask these questions:
1) What things are being compared or contrasted?
2) Which characteristics can be compared or con-trasted?
3) How are they similar, and how are they different?
4) Are there any signal words?

2 Practice It!

Read the passage and the directions below.

> Athens and Sparta, the two major city-states in ancient Greece, developed different governments that emphasized opposite aspects of society. Sparta focused on its military, while Athens focused on trade, culture, and democracy.
>
> — *from page 333*

Read to Write

Reread the passage labeled *Roles of Men and Women* in Section 4 of this chapter. Then write a short paragraph comparing and contrasting what life was like for men and women in ancient Athens.

Read Section 2 and use a chart like the one below to organize the similarities and differences between Sparta and Athens. In the first column, fill in the characteristics that you will compare and contrast. In the second and third columns, describe the characteristics of each city-state.

Characteristic	Sparta	Athens

▼ Spartan warrior

3 Apply It!

As you read the chapter, choose three pairs of subjects to compare and contrast. List the similarities and differences using a graphic organizer, such as the one above.

The Early Greeks

Guide to Reading

History Social Science Standards

WH6.4 Students analyze the geographic, political, economic, religious, and social structures of the early civilizations of Ancient Greece.

Looking Back, Looking Ahead

In Chapters 1 and 2, you learned about Mesopotamia and Egypt. These civilizations grew up in great river valleys with rich soil. Greece had no great river valleys. Instead, it had mountains, rocky soil, and many miles of seacoasts.

Focusing on the Main Ideas

- The geography of Greece influenced where people settled and what they did. *(page 337)*

- The Minoans earned their living by building ships and trading. *(page 338)*

- Mycenaeans built the first Greek kingdoms and spread their power across the Mediterranean region. *(page 339)*

- The idea of citizenship developed in Greek city-states. *(page 341)*

- Colonies and trade spread Greek culture and spurred industry. *(page 343)*

Meeting People

Agamemnon (A•guh•MEHM•nahn)

Locating Places

Crete (KREET)

Mycenae (my•SEE•nee)

Peloponnesus (PEH•luh•puh•NEE•suhs)

Content Vocabulary

peninsula (puh•NIHN•suh•luh)

polis (PAH•luhs)

agora (A•guh•ruh)

colony (KAH•luh•nee)

Academic Vocabulary

region (REE•juhn)

culture (KUHL•chuhr)

overseas (OH•vuhr•SEEZ)

community (kuh•MYOO•nuh•tee)

Reading Strategy

Finding Details Draw a diagram like the one below. In each oval write one detail about a polis.

polis

Where & When?

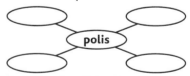

GREECE

Mycenae•

Crete— Knossos•

2000 B.C.	1250 B.C.	500 B.C.
c. 2000 B.C. Minoans control eastern Mediterranean	c. 1200 B.C. Mycenaean civilization declines	c. 750 B.C. Greece's Dark Age comes to an end

The Geography of Greece

Main Idea The geography of Greece influenced where people settled and what they did.

Reading Connection Do you rake leaves in the fall? Do you walk uphill to school? Your answers explain how geography shapes your life. Read to learn how geography shaped life in early Greece.

If you fly over Greece today, you will see a mountainous land framed by sparkling blue water. To the west is the Ionian (eye•OH•nee•uhn) Sea, to the south is the Mediterranean Sea, and to the east is the Aegean (ih•JEE•uhn) Sea. Hundreds of islands lie offshore, stretching across to Asia like stepping-stones. Mainland Greece is a peninsula (puh•NIHN•suh•luh)—a body of land with water on three sides.

Many ancient Greeks made a living from the sea. They became fishers, sailors, and traders. Others settled in farming communities. Greece's mountains and rocky soil were not ideal for growing crops. However, the climate was mild, and in some places people could grow wheat, barley, olives, and grapes. They also raised sheep and goats.

Ancient Greeks felt deep ties to the land, but the mountains and seas divided them from one another. As a result, early Greek communities grew up fiercely independent.

✓ Reading Check **Cause and Effect** How did geography discourage Greek unity?

Ancient Greece c. 750 B.C.

KEY
Ancient Greece

Sea of Marmara

MACEDONIA

Mt. Olympus ▲

• Troy

BALKAN PENINSULA

Aegean Sea

GREECE

Ionian Sea

ASIA MINOR

Delphi •

Gulf of Corinth

• Thebes

Corinth •
Mycenae •

• Athens

• Miletus

Mediterranean Sea

PELOPONNESUS

• Sparta

0   100 miles
0   100 kilometers
Lambert Azimuthal Equal-Area projection

40°N
20°E
30°E

Sea of Crete

Knossos
•
Crete •

Using Geography Skills

1. **Location** What body of water lies directly east of the Balkan Peninsula?
2. **Movement** What transportation was probably most useful to the early Greeks?

Find NGS online map resources @ www.nationalgeographic.com/maps

Mountains and seas played an important role in Greek history. ▶

WH6.4 Students analyze the geographic, political, economic, religious, and social structures of the early civilizations of Ancient Greece.

WH6.4.1 Discuss the connections between geography and the development of city-states in the region of the Aegean Sea, including patterns of trade and commerce among Greek city-states and within the wider Mediterranean region.

The Minoans

Main Idea The Minoans earned their living by building ships and trading.

Reading Connection Imagine what it would be like to uncover a building that is more than 5,000 years old. Read to learn how such a discovery unlocked clues to Greece's ancient past.

The island of **Crete** (KREET) lies southeast of the Greek mainland. There, in 1900, an English archaeologist by the name of Arthur Evans made the find of a lifetime. Evans uncovered the ruins of a grand palace that had been the center of Minoan (muh•NOH•uhn) civilization. The Minoans were not Greeks, but their civilization was the first to arise in the **region** that later became Greece.

The palace at Knossos (NAH•suhs) revealed the riches of an ancient society. Its twisting passageways led to many different rooms: private quarters for the royal family and storerooms packed with oil, wine, and grain. Other spaces were workshops for making jewelry, vases, and small ivory statues. The palace even had bathrooms.

The Minoans made their wealth from trade. They built ships from oak and cedar trees and sailed as far as Egypt and Syria. There they traded pottery and stone vases for ivory and metals. By 2000 B.C., Minoan ships controlled the eastern Mediterranean Sea. They carried goods to foreign ports and kept the sea secure from pirates.

About 1450 B.C., the Minoan civilization suddenly collapsed. Some historians think undersea earthquakes caused giant waves that washed away the Minoans' cities. Others think the cities were destroyed by a group of Greeks from the mainland. These invaders were called the Mycenaeans (MY•suh•NEE•uhns).

Reading Check **Explain** How did the Minoans become a trading civilization?

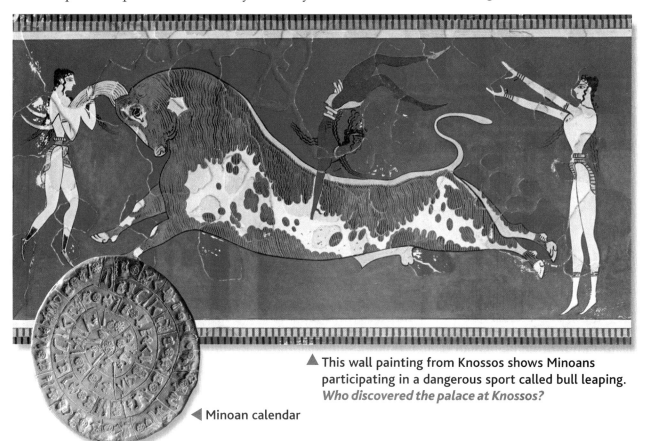

▲ This wall painting from Knossos shows Minoans participating in a dangerous sport called bull leaping.
Who discovered the palace at Knossos?

◀ Minoan calendar

WH6.4 Students analyze the geographic, political, economic, religious, and social structures of the early civilizations of Ancient Greece.

WH6.4.1 Discuss the connections between geography and the development of city-states in the region of the Aegean Sea, including patterns of trade and commerce among Greek city-states and within the wider Mediterranean region.

The First Greek Kingdoms

Main Idea Mycenaeans built the first Greek kingdoms and spread their power across the Mediterranean region.

Reading Connection What is the most important building in the area where you live? Is it a government building, a grocery store, or a hospital? Read to find out what building was most important in the Mycenaean civilization.

The Mycenaeans were originally from central Asia. They invaded the Greek mainland around 1900 B.C. and conquered the people living there. The Mycenaean leaders became the first Greek kings. Their warriors became nobles who ruled the people they had conquered. In the late 1800s, a German named Heinrich Schliemann (HYN• rihk SHLEE • MAHN) discovered one of their walled palaces in **Mycenae** (my • SEE • nee). He named the people of this civilization the Mycenaeans.

What Were Mycenaean Kingdoms Like?

The centerpiece of each Mycenaean kingdom was a fortified palace on a hill. The ruler lived there, surrounded by giant stone walls. Beyond the palace walls lay large farms, or estates, that belonged to the nobles. Slaves and farmers lived on the estates and took shelter inside the fortress in times of danger.

Mycenaean palaces hummed with activity. Artisans tanned leather, sewed clothes, and made jars for wine and olive oil. Other workers made bronze swords and ox-hide shields. Government officials kept track of the wealth of every person in the kingdom. Then they collected wheat, livestock, and honey as taxes and stored them in the palace.

Power From Trade and War

Soon after the Mycenaeans set up their kingdoms, Minoan traders began to visit from Crete.

▲ The ruins at Mycenae included this gate. *What lay outside the walls of a Mycenaean palace?*

Gold mask of Agamemnon ▶

As a result, Mycenaeans learned much about Minoan **culture.** They copied the ways Minoans worked with bronze and built ships. They learned how the Minoans used the sun and stars to find their way at sea. The Mycenaeans even started worshiping the Earth Mother, the Minoans' chief goddess.

Around 1400 B.C., the Mycenaeans replaced the Minoans as the major power on the Mediterranean. They traded widely, sailing to Egypt and southern Italy. Some historians think they conquered Crete and nearby islands.

Although trade made the Mycenaeans wealthy, they were prouder of their deeds in battle. Their most famous victory is probably the Trojan War. In the next chapter, you will learn the legend of how the Mycenaean king **Agamemnon** (A•guh•MEHM•nahn) used trickery to win that war.

What Was the Dark Age? By 1200 B.C., the Mycenaeans were in trouble. Earthquakes and fighting among the kingdoms had destroyed their hilltop forts. By 1100 B.C., Mycenaean civilization had collapsed.

The Greek Alphabet

Greek Letter	Written Name	English Sound
A	alpha	a
B	beta	b
Γ	gamma	g
Δ	delta	d
E	epsilon	e
Z	zeta	z
H	eta	e
Θ	theta	th
I	iota	i
K	kappa	c, k
Λ	lambda	l
M	mu	m
N	nu	n
Ξ	xi	x
O	omicron	o
Π	pi	p
P	rho	r
Σ	sigma	s
T	tau	t
Y	upsilon	y, u
Φ	phi	ph
X	chi	ch
Ψ	psi	ps
Ω	omega	o

▲ The Greek alphabet was based on the Phoenician alphabet. *What happened to Greek writing during the Dark Age?*

The years between 1100 B.C. and 750 B.C. were difficult for the Greeks. **Overseas** trade slowed, and poverty took hold. Farmers grew only enough food to meet their own family's needs. People also stopped teaching others how to write or do craftwork. Before long, the Greeks had forgotten their written language and how to make many things. As a result, historians call this time the Dark Age.

The changes that took place in the Dark Age were not all bad, however. One positive development was a huge population shift. Thousands of Greeks left the mainland and settled on islands in the Aegean Sea. Other Greeks moved to the western shores of Asia Minor, to what is now the country of Turkey. This wave of movement expanded the reach of Greek culture.

Meanwhile, a Greek-speaking people known as the Dorians (DOHR•ee•uhns), who lived in Greece's northern mountains, began to move south. Many settled in the southwest on the **Peloponnesus** (PEH•luh• puh•NEE•suhs). The Dorians brought iron weapons with them, giving Greece more advanced technology. Iron weapons and farm tools were stronger and cheaper than those made of bronze.

Gradually, farmers began to produce surplus food again. As a result, trade revived. One benefit of the increased trade was a new way of writing. As you read in Chapter 3, the Greeks picked up the idea of an alphabet from the Phoenicians, one of their trading partners who lived on the coast of the eastern Mediterranean.

The Greek alphabet had 24 letters that stood for different sounds. It made reading and writing Greek much simpler than ever before. Soon people were writing down tales that had been passed down by storytellers for generations.

Reading Check **Identify** Why were the Mycenaeans able to become a major power in the Mediterranean region?

WH6.4.1 Discuss the connections between geography and the development of city-states in the region of the Aegean Sea, including patterns of trade and commerce among Greek city-states and within the Mediterranean region.
WH 6.4.2 Trace the transition from tyranny and oligarchy to early democratic forms of government and back to dictatorship in ancient Greece, including the significance of the invention of the idea of citizenship (e.g., from *Pericles' Funeral Oration*).

The Polis

Main Idea The idea of citizenship developed in Greek city-states.

Reading Connection Did you know that the word "politics" comes from *polis*, the Greek term for a city-state? Read to find how the Greeks also created the idea of citizenship.

By the end of the Dark Age, many nobles who owned large estates had overthrown the Greek kings. They created city-states. Like the Mesopotamian city-states you read about in Chapter 1, those in Greece were made up of a town or city and the surrounding countryside. Each Greek city-state, known as a **polis** (PAH•luhs), was like a tiny independent country.

The main gathering place in the polis was usually a hill. A fortified area, called an acropolis (uh•KRAH•puh•luhs), stood at the top of the hill. It provided a safe refuge in case of attacks. Sometimes the acropolis also served as a religious center. Temples and altars were built there to honor the many Greek gods and goddesses.

Below the acropolis was an open area called an **agora** (A•guh•ruh). This space had two functions: it was both a market and a place where people could meet and debate issues. Just beyond the agora lay the farmland that belonged to the city-states.

City-states varied in size. Because of the mountains and seas, most city-states were small and very independent. A few were only a few square miles in size, but some covered hundreds of square miles. They also varied in population. Athens was by far the largest. By 500 B.C., nearly 300,000 people lived there. Most city-states were much smaller than Athens.

What Was Greek Citizenship? Each
Greek city-state was run by its citizens. When we speak of citizens, we mean mem-

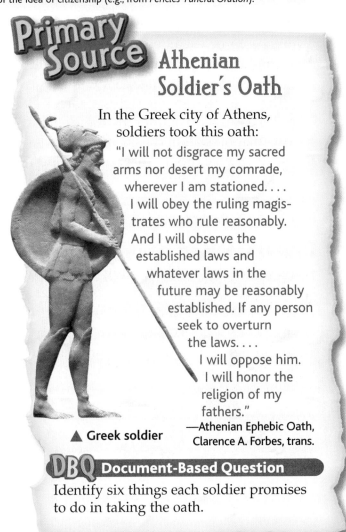

Primary Source Athenian Soldier's Oath

In the Greek city of Athens, soldiers took this oath:

"I will not disgrace my sacred arms nor desert my comrade, wherever I am stationed. . . . I will obey the ruling magistrates who rule reasonably. And I will observe the established laws and whatever laws in the future may be reasonably established. If any person seek to overturn the laws. . . . I will oppose him. I will honor the religion of my fathers."

—Athenian Ephebic Oath, Clarence A. Forbes, trans.

▲ Greek soldier

DBQ Document-Based Question
Identify six things each soldier promises to do in taking the oath.

bers of a political **community** who treat each other as equals and who have rights and responsibilities. This was very different from ancient Mesopotamia or Egypt. There, most people were subjects. They had no rights, no say in government, and no choice but to obey their rulers.

The Greeks were the first people to develop the idea of citizenship. Today, the word applies to almost everyone in a society. However, in most Greek city-states, only free native-born men who owned land could be citizens. From their point of view, the city-state was made up of their lands, and it was their responsibility to run it.

Some city-states, such as Athens, eventually dropped the land-owning requirement.

Slaves and foreign-born residents, however, continued to be excluded. Women and children might qualify for citizenship, but they had none of the rights that went with it.

What exactly were the rights of Greek citizens? They could gather in the agora to choose their officials and pass laws. They had the right to vote, hold office, own property, and defend themselves in court. In return, citizens had a duty to serve in government and to fight for their polis as citizen soldiers.

Citizens as Soldiers

In early Greece, wars were waged by nobles riding horses and chariots. As the idea of citizenship developed, however, the military system changed. By 700 B.C., the city-states had begun to depend on armies of ordinary citizens called hoplites (HAHP•LYTS).

Unable to afford horses, the hoplites fought on foot and went into battle heavily armed. Each soldier carried a round shield, a short sword, and a 9-foot (2.7-m) spear. Row upon row of soldiers marched forward together, shoulder to shoulder in a formation called a phalanx (FAY•langks). With their shields creating a protective wall, they gave their enemies few openings to defeat them.

Hoplites made good soldiers because, as citizens, they took pride in fighting for their city-state. However, "hometown" loyalties also divided the Greeks and caused them to distrust one another. A lack of unity always existed among the Greek city-states.

✓**Reading Check** **Explain** How did citizenship make the Greeks different from other ancient peoples?

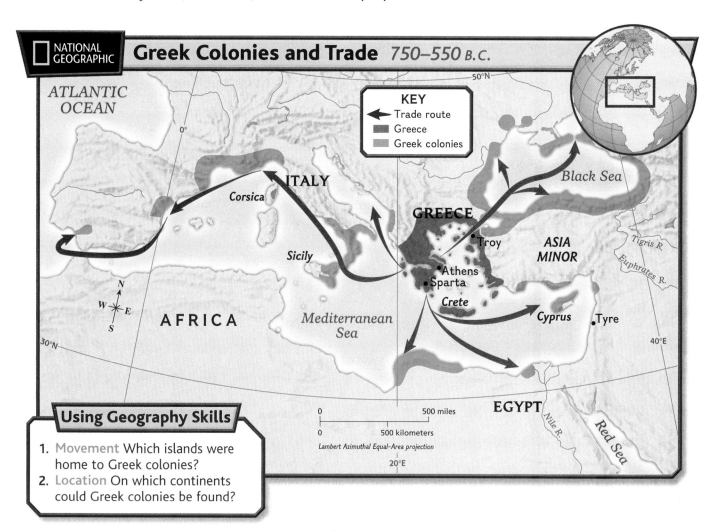

NATIONAL GEOGRAPHIC

Greek Colonies and Trade 750–550 B.C.

KEY
→ Trade route
■ Greece
■ Greek colonies

Using Geography Skills

1. **Movement** Which islands were home to Greek colonies?
2. **Location** On which continents could Greek colonies be found?

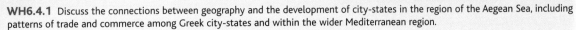
A Move to Colonize

Main Idea Colonies and trade spread Greek culture and spurred industry.

Reading Connection If you read labels, you know that your food and clothing come from all over the world. Read to find out where the early Greeks got their goods.

As Greece recovered from its Dark Age, its population rose quickly. By 700 B.C., city-states could no longer grow enough grain to feed everyone. As a result, cities began sending people outside Greece to start **colonies** (KAH•luh•nees). A colony is a settlement in a new territory that stays closely linked to its homeland.

Between 750 B.C. and 550 B.C., adventurous Greeks streamed to the coasts of Italy, France, Spain, North Africa, and western Asia. With each new colony, Greek culture spread farther.

Colonists traded regularly with their "parent" cities, shipping them grains, metals, fish, timber, and enslaved people. In return, the colonists received pottery, wine, and olive oil from the mainland. Overseas trade got an extra boost during the 600s B.C., when the Greeks began to mint coins. Merchants were soon exchanging goods for currency rather than for more goods.

By importing grain and other foods from their colonies, many city-states could support a much larger population. This made it very important to protect their colonies, otherwise people would starve. Trade also led to the growth of industry. As the demand for goods grew, producers had to keep pace. People in different areas began specializing in certain products. For example, pottery became popular in places with large amounts of clay.

✓ **Reading Check** **Cause and Effect** How did the founding of new colonies affect industry?

Study Central Need help understanding the importance of geography in ancient Greece? Visit ca.hss.glencoe.com and click on Study Central.

Section ① Review

Reading Summary

Review the Main Ideas

- Geography influenced the way Greek communities developed.

- The Minoan civilization on the island of Crete built ships and became wealthy from trade.

- The Mycenaeans created the first Greek kingdoms.

- After the Dark Age, the Greeks set up colonies and trade increased.

- The idea of citizenship developed in Greek city-states.

What Did You Learn?

1. What made the Minoans wealthy?

2. How was a Greek city-state different from a city?

Critical Thinking

3. **Compare** Create a Venn diagram to compare the Minoans and Mycenaeans. **CA 6RC2.2**

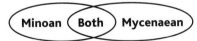

Minoan (Both) Mycenaean

4. **The Big Ideas** How did early Greek civilizations use their natural surroundings to prosper and grow? **CA CS3.**

5. **Citizenship Skills** Name three rights granted to Greek citizens that American citizens have today. **CA 6RC2.3**

6. **Economics Connection** Why did the use of money help trade to grow? **CA HI6.**

7. **Reading** **Comparing and Contrasting** Write an essay that compares and contrasts the Mycenaeans and the Dorians. Look for clues in the text that will help you make these comparisons. **CA 6WA2.2**

Section 2

Sparta and Athens

Guide to Reading

History Social Science Standards

WH6.4 Students analyze the geographic, political, economic, religious, and social structures of the early civilizations of Ancient Greece.

Looking Back, Looking Ahead

Although Greek city-states developed the idea of citizenship, they had many different types of government. This section describes their different governments and compares the best-known city-states, Athens and Sparta.

Focusing on the Main Ideas

• Tyrants were able to seize power from the nobles with the support of Greek farmers, merchants, and artisans. *(page 345)*

• The Spartans focused on military skills to control the people they conquered. *(page 346)*

• Unlike Spartans, Athenians were more interested in building a democracy than building a military force. *(page 348)*

Locating Places
Sparta (SPAHR•tuh)
Athens (A•thuhnz)

Meeting People
Solon (SOH•luhn)
Peisistratus (py•SIHS•truht•uhs)
Cleisthenes (KLYS•thuh•NEEZ)

Content Vocabulary
tyrant (TY•ruhnt)
oligarchy (AH•luh•GAHR•kee)
democracy (dih•MAH•kruh•see)
helot (HEH•luht)

Academic Vocabulary
enforce (ihn•FOHRS)
participate (pahr•TIH•suh•PAYT)

Reading Strategy
Compare and Contrast Use a Venn diagram to compare and contrast life in Sparta and Athens.

Sparta   Both   Athens

NATIONAL GEOGRAPHIC **Where&When?**

GREECE

Athens

PELOPONNESUS
Sparta

700 B.C.   **600** B.C.   **500** B.C.

c. 650 B.C.
Tyrants overthrow nobles in city-states

594 B.C.
Solon takes power in Athens

508 B.C.
Cleisthenes reforms Athenian government

Tyranny in the City-States

Main Idea Tyrants were able to seize power from the nobles with the support of Greek farmers, merchants, and artisans.

Reading Connection How do you feel when someone makes a decision that affects you without asking for your opinion? Read to find out how ancient Greeks who were shut out of governing made their voices heard.

As you read in the last section, kings ruled the first Greek communities. However, by the end of the Dark Age, the nobles who owned large farms had seized power from the kings.

Rule by the nobles would also be short-lived. The first challenge to their rule came from the owners of small farms. These farmers often needed money to live on until they could harvest and sell their crops. Many borrowed money from the nobles, promising to give up their fields if they could not repay the loans. Time and time again, farmers lost their land. Then they had to work for the nobles or become laborers in the city. In desperate cases, they sold themselves into slavery.

By 650 B.C., owners of small farms began to demand changes in the power structure. Merchants and artisans also wanted to share in governing. Both groups had become very wealthy from the trade between city-states. Because they did not own land, however, they were not citizens and had no say in running the polis.

The growing unhappiness led to the rise of tyrants. A **tyrant** (TY•ruhnt) is someone who takes power by force and rules with

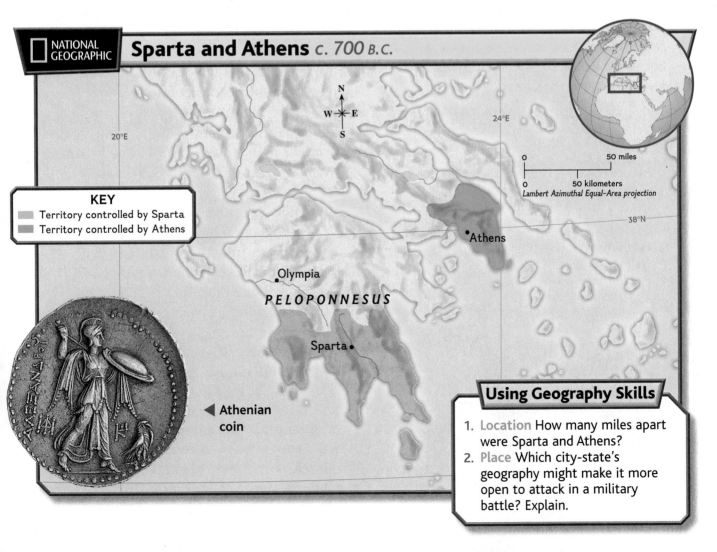

NATIONAL GEOGRAPHIC

Sparta and Athens c. 700 B.C.

KEY
- Territory controlled by Sparta
- Territory controlled by Athens

24°E

50 miles

50 kilometers
Lambert Azimuthal Equal-Area projection

38°N

Athens

20°E

Olympia

PELOPONNESUS

Sparta

◀ Athenian coin

Using Geography Skills

1. **Location** How many miles apart were Sparta and Athens?
2. **Place** Which city-state's geography might make it more open to attack in a military battle? Explain.

total authority. Today the word describes a harsh, oppressive ruler. Most early Greek tyrants, though, acted wisely and fairly.

During the 600s B.C., tyrants managed to overthrow the nobles because they had the backing of the common people. Key support came from the hoplites in the army, many of whom were also farmers.

Tyrants made themselves popular by building new marketplaces, temples, and walls. However, rule by one person was the opposite of what most Greeks wanted. They longed for rule by law with all citizens participating in the government.

By 500 B.C., tyrants had fallen out of favor in Greece. Most city-states became either oligarchies or democracies. In an **oligarchy** (AH•luh•GAHR•kee), a few people hold power. In a **democracy** (dih•MAH•kruh•see), all citizens share in running the government. The oligarchy of **Sparta** (SPAHR•tuh) and the democracy of **Athens** (A•thuhnz) became two of the most powerful governments of early Greece.

✓ **Reading Check** **Evaluate** Why were tyrants popular in the city-states?

Spartan Warrior

Spartan boys and men spent many years training for war.
At what age did Spartan boys leave their families for the military?

Sparta

Main Idea The Spartans focused on military skills to control the people they conquered.

Reading Connection What would it be like to leave home when you were only seven? Read to learn how Spartan boys faced this challenge.

As you read in the last section, Sparta was founded by the Dorians—Greeks who invaded the Peloponnesus in the Dark Age. Like other city-states, Sparta needed more land as it grew, but its people did not set up colonies. Instead, they conquered and enslaved their neighbors. The Spartans called their captive workers **helots** (HEH•luhts). This name comes from the Greek word for "capture."

Why Was the Military So Important?
Spartans feared that the helots might someday rebel. As a result, the government firmly controlled the people of Sparta and trained the boys and men for war.

At age seven, boys left their family to live in barracks. They were harshly treated to make them tough. The Greek historian Plutarch describes life for Spartan boys:

❝ After they were twelve years old, they were no longer allowed to wear any undergarment; they had one coat to serve them a year; . . . They lodged together in little bands upon beds made of the reeds [grasses] . . . which they were to break off with their hands without a knife. ❞

—Plutarch, "Spartan Discipline"

At age 20, Spartan men entered the regular army. The men remained in military barracks for 10 more years. They ate all their meals in dining halls with other soldiers.

Spartan girls were trained in sports. ▼

▲ Spartan boys began training for the military at age 7. *Why did the Spartan government want its young people to be physically fit?*

A typical meal was a vile-tasting dish called black broth—pork boiled in animal blood, salt, and vinegar.

Spartans returned home at age 30 but stayed in the army until age 60. They continued to train for combat. They expected to either win on the battlefield or die, but never to surrender. One Spartan mother ordered her son to "Come home carrying your shield or being carried on it."

Girls in Sparta were trained in sports—running, wrestling, and throwing the javelin. They kept fit to become healthy mothers. Wives lived at home while their husbands lived in the barracks. As a result, Spartan women were freer than other Greek women. They could own property and go where they wanted.

What Was Sparta's Government Like?

The Spartan government was an oligarchy. Two kings headed a council of elders. The council, which included 28 citizens over age 60, presented laws to an assembly.

All Spartan men over age 30 belonged to the assembly. They voted on the council's laws and chose five people to be ephors (EH•fuhrs) each year. The ephors **enforced** the laws and managed tax collection.

To keep anyone from questioning the Spartan system, the government discouraged foreign visitors. It also banned travel abroad for any reason but military ones. It even frowned upon citizens who studied literature or the arts.

The Spartans succeeded in keeping control over the helots for nearly 250 years. However, by focusing on military training, the Spartans fell behind other Greeks in trade. They also knew less about science and other subjects. However, their soldiers were especially strong and swift. The Spartans would play a key role in defending Greece.

✓ **Reading Check** **Cause and Effect** Why did the Spartans focus on military training?

WH6.4.2 Trace the transition from tyranny and oligarchy to early democratic forms of government and back to dictatorship in ancient Greece, including the significance of the invention of the idea of citizenship (e.g., from *Pericles' Funeral Oration*).
WH6.4.6 Compare and contrast life in Athens and Sparta, with emphasis on their roles in the Persian and Peloponnesian Wars.

Athens

> **Main Idea** Unlike Spartans, Athenians were more interested in building a democracy than building a military force.

Reading Connection When visiting a new city, does everything feel strange to you? Spartans who visited Athens probably felt the same way. Read to find out why.

Athens lay northeast of Sparta, at least a two-day trip away. The two city-states were also miles apart in their values and systems of government.

What Was Life in Athens Like? Athenian citizens raised their children very differently from Spartans. In Athenian schools, one teacher taught boys to read, write, and do arithmetic. Another teacher taught them sports. A third teacher taught them to sing and to play a stringed instrument called the lyre. This kind of instruction created well-rounded Athenians with good minds and bodies. At age 18, boys finished school and became citizens.

Athenian girls stayed at home. Their mothers taught them spinning, weaving,

Linking Past & Present

The Olympics

PAST In ancient Greece, only men could participate in and view the Olympic games. Athletes competed by themselves, not as part of a team. Contests included running, jumping, wrestling, and boxing. Each winning athlete won a crown of olive leaves and brought glory to his city.

▲ A warrior's race in the ancient Olympics

▼ **Modern Olympic athletes**

PRESENT In today's Olympic games, both men and women compete. These athletes come from all over the world. They may compete in either individual or team sporting events. Olympic athletes strive to win gold, silver, or bronze medals. *What did ancient Greek Olympic winners receive? What do present-day Olympic winners receive?*

◄ The city of Athens was named for the goddess Athena. *What group ruled Athens during the 600s B.C.?*

and other household duties. Only in some wealthy families did girls learn to read, write, and play the lyre. When they married, women stayed home to keep house and to teach their own daughters.

A Budding Democracy Early Athens, like other city-states, was ruled by landowning nobles during the 600s B.C. An assembly of all citizens existed, but it had few powers. Actually, the government was an oligarchy, as in Sparta.

Around 600 B.C., the Athenians began to rebel against the nobles. Most farmers owed the nobles money, and many sold themselves into slavery to pay their debts. Over and over, farmers demanded an end to all debts, along with land for the poor.

In 594 B.C. the nobles turned to the one man both sides trusted: a noble named **Solon** (SOH•luhn). Solon canceled all the farmers' debts and freed those who had become slaves. He also allowed all male citizens to **participate** in the assembly and law courts. A council of 400 wealthy citizens wrote the laws, but the assembly had to pass them.

Solon's reforms were popular among the common people. However, the farmers continued to press Solon to give away the wealthy nobles' land. This he refused to do.

After Solon, there were 30 years of turmoil. Finally, a tyrant named **Peisistratus** (py•SIHS•truht•uhs) seized power in 560 B.C. He won the support of the poor by dividing large estates among landless farmers. He also loaned money to poor people and gave them jobs building temples and other public works.

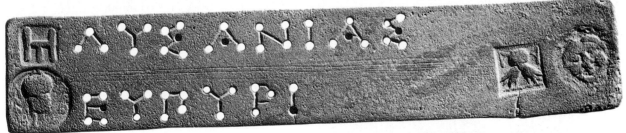

▲ Token used to select jurors for Athenian courts

The most important leader after Peisistratus died was **Cleisthenes** (KLYS•thuh•NEEZ). When he came to power in 508 B.C., he reorganized the assembly to play the central role in governing. As before, all male citizens could belong to the assembly and vote on laws. However, members had new powers. They could debate matters openly, hear court cases, and appoint army generals.

Most importantly, Cleisthenes created a new council of 500 citizens to help the assembly carry out daily business. The council proposed laws, dealt with foreign countries, and oversaw the treasury.

Athenians chose the members of the council each year in a lottery. They believed this system was fairer than an election, which might favor the rich.

Cleisthenes' reforms did not bring all Athenians into the political process.

◄ This stone carving shows Democracy crowning a figure that symbolizes Athens. *What leader is credited with making Athens a democracy?*

Noncitizens, which included all women, foreign-born men, and slaves, were still excluded. Nonetheless, Cleisthenes is credited with making the government of Athens a democracy.

✓ **Reading Check** **Explain** How did Cleisthenes build a democracy in Athens?

History Online

Study Central Need help comparing Athens and Sparta? Visit ca.hss.glencoe.com and click on Study Central.

Section ② Review

Reading Summary

Review the Main Ideas

- The support of wealthy merchants and artisans helped tyrants seize power from nobles in the city-states.

- Sparta was a powerful city-state. It created a military state to control the people it conquered and to prevent uprisings.

- Athens was a powerful democratic city-state. Athenians were more involved in government, education, and the arts than the Spartans.

What Did You Learn?

1. Who were the helots?

2. Why did tyrants fall out of favor with the Greeks?

Critical Thinking

3. **Persuasive Writing** Athenians chose officials by lottery. Write an essay arguing for or against this idea. **CA 6WA2.5**

4. **Classifying Information** Draw a diagram like the one below. In each oval write a fact about the Spartan oligarchy. **CA 6RC2.4**

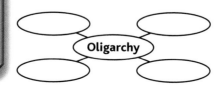

Oligarchy

5. **Explain** How did Greek nobles gain power? **CA 6RC2.0**

6. **Analyze** Why was Solon popular among some Athenian farmers and unpopular among others? **CA HR5.**

7. **The Big Ideas** To ensure stability, the Athenians set up their government to keep one person from gaining too much power. How did they do this? **CA 6RC2.4**

8. **Expository Writing** Imagine that you are a 28-year-old man living in Sparta in 700 B.C. Write a letter to your 6-year-old nephew telling him what to expect when he leaves home on his next birthday. **CA 6WS1.1**

3 Persia Attacks the Greeks

Guide to Reading

Looking Back, Looking Ahead

Section 2 explained how Greeks built strong but separate city-states. At the same time far to the east, the Persians were building a powerful empire. It was only a matter of time before Persia would try to invade Greece.

Focusing on the Main Ideas

- The Persian Empire united a wide area under a single government. *(page 352)*

- Both Sparta and Athens played roles in defeating the Persians. *(page 354)*

Locating Places

Persia (PUHR•zhuh)
Marathon (MAR•uh•THAHN)
Thermopylae
   (thuhr•MAH•puh•lee)
Salamis (SA•luh•muhs)
Plataea (pluh•TEE•uh)

Meeting People

Cyrus the Great (SY•ruhs)
Darius (duh•RY•uhs)
Xerxes (ZUHRK•SEEZ)
Themistocles
   (thuh•MIHS•tuh•KLEEZ)

Content Vocabulary

satrapies (SAY•truh•peez)
satrap (SAY•TRAP)
Zoroastrianism (ZOHR•uh•WAS•
   tree•uh•NIH•zuhm)

Academic Vocabulary

vision (VIH•zhuhn)
internal (ihn•TUHR•nuhl)

Reading Strategy

Organizing Information Create a chart like the one below to list the accomplishments of Cyrus, Darius, and Xerxes.

Ruler	Accomplishments

History Social Science Standards

WH6.4 Students analyze the geographic, political, economic, religious, and social structures of the early civilizations of Ancient Greece.

NATIONAL GEOGRAPHIC **Who & When?**

650 B.C.　　　550 B.C.　　　450 B.C.

660 B.C. Zoroaster born

559 B.C. Cyrus becomes ruler of Persia

480 B.C. Xerxes invades Greece

WH6.4.5 Outline the founding, expansion, and political organization of the Persian Empire.

The Persian Empire

Main Idea The Persian Empire united a wide area under a single government.

Reading Connection Have you ever seen soldiers marching through city streets on the news? Imagine the same thing happening in Asia in the 500s B.C. Read to learn what happened as Persian armies marched westward from Asia.

The people of **Persia** (PUHR•zhuh) lived in what is today southwestern Iran. Early Persians were warriors and nomads who herded cattle. For a time, they were dominated by others. Then one remarkable leader, **Cyrus the Great** (SY•ruhs), managed to unite the Persians into a powerful kingdom. Under Cyrus, who ruled from 559 B.C. to 530 B.C., Persia began building an empire larger than any yet seen in the world.

The Rise of the Persian Empire In 539 B.C. Cyrus's armies swept into Mesopotamia and captured Babylon. Then they took over northern Mesopotamia, Asia Minor, Syria, Canaan, and the Phoenician cities. Cyrus treated all his new subjects well. As you read in Chapter 3, he allowed the captive Jews in Babylon to return home. Cyrus's merciful rule helped hold his growing empire together.

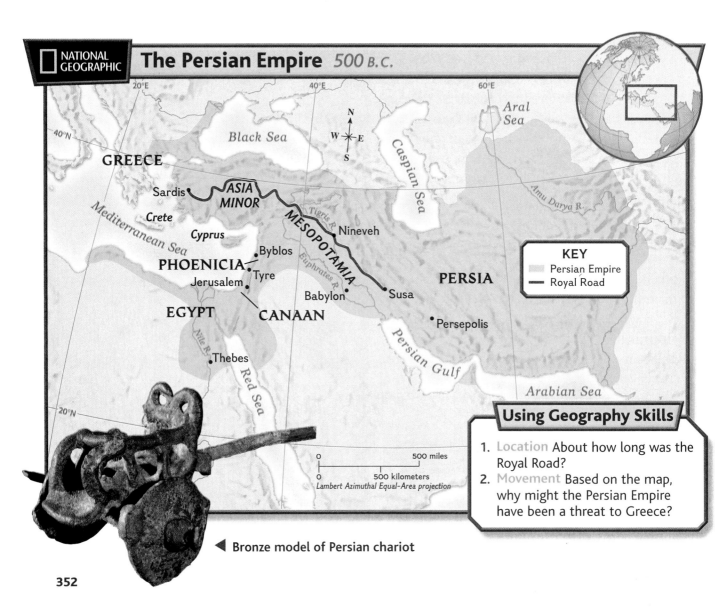

NATIONAL GEOGRAPHIC

The Persian Empire 500 B.C.

KEY
Persian Empire
— Royal Road

Using Geography Skills

1. **Location** About how long was the Royal Road?
2. **Movement** Based on the map, why might the Persian Empire have been a threat to Greece?

◀ Bronze model of Persian chariot

The leaders who followed Cyrus continued to add to Persian territory. They conquered Egypt, western India, and Thrace, a region northeast of Greece. From one end to the other, the Persian Empire was about the size of the continental United States today.

To connect their vast holdings, the Persians built miles of roads. The Royal Road stretched from Asia Minor to Susa, the Persian capital. Along the way, the Persians set up roadside stations to supply food, shelter, and fresh horses to the king's messengers.

What Was Persian Government Like?
As the Persian Empire grew bigger, it became very difficult to manage. When **Darius** (duh•RY•uhs) came to the throne in 521 B.C., he reorganized the government to make it work better.

Darius divided the empire into 20 provinces called **satrapies** (SAY•truh•peez). Each was ruled by an official with the title of **satrap** (SAY•TRAP), meaning "protector of the kingdom." The satrap acted as tax collector, judge, chief of police, and head recruiter for the Persian army. However, all the satraps answered to the Persian king.

The king's power depended upon his troops. By the time of Darius, Persia had a large army of professional soldiers. Unlike the Greek city-states, where the citizens took up arms in times of war, in Persia the government paid people to be full-time soldiers. Among them were 10,000 specially trained soldiers who guarded the king. They were called the Immortals because when a member died, he was immediately replaced.

The Persian Religion
The Persian religion was called **Zoroastrianism** (ZOHR•uh•WAS•tree•uh•NIH•zuhm). Its founder, Zoroaster, was born in 660 B.C. He began preaching after seeing **visions** as a young man.

Like the Jews, Zoroaster believed in one god. He viewed this supreme being as the creator of all things and a force of goodness. However, Zoroaster recognized evil in the world, too. He taught that humans had the freedom to choose between right and wrong, and that goodness would triumph in the end. The Persians practiced Zoroastrianism for centuries, and it still has a small number of followers today.

✓ **Reading Check** **Explain** What did Darius do to make his government work better?

King Darius

Darius helped to organize the Persian government. *What methods did he use?*

The Persian Wars

Main Idea Both Sparta and Athens played roles in defeating the Persians.

Reading Connection Have you and a rival ever set aside your differences to work for a common cause? This happened in ancient Greece when Sparta and Athens came together to fight the Persians. Read about the outcome.

As the Greeks set up colonies in the Mediterranean area, they often clashed with the Persians. By the mid-500s B.C., Persia already controlled the Greek cities in Asia Minor. In 499 B.C. the Athenian army helped the Greeks in Asia Minor rebel against their Persian rulers. The rebellion failed, but King Darius decided the mainland Greeks had to be stopped from interfering in the Persian Empire.

The Battle of Marathon In 490 B.C. a Persian fleet landed 20,000 soldiers on the plain of **Marathon** (MAR•uh•THAHN), only a short distance from Athens. For several days, the Persians waited there for the Athenians to advance. The Athenians, however, did not take the bait. They had only 10,000 soldiers compared to the Persians' 20,000. They knew that attacking was too dangerous. Instead they held back in the hills overlooking the plain.

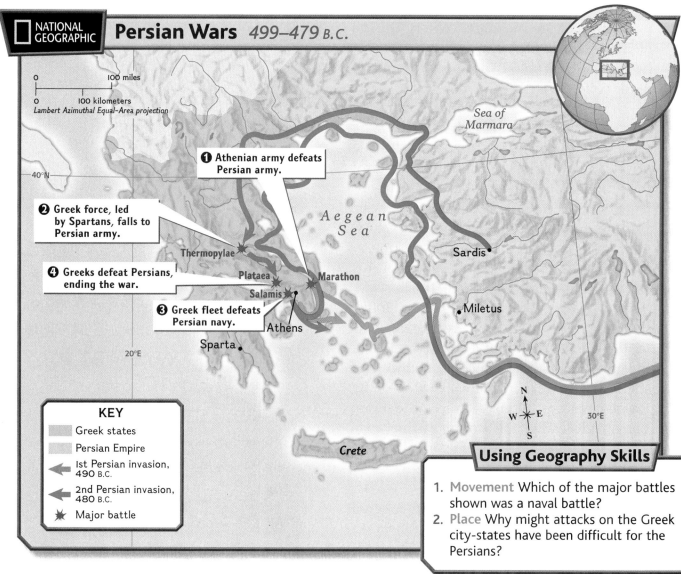

NATIONAL GEOGRAPHIC

Persian Wars 499–479 B.C.

0 100 miles
0 100 kilometers
Lambert Azimuthal Equal-Area projection

40°N

Sea of Marmara

❶ Athenian army defeats Persian army.

❷ Greek force, led by Spartans, falls to Persian army.

Aegean Sea

Thermopylae

Sardis

❹ Greeks defeat Persians, ending the war.

Plataea

Marathon

Salamis

❸ Greek fleet defeats Persian navy.

Athens

Miletus

Sparta

20°E

N
W—E
S

30°E

Crete

KEY

Greek states

Persian Empire

1st Persian invasion, 490 B.C.

2nd Persian invasion, 480 B.C.

✳ Major battle

Using Geography Skills

1. **Movement** Which of the major battles shown was a naval battle?
2. **Place** Why might attacks on the Greek city-states have been difficult for the Persians?

Tired of waiting, the Persian commander decided to sail south and attack Athens directly. He ordered his troops back onto the ships, and it was then that he made a big mistake. The first to board, he decided, would be the horsemen in the cavalry, the strongest part of the Persian army.

As soon as the cavalry was out of fighting range, the Greeks charged down from the hills and onto the plain of Marathon. They caught the Persian foot soldiers standing in the water, waiting their turn to board the ships. Unable to defend themselves, the Persians were easily defeated.

According to legend, the Athenians sent a messenger named Pheidippides (fy•DIHP•uh•DEEZ) home with the news. The runner raced nearly 25 miles (40.2 km) from Marathon to Athens. He collapsed from exhaustion and, with his last breath, announced, "Victory." Then he died. Modern marathon races are named for this famous run and are just over 26 miles long.

Another Persian Strike After Darius died in 486 B.C., his son **Xerxes** (ZUHRK•SEEZ) became the Persian king. Xerxes vowed revenge against the Athenians. In 480 B.C. he launched a new invasion of Greece, this time with about 180,000 troops and thousands of warships and supply vessels.

To defend themselves, the Greeks joined forces. Sparta sent the most soldiers, and their king, Leonidas (lee•AH•nuh•duhs), served as commander. Athens provided the navy. An Athenian general, **Themistocles** (thuh•MIHS•tuh•KLEEZ), created a plan to fight the Persians.

The Greeks knew that as the huge Persian army marched south, it depended on shipments of food brought in by boat. Themistocles argued that the Greeks' best strategy would be to attack the Persians' ships and cut off food supplies to the army.

To ready their fleet for battle, the Greeks needed to stall the Persian army before it reached Athens. The Greeks decided the best place to block the Persians was at **Thermopylae** (thuhr•MAH•puh•lee). Thermopylae was a narrow pass through the mountains that was easy to defend. About 7,000 Greek soldiers held off the Persians there for two days. The Spartans in the Greek army were especially brave. As one story has it, the Greeks heard that Persian arrows would darken the sky. A Spartan warrior responded, "That is good news. We will fight in the shade!"

Unfortunately for the Greeks, a traitor exposed a mountain path to the Persians that led them around the Greeks. As the Persians mounted a rear attack, King Leonidas sent most of his troops to safety. He and several hundred others, however, stayed behind and fought to the death. The Greeks lost the battle at Thermopylae, but their valiant stand gave Athens enough time to assemble 200 ships.

The Greek fleet attacked the Persian fleet in the strait of **Salamis** (SA•luh•muhs), not far from Athens. A strait is a narrow strip of water between two pieces of land. The Greeks expected to have the upper hand in the battle because their ships could maneuver well in tight spaces. Greek ships were smaller, faster, and easier to steer than the big Persian ships, which became easy targets.

The Greek plan worked. After a ferocious battle, the Greeks destroyed almost the entire Persian fleet. Still, the Persian army marched on. When their troops reached Athens, the Greeks had already fled.

The Persians burned the city. This only stiffened the resolve of the Greek city-states.

Battle of Salamis

At the Battle of Salamis, smaller, faster Greek ships defeated the Persian fleet. *Near what Greek city-state was the strait of Salamis located?*

In early 479 B.C., they came together to form the largest Greek army ever assembled. With solid body armor, longer spears, and better training, the Greek army crushed the Persian army at **Plataea** (pluh•TEE•uh), northwest of Athens.

The battle was a turning point for the Greeks, convincing the Persians to retreat to Asia Minor. By working together, the Greek city-states had saved their homeland from invasion.

What Caused the Persian Empire to Fall?

When the Greeks defeated the Persian army, they helped to weaken it. The empire was already affected by **internal** problems. As these problems worsened, the empire would gradually lose its strength.

Persia remained intact for almost 150 more years. However, after Darius and Xerxes, other Persian rulers raised taxes to gain more wealth. They spent the gold and silver that flowed into the treasuries on luxuries for the royal court.

The high taxes angered their subjects and caused many rebellions. At the same time, the Persian royal family fought over who was to be king. Many of the later Persian kings were killed by other family members who wanted the throne.

Persian kings had many wives and children. The sons had little, if any, power so they were constantly plotting to take over the throne. As a result of such plots, six of the nine rulers after Darius were murdered.

All of these problems made Persia vulnerable to attack. By the time a young Greek conqueror named Alexander invaded the empire in 334 B.C., the Persians were no match for his troops.

By 330 B.C., the last Persian king was dead and Alexander ruled over all his lands. You will learn more about Alexander the Great and his many achievements in Chapter 8.

✓ **Reading Check** **Cause and Effect** What led to the Persian Wars?

History Online

Study Central Need help understanding Persia or the Persian wars? Visit ca.hss.glencoe.com and click on Study Central.

Section 3 Review

Reading Summary

Review the **Main Ideas**

- The Persian Empire united its many lands under a single government.

- The Persian Empire attacked Greece several times. Despite their rivalry, Athens and Sparta joined forces to defeat the Persians.

What Did You Learn?

1. Why was Cyrus considered a fair ruler?

2. What was the Royal Road?

Critical Thinking

3. **Summarize** Draw a table like the one below. Then summarize what happened at each battle in the Persian Wars. **CA** 6RC2.4

Battle	Action
Marathon Thermopylae Salamis Plataea	

4. **The Big Ideas** Imagine you are an adviser to Xerxes and are alarmed about his plan for revenge on Greece. Compose a letter to him listing possible outcomes of the war. **CA** 6WS1.1; 6WA2.5

5. **Analysis** Determining Context Reread the Primary Source quote on page 355. Does it matter that the quote comes from a Greek? Write an essay discussing different ways the quote can be interpreted. **CA** HR5.

Section 4

The Age of Pericles

Guide to Reading

Looking Back, Looking Ahead

In Section 3, you learned how the Greeks defeated the Persians at Plataea. One lesson the Greeks drew from the war was that they needed each other for security. Athens and several other city-states soon banded together in a league for the common defense.

Focusing on the Main Ideas

- Under Pericles, Athens became very powerful and more democratic. **(page 359)**

- Athenian men and women had very different roles. **(page 362)**

- Sparta and Athens went to war for control of Greece. **(page 364)**

Locating Places

Delos (DEE•LAHS)

Meeting People

Pericles (PEHR•uh•KLEEZ)
Aspasia (as•PAY•zhuh)

Content Vocabulary

direct democracy (dih•MAH•kruh•see)
representative democracy (REH•prih•ZEHN•tuh•tihv)
philosopher (fuh•LAH•suh•fuhr)

Academic Vocabulary

behalf (bih•HAF)
economy (ih•KAH•nuh•mee)
framework (FRAYM•WUHRK)

Reading Strategy

Organizing Information Create a circle graph to show how many citizens, foreigners, and enslaved people lived in Athens in the 400s B.C.

History Social Science Standards

WH6.4 Students analyze the geographic, political, economic, religious, and social structures of the early civilizations of Ancient Greece.

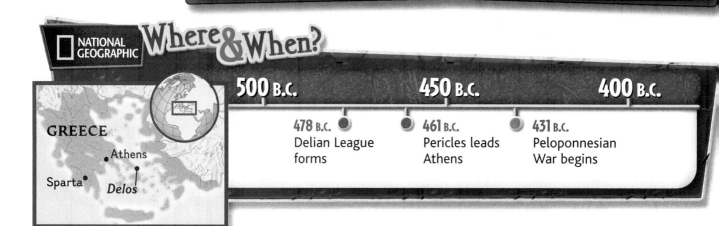

NATIONAL GEOGRAPHIC Where&When?

GREECE
Athens
Sparta•
Delos

500 B.C.	450 B.C.	400 B.C.
478 B.C. Delian League forms	**461 B.C.** Pericles leads Athens	**431 B.C.** Peloponnesian War begins

WH6.4.3 State the key differences between Athenian, or direct, democracy and representative democracy.

The Athenian Empire

Main Idea Under Pericles, Athens became very powerful and more democratic.

Reading Connection Do you vote in school elections? Why do you choose one classmate over another? Read to learn why Athenians kept electing Pericles.

As you read in Section 3, the Battle of Plataea in 479 B.C. put an end to the Persians' invasion of Greece. Although the Persians retreated, they still remained a threat. In 478 B.C. Athens joined with other city-states—but not Sparta—to form the Delian League.

The Delian League promised to defend its members against the Persians. It also worked to drive Persia out of Greek territories in Asia Minor. Eventually, the league freed almost all of the Greek cities under Persia's control.

At its start, the Delian League had headquarters on the island of **Delos** (DEE•LAHS). However, its chief officials—the treasurers in charge of its money and the commanders in charge of its fleet—were from Athens, as were most of the troops. Little by little, Athens gained control over the other city-states in the alliance. Soon the league was no longer a partnership to fight Persia but an Athenian empire.

In 454 B.C. the Athenians moved the Delian League's treasury from Delos to Athens. The Athenians also began sending troops to other Greek city-states, to help the common people rebel against the nobles in power.

Democracy in Athens Athenians had a strong faith in their democratic system. We call their system **direct democracy** (dih•MAH•kruh•see). In a direct democracy, people gather at mass meetings to decide on government matters. Every citizen can vote firsthand on laws and policies.

▲ These ruins are of the agora—an ancient marketplace in Athens where the assembly met. *What type of democracy did Athens have?*

Can you imagine such a system in the United States? A mass meeting of our millions of citizens would be impossible! Instead, in the United States we have a **representative democracy** (REH•prih•ZEHN•tuh•tihv). Under this type of democracy, citizens choose a smaller group to make laws and governmental decisions on their **behalf.** This is a much more practical system when the population is large.

What made direct democracy workable in ancient Athens was the relatively small number of citizens. In the mid-400s B.C., about 43,000 male citizens over 18 years old made up the assembly. Usually fewer than 6,000 attended the meetings, which were held every 10 days. The assembly passed all laws, elected officials, and made decisions on war and foreign affairs. Ten officials known as generals carried out the assembly's laws and policies.

Comparing Governments

	Athenian Democracy	American Democracy
Type of Democracy	Direct	Representative
Right to Vote	Only adult males born in Athens	All citizens, male and female age 18 or over
Laws	Proposed by the council and approved by a majority in the assembly	Approved by both houses of Congress and signed by the president
Citizen Involvement	Citizens with voting rights can vote for or against any law	Citizens with voting rights can vote for or against the officials who make the laws

Understanding Charts

The small number of citizens made a direct democracy possible in Athens.

1. In Athens, how was a law approved?
2. Compare Which government granted the right to vote to more of its population?

The Achievements of Pericles Athenians reelected their favorite generals again and again. After the Persian Wars, the leading figure in Athenian politics was a general named **Pericles** (PEHR•uh•KLEEZ). This great statesman guided Athens for more than 30 years, from 461 B.C., when he was first elected, until 429 B.C., shortly before his death.

Pericles helped Athens dominate the Delian League. He treated the other city-states like subjects, demanding strict loyalty and steady payments from them. He even insisted that they use Athenian coins and measures.

At the same time, Pericles made Athens more democratic at home. He believed that people's talents were more important than their social standing. For this reason, Pericles included more Athenians than ever before in government. He allowed lower-class male citizens to run for public office, and he also paid officeholders. As a result, even poor citizens could, for the first time, be part of the inner circle running the government.

Culture also blossomed under the rule of Pericles. The Age of Pericles was a period of tremendous creativity and learning that peaked in the mid-400s B.C. The Persians had destroyed much of the city during the Persian Wars. So Pericles started a major rebuilding program. He had new temples and statues built across the city.

Pericles supported artists, architects, writers, and **philosophers** (fuh•LAH•suh•fuhrs). Philosophers are thinkers who ponder questions about life. In Chapter 8, you will read more about the Greeks' achievements and understand why Pericles called Athens "the school of Greece."

Reading Check **Identify** What is the difference between a direct democracy and a representative democracy?

Biography

WH6.4.2 Trace the transition from tyranny and oligarchy to early democratic forms of government and back to dictatorship in ancient Greece, including the significance of the invention of the idea of citizenship (e.g., from *Pericles' Funeral Oration*).

PERICLES
c. 495–429 B.C.

Pericles was born just outside Athens, to a wealthy and powerful family. He received his education from philosophers. As a young man, he was known for his skill with words. Later, when he became a political leader, he strongly supported democracy.

Although he was from a wealthy family himself, he believed that citizenship should not be limited to the wealthy and powerful. He made changes to take power from the few and give it to the many. However, in describing Pericles' rule over Athens, Greek historian Thucydides wrote "In name democracy, but in fact the rule of one man."

The "Age of Pericles" was Athens's Golden Age, and the city blossomed under his leadership. Pericles wanted Athens to be a model for the world. He made it a centerpiece of art, philosophy, and democracy.

Pericles' goal was to make Athens a city that Greeks could be proud of. He hired hundreds of workers to construct public buildings in Athens. The most well known is the Parthenon. Based on the value of money today, it cost about $3 billion to build. Workers hauled 20,000 tons of marble from a nearby mountain and spent almost 15 years completing it.

Pericles ▶

> "Athens...is the school of Greece."
> —*Pericles*, as recorded by Thucydides

Pericles was a private person. He avoided being in public as much as possible. He spent most of his time alone, with family, or with close friends. He married and had three sons. In 429 B.C. Pericles died from the plague.

▲ The Parthenon sits at the top of the Acropolis.

Then and Now

Consider what Thucydides wrote about Pericles' rule in Athens. Do research to find out how the U.S. Constitution ensures that our government is not dominated by one leader.

Daily Life in Athens

Main Idea Athenian men and women had very different roles.

Reading Connection School may be difficult at times, but how would you feel if you could not go to school? Read on to learn about the limits placed on some Athenians.

In the 400s B.C., more people lived in Athens than in any other Greek city-state. Athens had about 285,000 residents in all. Some 150,000 were citizens, although only 43,000 of these were men with political rights. Foreigners in Athens numbered about 35,000. The population also included about 100,000 enslaved people.

Roles of Men and Women Athenian men usually worked in the morning and then exercised or attended meetings of the assembly. In the evenings, upper-class men enjoyed all-male gatherings where they drank, dined, and discussed politics and philosophy.

For Athenian women, life revolved around home and family. Girls married early—at 14 or 15—and were expected to

Athenian Homes

Many wealthy Athenians had large homes made of mud bricks and tiled roofs. They had many small windows to let light and air in the house. *Where are religious influences seen in the house?*

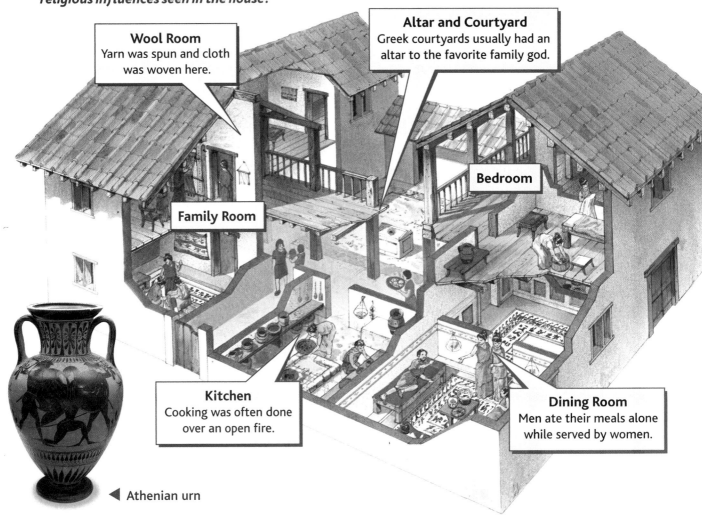

Wool Room
Yarn was spun and cloth was woven here.

Altar and Courtyard
Greek courtyards usually had an altar to the favorite family god.

Bedroom

Family Room

Kitchen
Cooking was often done over an open fire.

Dining Room
Men ate their meals alone while served by women.

◀ Athenian urn

have children and take care of household duties. Poor women might also work with their husbands in the fields or sell goods in the agora. Respectable upper-class women, however, stayed at home. They supervised the household servants and worked wool into cloth—spinning, dyeing, and weaving it. They rarely went out, except to funerals or festivals. Even then, they could leave the house only if a male relative went with them.

Although Athenian women could not attend school, many learned to read and to play music. Still, even educated women were not considered the equals of men. They had no political rights and could not own property. Fathers took charge of unmarried daughters. Husbands looked after their wives. Sons or other male relatives looked after the welfare of widows.

A few women did move more freely in public life. **Aspasia** (as•PAY•zhuh) is perhaps the most famous example. Aspasia was not a native Athenian. This gave her special status. She was well-educated and taught public speaking to many Athenians. Her writings have not survived, but Plato, the famous Greek philosopher, said her work helped shape his ideas. Pericles often consulted Aspasia, as did many other Athenian leaders. In this way, she became influential in politics even though she was not allowed to vote or hold office.

Slavery in Athens Most people in the ancient world considered slavery to be a normal way of life, even the enslaved people. Athens was no exception. Slavery was common even in the city of democracy.

Most Athenian homes had at least one enslaved person, and wealthy Athenian households often had many. Many of the enslaved were people Athenians had captured in battle with non-Greeks. Sometimes Greeks were also enslaved after being taken prisoner during a war by other Greeks.

Enslaved men usually worked on projects requiring heavy labor. Enslaved women and children become cooks and maids in Greek homes. Educated slaves sometimes became tutors to the children in the home. Others worked in the fields and in artisans' shops.

Enslaved people were treated differently from place to place. Those working in the mines often died at a young age. Skilled slaves often worked with citizens creating their crafts. A few held positions of privilege, such as overseers on farms. In some instances, they were able to earn money and even buy their freedom, but this did not happen very often. The Greek city-states depended on enslaved labor. Without it, Athens could not have supported its bustling **economy.**

What Drove the Athenian Economy?

Many Athenians depended on farming for a living. Herders raised sheep and goats for wool, milk, and cheese. Some farmers grew grains, vegetables, and fruit for local use. Others grew grapes and olives to make wine and olive oil to sell abroad.

Athens did not have enough farmland to grow crops for all its people. As a result, the city had to import grain from other places. This had much to do with Athens's geographic location. Athens was located near the coast of Greece in the middle of Greek civilization.

The city built a large fleet of ships to trade with colonies and other city-states in the Mediterranean. During the 400s B.C., Athens became an important crossroads for people, ideas, and goods traveling through the region. Merchants and artisans grew wealthy by making and selling pottery, jewelry, leather goods, and other items.

Reading Check **Describe** How did Athenian men and women spend their time?

WH6.4.2 Trace the transition from tyranny and oligarchy to early democratic forms of government and back to dictatorship in ancient Greece, including the significance of the invention of the idea of citizenship (e.g., from *Pericles' Funeral Oration*).

WH6.4.6 Compare and contrast life in Athens and Sparta, with emphasis on their roles in the Persian and Peloponnesian Wars.

NATIONAL GEOGRAPHIC — The Way It Was

Focus on Everyday Life

Women's Duties In ancient Athens, a woman's place was in the home. Her two main responsibilities were caring for the household and raising children. The Greek writer Xenophon (ZEH•nuh•fuhn) recorded a man's explanation of women's duties.

"Thus your duty will be to remain indoors and send out those servants whose work is outside, and superintend those who are to work indoors . . . . And when wool is brought to you, you must see that cloaks are made for those that want them. You must see too that the dry corn is in good condition for making food."

—Xenophon, *Memorabilia and Oeconomicus*

The second floor of each home was the women's quarters. An Athenian woman lived there with her children. She was expected to keep her children well and happy. She encouraged them to learn sports and play with toys, and taught them how to interact with friends and family members. Some boys went to school, while the girls stayed at home.

▲ Greek woman and servant

Connecting to the Past
1. Why do you think women and children lived on the second floor of the home?
2. Over what areas of life did an Athenian woman have authority?

The Peloponnesian War

Main Idea Sparta and Athens went to war for control of Greece.

Reading Connection Have you ever tried to get people to work together and been frustrated when they will not cooperate? Read to find out how the Greek city-states' refusal to cooperate nearly led to their destruction.

As the Athenian empire became rich and powerful, other city-states, especially Sparta, grew suspicious of Athenian aims. Sparta and Athens had built two very different kinds of societies, and neither state understood or trusted the other. After the Persian Wars, both city-states desired to be the major power in the Greek world. They clashed over this goal several times between 460 B.C. and 445 B.C. In this year, Athens and Sparta signed a peace treaty.

Conflict Between Athens and Sparta In the years following the Persian Wars, Sparta suffered from a major earthquake and the revolt of the helots. Both of these events weakened Sparta for some time. Meanwhile, Athens continued gaining more control over its empire, sometimes using its military to force other city-states to pay tribute. Between 460 B.C. and 450 B.C., Athens was able to gain a land empire near Thebes and Corinth. However, these city-states were able to throw off Athenian control by 446 B.C. Both Corinth and Thebes remained distrustful of Athens and became allies with Sparta.

Although Athens had lost some of its land in mainland Greece, it grew by gaining influence over other city-states and by settling colonies. Sometimes Athenian colonists fought with other Greeks who lived nearby because the Athenians were too aggressive. This angered Sparta, but the Spartans were not yet ready to declare war.

However, in 433 B.C. Athenian activities interfered directly with some of Sparta's allies. These allies began pushing Sparta to attack Athens. Finally, war broke out in 431 B.C. It would drag on until 404 B.C. and shatter any possibility of future cooperation among the Greeks. Historians call this conflict the Peloponnesian War because Sparta was located in the Peloponnesus.

Pericles' Funeral Oration In the first winter of the war, the Athenians held a public funeral. Its purpose was to honor those who had died in battle. The relatives of the dead wept for their loved ones. The rest of the citizens joined in a procession.

As was the custom, a leading Athenian addressed the crowd. On this day, Pericles spoke. He talked about the greatness of Athens and reminded the people that they made their government strong.

In this famous speech, called the Funeral Oration, Pericles pointed out that Athenians were part of a community. As citizens, they agreed to obey the rules in their constitution—their **framework** of government.

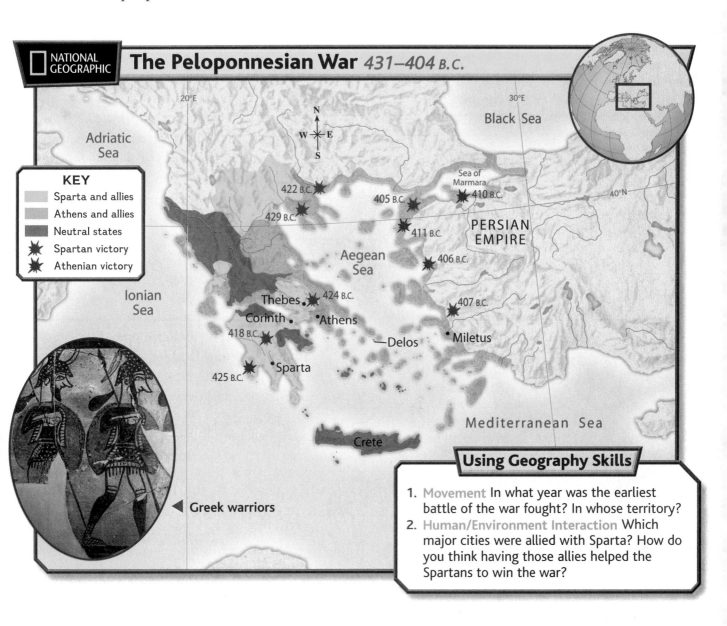

NATIONAL GEOGRAPHIC

The Peloponnesian War 431–404 B.C.

KEY
- Sparta and allies
- Athens and allies
- Neutral states
- ✳ Spartan victory
- ✳ Athenian victory

Adriatic Sea

Black Sea

Sea of Marmara

422 B.C.

405 B.C.

410 B.C.

429 B.C.

411 B.C.

PERSIAN EMPIRE

Aegean Sea

406 B.C.

Ionian Sea

Thebes • 424 B.C.

407 B.C.

Corinth • • Athens

418 B.C.

—Delos

• Miletus

425 B.C.

• Sparta

Mediterranean Sea

Crete

◄ Greek warriors

Using Geography Skills

1. **Movement** In what year was the earliest battle of the war fought? In whose territory?
2. **Human/Environment Interaction** Which major cities were allied with Sparta? How do you think having those allies helped the Spartans to win the war?

They accepted certain duties, such as paying taxes and defending the city. They also gained certain rights, such as the ability to vote and run for office. Pericles' speech reminded Athenians of the power of democracy and gave them the courage to keep fighting. Its ideas are still important for people living in democratic nations today.

Primary Source

Pericles' Funeral Oration

Pericles was a dominant figure in Athenian politics between 461 B.C. and 429 B.C., a period historians call the Age of Pericles. In his Funeral Oration, given during the Peloponnesian War, Pericles described democracy, the importance of the individual, and citizenship.

▲ Pericles

"Our constitution is called a democracy because power is in the hands not of a minority but of the whole people. When it is a question of settling private disputes, everyone is equal before the law; when it is a question of putting one person before another in positions of public responsibility, what counts is not membership of a particular class, but the actual ability which the man possesses. No one . . . is kept [out of government] because of poverty. And, just as our political life is free and open, so is our day-to-day life in our relations with each other."

—Pericles, as recorded by Thucydides, *History of the Peloponnesian War*

DBQ Document-Based Question

When Pericles said "everyone is equal before the law," what did he mean?

Why Was Athens Defeated? At the beginning of the Peloponnesian War, both Sparta and Athens thought they knew how to win. The Spartans and their allies surrounded Athens. They hoped that the Athenians would send out an army to fight. However, Pericles knew that Spartan forces could beat the Athenians in open battles. Believing his people would be safe behind the city walls, he urged farmers and others on the outskirts to move inside the city. There Athenians stayed put and had the navy deliver supplies from their colonies and allies. Because Sparta did not have a navy, it could not attack the Athenian ships.

Athens escaped serious harm for some time. Then, in the second year of the war, a deadly disease spread through the overcrowded city. It killed more than a third of the people, including Pericles himself in 429 B.C. Despite these terrible losses, the Athenians fought on. Over the next 25 years, each side won victories but did not have the strength to defeat the other city-state.

The historian Thucydides recorded what he saw:

❝ This, then, was the calamity which fell upon Athens, and the times were hard indeed, with men dying inside the city and the land outside being laid waste. ❞

—Thucydides, *History of the Peloponnesian War*

Finally, desperate to win, the Spartans made a deal with the Persian Empire. In exchange for enough money to build a navy, they gave the Persians some Greek territory in Asia Minor.

In 405 B.C. Sparta's new navy destroyed the Athenian fleet. The next year, after losing more battles on land, Athens surrendered.

The Spartans and their allies then tore down the city walls and broke up the Athenian empire.

The Results of the War The Peloponnesian War weakened all of the major Greek city-states, both the winners and the losers. Many people died in the fighting, and many farms were destroyed. Thousands of people were left without jobs. It was an extremely difficult time.

After defeating Athens, Sparta created its own empire. However, the Spartans soon began creating enemies among their allies, much as the Athenians had before. Over the next 30 years, Sparta fought Persia again and then tried to maintain control of rebellious allies. Finally, in 371 B.C., Sparta fell to an army led by Thebes. This city-state held a position of leadership in Greece for less than 10 years before collapsing.

◄ Thucydides is one of the greatest ancient historians. He fought in the Peloponnesian War for Athens and recorded the events he witnessed.

The Greek city-states continued to fight among themselves, growing progressively weaker. All the while, they failed to notice that to their north, the kingdom of Macedonia was growing in power. This would eventually cost them their freedom.

✓ **Reading Check** **Cause and Effect** What effects did the Peloponnesian War have on Greece?

Study Central Need help understanding the causes of the Peloponnesian War? Visit ca.hss.glencoe.com and click on Study Central.

Section 4 Review

Reading Summary

Review the Main Ideas

- Democracy and culture in Athens flourished under the leadership of Pericles.

- Athenian men worked as farmers, artisans, and merchants, while most women stayed secluded at home.

- Athens and Sparta fought each other in the Peloponnesian War. The fighting led to the defeat of Athens and the weakening of all the Greek states.

What Did You Learn?

1. What caused the Peloponnesian War?

2. According to Pericles, what duties did Athenian citizens have?

Critical Thinking

3. **Summarize** Use a chart like the one below to summarize what Athens was like in the Age of Pericles. **CA 6RC2.4**

Government	
Economy	
Culture	
Wars	

4. **Analyze** What caused the lack of trust between Sparta and Athens? **CA HI2.**

5. **The Big Ideas** Under Pericles' leadership, the economy of Athens grew. Which groups of workers were important to this growth? **CA 6RC2.0**

6. **Civics Link** How did the direct democracy of Athens differ from the democracy we have in the United States? **CA 6RC2.2**

7. **Expository Writing** Describe the role of the Delian League in the creation of the Athenian empire. **CA 6WA2.2**

Analyzing Primary Sources

WH6.4.4 Explain the significance of Greek mythology to the everyday life of people in the region and how Greek literature continues to permeate our literature and language today, drawing from Greek mythology and epics, such as Homer's *Iliad* and *Odyssey*, and from *Aesop's Fables*. **WH6.4.8** Describe the enduring contributions of important Greek figures in the arts and sciences (e.g., Hypatia, Socrates, Plato, Aristotle, Euclid, Thucydides).

Greek Historians

Writing history is not easy. The ancient Greeks wrote many histories, but their approach changed over time. Three of the most famous Greek writers are Homer, Herodotus, and Thucydides. They wrote at different times, and each explained historical events in a different way.

Read the passages on pages 368 and 369, and answer the questions that follow. Pay attention to how each writer explains events.

Homer ▶

Reader's Dictionary

Hector: a prince of Troy

Deïphobus (day•ee•FOH•buhs): a powerful fighter from Troy

Paris: brother of Hector and a prince of Troy

Priam (PREE•uhm): father of Hector and Paris

Helen: a beautiful Greek woman who was kidnapped by Paris, causing the Trojan War.

Medea (meh•DEE•uh): a woman the Greeks had kidnapped from the Persians

Homer's *Iliad*

Homer's Iliad *tells the story of the Trojan War and shows how early Greeks explained events. In this excerpt, the Trojan warrior Hector realizes that he will be killed by Achilles.*

And **Hector** let his heavy javelin fly,
A good throw, too, hitting Achilles' shield
Dead center, but it only rebounded away.
Angry that his throw was wasted, Hector
Fumbled about for a moment, reaching
For another spear. He shouted to
    Deïphobus,

But Deïphobus was nowhere in sight.
It was then that Hector knew in his heart
What had happened, and said to himself:

"I hear the gods calling me to my death.
I thought I had a good man here with me,
Deïphobus, but he's still on the wall.
Athena tricked me. Death is closing in
And there's no escape. Zeus and Apollo
Must have chosen this long ago, even though
They used to be on my side. My fate is here,
    But I will not perish without some great deed
    That future generations will remember."

—Homer, *Iliad*

The Histories by Herodotus

Herodotus often tried to provide sources for his history. Here he gives one of the reasons he believes the Greeks and the Persians did not like each other. the mythological story about how the Greeks had kidnapped the woman Medea from people in the land near Troy.

Paris, the son of **Priam,** was inspired . . . to steal a wife for himself out of Greece, being confident that he would not have to pay for the venture any more than the Greeks had done. And that was how he came to carry off **Helen.**

The first idea of the Greeks . . . was to send a demand for satisfaction and for Helen's return. The demand was met by a reference to the seizure of **Medea** and the injustice of expecting satisfaction from people to whom they themselves had refused it, not to mention the fact that they had kept the girl.

. . . [T]he Greeks, merely on account of a girl from Sparta, raised a big army, invaded Asia and destroyed the empire of Priam. From that root sprang their belief in the perpetual enmity of the Grecian world towards them—Asia with its various foreign-speaking peoples belonging to the Persians, Europe and the Greek states being, in their opinion, quite separate and distinct from them.

Such then is the Persian story. In their view it was the capture of Troy that first made them the enemies of the Greeks.

—Herodotus, *The Histories*

Thucydides' *History of the Peloponnesian War*

Thucydides took great care to analyze the causes of events and the sources for his history. In this passage, he discusses a terrible plague that hit Athens in 430 B.C.

▲ **Thucydides**

The most terrible thing of all was the despair into which people fell when they realized that they had caught the plague; for they would immediately adopt an attitude of utter hopelessness, and, by giving in this way, would lose their powers of resistance. Terrible, too, was the sight of people dying like sheep through having caught the disease as a result of nursing others. This indeed caused more deaths than anything else. For when people were afraid to visit the sick, then they died with no one to look after them; indeed, there were many houses in which all the inhabitants perished through lack of any attention. When, on the other hand, they did visit the sick, they lost their own lives.

—Thucydides, *History of the Peloponnesian War*

DBQ Document-Based Questions

Homer's Iliad
1. What does Hector think Athena did?
2. Why does Hector believe he is going to die?

The Histories *by Herodotus*
3. Why does Paris think he can get away with kidnapping Helen?
4. What does Herodotus's use of myths say about how he wrote his history?

Thucydides' History of the Peloponnesian War
5. According to Thucydides, what caused more deaths than anything else during the plague?
6. What caused people to lose their powers of resistance?

Read to Write
7. Which passage seems the most reliable? Why? How is Thucydides' approach to history different from the way Homer and Herodotus explain events? **CA 6RC2.6** **CA HR5.**

Review Content Vocabulary

Write the vocabulary word that completes each sentence. Write a sentence for each word not used.

a. satrap
b. agora
c. democracy
d. direct democracy
e. oligarchy
f. peninsula

1. In a(n) ___, a few wealthy people hold power.
2. The Greek mainland is a(n) ___, a body of land with water on three sides.
3. In a(n) ___, people at mass meetings make decisions for the government.
4. A(n) ___ acted as tax collector, judge, chief of police, and army recruiter.

Review the Main Ideas

Section 1 • The Early Greeks

5. How did the geography of Greece influence where people settled and how they made a living?
6. How did the building of ships affect Minoan civilization?
7. Which group built the first Greek kingdoms?
8. How did the Greek colonies help industry to grow?
9. What are Greek city-states also known as?

Section 2 • Sparta and Athens

10. Why were tyrants able to seize control from Greek nobles?
11. Who did the Spartans fear most within their city-states?
12. Describe the differences between Athens and Sparta.

Section 3 • Persia Attacks the Greeks

13. What system did Darius use to unite his large empire under one government?
14. Why did Sparta and Athens unite during the Persian Wars?

Section 4 • The Age of Pericles

15. How was democracy expanded during the Age of Pericles?
16. What were the main duties of women in Athens?
17. What was the result of the Peloponnesian War?

Critical Thinking

18. **Cause and Effect** How did the geography of Greece help to encourage trade? **CA CS3.**
19. **Conclude** Did the people of ancient Athens have a full democracy? Explain. **CA 6RC2.0**
20. **Explain** Do you think people would enjoy more freedom in an oligarchy or a tyranny? Explain. **CA 6RC2.2**

Geography Skills

Study the map below and answer the following questions.

21. **Place** What sea lies along the west coast of Greece? **CA CS3.**
22. **Location** Where was Knossos? **CA CS3.**
23. **Movement** If you traveled from Athens to Troy, in what direction would you be going? **CA CS3.**

NATIONAL GEOGRAPHIC **Ancient Greece**

Read to Write

24. **The Big Ideas** **Writing Research Reports**
Write an essay explaining how democracy helped create a strong and stable society in Greece. **CA 6WA2.3**

25. **Using Your FOLDABLES** Use the information from your completed chapter opener fold-ables to create a brief study guide for the chapter. Your study guide should include at least five questions for each section. Questions should focus on the main ideas. Exchange your study guide with a partner and answer each of the questions. **CA HR1.**

Using Academic Vocabulary

26. Separate the words below into three categories: Verbs, Nouns, and Adjectives. Keep in mind that some of the words can be placed in more than one column.

region	participate
culture	economy
overseas	vision
community	internal
enforce	framework

Linking Past and Present

27. **Making Comparisons** Choose a person mentioned in Chapter 7. Write a description of someone in the news today who has similar ideas or has acted in similar ways. List some of their similarities. **CA 6WA2.0**

Building Citizenship

28. **Analyze** Democracy is not easy to achieve or maintain. Make a chart like the one below to identify things that challenged or threatened democracy in Athens. **CA HI2.**

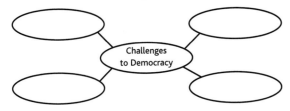

Reviewing Skills

29. **Reading Skill** **Comparing and Contrasting** Write an essay comparing and contrasting the Persian Empire to the Greek city-states. Explain how these similarities and differences affected the result of the Persian Wars. **CA WS1.3**

30. **Analysis Skill** **Facts and Opinions** Reread the quotations from Xenophon (page 364) and Pericles (page 366). Determine whether these statements are facts or opinions. Write a paragraph about each quotation explaining your decision. **CA HR2.; HR5.**

Standards Practice

Read the passage below and answer the following question.

> "My intent is to . . . march an army through Europe against Greece, that thereby I may obtain vengeance from the Athenians for the wrongs committed by them . . ."

31 **The above words were spoken by the leader of which group of people?**

A the Romans

B the Athenians

C the Persians

D the Minoans

Greek Civilization

The temple of Delphi was very important to ancient Greeks. Many people believed the priestess here could foretell the future. ▶

NATIONAL GEOGRAPHIC

Where & When?

400 B.C.	300 B.C.	200 B.C.
399 B.C. Socrates sentenced to death	**330** B.C. Alexander the Great conquers Persian Empire	**c. 287** B.C. Mathematician and inventor Archimedes is born

The Big Ideas

History Online
Chapter Overview Visit ca.hss.glencoe.com for a preview of Chapter 8.

Section 1 The Culture of Ancient Greece

Studying the past helps us to understand the present. The Greeks made great strides in the arts. Greek poetry, art, and drama are still part of our world today.

Section 2 Greek Philosophy and History

Civilizations are strengthened by a variety of advances. The Greeks' love of wisdom led to the study of history, politics, biology, and logic.

Section 3 Alexander the Great

Conflict often brings about great change. Alexander the Great was only 25 years old when he conquered the Persian Empire. As a result of his conquests, Greek art, ideas, language, and architecture spread throughout southwest Asia and North Africa.

Section 4 The Spread of Greek Culture

As different societies interact, they often bring about change in each other. Greek cities became centers of learning and culture. Greek scientists developed advanced ideas about astronomy and mathematics.

 View the Chapter 8 video in the Glencoe Video Program.

FOLDABLES™ Study Organizer

Organizing Information *Make the following foldable to help you organize information about Greek culture and philosophy.*

Step 1 *Fold two sheets of paper in half from top to bottom.*

Fold both sheets to leave $\frac{1}{2}$ inch tab on top.

Step 2 *Place glue or tape along both $\frac{1}{2}$ inch tabs.*

Step 3 *Fit both sheets of paper together to make a cube as shown.*

Step 4 *Turn the cube and label the foldable as shown.*

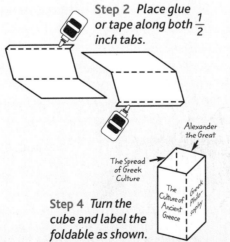

Alexander the Great

The Spread of Greek Culture

The Culture of Ancient Greece

Greek Philosophy

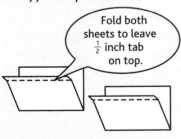

Reading and Writing
As you read the chapter, list the developments that occurred in ancient Greece. Write the developments under the correct foldable category.

Visualizing

Reading Skill

1 Learn It!

Authors use descriptive language to help readers create pictures of people, places, or events in their minds. Authors also use words to describe feelings or emotions to make the text come alive to the reader. Good readers visualize by forming mental images of the text as they read to help them understand.

As you read, you can visualize more easily by thinking of your five senses: sight, sound, touch, smell, and taste. Imagine how the text descriptions look, sound, feel, smell, or taste.

Read the following passage and answer the questions that follow.

> The Greeks believed that the gods and goddesses controlled nature. According to Greek myth, the god Zeus ruled the sky and threw lightning bolts, the goddess Demeter made the crops grow, and the god Poseidon caused earthquakes.
>
> — *from page 377*

Reading Tip

Visualizing will help you remember the information that you read.

- Which of the gods or goddesses above can you best visualize? Why?
- How do you picture them in your mind?
- Which of your senses most actively help you visualize each description above?

2 Practice It!

Read the following paragraph. Notice how the author uses the present tense to draw you into the story. Use the underlined details to make a picture in your mind as you read.

> The battle for Troy <u>drags</u> on for 10 years. Finally, the Greeks come up with a plan to capture the city. They <u>build</u> a <u>huge</u>, <u>hollow</u>, <u>wooden</u> horse. The best Mycenaean warriors <u>hide inside</u> the horse.
>
> The Trojans, thinking the horse was a gift from the Greeks, <u>celebrate</u> and <u>roll</u> the <u>giant</u> horse into the city. That night, the Greek warriors <u>quietly climb</u> from the horse and <u>capture</u> the city.
>
> *—from pages 379–380*

After you visualize what this event might have looked like, check the picture on page 379.

- How closely does it match your mental picture?
- Now reread the passage and look at the picture again. Did your ideas change?
- What other words would you use to describe the picture?
- Compare your image with what others in your class visualized. Discuss how your mental picture differed from theirs.

Read to Write

Visualizing can help you organize information before you write it down, especially when using graphic organizers. Choose five Greek writers from the chapter. Then create a table that shows their famous works.

Homer ▶

3 Apply It!

As you read the chapter, list three subjects or events that you were able to visualize. Then make a rough sketch or drawing showing how you picture these descriptions.

The Culture of Ancient Greece

Guide to Reading

History Social Science Standards

WH6.4 Students analyze the geographic, political, economic, religious, and social structures of the early civilizations of Ancient Greece.

Looking Back, Looking Ahead

You have read that under Pericles, Athens became a center of beauty and culture. During this Golden Age, Greek thinkers, writers, and artists contributed many new ideas to the world.

Focusing on the Main Ideas

- The Greeks believed that gods and goddesses controlled nature and shaped their lives. **(page 377)**

- Greek poetry and fables taught Greek values. **(page 379)**

- Greek drama still shapes entertainment today. **(page 382)**

- Greek art and architecture expressed Greek ideas of beauty and harmony. **(page 384)**

Meeting People

Homer (HOH•muhr)
Aesop (EE•SAHP)
Sophocles (SAH•fuh•KLEEZ)
Euripides (yu•RIH•puh•DEEZ)

Locating Places

Mount Olympus (uh•LIHM•puhs)
Delphi (DEHL•FY)

Content Vocabulary

myth (MIHTH)
oracle (AWR•uh•kuhl)
epic (EH•pihk)
fable (FAY•buhl)
drama (DRAH•muh)
tragedy (TRA•juh•dee)
comedy (KAH•muh•dee)

Academic Vocabulary

grant
generation (JEH•nuh•RAY•shuhn)
tradition (truh•DIH•shuhn)
conflict (KAHN•FLIHKT)

Reading Strategy

Compare and Contrast Create a Venn diagram showing similarities and differences between epics and fables.

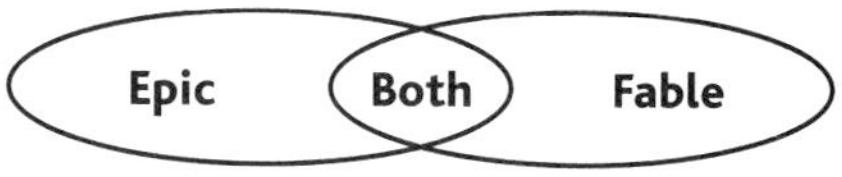

Epic — Both — Fable

NATIONAL GEOGRAPHIC Where&When?

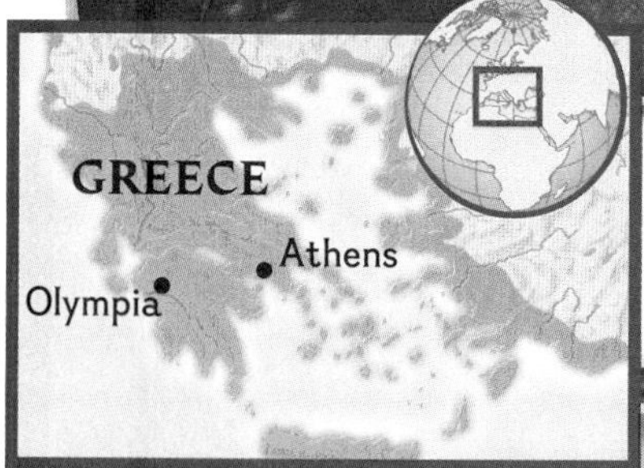

GREECE
Athens
Olympia

700 B.C.

600 B.C.

500 B.C.

c. 700s B.C.
Homer writes the *Iliad* and *Odyssey*

c. 550 B.C.
Aesop writes a series of fables

c. 500s B.C.
Greek architects begin using marble columns

Greek Mythology

Main Idea The Greeks believed that gods and goddesses controlled nature and shaped their lives.

Reading Connection Have you ever wondered why crops grow or why the sun rises and sets? To get the answer, you would read a science book. Read to learn how the Greeks used religion to explain nature.

Myths (MIHTHS) are traditional stories about gods and heroes. Greek mythology expressed the Greek people's religious beliefs. The Greeks believed in many gods and goddesses. They believed gods and goddesses affected people's lives and shaped events. That is why the most impressive buildings in Greek cities were religious temples.

Greek Gods and Goddesses The Greeks believed that the gods and goddesses controlled nature. According to Greek myth, the god Zeus ruled the sky and threw lightning bolts, the goddess Demeter made the crops grow, and the god Poseidon caused earthquakes.

The 12 most important gods and goddesses lived on **Mount Olympus** (uh•LIHM•puhs), the highest mountain in Greece. Among the 12 were Zeus, who was the chief god; Athena, the goddess of wisdom and crafts; Apollo, the god of the sun and poetry; Ares, the god of war; Aphrodite, the goddess of love; and Poseidon, the god of the seas and earthquakes.

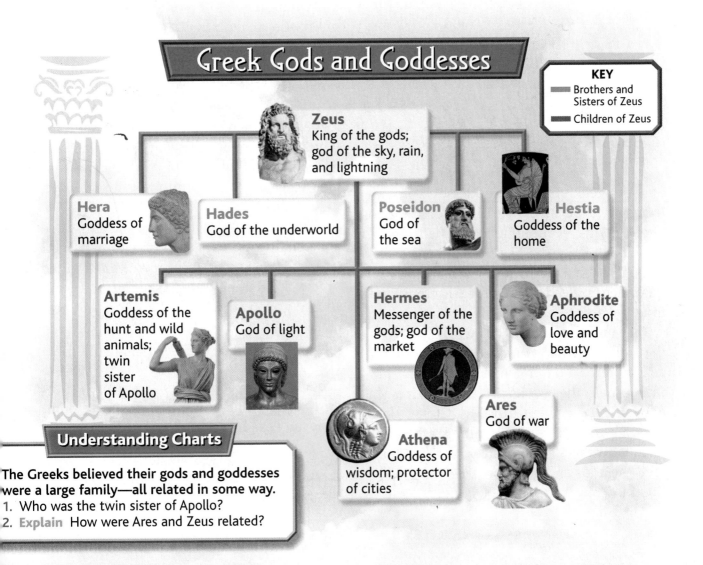

Greek Gods and Goddesses

KEY
- Brothers and Sisters of Zeus
- Children of Zeus

Zeus
King of the gods; god of the sky, rain, and lightning

Hera
Goddess of marriage

Hades
God of the underworld

Poseidon
God of the sea

Hestia
Goddess of the home

Artemis
Goddess of the hunt and wild animals; twin sister of Apollo

Apollo
God of light

Hermes
Messenger of the gods; god of the market

Aphrodite
Goddess of love and beauty

Ares
God of war

Athena
Goddess of wisdom; protector of cities

Understanding Charts

The Greeks believed their gods and goddesses were a large family—all related in some way.
1. Who was the twin sister of Apollo?
2. **Explain** How were Ares and Zeus related?

▲ This painting shows a Greek man at the oracle at Delphi receiving a prophecy. *Why were these prophecies often confusing?*

But Greek gods and goddesses were not thought to be all-powerful. According to Greek myths, even though gods had special powers, they looked like human beings and acted like them. They married, had children, quarreled, played tricks on each other, and fought wars.

Because Greeks sought their gods' favor, they followed many rituals. A ritual is a set of actions carried out in a fixed way. As part of their rituals, the Greeks prayed to their gods and also gave them gifts. In return, they hoped that the gods would **grant** good fortune to them. Many Greek festivals honored the gods and goddesses. Festivals dedicated to Zeus were held at Olympia.

The Greeks also believed in an afterlife. When people died, the Greeks believed their spirits went to a gloomy world beneath the earth ruled by a god named Hades.

What Was a Greek Oracle?

The Greeks believed that each person had a fate or destiny. They believed that certain events were going to happen no matter what they did. They also believed in prophecy. A prophecy is a prediction about the future. The Greeks believed that the gods gave prophecies to people to warn them about the future in time to change it.

To find out about the future, many Greeks visited an **oracle** (AWR•uh•kuhl). This was a sacred shrine where a priest or priestess spoke for a god or goddess. The most famous was the oracle at the Temple of Apollo at **Delphi** (DEHL•FY). The oracle chamber was deep inside the temple. The room had an opening in the floor where volcanic smoke hissed from a crack in the earth.

A priestess sat on a tripod—a three-legged stool—in the oracle chamber and listened to questions. The priests translated her answers. State leaders or their messengers traveled to Delphi to ask advice from the oracle of Apollo.

The priestess in the oracle often gave answers in riddles. When one king, named Croesus (KREE•suhs), sent messengers to the oracle at Delphi, they asked if the king should go to war with the Persians. The oracle replied that if Croesus attacked the Persians, he would destroy a mighty empire. Overjoyed to hear these words, Croesus declared war on the Persians. The Persian army crushed his army. The mighty empire King Croesus had destroyed was his own!

✔ **Reading Check** **Explain** Why did the Greeks have rituals and festivals for their gods and goddesses?

WH6.4.4 Explain the significance of Greek mythology to the everyday life of people in the region and how Greek literature continues to permeate our literature and language today, drawing from Greek mythology and epics, such as Homer's *Iliad* and *Odyssey*, and from *Aesop's Fables*.

Greek Poetry and Fables

Main Idea Greek poetry and fables taught Greek values.

Reading Connection Do you have favorite stories? Are the characters in the stories brave and clever? Read about the characters of the best-loved stories in early Greece.

Greek poems and stories are some of the oldest in Europe. For hundreds of years, Europeans and Americans have used these early works as models for their own poems and stories. Shakespeare, for example, borrowed many Greek plots and settings.

The earliest Greek stories were **epics** (EH•pihks). These long poems told about heroic deeds. The first great epics of early Greece were the *Iliad* and the *Odyssey*. The poet **Homer** (HOH•muhr) wrote these epics during the 700s B.C. He based them on stories of a war between Greece and the city of Troy, which once existed in the region that is today northwestern Turkey.

In the *Iliad*, a prince of Troy kidnaps the wife of the king of Sparta. The kidnapping outrages the Greeks. The king of Mycenae and the brother of the king of Sparta lead the Greeks in an attack on Troy.

The battle for Troy drags on for 10 years. Finally, the Greeks come up with a plan to capture the city. They build a huge, hollow, wooden horse. The best Mycenaean warriors hide inside the horse.

The Trojan Horse

After building the Trojan horse, the Greeks returned to their ships and pretended to retreat. Despite warnings, the Trojans brought the horse within their city as a war trophy. The Greeks inside the horse opened the city gates for their fellow soldiers and captured the city. *What epic included the story of the Trojan horse?*

▲ Clay carving of the Trojan horse

The Greek soldiers hid in the belly of the horse.

Troops left the horse through a trapdoor.

The wooden horse was placed on a platform with wheels.

Aesop

▲ According to legend, Aesop was freed from slavery and became an adviser to Greek rulers. *What is a fable?*

The Trojans, thinking the horse was a gift from the Greeks, celebrate and roll the giant horse into the city. That night, the Greek warriors quietly climb from the horse and capture the city.

The *Odyssey* tells the story of Odysseus, another Greek hero. It describes his journey home from the Trojan War. Odysseus faces storms, witches, and giants before returning to his wife. Because it took Odysseus 10 years to get home, we use the word *odyssey* today to mean a long journey with many adventures.

Greeks believed the *Iliad* and the *Odyssey* were more than stories. They looked on the epics as real history. These poems gave the Greeks an ideal past with a cast of heroes. **Generations** of Greeks read Homer's works. One Athenian wrote, "My father was anxious to see me develop

into a good man . . . [so] he compelled me to memorize all of Homer."

Homer's stories promoted courage and honor. They also taught that it was important to be loyal to your friends and to value the relationship between husband and wife. The stories showed heroes striving to be the best they could be. Heroes fought to protect their own honor and their family's honor. Homer's heroes became role models for Greek boys.

Who Was Aesop? About 550 B.C., a Greek slave named **Aesop** (EE•SAHP) made up his now famous fables. A **fable** (FAY•buhl) is a short tale that teaches a lesson. In most of Aesop's fables, animals talk and act like people. These often funny stories expose human flaws as well as strengths. Each fable ends with a message, or moral.

One of the best-known fables is "The Tortoise and the Hare." In this fable, a tortoise and a hare decide to race. More than halfway into the race, the hare is way ahead. He stops to rest and falls asleep. Meanwhile, the tortoise keeps going at a slow but steady pace and finally wins the race.

The moral of the story is "slow and steady wins the race." Some of the phrases we hear today came from Aesop's fables. "Sour grapes," "a wolf in sheep's clothing," and "appearances often are deceiving" are examples.

For about 200 years, Aesop's fables were a part of Greece's oral **tradition**. This means they were passed from person to person by word of mouth long before they were ever written down. Since then, countless writers have retold the stories in many different languages.

✔ **Reading Check** **Describe** What are the characteristics of a fable?

Biography

WH6.4.4 Explain the significance of Greek mythology to the everyday life of people in the region and how Greek literature continues to permeate our literature and language today, drawing from Greek mythology and epics, such as Homer's *Iliad* and *Odyssey*, and from *Aesop's Fables*.

HOMER
c. 750 B.C.

Homer ▶

Homer's epic poems—the *Iliad* and the *Odyssey*—are famous, but until the 1900s, historians believed that Homer never existed. Historians now know Homer was a real person, but they still debate whether he wrote his poems alone or with the help of other poets.

Many historians have speculated, or made educated guesses, about Homer's personal life. Some say that Homer came from Ionia and seven cities claim to be his birthplace. Some believe that he was blind. Others believe that he wandered from town to town.

Legends tell of Homer's strong influence on his readers. For example, as a young child, Alexander the Great is said to have slept with a copy of the *Iliad* under his pillow.

Homer used the term *aoidos* for a poet. This word means "singer," which tells us that the poetry created during Homer's time was memorized and recited, not written down. Usually, short, simple poems that were easy to remember were told to an audience as entertainment.

Homer created a different style of poetry that influenced all Western literature that followed. His epics are long and involve complex characters, dramatic action, and interesting events. Because each section of the *Iliad* and the *Odyssey* has these characteristics, most historians today think that only one poet could have created both epics. Whoever Homer was, his two epics have influenced readers for nearly 3,000 years.

> "I hate as I hate [Hades'] own gate that man who hides one thought within him while he speaks another."
>
> —Homer, the *Iliad*

Then and Now

Review the characteristics of an epic. Then do research to identify a modern epic.

WH6.4.4 Explain the significance of Greek mythology to the everyday life of people in the region and how Greek literature continues to permeate our literature and language today, drawing from Greek mythology and epics, such as Homer's *Iliad* and *Odyssey,* and from *Aesop's Fables.* **WH6.4.8** Describe the enduring contributions of important Greek figures in the arts and sciences (e.g., Hypatia, Socrates, Plato, Aristotle, Euclid, Thucydides).

Greek Drama

Main Idea Greek drama still shapes entertainment today.

Reading Connection Think about your favorite movie. How would you describe it? Is it a tragedy? Is it a comedy? Read to find out how Greek plays still influence our entertainment.

What is **drama** (DRAH•muh)? Drama is a story told by actors who pretend to be characters in the story. In a drama, actors speak, show emotion, and imitate the actions of the characters they represent.

Today's movies, plays, and television shows are all examples of drama.

Tragedies and Comedies The Greeks performed plays in outdoor theaters as part of their religious festivals. They developed two kinds of dramas—comedies and tragedies.

In a **tragedy** (TRA•juh•dee), a person struggles to overcome difficulties but fails. As a result, the story has an unhappy ending. Early Greek tragedies presented people in a struggle against their fate. Later Greek tragedies showed how a person's character flaws caused him or her to fail.

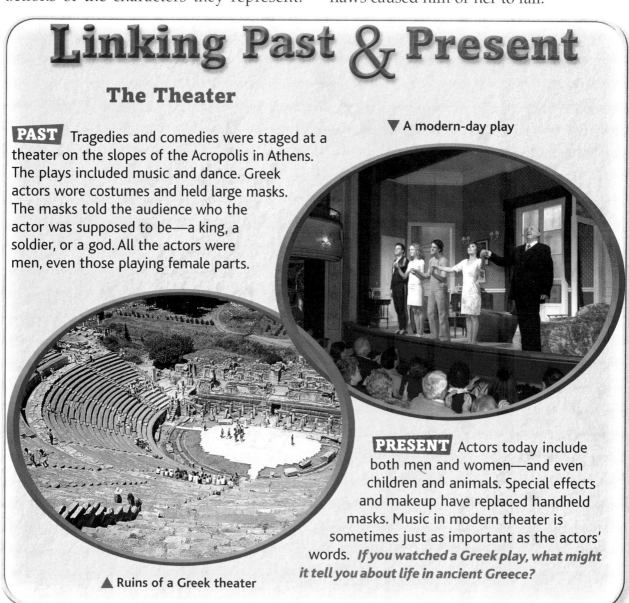

Linking Past & Present

The Theater

PAST Tragedies and comedies were staged at a theater on the slopes of the Acropolis in Athens. The plays included music and dance. Greek actors wore costumes and held large masks. The masks told the audience who the actor was supposed to be—a king, a soldier, or a god. All the actors were men, even those playing female parts.

▼ A modern-day play

PRESENT Actors today include both men and women—and even children and animals. Special effects and makeup have replaced handheld masks. Music in modern theater is sometimes just as important as the actors' words. *If you watched a Greek play, what might it tell you about life in ancient Greece?*

▲ Ruins of a Greek theater

In a **comedy** (KAH•muh•dee), the story ends happily. Today we use the word *comedy* to mean a story filled with humor. The word actually means any drama that has a happy ending.

Greek stories dealt with big questions, such as:

- What is the nature of good and evil?
- What rights should people have?
- What role do gods play in our lives?

The three best-known writers of Greek tragedies were Aeschylus (EHS•kuh•luhs), **Sophocles** (SAH•fuh•KLEEZ), and **Euripides** (yu•RIH•puh•DEEZ). The best-known writer of Greek comedies was Aristophanes (ar•uh•STAH•fuh•NEEZ).

Early Greek tragedies had only one actor who gave speeches and a chorus that sang songs describing the events. Aeschylus was the first to introduce the idea of having two actors. This let the writer tell a story involving **conflict** between the two people. Aeschylus also introduced costumes, props, and stage decorations—all items we still use today.

One of Aeschylus's best-known plays is a group of three plays called the *Oresteia* (ohr•eh•STY•uh). Aeschylus wrote the plays in 458 B.C. They describe what happens when the king of Mycenae returns home from the Trojan War. The *Oresteia* teaches that evil acts cause more evil acts and suffering. In the end, however, reason triumphs over evil. The moral of these plays is that people should not seek revenge.

Sophocles, a general and a writer of plays, developed drama even further. He used three actors in his stories instead of one or two. He also placed painted scenes behind the stage as a backdrop to the action. Two of Sophocles' most famous plays are *Oedipus Rex* (EH•duh•puhs REHKS) and *Antigone* (an•TIH•guh•nee) In *Antigone,* Sophocles

▲ This artwork shows actors preparing for a play. *When and where were Greek plays performed?*

◄ Comedy and tragedy masks

asks the question "Is it better to follow orders or to do what is right?"

Euripides, a later playwright, tried to take Greek drama beyond heroes and gods. His characters were more down-to-earth. Euripides' plots show a great interest in real-life situations. He questioned traditional thinking, especially about war. He showed war as cruel and women and children as its victims.

The works of Aristophanes are good examples of comedies. They make fun of leading politicians and scholars. They encourage the audience to think as well as to laugh. Many of Aristophanes' plays included jokes, just like popular television comedies do today.

✓ Reading Check **Summarize** What two types of drama did the Greeks create?

WH6.4.8 Describe the enduring contributions of important Greek figures in the arts and sciences (e.g., Hypatia, Socrates, Plato, Aristotle, Euclid, Thucydides).

Greek Art and Architecture

Main Idea Greek art and architecture expressed Greek ideas of beauty and harmony.

Reading Connection Do you consider any building in your neighborhood a work of art? Read on to find out about buildings that people have admired as art for centuries.

Artists in ancient Greece believed in certain ideas and tried to show those ideas in their work. These ideas have never gone out of style. Greek artists wanted people to see reason, moderation, balance, and harmony in their work. They hoped their art would inspire people to base their lives on these same ideas.

We know that the Greeks painted murals, but none of them have survived. However, we can still see examples of Greek painting on Greek pottery. The pictures on most Greek pottery are either red on a black background or black on a red background. Large vases often had scenes from Greek myths. Small drinking cups showed scenes from everyday life.

The Parthenon

Standing at almost 230 feet long and 100 feet wide, the Parthenon was the glory of ancient Athens. It was built between 447 and 432 B.C. *What was the purpose of the Parthenon?*

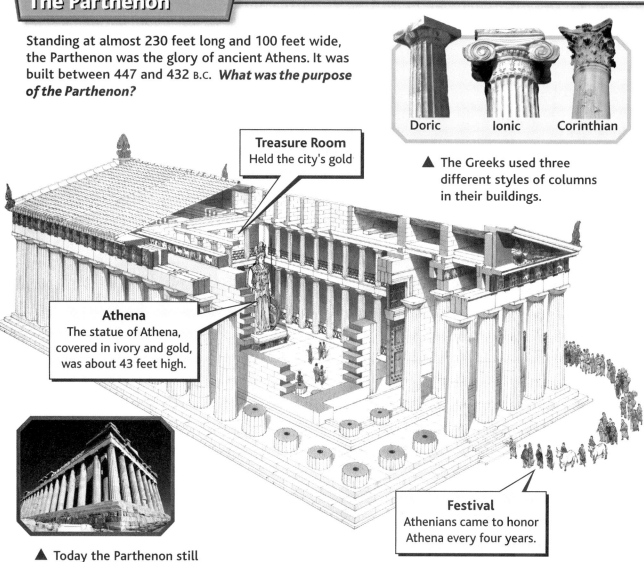

Doric   Ionic   Corinthian

▲ The Greeks used three different styles of columns in their buildings.

Treasure Room
Held the city's gold

Athena
The statue of Athena, covered in ivory and gold, was about 43 feet high.

Festival
Athenians came to honor Athena every four years.

▲ Today the Parthenon still rises above Athens.

In addition to making pottery, the Greeks were skilled architects. Architecture is the art of designing and building structures. In Greece, the most important architecture was the temple dedicated to a god or goddess. The best-known example is the Parthenon. Temples, such as the Parthenon, had a walled room in their centers. Statues of gods and goddesses and the gifts offered to them were kept in these central rooms.

Large columns supported many Greek buildings. The first Greek columns were carved from wood. Then, in 500 B.C., the Greeks began to use marble. Marble columns were built in sections. Large blocks of marble were chiseled from stone quarries and brought by oxen-drawn wagon to the building site. The sections were stacked on top of each other. To keep them from toppling, the column's sections were joined with wooden pegs. Today, marble columns are common features of churches and government buildings. Some of the best-known buildings in our nation's capital, such as the White House and the Capitol, have Greek columns.

Many Greek temples were decorated with sculpture. Greek sculpture, like Greek architecture, was used to express Greek ideas. The favorite subject of Greek artists was the human body. Greek sculptors did not copy their subjects exactly, flaws and all. Instead, they tried to show their ideal version of perfection and beauty.

✔ **Reading Check** **Identify** What was the most important type of building in Greece?

Study Central Need help understanding Greek culture? Visit ca.hss.glencoe.com and click on Study Central.

Section 1 Review

Reading Summary

Review the Main Ideas

- The Greeks believed gods and goddesses influenced their lives. They believed oracles spoke for the gods and goddesses.

- The Greeks wrote long poems, called epics, and short tales, called fables, to pass on Greek values.

- The Greeks created the ideas of tragedy and comedy that are still used in drama today.

- Greek art forms, such as painting, architecture, and sculpture, expressed Greek ideas of beauty, harmony, and moderation.

What Did You Learn?

1. How and why did the Greeks honor their gods?

2. What values did the epic poems of Homer teach Greeks?

Critical Thinking

3. **The Big Ideas** What are the main themes of Euripedes' plays? Would they be popular today? **CA 6RL3.6**

4. **Summarizing Information** Draw a table like the one below to describe the characteristics of Greek architecture and pottery. **CA 6RC2.4**

Greek Architecture	
Greek Pottery	

5. **Contrast** How do Greek tragedies and comedies differ? **CA 6RL3.1**

6. **Evaluate** Why did Greek artists include the ideas of reason, moderation, balance, and harmony in their works? **CA 6RC2.3**

7. **Expository Writing** Greek literature tells us about Greek society. Choose a modern book or movie. Write a paragraph to explain what it would tell others about our society. **CA 6WA2.2**

8. **Reading Visualizing** Write a description of Greek architecture. Give details so readers can visualize them. **CA 6RC2.4**

ICARUS AND DAEDALUS

Retold by Geraldine McCaughrean

Before You Read

The Scene: This story takes place on the Greek island of Crete in the legendary time when both humans and gods lived in ancient Greece.

The Characters: Daedalus is the master architect for King Minos of Crete. Icarus is the son of Daedalus.

The Plot: King Minos summons Daedalus and Icarus to build him a palace and then keeps them captive in their own creation. Daedalus plans to escape.

Vocabulary Preview

labyrinth: an extremely complicated maze

luxurious: characterized by comfort or pleasure

astonishment: sudden wonder or surprise

taunt: to mock in an insulting manner

daub: to cover with a sticky matter

plume: a large and showy feather of a bird

Have you ever known someone who ignored warnings and did something dangerous? This is the story of a young boy who does not listen to his father and suffers the consequences.

As You Read

Keep in mind that a myth is a special kind of story, usually involving gods or goddesses. Greek myths, like this one, were told and retold over many hundreds of years. Try to figure out why the Greeks told this story. What lesson does it teach?

The island of Crete was ruled by King Minos,[1] whose reputation for wickedness had spread to every shore. One day he summoned to his country a famous inventor named Daedalus.[2] "Come, Daedalus, and bring your son Icarus,[3] too. I have a job for you, and I pay well."

King Minos wanted Daedalus to build him a palace, with soaring towers and a high, curving roof. In the cellars there was to be a maze of many corridors—so twisting and dark that any man who once ventured in there would never find his way out again.

"What is it for?" asked Daedalus. "Is it a treasure vault? Is it a prison to hold criminals?"

But Minos only replied, "Build my labyrinth as I told you. I pay you to build, not to ask questions."

So Daedalus held his tongue and set to work. When the palace was finished, he looked at it with pride, for there was nowhere in the world so fine. But when he found out the purpose of the maze in the cellar, he shuddered with horror.

For at the heart of that maze, King Minos put a creature that was half man, half beast—a thing almost too horrible to describe. He called it the Minotaur,[4] and he fed it on men and women!

Then Daedalus wanted to leave Crete at once, and forget both maze and Minotaur. So he went to King Minos to ask for his money.

"I regret," said King Minos, "I cannot let you leave Crete, Daedalus. You are the only man who knows the secret of the maze and how to escape from it. The secret must never leave this island. So I'm afraid I must keep you and Icarus here a while longer."

"How much longer?" gasped Daedalus.

---

[1] **King Minos:** the king of Crete
[2] **Daedalus** (DEH • duhl • uhs): architect for King Minos
[3] **Icarus** (IH • kuh • ruhs): son of Daedalus
[4] **Minotaur:** the half man, half beast that lived in the king's palace

"Oh—just until you die," replied Minos cheerfully. "But never mind. I have plenty of work for a man as clever as you."

Daedalus and Icarus lived in great comfort in King Minos's palace. But they lived the life of prisoners. Their rooms were in the tallest palace tower, with beautiful views across the island. They ate delectable food and wore expensive clothes. But at night the door of their fine apartment was locked, and a guard stood outside. It was a comfortable prison, but it was a prison, even so. Daedalus was deeply unhappy.

Every day he put seed out on the windowsill, for the birds. He liked to study their brilliant colors, the clever overlapping of their feathers, the way they soared on the sea wind. It comforted him to think that they at least were free to come and go. The birds had only to spread their wings and they could leave Crete behind them, whereas Daedalus and Icarus must stay forever in their luxurious cage.

Young Icarus could not understand his father's unhappiness. "But I like it here," he said. "The king gives us gold and this tall tower to live in."

Daedalus groaned. "But to work for such a wicked man, Icarus! And to be prisoners all our days!...We shan't stay. We shan't"

"But we can't get away, can we?" said Icarus. "How can anybody escape from an island? Fly?" He snorted with laughter.

Daedalus did not answer. He scratched his head and stared out of the window at the birds pecking seed on the sill.

From that day onward, he got up early each morning and stood at the open window. When a bird came for the seed, Daedalus begged it to spare him one feather.

Then each night, when everyone else had gone to bed, Daedalus worked by candlelight on his greatest invention of all.

Early mornings. Late nights. A whole year went by. Then one morning Icarus was awakened by his father shaking his shoulder. "Get up, Icarus, and don't make a sound. We are leaving Crete."

"But how? It's impossible!"

Daedalus pulled out a bundle from under his bed. "I've been making something, Icarus." Inside were four great folded fans of feathers. He stretched them out on the bed. They were wings! "I sewed the feathers together with strands of wool from my blanket. Now hold still."

Daedalus melted down a candle and daubed his son's shoulders with sticky wax. "Yes, I know it's hot, but it will soon cool." While the wax was still soft, he stuck two of the wings to Icarus's shoulder blades.

"Now you must help me put on my wings, Son. When the wax sets hard, you and I will fly away from here, as free as birds!"

"I'm scared!" whispered Icarus as he stood on the narrow window ledge, his knees knocking and his huge wings drooping down behind. The lawns and courtyards of the palace lay far below. The royal guards looked as small as ants. "This won't work!"

"Courage, Son!" said Daedalus. "Keep your arms out wide and fly close to me. Above all—are you listening, Icarus?"

"Y-y-yes, Father."

"Above all, don't fly too high! Don't fly too close to the sun!"

"Don't fly too close to the sun," Icarus repeated, with his eyes tight shut. Then he gave a cry as his father nudged him off the windowsill.

He plunged downward. With a crack, the feathers behind him filled with wind, and Icarus found himself flying. Flying!

"I'm flying!" he crowed.

The guards looked up in astonishment, and wagged their swords, and pointed and shouted, "Tell the king! Daedalus and Icarus are…are…flying away!"

By dipping first one wing, then the other, Icarus found that he could turn to the left and to the right. The wind tugged at his hair. His legs trailed out behind him. He saw the fields and streams as he had never seen them before!

Then they were out over the sea. The sea gulls pecked at him angrily, so Icarus flew higher, where they could not reach him.

He copied their shrill cry and taunted them: "You can't catch me!'

"Now remember, don't fly too high!" called Daedalus, but his words were drowned by the screaming of the gulls.

I'm the first boy ever to fly! I'm making history! I shall be famous! thought Icarus, as he flew up and up, higher and higher.

At last Icarus was looking the sun itself in the face, "Think you're the highest thing in the sky, do you?" he jeered. "I can fly just as high as you! Higher, even!" He did not notice the drops of sweat on his forehead: He was so determined to outfly the sun.

Soon its vast heat beat on his face and on his back and on the great wings stuck on with wax. The wax softened. The wax trickled. The wax dripped. One feather came unstuck. Then a plume of feathers fluttered slowly down.

Icarus stopped flapping his wings. His father's words came back to him clearly now: *"Don't fly too close to the sun!"*

With a great sucking noise, the wax on his shoulders came unstuck. Icarus tried to catch hold of the wings, but they just folded up in his hands. He plunged down, his two fists full of feathers—down and down and down.

The clouds did not stop his fall.

The sea gulls did not catch him in their beaks.

His own father could only watch as Icarus hurtled head first into the glittering sea and sank deep down among the sharks and eels and squid. And all that was left of proud Icarus was a litter of waxy feathers floating on the sea.

Responding to the Literature

1. What does Daedalus build for King Minos?

2. What does King Minos do to keep Daedalus and Icarus from escaping from Crete?

3. **Drawing Conclusions** Do you think Daedalus is a concerned father? Why or why not? Support your opinion with examples. **CA 6RL3.2**

4. **Analyze** How does the setting of the story influence the plot? Support your ideas with details from the story. **CA 6RL3.3**

5. **Read to Write** Imagine you are Icarus. Would you listen to your father's advice? Write two or three paragraphs explaining what you would have done and why. **CA 6WA2.4**

Reading on Your Own...

Do you want to learn more about the ancient Greeks?
If so, check out these other great books.

Nonfiction

Trade and Warfare by Robert Hull explores the history of Greece through trading and conflict. It looks at the different types of ships the Greeks used and the battles on both land and sea. *The content of this book is related to History–Social Science Standard WH6.4.*

Biography

Archimedes and the Door of Science by Jeanne Bendick follows the life of the Greek scientist Archimedes. Learn about the different discoveries and inventions of one of the greatest minds of the ancient world. *The content of this book is related to History–Social Science Standard WH6.4.*

Mythology

Adventures of the Greek Heroes by Mollie McLean and Anne Wiseman is a book written by two teachers who love the tales of action and adventure in ancient Greece. Exciting tales give the reader a glimpse into the lives of heroic Greeks. *The content of this book is related to History–Social Science Standard WH6.4.*

Mythology

D'Aulaires' Book of Greek Myths by Edgar and Ingri D'Aulaire is a retelling of the most significant stories of ancient Greece. The book is filled with adventures and stories of the gods and goddesses and men and women who influenced Greek mythology. *The content of this book is related to History–Social Science Standard WH6.4.*

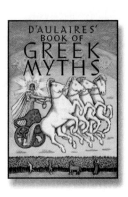

Greek Philosophy and History

Guide to Reading

History Social Science Standards

WH6.4 Students analyze the geographic, political, economic, religious, and social structures of the early civilizations of Ancient Greece.

Looking Back, Looking Ahead

Section 1 discussed early Greek artists and writers. Many of them made the years between 500 and 350 B.C. the Golden Age for Greece. Greek thinkers and historians produced works that shape people's views of the world today.

Focusing on the **Main Ideas**

- Greek philosophers developed ideas that are still used today. *(page 393)*

- Greeks wrote the first real histories in Western civilization. *(page 397)*

Meeting People

Pythagoras (puh•THA•guh•ruhs)
Socrates (SAH•kruh•TEEZ)
Plato (PLAY•TOH)
Aristotle (AR•uh•STAH•tuhl)
Herodotus (hih•RAH•duh•tuhs)
Thucydides (thoo•SIH•duh•DEEZ)

Content Vocabulary

philosophy (fuh•LAH•suh•fee)
philosopher (fuh•LAH•suh•fuhr)
Sophist (SAH•fihst)
Socratic method (suh•KRA•tihk)

Academic Vocabulary

reject (ree•JEHKT)
accurate (A•kyuh•ruht)

Reading Strategy

Categorizing Information Use diagrams like the one below to show the basic philosophies of Socrates, Plato, and Aristotle.

(Socrates)

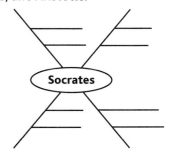

NATIONAL GEOGRAPHIC **Who & When?**

500 B.C.

435 B.C. Herodotus writes history of Persian Wars

400 B.C.

399 B.C. Socrates sentenced to death

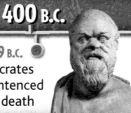

300 B.C.

335 B.C. Aristotle opens the Lyceum in Athens

Greek Philosophers

Main Idea Greek philosophers developed ideas that are still used today.

Reading Connection What is right? What is wrong? What makes a government good? Read to learn how the ancient Greeks tried to answer similar "big" questions.

The word **philosophy** (fuh•LAH•suh•fee) comes from the Greek word for "love of wisdom." Greek philosophy led to the study of history, political science, science, and mathematics. Greek thinkers who believed the human mind could understand everything were called **philosophers** (fuh•LAH•suh•fuhrs).

Many philosophers were teachers. One Greek philosopher, **Pythagoras** (puh•THA•guh•ruhs), taught his pupils that the universe followed the same laws that governed music and numbers. He believed that all relationships in the world could be expressed in numbers. As a result, he developed many new ideas about mathematics. Most people know his name because of the Pythagorean theorem that is still used in geometry. It is a way to determine the length of the sides of a triangle.

Who Were the Sophists? The **Sophists** (SAH•fihsts) were professional teachers in ancient Greece. They traveled from city to

▲ This artwork shows Greek philosophers involved in a discussion. *Where does the word* philosophy *come from?*

Greek Philosophers

Thinker or Group	Sophists	Socrates	Plato	Aristotle
Main Idea	Sophists like Libanius (above) thought that people should use knowledge to improve themselves. They believed that there is no absolute right or wrong.	He was a critic of the Sophists. Socrates believed that there was an absolute right and wrong.	He rejected the idea of democracy as a form of government. Plato believed that philosopher-kings should rule society.	Aristotle taught the idea of the "golden mean." He believed observation and comparison were necessary to gain knowledge.
Important Contribution	They developed the art of public speaking and debate.	He created the Socratic method of teaching.	He described his vision of the ideal government in his work the *Republic*.	He wrote over 200 books on philosophy and science. He divided all governments into three basic types.
Influence on Today	The importance of public speaking can be seen in political debates between candidates.	His methods influenced the way teachers interact with their students.	He introduced the idea that government should be fair and just.	His political ideas still shape political ideas today.

city and made a living by teaching others. They believed students should use their time to improve themselves. Many taught their students how to win an argument and make good political speeches.

Sophists did not believe that gods and goddesses influenced people. They also **rejected** the concept of absolute right or wrong. They believed that what was right for one person might be wrong for another.

The Ideas of Socrates

One critic of the Sophists was **Socrates** (SAH•kruh•TEEZ). Socrates was an Athenian sculptor whose true love was philosophy. Socrates left no writings behind. What we know about him we have learned from the writings of his students.

Socrates believed that an absolute truth existed and that all real knowledge was within each person. He invented the **Socratic method** (suh•KRA•tihk) of teaching still used today. He asked pointed questions to force his pupils to use their reason and to see things for themselves.

Some Athenian leaders considered the Socratic method a threat to their power. At one time, Athens had a tradition of questioning leaders and speaking freely. However, their defeat in the Peloponnesian War changed the Athenians. They no longer trusted open debate. In 399 B.C. the leaders accused Socrates of teaching young Athenians to rebel against the state. A jury found Socrates guilty and sentenced him to death. Socrates could have fled the city, but he chose to remain. He argued that he had lived under the city's laws, so he had to obey them. He then drank poison to carry out the jury's sentence.

The Ideas of Plato One of Socrates' students was **Plato** (PLAY•TOH). Unlike Socrates, we are able to learn a lot about Plato from his writings. One work Plato wrote is called the *Republic.* It explains his vision of government. Based on life in Athens, Plato decided that democracy was not a good system of government. He did not think that rule by the people produced fair or sensible policies. To him, people could not live good lives unless they had a just and reasonable government.

In the *Republic,* Plato described his ideal government. He divided people into three basic groups. At the top were philosopher-kings, who ruled using logic and wisdom. Warriors made up the second group. They defended the state from attack.

The third group included the rest of the people. They were driven by desire, not by wisdom like the first group or courage like the second. These people produced the state's food, clothing, and shelter. Plato also believed that men and women should have the same education and an equal chance to have the same jobs.

Who Was Aristotle? Plato established a school in Athens known as the Academy. His best student was **Aristotle** (AR•uh•STAH•tuhl). Aristotle wrote more than 200 books on topics ranging from government to the planets and stars.

In 335 B.C. Aristotle opened his own school called the Lyceum. At the Lyceum, Aristotle taught his pupils the "golden mean." This idea holds that a person should do nothing in excess. For example, a person should not eat too little or too much but just enough to stay well.

Aristotle also helped to advance science. He urged people to use their senses to make observations, just as scientists today make observations. Aristotle was the first person to group observations according to their similarities and differences. Then he made generalizations based on the groups of facts.

Like Plato, Aristotle wrote about government. He studied and compared the governments of 158 different places to find the best form of government. In his book *Politics,* Aristotle divided the governments into three types:

- Government by one person, such as a monarch (king or queen) or a tyrant
- Government by a few people, which might be an aristocracy or an oligarchy
- Government by many people, as in a democracy

Aristotle noticed that governments run by a few people were usually run by the rich. He noticed that most democracies were run by the poor. He thought the best government was a mixture of the two.

Aristotle's ideas shaped the way Europeans and Americans thought about government. The founders of the United States Constitution tried to create a mixed government that balanced the different types Aristotle had identified.

✓ **Reading Check** **Contrast** How did Aristotle's idea of government differ from Plato's?

History Online

Web Activity Visit ca.hss.glencoe.com and click on *Chapter 8—Student Web Activity* to learn more about ancient Greece.

Biography

WH6.4.8 Describe the enduring contributions of important Greek figures in the arts and sciences (e.g., Hypatia, Socrates, Plato, Aristotle, Euclid, Thucydides).

PLATO AND ARISTOTLE

Plato c. 428–347 B.C.
Aristotle 384–322 B.C.

Plato was from a noble Greek family and had planned a career in politics. However, he was so horrified by the death of his teacher, Socrates, that he left politics and spent many years traveling and writing. When Plato returned to Athens in 387 B.C., he founded an academy, where he taught using Socrates' method of questioning. His academy drew bright young students from Athens and other Greek city-states. Plato looked for truth beyond the appearances of everyday objects and reflected this philosophy in his writing and teaching. He believed the human soul was the connection between the appearance of things and ideas.

Plato ▲

Plato and Aristotle—two of the greatest ancient Greek philosophers—met as teacher and student at Plato's Academy in Athens. Aristotle left his home in Stagira and arrived on the Academy's doorstep when he was eighteen years old. He remained at Plato's Academy for 20 years, until the death of his teacher. Unlike Plato, Aristotle did not come from a noble family. His father was the court physician to the king of Macedonia. At an early age, Aristotle's father introduced him to the topics of medicine and biology, and these became his main interests of study. Aristotle sought truth through a systematic, scientific approach. He liked to jot down notes and details about different topics—from weather to human behavior—and arrange them in categories. He did not trust the senses' ability to understand the universe.

After Plato's death, Aristotle traveled for about 12 years. He also tutored the future Alexander the Great. Later in his life, he returned to Athens and opened his own school, the Lyceum. He made his school the center for research in every area of knowledge known to the Greeks.

Then and Now

Aristotle spent 20 years at Plato's Academy. What present-day careers or subjects of study require lifelong learning?

▲ Aristotle

WH6.4.8 Describe the enduring contributions of important Greek figures in the arts and sciences (e.g., Hypatia, Socrates, Plato, Aristotle, Euclid, Thucydides).

Greek Historians

Main Idea Greeks wrote the first real histories in Western civilization.

Reading Connection How would the United States be different if we did not know our history? Read to learn how the Greeks began to write history.

In most places in the ancient world, people used legends and myths to explain their past. No one tried to explain the past by studying events. Then, in 435 B.C., a Greek named **Herodotus** (hih•RAH•duh•tuhs) wrote the history of the Persian Wars.

In his book, Herodotus tried to separate fact from legend. He asked questions, recorded answers, and checked the truthfulness of his sources. Although his history includes some errors and uses gods and goddesses to explain some events, many European and American historians consider him the "father of history."

Many historians consider **Thucydides** (thoo•SIH•duh•DEEZ) the greatest historian of the ancient world. Thucydides fought in the Peloponnesian War. Afterward, he wrote his *History of the Peloponnesian War.*

Unlike Herodotus, Thucydides saw war and politics as the activities of human beings, not gods. He also stressed the importance of having **accurate** facts:

> 66 **Either I was present myself at the events which I have described or else I heard of them from eyewitnesses whose reports I have checked with as much thoroughness as possible.** 99

—Thucydides, *History of the Peloponnesian War*

✓ Reading Check **Identify** How did Thucydides view war and politics?

History Online

Study Central Need help with Greek philosophy and history? Visit ca.hss.glencoe.com and click on Study Central.

Section ② Review

Reading Summary

Review the Main Ideas

- The ideas of Greek philosophers, including Socrates, Plato, and Aristotle, still affect modern thinking about education, government, and science.

- Herodotus and Thucydides are considered western civilization's first historians. They believed that people could understand the present by studying the past.

What Did You Learn?

1. Who were the Sophists and what were their beliefs?

2. Before Herodotus, how did Greeks explain the past?

Critical Thinking

3. **Organizing Information** Draw a diagram like the one below. Use the diagram to organize Plato's ideas about an ideal government. **CA 6RC2.4**

4. **Science Connection** How are Aristotle's teachings related to the scientific method used by scientists today? **CA 6RC2.3**

5. **Contrast** What is different about the works of Herodotus and Thucydides? **CA 6RC2.2**

6. **The Big Ideas** How did the ideas of Greek philosophers affect Greek society? **CA HI2.**

7. **Persuasive Writing** Do you agree with Plato's vision of the ideal state in the *Republic?* Write an editorial expressing your viewpoint. **CA 6WA2.5**

Alexander the Great

Guide to Reading

History Social Science Standards

WH6.4 Students analyze the geographic, political, economic, religious, and social structures of the early civilizations of Ancient Greece.

Looking Back, Looking Ahead

In Section 2, you learned that the Greek philosopher Aristotle was also a teacher. The king of Macedonia admired Greek culture and hired Aristotle to tutor his son, Alexander. Years later, his son would take control of the Greek world.

Focusing on the Main Ideas

- Philip II of Macedonia united the Greek states. *(page 399)*

- Alexander the Great conquered the Persian Empire and spread Greek culture throughout southwest Asia. *(page 400)*

Locating Places

Macedonia (MA•suh•DOH•nee•uh)
Chaeronea (KEHR•uh•NEE•uh)
Syria (SIHR•ee•uh)
Alexandria (A•lihg•ZAN•dree•uh)

Meeting People

Philip II
Alexander the Great

Content Vocabulary

legacy (LEH•guh•see)
Hellenistic Era (HEH•luh•NIHS•tihk)

Academic Vocabulary

achieve (uh•CHEEV)
military (MIH•luh•TEHR•ee)

Reading Strategy

Sequencing Create a diagram like the one below to track the achievements of Alexander the Great.

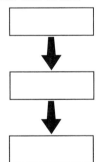

NATIONAL GEOGRAPHIC Where&When?

MACEDONIA
Gaugamela•
Babylon•

360 B.C.

359 B.C.
Philip II becomes king of Macedonia

340 B.C.

331 B.C.
Alexander defeats Darius at Gaugamela

320 B.C.

323 B.C.
Alexander dies

WH6.4 Students analyze the geographic, political, economic, religious, and social structures of the early civilizations of Ancient Greece.

WH6.4.7 Trace the rise of Alexander the Great and the spread of Greek culture eastward and into Egypt.

Macedonia Attacks Greece

Main Idea) **Philip II of Macedonia united the Greek states.**

Reading Connection Have you ever wanted something because your neighbor had it? Read to find what the king of Macedonia wanted from his neighbors, the Greeks.

Macedonia (MA•suh•DOH•nee•uh) lay north of Greece. The Macedonians raised sheep and horses and grew crops in their river valleys. They were a warrior people who fought on horseback. The Greeks looked down on them, but by 400 B.C., Macedonia had become a powerful kingdom.

A Plan to Win Greece
In 359 B.C. **Philip II** rose to the throne in Macedonia. Philip had lived in Greece as a young man. He admired everything about the Greeks—their art,

their ideas, and their armies. Although Macedonia was influenced by Greek ideas, Philip wanted to make his kingdom strong enough to defeat the mighty Persian Empire. In order to **achieve** this goal, Philip needed to unite the Greek city-states with his own kingdom.

Philip trained a vast army of foot soldiers to fight like the Greeks. He took over the city-states one by one. He took some city-states by force and bribed the leaders of others to surrender. Some united with his kingdom voluntarily.

Demosthenes (dih•MAHS•thuh•NEEZ) was a lawyer and one of Athens's great public speakers. He gave several powerful speeches warning Athenians that Philip was a threat to Greek freedom. He urged Athens and other city-states to join together to fight the Macedonians.

Primary Source

Demosthenes' Warning

As King Philip II of Macedonia became more powerful, he began to take part in the affairs of Greece. Demosthenes realized that Macedonia's powerful army would eventually be a threat to Greece. He tried to warn the Greeks to take action.

"Remember only that Philip is our enemy, that he has long been robbing and insulting us, that wherever we have expected aid from others we have found hostility, that the future depends on ourselves, and that unless we are willing to fight him there we shall perhaps be forced to fight here.... You need not speculate [guess] about the future except to assure yourselves that it will be disastrous unless you face the facts and are willing to do your duty."

—Demosthenes, *"The First Philippic"* in *Orations of Demosthenes*

▼ **Demosthenes**

DBQ **Document-Based Question**

Which line of Demosthenes' speech tells what he thinks will happen if the Greeks ignore Philip?

However, by the time the Greeks saw the danger, it was too late. The Peloponnesian War had left the Greeks weak and divided. In many Greek city-states, the population had declined after the Peloponnesian War. Fighting had destroyed many farms and left people with no way to earn a living. As a result, thousands of young Greeks left Greece to join the Persian army. Many who stayed behind began fighting among themselves. The city-states grew weaker.

Although the Athenians joined some other Greek states to fight Philip's army, they could not stop the invasion. In 338 B.C. the Macedonians crushed the Greek allies at the Battle of **Chaeronea** (KEHR•uh•NEE•uh) near Thebes. Philip now controlled most of Greece.

Reading Check **Summarize** Why did Philip II invade Greece?

Alexander Builds an Empire

Main Idea Alexander the Great conquered the Persian Empire and spread Greek culture throughout southwest Asia.

Reading Connection What will you be doing at age 20? Read to learn what Philip's son Alexander achieved.

Philip planned to conquer the Persian Empire with the Greeks' help. Before Philip could carry out his plan, however, he was murdered. As a result, the invasion of Asia fell to his son.

Alexander was only 20 when he became king of Macedonia. Philip had carefully trained his son for leadership. While still a boy, Alexander often went with his father to the battlefront. At age 16 he rose to commander in the Macedonian army. After his

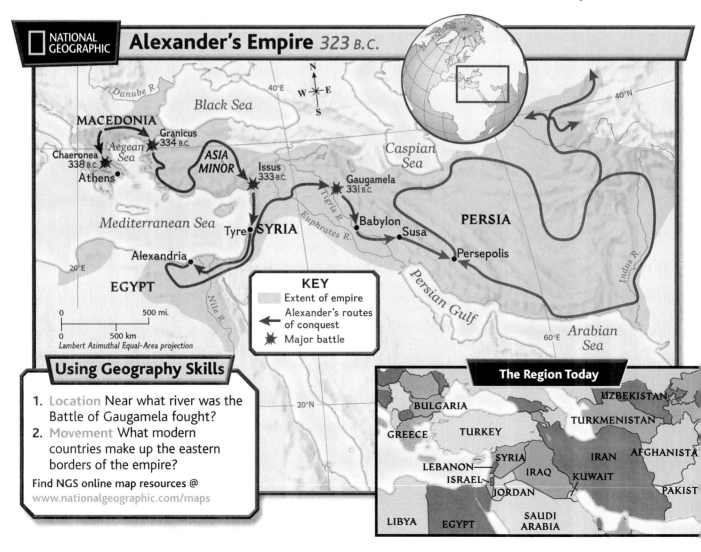

NATIONAL GEOGRAPHIC **Alexander's Empire** 323 B.C.

KEY
Extent of empire
⬅ Alexander's routes of conquest
✴ Major battle

0 — 500 mi.
0 — 500 km
Lambert Azimuthal Equal-Area projection

Using Geography Skills

1. **Location** Near what river was the Battle of Gaugamela fought?
2. **Movement** What modern countries make up the eastern borders of the empire?

Find NGS online map resources @ www.nationalgeographic.com/maps

The Region Today

father's death, Alexander was ready to fulfill his father's dream—the invasion of the Persian Empire.

What Did Alexander Conquer?

In the spring of 334 B.C., Alexander invaded Asia Minor with about 37,000 foot soldiers. He also took along 5,000 mounted warriors. With Alexander at their head, the cavalry destroyed the forces of the local Persian satraps at the Battle of Granicus.

By the next year, Alexander had freed the Greek cities in Asia Minor from Persian rule and defeated a large Persian army at Issus. He then turned south. By the winter of 332 B.C., he had captured **Syria** (SIHR•ee•uh) and Egypt. Then he built the city of **Alexandria** (A•lihg•ZAN•dree•uh) in Egypt as a center of business and trade. The city became one of the most important cities in the ancient world.

In 331 B.C. Alexander headed east and defeated the Persians at Gaugamela, near Babylon. After this victory, his army easily overran the rest of the Persian Empire. However, Alexander did not stop at Persia. Over the next three years, he marched east as far as modern Pakistan. In 326 B.C. he crossed the Indus River and entered India. There he fought a number of bloody battles. Weary of continuous war, his soldiers refused to go farther. Alexander agreed to lead them home.

On the return march, the troops crossed a desert in what is now southern Iran. Heat and thirst killed thousands of soldiers. At one point, a group of soldiers found a little water and scooped it up in a helmet. Then they offered the water to Alexander. According to a Greek historian, Alexander, "in full view of his troops, poured the water on the ground. So extraordinary was the effect of this action that the water wasted by Alexander was as good as a drink for every man in the army."

In 323 B.C. Alexander returned to Babylon. He wanted to plan an invasion of southern Arabia but was very tired and weak from wounds. He came down with a bad fever. Ten days later he was dead at age 32.

Alexander's Legacy

Alexander was a great **military** leader. He was brave and even reckless. He often rode into battle ahead of his men and risked his own life. He inspired his armies to march into unknown lands and risk their lives in difficult situations.

The key to Alexander's courage may have been his childhood education. Alexander kept a copy of the *Iliad* under his pillow. Most likely his inspiration was Homer's warrior-hero Achilles. In the end, Alexander's reputation outstripped even Achilles', and today he is called **Alexander the Great.**

Alexander the Great

▲ This carving of Alexander the Great on his horse decorated the side of a tomb. *Was Alexander able to fulfill his plans of conquest? Explain.*

A **legacy** (LEH•guh•see) is what a person leaves behind when he or she dies. Alexander's skill and daring created his legacy. He helped extend Greek and Macedonian rule over a vast region. At the same time, he and his armies spread Greek art, ideas, language, and architecture wherever they went in southwest Asia and northern Africa. Greeks, in turn, brought new ideas back from Asia and Africa.

Alexander's conquests marked the beginning of the **Hellenistic Era** (HEH•luh•NIHS•tihk). The word *Hellenistic* comes from a Greek word meaning "like the Greeks." It refers to a time when the Greek language and Greek ideas spread to the non-Greek people of southwest Asia.

The Empire Breaks Apart Alexander the Great planned to unite Macedonians, Greeks, and Persians in his new empire. He used Persians as officials and encouraged his soldiers to marry Asian women. After Alexander died, however, his generals fought one another for power. As a result, the empire that Alexander had created fell apart. Four kingdoms took its place: Macedonia, Pergamum (PUHR•guh•muhm), Egypt, and the Seleucid Empire (suh•LOO•suhd). Look at the map on page 403 to see where these kingdoms were located.

All government business in the Hellenistic kingdoms was conducted in the Greek language. Only those Asians and Egyptians who spoke Greek could apply

Alexandria, Egypt

Alexandria

▼ **Modern Alexandria**

◄ **The Lighthouse of Alexandria was one of the Seven Wonders of the Ancient World. A fire in its tall tower guided ships into harbor. *What was special about Alexandria in 100 B.C.?***

for government posts. The kings preferred to give the jobs to Greeks and Macedonians. In this way, Greeks managed to stay in control of the governments.

By 100 B.C., the largest city in the Mediterranean world was Alexandria, which Alexander had founded in Egypt. In addition, the Hellenistic kings created many new cities and military settlements.

These new Greek communities needed architects, engineers, philosophers, artisans, and artists. For this reason, Hellenistic rulers encouraged Greeks and Macedonians to settle in southwest Asia. These colonists provided new recruits for the army and a pool of government officials. They helped spread Greek culture into Egypt and as far east as modern-day Afghanistan and India.

Reading Check **Explain** What was Alexander's legacy?

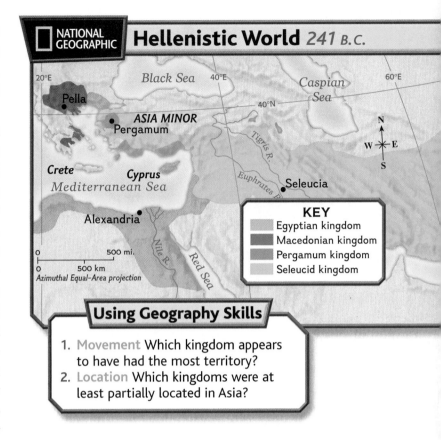

NATIONAL GEOGRAPHIC

Hellenistic World 241 B.C.

KEY
- Egyptian kingdom
- Macedonian kingdom
- Pergamum kingdom
- Seleucid kingdom

Using Geography Skills

1. **Movement** Which kingdom appears to have had the most territory?
2. **Location** Which kingdoms were at least partially located in Asia?

History Online

Study Central Need help understanding the conquests of Alexander the Great? Visit ca.hss.glencoe.com and click on Study Central.

Section 3 Review

Reading Summary

Review the Main Ideas

- Following the Battle of Chaeronea in 338 B.C., King Philip of Macedonia ruled all of Greece.

- Alexander the Great, King Philip's son, conquered an empire that stretched to Africa in the south and India in the east. After Alexander's death, his empire split into several kingdoms.

What Did You Learn?

1. How did Philip II of Macedonia feel about the Greeks?

2. What ended Alexander's conquest of India?

Critical Thinking

3. **Analyze** Why was Alexander a good leader? **CA 6RC2.0**

4. **Summarize** Draw a table to summarize what you know about each topic. **CA 6RC2.4**

Philip of Macedonia	Alexander the Great	Alexander's Empire After His Death

5. **Points of View** Why did some Greeks ignore the rise of Macedonia? Who tried to warn them? **CA HR5.**

6. **The Big Ideas** What changes to Greek civilization did Philip and Alexander bring about through war? **CA HI3.**

7. **Geography Skills** How many continents did Alexander's empire reach? **CA CS3.**

8. **Analysis** **Predicting** How might history be different if Alexander had not died at such a young age? **CA HI4.**

You Decide . . .

Alexander the Great: Villain or Hero?

Villain

Was Alexander the Great really great? Or was he an evil conqueror? Those who see him as bloodthirsty and cruel give this as evidence against Alexander. They say he

- destroyed Persepolis
- attacked Tyre, killing 10,000 people and enslaving 30,000
- treated his slaves harshly
- ordered the murder of several close advisers.

Many legends about Alexander have been told. One historian found this account to support the "villain theory."

"The following is my favourite [story] which is found all the way from Turkey to Kazakhstan: Iskander [Alexander] was actually a devil and he had horns. But his hair was long and wavy and the horns were never seen. Only his barbers knew. But he feared they could not keep the secret. So, he killed them when they discovered. His last barber pretended not to notice and kept the secret. Eventually though he could bear it no longer and, as he could tell no one, he ran to a well and called down the well: 'Iskander has horns!' But in the bottom of the well were whispering reeds [used in flutes] and they echoed the story until it went round the whole world."

—Michael Wood,
"In the Footsteps of
Alexander the Great"

▲ Alexander the Great (at far left)

Arrian, a Greek historian who lived in the A.D. 100s, wrote about Alexander this way:

"For my own part, I think there was at that time no race of men, no city, nor even a single individual to whom Alexander's name and fame had not penetrated. For this reason it seems to me that a hero totally unlike any other human being could not have been born without the agency [help] of the deity [gods]."

—Arrian, *The Anabasis of Alexander*

On two points all historians agree: Alexander was a brilliant general and he was a brave fighter. He once boasted to his men:

"For there is no part of my body, in front at any rate, remaining free from wounds; nor is there any kind of weapon used either for close combat or for hurling at the enemy, the traces of which I do not bear on my person. For I have been wounded with the sword in close fight, I have been shot with arrows, and I have been struck with missiles projected from engines of war; and though oftentimes I have been hit with stones and bolts of wood for the sake of your lives, your glory, and your wealth, I am still leading you as conquerors over all the land and sea, all rivers, mountains, and plains. I have celebrated your weddings with my own, and the children of many of you will be akin to my children."

—Arrian, *The Anabasis of Alexander*

▲ Alexander the Great

Hero

Other historians consider Alexander the Great to be a hero. They claim he brought progress, order, and culture to each new land he conquered. In support of him, they say Alexander

- tried to promote learning
- visited all of his wounded men after each battle
- spared the lives of the queen and princess of Persia
- built new cities where others had been destroyed.

You Be the Historian

DBQ Document-Based Questions

1. Why do some historians view Alexander as a villain? **CA HR5.**

2. Why do others view him as a hero? **CA HR5.**

3. Was Alexander wicked or heroic? Take the role of a historian. Write a persuasive essay that explains how you see Alexander the Great. Be sure to use facts to support your position. **CA 6WA2.5**

The Spread of Greek Culture

Guide to Reading

Looking Back, Looking Ahead

In Section 3, you read that Alexander's conquests helped to spread Greek culture. The kings who came after Alexander also tried to attract the best and brightest Greeks to Asia and Egypt. They hoped to re-create the glory of Greece's Golden Age in their own kingdoms.

Focusing on the **Main Ideas**

• Hellenistic cities became centers of learning and culture. *(page 407)*

• Philosophers and scientists in the Hellenistic Era introduced new ideas and made major discoveries. *(page 408)*

• Greek power declined as a new power in the Mediterranean arose: Rome. *(page 411)*

Meeting People

Euclid (YOO•kluhd)
Archimedes (AHR•kuh•MEE•deez)
Hypatia (hy•PAY•shuh)

Locating Places

Rhodes (ROHDZ)
Syracuse (SIHR•uh•KYOOS)

Content Vocabulary

Epicureanism
    (EH•pih•kyu•REE•uh•NIH•zuhm)
Stoicism (STOH•uh•SIH•zuhm)
astronomer (uh•STRAH•nuh•muhr)
plane geometry (jee•AH•muh•tree)
solid geometry (jee•AH•muh•tree)

Academic Vocabulary

goal (GOHL)
lecture (LEHK•chuhr)
major (MAY•juhr)

Reading Strategy

Summarizing Information Create a diagram to show the major Greek contributions to Western civilization.

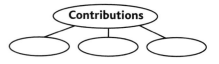

History Social Science Standards

WH6.4 Students analyze the geographic, political, economic, religious, and social structures of the early civilizations of Ancient Greece.

NATIONAL GEOGRAPHIC Where&When?

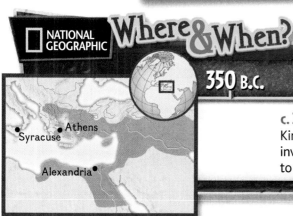

350 B.C.		275 B.C.	200 B.C.
	c. 300 B.C. King Ptolemy I invites Euclid to Alexandria	291 B.C. Menander, the playwright, dies	212 B.C. Archimedes killed by Romans

Greek Culture Spreads

Main Idea Hellenistic cities became centers of learning and culture.

Reading Connection Imagine you are a leading citizen in a new city. How would you make it the best city possible? Read to find out how leaders in the Hellenistic Era improved their cities.

During the Hellenistic Era, philosophers, scientists, poets, and writers flocked to the new Greek cities in southwest Asia and Egypt, especially Alexandria. Many came to take advantage of Alexandria's library. Its more than 500,000 scrolls were useful to students of literature and language. Alexandria also had a museum where researchers went to do their work.

Architecture and Sculpture The Hellenistic kingdoms were lands of opportunity for Greek architects. New cities were being founded, and old ones were being rebuilt. The Hellenistic kings wanted to make these cities like the cultural centers of Greece. They paid handsome fees to line the streets with baths, theaters, and temples.

Hellenistic kings and other wealthy citizens hired Greek sculptors to fill their towns and cities with thousands of statues. These statues showed the same level of workmanship as the statues from Greece's Golden Age.

Literature and Theater Hellenistic leaders also admired talented writers. Kings and leading citizens spent generous sums of money supporting writers' work. As a result, the Hellenistic Age produced a large body of literature. Sadly, very little of this writing has survived.

One of the works we know about is an epic poem by Appolonius (A•puh•LOH•nee•uhs) of **Rhodes** (ROHDZ). Called *Argonautica*, it tells the legend of Jason and his band of heroes. They sail the seas in search of a ram

with golden fleece. Another poet, Theocritus (thee•AH•kruh•tuhs), wrote short poems about the beauty of nature.

Athens remained the center of Greek theater. Playwrights in Athens created a new kind of comedy. The stories had happy endings and still make people laugh. However, unlike the comedies of Greece's Golden Age, they did not poke fun at political leaders. Instead the plays told stories about love and relationships. One of the best known of the new playwrights was Menander (muh•NAN•duhr), who lived from 343 B.C. to 291 B.C.

✔ Reading Check **Explain** How did the Hellenistic kingdoms spread Greek culture?

 **The Poetry of Theocritus**

Theocritus is considered the creator of pastoral poetry. Pastoral poetry deals with rural life, especially the lives of shepherds. It often compares rural and city life. In this selection, he talks about shepherding as a way of life.

"Shepherd, your song is sweeter than the water that tumbles and splashes down from the rocks.

If the Muses get the ewe for their prize,

▲ Sculpture of shepherd

you'll win the [baby] lamb. But if they choose

the lamb, you'll carry away the ewe."
—Theocritus, "First Idyll"

 Document-Based Question

How does Theocritus describe the song of the shepherd?

WH6.4.7. Trace the rise of Alexander the Great and the spread of Greek culture eastward and into Egypt.

WH6.4.8. Describe the enduring contributions of important Greek figures in the arts and sciences (e.g., Hypatia, Socrates, Plato, Aristotle, Euclid, Thucydides).

NATIONAL GEOGRAPHIC — The Way It Was

Science and Inventions

Greek Medicine The ancient Greeks believed that their gods had the power to cure them of illnesses and injuries. Greek temples were places of healing as well as places of worship. In temples, priests treated patients with herbs, prayers and sacrifices to the gods.

In the 400s B.C., Hippocrates (hih • PAH • kruh • TEEZ), a doctor and pioneer of medical science, began to separate medicine from religion. He stressed that it was important to examine the body and look at a patient's symptoms.

Hippocrates asked his students to recite an oath, or pledge, promising never to harm and always to care for their patients. Doctors today still take a version of the Hippocratic Oath when they graduate from medical school.

▲ Greek doctor treating patients

Connecting to the Past

1. How were illnesses and injuries treated before Hippocrates?

2. How did Hippocrates change the way medicine was practiced in ancient Greece?

New Philosophy and Science

Main Idea Philosophers and scientists in the Hellenistic Era introduced new ideas and made major discoveries.

Reading Connection What makes you happy? Read on to learn different Greek ideas about happiness.

During the Hellenistic Era, Athens continued to attract the most famous philosophers in the Greek world. The two most important philosophers were Epicurus and Zeno.

Epicureans Epicurus founded a philosophy we now know as **Epicureanism** (EH • pih • kyu • REE • uh • NIH • zuhm). He taught his students that happiness was the **goal** of life. He believed that the way to be happy was to seek out pleasure.

Today the word *epicurean* means the love of physical pleasure, such as good food or comfortable surroundings. However, to Epicurus, pleasure meant spending time with friends and learning not to worry about things. Epicureans avoided worry by staying out of politics and public service.

Who Were the Stoics? A Phoenician named Zeno developed **Stoicism** (STOH • uh • SIH • zuhm). It became a very popular philosophy in the Hellenistic world. When Zeno came to Athens, he could not afford to rent a **lecture** hall. So he taught at a building known as the "painted porch" near the city market. "Stoicism" comes from *stoa*, the Greek word for "porch."

For Stoics, happiness came from following reason, not emotions, and doing your duty. Today the word *stoic* is used to describe someone who is not affected by joy or grief. Unlike Epicureans, Stoics thought people had a duty to serve their city. The ideas of the Stoic philosophers would later influence Roman philosophers.

Greek Science and Math Scientists, especially mathematicians and astronomers, made **major** contributions during the Hellenistic Era. **Astronomers** (uh•STRAH•nuh•muhrs) study stars, planets, and other heavenly bodies. Aristarchus (AR•uh•STAHR•kuhs), an astronomer from Samos, claimed that the sun was at the center of the universe and that Earth circled the sun. At the time, other astronomers rejected his ideas. They thought that Earth was the center of the universe.

Another astronomer, Eratosthenes (EHR•uh•TAHS•thuh•NEEZ), was in charge of the library at Alexandria. Eratosthenes concluded that Earth is round. He then used his knowledge of geometry and astronomy to measure Earth's circumference—the distance around Earth.

Eratosthenes put two sticks in the ground far apart from each other. When the sun was directly over one stick, the shadow was shorter than the shadow at the other stick. By measuring the shadows, he was

Greek Scientists and Their Contributions

Scientist	Scientific "Firsts"
Archimedes	Established the science of physics Explained the lever and compound pulley
Aristarchus	Established that Earth revolves around the sun
Eratosthenes	Figured out that Earth is round
Euclid	Wrote a book that organized information about geometry
Hipparchus	Created a system to explain how planets and stars move
Hippocrates	Known as the "Father of Medicine" First to write a medical code of good behavior
Hypatia	Expanded knowledge of mathematics and astronomy
Pythagoras	First to establish the principles of geometry

▲ Hippocrates

◄ Hypatia

◄ Pythagoras

Understanding Charts

The ancient Greeks made advances in science.
1. What were Archimedes' achievements?
2. Identify Who wrote a code of behavior that doctors still follow today?

▲ Euclid

▼ Archimedes

able to calculate the curve of Earth's surface and Earth's diameter.

Using his measurements, Eratosthenes estimated that the distance around Earth equaled 24,675 miles (39,702 km). Amazingly, his estimate was within 185 miles (298 km) of the actual distance. Using similar methods, he measured the distance to the sun and to the moon. His measurements were quite accurate for the time.

Euclid (YOO•kluhd) is probably the most famous Greek mathematician. His best-known book *Elements* describes plane geometry. **Plane geometry** (jee•AH•muh•tree) is the branch of mathematics that shows how points, lines, angles, and surfaces relate to one another.

Around 300 B.C., King Ptolemy I (TAH•luh•mee) of Egypt asked Euclid if he knew an easier way to learn geometry than by reading *Elements.* Euclid answered that "there is no royal way" to learn geometry. In other words, if the king wanted to understand Euclid's teachings, he would have to study the same as everyone else. Euclid's theories have influenced mathematicians up to the present day.

The most famous scientist of the Hellenistic Era was **Archimedes** (AHR•kuh•MEE•deez) of **Syracuse** (SIHR•uh•KYOOS). He worked on **solid geometry** (jee•AH•muh•tree)—the study of ball-like shapes called spheres and tubelike shapes called cylinders. He also figured out the value of *pi.* This number is used to measure the area of circles and is usually represented by the symbol π.

Archimedes was also an inventor. One story about Archimedes tells how he came to invent weapons for a war. It all happened because Archimedes had been bragging. "Give me a lever and a place to stand on," Archimedes said to the king of Syracuse, "and I will move the earth."

The king of Syracuse was impressed. He asked Archimedes to use his levers to defend the city. So Archimedes designed catapults—machines that hurled arrows, spears, and rocks.

When the Romans attacked Syracuse in 212 B.C., Archimedes' catapults drove them back. It took the Romans three years to capture Syracuse. During the massacre that followed, Archimedes was killed.

Hellenistic thought and culture had long-lasting effects. The mathematician **Hypatia** (hy•PAY•shuh) is a good example. She lived in Alexandria in Egypt around A.D. 400, over 700 years after Alexander the Great first spread Hellenism. Hypatia continued the Greek tradition of studying philosophy and mathematics. In fact, she is one of the first women mathematicians whose records survive. In addition, she also wrote about astronomy. Her commentaries on other writers provided important information for later generations of historians and scientists.

Reading Check **Explain** Who was the most famous scientist of the Hellenistic Era? What did he contribute?

Greece Falls to Rome

Main Idea Greek power declined as a new power in the Mediterranean arose: Rome.

Reading Connection Think about what makes your country strong. What would happen if you took those things away? Read on to find out what happened to Greece when it grew weak.

The four Greek kingdoms that developed from Alexander's empire shared Hellenistic culture. Despite their common culture, they were unable to work together and often fought wars with one another.

Macedonia dominated Greece for a time but could not keep the various city-states permanently under control. Sparta and many other city-states gained their freedom. These states were Hellenistic in culture but did not have a strong military, so they could not keep their independence long.

In the late 200s B.C., a city-state in Italy called Rome conquered the Italian peninsula. The Romans then began expanding into Greece in order to secure their shipping lanes from pirates. This gave the Romans the excuse to interact directly with the Greeks.

As Roman power grew, both the Greeks and Macedonians began supporting Rome's enemies in times of war. The Romans proved victorious, however. They defeated the Greeks and their allies, invaded Macedonia, and divided it into four kingdoms.

By 146 B.C., Rome had conquered all of Greece. Although Greece was no longer free, Greek ideas and culture continued to influence societies in Europe and Asia for hundreds of years.

✓ **Reading Check** **Explain** Why did Rome conquer the Greek city-states?

 **Study Central** Need help understanding the Hellenistic Era? Visit ca.hss.glencoe.com and click on Study Central.

Section 4 Review

Reading Summary

Review the **Main Ideas**

- Hellenistic cities, such as Alexandria, attracted some of the Greek world's best architects, sculptors, and writers.

- During the Hellenistic Era, new philosophies developed, such as Stoicism and Epicureanism, and scientists made important advances in the fields of astronomy and mathematics.

- The Hellenistic kingdoms fought constantly and were eventually conquered by Rome.

What Did You Learn?

1. Why did the city of Alexandria attract scholars?

2. Describe the form of philosophy developed by Zeno.

Critical Thinking

3. **Summarize** Draw a table like the one below. Write several facts about each scientist in the correct column. **CA 6RC2.4**

Aristarchus	
Eratosthenes	
Euclid	
Archimedes	

4. **The Big Ideas** How were the comedies of the Hellenistic Era influenced by Greece's Golden Age? **CA 6RC2.2**

5. **Analyze** How would knowledge of geometry be helpful to the Greeks? **CA HI2.**

6. **Identify** What did the Epicureans believe about happiness? **CA 6RC2.0**

7. **Writing Poetry** Reread the Primary Source on page 407. How do the author's words create a picture of the shepherd? Use these writing tools to write a poem about Greece. **CA 6RL3.4; 6WA2.1**

Analyzing Primary Sources

WH6.4.4 Explain the significance of Greek mythology to the everyday life of people in the region and how Greek literature continues to permeate our literature and language today, drawing from Greek mythology and epics, such as Homer's *Iliad* and *Odyssey*, and from *Aesop's Fables*. **WH6.4.8** Describe the enduring contributions of important Greek figures in the arts and sciences (e.g., Hypatia, Socrates, Plato, Aristotle, Euclid, Thucydides).

Words of Wisdom

Like many ancient societies, the ancient Greeks admired and wrote about their heroes and military leaders. However, their great thinkers also wrote about many other subjects, from government and religion to science and culture. Many of their works were intended to convey an idea or message, or to convince people of their point of view.

Read the passages on pages 412 and 413, and answer the questions that follow.

Plato ▶

Reader's Dictionary

Glaucon: a man the narrator is addressing

compelling: persuading

dissension (dih•SEHN•shuhn): conflict

destined: decided beforehand

refute (rih•FYOOT): prove wrong

imputation (IHM•pyuh•TAY•shuhn): accusation

The *Republic* of Plato

Plato was one of the great philosophers of ancient Athens. In his Republic Plato argues that the ideal government is one ruled by philosopher-kings. Here he discusses what kind of person should be a ruler.

You will see then, **Glaucon,** that there will be no real injustice in **compelling** our philosophers to watch over and care for the other citizens. We can fairly tell them . . . we have brought you into existence for your country's sake . . . you have been better and more thoroughly educated than those others and hence you are more capable of playing your part both as men of thought and as men of action . . . in truth, government can be at its best and free from

dissension only where the **destined** rulers are least desirous of holding office.

. . . All goes wrong when, starved for lack of anything good in their own lives, men turn to public affairs hoping to snatch from thence the happiness they hunger for. They set about fighting for power, and this conflict ruins them and their country. The life of true philosophy is the only one that looks down upon offices of state. . . . So whom else can you compel to **undertake** the guardianship of the **commonwealth,** if not those who, besides understanding best the principles of government, enjoy a nobler life than the politician's and look for rewards of a different kind?

—Plato, *Republic*

Aesop's Fables

Fables are short tales with the purpose of teaching a lesson. The most famous author of Greek fables is Aesop. His fables were passed down by word of mouth for hundreds of years before finally being collected into written volumes.

The Father and His Sons

A FATHER had a family of sons who were perpetually quarreling among themselves. When he failed to heal their disputes by his exhortations, he determined to give them a practical illustration of the evils of disunion; and for this purpose he one day told them to bring him a bundle of sticks. When they had done so, he placed the [bundle of sticks] into the hands of each of them in succession, and ordered them to break it in pieces. They tried with all their strength, and were not able to do it. He next . . . took the sticks separately, one by one, and again put them into his sons' hands, upon which they broke them easily. He then addressed them in these words: "My sons, if you are of one mind, and unite to assist each other, you will be as this [bundle of sticks], uninjured by all the attempts of your enemies; but if you are divided among yourselves, you will be broken as easily as these sticks."

The Wolf and the Lamb

WOLF, meeting with a Lamb astray from the fold, resolved not to lay violent hands on him, but to find some plea to justify to the Lamb the Wolf's right to eat him. He thus addressed him: "Sirrah, last year you grossly insulted me." "Indeed," bleated the Lamb in a mournful tone of voice, "I was not then born." Then said the Wolf, "You feed in my pasture." "No, good sir," replied the Lamb, "I have not yet tasted grass." . . . Upon which the Wolf seized him and ate him up, saying

▲ Aesop

"Well! I won't remain supperless, even though you **refute** every one of my **imputations**." The tyrant will always find a pretext for his tyranny.

—*Aesop's Fables*, George Fyler Townsend, trans.

DBQ Document-Based Questions

The Republic of Plato

1. Why do you think the best ruler is someone who does not want power?

2. Why does Plato believe that philosophers would make the best rulers?

3. What kind of men make the worst rulers?

Aesop's Fables

4. Explain the moral of the first fable.

5. Explain the moral of the second fable.

6. Give a modern example of the moral of the first fable.

Read to Write

7. Explain how Aesop's fables are related to creating a strong government. Do you think Plato would have agreed with the morals in Aesop's fables? Why? **CA HR5.**

Review Content Vocabulary

1. Write a brief paragraph that defines and compares the following terms.

   epic   fable   myth

Decide if each statement is *True* or *False*.

____ 2. An oracle was a shrine Greeks visited to receive prophecies.

____ 3. Sophists were professional teachers.

____ 4. The death of Socrates marks the beginning of the Hellenistic Era.

____ 5. Astronomers study stars, planets, and other heavenly bodies.

____ 6. Euclid developed plane geometry.

Review the Main Ideas

Section 1 • The Culture of Ancient Greece

7. What did the Greeks believe about their gods and goddesses?

8. How did the Greeks use poetry and fables to teach values?

9. What are two types of Greek dramas?

10. What did Greek art and architecture express?

Section 2 • Greek Philosophy and History

11. How have the ideas of Greek philosophers influenced our world today?

12. Why are Greek historians so important?

Section 3 • Alexander the Great

13. Which leader united the Greek states?

14. What are the two main accomplishments of Alexander the Great?

Section 4 • The Spread of Greek Culture

15. Why were Hellenistic cities important?

16. In what fields did Hellenistic scientists make advances?

17. What new power arose in the Mediterranean and threatened Greece?

Critical Thinking

18. **Understanding Cause and Effect** How did the Peloponnesian War weaken the Greek states? **CA HI2.**

19. **Analyze** Why would knowing the circumference of Earth have been helpful to the Greeks? **CA 6RC2.0**

20. **Compare** How was religion in ancient Greece similar to religion in ancient Egypt? **CA 6RC2.2**

21. **Analyze** Why do you think the development of written history is important? **CA 6RL3.0**

Geography Skills

Study the map below and answer the following questions.

22. **Location** Analyze the location of the Hellenistic kingdoms. What present-day countries control territory that was controlled by the Seleucid empire? **CA CS3.**

23. **Human/Environment Interaction** Which kingdom do you think was the most difficult to govern based on its geography? **CA CS3.**

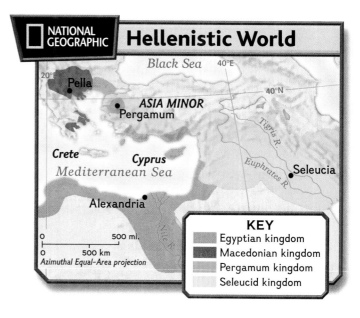

NATIONAL GEOGRAPHIC
Hellenistic World

Black Sea   40°E

Pella

ASIA MINOR
Pergamum

Crete

Cyprus

Mediterranean Sea

Tigris R.

Euphrates R.

Seleucia

Alexandria

Nile R.

500 mi.
500 km
Azimuthal Equal-Area projection

KEY
Egyptian kingdom
Macedonian kingdom
Pergamum kingdom
Seleucid kingdom

Read to Write

24. The Big Ideas Understanding Cultures As Hellenistic cities became centers of learning and trade, they were influenced by Greek culture. Write a three-paragraph essay describing how Greek culture affected people in Asia in the Hellenistic Era. **CA CS3.**

25. Using Your FOLDABLES Review the developments in early Greece that you listed on your foldable. Using numbers, rank each development from the most valuable to the least valuable. Explain the reason for your highest and lowest ranking. **CA CS1.**

Using Academic Vocabulary

26. Review the list of words below. Write a paragraph that uses all of these words in the past tense. Then rewrite that same paragraph using the words in the present and future tenses.

grant	achieve
conflict	lecture
reject	major

Linking Past and Present

27. Expository Writing The Nobel Prize is awarded yearly to people who have made great achievements. Do research to find out more about the award. Then choose one Greek philosopher, writer, scientist, or leader you think deserves the Nobel Prize. Write a short speech to explain why. Present your speech to the class. **CA 6WA2.5**

Economics Connection

28. Writing Research Reports The vast empire established during the reign of Alexander the Great allowed many different cultures and people to more easily reach one another. Write a research report that explains how this joining of cultures affected the economies of people in the empire. Use evidence from your local library and the Internet to support your position. **CA 6WA2.3**

Reviewing Skills

29. Reading Skill Visualizing Using the visualizing techniques that were introduced in this chapter, create a story describing Alexander the Great's soldiers during their march across Iran's southern desert. Reread page 401 to help you visualize the scene. Write your story from a soldier's point of view. Use visualization to help you describe the setting of the story. **CA 6WA2.1**

30. Analysis Skill Building a Time Line Using information from the chapter, create a time line that shows the major authors, artists, and philosophers of ancient Greece. Include each person's most important contributions and works. **CA CS2.**

Standards Practice

Select the best answer for each of the following questions.

31 The *Iliad* and the *Odyssey* are

- **A** two ships that traveled to Troy.
- **B** poems by Aesop.
- **C** epics by Homer.
- **D** Greek comedies performed in outdoor theaters.

32 What do Sophists, Socrates, Plato, and Aristotle have in common?

- **A** all were Greek philosophers
- **B** they agreed that democracy was the best system of government
- **C** they were pupils of Libanius
- **D** they all wrote histories

The Rise of Rome

◀ Ruins of the Forum in Rome, Italy

NATIONAL GEOGRAPHIC *Where&When?*

500 B.C.	300 B.C.	100 B.C.	A.D. 100
451 B.C.	**267** B.C.	**27** B.C.	**A.D. 96**
Romans adopt the Twelve Tables	Rome controls most of Italy	Octavian becomes Rome's first emperor	Rule of the Good Emperors begins

The Big Ideas

History Online
Chapter Overview Visit ca.hss.glencoe.com for a preview of Chapter 9.

Section 1 Rome's Beginnings

Physical geography plays a role in how civilizations develop and decline. The civilization of Rome began on a river in Italy. Surrounded by hills, its location in central Italy helped it become an economic and military power.

Section 2 The Roman Republic

Systems of order, such as law and government, contribute to stable societies. Rome was a republic that developed written laws and a strong government. This helped Rome survive wars and expand into the Mediterranean.

Section 3 The Fall of the Republic

All civilizations depend upon leadership for survival. As Rome's territory grew, generals in the army gained political power. Eventually, they seized power and turned the republic into the Roman Empire.

Section 4 The Early Empire

Civilizations with strong economies prosper and grow. Augustus and many of his successors helped improve Rome's economy. As Rome prospered, its empire grew larger and wealthier.

View the Chapter 9 video in the Glencoe Video Program.

FOLDABLES™ Study Organizer

Know-Want-Learn *Make this foldable to help you organize what you know, what you want to know, and what you learn about the rise of Rome.*

Step 1 *Fold four sheets of paper in half from top to bottom.*

Step 2 *On each folded paper, make a cut 1 inch from the side on the top flap.*

Cut 1 inch from the edge through the top flap only.

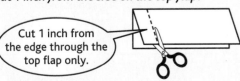

Step 3 *Place the folded papers one on top of the other. Staple the four sections together and label the top four tabs: Rome's Beginnings, The Roman Republic, The Fall of the Republic, and The Early Empire.*

Staple here.

Rome's Beginnings

Reading and Writing *Before reading the chapter, write under the tabs of your foldable what you already know about the beginning of Rome, the rise and fall of its republic, and the early Roman Empire. Also write one question you have on each tab. As you read, summarize what you learn under each tab.*

Making Inferences

Reading Skill

1 Learn It!

When you make inferences, you draw conclusions that are not directly stated in the text. This means you "read between the lines." You interpret clues and details in the text and draw upon your prior knowledge and experience. Authors rely on a reader's ability to infer because all the details are not always given. Read this paragraph about Roman law from Section 2.

> In many lands, **people at the top of society** often had **special privileges** and did not have to obey the same laws or use the same courts as people lower down. In some places, **people at the bottom of society** did not have any legal rights at all.
>
> *— from page 431*

Use this Think-Through chart to help you make inferences.

Text	Question	Inferences
people at the top of society	Who were they?	Rich landowners, nobility, aristocracy?
special privileges	What kind of privileges?	Right to own land? Right to vote?
people at the bottom of society	Who were they?	Poor farmers, artisans, enslaved peoples, non-military people, women?

Reading Tip

Sometimes you make inferences by using other reading skills, such as questioning and predicting.

2 Practice It!

Read the excerpt below about the five "good emperors" and pay attention to highlighted words as you make inferences.

Read to Write ·····

Read the first paragraph of Section 4 under the label **The Emperor Augustus.** Write down inferences about what kind of person you think Augustus was. Then read the biography of Augustus on page 447 to see if your inferences were correct.

They presided over nearly **a century of prosperity,** from A.D. 96 to A.D. 180. **Agriculture flourished, trade increased, and the standard of living rose.**

During this time, the **emperor came to overshadow the Senate** more than ever before. The **five "good emperors" did not abuse their power,** however. They were among the most devoted and capable rulers in Rome's history.

—from page 448

▲ Roman coins

Create your own Think-Through chart to help you make further inferences about the "good emperors." You might want to use a chart similar to the one on the previous page, with the same labels: *Text, Questions,* and *Inferences.* Read the rest of page 448 to see if your inferences were correct.

3 Apply It!

Inferring can help you understand an author's point of view. With a partner, read the excerpt from Cicero's speech on page 440. Discuss what inferences you both made.

Rome's Beginnings

Guide to Reading

History Social Science Standards

WH6.7 Students analyze the geographic, political, economic, religious, and social structures during the development of Rome.

Looking Back, Looking Ahead

In previous chapters, you learned about the civilization of ancient Greece. Greek ways did not die with the end of Greece's freedom. They were adopted and spread widely by another civilization, Rome.

Focusing on the Main Ideas

- Geography played an important role in the rise of Roman civilization. *(page 421)*

- The Romans created a republic and conquered Italy. By treating people fairly, they built Rome from a small city into a great power. *(page 423)*

Locating Places

Sicily (SIH•suh•lee)
Apennines (A•puh•NYNZ)
Latium (LAY•shee•uhm)
Tiber River (TY•buhr)
Etruria (ih•TRUR•ee•uh)

Meeting People

Romulus (RAHM•yuh•luhs)
Remus (REE•muhs)
Aeneas (ih•NEE•uhs)
Latins (LA•tuhnz)
Etruscans (ih•TRUHS•kuhnz)
Tarquins (TAHR•kwihnz)

Content Vocabulary

republic (rih•PUH•blihk)
legion (LEE•juhn)

Academic Vocabulary

isolate (EYE•suh•LAYT)
capacity (kuh•PA•suh•tee)
chapter (CHAP•tuhr)
status (STA•tuhs)

Reading Strategy

Summarizing Information Use a diagram to show how the Etruscans affected the development of Rome.

Etruscans	

Where & When?

NATIONAL GEOGRAPHIC

ITALY
• Rome
Sicily
AFRICA

650 B.C.	450 B.C.	250 B.C.
c. 650 B.C. Etruscans rule Rome	509 B.C. Rome becomes a republic	267 B.C. Rome controls most of Italy

The Origins of Rome

Main Idea Geography played an important role in the rise of Roman civilization.

Reading Connection If you were founding a new city, what natural features would influence your choice of a building site? As you read this section, think about the choices that the early Romans made.

Italy is in an important location in the middle of the Mediterranean region. It is a long, narrow peninsula with a distinctive shape: it looks like a high-heeled boot extending into the sea. The heel points toward Greece and the toe toward the island of **Sicily** (SIH•suh•lee). Across the top of the boot are the Alps, high mountains that separate Italy from European lands to the north. Another mountain range, the **Apennines** (A•puh•NYNZ), runs all the way down the boot from north to south.

The landscape of Italy is similar to that of Greece, but the Apennines are not as rugged as Greece's mountains. They can be crossed much more easily. As a result, the people who settled in Italy were not split up into small, **isolated** communities as the Greeks were. In addition, Italy had better farmland than Greece. Its mountain slopes level off to large flat plains that are ideal for growing crops. With more **capacity** to produce food, Italy could support more people than Greece could.

Historians know little about the first people to live in Italy. There is evidence, however, that groups from the north slipped through Italy's mountain passes between about 1500 B.C. and 1000 B.C. Attracted by the mild climate and rich soil, a small but steady stream of newcomers settled in the hills and on the plains. One group of Latin-speaking people built the city of Rome on the plain of **Latium** (LAY•shee•uhm) in central Italy. They became known as Romans.

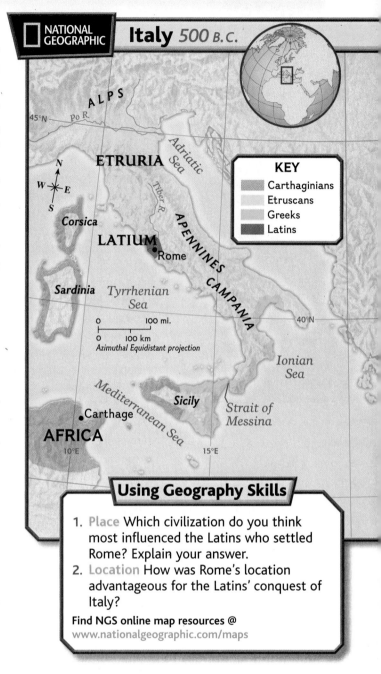

NATIONAL GEOGRAPHIC **Italy** 500 B.C.

KEY
- Carthaginians
- Etruscans
- Greeks
- Latins

0 — 100 mi.
0 — 100 km
Azimuthal Equidistant projection

Using Geography Skills

1. **Place** Which civilization do you think most influenced the Latins who settled Rome? Explain your answer.
2. **Location** How was Rome's location advantageous for the Latins' conquest of Italy?

Find NGS online map resources @
www.nationalgeographic.com/maps

Where Was Rome Located? Geography played a major part in the location of Rome. The site chosen for Rome was about 15 miles (24 km) up the **Tiber River** (TY•buhr) from the Mediterranean Sea. The Tiber River gave the Romans a source of water and a way to get to the rest of the Mediterranean world. At the same time, Rome was far enough from the sea to escape raids by pirates.

The *Aeneid*

Two legends describe the beginning of Rome. One says that after Troy was destroyed, Aeneas and the other Trojans went in search of another place to live.

▲ Virgil

"Weeping, I drew away from our old country. . . . I took to the open sea, borne outward into exile with my people, my son, my hearth gods, and the greater gods. . . . Now making landfall under the southwind there, I plotted out on that curved shore the walls of a colony—though fate opposed it—and I devised the name Aeneadae for the people, from my own."

—adapted from Virgil, *Aeneid*

DBQ Document-Based Question

What type of person do you think Aeneas was to build a new city after having the first one destroyed?

In addition, Rome was built on a series of seven hills. The Romans did this on purpose. The hills were very steep, making it easy to defend the city against enemy attack. Rome was also located at a place where people could easily cross the Tiber River. As a result, Rome became a stopping place for people traveling north and south in western Italy and for merchant ships sailing in the Mediterranean.

How Did Rome Begin?

Two different legends describe how Rome began. The traditional story is that twin brothers named **Romulus** (RAHM•yuh•luhs) and **Remus** (REE•muhs) founded the city. As babies, the boys were abandoned near the Tiber River. Rescued by a wolf and raised by a shepherd, they decided to build a city in 753 B.C. The twins quarreled, however, and Remus made fun of the wall his brother was building. In a fury, Romulus attacked Remus and killed him. Romulus went on to become the first king of Rome, the new city he named after himself.

The seeds of Rome are traced even farther back in the *Aeneid,* a famous epic by the Roman poet Virgil. The *Aeneid* is the story of the Trojan hero **Aeneas** (ih•NEE•uhs). He and a band of followers are said to have sailed the Mediterranean Sea after the Greeks captured Troy. After many adventures, the Trojans landed at the mouth of the Tiber. Through warfare and then marriage to the local king's daughter, Aeneas united the Trojans and some of the **Latins** (LA•tuhnz), the local people. He thus became the "father" of the Romans.

Historians are not sure how Rome began. They think that Latins lived in the area of Rome as early as 1000 B.C. They built huts on Rome's hills, tended herds, and grew crops. Sometime between 800 B.C. and 700 B.C., they decided to band together for protection. It was this community that became known as Rome.

Early Influences

After about 800 B.C., other groups came to Italy. Two of these groups, the Greeks and the **Etruscans** (ih•TRUHS•kuhnz), played a major role in shaping the framework of the Roman civilization.

Many Greeks came to southern Italy and Sicily between 750 B.C. and 550 B.C., when Greece was busily building overseas colonies. From the Greeks, Romans learned to grow olives and grapes. They also adopted the Greek alphabet, and they would eventually model their architecture, sculpture, and literature after the Greeks.

▲ The Etruscans used a variety of metals, including copper, lead, iron, and tin to make beautiful jewelry like the piece shown above.

Rome's early growth was influenced most, however, by the Etruscans. The Etruscans lived north of Rome in **Etruria** (ih•TRUR•ee•uh). After 650 B.C., they moved south and took control of Rome and most of Latium.

The Etruscans were skilled metalworkers who became rich from mining and trade. They forced enslaved people to do the heaviest work and made their own lives comfortable. Their tomb paintings show men and women feasting, dancing, and playing music and sports. Some murals also show bloody battle scenes, revealing the Etruscans' military achievements.

The Etruscans changed Rome from a village of straw-roofed huts into a city of wood and brick buildings. They laid out streets, temples, and public buildings around a central square. Etruscans also exposed the Romans to a new style of dress, featuring short cloaks and togas—loose garments draped over one shoulder. More importantly, the Etruscan army would serve as a model for the mighty army the Romans eventually assembled.

✓ **Reading Check** **Explain** How did geography help the Romans prosper?

The Birth of a Republic

Main Idea The Romans created a republic and conquered Italy. By treating people fairly, they built Rome from a small city into a great power.

Reading Connection Have you heard the phrase "winning hearts and minds"? It means convincing people to support you rather than just forcing them to obey. Read on to learn how the Romans not only conquered other people in Italy but also won their hearts and minds.

The Etruscans ruled Rome for more than 100 years. Under the Etruscans, Rome became wealthy and powerful. However, the ruling family, called the **Tarquins** (TAHR•kwihnz), grew more and more cruel.

Finally, in 509 B.C., the Romans rebelled. They overthrew the Tarquins and set up a **republic** (rih•PUH•blihk). A republic is a form of government in which the leader is not a king or queen but someone put in office by citizens with the right to vote. In a republic, the citizens have the power. The rise of the Roman Republic marked the beginning of a new **chapter** in Rome's history.

▲ Etruscan murals often showed lively scenes of daily life, such as religious ceremonies or people enjoying music and feasts. *How did the Etruscans become wealthy?*

At the time Rome became a republic, it was still a small city, surrounded by enemies. Over the next 200 years, the Romans fought war after war against their neighbors. In 338 B.C. they finally defeated the other Latins living nearby. Next they attacked the Etruscans and defeated them in 284 B.C. By 267 B.C., the Romans had also conquered the Greeks in southern Italy. With this victory, the Romans became the masters of almost all of Italy.

Roman Legionary

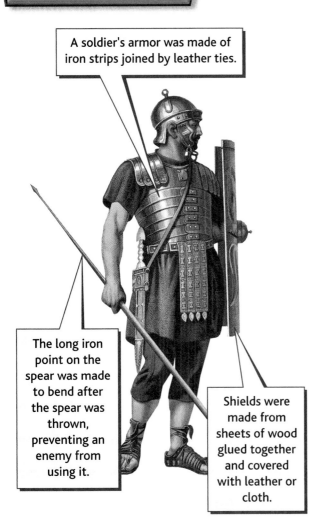

A soldier's armor was made of iron strips joined by leather ties.

The long iron point on the spear was made to bend after the spear was thrown, preventing an enemy from using it.

Shields were made from sheets of wood glued together and covered with leather or cloth.

At first, the Roman army was made up of ordinary citizens. Later the army contained well-trained professional soldiers and was one of the best fighting forces in the world. *What was a standard, and why did the army carry them?*

Why Was Rome So Strong? Rome was able to conquer Italy because the Romans were excellent soldiers. In the republic's early days, every male citizen who owned land had to serve in the army. Discipline was harsh, and deserters were punished by death. The tough discipline helped mold Roman soldiers into fighters who did not give up easily. In addition, they were practical problem solvers.

For example, Roman armies at first fought like Greek armies. Row upon row of soldiers marched shoulder to shoulder, keeping their shields together and holding long spears. Roman generals accurately assessed that this way of fighting was slow and hard to control. They reorganized their soldiers into smaller groups called **legions** (LEE•juhnz). Each legion had about 6,000 men and was further divided into groups of 60 to 120 soldiers. These small groups could quickly cut through enemy lines.

Roman soldiers, or legionaries, were armed with a short sword called a *gladius* and a spear called a *pilum.* Each unit also carried its own standard—a tall pole topped with a symbol. In battle, standards helped keep units together because the soldiers could see them above the conflict.

Shrewd Rulers The Romans were not only good fighters but also smart planners. As they expanded throughout Italy, they built permanent military settlements in the areas they conquered. Then they built roads between these towns. These roads allowed troops to travel swiftly to any place in their growing territory.

To rule their new conquests, the Romans created the Roman Confederation. Under this system, Romans granted full citizenship to some peoples, especially other Latins. They could vote and participate in the government, and they were treated the same as other citizens under the law. The Romans granted other peoples the **status** of allies.

Allies were free to run their own local affairs, but they had to pay taxes to the republic and provide soldiers for the army. The Romans made it clear that loyal allies could improve their position and even become Roman citizens.

With these policies, the Romans proved themselves clever rulers. They were aware that conquered peoples were more loyal to the government if they were well treated. Rome's generosity paid off. As a result, the republic grew stronger and more unified.

All the same, Rome was not afraid to use force if necessary. If conquered peoples revolted against Roman rule, their resistance was swiftly put down.

✓ Reading Check **Describe** How did Rome rule its new conquests?

▲ This mosaic, or picture made from bits of stone, shows a group of Roman legionaries. *How many soldiers made up a legion?*

History Online
Study Central Need help understanding Rome's beginnings? Visit ca.hss.glencoe.com and click on Study Central.

Section ① Review

Reading Summary

Review the **Main Ideas**

- The Romans, a Latin-speaking people, settled the region of Rome on the west side of Italy. The region's geography, as well as Etruscan and Greek ideas, helped Rome grow.

- In 509 B.C. the Romans overthrew Etruscan rule and established a republic. By about 275 B.C., Roman legions had conquered most of Italy.

What Did You Learn?

1. Where did the Greeks live in Italy, and how did they influence Roman civilization?

2. Describe the two legends that tell of the founding of Rome. Then describe how and when Rome was actually founded.

Critical Thinking

3. **Geography Skills** Draw a diagram like the one below. List examples of how geography determined Rome's location.
CA 6RC2.4 **CA CS3.**

Rome's Location

4. **The Big Ideas** How did geography affect the development of civilization in Greece and Italy?
CA CS3.

5. **Expository Writing** Write a short essay discussing the reasons Rome was so successful in its conquest of Italy.
CA 6WA2.2

6. **Reading** **Making Inferences** After reading this section, what can you infer about the reasons for Rome's success? **CA 6RC2.0**

Section 2

The Roman Republic

History Social Science Standards

WH6.7 Students analyze the geographic, political, economic, religious, and social structures during the development of Rome.

Guide to Reading

Looking Back, Looking Ahead

Romans had suffered under cruel Etruscan kings. When they had the chance to create their own government, they chose something very different.

Focusing on the Main Ideas

- Rome's republic was shaped by a struggle between wealthy landowners and regular citizens as it gradually expanded the right to vote. *(page 427)*

- The Roman Republic's legal system was based on the rule of law. *(page 431)*

- Rome slowly destroyed the Carthaginian Empire and took control of the entire Mediterranean region. *(page 432)*

Locating Places

Carthage (KAHR•thihj)
Cannae (KA•nee)
Zama (ZAY•muh)

Meeting People

Cincinnatus (SIHN•suh•NA•tuhs)
Hannibal (HA•nuh•buhl)

Content Vocabulary

patrician (puh•TRIH•shuhn)
plebeian (plih•BEE•uhn)
consul (KAHN•suhl)
veto (VEE•toh)
praetor (PREE•tuhr)
dictator (DIHK•TAY•tuhr)

Academic Vocabulary

legislate (LEH•juhs•LAYT)
accommodate (uh • KAH • muh • DAYT)
challenge (CHA•luhnj)

Reading Strategy

Categorizing Information Complete a chart like the one below describing the government of Rome.

Officials	Legislative Bodies

Where&When?

NATIONAL GEOGRAPHIC

450 B.C.   300 B.C.   150 B.C.

451 B.C. Romans adopt the Twelve Tables

264 B.C. Punic Wars begin

146 B.C. Rome destroys Carthage

SPAIN ITALY •Rome Carthage• GREECE

WH6.7.1 Identify the location and describe the rise of the Roman Republic, including the importance of such mythical and historical figures as Aeneas, Romulus and Remus, Cincinnatus, Julius Caesar, and Cicero.

WH6.7.2 Describe the government of the Roman Republic and its significance (e.g., written constitution and tripartite government, checks and balances, civic duty).

Rome's Government

Main Idea Rome's republic was shaped by a struggle between wealthy landowners and regular citizens as it gradually expanded the right to vote.

Reading Connection Do you know where our word *republic* comes from? It is made up of two Latin words meaning "thing of the people." Read on to learn about the republican government that early Romans created.

Early Romans were divided into two classes: patricians and plebeians. The **patricians** (puh•TRIH•shuhnz) were wealthy landowners. These nobles made up Rome's ruling class. Most of Rome's people, however, were **plebeians** (plih•BEE•uhnz). This group consisted of artisans, shopkeepers, and owners of small farms.

Both patrician and plebeian men were Roman citizens. They had the right to vote and the duty to pay taxes and serve in the army. However, plebeians had less social status. They could not marry patricians and could not hold public office.

How Did Rome's Government Work?

Rome had a tripartite, or three part, government. One group of people ran the government, another group made laws, and a third group acted as judges. It had checks and balances so that one group could not get too strong, but it did not separate powers like our goverment does today. Judges also helped run the government, and some leaders who ran the government also helped make laws.

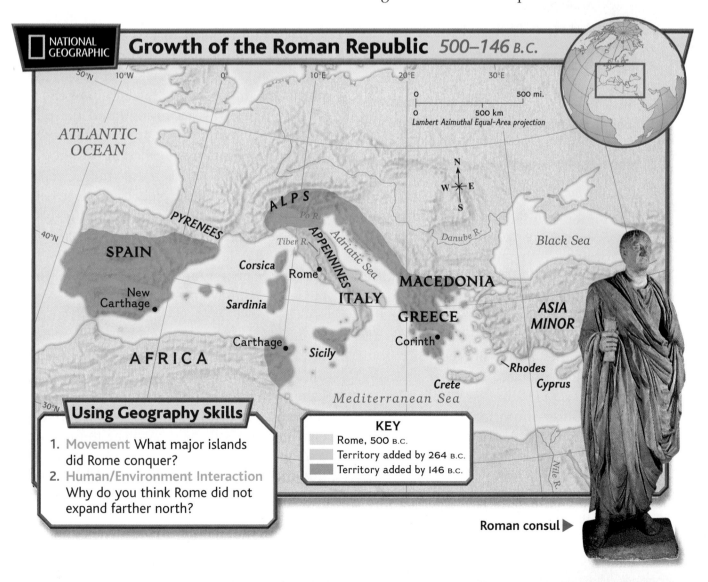

NATIONAL GEOGRAPHIC

Growth of the Roman Republic 500–146 B.C.

ATLANTIC OCEAN

SPAIN

PYRENEES

New Carthage

AFRICA

Carthage

Sardinia

Corsica

ALPS

Po R.

Tiber R.

Rome

APPENNINES

ITALY

Sicily

Adriatic Sea

Danube R.

MACEDONIA

GREECE

Corinth

Crete

Mediterranean Sea

Black Sea

ASIA MINOR

Rhodes

Cyprus

Nile R.

500 mi.

500 km

Lambert Azimuthal Equal-Area projection

Using Geography Skills

1. **Movement** What major islands did Rome conquer?
2. **Human/Environment Interaction** Why do you think Rome did not expand farther north?

KEY

Rome, 500 B.C.
Territory added by 264 B.C.
Territory added by 146 B.C.

Roman consul ▶

A Roman Triumph

Sometimes military leaders returning to Rome after a victory took part in a great parade called a triumph.

"Thus arrayed [decoratively dressed], they entered the city, having at the head of the procession the spoils and trophies and figures representing the captured forts, cities, mountains, rivers, lakes, and seas—everything, in fact, that they had taken. . . . [When] . . . the victorious general arrived at the Roman Forum . . . he rode up to the Capitol. There he performed certain rites and made offerings."

▲ Roman soldiers

—Zonaras, "A Roman Triumph"

DBQ Document-Based Question

Why do you think the military leaders and their troops were dressed decoratively before the triumph?

In the Roman Republic, the top government officials were the **consuls** (KAHN•suhlz). Two consuls—both patricians—were chosen every year. They headed the army and ran the government. Because they served such short terms, there was little risk that they would abuse their power. The consuls also kept each other in line because each could **veto** (VEE•toh), or reject, the other's decision. The word *veto* is Latin for "I forbid." Rome also had other important officials called **praetors** (PREE•tuhrz). Their core task was to interpret the law and act as judges in court cases.

Rome's most important **legislative,** or lawmaking, body was the Senate. This was a select group of 300 patrician men who served for life. In the beginning, the Senate only gave advice to the consuls. Over time, the power of the Senate grew. By the 200s B.C., it could propose laws, hold debates, and approve building programs.

Another legislative body was the Assembly of Centuries. It elected the consuls and praetors, and passed laws. Like the Senate, the Assembly of Centuries was controlled by the patricians.

Plebeians Against Patricians As you might predict, plebeians complained about having so little power in the Roman Republic. After all, they fought alongside patricians in the army, and their tax payments helped the republic thrive.

In 494 B.C. many plebeians went on strike. They refused to serve in the army. They also left the city to set up a republic of their own. These moves frightened the patricians into agreeing to share power.

The patricians **accommodated** the plebeians by allowing them to have their own body of representatives, called the Council of the Plebs in 471 B.C. The assembly elected tribunes who brought plebeian concerns to the government's attention. The tribunes also won the right to veto government decisions. In 455 B.C. plebeians and patricians were allowed to marry, and in the 300s B.C., plebeians were allowed to become consuls.

The most far-reaching political reform came in 287 B.C. In that year, the Council of the Plebs finally was granted the power to pass laws for all Romans. Now all male citizens had equal political standing, at least in theory. In practice, a few wealthy patrician families still held most of the power, and women remained without a voice in government. The Roman Republic had become more representative, but it was far from a full-fledged democracy.

Who Was Cincinnatus? An unusual feature of the Roman Republic was the office of **dictator** (DIHK•TAY•tuhr). Today we define a dictator as an oppressive ruler with complete control over the state. Roman dictators also had complete control, but they only ruled on a temporary basis during emergencies. The Senate appointed a dictator in times of great danger. As soon as the danger was past, Roman dictators gave up their power.

The best-known early Roman dictator is **Cincinnatus** (SIHN•suh•NA•tuhs). About 460 B.C., a powerful enemy had surrounded a Roman army. Officials decided that Rome needed a dictator and that Cincinnatus was the man for the job. Cincinnatus left his farm and gathered an army. He defeated the enemy in short order and returned to Rome in triumph. Although he probably could have continued ruling, Cincinnatus did not want power. Having done his duty, he returned to his farm and gave up his dictatorship.

Romans strongly believed in civic duty, or the idea that citizens have a responsibility to help their country. Cincinnatus was a popular example of someone doing his duty as a citizen. He was widely admired in his generation and in later ages. George Washington, for one, took inspiration from his example. Like Cincinnatus, Washington was a farmer when he was asked to head an army: the Continental Army in the American War for Independence. After leading the Americans to victory, Washington returned to his plantation home. Only later, and with some reluctance, did he agree to become the first president of the United States.

✓ Reading Check **Explain** What checks and balances existed in the Roman Republic's government?

The Way It Was

Focus on Everyday Life

Roman Dinner Parties Before Rome became a powerful empire, Romans ate simple meals of porridge, dried vegetables, and greens. People rarely ate meat or seafood. After Rome's conquests, the dining habits of wealthy Romans changed. Newly rich Romans showed off their wealth with expensive feasts that included exotic foods and lively entertainment for their guests.

At Roman dinner parties, guests reclined on couches. The enslaved servants served the food, which would be carried into the banquet room on great silver platters. Roman dishes might include boiled stingray garnished with hot raisins; boiled crane with turnips; or roast flamingo cooked with dates, onions, honey, and wine.

▼ A wealthy Roman woman reclining on a couch

Connecting to the Past
1. Whose eating habits changed after Rome became wealthy and powerful?
2. Describe how their eating habits changed.

Biography

WH6.7.1 Identify the location and describe the rise of the Roman Republic, including the importance of such mythical and historical figures as Aeneas, Romulus and Remus, Cincinnatus, Julius Caesar, and Cicero.

LUCIUS QUINCTIUS CINCINNATUS

c. 519–438 B.C.

▲ Cincinnatus is asked to lead Rome.

The loyal devotion of Cincinnatus greatly impressed the Roman historian Livy. In his *History of Rome,* Livy advised his readers to listen to the worthwhile story of Cincinnatus, whose virtue rose high above any rewards that wealth could bring.

According to Livy, Cincinnatus lived in Rome but owned and worked a four-acre field on the other side of the Tiber River. On the day that the officials looked for Cincinnatus, they found him hard at work in his field, covered with dirt and sweat. Cincinnatus was surprised when the officials asked him to put on his toga and listen as they explained the wishes of the Roman Senate.

The officials explained the emergency situation to Cincinnatus. He agreed to the Senate's request that he become a dictator. Cincinnatus and the officials crossed the Tiber River to Rome. The next morning, before daylight, Cincinnatus went to the Forum and gathered his forces to attack the enemy.

The story of Cincinnatus was important to the ancient Romans for several reasons. He was victorious in battle and quickly gave up the dictatorship. Perhaps more importantly, he did his civic duty by responding to a call to serve.

"The city was in the grip of fear."
–Livy, *The Rise of Rome*

Then and Now

Name a modern-day leader that you think historians will write about with great admiration. Explain why.

WH6.7.2 Describe the government of the Roman Republic and its significance (e.g., written constitution and tripartite government, checks and balances, civic duty).

WH6.7.8 Discuss the legacies of Roman art and architecture, technology and science, literature, language, and law.

Roman Law

Main Idea The Roman Republic's legal system was based on the rule of law.

Reading Connection Have you ever heard the phrase "innocent until proven guilty"? Read to learn how Rome introduced this idea that we still use in our courts today.

One of Rome's major gifts to the world was its system of law. The legal system of the United States owes much to the Roman system.

Rome's first code of laws was the Twelve Tables, adopted about 451 B.C. Before this time, Rome's laws were not written down. As a result, plebeians claimed that patrician judges often favored their own class. They demanded that the laws be put in writing for everyone to see.

The patricians finally agreed. They had the laws carved on bronze tablets that were placed in Rome's marketplace, or the Forum (FOHR•uhm). The Twelve Tables became the basis for all future Roman laws. They established the principle that all free citizens had the right to be treated equally by the legal system.

The Twelve Tables, however, applied only to Roman citizens. As the Romans took over more lands, they realized that new rules were needed to solve legal disputes between citizens and noncitizens. They created a collection of laws called the Law of Nations. It stated principles of justice that applied to all people everywhere.

These standards of justice included ideas that we still accept today. A person was seen as innocent until proven guilty. People accused of crimes could defend themselves before a judge. A judge had to look at the evidence carefully before making a decision.

The idea that the law should apply to everyone equally and that all people should be treated the same way by the legal system is called the "rule of law." In the age of

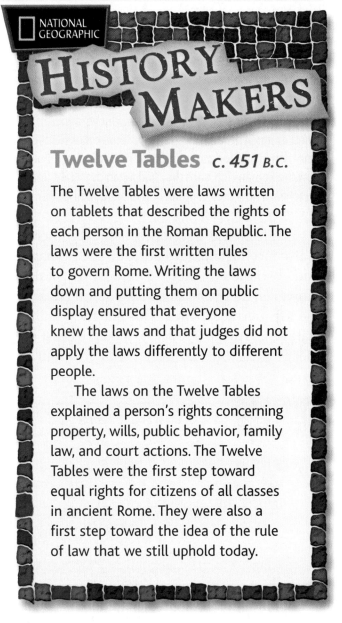

NATIONAL GEOGRAPHIC

HISTORY MAKERS

Twelve Tables c. 451 B.C.

The Twelve Tables were laws written on tablets that described the rights of each person in the Roman Republic. The laws were the first written rules to govern Rome. Writing the laws down and putting them on public display ensured that everyone knew the laws and that judges did not apply the laws differently to different people.

The laws on the Twelve Tables explained a person's rights concerning property, wills, public behavior, family law, and court actions. The Twelve Tables were the first step toward equal rights for citizens of all classes in ancient Rome. They were also a first step toward the idea of the rule of law that we still uphold today.

Rome, the rule of law was still a new concept. In many lands, people at the top of society often had special privileges and did not have to obey the same laws or use the same courts as people lower down. In some places, people at the bottom of society did not have any legal rights at all.

The rule of law is one of the key ideas that the Romans gave to the world. It remains the basis of our legal system today.

Reading Check **Identify** What is the "rule of law" and why is it important?

Rome Expands

Main Idea Rome slowly destroyed the Carthaginian Empire and took control of the entire Mediterranean region.

Reading Connection When you achieve a victory–whether it is in academics, sports, or some other field–do you then strive for more success? That may have been how the Romans felt once they had taken over Italy. Read on to learn how they continued to expand their power.

While Rome developed its government, it also faced **challenges** abroad. The Romans had completed their conquest of Italy. However, they now faced a powerful rival in the Mediterranean area. This enemy was the state of **Carthage** (KAHR•thihj) on the coast of North Africa. It had been founded around 800 B.C. by the Phoenicians. As you learned earlier, the Phoenicians were sea traders from the Middle East.

Carthage ruled a great trading empire that included parts of northern Africa and southern Europe. By controlling the movement of goods in this region, Carthage made itself the largest and richest city in the western Mediterranean.

The First Punic War Both Carthage and Rome wanted to control the island of Sicily. In 264 B.C. the dispute led to war. The war that began in 264 B.C. is called the First Punic War. *Punicus* is the Latin word for "Phoenician." The war started when the Romans sent an army to Sicily to prevent a Carthaginian takeover. The Carthaginians,

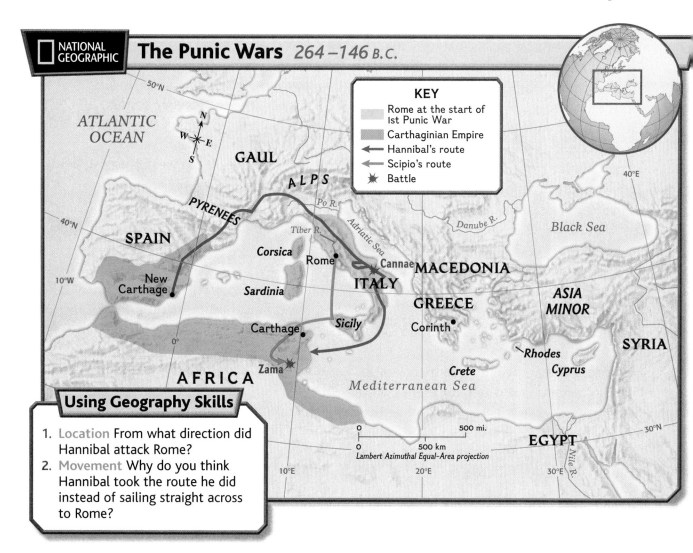

NATIONAL GEOGRAPHIC

The Punic Wars 264–146 B.C.

KEY
- Rome at the start of 1st Punic War
- Carthaginian Empire
- ← Hannibal's route
- ← Scipio's route
- ✳ Battle

Using Geography Skills

1. **Location** From what direction did Hannibal attack Rome?
2. **Movement** Why do you think Hannibal took the route he did instead of sailing straight across to Rome?

who already had colonies on the island, were determined to stop this invasion.

Up until then, the Romans had fought their wars on land. They soon realized they could not defeat a sea power like Carthage without a navy. They quickly built a large fleet of ships and confronted their enemy at sea. The war dragged on for more than 20 years. Finally, in 241 B.C., Rome crushed Carthage's navy off the coast of Sicily. Carthage was forced to leave Sicily and pay a huge fine to the Romans. The island then came under Roman rule.

The Second Punic War
To make up for its loss of Sicily, Carthage expanded its empire into southern Spain. Roman leaders were not happy about Carthage gaining land near Rome's northern border. They helped the people living in Spain rebel against Carthage. Of course, Carthaginians were angry. To punish Rome, Carthage sent its greatest general, **Hannibal** (HA•nuh•buhl), to attack Rome in 218 B.C. This started the Second Punic War.

Hannibal's strategy was to take the fighting into Italy itself. To do this, Hannibal gathered an army of about 46,000 men, many horses, and 37 elephants. He landed his forces in Spain and then marched east to attack Italy.

Even before reaching Italy, Hannibal's forces suffered severe losses crossing the steep, snowy Alps into Italy. The brutal cold, gnawing hunger, and attacks by mountain tribes killed almost half of the

▼ In December 218 B.C., Hannibal's forces and the Roman army met in battle near the Trebbia River in northern Italy. In a well-planned attack, the Carthaginian forces badly defeated the Romans. Hannibal made good use of his elephants in the attack, but most died following the battle. *At what other battle in Italy were the Romans defeated by Hannibal?*

433

soldiers and most of the elephants. The remaining army, however, was still a powerful fighting force when it reached Italy.

The Romans suffered a severe loss in 216 B.C. at the Battle of **Cannae** (KA•nee) in southern Italy. Even though Hannibal's army was outnumbered, it overpowered the Roman force and began raiding much of Italy.

The Romans, however, raised another army. In 202 B.C. a Roman force led by a general named Scipio (SIH•pee•OH) invaded Carthage. Almost all of Carthage's troops were with Hannibal. Scipio's invasion forced Hannibal to head home to defend his city.

At the Battle of **Zama** (ZAY•muh), Scipio's troops defeated the Carthaginians. Carthage gave up Spain to Rome. It also had to give up its navy and pay a large fine. Rome now ruled the western Mediterranean.

More Conquests While Carthage was no longer a military power, it remained a trading center. In 146 B.C. Rome finally destroyed its great rival in the Third Punic War. Roman soldiers burned Carthage and enslaved 50,000 men, women, and children. Legend says that the Romans even spread salt on the earth so no crops would grow. Carthage became a Roman province, or regional district.

During the Punic Wars, Rome successfully battled states in the eastern Mediterranean. In 148 B.C. Macedonia came under Roman rule. Two years later, the rest of Greece became Roman. In 129 B.C. Rome gained its first province in Asia. It was no wonder that the Romans began to call the Mediterranean *mare nostrum*—"our sea."

✓ **Reading Check** **Describe** How did Rome punish Carthage at the end of the Third Punic War?

History Online

Study Central Need help understanding how Rome expanded? Visit ca.hss.glencoe.com and click on Study Central.

Section 2 Review

Reading Summary

Review the Main Ideas

• During the Roman Republic, the government changed as the plebeians, or lower classes, and the patricians, or ruling class, struggled for power.

• Rome introduced the idea of the rule of law treating all citizens equally in court.

• Beginning in 264 B.C., Rome fought and won a series of wars with Carthage and other powers and gained control of the Mediterranean region.

What Did You Learn?

1. Who were the top government officials in the Roman Republic, and what were their duties?

2. What does *mare nostrum* mean, and why did the Romans use the term?

Critical Thinking

3. **Sequencing Information** Draw a diagram to describe the sequence of events from the start of the First Punic War to the start of the Second Punic War. **CA CS1.**

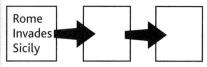

4. **Geography Skills** Where was Carthage located, and why did it compete with Rome? **CA 6RC2.0** **CA CS3.**

5. **Summarize** What other conquests did Rome carry out during the period of the Punic Wars? **CA 6RC2.4**

6. **The Big Ideas** How did the creation of the Twelve Tables change the legal system in Rome? **CA HI2.**

7. **Persuasive Writing** Write a speech demanding equal rights for plebeians in the early republic. **CA 6WA2.5**

The Fall of the Republic

Guide to Reading

Looking Back, Looking Ahead
By the end of the Third Punic War, Rome ruled the Mediterranean world. All was not well, however. Closer to home, the republic faced increasing dangers that would soon lead to its end.

Focusing on the Main Ideas
- The use of enslaved labor hurt farmers, increased poverty and corruption, and brought the army into politics. *(page 436)*
- Military hero Julius Caesar seized power and made reforms. *(page 438)*
- The Roman Republic, weakened by civil wars, became an empire under Augustus. *(page 440)*

Meeting People
Julius Caesar (jool•yuhs SEE•zuhr)
Octavian (ahk•TAY•vee•uhn)
Antony (AN•tuh•nee)
Cicero (SIH•suh•ROH)
Augustus (aw•GUHS•tuhs)

Locating Places
Rubicon (ROO•bih•KAHN)
Actium (AK•shee•uhm)

Content Vocabulary
latifundia (LA•tuh•FUHN•dee•uh)
triumvirate (try•UHM•vuh•ruht)

Academic Vocabulary
despite (dih•SPYT)
estate (ihs•TAYT)
sole (SOHL)
foundation (fown•DAY•shuhn)

Reading Strategy
Finding the Main Idea Use a chart like the one below to identify the main ideas of Section 3 and supporting details.

Main Idea		
Supporting Detail	Supporting Detail	Supporting Detail
Supporting Detail	Supporting Detail	Supporting Detail

History Social Science Standards
WH6.7 Students analyze the geographic, political, economic, religious, and social structures during the development of Rome.

NATIONAL GEOGRAPHIC Where&When?

GAUL	ITALY	ASIA MINOR
SPAIN	Rome	GREECE

100 B.C. — **60 B.C.** — **20 B.C.**

82 B.C. Sulla becomes dictator of Rome

44 B.C. Group of senators murder Julius Caesar

27 B.C. Octavian becomes Rome's first emperor

WH6.7.1 Identify the location and describe the rise of the Roman Republic, including the importance of such mythical and historical figures as Aeneas, Romulus and Remus, Cincinnatus, Julius Caesar, and Cicero.

Trouble in the Republic

Main Idea The use of enslaved labor hurt farmers, increased poverty and corruption, and brought the army into politics.

Reading Connection Poverty, corruption, unemployment, crime, and violence are problems we hear about today. Read on to learn how the Romans struggled with these same issues 2,000 years ago.

Rome's armies were victorious wherever they went. Yet problems were building at home. As you read in Section 2, most of the people who ruled Rome were patricians—rich people who owned large farms. These rich landowners ran the Senate and held the most powerful government jobs. They handled Rome's finances and directed its wars. **Despite** some gains for the plebeians, many people became very unhappy about this situation.

Problems for Farmers

Rome had few privileged citizens compared with the many Romans who farmed small plots of land. In the 100s B.C., however, these farmers were sinking into poverty and debt. Why? Many of them had been unable to farm because they were fighting in Rome's wars. Others had suffered damage to their farms during Hannibal's invasion of Italy.

Moreover, owners of small farms could not compete with the new **latifundia** (LA•tuh•FUHN•dee•uh), or large farming **estates** created by wealthy Romans. The latifundia were tended by a new source of labor—the thousands of prisoners captured during Rome's wars. By using enslaved labor, the latifundia could produce cheap crops and drive small farms out of business.

Faced with debts they could not pay off, many farmers sold their land and headed to the cities, desperate for work. However, jobs were hard to find, and wages were low. Enslaved people did most of the work. These conditions created widespread anger.

Roman politicians quickly turned the situation to their advantage. To win the votes of the poor, they began providing cheap food and entertainment. This policy of "bread and circuses" helped many dishonest rulers come to power.

Why Did Reform Fail?

Not all wealthy people ignored the problems facing the Roman Republic. Two prominent officials who worked for reforms were Tiberius and Gaius Gracchus (GRA•kuhs). These brothers thought that many of Rome's problems were caused by the loss of small farms. They asked the Senate to take back public land from the rich and divide it among landless Romans.

This issue concerned many senators who had claimed parcels of public land. Putting their own interests above the general welfare, they rejected the Gracchus brothers' proposals. A band of senators even went so far as to kill Tiberius in 133 B.C. Twelve years later, Gaius met the same fate.

The Army Enters Politics

For most of Rome's history, the army had stayed out of politics. This changed when a general named Marius became consul in 107 B.C. Previously, most soldiers were owners of small farms. Now because this type of farmer was disappearing, Marius began to recruit soldiers from the poor. In return for their service, he paid them wages and promised them the one thing they desperately wanted—land.

History Online

Web Activity Visit ca.hss.glencoe.com and click on *Chapter 9—Student Web Activity* to learn more about the rise of Rome.

Marius changed the Roman army from citizen volunteers to paid professional soldiers. The new troops, however, felt loyal to their general, not to the Roman Republic. This gave individual generals a great deal of influence and good reason to become involved in politics. Their goal was to get laws passed that would provide the land they had promised their soldiers.

Marius's new military system led to new power struggles. It was not long before Marius faced a challenge from a rival general with his own army, a man named Sulla.

In 82 B.C. Sulla drove his enemies out of Rome and made himself dictator.

Over the next three years, Sulla changed the government. He weakened the Council of the Plebs and strengthened the Senate. After he left power, Rome plunged into an era of civil wars for the next 50 years. Ambitious men saw how Sulla used an army to seize power. They decided to follow the same path.

✓ **Reading Check** **Explain** What change did Marius make to the Roman army?

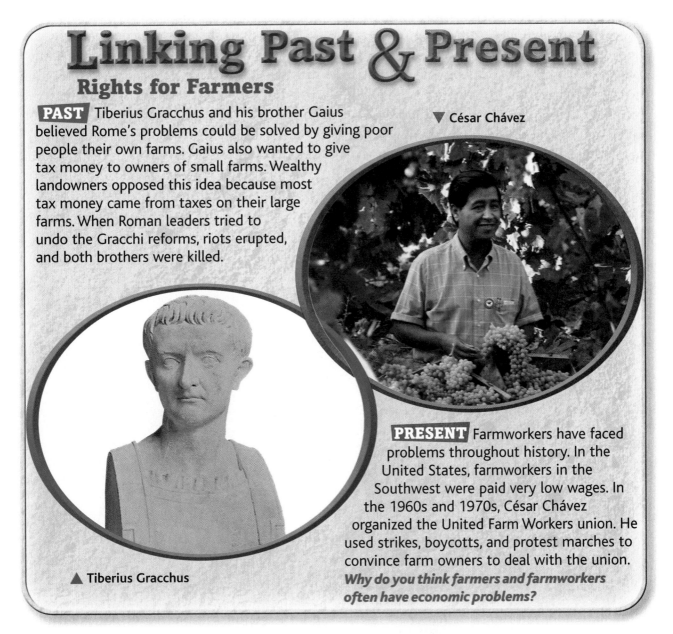

Linking Past & Present

Rights for Farmers

PAST Tiberius Gracchus and his brother Gaius believed Rome's problems could be solved by giving poor people their own farms. Gaius also wanted to give tax money to owners of small farms. Wealthy landowners opposed this idea because most tax money came from taxes on their large farms. When Roman leaders tried to undo the Gracchi reforms, riots erupted, and both brothers were killed.

▼ César Chávez

▲ Tiberius Gracchus

PRESENT Farmworkers have faced problems throughout history. In the United States, farmworkers in the Southwest were paid very low wages. In the 1960s and 1970s, César Chávez organized the United Farm Workers union. He used strikes, boycotts, and protest marches to convince farm owners to deal with the union.
Why do you think farmers and farmworkers often have economic problems?

WH6.7.1 Identify the location and describe the rise of the Roman Republic, including the importance of such mythical and historical figures as Aeneas, Romulus and Remus, Cincinnatus, Julius Caesar, and Cicero.

WH6.7.4 Discuss the influence of Julius Caesar and Augustus in Rome's transition from republic to empire.

Julius Caesar

Main Idea Military hero Julius Caesar seized power and made reforms.

Reading Connection Did you know that George Washington, Andrew Jackson, William H. Harrison, Zachary Taylor, Ulysses S. Grant, and Dwight D. Eisenhower all commanded armies before becoming president? Read to learn about a famous Roman who made a similar jump from military leader to political leader.

After Sulla left office, different Roman leaders battled for power, supported by their loyal armies. In 60 B.C. three men were on top: Crassus, Pompey, and **Julius Caesar** (jool•yuhs SEE•zuhr). Crassus was a military leader and one of the richest men in Rome. Pompey and Caesar were not as rich, but both were successful military men. Drawing on their wealth and power, they formed the First Triumvirate to rule Rome. A **triumvirate** (try•UHM•vuh•ruht) is a political alliance of three people.

Caesar's Military Campaigns The members of the Triumvirate each had a military command in a remote area of the republic. Pompey was in Spain, Crassus in Syria, and Caesar in Gaul (modern France). While in Gaul, Caesar battled foreign tribes and invaded Britain. He became a hero to Rome's lower classes. Senators and others back home in Rome feared that Caesar was becoming too popular and might seize power like Sulla or Marius.

After Crassus was killed in battle in 53 B.C., the Senate decided that Pompey should return to Italy and rule alone. In 49 B.C. the Senate ordered Caesar to give up his army and come home. Caesar faced a difficult choice. He could obey the Senate and perhaps face prison or death at the hands of his rivals, or he could march on Rome with his army and risk a civil war.

Caesar decided to hold on to his 5,000 loyal soldiers. He marched into Italy by crossing the **Rubicon** (ROO•bih•KAHN), a

Caesar's Rise to Power

Caesar was part of the First Triumvirate, whose members are shown below.

Caesar ▶

▼ A scene showing a battle between Romans and Gauls

▲ Crassus

▲ Pompey

small river at the southern boundary of his command area. By doing so, Caesar knew that he was starting a civil war and that there was no turning back. The phrase "crossing the Rubicon" is used today to mean making a decision that you cannot take back.

Pompey tried to stop Caesar, but Caesar was the better general. He drove Pompey's forces from Italy and then destroyed Pompey's army in Greece in 48 B.C.

Caesar's Rise to Power

In 44 B.C. Caesar had himself declared dictator of Rome for life. This broke with the Roman tradition that allowed dictators to hold power for only short periods of time. To strengthen his hold on power, Caesar filled the Senate with new members who were loyal to him.

At the same time, Caesar knew that reforms were needed. He granted citizenship to people living in Rome's territories outside the Italian peninsula. He started new colonies to provide land for the landless and created work for Rome's jobless people. He ordered landowners using slave labor to hire more free workers. These measures made Caesar popular with Rome's poor.

Caesar also created a new calendar with 12 months, 365 days, and a leap year. The Julian calendar, as it was called, was used throughout Europe until A.D. 1582. That year it was modified slightly to become the Gregorian calendar. This calendar, based on the birth of Christ, has been used in the United States since its beginning and is used by most countries in the world today.

While many Romans supported Caesar, others did not. His supporters believed he was a strong leader who brought peace and order to Rome. His enemies, however, feared that Caesar wanted to be king. These opponents, led by the senators Brutus and Cassius, plotted to kill him. Caesar ignored a famous warning to "beware the Ides of March" (March 15). On that date in 44 B.C., Caesar's enemies surrounded him and stabbed him to death.

✓ **Reading Check** **Explain** Why did Brutus, Cassius, and others kill Caesar?

▼ Caesar crossing the Rubicon

Brutus (left) was one of the senators who killed Caesar. Antony (above) supported Caesar and his nephew Octavian and fought against Caesar's assassins.

WH6.7.1 Identify the location and describe the rise of the Roman Republic, including the importance of such mythical and historical figures as Aeneas, Romulus and Remus, Cincinnatus, Julius Caesar, and Cicero.

WH6.7.4 Discuss the influence of Julius Caesar and Augustus in Rome's transition from republic to empire.

Rome Becomes an Empire

Main Idea The Roman Republic, weakened by civil wars, became an empire under Augustus.

Reading Connection Have you ever been in a traffic jam and wished that a police officer would show up to get things moving? Read on to learn how Romans welcomed the arrival of a strong new ruler.

Caesar's death plunged Rome into another civil war. On one side were forces led by the men who had killed Caesar. On the other side was Caesar's grandnephew **Octavian** (ahk•TAY•vee•uhn), who had inherited Caesar's wealth, and two of Caesar's top generals, **Antony** (AN•tuh•nee) and Lepidus. After defeating Caesar's assassins, these three men created the Second Triumvirate in 43 B.C.

The Second Triumvirate The members of the Second Triumvirate began quarreling almost at once. Octavian soon forced Lepidus to retire from politics. Then the two remaining leaders divided the Roman world between themselves. Octavian took the west; Antony took the east.

In short order, though, Octavian and Antony came into conflict. Antony fell in love with the Egyptian queen Cleopatra VII and formed an alliance with her. Octavian told the Romans that Antony, with Cleopatra's help, planned to make himself the **sole** ruler of the republic. This alarmed many Romans and enabled Octavian to declare war on Antony.

In 31 B.C., at the Battle of **Actium** (AK•shee•uhm) off the west coast of Greece, Octavian crushed the army and navy of

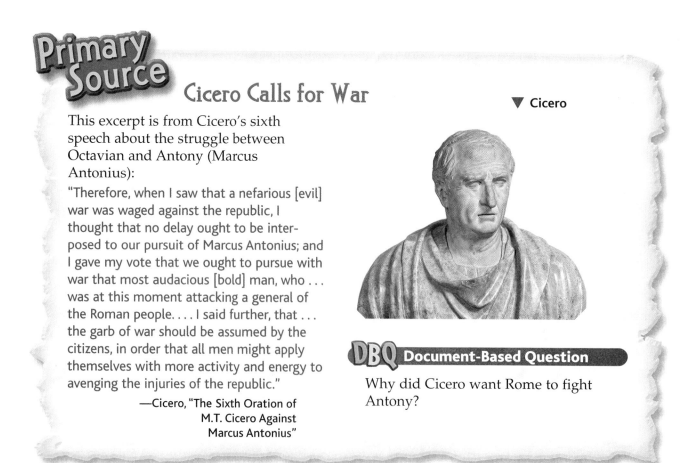

Cicero Calls for War

This excerpt is from Cicero's sixth speech about the struggle between Octavian and Antony (Marcus Antonius):

"Therefore, when I saw that a nefarious [evil] war was waged against the republic, I thought that no delay ought to be interposed to our pursuit of Marcus Antonius; and I gave my vote that we ought to pursue with war that most audacious [bold] man, who . . . was at this moment attacking a general of the Roman people. . . . I said further, that . . . the garb of war should be assumed by the citizens, in order that all men might apply themselves with more activity and energy to avenging the injuries of the republic."

—Cicero, "The Sixth Oration of M.T. Cicero Against Marcus Antonius"

▼ Cicero

DBQ **Document-Based Question**

Why did Cicero want Rome to fight Antony?

Antony and Cleopatra. The couple then fled to Egypt. A year later, as Octavian closed in, they killed themselves. Octavian, at the age of 32, now stood alone at the top of the Roman world. The period of civil wars was over, but so was the republic. Octavian would lay the **foundation** for a new system of government—the Roman Empire.

Who Was Augustus? Octavian could have made himself dictator for life, like Julius Caesar did. He knew, though, that many people favored a republican form of government. One such person was **Cicero** (SIH•suh•ROH), a political leader, writer, and Rome's greatest public speaker. Cicero had argued against dictators and called for a representative government with limited powers.

Cicero's speeches and books swayed many Romans. Centuries later, his ideas would also influence the writers of the United States Constitution.

Although Cicero did not live to see Octavian rule, he had supported him, hoping he would restore the republic. In 27 B.C. Octavian announced that he was doing just that.

He knew the Senate wanted this form of government. However, Octavian also knew that the republic had been too weak to solve Rome's problems. Although he gave some power to the Senate, he really put himself in charge. His title, *imperator*, translates to "commander in chief," but it came to mean "emperor." Octavian also took the title of **Augustus** (aw•GUHS•tuhs)—"the revered or majestic one." From this point on, he was known by this name.

✓ **Reading Check** **Explain** How did the Battle of Actium affect the history of Rome?

History Online

Study Central Need help understanding how the republic collapsed? Visit ca.hss.glencoe.com and click on Study Central.

Section 3 Review

What Did You Learn?

Reading Summary

Review the Main Ideas

- As the gap between the ruling class and the poor in Rome increased, a number of reforms failed, and generals began to gather power.

- Julius Caesar became dictator and carried out reforms to aid Rome's poor. Later he was assassinated by members of the Senate.

- Caesar's grandnephew Octavian defeated Antony and Cleopatra and became Augustus, the first Roman emperor.

1. What is a triumvirate?

2. Who was Cicero, and how did he influence the writers of the United States Constitution?

Critical Thinking

3. **Understanding Cause and Effect** Draw a diagram like the one below. Fill in the chain of events that led to Julius Caesar taking power. **CA CS2.**

4. **Summarize** What reforms did the Gracchus brothers suggest? **CA 6RC2.4**

5. **The Big Ideas** How did failures in leadership help bring about the fall of the republic? What new leaders took power as a result? **CA HR5.; HI3.**

6. **Analyze** What reforms did Julius Caesar put in place that increased his popularity with poor and working-class Romans? **CA 6RC2.0**

7. **Persuasive Writing** Imagine you are a Roman citizen. Decide whether you would have been for or against Julius Caesar's rise to power and his reforms. Then write a newspaper editorial explaining your views. **CA 6RC2.1; 6WA2.5**

You Decide . . .

WH6.7.4 Discuss the influence of Julius Caesar and Augustus in Rome's transition from republic to empire.

Was Caesar a Reformer or a Dictator?

Great Reformer

During his life, Julius Caesar was greatly admired by many people. He was also hated and feared by many others. Some believed he was too ambitious—exceptionally eager for fame and power—and that his ambition would keep him from acting in Rome's best interest.

Was Caesar a great reformer or an ambitious dictator? Those who saw him as a great leader and reformer said that he

- won the support of his soldiers through his military leadership and strategy
- treated many of his defeated enemies generously and appointed some of them—including Brutus—to government positions
- ended the rule of corrupt Roman nobles
- brought order and peace to Rome
- restored cities that had been destroyed by the republic
- strengthened and expanded the state of Rome
- started public jobs programs to aid the poor
- granted Roman citizenship to people from foreign countries or states.

▲ The assassination of Julius Caesar

Ambitious Dictator

Caesar also had many enemies, including some who had been his friends. They saw Caesar as a dangerous dictator and thought he was taking advantage of his growing power.

They said that he

- became an enemy when he refused to follow the Senate's order to return to Rome
- started a civil war that led to the destruction of the republic
- increased the number of senators to add to his number of supporters
- treated his defeated enemies with cruelty
- punished those who wanted to uphold the traditions and laws of the republic
- weakened the Senate to gain absolute power over Rome
- kept hidden any facts that did not make him look brave and intelligent
- sought glory for himself at the expense of the republic.

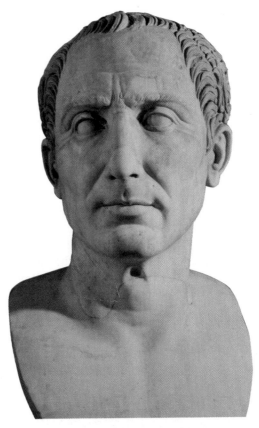

▲ Julius Caesar

You Be the Historian

Checking for Understanding

1. Define *ambition*. Identify some ways ambition can be a positive characteristic and some ways it can be a negative characteristic. **CA** 6RW1.2

2. What could Caesar have done to show his enemies that he was not abusing his power? **CA** HI2.

3. Do you think Caesar was a great leader and reformer or an ambitious dictator? Write a brief essay that explains how you view Caesar. Use facts to support your position. **CA** HR5. **CA** 6WA2.5

The Early Empire

Guide to Reading

Looking Back, Looking Ahead

You learned in Section 3 that when Octavian became Augustus, the Roman world began to change. The republic gave way to an empire, and peace and prosperity spread throughout the Mediterranean.

Focusing on the Main Ideas

- By expanding the empire and reorganizing the military and government, Augustus created a new era of prosperity. *(page 445)*

- Rome's system of roads, aqueducts, ports, and common currency made the empire rich and prosperous. *(page 446)*

Locating Places

Rhine River (RYN)
Danube River (DAN•YOOB)
Puteoli (pyu•TEE•uh•LY)
Ostia (AHS•tee•uh)

Meeting People

Caligula (kuh•LIH•gyuh•luh)
Nero (NEE•roh)
Hadrian (HAY•dree•uhn)

Content Vocabulary

Pax Romana
  (pahks   roh•MAH•nah)
aqueduct (A•kwuh•DUHKT)
currency (KUHR•uhn•see)

Academic Vocabulary

successor (suhk•SEH•suhr)
commit (kuh•MIHT)
capable (KAY•puh •buhl)

Reading Strategy

Cause and Effect Use a chart like the one below to show the changes Augustus made in the Roman Empire and the effect of each change.

Causes		Effects
	→	
	→	

History Social Science Standards

WH6.7 Students analyze the geographic, political, economic, religious, and social structures during the development of Rome.

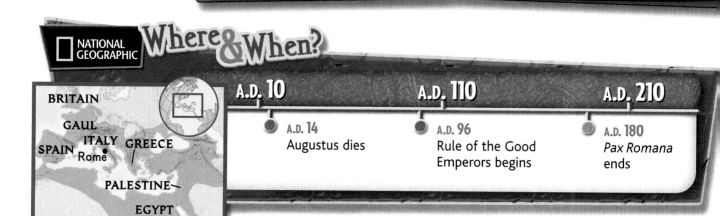

NATIONAL GEOGRAPHIC Where & When?

A.D. 10

A.D. 14
Augustus dies

A.D. 110

A.D. 96
Rule of the Good Emperors begins

A.D. 210

A.D. 180
Pax Romana ends

BRITAIN
GAUL
ITALY GREECE
SPAIN Rome
PALESTINE
EGYPT

The Emperor Augustus

Main Idea By expanding the empire and reorganizing the military and government, Augustus created a new era of prosperity.

Reading Connection What makes a good or bad leader? Think about this question as you read about Augustus and other Roman emperors.

Augustus paved the way for 200 years of peace and prosperity in Rome. The emperors who followed him were not all good rulers, but they helped the Roman Empire reach its peak. For centuries, the Mediterranean region had been filled with conflict. Under Augustus and his **successors,** the region was under the control of one empire. A long era of peace began with Augustus and lasted until A.D. 180. It was called the *Pax Romana* (pahks roh•MAH•nah), or "Roman Peace."

What Did Augustus Achieve? Upon becoming emperor in 27 B.C., Augustus set a goal to make the empire strong and safe. To provide security, he built a permanent, professional army of about 150,000 men—all Roman citizens. Augustus also created a special unit called the Praetorian Guard.

This force consisted of about 9,000 men in charge of guarding the emperor. The Praetorian Guard later became very influential in Roman politics.

Augustus's legions conquered new territories and added vast stretches of northern Europe to the empire. All of Spain and Gaul came under Roman rule, as did land in what is today Austria, Hungary, Romania, and Bulgaria.

Meanwhile, Augustus rebuilt Rome with stately palaces, fountains, and splendid public buildings. "I found Rome a city of brick," he boasted, "and left it a city of marble." The arts flourished as never before, and Augustus also imported grain from Africa to feed the poor. He knew that a well-fed population would be less likely to cause trouble.

Augustus devoted much of his energy to improving Rome's government. During his reign, more than 50 million people lived in the Roman Empire. To rule this huge population, Augustus appointed a proconsul, or governor, for each of Rome's provinces.

Augustus also reformed the Roman tax system. Previously, individual tax collectors paid the government for the right to do the job. To make their investment worthwhile,

▲ The city of Rome at the height of the Roman Empire

WH6.7.3 Identify the location of and the political and geographic reasons for the growth of Roman territories and expansion of the empire, including how the empire fostered economic growth through the use of currency and trade routes.

tax collectors were allowed to keep some of the money they gathered. Many of them, however, were dishonest and took too much. Augustus solved this problem by making tax collectors permanent government workers. This change made the tax system fairer.

Augustus also reformed the legal system. He created a set of laws for people in the provinces who were not citizens. As time passed, however, most of these people gained citizenship. The laws of Rome then applied to everyone, although the legal system traditionally stressed the authority of the government over the rights of the individual.

Who Came After Augustus?

After ruling nearly 40 years, Augustus died in A.D. 14. No law stated how the next emperor was to be chosen. Augustus, however, had trained a relative, Tiberius, to follow him. The next three emperors—**Caligula** (kuh•LIH•gyuh•luh), Claudius, and **Nero** (NEE•roh)—also came from Augustus's family. They are called the Julio-Claudian emperors. Unfortunately, they were not all fit to lead. Tiberius and Claudius ruled capably. Caligula and Nero, however, proved to be cruel leaders.

Mental illness caused Caligula to act strangely and to treat people cruelly. He had many people murdered, wasted a lot of money, and even gave his favorite horse the position of consul. Eventually, the Praetorian Guard killed him and put Claudius on the throne.

Nero was also a vicious man. Among those he had killed were his mother and two wives. He is best remembered for having "fiddled while Rome burned." According to legend, he was playing music miles from Rome when a fire destroyed much of the city in A.D. 64. Eventually, he **committed** suicide.

Reading Check **Explain** What did Augustus do to make the empire safer and stronger?

Unity and Prosperity

Main Idea Rome's system of roads, aqueducts, ports, and common currency made the empire rich and prosperous.

Reading Connection Do you find that you are more productive when you are not worried about conflicts at home or school? Read to learn how the Roman Empire prospered during its time of peace.

After Nero committed suicide, Rome passed through a period of serious disorder. In not much more than a year, four different men had taken the title of emperor.

At first the senate tried to appoint Nero's successor. However, the new emperor did not pay his personal troops enough money, and they assassinated him. The leader of this conspiracy, a man named Otho, became the next emperor. Many of the legions outside of Italy did not support him. The troops in Gaul picked one of their own generals to rule, a man named Vitellius. After Vitellius defeated Otho in battle, Otho committed suicide and Vitellius became emperor.

However, the troops in Palestine did not support Otho or Vitellius. In July of A.D. 69, they declared the general Vespasian to be emperor. Vespasian led his soldiers back to Italy, where he defeated Vitellius and took the throne. Unlike the other generals, Vespasian restored peace and order. He put down several rebellions in the empire, including the Jewish rebellion in Palestine. Troops commanded by his son Titus defeated the Jews and destroyed the Jewish temple in Jerusalem in A.D. 70.

During his reign, Vespasian began construction of the Colosseum—a huge amphitheater—in central Rome. His son Titus, then his other son Domitian, ruled Rome after he died. Both sons oversaw an era of recovery and growth in Rome.

Biography

AUGUSTUS
63 B.C.–A.D. 14

Augustus ▶

Octavian was born to a wealthy family in a small Italian town southeast of Rome. During his youth, Octavian suffered a number of illnesses. He refused to let his illnesses interfere with his life, however, showing the determination that would later make him Rome's first emperor.

Octavian's father was a Roman senator, but it was Octavian's great-uncle—Julius Caesar—who first introduced Octavian to public life in Rome. In his late teens, Octavian joined Caesar in Africa and then the following year in Spain. At the age of 18, while Octavian was studying at school, he learned that his great-uncle had been murdered. In his will, Caesar had adopted Octavian as his son. Caesar had also made Octavian his heir—a position that Antony had assumed would be his. Against his family's advice, Octavian went to Rome to claim his inheritance. By the time he reached Rome, however, Antony had seized Caesar's papers and money and refused to give them to Octavian. With remarkable political savvy for someone so young, Octavian turned the situation around in his favor. He won the hearts of Caesar's soldiers and the people of Rome by celebrating the public games that Caesar had started.

In his rise to power and during his reign as Emperor Augustus, Octavian pushed himself and his loyal followers with relentless energy. In his private life, however, he lived simply and quietly and shunned personal luxury. He was devoted to his wife, Livia Drusilla, and spent his spare time with her at their home on the outskirts of Rome.

> **"I extended the frontiers of all the provinces of the Roman people."**
>
> —Augustus, "Res Gestae: The Accomplishments of Augustus"

Then and Now

Augustus overcame the obstacles of illness and political enemies to become a great emperor. Can you think of any present-day individuals who overcame obstacles to excel at something?

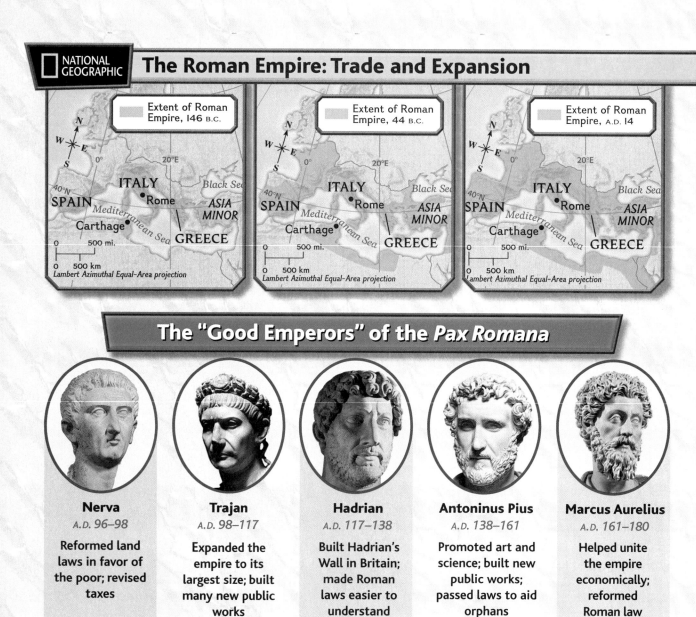

The Roman Empire: Trade and Expansion

Extent of Roman Empire, 146 B.C.

Extent of Roman Empire, 44 B.C.

Extent of Roman Empire, A.D. 14

The "Good Emperors" of the *Pax Romana*

Nerva
A.D. *96–98*
Reformed land laws in favor of the poor; revised taxes

Trajan
A.D. *98–117*
Expanded the empire to its largest size; built many new public works

Hadrian
A.D. *117–138*
Built Hadrian's Wall in Britain; made Roman laws easier to understand

Antoninus Pius
A.D. *138–161*
Promoted art and science; built new public works; passed laws to aid orphans

Marcus Aurelius
A.D. *161–180*
Helped unite the empire economically; reformed Roman law

The "Good Emperors" At the beginning of the A.D. 100s, a series of rulers who were not related to Augustus or Vespasian came to power. These five emperors—Nerva, Trajan, **Hadrian** (HAY•dree•uhn), Antoninus Pius, and Marcus Aurelius—are known as the "good emperors." They presided over nearly a century of prosperity, from A.D. 96 to A.D. 180. Agriculture flourished, trade increased, and the standard of living rose.

During this time, the emperor came to overshadow the Senate more than ever before. The five "good emperors" did not abuse their power, however. They were among the most devoted and **capable** rulers in Rome's history.

Among the achievements of these emperors were programs to help ordinary people. Trajan gave money to help poor parents raise and educate their children. Hadrian made Roman law easier to interpret and apply. Antoninus Pius passed laws to help orphans. All the emperors supported public building projects. They built arches and monuments, bridges and roads, and harbors and aqueducts. An **aqueduct** (A•kwuh•DUHKT) is a human-made channel for carrying water long distances.

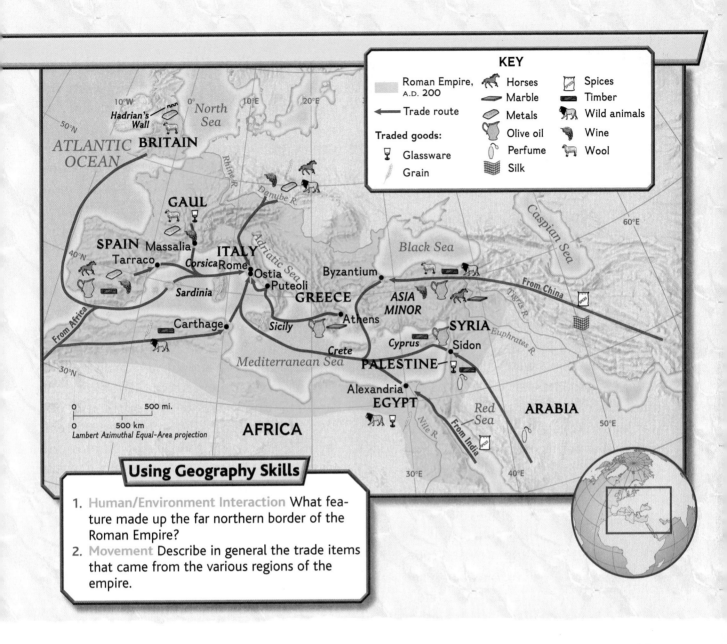

KEY

Roman Empire, A.D. 200

← Trade route

Traded goods:

Glassware

Grain

Horses

Marble

Metals

Olive oil

Perfume

Silk

Spices

Timber

Wild animals

Wine

Wool

Using Geography Skills

1. **Human/Environment Interaction** What feature made up the far northern border of the Roman Empire?
2. **Movement** Describe in general the trade items that came from the various regions of the empire.

A Unified Empire Later emperors continued to conquer new territory for Rome. The empire reached its largest size under Trajan. It spread well beyond the Mediterranean, including Britain in the north and part of Mesopotamia in the east.

Trajan's successors, however, realized that the empire had grown too big to rule effectively. Hadrian began to pull back. He removed troops from most of Mesopotamia. In Europe, he set the empire's eastern boundaries at the **Rhine River** (RYN) and **Danube River** (DAN•YOOB). He also built Hadrian's Wall across northern Britain to keep out the Picts and Scots—two warlike people who lived in northern Britain.

In the A.D. 100s, the Roman Empire was one of the greatest empires in history. It included about 3.5 million square miles (9.1 million square km). Its people spoke different languages—mostly Latin in the west and Greek in the east. They also practiced different local customs. What unified the empire, though, were Roman law, Roman rule, and a shared identity as Romans. The Romans were also generous in granting citizenship. In A.D. 212 every free person was made a Roman citizen.

The Way It Was

Science and Inventions

Roman Aqueducts

Transporting water is a complex problem. Roman engineers solved it by building aqueducts. Roman aqueducts carried water across a valley or hillside using gravity, aboveground stone arches, and underground pipes made of stone or clay. Between 312 B.C. and A.D. 226, 11 aqueducts were built to bring water to Rome from as far away as 57 miles. Once the water made it to Rome, it was held in collecting tanks. Most people gathered water from these public tanks. Only the rich and high-ranking officials had private water tanks in their homes.

Many Roman aqueducts still stand and are used today. Engineers in ancient Persia, India, and Egypt built similar water systems hundreds of years before the Romans. However, historians agree that the Romans were the greatest aqueduct builders of the ancient world.

▲ Roman aqueduct

Connecting to the Past

1. How did the Romans transport water to the city of Rome?
2. Why do you think that only the rich and powerful had private water supplies?

A Booming Economy

Most people in the Roman Empire made a living from the land. Small farms dotted northern Italy. In southern and central Italy, latifundia, or large estates worked by enslaved people, were common. On these estates and in the provinces of Gaul and Spain, farmers produced grapes, olives, wine, and olive oil. In Britain and Egypt, the chief crops were grains. Bountiful harvests from these regions kept Rome's people well fed.

Agriculture was the most important part of the economy, but industry was important too. Potters, weavers, and jewelers produced goods, and cities became centers for making glass, bronze, and brass.

Traders came from all over the empire—and beyond—to ports in Italy. Two of the largest port cities were **Puteoli** (pyu•TEE•uh•ly) on the Bay of Naples and **Ostia** (AHS•tee•uh) at the mouth of the Tiber. The docks were lively places. Luxury items, including silk goods from China and spices from India, poured in to satisfy the rich. Raw materials, such as British tin, Spanish lead, and iron from Gaul, went to the workshops of Roman cities.

Roads and Money

A good transportation network was vital to the empire's trade. During the *Pax Romana*, Rome's system of roads reached a total length of 50,000 miles (80,000 km). On the seas, the Roman navy helped to rid the Mediterranean of pirates, allowing goods to be shipped more safely.

Rome's trade was helped by a common **currency** (KUHR • uhn • see), or system of money. For many years, Romans had minted coins so that merchants, traders, and others could buy and sell products with money rather than bartering.

Roman coins were accepted throughout the Mediterranean region by A.D. 100.

Merchants could use the same money in Gaul or Greece as they did in Italy. The Romans also created a standard system of weights and measures. This made it easier for people to price goods, trade, and ship products.

The Romans also stamped images on coins as a way to share a message. For example, Augustus had coins made with images of himself and references to Julius Caesar or images of his military victories. He wanted people to believe that he was a good leader.

Ongoing Inequality Roman culture had been carried into every province by Roman soldiers and officials sent to govern. However, the Roman Empire's prosperity did not reach all of its people. Shopkeepers, merchants, and skilled workers benefited

▲ Roman coins could be used throughout most of the empire, making trade much easier. *How else did Rome improve trade during the empire?*

and rich Romans lived in luxury. However, most city dwellers and farmers were poor, and many were enslaved.

✓ **Reading Check** **Identify** Who were the "good emperors," and what did they accomplish?

Study Central Need help understanding the prosperity of the empire? Visit ca.hss.glencoe.com and click on Study Central.

Section 4 Review

Reading Summary

Review the Main Ideas

- Augustus conquered new lands and created a professional military and a system of proconsuls. He improved the tax system and the legal system, ushering in the *Pax Romana*.

- Under Vespasian, his sons, and the five good emperors, Romans continued to be prosperous. They built an elaborate system of roads and developed a common currency that promoted trade and economic growth.

What Did You Learn?

1. What was the *Pax Romana*?

2. What products came from the farms of Italy, Gaul, and Spain?

Critical Thinking

3. **Organizing Information** Draw a diagram like the one below. Add details about the improvements and changes Augustus made to the Roman Empire during his reign. **CA 6RC2.4**

Changes Under Augustus

4. **Sequencing Information** Describe the sequence of emperors who ruled Rome, from Augustus through the "good emperors." **CA CS2.**

5. **The Big Ideas** Why was Rome's creation of a common currency important? **CA HI6.**

6. **Creative Writing** Write a short play in which several Roman citizens compare the accomplishments of Rome's emperors. **CA 6WA2.1**

7. **Analysis** Reading Maps Look at the maps on pages 448 and 449. What natural features shaped the growth of the Roman Empire and its trade? **CA CS3.**

Analyzing Primary Sources

Roman Propaganda

The Romans knew the power of the written word. They believed that history could be preserved by written records. Because of this, they often wrote their letters, histories, and other documents in a way to make themselves look good. For example, after Cicero had given some speeches, he rewrote the text of those speeches so that they were even better than the original. Each of the following passages is about a great Roman person.

Read the passages on pages 452 and 453, and answer the questions that follow.

▲ **Cicero**

Reader's Dictionary

posterity (pah•STEHR•uh•tee): future time

allay: calm

principate: rule or reign

detention: imprisonment

allot (uh•LAHT): give

expenditures (ihk•SPEHN•dih•chuhrs): the spending of money

excel: be better than

magistracy (MAH•juh•struh•see): official duty

A Heroic Rescue Attempt

Pliny the Elder—a Roman admiral and well-known author and scientist—died attempting to rescue people after Mt. Vesuvius erupted in A.D. 79. His nephew, Pliny the Younger, recorded his uncle's death in a letter written to a Roman historian named Tacitus.

Thank you for asking me to send you a description of my uncle's death so that you can leave an accurate account of it for **posterity;** . . .

As he was leaving the house he was handed a message from Rectina, . . . whose house was at the foot of the mountain, so that escape was impossible except by boat. She was terrified by the danger threatening her and implored him to rescue her. . . . For

a moment my uncle wondered whether to turn back, but when the helmsman advised this he refused, telling him that Fortune stood by the courageous. . . .

. . . My uncle tried to **allay** the fears of his companions. . . . They debated whether to stay indoors or take their chance in the open, for the buildings were now shaking with violent shocks. . . .

. . . Then the flames and smell of sulphur which gave warning of the approaching fire drove the others to take flight. . . . He stood . . . and then suddenly collapsed, I imagine because the dense fumes choked his breathing.

—Pliny, *Letters and Panegyricus*

Caesar's Story

Julius Caesar's military victories helped to bring him to power. In the following passage, Caesar explains why he thought it was important to keep the people of Gaul under control.

"In spite of the difficulties, Caesar had several strong reasons for undertaking this campaign: the unlawful detention of Roman knights, the revolt and renewal of hostilities by enemies who had submitted and given hostages, the large number of tribes leagued against him, and above all the danger that if these were left unpunished others might think themselves entitled to follow their example."

—"Julius Caesar in Gaul," J.M. Roberts,
Rome and the Classical West

▲ **Caesar crossing the Rubicon River**

The Emperor Augustus

Shortly before his death in A.D. 14, Augustus wrote a document called the Res Gestae to summarize his career.

5. . . . In the midst of a critical scarcity of grain I did not decline the supervision of the grain supply, which I so administered that within a few days I freed the whole people from the imminent panic and danger by my **expenditures** and efforts. The consulship, too, which was offered to me at that time as an annual office for life, I refused to accept. . . . I refused to accept any office offered me which was contrary to the traditions of our ancestors.

13. The temple of Janus Quirinus, which our ancestors desired to be closed whenever peace with victory was secured . . . which before I was born is recorded to have been closed only twice since the founding of the city, was during my principate three times ordered by the senate to be closed.

34. . . . I transferred the state from my own power to the control of the Roman senate and people. . . . After that time I **excelled** all in authority, but I possessed no more power than the others who were my colleagues in each **magistracy.**

—Augustus, "Res Gestae:
The Accomplishments of Augustus"

DBQ Document-Based Questions

A Heroic Rescue Attempt

1. Why did Pliny the Elder sail to Mt. Vesuvius?

2. Does Pliny the Younger consider his uncle a hero? Why or why not?

Caesar's Story

3. How does Caesar justify his attack on the Gauls?

4. How does this passage show Caesar's abilities as a leader?

The Emperor Augustus

5. Why was it important that the temple doors be closed?

6. Do you think Augustus was being honest? Why or why not?

7. Think about what you have read in this chapter about Augustus's authority. Why do you think he declined to be the consul? How did he transfer all power back to the Senate but still excel others in authority?

Read to Write

8. Use all of these passages to answer the following question: How are the stories of Pliny, Caesar, and Augustus exaggerated? Give examples of words and sentences that create the impression these three men had good character. **CA HR5.**

Review Content Vocabulary

Each of the following statements is false. Replace each word in italics with a word that makes the statement true. Write the correct words on a separate sheet of paper.

____ 1. A *legion* is a form of government in which the citizens choose their leader.

____ 2. *Patricians* included artisans and shopkeepers.

____ 3. The judge in a Roman court case was a *consul*.

____ 4. In early Rome, the role of *praetor* lasted only until a crisis had passed.

____ 5. Large farming estates that used enslaved people to tend crops were called *aqueducts*.

____ 6. A *veto* was a human-made channel for carrying water.

Review the Main Ideas

Section 1 • Rome's Beginnings

7. Describe the role geography played in the rise of Roman civilization.

8. How did treating people fairly help Rome to increase its power?

Section 2 • The Roman Republic

9. How did the roles of patricians and plebeians differ in Roman society?

10. Explain how Rome gradually defeated the Carthaginians.

Section 3 • The Fall of the Republic

11. How did slavery weaken the Roman Republic?

12. Who were the members of the First Triumvirate?

13. How did Augustus change the Roman Republic?

Section 4 • The Early Empire

14. Was Augustus a successful ruler? Explain your answer.

15. What advances helped make Rome wealthy and prosperous?

Critical Thinking

16. **Compare** Cincinnatus is often compared to George Washington. Think of another person who is similar to Cincinnatus. Explain how they are similar. **CA 6RC2.2**

17. **Explain** Why did Caesar fight Pompey? **CA 6RC2.0**

18. **Predict** What do you think would have happened if Hadrian had tried to further expand the Roman Empire? **CA HI2.**

Geography Skills

Study the map below and answer the following questions.

19. **Place** Which areas did Rome control after the Punic Wars? **CA CS3.**

20. **Human/Environment Interaction** What does Hadrian's Wall reveal about the people north of it? **CA CS3.**

21. **Region** Why was control of the Mediterranean important to Rome? **CA CS3.**

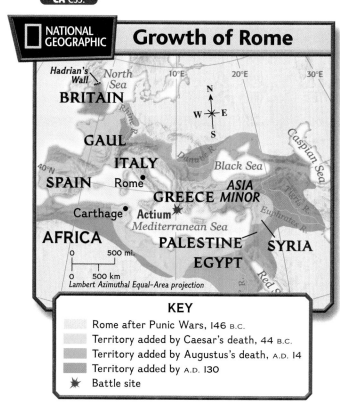

NATIONAL GEOGRAPHIC
Growth of Rome

KEY
- Rome after Punic Wars, 146 B.C.
- Territory added by Caesar's death, 44 B.C.
- Territory added by Augustus's death, A.D. 14
- Territory added by A.D. 130
- ✳ Battle site

Read to Write

22. **The Big Ideas** **Persuasive Writing** Suppose you were working with Tiberius and Gaius Gracchus to reform Rome. Prepare a speech that explains why reform is needed, what types of reforms should occur, and why Rome needs strong leaders like the Gracchus brothers. **CA 6WA2.5**

23. **Using Your FOLDABLES** Use your foldable to write a series of questions about the chapter. With a partner, take turns asking and answering questions until you have reviewed the entire chapter. **CA HR1.**

Using Academic Vocabulary

24. Match the word in Column A with its opposite in Column B.

A	B
challenge	unable
capable	many
sole	together
isolate	easy

Building Citizenship

25. **Making Connections** Use the Internet and your local library to research the Twelve Tables. Work with your classmates to design a similar series of laws, and record them, using modern language. How is your law code similar to and different from the Twelve Tables? **CA 6WA2.3**

Reviewing Skills

26. **Analysis Skill** **Analyzing Primary Sources** Reread the Primary Source feature on page 440. Write a paragraph that answers the following questions. Is this a speech of fact or opinion? Who is Cicero attacking in his speech? How might the speech be different if Cicero were a friend of Antony? Is the speech effective in changing your opinion of Antony? **CA HR5.; HR2.**

27. **Reading Skill** **Making Inferences** Read the following passage from page 439:

". . . Caesar knew that reforms were needed. He granted citizenship to people living in Rome's territories. . . . He started new colonies to provide land for the landless and created work for Rome's jobless people. He ordered landowners using slave labor to hire more free workers."

What can you infer about Caesar's leadership from these sentences? Write an essay describing his leadership. **CA 6WA2.2**

Standards Practice

Select the best answer for each of the following questions.

28 One of Rome's most significant influences on the world is its _____

A invention of paper.
B creation of democracy.
C establishment of the Silk Road.
D system of law.

29 Caesar granted Roman citizenship to

A people living in Rome's territories outside the Italian peninsula.
B people living in the eastern provinces only.
C just the people who lived in Italy.
D members of the Senate.

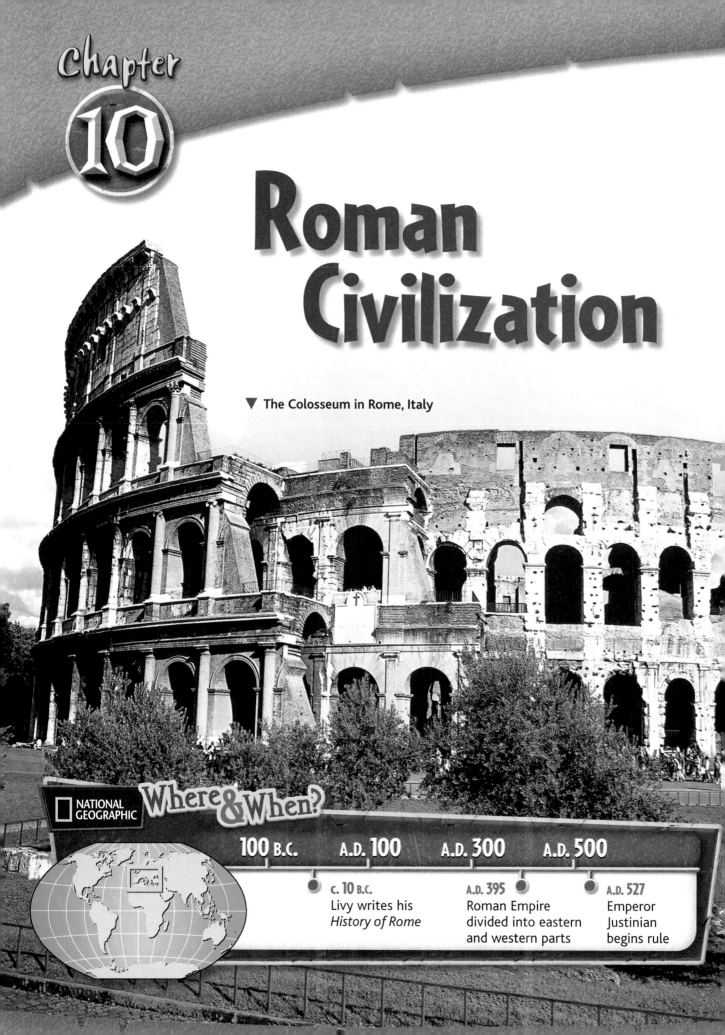

Chapter 10

Roman Civilization

▼ The Colosseum in Rome, Italy

NATIONAL GEOGRAPHIC **Where & When?**

100 B.C.	A.D. 100	A.D. 300	A.D. 500

c. 10 B.C.
Livy writes his
History of Rome

A.D. 395
Roman Empire
divided into eastern
and western parts

A.D. 527
Emperor
Justinian
begins rule

The Big Ideas

History Online
Chapter Overview Visit ca.hss.glencoe.com for a preview of Chapter 10.

Section 1 Life in Ancient Rome

As different societies interact, they often bring about change in each other. The Romans learned from the Greeks but changed what they borrowed to suit their own needs. The lives of rich and poor Romans were very different.

Section 2 The Fall of Rome

Studying the past helps us to understand the present. Rome finally fell when Germanic invaders swept through the empire in the A.D. 400s. Despite this, Roman achievements in government, law, language, and the arts are still important today.

Section 3 The Byzantine Empire

Physical geography plays a role in how civilizations develop and decline. Because it was centered at Constantinople, the Byzantine Empire developed a culture based on Roman, Greek, and Christian ideas. It also established a powerful trading economy.

View the Chapter 10 video in the Glencoe Video Program.

Organizing Information *Make this foldable to help you organize and analyze information by asking yourself questions about Roman civilization.*

Step 1 *Fold a sheet of paper into thirds from top to bottom.*

Step 2 *Turn the paper horizontally, unfold, and label the three columns as shown.*

| Life in Ancient Rome | The Fall of Rome | The Byzantine Empire |

Reading and Writing *As you read the chapter, write the main ideas for each section in the appropriate columns of your foldable. Then write one statement that summarizes the main ideas in each column.*

Chapter 10 Get Ready to Read

Making Predictions

1 Learn It!

A prediction is a guess based on what you already know. One way to predict while reading is to guess what you believe the author will tell you next. As you are reading, each new topic should make sense because it is related to the previous paragraph or passage. Read the excerpt below from Section 2. Based on what you have read, make predictions about what you will read in the rest of the section. After you read Section 2, go back to your predictions to see if they were correct.

> Predict how different our world may have been without the Romans.

> What ideas from our system of law do you predict came from the Romans?

Our world would be very different if the Romans had never existed. Many words in the English language and many of our ideas about government come from the Romans. The same is true for our code of laws and our knowledge about building.

— from page 482

> Can you predict which Roman building influences will be discussed in the text that follows?

Reading Tip

As you read, check your predictions to see if they were correct.

2 Practice It!

Read the excerpt below from Section 1 of this chapter.

Family life was important to the Romans. Their families were large. They included not only parents and young children but also married children and their families, other relatives, and enslaved servants. The father was the head of the household. Called the pater-familias (PA • tuhr • fuh • MIH • lee • uhs), or "father of the family," he had complete control over family members.

— from page 465

Read to Write ⋯⋯

Select one blue subhead in this chapter. Without reading the text under that subhead, write a paragraph that you think might appear there. Check the facts in your paragraph to see if they are correct.

Predict what information will be discussed throughout this section, and write down your predictions. Then as you read this section, discuss your predictions with a partner, and decide if they were correct.

▶ A Roman family at the dinner table

3 Apply It!

Before you read the chapter, skim the questions on pages 494–495 in the Chapter Assessment. Choose three questions and predict what the answers will be.

Section 1

Life in Ancient Rome

Guide to Reading

History Social Science Standards

WH6.7 Students analyze the geographic, political, economic, religious, and social structures during the development of Rome.

WH7.1 Students analyze the causes and effects of the vast expansion and ultimate disintegration of the Roman Empire.

Looking Back, Looking Ahead

You have already learned about Rome's rise to power. Life in Rome was not easy, but as the empire grew, its people accomplished many things in art, science, and engineering.

Focusing on the Main Ideas

- In addition to their own developments in science and engineering, the Romans borrowed many Greek ideas about art and literature. **(page 461)**

- The rich and poor had very different lives in Rome, as did men and women. **(page 464)**

Meeting People

Virgil (VUHR•juhl)
Horace (HAWR•uhs)
Galen (GAY•luhn)
Ptolemy (TAH•luh•mee)
Spartacus (SPAHR•tuh•kuhs)

Content Vocabulary

vault (VAWLT)
satire (SA•TYR)
ode (OHD)
anatomy (uh•NA•tuh•mee)
Forum (FOHR•uhm)
gladiator (GLA•dee•AY•tuhr)
paterfamilias (PA•tuhr•fuh•MIH•lee•uhs)
rhetoric (REH•tuh•rihk)

Academic Vocabulary

technique (tehk•NEEK)
constant (KAHN•stuhnt)

Reading Strategy

Compare and Contrast Use a Venn diagram like the one below to show similarities and differences between the rich and the poor in Rome.

Roman Rich | Roman Poor

NATIONAL GEOGRAPHIC Where & When?

BRITAIN
GAUL GREECE
SPAIN ITALY
Rome • • Constantinople
EGYPT

100 B.C.

73 B.C. Spartacus leads revolt of enslaved people

A.D. 1

c. 10 B.C. Livy writes his *History of Rome*

A.D. 100

c. A.D. 80 Colosseum completed

WH6.7.8 Discuss the legacies of Roman art and architecture, technology and science, literature, language, and law.
WH7.1.1 Study the early strengths and lasting contributions of Rome (e.g., significance of Roman citizenship; rights under Roman law; Roman art, architecture, engineering, and philosophy; preservation and transmission of Christianity) and its ultimate internal weaknesses (e.g., rise of autonomous military powers within the empire, undermining of citizenship by the growth of corruption and slavery, lack of education, and distribution of news).

Roman Culture

Main Idea In addition to their own developments in science and engineering, the Romans borrowed many Greek ideas about art and literature.

Reading Connection Are there people in your life that you admire? What have you learned from them? Read to find out what the Romans learned from the Greeks.

The Romans admired and studied Greek statues, buildings, and ideas. They copied the Greeks in many ways. However, they changed what they borrowed to accomodate their own needs.

What Was Roman Art Like?

The Romans admired Greek art and architecture. They placed Greek-style statues in their homes and public buildings. Roman artists, however, carved statues that looked different from those of the Greeks. Greek statues were made to look perfect. People were shown young, healthy, and with beautiful bodies. Roman statues were more realistic and included wrinkles, warts, and other less attractive features.

In building, the Romans also turned to the Greeks for ideas. They used Greek-style porches and rows of columns called colonnades. But they also added their own features, such as arches and domes. Roman builders were the first to make full use of the arch. Arches supported bridges, aqueducts, and buildings. Rows of arches were often built against one another to form a **vault** (VAWLT), or curved ceiling. Using this **technique,** the Romans were also able to build domes.

The Romans were the first people to invent and use concrete, a mixture of volcanic ash, lime, and water. When it dried, this mix was as hard as rock. Concrete made buildings sturdier and allowed them to be built taller.

Rome's concrete buildings were so well built that many still stand. One of the most famous is the Colosseum, completed about A.D. 80. It was a huge arena that had a seating capacity of about 60,000 people. Another famous building is the Pantheon, a temple built to honor Rome's gods. The Pantheon's domed roof was the largest of its time.

▼ **This Roman bridge still stands in Spain.**
In what other structures were arches used?

The Book of Epodes

In this poem excerpt, Horace praises the lifestyle of those who farm their family's land.

"Happy the man who, far from business and affairs

Like mortals of the early times,

May work his father's fields with oxen of his own,

Exempt [free] from profit, loss, and fee,

Not like the soldier roused by savage trumpet's blare,

Not terrified by seas in rage,

Avoiding busy forums and the haughty doors

Of influencial citizens."

—Horace, *The Book of Epodes*

▲ Horace

DBQ Document-Based Question

According to Horace, what kinds of things does the farmer avoid?

Roman Literature

Roman authors based much of their writing on Greek works. For example, the Roman writer **Virgil** (VUHR•juhl) drew some of his ideas from Homer's *Odyssey*. Virgil's epic poem, the *Aeneid* (uh•NEE•uhd), describes the adventures of the Trojan prince Aeneas and how he came to Italy. Virgil presents Aeneas as the ideal Roman—brave, self-controlled, and loyal to the gods.

Rome's other famous writers also looked to the Greeks for inspiration. Using Greek models, the poet **Horace** (HAWR•uhs) wrote **satires** (SA•TYRZ). These works poked fun at human weaknesses. Horace also composed **odes** (OHDZ), or poems that express strong emotions about life. The

Roman writer Ovid wrote works that were based on the Greek myths. The poet Catullus also admired Greek writings. He wrote short poems about love, sadness, and envy.

Like the Greeks, Rome's historians recorded the events of their civilization. One of Rome's most famous historians was Livy. He wrote his *History of Rome* about 10 B.C. In this book, Livy describes Rome's rise to power. Livy greatly admired the deeds of the early Romans, and he believed that history had important moral lessons to teach people.

Livy celebrated Rome's greatness, but the Roman historian Tacitus took a darker view. He believed that Rome's emperors had taken people's freedom. Tacitus also thought Romans were not committed to the values that made them strong. He accused them of wasting time on sports and other pleasures.

Also like the Greeks, the Romans enjoyed plays. Roman plays were often based on Greek tragedies and comedies. Playwrights such as the tragedy writer Seneca and the comedy writers Plautus and Terence wrote plays for religious festivals. Romans especially liked plays with humor.

Roman authors influenced later writers in Europe and America, but the language of the Romans, Latin, had an even bigger impact on future generations. Latin became Europe's language for government, trade, and instruction until about A.D. 1500. Latin became the foundation for many modern European languages, such as Italian, French, and Spanish, and shaped many others. Many of the English words we use today come from Latin as well.

Roman Science and Engineering

The Romans also learned from Greek science. A Greek doctor named **Galen** (GAY•luhn)

brought many medical ideas to Rome. For example, he emphasized the importance of **anatomy** (uh•NA•tuh•mee), the study of body structure. To learn about internal organs, Galen cut open dead animals and recorded his findings. Doctors in the West studied Galen's books and drawings for more than 1,500 years.

Another important scientist of the Roman Empire was **Ptolemy** (TAH•luh•mee). Ptolemy lived in Alexandria, in Egypt. He studied the sky and carefully mapped over 1,000 different stars. He also studied the motion of planets and stars and created rules explaining their movements. Even though Ptolemy inaccurately placed Earth at the center of the universe, educated people in Europe accepted his ideas for centuries.

While Roman scientists tried to understand how the world worked, Roman engineers built an astonishing system of roads and bridges to connect the empire. Have you ever heard the saying "All roads lead to Rome"? Roman engineers built roads from Rome to every part of the empire. These roads were well built and made travel and trade more accessible.

The Romans also used advanced engineering to supply their cities with freshwater. Engineers built aqueducts to bring water from the hills into the cities. Aqueducts were long troughs supported by rows of arches. They carried water over long distances. At one time, 11 great aqueducts fed Rome's homes, bathhouses, fountains, and public bathrooms. Roman cities also had sewers to remove waste.

✔ Reading Check **Explain** How did the Romans improve on Greek ideas in architecture?

The Roman Colosseum

The Colosseum in Rome could hold 60,000 people. It was made of concrete and had a removable canvas awning to protect spectators from the hot sun. *What was concrete made from?*

A system of cages, ropes, and pulleys brought wild animals up to the Colosseum floor from rooms underground. ▼

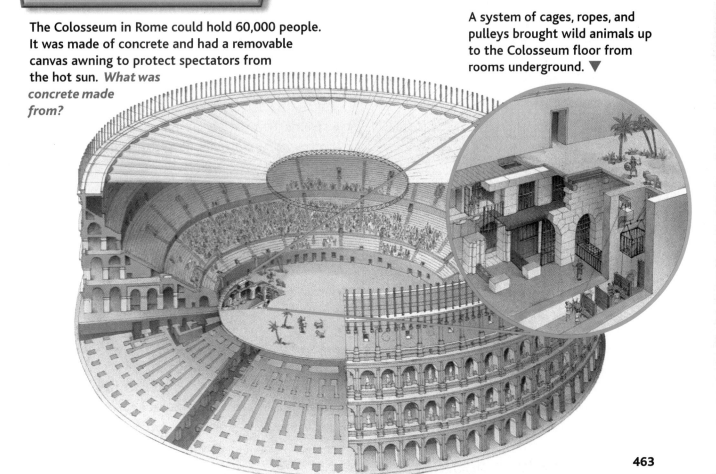

WH6.7 Students analyze the geographic, political, economic, religious, and social structures during the development of Rome.

WH7.1 Students analyze the causes and effects of the vast expansion and ultimate disintegration of the Roman Empire.

NATIONAL GEOGRAPHIC

The Way It Was

Sports & Contests

Ancient Roman Sports Sports were important to the Romans. Paintings on vases, frescoes [moist plaster], and stone show Romans playing ball, including a version of soccer. Roman girls are shown exercising with handheld weights and throwing an egg-shaped ball.

Some Roman sporting events took place in the Colosseum. Wild beast fights, battles between ships, and gladiator contests attracted Roman spectators by the thousands. Chariot racing was held in the Circus Maximus, and the drivers wore team colors of red, white, green, and blue.

▲ Scene showing gladiators in battle

Connecting to the Past

1. How do we know sports were important to the Romans?

2. How are today's sports different from Roman sports? How are they similar?

Daily Life in Rome

Main Idea The rich and poor had very different lives in Rome, as did men and women.

Reading Connection Do you think there is a big difference in the lives of boys and girls you know today? Why or why not? Read to learn how the lives of Roman boys and girls were very different from each other.

What was it like to live in Rome over 2,000 years ago? Rome was one of the largest cities in the ancient world. By the time of Augustus, over a million people lived there. Rome was carefully planned, as were many Roman cities. It was laid out in a square with the main roads crossing at right angles. At its center was the **Forum** (FOHR•um). This was an open space that served as a marketplace and public square. Temples and public buildings were built around it.

Wealthy Romans lived in large, comfortable houses. Each home had large rooms, fine furniture, and beautiful gardens. In the center was an inner court called an atrium. Wealthy Romans also had homes called villas on their country estates.

The city of Rome was crowded, noisy, and dirty. People tossed garbage into the streets from their apartments, and thieves prowled the streets at night. Most people in Rome were poor. They lived in apartment buildings made of stone and wood. High rent forced families to live in one room.

Roman apartments were up to six stories high. They often collapsed because they were so poorly built. Fire was a **constant** danger because people used torches and lamps for lighting and cooked with oil. Once started, a fire could destroy entire blocks of apartments.

To keep the people from rioting, the Roman government provided "bread and circuses," or free grain and shows. Romans of all classes flocked to the chariot races and gladiator contests. **Gladiators** (GLA•dee•AY•tuhrz)

▲ Chariot races were held in an arena called the Circus Maximus, one of the largest arenas ever made. *Besides chariot races, what other types of shows attracted Romans?*

fought animals and each other. Most gladiators were enslaved people, criminals, or poor people. Gladiators were admired, much like sports heroes are today.

What Was Family Life Like?
Family life was important to the Romans. Their families were large. They included not only parents and young children but also married children and their families, other relatives, and enslaved servants. The father was the head of the household. Called the **paterfamilias** (PA•tuhr•fuh•MIH•lee•uhs), or "father of the family," he had complete control over family members. For example, he punished children severely if they disobeyed. He also arranged their marriages.

In some cases, the paterfamilias made sure his children were educated. Poor Romans could not afford to send their children to school. Wealthy Romans, however, hired tutors to teach their young children at home. Some older boys went to school, where they learned reading, writing, and **rhetoric** (REH•tuh•rihk), or public speaking.

Older girls did not go to school. Instead, they studied reading and writing at home. They also learned household duties such as cooking, weaving and cleaning.

Between the ages of 14 and 16, a Roman boy celebrated becoming a man. He would burn his toys and put on a toga, a loose-fitting robe that Roman men wore. Once he came of age, a man might join his family's business, become a soldier, or begin a career

▲ A Roman teacher and student

in the government. Roman women did not become adults until they married. A woman usually wore a long flowing robe with a cloak called a *palla.*

Women in Rome

Women in early Rome had some rights, but they did not have the same status as men. The paterfamilias controlled his wife's activities. However, he often sought her advice in private. Women had a strong influence on their families, and some wives of famous men, including emperors, became well-known themselves. For example, the empress Livia (LIHV•ee•uh), wife of Augustus, had a say in Rome's politics. She was later honored as a goddess.

The freedoms a Roman woman enjoyed depended on her husband's wealth and status. Wealthy women had a great deal of independence. They could own land, run businesses, and sell property. They managed the household and had enslaved people do the housework. This left the women free to study literature, art, and fashion. Outside the home, they could go to the theater or the amphitheater, but in both places they had to sit in areas separate from men.

Women with less money had less freedom. They spent most of their time working in their houses or helping their husbands in family-run shops. They were allowed to leave home to shop, visit friends, worship at temples, or go to the baths. A few women did work independently outside the home. Some served as priestesses, while others worked as hairdressers and even doctors.

A Roman House

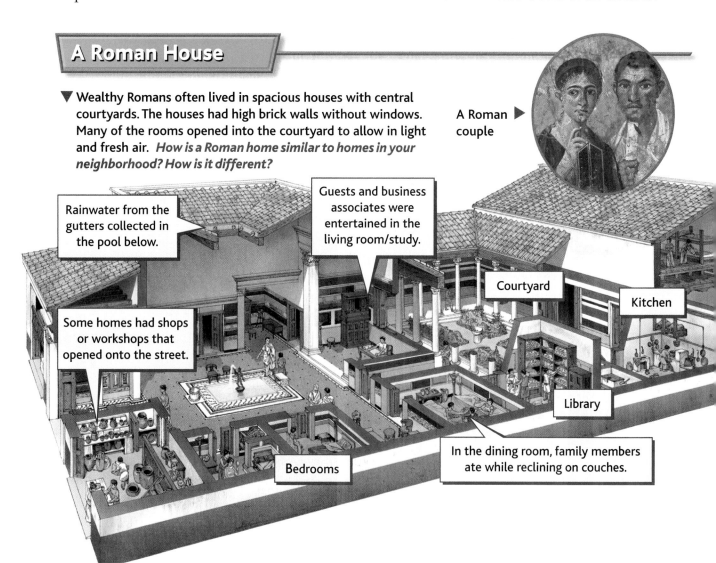

▼ Wealthy Romans often lived in spacious houses with central courtyards. The houses had high brick walls without windows. Many of the rooms opened into the courtyard to allow in light and fresh air. *How is a Roman home similar to homes in your neighborhood? How is it different?*

A Roman ▶ couple

Rainwater from the gutters collected in the pool below.

Guests and business associates were entertained in the living room/study.

Courtyard

Kitchen

Some homes had shops or workshops that opened onto the street.

Library

Bedrooms

In the dining room, family members ate while reclining on couches.

▼ A Roman family at the dinner table

▲ These apartments were built of brick and stone for wealthy Romans. *What sort of buildings did poor Romans live in?*

How Did Romans Treat Enslaved People?

Historians can trace slavery to early times in Roman history. But the use of slave labor grew as Rome took over more territory. Thousands of prisoners from conquered lands were brought to Italy. By 100 B.C., an estimated 40 percent of the people in Italy were enslaved.

Enslaved people did many different jobs. They worked in homes, fields, mines, and workshops. They helped build roads, bridges, and aqueducts. Many enslaved Greeks were well educated. They served as teachers, doctors, and artisans.

For most enslaved people, life was miserable. They were punished severely for poor work or for running away. To escape their hardships, enslaved people often rebelled.

In 73 B.C. a slave revolt broke out in Italy. It was led by a gladiator named **Spartacus** (SPAHR•tuh•kuhs). Under Spartacus, a force of 70,000 enslaved people defeated several Roman armies. The revolt was finally crushed two years later. Spartacus and 6,000 of his followers were crucified, or put to death by being nailed to a cross.

Roman Religion and Philosophy

The ancient Romans worshiped many gods and goddesses. They also believed that spirits lived in natural things, such as trees and rivers. Greek gods and goddesses were popular in Rome, although they were given Roman names. For example, Zeus became Jupiter, the sky god, and Aphrodite became Venus, the goddess of love and beauty. Roman emperors also were worshiped. This practice strengthened support for the government.

Romans honored their gods and goddesses by praying and offering food. Every Roman home had an altar for the family's household gods. Government officials made offerings in temples. There the important gods and goddesses of Rome were honored. Some Roman priests looked for messages from the gods. They studied the insides of dead animals or watched the flight of birds, looking for meaning.

The Romans also borrowed ideas from Greek philosophy. For example, they borrowed and modified, or changed slightly, the Greek philosophy of Stoicism. For Romans, Stoicism was not about finding happiness through reason like it was for the Greeks. Instead, Stoicism encouraged Romans to live in a practical way. Stoic philosophers urged people to participate in public affairs, to do their civic duty, and to treat conquered peoples well.

As the empire grew larger, Romans came into contact with other religions. These religions were allowed, as long as they did not threaten the government. Those that did faced severe hardships. You will read about one of these religions—Christianity—in the next chapter.

Reading Check **Contrast** Compare the life of upper-class women to women of other classes.

Greek and Roman Gods

Greek God	Roman God	Role
Ares	Mars	god of war
Zeus	Jupiter	chief god
Hera	Juno	wife of chief god
Aphrodite	Venus	goddess of love
Artemis	Diana	goddess of the hunt
Athena	Minerva	goddess of wisdom
Hermes	Mercury	messenger god
Hades	Pluto	god of the underworld
Poseidon	Neptune	god of the sea
Hephaestus	Vulcan	god of fire

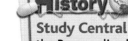

History Online

Study Central Need help understanding how the Romans lived? Visit ca.hss.glencoe.com and click on Study Central.

Section 1 Review

Reading Summary

Review the Main Ideas

- Roman art, literature, and science borrowed much from the Greeks. Roman engineers made advances, including the development of cement, the arch, aqueducts, and domes.

- Religion and family were important parts of Roman life. Enslaved people carried out many different tasks in Roman society.

What Did You Learn?

1. What were some of Ptolemy's scientific achievements?

2. How were the Roman and Greek religions similar?

Critical Thinking

3. **Compare and Contrast** Draw a chart like the one below. Fill in details comparing Roman and Greek art and architecture. **CA 6RC2.4**

Greek Art	Roman Art
Greek Architecture	Roman Architecture

4. **Analyze** Why is the Roman language important? **CA 6RC2.0**

5. **Describe** Describe Roman education. **CA 6RC2.0**

6. **The Big Ideas** The Romans borrowed ideas from other peoples. Do you think our culture today borrows ideas from other peoples? Explain your answer. **CA 6RC2.3**

7. **Reading** **Making Predictions** Reread the text on Roman literature on page 462. How might Roman writing have been different without the influence of Greek writers? **CA 6RC2.3**

BAUCIS AND PHILEMON

By Don Nardo

Before You Read

The Scene: This story takes place in ancient Rome in the legendary time when gods visited Earth to interact with humans in person.

The Characters: Baucis and Philemon are a woman and man who welcome guests into their home. Jupiter and Mercury are two ancient Roman gods.

The Plot: A husband and wife welcome two guests into their cottage. As the pair try to provide for their guests with food, the guests reveal their identities and reward the host and hostess for their generosity.

Vocabulary Preview

diversion: something that relaxes, amuses, or entertains

descend: to pass from a higher level to a lower level

hospitality: kind treatment of guests and visitors

thatch: a plant material used to cover the roof of a building

burden: something taken as a duty or responsibility

edible: safe to eat

replenish: to make full or complete again

vantage: a position giving a total view

deluge: flood

unscathed: unharmed

transform: to change completely

ensure: to make certain

eternity: endless time

foliage: leaves from a tree

peasant: farm laborer

Do you know a person who is always friendly and generous, no matter what the circumstances? In this story, a good-natured husband and wife are rewarded when they receive special guests into their home.

As You Read

Keep in mind that this story is a myth. Like the Greeks, Romans passed myths from one generation to the next to explain some aspect of the world. Often, the stories involved gods and goddesses as well as humans.

One of Jupiter's favorite pastimes was disguising himself as a mortal and roaming the earth in search of diversions and adventures. On one particular day, he and his messenger, Mercury, dressed themselves as lowly beggars and descended to the land of Phrygia[1] (in central Asia Minor) to test the hospitality of the local people. To their dismay, the gods encountered much rudeness and selfishness. As they went from house to house, rich ones and poor ones alike, asking humbly for a scrap of food and a place to sleep, one owner after another told them to go away and barred the door against them. They tried a thousand houses and always received the same poor treatment.

Finally, Jupiter and Mercury came to a small hut thatched with straw and reeds, the humblest and poorest hovel[2] they had seen so far. This time, an elderly couple, Baucis and Philemon by name, welcomed them in. As Ovid[3] told it: They had married young and were deeply in love.

---

[1]**Phrygia:** an area of the Roman Empire in present-day Turkey
[2]**hovel:** a small, poorly built house
[3]**Ovid:** Roman poet, author of tales of Roman mythology

They had grown old together in the same cottage; they were very poor, but faced their poverty with cheerful spirit and made its burden light by not complaining. It would do you little good to ask for servants or masters in that household, for the couple were all the house; both gave and followed orders.

The two old people went out of their way to make the strangers comfortable. Baucis carefully washed her wobbly wooden table, and she and her husband prepared a supper of cabbage, olives, radishes, eggs, and whatever else edible they could find. As they and their guests ate the meal, Baucis and Philemon noticed that each time their mixing bowl was near to empty, it suddenly filled up again; and the wine kept on replenishing itself, too. Not realizing that this was the work of their superhuman guests, the two humans became afraid and raised their hands high in prayer.

At this moment, Jupiter and Mercury revealed themselves to the old people. They told them not to fear and led them to a mountaintop. From that vantage, Baucis and Philemon watched as a great flood drowned all their neighbors, the ones who had treated the gods so badly, a deluge that left only their own hut standing unscathed. Jupiter then

transformed the hut into a magnificent temple, and the two mortals thereafter resided in it as his devoted priests.

The king of the gods did the two aging lovers a further kindness, ensuring that neither would have to endure the sadness and loneliness of outliving the other and also that they would remain together for eternity. On the last day of their lives each suddenly saw leaves sprouting from the other.

Philemon watched Baucis changing, Baucis watched Philemon, and as the foliage spread, they still had time to say "Farewell, my dear!" and the bark closed over sealing their mouths. And even to this day the peasants in that district show the stranger the two trees close together, and the union of oak and linden[4] in one [trunk].

---

[4]**linden:** a type of tree with large heart-shaped leaves

Responding to the Literature

1. Who comes to visit Baucis and Philemon?

2. What did Baucis and Philemon notice was happening to their food?

3. **Cause and Effect** What reward was given to the two hosts by Jupiter and Mercury? Why were Baucis and Philemon rewarded in such a way? **CA 6RL3.0**

4. **Analyze** How does the setting of the story influence the plot? Support your ideas with details from the story. **CA 6RL3.3**

5. **Read to Write** Imagine that you are Baucis or Philemon. What would your reaction be to discovering that Jupiter and Mercury were guests in your house? How would you treat them once you knew who they were? Write a journal entry that describes your reaction. **CA 6WA2.4**

From the California Reading List

Do you want to learn more about the ancient Romans or the history of Christianity? If so, check out these other great books.

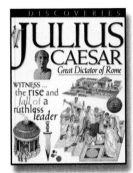

Biography

Julius Caesar: Great Dictator of Rome by Richard Platt follows the life and times of Rome's most famous leader. The book explains Caesar's rise to power, his achievements, and his death. *The content of this book is related to* *History–Social Science Standard WH6.7.*

Nonfiction

Science in Ancient Rome by Jacqueline L. Harris provides details and descriptions of the important scientific contributions made by the ancient Romans. It gives specific examples of the significant people and events in Roman history that helped make these advancements. *The content of this book is related to* *History–Social Science Standard WH6.7.*

Fiction

The Thieves of Ostia by Caroline Lawrence tells the story of Flavia Gemina, a young girl living in ancient Rome. The book follows Flavia and her friends as they try to solve a crime in the Roman city of Ostia. *The content of this book is related to* *History–Social Science Standard WH6.7.*

Nonfiction

The Story of Christianity by Michael Collins and Matthew A. Price covers the historical background of Christianity. The book takes the reader from the birth of Christ to the present day, detailing the important people and events that helped shape the religion along the way. *The content of this book is related to* *History–Social Science Standard WH6.7.*

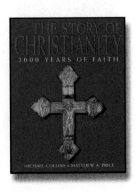

Section 2

The Fall of Rome

Guide to Reading

Looking Back, Looking Ahead

In Section 1, you learned about Roman life and achievements when the empire was at its height. Over time, however, the Roman Empire began to have problems, and it gradually grew weaker. Eventually, Rome fell to outside invaders.

Focusing on the Main Ideas

- Poor leadership, a declining economy, and attacks by Germanic tribes weakened the Roman Empire. *(page 475)*

- Rome finally fell when invaders swept through the empire during the A.D. 400s. *(page 479)*

- Rome passed on many achievements in government, law, language, and the arts. *(page 482)*

Locating Places

Constantinople
(KAHN•STAN•tuhn•OH•puhl)

Meeting People

Diocletian (DY•uh•KLEE•shuhn)
Constantine (KAHN•stuhn•TEEN)
Theodosius
(THEE•uh•DOH•shuhs)
Alaric (A•luh•rihk)
Odoacer (OH•duh•WAY•suhr)

Content Vocabulary

inflation (ihn•FLAY•shuhn)
barter (BAHR•tuhr)
reform (rih•FAWRM)

Academic Vocabulary

authority (uh•THAHR•uh•tee)
expand (ihk•SPAND)

Reading Strategy

Sequencing Information Create a diagram to show the events that led up to the fall of the Roman Empire.

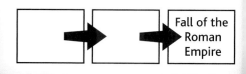

Fall of the Roman Empire

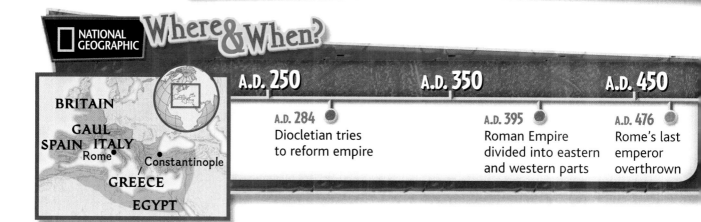

NATIONAL GEOGRAPHIC Where & When?

BRITAIN
GAUL
SPAIN ITALY
Rome
Constantinople
GREECE
EGYPT

A.D. 250

A.D. 284 Diocletian tries to reform empire

A.D. 350

A.D. 395 Roman Empire divided into eastern and western parts

A.D. 450

A.D. 476 Rome's last emperor overthrown

History Social Science Standards

WH6.7 Students analyze the geographic, political, economic, religious, and social structures during the development of Rome.
WH7.1 Students analyze the causes and effects of the vast expansion and ultimate disintegration of the Roman Empire.

WH7.1.1 Study the early strengths and lasting contributions of Rome (e.g., significance of Roman citizenship; rights under Roman law; Roman art, architecture, engineering, and philosophy; preservation and transmission of Christianity) and its ultimate internal weaknesses (e.g., rise of autonomous military powers within the empire, undermining of citizenship by the growth of corruption and slavery, lack of education, and distribution of news).

The Decline of Rome

Main Idea Poor leadership, a declining economy, and attacks by Germanic tribes weakened the Roman Empire.

Reading Connection What do you do when you face a difficult problem? Do you try to solve it yourself? Do you ask other people for help? Read to learn about the problems the Roman Empire faced and how its leaders responded.

In A.D. 180 Marcus Aurelius died. His son, Commodus (KAH•muh•duhs), became emperor. Commodus was cruel and wasted money. Instead of ruling Rome, Commodus spent much of his time fighting as a gladiator. In A.D. 192 the emperor's bodyguard killed him. Many decades of confusion and conflict followed.

After Commodus, emperors called the Severans ruled Rome. Much of their time was spent putting down revolts and protecting Rome's borders. The Severans stayed in power by paying the army well, but they ignored the growing problems of crime and poverty.

Political and Social Problems When the last Severan ruler died in A.D. 235, Rome's government became very weak. For almost 50 years, army leaders constantly fought each other for the throne. During this time, Rome had 22 different emperors.

Poor leadership was not Rome's only difficulty. Fewer Romans honored the old ideals of duty, courage, and honesty. Many government officials took bribes. As problems

The Decline of Rome

Weak Roman Government
- Dishonest government officials provide poor leadership.

Social Problems
- Famine and disease spread throughout the empire.

Declining Economy
- Income and wages fall.
- Wealthy fail to pay taxes.

Reform Fails and Rome Divides in Two
- Government fails to keep order.
- Violence and tension increase.
- Diocletian divides the empire.

Eastern Roman Empire
- Constantinople becomes the new capital.
- The empire survives attacks and prospers.

Western Roman Empire
- Numerous attacks threaten the empire.
- Territory is slowly lost to invaders.

Byzantine Empire
- This empire is created from the Eastern Roman Empire and lasts nearly 1,000 years.

Rome Falls
- The city of Rome falls in A.D. 476.
- The Western Roman Empire is divided into Germanic kingdoms by A.D. 550.

Understanding Charts

Many issues, including a weak government, lack of food, and fewer jobs, led to Rome's decline.

1. According to the flow chart, what occurs after reform fails?
2. **Cause and Effect** What were the final effects of the Roman Empire being split in two?

increased, talented people often refused to serve in government. Many wealthy citizens even stopped paying taxes. Fewer people attended schools, and a large number of the empire's people were now enslaved. Wealthy Romans supported slavery because it was a cheap way to get work done.

Economic and Military Problems During the A.D. 200s, Rome's economy began to fall apart. As government weakened, law and order broke down. Roads and bridges were destroyed, and trade routes became unsafe. Information could not be sent quickly across the empire, and Rome's army could no longer organize quickly enough to drive out invaders. Roman soldiers and invaders seized crops and destroyed fields. Farmers grew less food, and hunger began to spread.

As the economy worsened, people bought fewer goods. Artisans produced less, and shopkeepers lost money. Many businesses closed, and the number of workers dropped sharply. Many workers had to leave jobs and serve in the military.

Rome also began to suffer from **inflation** (ihn•FLAY•shuhn), or rapidly increasing prices. Inflation happens when money loses its value. How did this happen? The weak economy meant fewer taxes were paid. With less money coming in, the Roman government could not afford to defend its territories and had to find a way to pay its soldiers and officials. One way for the government to get the money it needed was to put less gold in its coins.

By putting less gold in each coin, the government could make extra coins and pay for more things. People soon learned that the coins did not have as much gold in them, and the coins began losing value. Prices went up, and many people stopped using money altogether. They began to **barter** (BAHR•tuhr), or exchange goods without using currency.

Meanwhile, invaders swept into the empire. In the west, Germanic tribes raided Roman farms and towns. In the east, armies from Persia pushed into the empire's territory. As fighting increased, the government could no longer enlist and pay Romans as soldiers. It began using Germanic warriors in the army. However, these Germanic soldiers were not loyal to Rome.

Primary Source — Distrust of Money

As the Roman Empire declined, people stopped trusting the value of money.

"Whereas [because] the public officials have assembled and have accused the bankers of the exchange banks of having closed them because of their unwillingness to accept the divine coin of the emperors, it has become necessary to issue an order to all owners of the banks to open them and to accept and exchange all coin except the absolutely spurious [false] and counterfeit—and not alone to them but to those who engage in business transactions of any kind."

▲ Roman coins

—"Distrust of Imperial Coinage," *Oxyrhynchus Papyrus*, no. 1411, Vol. 2, A.S. Hunt, trans.

DBQ Document-Based Question

What do you think was happening to the economy of the empire as people stopped using the official money?

What Were Diocletian's Reforms?

In A.D. 284 a general named **Diocletian** (DY•uh•KLEE•shuhn) became emperor. To stop the empire's decline, he introduced **reforms** (rih•FAWRMZ), or political changes to make things better. Believing the empire to be too large to rule by himself, Diocletian changed its framework by dividing it into four parts. He named officials to rule these areas but kept **authority** over all.

Diocletian also worked to boost the economy. To slow inflation, he issued rules that set the prices of goods and the wages to be paid to workers. To make sure more goods were produced, he ordered workers to occupy the same jobs until they died. Diocletian's reforms failed. The people ignored the new rules, and Diocletian did not have enough power to enforce them.

Who Was Constantine?

In A.D. 305 Diocletian retired from office. After an interval of conflict, another general named **Constantine** (KAHN•stuhn•TEEN) became emperor in A.D. 312. To aid the economy, Constantine issued several orders and passed important legislation. The sons of workers had to follow their fathers' trades, the sons of farmers had to work the land their fathers worked, and the sons of soldiers had to serve in the army.

Constantine's changes did not halt the empire's decline in the west. As a result, Constantine moved the capital from a dying Rome to a new city in the east. He chose the site of the Greek city of Byzantium (buh•ZAN •tee•uhm). There he built a forum, an amphitheater called the Hippodrome, and many palaces. The city became known as **Constantinople** (KAHN•STAN•tuhn•OH•puhl). Today, Constantinople is called Istanbul.

Reading Check **Explain** How did Diocletian try to reverse the decline of Rome?

The Way It Was

Focus on Everyday Life

Slavery in the Roman Empire Public and private slavery were common in Roman society. Public slaves were owned by the state. They took care of important buildings and served government officials. Educated public slaves were used to help organize the governments of conquered areas.

Private slaves were owned by individuals. They were often forced to work long hours and could be sold at any time. Wealthy Romans had hundreds or even thousands of enslaved people. Most enslaved people worked on farms.

Most enslaved people were men. This was probably because their work required great strength. Some enslaved men also became gladiators. Enslaved women made clothing and cooked for their owner's family.

▼ Roman slaves at work

Connecting to the Past

1. What was the main difference between public and private enslavement?

2. Which jobs were probably considered the most desirable by enslaved people?

CONSTANTINE THE GREAT

c. A.D. 280–337

First Christian Roman Emperor

Constantine was the first Roman Emperor to become a Christian, although he was not baptized until near his death in A.D. 337. He first came to believe in Christianity many years earlier, when he was a military leader. Constantine believed he had seen a flaming cross in the sky inscribed with these words: "By this sign thou shall conquer." The next day his army was victorious in an important battle. He believed that the cross was a call to the Christian God.

During his reign, Constantine granted new opportunities to Christians and helped advance the power of the early Catholic Church. At the Council of Nicea in A.D. 325, he encouraged discussion about the acceptance of the Trinity (Father, Son, and Holy Spirit). He also boosted the political positions and power of bishops within the Roman government.

Even though Constantine had many political and religious successes, his life was filled with controversy and tragedy. Constantine married a woman named Fausta. His eldest son from a previous marriage was named Crispus. Fausta accused Crispus of crimes and claimed that he was planning to seize the throne.

▲ Constantine

Constantine was so shocked that he had his son killed. Constantine later discovered that Fausta had lied because she wanted her own son to be in line for the throne. He then had Fausta killed.

▲ Modern-day Constantinople

Then and Now

Constantine believed freedom of religion was important for the success of his empire and made sure that Christians could no longer be persecuted. What part of the U.S. Constitution protects freedom of religion?

WH7.1.1 Study the early strengths and lasting contributions of Rome (e.g., significance of Roman citizenship; rights under Roman law; Roman art, architecture, engineering, and philosophy; preservation and transmission of Christianity) and its ultimate internal weaknesses (e.g., rise of autonomous military powers within the empire, undermining of citizenship by the growth of corruption and slavery, lack of education, and distribution of news). **WH7.1.2** Discuss the geographic borders of the empire at its height and the factors that threatened its territorial cohesion.

Rome Falls

Main Idea Rome finally fell when invaders swept through the empire during the A.D. 400s.

Reading Connection How would you feel if a favorite place—a shop, park, or recreation center—was closed after being open for many years? Read to learn how the Romans had to face an even greater loss when their city and empire fell.

Both Diocletian and Constantine failed to save the Roman Empire. When Constantine died in A.D. 337, fighting broke out again. A new emperor called **Theodosius** (THEE•uh•DOH•shuhs) finally gained control and ended the fighting.

Ruling the empire proved to be difficult. Theodosius decided to divide the empire after his death. In A.D. 395, the Roman Empire split into two separate empires. One was the Western Roman Empire, with its capital at Rome. The other was the Eastern Roman Empire, with its capital at Constantinople.

Rome Is Invaded As Rome declined, it was no longer able to hold back the Germanic tribes on its borders. Many different Germanic groups existed—Ostrogoths, Visigoths, Franks, Vandals, Angles, and Saxons. They came from the forests and marshes of northern Europe.

These Germanic groups were in search of warmer climates and better grazing land for their cattle. They also were drawn by Rome's wealth and culture. In addition, many were fleeing the Huns, fierce warriors from Mongolia in Asia.

In the late A.D. 300s, the Huns entered Eastern Europe and defeated the Ostrogoths (AHS•truh•GAHTHS). The Visigoths, fearing for their own welfare, asked the Eastern Roman emperor for protection. He let them settle

Primary Source — Rome Is Attacked

In this excerpt from one of his letters, the Christian leader Jerome describes attacks on the Roman provinces.

▲ Saint Jerome

"Who would believe that Rome, victor over all the world, would fall, that she would be to her people both the womb and the tomb.... Where we cannot help we mourn and mingle with theirs our tears.... There is not an hour, not even a moment, when we are not occupied with crowds of refugees, when the peace of the monastery is not invaded by a horde of guests so that we shall either have to shut the gates or neglect the Scriptures for which the gates were opened."

—Jerome, "News of the Attacks"

DBQ Document-Based Question

Does Jerome think the gates of the monastery should be shut? Explain.

just inside the empire's border. In return they promised to be loyal to Rome.

Before long, trouble broke out between the Visigoths and Romans. The empire forced the Visigoths to buy food at very high prices. The Romans also kidnapped and enslaved many Visigoths.

Finally, the Visigoths rebelled against the Romans. In A.D. 378 they defeated Roman legions at the Battle of Adrianople (AY•dree•uh•NOH•puhl). After that defeat, Rome was forced to surrender land to the Visigoths inside Roman territory.

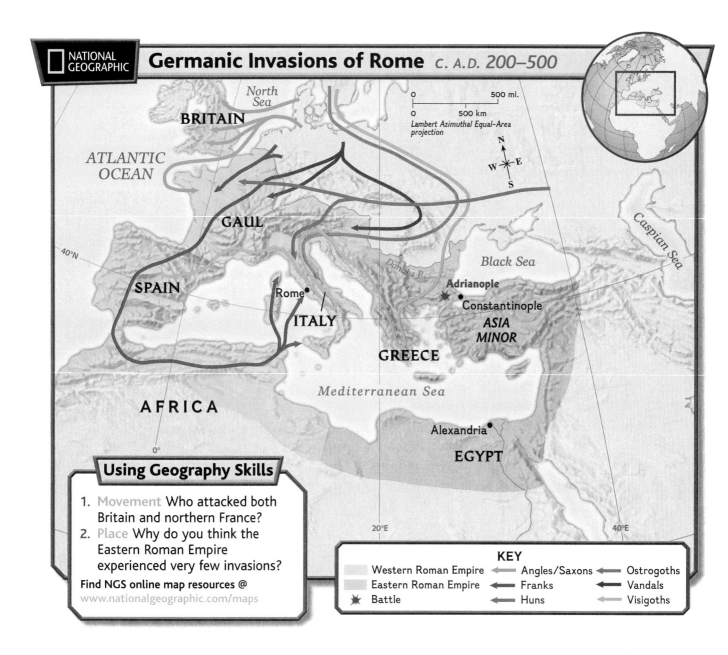

Germanic Invasions of Rome c. a.d. 200–500

North Sea

BRITAIN

ATLANTIC OCEAN

GAUL

40°N

SPAIN

Rome

ITALY

AFRICA

Mediterranean Sea

0°

Danube R.

Black Sea

Adrianople

Constantinople

ASIA MINOR

GREECE

Alexandria

EGYPT

Caspian Sea

0   500 mi.
0   500 km
Lambert Azimuthal Equal-Area projection

N
W E
S

20°E   40°E

Using Geography Skills

1. Movement Who attacked both Britain and northern France?
2. Place Why do you think the Eastern Roman Empire experienced very few invasions?

Find NGS online map resources @
www.nationalgeographic.com/maps

KEY

Western Roman Empire   ← Angles/Saxons   ← Ostrogoths
Eastern Roman Empire   ← Franks   ← Vandals
★ Battle   ← Huns   ← Visigoths

The Germanic tribes now knew that Rome was not capable of defending itself. More and more Germanic warriors crossed the borders in search of land. In the winter of A.D. 406, the Rhine River in Western Europe froze. Germanic groups crossed the frozen river and entered Gaul, which is today France. The Romans were too weak to force them back across the border.

In A.D. 410 the Visigoth leader **Alaric** (A•luh•rihk) and his soldiers captured Rome. They burned records and looted the treasury. Rome's capture shocked the empire's people. It was the first time Rome had been conquered in 800 years.

Another Germanic group known as the Vandals overran Spain and northern Africa. They enslaved some Roman landowners and drove others away. Then the Vandals sailed to Italy. In A.D. 455 they entered Rome. They spent 12 days stripping buildings of everything valuable and burning them. From these attacks came the English word *vandalism*, which means "the willful destruction of property."

▲ An image showing the Visigoths invading Rome. *What leader did the Visigoths overthrow to take control of Rome?*

Rome Falls By the mid-A.D. 400s, several Germanic leaders held high posts in Rome's government and army. In A.D. 476 a Germanic general named **Odoacer** (OH•duh•WAY•suhr) took control, overthrowing the western emperor, a 14-year-old boy named Romulus Augustulus (RAHM•yuh•luhs aw•GUHS•chah•luhs). After Romulus Augustulus, no emperor ever again ruled from Rome. Historians often use this event to mark the end of the Western Roman Empire.

Odoacer controlled Rome for almost 15 years. Then a group of Visigoths seized the city and killed Odoacer. They set up a kingdom in Italy under their leader, Theodoric (thee•AH•duh•rihk). Elsewhere in Europe, other Germanic kingdoms arose. For example, in the Roman province of Gaul, a Germanic people called the Franks took power in A.D. 486. About 10 years later, Clovis, the Frankish king, converted to Christianity and became a Catholic. Before long, nearly all of the Franks became Catholic, helping to spread Christianity in Europe.

By A.D. 550, the Western Roman Empire had faded away. Many Roman beliefs and practices remained in use, however. For example, Europe's new Germanic rulers adopted the Latin language, Roman laws, and Christianity. Despite the Western Roman Empire's fall to Germanic invaders, the Eastern Roman Empire prospered. It became known as the Byzantine Empire and lasted nearly 1,000 more years.

✓ Reading Check **Identify** Which event usually marks the fall of the Western Roman Empire?

WH6.7.8 Discuss the legacies of Roman art and architecture, technology and science, literature, language, and law.
WH7.1.1 Study the early strengths and lasting contributions of Rome (e.g., significance of Roman citizenship; rights under Roman law; Roman art, architecture, engineering, and philosophy; preservation and transmission of Christianity) and its ultimate internal weaknesses (e.g., rise of autonomous military powers within the empire, undermining of citizenship by the growth of corruption and slavery, lack of education, and distribution of news).

The Legacy of Rome

Main Idea Rome passed on many achievements in government, law, language, and the arts.

Reading Connection Did you know that the words *doctor*, *animal*, *circus*, and *family* come from Latin, the Roman language? Read to discover other things we have borrowed from the Romans.

A legacy is something that someone leaves to future generations of people. The Romans left a large legacy. Our world would be very different if the Romans had never existed. Many words in the English language and many of our ideas about government come from the Romans. The same is true for our code of laws and our knowledge about building. Roman rule also allowed the Christian religion to spread.

Roman Ideas and Government Today

Roman ideas about law, as first written in the Twelve Tables, are with us today. We, like the Romans, believe that all people are equal under the law. We expect our judges to

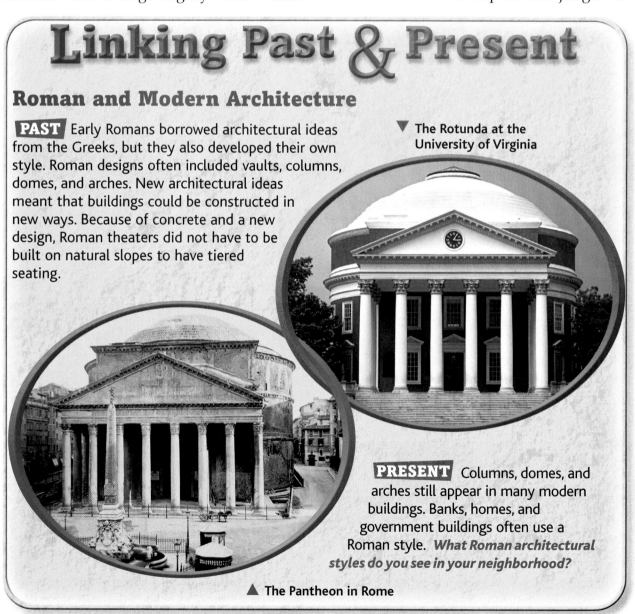

Linking Past & Present

Roman and Modern Architecture

PAST Early Romans borrowed architectural ideas from the Greeks, but they also developed their own style. Roman designs often included vaults, columns, domes, and arches. New architectural ideas meant that buildings could be constructed in new ways. Because of concrete and a new design, Roman theaters did not have to be built on natural slopes to have tiered seating.

▼ The Rotunda at the University of Virginia

PRESENT Columns, domes, and arches still appear in many modern buildings. Banks, homes, and government buildings often use a Roman style. *What Roman architectural styles do you see in your neighborhood?*

▲ The Pantheon in Rome

decide cases fairly, and we consider a person innocent until proven guilty.

Roman ideas about government and citizenship are also important in many countries today. For example, like the early Romans, Americans believe that a republic made up of equal citizens is the best form of government. We also believe that a republic works best if citizens do their duty, participate in government, and work to make their society better.

Roman Influence on Culture

Today we use the Latin alphabet, **expanded** from 22 to 26 letters. Latin shaped the languages of Italy, France, Spain, Portugal, and Romania. Many English words also come from Latin. Scientists, doctors, and lawyers still use Latin phrases. Every known species of plant and animal has a Latin name. Today, we also still read the works of Romans such as Virgil, Horace, Livy, Cicero, Suetonius, and Tacitus.

Ancient Rome also left a lasting mark on architecture. We still use concrete for construction, and Roman architectural styles are still seen in public buildings today. When you visit Washington, D.C., or the capital city of most states, you will see capitols with domes and arches inspired by Roman architecture.

Christianity

As you probably know, Christianity is one of the major religions in the world today. Christianity began in the Roman Empire. When Rome's government adopted Christianity in the A.D. 300s, it helped the new religion to grow and spread.

✓ **Reading Check** **Compare** Which aspects of Rome are reflected in present-day cultures?

History Online

Study Central Need help with the fall of Rome? Visit ca.hss.glencoe.com and click on Study Central.

Section 2 Review

Reading Summary

Review the Main Ideas

- A series of weak emperors, invasions by outsiders, disease, and a number of other factors led to a greatly weakened Roman Empire.

- Numerous invasions by Germanic peoples led to the fall of Rome in A.D. 476.

- Roman ideas about government and Roman architecture are just some of the legacies of ancient Rome.

What Did You Learn?

1. What social problems helped cause the empire's decline?

2. Why did the Roman government use Germanic warriors in its army?

Critical Thinking

3. **Summarizing Information** Draw a diagram like the one below. Fill in details about Rome's legacy. **CA 6RC2.4**

Roman Legacies

4. **Cause and Effect** What caused Rome's economy to weaken? How did inflation affect Rome? **CA HI6.**

5. **Describe** Who were the Visigoths, and why are they important? **CA HI2.**

6. **The Big Ideas** What is the influence of Rome's language and architecture today? **CA 6RC2.3**

7. **Persuasive Writing** Write an essay explaining what you think is the main reason for the decline and fall of the Roman Empire, and what might have been done to prevent it. **CA 6WS1.1; 6WA2.5**

Section 3

The Byzantine Empire

Guide to Reading

History Social Science Standards

WH7.1 Students analyze the causes and effects of the vast expansion and ultimate disintegration of the Roman Empire.

Looking Back, Looking Ahead

In the last section, you learned that even though the Roman Empire in the West fell, the Eastern Roman Empire survived and prospered. It became known as the Byzantine Empire. The Byzantines developed a new civilization based on Greek, Roman, and Christian ideas.

Focusing on the Main Ideas

- The Eastern Roman Empire grew rich and powerful as the Western Roman Empire fell. *(page 485)*

- The policies and reforms of Emperor Justinian and Empress Theodora helped make the Byzantine Empire strong. *(page 486)*

- The Byzantines developed a rich culture based on Roman, Greek, and Christian ideas. *(page 489)*

Locating Places

Black Sea

Aegean Sea (ih•JEE•uhn)

Meeting People

Justinian (juh•STIH•nee•uhn)

Theodora (THEE•uh•DOHR•uh)

Belisarius (BEH•luh•SAR•ee•uhs)

Tribonian (truh•BOH•nee•uhn)

Content Vocabulary

mosaic (moh•ZAY•ihk)

saint (SAYNT)

regent (REE•juhnt)

Academic Vocabulary

income (IHN•KUHM)

rely (rih•LY)

enormous (ih•NAWR•muhs)

Reading Strategy

Cause and Effect Complete a chart to show the causes and effects of Justinian's new law code.

```
    Causes
      |
New Code of Laws
      |
    Effects
```

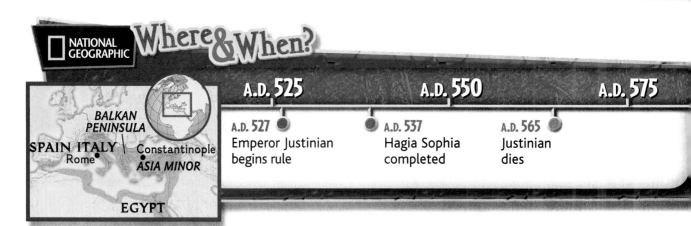

NATIONAL GEOGRAPHIC Where&When?

BALKAN PENINSULA

SPAIN ITALY
Rome• Constantinople•
ASIA MINOR

EGYPT

A.D. 525 — A.D. 550 — A.D. 575

A.D. 527 Emperor Justinian begins rule

A.D. 537 Hagia Sophia completed

A.D. 565 Justinian dies

The Rise of the Byzantines

Main Idea The Eastern Roman Empire grew rich and powerful as the Western Roman Empire fell.

Reading Connection Think of your own community. How have groups of people from different backgrounds contributed to its character? What would your town or city be like without these contributions from all the different groups? Read to learn about the different groups that made up the Byzantine Empire.

The Eastern Roman, or Byzantine, Empire reached a high point in the A.D. 500s. At this time, the empire stretched west to Italy, south to Egypt, and east to the border with Arabia. Greeks made up the empire's largest group, but many other peoples were found within the empire. They included Egyptians, Syrians, Arabs, Armenians, Jews, Persians, Slavs, and Turks.

Why Is Constantinople Important?
In the last section, you learned that Emperor Constantine moved the capital of the Roman Empire from Rome to a new city called Constantinople. Constantine's city became the capital of the Byzantine Empire. By the A.D. 500s, Constantinople had become one of the world's great cities.

One reason for Constantinople's success was its location. It lay on the waterways between the **Black Sea** and the **Aegean Sea** (ih•JEE•uhn). Its harbors offered a safe shelter for fishing boats, trading ships, and warships. Constantinople also sat at the crossroads of trade routes between Europe and Asia. The trade that passed through made the city extremely wealthy.

Constantinople had a secure land location. Residing on a peninsula, Constantinople was easily defended. Seas protected it on three sides, and on the fourth side, a huge wall guarded the city. Invaders could not easily take Constantinople.

▲ The ancient walled city of Constantinople

Influence of Greek Culture The Byzantines at first followed Roman ways. Constantinople was known as the "New Rome." Its public buildings and palaces were built in the Roman style. The city even had an oval arena called the Hippodrome, where chariot races and other events were held.

Byzantine political and social life also were based on that of Rome. Emperors spoke Latin and enforced Roman laws. The empire's poor people received free bread and shows. Wealthy people lived in town or on large farming estates. In fact, many of them had once lived in Rome.

History Online

Web Activity Visit ca.hss.glencoe.com and click on **Chapter 10—Student Web Activity** to learn more about Roman civilization.

WH7.1.3 Describe the establishment by Constantine of the new capital in Constantinople and the development of the Byzantine Empire, with an emphasis on the consequences of the development of two distinct European civilizations, Eastern Orthodox and Roman Catholic, and their two distinct views on church-state relations.

As time passed, the Byzantine Empire became less Roman and more Greek. Most Byzantines spoke Greek and honored their Greek past. Byzantine emperors and officials began to speak Greek too. The ideas of non-Greek peoples, like the Egyptians and the Slavs, also shaped Byzantine life. Still other customs came from Persia to the east. All of these cultures blended together to form the Byzantine civilization. Between A.D. 500 and A.D. 1200, the Byzantines had one of the world's richest and most-advanced empires.

Reading Check **Explain** Why did the Byzantine Empire have such a blending of cultures?

Emperor Justinian

Main Idea The policies and reforms of Emperor Justinian and Empress Theodora helped make the Byzantine Empire strong.

Reading Connection Do you sometimes rewrite reports to make them easier to understand? Read to learn how Justinian rewrote and reorganized the Byzantine law code.

Justinian (juh•STIH•nee•uhn) became emperor of the Byzantine Empire in A.D. 527 and ruled until A.D. 565. Justinian was a strong leader. He controlled the military, made laws, and was supreme judge. His order could not be challenged.

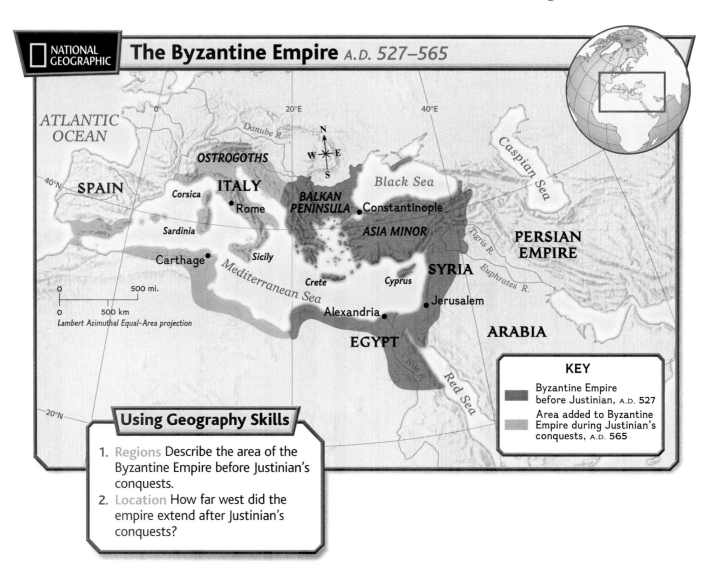

NATIONAL GEOGRAPHIC

The Byzantine Empire A.D. 527–565

KEY

Byzantine Empire before Justinian, A.D. 527

Area added to Byzantine Empire during Justinian's conquests, A.D. 565

Using Geography Skills

1. Regions Describe the area of the Byzantine Empire before Justinian's conquests.
2. Location How far west did the empire extend after Justinian's conquests?

Justinian's wife, the empress **Theodora** (THEE•uh•DOHR•uh), helped him run the empire. Theodora, a former actress, was intelligent and strong-willed, and she helped Justinian choose government officials. Theodora also convinced him to give women more rights. For the first time, a Byzantine wife could own land. If she became a widow, she now had the **income** to take care of her children.

In A.D. 532 Theodora helped save Justinian's throne. Angry taxpayers threatened to overthrow Justinian and stormed the palace. Justinian's advisers urged him to leave Constantinople. Theodora, however, told him to stay and fight. Justinian took Theodora's advice. He stayed in the city and crushed the uprising. By doing this, Justinian not only restored order but also strengthened his power to rule.

Justinian's Conquests

Justinian wanted to reunite the Roman Empire and bring back Rome's glory. To do this, he had to conquer Western Europe and northern Africa. He ordered a general named **Belisarius** (BEH•luh•SAR•ee•uhs) to strengthen and lead the Byzantine army.

When Belisarius took command, he reorganized the Byzantine army. Instead of foot soldiers, the Byzantine army came to **rely** on cavalry—soldiers mounted on horses. Byzantine cavalry wore armor and carried bows and lances, which were long spears.

During Justinian's reign, the Byzantine military conquered most of Italy and northern Africa and defeated the Persians in the east. However, Justinian conquered too much too quickly. After he died, the empire did not have the money to maintain an army large enough to hold all of the territory in the west. About three years after he died, much of northern Italy was lost to an invading tribe of Germans.

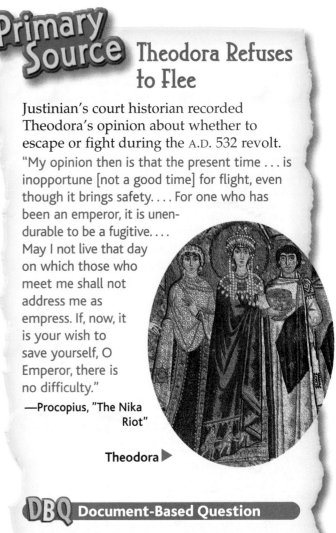

Primary Source — Theodora Refuses to Flee

Justinian's court historian recorded Theodora's opinion about whether to escape or fight during the A.D. 532 revolt. "My opinion then is that the present time . . . is inopportune [not a good time] for flight, even though it brings safety. . . . For one who has been an emperor, it is unendurable to be a fugitive. . . . May I not live that day on which those who meet me shall not address me as empress. If, now, it is your wish to save yourself, O Emperor, there is no difficulty."

—Procopius, "The Nika Riot"

Theodora ▶

DBQ **Document-Based Question**

Why did the empress not wish to escape?

Justinian's Law Code Justinian decided that the empire's laws were disorganized and too difficult to understand. He ordered a group of legal scholars headed by **Tribonian** (truh•BOH•nee•uhn) to interpret and reform the law code.

The group's new simplified code became known as the Justinian Code. Officials, businesspeople, and individuals could now more easily understand the empire's laws. Over the years, the Justinian Code has had a great influence on the laws of almost every country in Europe.

✓ **Reading Check** **Explain** What did Justinian accomplish during his reign?

WH7.1.3 Describe the establishment by Constantine of the new capital in Constantinople and the development of the Byzantine Empire, with an emphasis on the consequences of the development of two distinct European civilizations, Eastern Orthodox and Roman Catholic, and their two distinct views on church-state relations.

EMPRESS THEODORA
c A.D. 500–548

Theodora began life in the lower class of Byzantine society but rose to the rank of empress. The historian Procopius recorded the events of her early life. According to Procopius, Theodora's father worked as a bear keeper at the Hippodrome. After his death, Theodora followed her mother's advice and became an actress. A career in acting was not as glamorous then as it is now. It was a job of the lower class, like wool spinning, which was Theodora's other job.

Even though Theodora was of the lower class, she began dating Justinian. Justinian was attracted to Theodora's beauty and intelligence. Because Justinian wanted to marry Theodora, his uncle, the emperor, changed the law that prevented upper-class nobles from marrying actresses. The two were married in A.D. 525.

Justinian considered Theodora his intellectual equal. In his writings, Justinian said he asked for Theodora's advice on laws and policies. At Theodora's urging, he granted more rights to women. Some historians believe Theodora had great power within the royal court, perhaps more than Justinian. For example, nearly all the laws passed during Theodora's reign as empress mention her name. Theodora and Justinian had no children together. When Theodora died from cancer in A.D. 548, Justinian was overcome with grief. He had her portrait incorporated into many works of art, including numerous Byzantine mosaics.

▲ Empress Theodora advises Emperor Justinian.

> "She was extremely clever and had a biting wit."
> –Procopius, *The Secret History*

Then and Now

Name a modern-day female political leader that you think has great influence in making and changing laws. Explain your choice.

WH7.1.3 Describe the establishment by Constantine of the new capital in Constantinople and the development of the Byzantine Empire, with an emphasis on the consequences of the development of two distinct European civilizations, Eastern Orthodox and Roman Catholic, and their two distinct views on church-state relations.

Byzantine Civilization

Main Idea The Byzantines developed a rich culture based on Roman, Greek, and Christian ideas.

Reading Connection Do you think a multicultural population adds to a country's interest and success? Read to learn how the diverse groups of the Byzantine Empire contributed to its culture.

From the A.D. 500s to the A.D. 1100s, the Byzantine Empire was the center of trade between Europe and Asia. Trade goods from present-day Russia in the north, Mediterranean lands in the south, Latin Europe in the west, and Persia and China in the east passed through the empire. From Asia, ships and caravans brought luxury goods—spices, gems, metals, and cloth—to Constantinople. For these items, Byzantine merchants traded farm goods as well as furs, honey, and enslaved people from northern Europe.

This **enormous** trade made the Byzantine Empire very rich. However, most Byzantines were not merchants. Instead they were farmers, herders, laborers, and artisans. One of the major Byzantine industries was weaving silk. It developed around A.D. 550. At that time, Byzantine travelers smuggled silkworm eggs out of China. Brought to Constantinople, the silkworms fed on mulberry leaves and produced silk threads. Weavers then used the threads to make the silk cloth that brought wealth to the empire.

▲ Sculpture showing chariot racing at the Hippodrome

▲ Byzantine jewelry

▲ The style of the Hagia Sophia, shown here, and other Byzantine churches influenced the architecture of churches throughout Russia and Eastern Europe.
What does the name Hagia Sophia mean?

The Way It Was

Focus on Everyday Life

Byzantine Mosaics Imagine taking bits of glass and turning them into beautiful masterpieces. Byzantine artists did just that starting around A.D. 330. Roman mosaics were made of natural-colored marble pieces and decorated villas and buildings. Byzantine mosaics were different. They were made of richly colored, irregular pieces of glass and decorated the ceilings, domes, and floors of Byzantine churches.

Byzantine mosaics were created to honor religious or political leaders. The centers of domes—because they were the highest points of the churches—were commonly reserved for images of Jesus.

Mosaics were expensive. They were ordered and paid for by emperors, state officials, or church leaders. Many mosaics are still intact and can be seen today inside churches, monasteries, and museums.

Mosaic from the Byzantine Empire ▶

Connecting to the Past

1. Why do you think the name of the person who paid for the mosaic—rather than the name of the person who made the mosaic—was often recorded in the inscription?
2. What types of art do present-day artists make with glass?

Byzantine Art and Architecture The Byzantine Empire lasted approximately 1,000 years. For much of that chapter in history, Constantinople was the largest and richest city in Europe. The Byzantines were highly educated and creative. They preserved and passed on Greek culture and Roman law to other peoples. They gave the world new techniques in the arts.

Justinian and many of his successors supported artists and architects. They ordered the building of churches, forts, and public buildings throughout the empire. Constantinople was known for its hundreds of churches and palaces. One of Justinian's greatest achievements was building the huge church called Hagia Sophia (HAH•jee•uh soh•FEE•uh), or "Holy Wisdom." It was completed in A.D. 537 and became the religious center of the Byzantine Empire. It still stands today in Istanbul.

Inside Hagia Sophia, worshipers could see walls of beautiful marble and mosaics. **Mosaics** (moh•ZAY•ihks) are pictures made from many bits of colored glass or stone. They were an important type of art in the Byzantine Empire. Mosaics mainly showed figures of **saints** (SAYNTS), or Christian holy people.

Byzantine Women The family was the foundation of social life for most Byzantines. Religion and the government stressed the importance of marriage and family life. Divorces were rare and difficult to get.

Byzantine women were not encouraged to lead independent lives. They were expected to stay home and take care of their families. Despite this tradition, women did gain some important rights, thanks to Empress Theodora. Some

Byzantine women became well educated and involved in politics. Several royal women served as regents. A **regent** (REE•juhnt) is a person who stands in for a ruler who is too young or too ill to govern. A few ruled the empire in their own right.

Byzantine Education The Byzantines valued education. In Byzantine schools, boys studied religion, medicine, law, arithmetic, grammar, and other subjects. Wealthy Byzantines sometimes hired tutors to teach their children. Girls usually did not attend schools and were taught at home.

Most Byzantine authors wrote about religion. They stressed the need to obey God and save one's soul. To strengthen faith, they wrote about the lives of saints. Byzantine writers gave an important gift to the world. They copied and passed on the

▲ This Byzantine religious text is beautifully illustrated. *What did Byzantine boys study at school?*

writings of the ancient Greeks and Romans. Without Byzantine copies, many important works from the ancient world would have disappeared forever.

Reading Check **Identify** What church is one of Justinian's greatest achievements?

History Online

Study Central Need help understanding the rise of the Byzantine Empire? Visit ca.hss.glencoe.com and click on Study Central.

Section 3 Review

Reading Summary
Review the Main Ideas

- With its capital at Constantinople and strong Greek influences, the Byzantine Empire grew powerful and wealthy.

- The Byzantine emperor, Justinian, reconquered much of the land that had been held by the old Roman Empire in the Mediterranean. It also issued a new law code known as the Justinian Code.

- As the Byzantine Empire grew wealthy from trade, art, architecture, and education flourished.

What Did You Learn?

1. What is a mosaic, and where were mosaics found in the Byzantine Empire?

2. How did silk weaving develop in the Byzantine Empire?

Critical Thinking

3. **Organizing Information** Draw a diagram like the one below. Fill in details about Constantinople's location.
CA 6RC2.4

Location of Constantinople

4. **Describe** What were the consequences of Justinian's wars in Italy, North Africa, and Persia?
CA 6RC2.4

5. **The Big Ideas** How did geography influence Byzantine trade?
CA CS3.

6. **Analyze** What important service did Byzantine writers provide to the rest of the world? Explain its significance.
CA HI2.

7. **Analysis** Geography Study the map on page 486. Explain why geography made it hard for the Byzantine Empire to expand north or west.
CA CS3.

Analyzing Primary Sources

WH7.1 Students analyze the causes and effects of the vast expansion and ultimate disintegration of the Roman Empire.

Problems in Rome

You have read about many of the problems of the Roman Empire. These included poor leadership, a declining economy, and attacks by Germanic tribes. Other problems also faced Rome, including the unemployed poor in Rome who did not have enough to eat and emperors who did not have a plan for choosing the next ruler of Rome. Roman rulers tried to address these problems, but they were not always successful.

Read the passages on pages 492 and 493, and answer the questions that follow.

▲ **Roman coin**

Reader's Dictionary

entail: to be involved in something
detriment (DEH•truh•muhnt): damage
largess (lahr•JEHS): gift
dole: a government gift

plebs (PLEHBS): the common people
vied: competed
sesterce (SEHS•TUHRS): a Roman coin roughly equivalent to one U.S. dollar

"Bread and Circuses"

The city of Rome may have had over one million people at its height. Many people were unemployed and could not buy food. They were also bored and restless. Unhappy hungry people might rebel. The following passage by the Roman writer Fronto explains how emperors tried to solve these problems.

It was the height of political wisdom for the emperor not to neglect even actors and the other performers of the stage, the circus, and the arena, since he knew that the Roman people is held fast by two things above all, the grain supply and the shows, that the success of the government depends

▲ **Gladiators in battle**

on amusements as much as on serious things. Neglect of serious matters **entails** the greater **detriment,** of amusements the greater unpopularity. The money **largesses** are less eagerly desired than the shows; the largesses appease only the grain-**doled plebs** singly and individually, while the shows keep the whole population happy.

—Fronto, "Bread and Circuses"

"Empire for Sale"

One of the main problems that faced Rome was how to choose a new emperor. The following passage by Dio Cassius describes the imperial crisis of A.D. 193.

Didius Julianus . . . when he heard of the death of [Emperor] Pertinax, hastily made his way to the [Praetorian] camp and, standing at the gates of the enclosure, made bids to the soldiers for the rule over the Romans. . . . For, just as if it had been in some market or auction room, both the city and its entire Empire were auctioned off. The sellers were the ones who had slain their emperor, and the would-be buyers were Sulpicianus and Julianus, who **vied** to outbid each other. . . . They gradually raised their bids up to 20,000 **sesterces** per soldier. Some of the soldiers would carry word to Julianus, "Sulpicianus offers so much; how much more do you bid?" And to Sulpicianus in turn, "Julianus promises so much; how much do you raise him?" Sulpicianus would have won the day. . . . had not Julianus raised his bid no longer by a small amount but by 5,000 at one time. . . . So the soldiers, captivated by this extravagant bid . . . received Julianus inside and declared him emperor.

—Dio Cassius, "Empire for Sale"

Justinian's Laws

Slavery was common in both the Roman Empire and the Byzantine Empire. The use of enslaved workers during a time of high unemployment helped weaken the Roman Empire. When the Byzantine emperor Justinian created his law codes, he included regulations about slavery based on the old Roman slave laws. The following laws come from the Institutes, a collection of some of Justinian's laws.

Book I, Chapter III

4. Slaves either are born or become so. They are born so when their mother is a slave; they become so either by the law of nations, that is, by captivity, or by the civil law, as when a free person, above the age of twenty, suffers himself to be sold, that he may share the price given for him.

Book I, Chapter VIII

1. Slaves are in the power of masters, a power derived from the law of nations: for among all nations it may be remarked that masters have the power of life and death over their slaves, and that everything acquired by the slave is acquired for the master.

2. But at the present day none of our subjects may use unrestrained violence towards their slaves, except for a reason recognized by law.

—The Institutes

DBQ Document-Based Questions

"Bread and Circuses"
1. How did the grain doles help keep order?
2. Why was it important for emperors not to neglect actors? Why was this more important than the grain dole?

"Empire for Sale"
3. How did Julianus become emperor?
4. What does this process of choosing an emperor say about the loyalty and power of the soldiers?

Justinian's Laws
5. Besides being born enslaved, what other ways could a person become enslaved?
6. Based on the laws shown, how do you think enslaved people were treated? Explain.

Read to Write
7. Write a short essay using these primary sources to answer this question: What problems do these sources reveal that may have helped cause the Roman Empire to fall?
   CA HR4.

Review Content Vocabulary

Match the definitions in the second column to the terms in the first column.

____ 1. anatomy   a. pictures made of many bits of colored glass or stone

____ 2. inflation   b. rapidly increasing prices

____ 3. gladiator   c. father of a family

____ 4. regent   d. emotional poem about life's ups and downs

____ 5. mosaic   e. study of the body's structure

____ 6. paterfamilias   f. a person who stands in for a ruler who cannot govern

____ 7. ode   g. a warrior who fought animals and people in public arenas

Review the Main Ideas

Section 1 • Life in Ancient Rome

8. What did the Romans borrow from the Greeks? What did they develop on their own?

9. What were the lives of the rich and poor like in Rome?

Section 2 • The Fall of Rome

10. What weakened the Roman Empire?

11. What caused the fall of Rome?

12. In what areas of today's society can we see Roman influence?

Section 3 • The Byzantine Empire

13. Which half of the former Roman Empire was most successful?

14. What policies and reforms helped make the Byzantine Empire strong?

15. What different groups of people contributed to the Byzantine culture?

Critical Thinking

16. **Cause and Effect** Why did Alaric's capture of Rome shock the Roman people? **CA HR5.**

17. **Predict** How do you think history would have been different if Theodosius had not divided the Roman Empire? **CA HI2.**

Geography Skills

Study the map below and answer the following questions.

18. **Place** Which areas were conquered by Justinian's military? **CA CS3.**

19. **Human/Environment Interaction** Why do you think Justinian decided to conquer lands to the west of his empire? **CA CS3.**

20. **Movement** What made it difficult for the Byzantine Empire to hold on to Justinian's conquests? **CA CS3.**

NATIONAL GEOGRAPHIC

Byzantine Empire

ATLANTIC OCEAN

Danube R.

SPAIN

40°N

Corsica

ITALY

Rome

Sardinia

Carthage

Sicily

Constantinople

Mediterranean Sea

Crete

30°N

0   500 mi.

0   500 km

Lambert Azimuthal Equal-Area projection

KEY

Byzantine Empire before Justinian, A.D. 527

Byzantine Empire after Justinian's conquests, A.D. 565

N W E S

Read to Write

21. **The Big Ideas** **Writing Reports** You have learned that Byzantine culture was greatly influenced by the Romans, Greeks, Egyptians, Slavs, and Persians. Think about the culture of the United States. Work with a classmate to prepare a report identifying parts of U.S. culture that were originally part of other cultures. **CA HI2.**

22. **Using Your FOLDABLES** Use the information in your foldable to create a study guide. For each section, your study guide should include five questions that focus on the main ideas. **CA 6RC2.0**

Using Academic Vocabulary

23. Use five of the following vocabulary words to write a short essay about the fall of Rome. Make sure that the words are used correctly.

constant	income
authority	enormous
expand	rely

Building Citizenship

24. **Analyze** Traditional Roman ideas of duty, courage, and honesty lost their importance before Rome fell. Why do you think duty, courage, and honesty are important in keeping a society strong? **CA 6RC2.3**

Linking Past and Present

25. **Language Connections** Use your local library to research some of the words from the Roman language, Latin, that we still use today. Create a list of these words as well as the Latin words from which they come. Be sure to include a definition with each entry. **CA 6RC2.3**

Economics Connection

26. **Explain** What role did taxation play in the fall of Rome? What would be some possible solutions to solving the tax problems? Write an essay explaining your solution to the problem. **CA HI6.**

History Online

Self-Check Quiz To help you prepare for the Chapter Test, visit ca.hss.glencoe.com

Reviewing Skills

27. **Reading Skill** **Predicting** Write an essay in which you predict the fall of the Roman Empire. What are some of the things that you notice as signs of the fall? **CA 6WA2.2**

28. **Analysis Skill** **Making Choices** How did Rome's leaders try to strengthen the empire? How well did these methods work? Write a short story describing how you would make Rome strong. **CA HI1.** **CA 6WA2.1**

Standards Practice

Select the best answer for each of the following questions.

29 Which of the following contributed to the instability of the Roman Empire and its eventual fall?

A dishonest government officials

B attacks by the Greeks

C the death of Julius Caesar

D the rise of the Byzantines

30 The Eastern Roman Empire was able to avoid many Germanic invasions because

A it was protected by the Spartans.

B the Western Roman Empire had more wealth.

C the Mediterranean and Black Seas offered protection from invaders.

D Constantine moved the capital to Constantinople.

The Rise of Christianity

▼ Mount of the Beatitudes on the Sea of Galilee in Israel

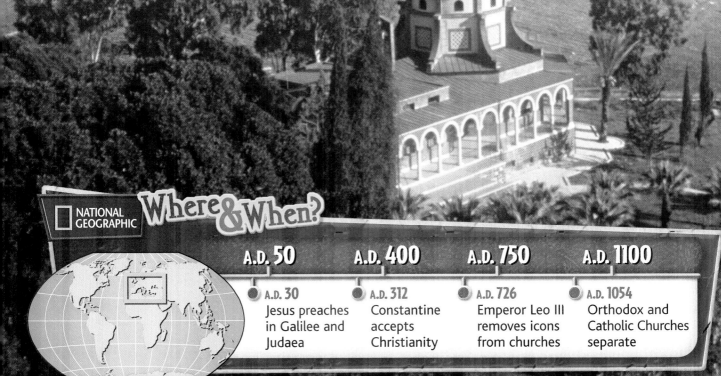

NATIONAL GEOGRAPHIC *Where & When?*

A.D. 50	A.D. 400	A.D. 750	A.D. 1100
A.D. 30 Jesus preaches in Galilee and Judaea	A.D. 312 Constantine accepts Christianity	A.D. 726 Emperor Leo III removes icons from churches	A.D. 1054 Orthodox and Catholic Churches separate

The Big Ideas

History Online

Chapter Overview Visit ca.hss.glencoe.com for a preview of Chapter 11.

Section 1 The First Christians

Studying the past helps us to understand the present. During the Roman Empire, Jesus of Nazareth began preaching a message of love and forgiveness. His life and teachings led to the rise of Christianity. This religion had a great influence on the Roman Empire and on people throughout the world.

Section 2 The Christian Church

Religion shapes how culture develops, just as culture shapes how religion develops. Although the Romans at first persecuted the Christians, in time, Christianity became the official religion of Rome. Early Christians organized the church and collected the New Testament of the Bible.

Section 3 The Spread of Christian Ideas

As different societies interact, they often bring about change in each other. The church and government worked closely together in the Byzantine Empire. Christians founded new communities and spread their faith throughout Europe.

View the Chapter 11 video in the Glencoe Video Program.

Sequencing Information *Make this foldable to help you sequence information about the rise of Christianity.*

Step 1 *Fold a piece of paper from top to bottom.*

Step 2 *Then fold back each half to make quarter folds.*

This makes an accordian shape.

Reading and Writing *As you read the chapter, write the important events that occurred in the rise of Christianity.*

Step 3 *Unfold and label the time line as shown.*

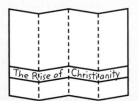

Step 4 *Fill in important dates as you read like those shown.*

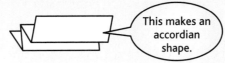

A.D. 30	Jesus begins to preach
A.D. 64	Romans persecute Christians
A.D. 313	Constantine's conversion
A.D. 726	Emperor Leo III removes icons

Identifying Cause and Effect

Reading Skill

1 Learn It!

A *cause* is the reason that something happens. The result of what happens is called an *effect*. Learning to identify causes and effects helps you understand why things happen in history. By using graphic organizers, you can sort and analyze causes and effects as you read. As shown below, a single cause can have several effects. A single effect can also be the result of several causes.

Cause

Effects

> In A.D. 313 Constantine issued an order called the Edict of Milan. It gave religious freedom to all people and made Christianity legal. Constantine began giving government support to Christianity. With the help of his mother, Helena (HEHL • uh • nuh), he built churches in Rome and Jerusalem. He also let church officials serve in government and excused them from paying taxes.
>
> — *from page 512*

Reading Tip

Create different types of graphic organizers to help you understand what you are reading.

CAUSE
Constantine began supporting Christianity.

EFFECT
built churches in Rome and Jerusalem

EFFECT
let church officials serve in government

EFFECT
excused church officials from paying taxes

② Practice It!

Read the following paragraph. Then use the graphic organizer below or create your own to show what happened as monks and nuns began to play more important roles.

> Monks and nuns began to serve in many capacities in Roman Catholic and Eastern Orthodox life. They ran hospitals and schools and aided the poor. They also helped preserve Greek and Roman writings. One important duty was to serve as missionaries (MIH • shuh • NEHR • eez). Missionaries teach their religion to those who do not believe.
>
> — *from page 519*

Read to Write

History is often a chain of causes and effects. The result, or effect, of an event can also be the cause of another effect. Find examples of cause-and-effect chains in the chapter, and show your findings in a graphic organizer.

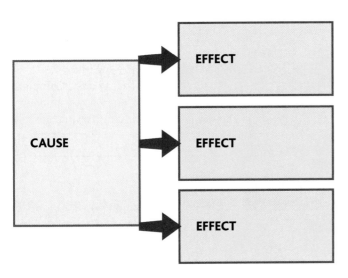

CAUSE → EFFECT

CAUSE → EFFECT

CAUSE → EFFECT

▲ Benedictine monks

③ Apply It!

As you read the chapter, be aware of causes and effects in the history of Christianity. Find at least five causes and their effects, and create graphic organizers to record them.

The First Christians

Guide to Reading

History Social Science Standards

WH6.7.5 Trace the migration of Jews around the Mediterranean region and the effects of their conflict with the Romans, including the Romans' restrictions on their right to live in Jerusalem.

WH6.7.6 Note the origins of Christianity in the Jewish Messianic prophecies, the life and teachings of Jesus of Nazareth as described in the New Testament, and the contribution of St. Paul the Apostle to the definition and spread of Christian beliefs (e.g., belief in the Trinity, resurrection, salvation).

Looking Back, Looking Ahead

You learned that the Romans ruled many areas of the Mediterranean. In one of these areas, Judaea, a new religion, Christianity, began.

Focusing on the Main Ideas

- Roman rule of Judaea led some Jews to oppose Rome peacefully, while others rebelled. *(page 501)*

- Jesus of Nazareth preached of God's love and forgiveness. He was eventually crucified and then reported to have risen from the dead. *(page 502)*

- Jesus' life and a belief in his resurrection led to a new religion called Christianity. *(page 506)*

Locating Places

Jerusalem (juh•ROO•suh•luhm)
Judaea (ju•DEE•uh)
Nazareth (NA•zuh•ruhth)
Galilee (GA•luh•LEE)

Meeting People

Jesus (JEE•zuhs)
Peter
Paul

Content Vocabulary

messiah (muh•SY•uh)
disciple (dih•SY•puhl)
parable (PAR•uh•buhl)
resurrection (REH•zuh•REHK•shuhn)
apostle (uh•PAH•suhl)
salvation (sal•VAY•shuhn)

Academic Vocabulary

decade (DEH•KAYD)
reside (rih•ZYD)

Reading Strategy

Summarizing Information Complete a diagram like the one below showing the purposes of early Christian churches.

Purposes of Churches

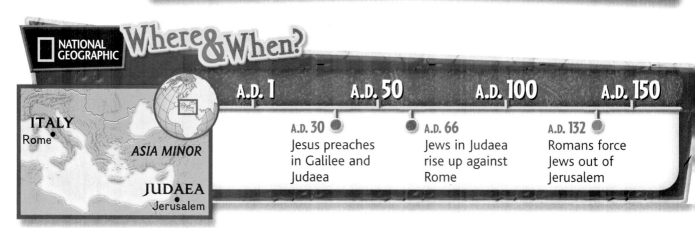

NATIONAL GEOGRAPHIC Where&When?

| A.D. 1 | A.D. 50 | A.D. 100 | A.D. 150 |

ITALY
Rome

ASIA MINOR

JUDAEA
Jerusalem

A.D. 30 Jesus preaches in Galilee and Judaea

A.D. 66 Jews in Judaea rise up against Rome

A.D. 132 Romans force Jews out of Jerusalem

The Jews and the Romans

Main Idea Roman rule of Judaea led some Jews to oppose Rome peacefully, while others rebelled.

Reading Connection Suppose you were separated from your home and could not easily return to it. What effect might this have on you? Read to learn how the Jews were forced to leave their capital city.

As you learned earlier, during the 900s B.C., two great kings, David and Solomon, united the Israelites and created the kingdom of Israel. Its capital was **Jerusalem** (juh•ROO•suh•luhm). This unity did not last long, however. Israel divided into two kingdoms: Israel and Judah. These small kingdoms were later taken over by more powerful neighbors. Israel was destroyed, and its people scattered. But the Jews, the people of Judah, survived.

Roman Rule In 63 B.C. the Romans took over Judah. At first, they ruled through Jewish kings. Then, in A.D. 6, Emperor Augustus turned Judah into a Roman province called **Judaea** (ju•DEE•uh). Instead of a king, a Roman governor called a procurator (PRAH•kyuh•RAY•tuhr) ruled the new province on the emperor's behalf.

The Jews argued among themselves over what to do about the Romans. Some favored working with the Romans. Others opposed Roman authority by closely following Jewish traditions. Still others turned their backs on the Romans. They settled in isolated areas and shared their belongings.

The Jews Rebel Some Jews believed that they should fight the Romans and take back control of their kingdom. These people, called Zealots, convinced many Jews to take up arms against the Romans in A.D. 66. The rebellion was brutally crushed. The Romans destroyed the temple and killed thousands of Jews. A Jewish general named Josephus (joh•SEE•fuhs) fought in the war but later sided with the Romans. He wrote about the horrors of Jerusalem's fall in his work *History of the Jewish War.*

The Jews rebelled again in A.D. 132 and were again defeated. This time the Romans forced all Jews to leave Jerusalem and banned them from ever returning to the city. Saddened by the loss of Jerusalem, many Jews found new homes elsewhere.

By A.D. 700, the Jews had set up communities as far west as Spain and as far east as central Asia. In later centuries, they settled throughout Europe and the Americas. In their scattered communities, the Jews remained commited to their faith by studying and following their religious laws.

✓ **Reading Check** **Explain** Why did many Jews leave Judaea after the A.D. 132 revolt?

These ruins are of the mountaintop Jewish fortress at Masada in Israel. Jewish rebels were defeated by Roman troops here in A.D. 73. *What were the Jewish rebels called?*

WH6.7.6 Note the origins of Christianity in the Jewish Messianic prophecies, the life and teachings of Jesus of Nazareth as described in the New Testament, and the contribution of St. Paul the Apostle to the definition and spread of Christian beliefs (e.g., belief in the Trinity, resurrection, salvation).

The Life of Jesus

Main Idea Jesus of Nazareth preached of God's love and forgiveness. He was eventually crucified and then reported to have risen from the dead.

Reading Connection If you could give people advice on how to behave, what would you tell them? Why? Read to learn how Jesus thought people should behave.

During Roman times, many Jews hoped that God would send a **messiah** (muh•SY•uh), or deliverer. This leader would help them win back their freedom. The Israelite prophets had long ago predicted that a messiah would come. Many Jews expected the messiah to be a great king, like David. They thought the messiah would restore the past glories of the Israelite kingdom.

A few **decades** before the first Jewish revolt against Rome, a Jew named **Jesus** (JEE•zuhs) left his home in **Nazareth** (NA•zuh•ruhth) and began preaching. From about A.D. 30 to A.D. 33, Jesus traveled throughout Judaea and **Galilee** (GA•luh•LEE), the region just north of Judaea, preaching his ideas. Crowds gathered to hear him teach and lecture. He soon assembled a small band of 12 close followers called **disciples** (dih•SY•puhlz).

What Did Jesus Teach? According to the Christian Bible, Jesus preached that God was coming soon to rule the world. He urged people to turn from their sins. He also told them that following Jewish religious laws was not as important as having a relationship with God, whom Jesus referred to as his Father.

The main points of Jesus' message are given in a group of sayings known as the Sermon on the Mount. In them, Jesus made it clear that a person had to love and forgive

The Teachings of Jesus

▼ Jesus traveled throughout the regions of Judaea and Galilee, preaching to all who would listen to his religious message. In the Sermon on the Mount, illustrated below, Jesus described God's love and how to be a good person. At right, Jesus is shown as the Good Shepherd, a popular image in early Christian art. *What did Jesus teach about Jewish religious laws?*

from the heart and not just go through the motions of following religious laws. Among Jesus' sayings were "Blessed are the merciful, for they will obtain mercy" and "Blessed are the peacemakers, for they will be called the children of God."

Jesus told his listeners to love and forgive each other because God loves and forgives people. According to Jesus, God's command was simple. He repeated the age-old Jewish teaching: "Love the Lord your God with all your heart and with all your soul and with all your mind and with all your strength." Jesus also stressed another teaching: "Love your neighbor as yourself." Jesus' message of love and forgiveness helped shape the values many people in Europe and America hold today.

To present his message, Jesus often used **parables** (PAR•uh•buhlz). These were stories that used events from everyday life to express spiritual ideas. In the story of the Prodigal (wasteful) Son, Jesus told how a father welcomed back his reckless son with open arms. He forgave his son's mistakes. In another parable, he told of a shepherd who left his flock unguarded to go after one lost sheep. Both stories taught that God forgives mistakes and wants all people to turn away from bad deeds and be saved.

The parable of the Good Samaritan is one of the best known. In this story, a man is beaten by robbers. A priest and another religious leader refuse to help the injured man. However, a Samaritan, a member of a group looked down upon by Jesus' listeners, stops to help the victim. He treats the man's wounds and pays for his stay at an inn. Jesus asked his followers, "Which man do you think truly showed love to his neighbor?"

▼ Jesus used stories, called parables, to describe correct behaviors to his followers. The parables of the Prodigal Son (left) and the Good Samaritan (right) are shown here. *What lesson was taught by the parable of the Prodigal Son?*

Biography

WH6.7.6. Note the origins of Christianity in the Jewish Messianic prophecies, the life and teachings of Jesus of Nazareth as described in the New Testament, and the contribution of St. Paul the Apostle to the definition and spread of Christian beliefs (e.g., belief in the Trinity, resurrection, salvation).

Jesus of Nazareth

c. 6 B.C.–A.D. 33

Much of what we know about Jesus, whose life and teachings established the Christian religion, is based on accounts found in the Bible. According to the Bible, Jesus' birth was guided by God. An angel visited Mary, Jesus' mother, to tell her she was going to have a baby. The angel told Mary her baby would be the Son of God. An angel also visited Joseph, Mary's fiancé, and instructed him to marry her.

Jesus was humbly born in a stable beside barn animals in the town of Bethlehem. Mary and Joseph had traveled there to take part in a census ordered by the Romans. Shepherds and wise men, possibly princes from neighboring kingdoms, followed a brightly shining star to find and honor Jesus in the stable. Christmas is a celebration of Jesus' birth.

The Bible tells very little about the middle years of Jesus' life. He grew up in Nazareth, a small town in Galilee, where he learned the carpenter's trade from Joseph. Later in life, Jesus set out to share his religious teachings. At this point, the Bible provides many stories of Jesus' travels and the miracles he performed. The accounts of Jesus' miracles, such as giving a blind man sight, raising a man from the dead, and calming a storm at sea, brought many followers to his teachings. When Jesus entered Jerusalem the week before his death, he was greeted by cheering crowds. One of Jesus' closest followers, however, betrayed him and turned him over to Roman authorities. Jesus was questioned by Jewish and Roman officials and sentenced to death. Soon afterwards, reports that he had risen from the dead would lead to a new religion—Christianity.

▲ **Jesus entering Jerusalem**

> **"I am the light that has come into the world."**
> —Jesus of Nazareth, John 13:46

Then and Now

What event does Christmas celebrate? What aspects of Christmas today are not related to its traditional meaning?

What Is the Crucifixion? Jesus and his message drew strong responses from people. His followers spoke of instances in which they believed he healed the sick and performed other miracles. They said he was the long-awaited messiah. Other Jews rejected him and said he was a deceiver. Above all, Judaea's Roman rulers feared the effects of Jesus' preaching. A person who could spark such strong reactions was capable of threatening law and order.

About A.D. 33, Jesus went to Jerusalem to celebrate Passover, an important Jewish holiday. There he was greeted by large, cheering crowds. In an event known as the Last Supper, Jesus celebrated the holiday with his 12 disciples. Fearing trouble, leaders in Jerusalem arrested Jesus and charged him with treason, or disloyalty to the government. As punishment, Jesus was crucified, or hung from a cross until dead. This was Rome's way of punishing political rebels and lower-class criminals.

After Jesus' death, his followers made a startling claim. They announced that Jesus had risen from the dead. Christian tradition states that Mary Magdalene, one of Jesus' followers, was the first to see Jesus alive again. Others, including Jesus' disciples, reported seeing him as well. The disciples also pointed to his empty tomb as proof that Jesus was the messiah. These reports of Jesus' **resurrection** (REH•zuh•REHK•shuhn), or rising from the dead, led to a new religion called Christianity.

Reading Check **Describing** What were the main ideas Jesus taught during his life?

▲ According to the Bible, just before his death, Jesus gathered his disciples together for a meal known as the Last Supper. *Why did the Romans fear Jesus?*

WH6.7.6 Note the origins of Christianity in the Jewish Messianic prophecies, the life and teachings of Jesus of Nazareth as described in the New Testament, and the contribution of St. Paul the Apostle to the definition and spread of Christian beliefs (e.g., belief in the Trinity, resurrection, salvation). **WH6.7.7** Describe the circumstances that led to the spread of Christianity in Europe and other Roman territories.

The First Christians

Main Idea Jesus' life and a belief in his resurrection led to a new religion called Christianity.

Reading Connection Have you ever read news stories about people sacrificing their lives to help others? Read to learn about the sacrifice Christians believe Jesus made for everyone.

Jesus' disciples began to spread the message of Jesus and his resurrection. Small groups in the Greek-speaking cities of the eastern Mediterranean accepted this message. Some were Jews, but others were not.

Primary Source

Sermon on the Mount

Jesus encouraged his disciples with the Sermon on the Mount.

"Happy are you when men insult you and persecute you and tell all kinds of evil lies against you because you are my followers. Be happy and glad, for a great reward is kept for you in heaven. This is how the prophets who lived before you were persecuted."

—Matthew 5:11–12

▲ Jesus and his followers

DBQ Document-Based Question

Why does Jesus tell his followers to ignore—even rejoice in—persecution?

Those who accepted Jesus Christ and his teachings became known as Christians. The word *Christ* comes from *Christos,* the Greek word for "messiah."

The early Christians formed churches, or communities for worship and instruction. They met in people's houses, many of which were owned by women. At these gatherings, Christians prayed and studied the Hebrew Bible. They also shared in a ritual meal like the Last Supper to remember Jesus' death and resurrection.

Who Were Peter and Paul? Apostles

(uh•PAH•suhlz), or early Christian leaders who helped set up churches and spread the message of Jesus, played an important role in the growth of Christianity. Perhaps the two most important were **Peter** and **Paul.**

Peter was a Jewish fisher. He had known Jesus while he was alive and had been one of the original 12 people Jesus had called to preach his message. Christian tradition states that he went to Rome after the death of Jesus and helped establish a church there. Today, the leader of Catholic Christians **resides** in Rome.

Paul of Tarsus was another important Christian leader. He was a well-educated Jew and a Roman citizen. Paul at first hated Christianity and persecuted Christians in Jerusalem. The chief Jewish priest in Jerusalem then sent him to Damascus (duh•MAS•kuhs), a city in Syria, to stop Christians in the city from spreading their ideas.

While on the road to Damascus, Paul had an unusual experience. According to Christian belief, he had a vision of a great light and heard Jesus' voice. Paul became a Christian and spent the rest of his life spreading Jesus' message. Paul traveled widely, founding churches throughout the eastern Mediterranean.

Section 2

The Christian Church

Guide to Reading

Looking Back, Looking Ahead
In the last section, you read about the origins of Christianity. In this section, you will discover how Christianity grew and was organized.

Focusing on the **Main Ideas**
- Christianity won many followers and eventually became the official religion of the Roman Empire. *(page 510)*

- Early Christians set up a church organization and explained their beliefs. *(page 513)*

Locating Places
Rome

Meeting People
Constantine (KAHN•stuhn•TEEN)
Helena (HEHL•uh•nuh)
Theodosius I (THEE•uh•DOH•shuhs)

Content Vocabulary
persecute (PURH•sih•KYOOT)
martyr (MAHR•tuhr)
hierarchy (HY•uhr•AHR•kee)
clergy (KLUHR•jee)
laity (LAY•uh•tee)
doctrine (DAHK•truhn)
gospel (GAHS•puhl)
pope

Academic Vocabulary
establish (ihs•TAH•blihsh)
issue (IH•shoo)
unify (YOO•nuh•FY)

Reading Strategy
Organizing Information Complete a diagram like the one below showing reasons for the growth of Christianity.

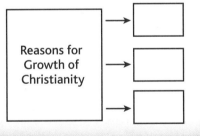

Reasons for Growth of Christianity →
→
→

History Social Science Standards

WH6.7.7 Describe the circumstances that led to the spread of Christianity in Europe and other Roman territories.

WH7.1.3 Describe the establishment by Constantine of the new capital in Constantinople and the development of the Byzantine Empire, with an emphasis on the consequences of the development of two distinct European civilizations, Eastern Orthodox and Roman Catholic, and their two distinct views on church-state relations.

NATIONAL GEOGRAPHIC — Where & When?

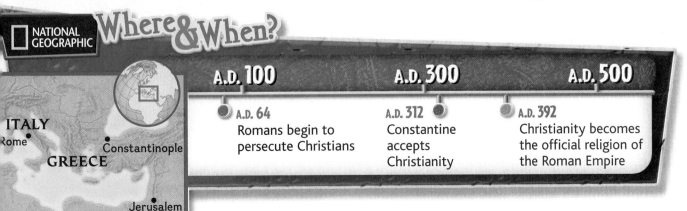

A.D. 100

A.D. 300

A.D. 500

A.D. 64 Romans begin to persecute Christians

A.D. 312 Constantine accepts Christianity

A.D. 392 Christianity becomes the official religion of the Roman Empire

ITALY
Rome
Constantinople
GREECE
Jerusalem

WH6.7.7 Describe the circumstances that led to the spread of Christianity in Europe and other Roman territories.

WH7.1.3 Describe the establishment by Constantine of the new capital in Constantinople and the development of the Byzantine Empire, with an emphasis on the consequences of the development of two distinct European civilizations, Eastern Orthodox and Roman Catholic, and their two distinct views on church-state relations.

A Growing Faith

Main Idea Christianity won many followers and eventually became the official religion of the Roman Empire.

Reading Connection Why do you think people like to belong to a community? Read to learn about early Christian communities.

During the 100 years after Jesus' death, Christianity won followers throughout the Roman world. The empire itself helped spread Christian ideas. The peace and order **established** by **Rome** allowed people to travel in safety. Christians used well-paved

Roman roads to carry their message from place to place. Since most of the empire's people spoke either Latin or Greek, Christians could talk with them directly.

Why did Christianity attract followers? First, the Christian message gave meaning to people's lives. Rome's official religion urged people to honor the state and the emperor. Christianity instead reached out to the poor and the powerless who led very hard lives. It offered hope and comfort.

Second, some ideas of Christianity were familiar to many Romans. They were already aware of many other eastern Mediterranean religions. Like these faiths, Christianity

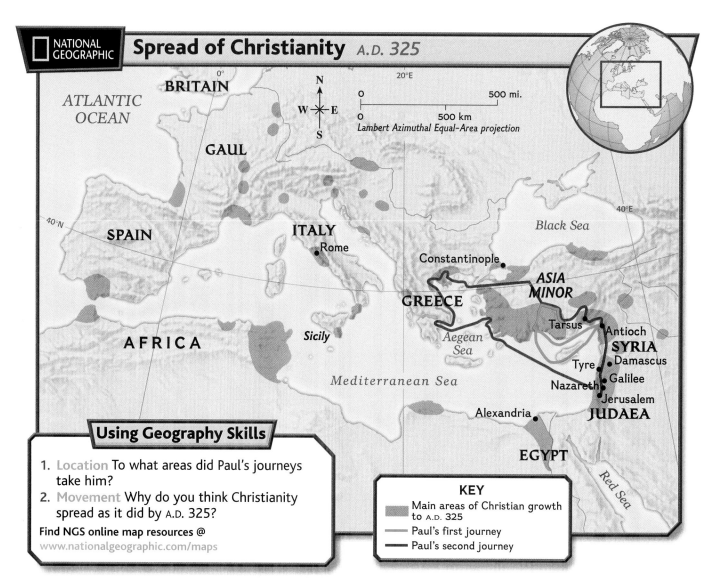

NATIONAL GEOGRAPHIC

Spread of Christianity A.D. 325

BRITAIN

ATLANTIC OCEAN

GAUL

SPAIN

ITALY
Rome

AFRICA

Sicily

Mediterranean Sea

Constantinople

GREECE

Aegean Sea

ASIA MINOR

Black Sea

Tarsus

Antioch

SYRIA

Tyre · Damascus

Nazareth · Galilee

Jerusalem

JUDEA

Alexandria

EGYPT

Red Sea

500 mi.

500 km

Lambert Azimuthal Equal-Area projection

Using Geography Skills

1. **Location** To what areas did Paul's journeys take him?
2. **Movement** Why do you think Christianity spread as it did by A.D. 325?

Find NGS online map resources @
www.nationalgeographic.com/maps

KEY

Main areas of Christian growth to A.D. 325
Paul's first journey
Paul's second journey

appealed to the emotions and promised happiness after death.

Finally, Christianity gave people the chance to be part of a caring group. Within their churches, Christians not only worshiped together but helped each other. They took care of the sick, the elderly, widows, and orphans. Many women found that Christianity offered them new roles. They ran churches from their homes, spread Jesus' message, and helped care for those in need.

How Did the Romans Treat Christians?

Over time, Roman officials began to see the Christians as a threat to the government. All people in the empire were usually allowed to worship freely, but the Romans expected everyone to honor the emperor as a god. Christians, like the Jews, refused to do this. They claimed that only God could be worshiped. Christians also refused to serve in the army or hold public office. They criticized Roman festivals and games. As a result, the Romans saw the Christians as traitors who should be punished.

In A.D. 64 the Roman government began to **persecute** (PURH•sih•KYOOT), or mistreat, Christians. At this time, the emperor Nero accused Christians of starting a terrible fire that burned much of Rome. Christianity was made illegal, and many Christians were killed.

Other persecutions followed. During these difficult times, many Christians became **martyrs** (MAHR•tuhrz), people willing to die rather than give up their beliefs. At that time, Romans required dead people to be cremated, or burned to ashes. Christians wanted to bury their dead. They were forced to bury their dead outside Rome in catacombs, or underground burial places. Catacombs were also used for religious services during times of persecution.

Focus on Everyday Life

Christian Catacombs Christians believed in resurrection, the idea that the body would one day reunite with the soul. For this reason, they would not allow their dead bodies to be burned, which was the Roman custom. Also, Roman law did not allow bodies to be buried aboveground. Therefore, starting in the A.D. 100s, Christians buried their dead beneath the city of Rome in a series of dark, cold, stench-filled tunnels called catacombs.

Each tunnel was about 8 feet (2.4 m) high and less than 3 feet (1 m) wide. Bodies were stacked in slots along the sides of the tunnels. The catacomb walls were painted with images from the Bible or from Greek or Roman mythology.

More than five million bodies were buried under Roman streets and buildings. Many of the Christians buried there were martyrs who had been killed for their beliefs.

◀ Christian catacombs in Rome

Connecting to the Past
1. Why did Christians bury their dead in catacombs?
2. What skills do you think would be necessary to dig and plan catacombs?

511

Rome Adopts Christianity Despite the enormous challenges, Christianity spread. Over time it even began to draw people from all classes. In the A.D. 200s as invaders attacked the empire, many Romans became worried. They admired the faith and courage of the Christians. At the same time, many Christians started to accept the empire.

In the early A.D. 300s the emperor Diocletian carried out the last great persecution of Christians. Diocletian failed, and Roman officials began to realize that Christianity had grown too strong to be destroyed by force.

Then, in A.D. 312, the Roman emperor **Constantine** (KAHN•stuhn•TEEN) accepted Christianity. According to tradition, Constantine saw a flaming cross in the sky as he was about to go into battle. Written beneath the cross were the words "In this sign you will conquer." Constantine won the battle and believed that the Christian God had helped him.

In A.D. 313 Constantine **issued** an order called the Edict of Milan. It gave religious freedom to all people and made Christianity legal. Constantine began giving government support to Christianity. With the help of his mother, **Helena** (HEHL•uh•nuh), he built churches in Rome and Jerusalem. He also let church officials serve in government and excused them from paying taxes.

Constantine's successor, the emperor **Theodosius I** (THEE•uh•DOH•shuhs), made Christianity Rome's official religion in A.D. 392. At the same time, he outlawed other religions.

✓ **Reading Check** **Explain** Why did the Romans see the Christians as traitors?

Constantine's Conversion

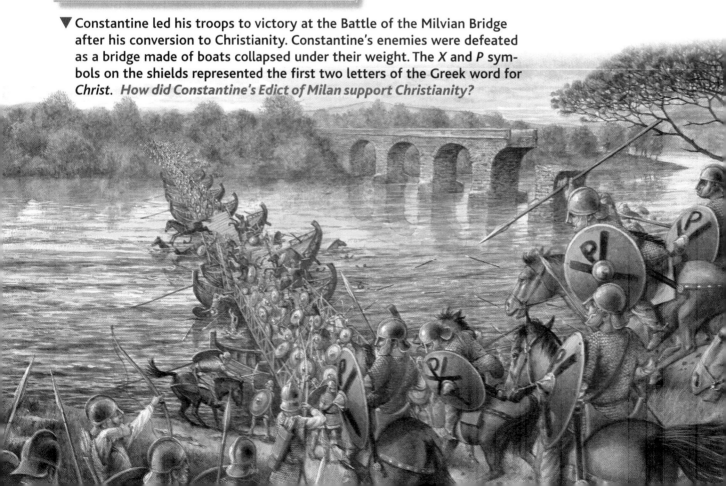

▼ Constantine led his troops to victory at the Battle of the Milvian Bridge after his conversion to Christianity. Constantine's enemies were defeated as a bridge made of boats collapsed under their weight. The *X* and *P* symbols on the shields represented the first two letters of the Greek word for *Christ.* *How did Constantine's Edict of Milan support Christianity?*

WH6.7.7 Describe the circumstances that led to the spread of Christianity in Europe and other Roman territories.

WH7.1.3 Describe the establishment by Constantine of the new capital in Constantinople and the development of the Byzantine Empire, with an emphasis on the consequences of the development of two distinct European civilizations, Eastern Orthodox and Roman Catholic, and their two distinct views on church-state relations.

The Early Church

Main Idea Early Christians set up a church organization and explained their beliefs.

Reading Connection How can good organization make the difference between whether a plan or project fails or succeeds? Read how early Christians organized their churches and chose what to include in the Bible.

In its early years, Christianity was loosely organized. Leaders like Paul traveled from one Christian community to another. They tried to **unify** the isolated groups. In their teaching, they emphasized that all the individual groups of Christians were part of one body called the church. Early Christians, however, faced a challenge. How were they to unite?

Organizing the Church The early Christians turned to a surprising model to organize the church—the Roman Empire itself. Like the Roman Empire, the church came to be ruled by a **hierarchy** (HY•uhr•AHR•kee). A hierarchy is an organization with different levels of authority.

The **clergy** (KLUHR•jee) were the leaders of the church. They had different roles from the **laity** (LAY•uh•tee), or regular church members. As the church's organization grew, women were not permitted to serve in the clergy. However, as members of the laity, they were relied upon to care for the sick and needy.

By around A.D. 300, local churches were led by clergy called priests. Several churches formed a **diocese** (DY•uh•suhs), led by a bishop. A bishop in charge of a city diocese was sometimes also put in charge of an entire region. This made him an archbishop. The five leading archbishops became known as **patriarchs** (PAY•tree•AHRKS). They led churches in large cities and were in charge of large areas of territory.

Early Church Hierarchy

Patriarchs → Archbishops → Bishops → Priests → Laity

The bishops explained Christian beliefs. They also took care of church business on behalf of the laity and met to discuss questions about Christian faith. Decisions they reached at these meetings came to be accepted as **doctrine** (DAHK•truhn), or official church teaching.

What Is the New Testament? Along with explaining Christian ideas, church leaders preserved a written record of the life of Jesus and put together a group of writings to help guide Christians. Jesus himself left no writings. His followers, however, passed on what they knew about him. By A.D. 300, four accounts of Jesus' life, teachings, and resurrection had become well-known. Christians believed these accounts were written by early followers of Jesus named Matthew, Mark, Luke, and John.

Each work was called a **gospel** (GAHS•puhl), which means "good news." Christians later combined the four gospels with the writings of Paul and other early Christian leaders. Together, these works form the New Testament of the Bible.

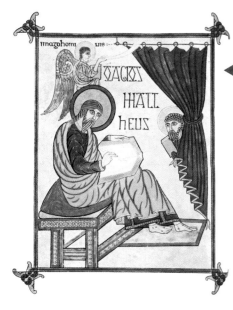

◀ Saint Matthew wrote one of the four gospels in the New Testament of the Bible. *What is the subject of the gospels of Matthew, Mark, Luke, and John?*

Other important writings also influenced early Christians. Scholars known as the Church Fathers wrote books to explain church teachings. One leading Church Father was a bishop in North Africa named Augustine. In his writings, Augustine defended Christianity against its opponents. He wrote *The City of God*—one of the first history books written from a Christian viewpoint. He also wrote a work called *Confessions.* It was an account of his personal journey to the Christian faith.

Who Is the Pope? As the church grew, the bishop of Rome, who was also the patriarch of the West, claimed power over the other bishops. He believed that he had the authority of Peter, Jesus' disciple. Also, his diocese was in Rome, the empire's capital.

By A.D. 600, the bishop of Rome had gained a special title—**pope**. The title comes from a Latin word meaning "father." Latin-speaking Christians accepted the pope as head of the church. Their churches became known as the Roman Catholic Church. Greek-speaking Christians rejected the pope's authority over them. As you will learn, they formed their own church in the Eastern Roman Empire.

 **Reading Check** **Identify** What are the gospels, and why are they significant?

History Online

Study Central Need help understanding the early Christian church? Visit ca.hss.glencoe.com and click on Study Central.

Section 2 Review

Reading Summary

Review the Main Ideas

- After its followers suffered Roman persecution for several hundred years, Christianity became the official religion of the Roman Empire under Emperor Theodosius.

- As Christianity grew, the church became more united under a hierarchy of leaders. Christian writings were gathered into the New Testament of the Bible.

What Did You Learn?

1. What is a martyr?
2. What writings are included in the New Testament?

Critical Thinking

3. **Organizing Information** Draw a chart like the one below. Fill in details describing how each emperor helped Christianity to grow. **CA 6RC2.4**

Roman Emperors		
Diocletian	Constantine	Theodosius

4. **Analyze** Following Jesus' death, why was Christianity able to attract followers? **CA HI2.**

5. **Analyze** Why do you think the Christian church became a hierarchy? **CA 6RC2.0**

6. **The Big Ideas** How did the Christian religion affect the Roman Empire? **CA HI2.**

7. **Analysis** **Writing Questions** Write five questions that you might have asked Constantine about Christianity. **CA HR1.** **CA 6RC2.1**

The Spread of Christian Ideas

Guide to Reading

Looking Back, Looking Ahead

In the last section, you read about the growth of the Christian church. In this section, you will learn how the church underwent a great division and how Christians spread their faith to new lands.

Focusing on the Main Ideas

- Church and government worked closely together in the Byzantine Empire.
  (page 516)

- Christians founded new communities and spread their faith to various parts of Europe.
  (page 518)

Locating Places

Byzantine Empire
(BIH•zuhn•TEEN   EHM•PYR)
Britain (BRIH•tuhn)
Ireland (EYER•luhnd)

Meeting People

Charlemagne (SHAHR•luh•MAYN)
Basil (BAY•zuhl)
Benedict (BEH•nuh•DIHKT)
Cyril (SIHR•uhl)
Patrick

Content Vocabulary

icon (EYE•KAHN)
iconoclast (eye•KAH•nuh•KLAST)
excommunicate
(EHK•skuh•MYOO•nuh•KAYT)
schism (SKIH•zuhm)
monastery (MAH•nuh•STEHR•ee)
missionary (MIH•shuh•NEHR•ee)

Academic Vocabulary

survive (suhr•VYV)

Reading Strategy

Organizing Information Create a diagram to show the reach of Christian missionaries.

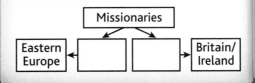

Missionaries → Eastern Europe | Britain/Ireland

History Social Science Standards

WH6.7.7 Describe the circumstances that led to the spread of Christianity in Europe and other Roman territories.

WH7.1.3 Describe the establishment by Constantine of the new capital in Constantinople and the development of the Byzantine Empire, with an emphasis on the consequences of the development of two distinct European civilizations, Eastern Orthodox and Roman Catholic, and their two distinct views on church-state relations.

NATIONAL GEOGRAPHIC Where & When?

IRELAND
BRITAIN
GAUL
SPAIN ITALY Constantinople
Rome• •ASIA MINOR
GREECE
AFRICA Jerusalem•

A.D. 400	A.D. 800	A.D. 1200

c. A.D. 450
Patrick preaches Christianity in Ireland

A.D. 726
Emperor Leo III removes icons from churches

A.D. 1054
Eastern Orthodox and Roman Catholic Churches separate

WH6.7.7 Describe the circumstances that led to the spread of Christianity in Europe and other Roman territories.
WH7.1.3 Describe the establishment by Constantine of the new capital in Constantinople and the development of the Byzantine Empire, with an emphasis on the consequences of the development of two distinct European civilizations, Eastern Orthodox and Roman Catholic, and their two distinct views on church-state relations.

The Byzantine Church

Main Idea Church and government worked closely together in the Byzantine Empire.

Reading Connection In our country, religion and government are separated. Read to learn about the relationship between religion and government in the Byzantine Empire.

As you learned earlier, the church of Rome **survived** the fall of the Western Roman Empire. Its head, the pope, became the strongest leader in Western Europe. Under the pope, the Latin churches of the region became known as the Roman Catholic Church. In the East, however, the Roman Empire continued. It developed into the **Byzantine Empire** (BIH•zuhn•TEEN EHM•PYR). Like Roman Catholics in the West, the Byzantines developed their own version of Christianity that accommodated their Greek heritage. It was known as the Eastern Orthodox Church.

Church and State

Church and government worked closely together in the Byzantine Empire. The Byzantines believed their emperor represented Jesus Christ on Earth. The emperor was crowned in a religious ceremony.

The emperor also chose the patriarch of Constantinople, the leading Church official in the Byzantine Empire. In this way, the emperor controlled the Church as well as the government. Byzantines believed that God wanted them to preserve and spread Christianity. All Church and government officials were united in this goal.

History **O**nline

Web Activity Visit ca.hss.glencoe.com and click on *Chapter 11—Student Web Activity* to learn more about the rise of Christianity.

Religious Arguments

Byzantines, from the emperor down to the poorest farmer, were very interested in religious matters. In homes and shops, they argued about religious questions. For example, Byzantines loved to discuss the exact relationship between Jesus and God.

In the A.D. 700s, a major dispute divided the Church in the Byzantine Empire. The argument was over the use of **icons** (EYE• KAHNZ). Icons are pictures or images of Jesus, Mary (the mother of Jesus), and the saints, or Christian holy people. Many Byzantines honored icons. They covered the walls of their churches with them. A few important icons were even believed to work miracles.

Some Byzantines, however, wanted an end to the use of icons. They thought that honoring them was a form of idol worship forbidden by God. Supporters of icons,

▼ This gold Byzantine incense burner is in the shape of a church. *What was the Christian church that developed in the Byzantine Empire called?*

however, claimed that icons were symbols of God's presence in daily life. These images, they also said, helped explain Christianity to people.

Emperor Leo III did not approve of icons. In A.D. 726 he ordered all icons removed from the churches. Government officials who carried out his orders were known as **iconoclasts** (eye•KAH•nuh•KLASTS), or image breakers. We use this word today to mean someone who attacks traditional beliefs or institutions.

Most Byzantines, many church leaders, and even the pope in Rome opposed the emperor's order. In fact, the dispute over icons damaged ties between the churches of Rome and Constantinople. Over the next 100 years, the argument cooled, and the use of icons became accepted once again. They are still an important part of Eastern Orthodox religious practice.

Conflicts Between Churches Icons were not the only issue that caused bitterness between the churches of Constantinople and Rome. The most serious argument was about how churches were to be run. The pope claimed that he was the sole head of all Christian churches. The Byzantines did not accept the pope's claim. They believed the patriarch of Constantinople and other bishops were equal to the pope.

Making matters worse was the fact that each church sometimes refused to help the other when outsiders attacked. In the late A.D. 700s, the Byzantine emperor refused to help the pope when Italy was invaded. The pope turned instead to a Germanic people called the Franks for help. The Franks were Roman Catholics and loyal to the pope.

The pope was grateful to the Franks for stopping the invasion. In A.D. 800 he gave the Frankish king, **Charlemagne** (SHAHR•luh•MAYN), the title of emperor. This

▲ This icon on wood shows the archangel Gabriel, who served as a messenger for God according to the Bible. *What reasons were given to support the use of icons?*

Byzantine cross ▶

angered the Byzantines. They believed the leader of the Byzantines was the only true Roman emperor.

This conflict pointed out the differences in how each church felt about relations with the government. In the Byzantine Empire, the emperor was in control, with church leaders accommodating his wishes. In the West, however, the pope claimed both spiritual and political power. He often quarreled with kings over church and government affairs.

Finally, after centuries of tension, the pope and the patriarch of Constantinople took a drastic step in their constant feud. In A.D. 1054 they **excommunicated** (EHK•skuh•MYOO•nuh•KAY•tuhd) each other. Excommunication means to declare that a person or group no longer belongs to the church. This began a formal **schism** (SKIH•zuhm), or separation, of the two most important branches of Christianity. The split between the Roman Catholic and Eastern Orthodox Churches has lasted to this day.

✓ **Reading Check** **Describe** How did church and government work together in the Byzantine Empire?

Christian Ideas Spread

Main Idea Christians founded new communities and spread their faith to various parts of Europe.

Reading Connection Have you ever tried to get someone to believe something you believe? Read to learn how Christians spread their faith across Europe.

After the fall of Rome, the people of Western Europe faced confusion and conflict. As a result, people were looking for order and unity. Christianity helped to meet this need. It spread rapidly into lands that had once been part of the Roman Empire.

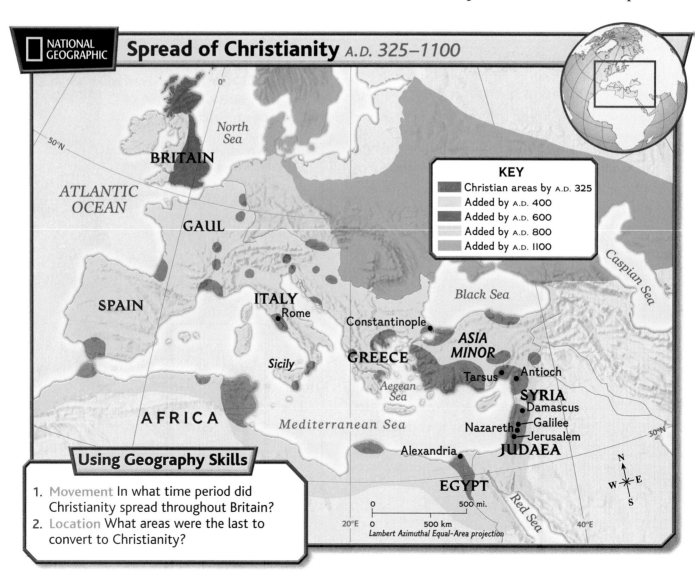

NATIONAL GEOGRAPHIC

Spread of Christianity A.D. 325–1100

KEY
- Christian areas by A.D. 325
- Added by A.D. 400
- Added by A.D. 600
- Added by A.D. 800
- Added by A.D. 1100

Using Geography Skills

1. **Movement** In what time period did Christianity spread throughout Britain?
2. **Location** What areas were the last to convert to Christianity?

0   500 mi.

20°E   0   500 km

Lambert Azimuthal Equal-Area projection

What Are Monasteries? As Christianity spread, it also brought new ways of thinking and living. During the A.D. 300s, a new kind of religious group was born in the Eastern Roman Empire. Men called monks banded together in religious communities called **monasteries** (MAH•nuh•STEHR•eez). Some monasteries were built near cities, while others arose in isolated areas.

One of the earliest monks was Anthony, who founded a monastery in the deserts of Egypt. Monks tried to live a spiritual life apart from the temptations of the world. Many also tried to do good deeds and be examples of Christian living.

Women soon followed the monks' example and formed communities of their own. These women were called nuns, and they lived in convents.

In the early A.D. 400s, Paula, a Roman widow, gave up her wealth and went to Palestine. There she built churches, a hospital, and a convent. Being well-educated, Paula helped a scholar named Jerome translate the Bible from Hebrew and Greek into Latin.

A bishop called **Basil** (BAY•zuhl) drew up a list of rules for monks and nuns to follow. This list, called the Basilian (buh•ZIH•lee•uhn) Rule, became the model for Eastern Orthodox religious life.

In the West, another set of rules was followed. It was written by an Italian monk named **Benedict** (BEH•nuh•DIHKT). Monks who followed the Benedictine Rule gave up their belongings, lived simply, and occupied their time with work and prayer. Like Basil's rule in the East, Benedict's rule became the model for monasteries and convents in the West. Basilian and Benedictine communities still exist today.

Monks and nuns began to serve in many capacities in Roman Catholic and Eastern Orthodox life. They ran hospitals and

The Cyrillic Alphabet

Cyrillic Letter	Written Name	English Sound
Б	beh	B
Г	gey	G
Ж	zheh	ZH
М	em	M
П	pey	P
С	ess	S
Ф	ef	F
Ч	cheh	CH

Cyril, a Byzantine missionary, developed the Cyrillic alphabet, part of which is shown above. *What peoples still use the Cyrillic alphabet today?*

schools and aided the poor. They also helped preserve Greek and Roman writings. One important duty was to serve as **missionaries** (MIH•shuh•NEHR•eez). Missionaries teach their religion to those who do not believe.

Christianity Spreads North Among the most successful Byzantine missionaries were two brothers, **Cyril** (SIHR•uhl) and Methodius (mih•THOH•dee•uhs). They carried the Christian message to the Slavs, a people of Eastern Europe.

About A.D. 863, Cyril invented a new alphabet. He wanted to present the Christian message in the Slavic languages. He believed that people would be more interested in Christianity if they could worship and read the Bible in their own languages. The Cyrillic (suh•RIH•lihk) alphabet was based on Greek letters. It is still used today by Russians, Ukrainians, Serbs, and Bulgarians.

Eastern Orthodox missionaries traveled in northern lands that bordered the Byzantine Empire. At the same time, other missionaries from Rome were also busy.

Christianity Spreads West In the West, Christian missionaries looked to the islands of **Britain** (BRIH•tuhn) and **Ireland** (EYER•luhnd). In the A.D. 300s, Roman soldiers in Britain were called home to defend the empire against Germanic invaders. When the Romans left, Britain was opened to attack by others.

Starting in the A.D. 400s, tribes from what are today Germany and Denmark invaded Britain. These people were the Angles and the Saxons. These groups united to become the Anglo-Saxons. They built settlements and set up several small kingdoms. The southern part of Britain soon became known as Angleland, or England.

While invading Britain, the Angles and Saxons pushed aside the people already living there. These people were called the Celts (KEHLTS). Some Celts fled to the mountainous regions of Britain. Others went to Ireland.

In the A.D. 400s, a priest named **Patrick** brought Christianity to Ireland. He set up a number of monasteries and churches. Over

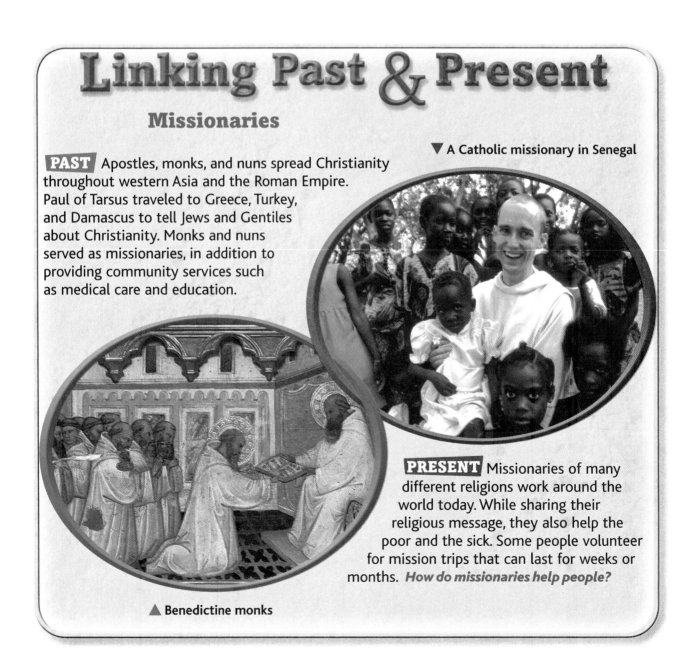

Linking Past & Present

Missionaries

PAST Apostles, monks, and nuns spread Christianity throughout western Asia and the Roman Empire. Paul of Tarsus traveled to Greece, Turkey, and Damascus to tell Jews and Gentiles about Christianity. Monks and nuns served as missionaries, in addition to providing community services such as medical care and education.

▼ **A Catholic missionary in Senegal**

PRESENT Missionaries of many different religions work around the world today. While sharing their religious message, they also help the poor and the sick. Some people volunteer for mission trips that can last for weeks or months. *How do missionaries help people?*

▲ **Benedictine monks**

the next centuries, Irish monks played an important role in preserving Christian and Roman learning.

The Anglo-Saxon kingdoms of Britain were slower than Ireland to accept the new religion. In A.D. 597 Pope Gregory I sent about 40 monks from Rome to take Christianity to England.

The missionaries converted Ethelbert, the ruler of the English kingdom of Kent. Ethelbert allowed the missionaries to build a church in his capital city of Canterbury. In about 100 years, most of England was Christian. Today, Canterbury is still an important center of Christianity in England.

✓ **Reading Check** **Analyze** Why were Basil and Benedict important?

Gregory was a monk before he became ▶ Pope Gregory I in the late 500s. *How did Gregory impact Christianity in England?*

History **O**nline

Study Central Need help understanding how Christian ideas spread? Visit ca.hss.glencoe.com and click on Study Central.

Section 3 Review

What Did You Learn?

Reading Summary

Review the Main Ideas

- In the Byzantine Empire, Christianity developed into the Eastern Orthodox Church, which in time split with the Roman Catholic Church in the West.

- Eastern Orthodox and Catholic missionaries helped spread Christianity to areas such as Eastern Europe, Ireland, and Britain.

1. What are icons, and why was their use controversial?

2. What roles did monks and nuns play in Roman Catholic and Eastern Orthodox life?

Critical Thinking

3. **Cause and Effect** Draw a diagram to show the causes of the schism between the Roman Catholic and Eastern Orthodox Churches. **CA HI2.**

Cause:		Effect: Roman Catholic and Eastern Orthodox Churches split
Cause:		
Cause:		

4. **The Big Ideas** How did Cyril change Slavic society? **CA 6RC2.3**

5. **Explain** What role did Charlemagne play in the schism between the Catholic and Orthodox Churches? **CA CS2.**

6. **Analyze** Why do you think the Basilian and Benedictine Rules were put in place for monks? **CA 6RC2.0**

7. **Creating Time Lines** Create a time line that traces the spread of Christianity. Use your time line to write a report on this topic. **CA CS1.**

Analyzing Primary Sources

WH6.7.6 Note the origins of Christianity in the Jewish Messianic prophecies, the life and teachings of Jesus of Nazareth as described in the New Testament, and the contribution of St. Paul the Apostle to the definition and spread of Christian beliefs (e.g., belief in the Trinity, resurrection, salvation).

The Message of Jesus

As you have learned, Jesus often spread his message by speaking in parables. These stories conveyed spiritual messages. Through them, Jesus taught people the importance of being good, of having compassion, and loving one another instead of fighting or hurting each other.

Read the following passages on pages 522 and 523, and answer the questions that follow.

Parable of the ▶
Prodigal Son

Reader's Dictionary

Levite (LEE•vyt): a member of the Biblical tribe of Levi, who had special duties to care for the temple.

denarii (DEH•nah•REE): money equal to two days wages

repents: feels sorry for one's sins and changes one's ways

prodigal (PRAH•dih•guhl): wasteful person

entreat: to encourage

The Good Samaritan

Before telling this parable, Jesus first explained that in order to have life after death, you must not only love God but also love your neighbor as yourself.

"A man was going down from Jerusalem to Jericho, and he fell among robbers, who stripped him and beat him and departed, leaving him half dead. Now by chance a priest was going down that road, and when he saw him he passed by on the other side. So likewise a **Levite,** when he came to the place and saw him, passed by on the other side. But a Samaritan, . . . when he saw him, he had compassion. He went to him and bound up his wounds. . . . Then he set him on his own animal and brought him to an inn and took care of him. And the next day he took out two **denarii** and gave them to the innkeeper, saying, 'Take care of him, and . . . I will repay you when I come back.' Which of these three, do you think, proved to be a neighbor to the man who fell among the robbers?" He said, "The one who showed him mercy." And Jesus said to him, "You go, and do likewise."

—Luke 10:30–37

The Prodigal Son

Jesus gave this parable shortly after the parable of the Lost Sheep.

"There was a man who had two sons. And the younger of them said to his father; 'Father, give me the share of property that is coming to me.' . . . Not many days later, the younger son gathered all he had and took a journey into a far country, and there he squandered his property in reckless living. . . .

"But when he came to himself, he said . . . I will arise and go to my father. . . . But while he was still a long way off, his father saw him and . . . ran and embraced him and kissed him. . . . [T]he father said to his servants, 'Bring quickly the best robe, and put it on him, and . . . bring the fattened calf and kill it, and let us eat and celebrate. . . .

"Now his older son was in the field, and as he came and drew near to the house, he . . . refused to go in. His father came out and **entreated** him, but he answered his father, 'Look, these many years I have served you, . . . yet you never gave me a young goat, that I might celebrate with my friends. . . . And [his father] said to him, 'Son, you are always with me, and all that is mine is yours. It was fitting to celebrate and be glad, for this your brother was dead, and is alive; he was lost, and is found.'"

—Luke 15:11–32

The Lost Sheep

Jesus gave this parable to explain to the Pharisees why he spent time with sinners.

Now the tax collectors and sinners were all drawing near to hear him. And the Pharisees and the scribes grumbled, saying, "This man receives sinners and eats with them."

So he told them this parable:

▲ Jesus as the Good Sheperd

"What man of you, having a hundred sheep, if he has lost one of them, does not leave the ninety-nine in the open country, and go after the one that is lost, until he finds it? And when he has found it, he lays it on his shoulders, rejoicing. And when he comes home, he calls together his friends and his neighbors, saying to them, 'Rejoice with me, for I have found my sheep that was lost.' Just so, I tell you, there will be more joy in heaven over one sinner who **repents** than over ninety-nine righteous persons who need no repentance.

—Luke 15:1–7

DBQ Document-Based Questions

The Good Samaritan

1. Priests and Levites were important leaders in Jewish society. Samaritans and Jews hated each other. The man attacked by robbers was a Jew. Knowing this, what does the parable teach about being a good neighbor?

The Prodigal Son

2. Why was the older brother not happy about his brother's return?

3. What was the father's reply to his oldest son?

The Lost Sheep

4. To whom are the ninety-nine sheep compared? The one lost sheep?

5. The Pharisees and scribes grumbled because Jesus was talking to sinners. How does Jesus' parable explain his actions to them?

Read to Write

6. What ideas do these three parables have in common? What do these parables reveal about Jesus' teachings? **CA HR5.**

Review Content Vocabulary

1. Write a paragraph about the basic beliefs of Christianity using the following words.

   messiah   **salvation**

   resurrection   **gospel**

Write the vocabulary word that completes each sentence. Then write a sentence for each word not chosen.

a. laity	e. parables
b. missionaries	f. schism
c. martyrs	g. apostle
d. iconoclasts	h. pope

2. Jesus told symbolic stories called ___.

3. The bishop of Rome was called the ___.

4. The ___ in the Christian churches happened in A.D. 1054.

5. Christians who died for their faith were ___.

Review the Main Ideas

Section 1 • The First Christians

6. How did Jews react to Roman rule?

7. When did Jesus begin preaching?

8. On what is Christianity based?

Section 2 • The Christian Church

9. How did the Roman Empire eventually recognize Christianity?

10. What did early Christians do to organize their religion?

Section 3 • The Spread of Christian Ideas

11. What was the relationship between the church and the government in the Byzantine Empire?

12. How and where did Christianity spread?

Critical Thinking

13. **Explain** What message did Jesus teach in the Sermon on the Mount? How was his message received? **CA 6RC2.0**

14. **Contrast** How did Jews and Christians differ in their belief about Jesus and his message? **CA HI2.**

15. **Predict** How would the growth of Christianity have been affected if the emperor Constantine had not become a Christian? **CA HI2.**

Geography Skills

Study the map below and answer the following questions.

16. **Human/Environment Interaction** What geographical feature do you think most helped the spread of Christianity? **CA CS3.**

17. **Location** By A.D. 325, Christianity had spread to which continents? **CA CS3.**

18. **Region** Why do you think the cities of Judaea were all important centers of Christianity? **CA CS3.**

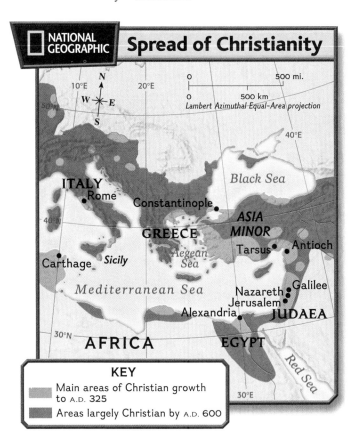

NATIONAL GEOGRAPHIC **Spread of Christianity**

KEY
Main areas of Christian growth to A.D. 325
Areas largely Christian by A.D. 600

Read to Write

19. **The Big Ideas** **Narrative Writing** Rewrite the parable of the Good Samaritan as if the events took place in the present day. Explain how the story helps you understand today's society. Read your parable to your classmates, and explain any changes in the meaning that occurred as you modernized it. **CA 6WA2.1**

20. **Using Your** **FOLDABLES** Use your foldable to write three sentences that summarize the main ideas of this chapter. Share your sentences with the class, and listen to their sentences. Then vote for the one you think best summarizes the chapter. **CA 6RC2.0**

Using Academic Vocabulary

Fill in the blank spaces in the following sentences. Keep in mind that the word might need to be changed slightly in order to fit properly in the sentence.

a. decade
b. reside
c. establish
d. issue
e. unify
f. survive

21. Before he left home, Jesus _____ in Nazareth.

22. Roman leaders _____ a death sentence for Jesus.

23. The Twelve Apostles helped _____ the Christian church.

24. The creation of the position of the pope _____ the church.

25. Ten years are known as a _____.

Linking Past and Present

26. **Recognizing Patterns** Conduct research to find out the number of people worldwide who are Christian, Jewish, Buddhist, Hindu, and Muslim. Also record the countries where people of each religion live. Write an essay describing the patterns you noticed about religions in different regions of the world. **CA 6WA2.3**

Reviewing Skills

27. **Reading Skill** **Identifying Cause and Effect** Review Section 3, The Spread of Christian Ideas. Use a graphic organizer to show the causes and effects of the spread of Christianity. **CA HI2.**

28. **Analysis Skill** **Understanding Narratives** Search your local library for a book on Christian parables. What are the stories trying to teach? What information from the parables is useful to learning what they teach? What information is not needed? Write an essay that answers these questions. **CA HR2.** **CA HR3.**

 Standards Practice

Select the best answer for each of the following questions.

29 Why was Paul important to the spread of Christianity?

A He wrote one of the gospels.

B He wrote epistles and preached to Gentiles.

C He formed the Catholic Church in Rome.

D He convinced Constantine to become Christian.

30 What two important actions led to the acceptance of Christianity in Rome?

A Jesus' crucifixion and Paul's preaching throughout Asia

B Christian persecutions and the conversion of Saul

C Constantine's conversion and Theodosius outlawing other religions

D fires in Rome and the Battle of the Milvian Bridge

Making Comparisons

Compare ancient Greece, ancient Rome, and early Christianity by reviewing the information below. Can you see how the people during this time had lives that were very much like yours?

Where in the World?

NATIONAL GEOGRAPHIC

- Chapters 7 & 8
- Chapters 9 & 10
- Chapter 11

	Ancient Greece Chapters 7 & 8	**Ancient Rome** Chapters 9 & 10	**Early Christianity** Chapter 11
Where did these groups develop?	• On Mediterranean islands and the Balkan Peninsula	• Began on Italian peninsula • Won control of Mediterranean world	• Began in Palestine • Spread throughout the Roman Empire
Who were some important people?	• Homer, c. 750 B.C. • Pericles, c. 495–429 B.C. • Socrates, c. 470–399 B.C. • Alexander the Great, c. 356–323 B.C.	• Cincinnatus c. 519–438 B.C. • Augustus, ruled 27 B.C.–A.D. 14 • Theodora c. A.D. 500–548	• Jesus c. 6 B.C.–A.D. 33 • Helena c. A.D. 248–328 • Augustine A.D. 354–430
Where did most of the people live?	• Early Greeks lived on estates near walled palaces • Later Greeks lived in a polis and in nearby farms and villages	• Farming villages • Major cities included Rome and Alexandria	• Ports and cities of Mediterranean area

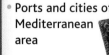

	Ancient Greece Chapters 7 & 8	Ancient Rome Chapters 9 & 10	Early Christianity Chapter 11
What were these people's beliefs?	• Greeks worshiped many gods and goddesses and believed in fate 	• Belief in many gods and goddesses • Emperors honored as gods • Many local religions	• Belief in one God and Jesus as Son of God and the Savior • Major groups: Eastern Orthodox and Roman Catholic
What was their government like?	• Early Greeks were ruled by kings • Later, some Greeks developed governments run by citizens	• Rome developed from a republic into an empire • An emperor was the chief leader • Army played role in government 	• Ranked order of priests, bishops, and archbishops • Bishop of Rome became head of the Roman Catholic Church
What was their language and writing like?	• Greek: used characters to form letters and words	• Latin was official language; Greek spoken in empire's eastern part • Many local languages	• New Testament of Bible written in Greek • Latin became language of Roman Catholic Church
What contributions did they make?	• Introduced democracy • Architecture was copied by others • Developed the idea of theater and drama	• Introduced ideas about law and government • Developed new styles of building	• Christianity became a world religion • Shaped beliefs and values of Western civilization
How do these contributions affect me? _Can you add any?_	• We have a democratic government in the United States • Modern plays, movies, and television shows have their roots in Greek theater	• Latin contributed many words to English language • Rome's idea of a republic followed by governments today	• Christianity is major religion of the West today • Birth date of Jesus is starting date for Western calendar

Appendix

What Is an Appendix?

An appendix is the additional material you often find at the end of books. The following information will help you learn how to use the Appendix in Discovering Our Past: Ancient Civilizations.

SkillBuilder Handbook

The **SkillBuilder Handbook** offers you information and practice using critical thinking and social studies skills. Mastering these skills will help you in all your courses.

California Standards Handbook

Take time to review what you have learned in this book by using the **California Standards Handbook.** The handbook lists all the content standards listed in each chapter and challenges you with a **Standards Practice** question about each.

Glossary

The **Glossary** is a list of important or difficult terms found in a textbook. Since words sometimes have other meanings, you may wish to consult a dictionary to find other uses for the term. The glossary gives a definition of each term as it is used in the book. The glossary also includes page numbers telling you where in the textbook the term is used.

Spanish Glossary

The **Spanish Glossary** contains everything that an English glossary does, but it is written in Spanish. A Spanish glossary is especially important to bilingual students, or those Spanish-speaking students who are learning the English language.

Gazetteer

The **Gazetteer** (GA•zuh•TIHR) is a geographical dictionary. It lists some of the largest countries, cities, and several important geographic features. Each entry also includes a page number telling where this place is talked about in your textbook.

Index

The **Index** is an alphabetical listing that includes the subjects of the book and the page numbers where those subjects can be found. The index in this book also lets you know that certain pages contain maps, graphs, photos, or paintings about the subject.

Acknowledgements and Photo Credits

This section lists photo credits and/or literary credits for the book. You can look at this section to find out where the publisher obtained the permission to use a photograph or to use excerpts from other books.

Test Yourself

Find the answers to these questions by using the Appendix on the following pages.

1. **What does *dynasty* mean?**
2. **On what page can I find out about Julius Caesar?**
3. **Where exactly is Rome located?**
4. **What skill is discussed on page 535?**
5. **What main standard is explained on page 549?**

SkillBuilder Handbook

Contents

Finding the Main Idea

Why Learn This Skill?

Understanding the main idea allows you to grasp the whole picture and get an overall understanding of what you are reading. Historical details, such as names, dates, and events, are easier to remember when they are connected to a main idea.

1 Learning the Skill

Follow these steps when trying to find the main idea:

- Read the material and ask, "Why was this written? What is its purpose?"

- Read the first sentence of the first paragraph. The main idea of a paragraph is often found in the topic sentence. The main idea of a large section of text is often found in a topic paragraph.

- Identify details that support the main ideas.

- Keep the main idea clearly in your mind as you read.

2 Practicing the Skill

Read the paragraph at the top of the next column that describes how the culture of the world is changing. Answer the questions, and then complete the activity that follows. If you have trouble, use the graphic organizer to help you.

Cultural diffusion has increased as a result of technology. Cultural diffusion is the process by which a culture spreads its knowledge and skills from one area to another. Years ago, trade—the way people shared goods and ideas—resulted in cultural diffusion. Today communication technology, such as television and the Internet, links people throughout the world.

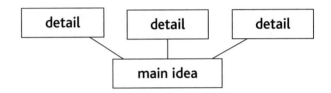

1. What is the main idea of this paragraph?

2. What are some details that support that main idea?

3. Do you agree or disagree with the main idea presented above? Explain.

4. Practice the skill by reading three paragraphs in your textbook and identifying their main ideas.

3 Applying the Skill

Bring a newspaper or magazine to class. With a partner, identify the main ideas in three different articles. Then describe how other sentences or paragraphs in the article support the main idea.

Taking Notes and Outlining

Why Learn This Skill?

If you asked someone for his or her phone number or e-mail address, how would you best remember it? Most people would write it down. Making a note of it helps you remember. The same is true for remembering what you read in a textbook.

1 Learning the Skill

Taking notes as you read your textbook will help you remember the information. As you read, identify and summarize the main ideas and details and write them in your notes. Do not copy material directly from the text.

Using note cards—that you can reorder later—can also help. First write the main topic or main idea at the top of the note card. Then write the details that support or describe that topic. Number the cards to help you keep them in order.

Ancient Egypt—The Middle Kingdom ③
• Pharaohs moved their capital to Thebes

• The Middle Kingdom lasted from about 2050 B.C. to 1670 B.C.

You also may find it helpful to use an outline when writing notes. Outlining can help you organize your notes in a clear and orderly way.

First read the material to identify the main ideas. In this textbook, section headings and subheadings provide clues to the main ideas. Supporting details can then be placed under each heading. Each level of an outline must contain at least two items. The basic pattern for outlines is as follows:

Main Topic
   I. First idea or item
  II. Second idea or item
     A. first detail
     B. second detail
       1. subdetail
       2. subdetail
  III. Third idea or item
     A. first detail
     B. second detail

2 Practicing the Skill

Look back at Chapter 2, Section 1. Outline the main ideas of the section as shown above.

3 Applying the Skill

Use the outline that you created in step 2 to write a paragraph with a main idea and at least three supporting details.

Reading a Time Line

Why Learn This Skill?

Have you ever had to remember events and their dates in the order in which they happened? A time line is an easy way to make sense of the flow of dates and events. It is a simple diagram that shows how dates and events relate to one another. On most time lines, years are evenly spaced. Events on time lines are placed beside the date they occurred.

1 Learning the Skill

To read a time line, follow these steps:

- Find the dates on the opposite ends of the time line. They show the period of time that the time line covers.

- Note the equal spacing between dates on the time line.

- Study the order of events.

- Look to see how the events relate to each other.

2 Practicing the Skill

Examine the time line below. It shows major events in the history of early Egypt. Then answer the questions and complete the activity that follows.

1. When does the time line begin? When does it end?

2. What major event happened around 1550 B.C.?

3. How long did the Hyksos rule Egypt?

4. What happened to Egypt around 670 B.C.?

3 Applying the Skill

List 10 key events found in Unit 1 and the dates on which these events took place. Write the events in the order in which they occurred on a time line.

Ancient Egypt

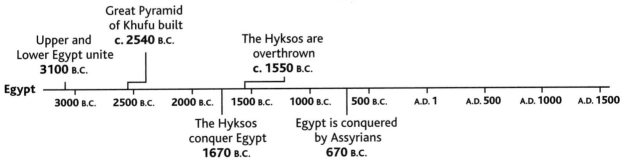

Great Pyramid of Khufu built **c. 2540** B.C.

Upper and Lower Egypt unite **3100** B.C.

The Hyksos are overthrown **c. 1550** B.C.

Egypt 3000 B.C. | 2500 B.C. | 2000 B.C. | 1500 B.C. | 1000 B.C. | 500 B.C. | A.D. 1 | A.D. 500 | A.D. 1000 | A.D. 1500

The Hyksos conquer Egypt **1670** B.C.

Egypt is conquered by Assyrians **670** B.C.

Sequencing and Categorizing Information

Why Learn This Skill?

Sequencing means placing facts in the order in which they happened. *Categorizing* means organizing information into groups of related facts and ideas. Both actions help you deal with large quantities of information in an understandable way.

1 Learning the Skill

Follow these steps to learn sequencing and categorizing skills:

- Look for dates or clue words that provide you with a chronological order: *in 2004, the late 1990s, first, then, finally, after the Great Depression,* and so on.

- Sequencing can be seen in unit and chapter time lines or on graphs where information covers several years.

- If the sequence of events is not important, you may want to categorize the information instead. To categorize information, look for topics and facts that are grouped together or have similar characteristics. If the information is about farming, one category might be *tools of farming.*

- List these categories, or characteristics, as the headings on a chart.

- As you read, look for details. Fill in these details under the proper categories on the chart.

2 Practicing the Skill

Read the paragraph below and then answer the questions that follow.

Buddhism started in India about 500 B.C. but was mostly driven out by 300 B.C. The religion of Islam also influenced India's history. In the A.D. 700s, Muslims from southwest Asia brought Islam to India. In the 1500s, they founded the Mogul empire and ruled India for the next 200 years.

1. What information can be organized by sequencing?

2. What categories can you use to organize the information? What facts could be placed under each category?

3 Applying the Skill

Look at the Geographic Dictionary on pages 90 and 91. Record any terms that would fit into the category "bodies of water." Also, find two newspaper or magazine articles about an important local issue. Sequence or categorize the information on note cards or in a chart.

Recognizing Point of View

Why Learn This Skill?

If you say, "Cats make better pets than dogs," you are expressing a point of view. You are giving your personal opinion. Knowing when someone is giving you his or her personal point of view can help you judge the truth of what is being said.

1 Learning the Skill

Most people have feelings and ideas that affect their point of view. A person's point of view is often influenced by his or her age, background, or position in a situation.

To recognize point of view, follow these steps:

- Identify the speaker or writer and examine his or her views on an issue. Think about his or her position in life and relationship to the issue.

- Look for language that shows an emotion or an opinion. Look for words such as *all, never, best, worst, might,* or *should.*

- Examine the speech or writing for imbalances. Does it have only one viewpoint? Does it fail to provide equal coverage of other viewpoints?

- Identify statements of fact. Factual statements usually answer the *Who? What? When?* and *Where?* questions.

- Determine how the person's point of view is reflected in his or her statements or writing.

2 Practicing the Skill

Read the following statement about wildlife in Africa, and answer the questions below.

Mountain gorillas live in the misty mountain forests of East Africa. Logging and mining, however, are destroying the forests. Unless the forests are protected, all of the gorillas will lose their homes and disappear forever. As a concerned African naturalist, I must emphasize that this will be one of the worst events in Africa's history.

1. What problem is the speaker addressing?
2. What reasons does the speaker give for the loss of the forests?
3. What is the speaker's point of view about the problem facing the gorillas in East Africa?

3 Applying the Skill

Choose a "Letter to the Editor" from a newspaper. Summarize the issue being discussed and the writer's point of view about that issue. State what an opposing point of view to the issue might be. Describe who might hold this other viewpoint in terms of their age, occupation, and background.

Distinguishing Fact From Opinion

Why Learn This Skill?

Suppose a friend says, "Our school's basketball team is awesome. That's a fact." Actually, it is not a fact; it is an opinion. Knowing how to tell the difference between a fact and an opinion can help you analyze the accuracy of political claims, advertisements, and many other kinds of statements.

1 Learning the Skill

A **fact** answers a specific question such as: What happened? Who did it? When and where did it happen? Why did it happen? Statements of fact can be checked for accuracy and proven.

An **opinion,** on the other hand, expresses beliefs, feelings, and judgments. It may reflect someone's thoughts, but it cannot be proven. An opinion often begins with a phrase such as *I believe, I think, probably, it seems to me,* or *in my opinion.*

To distinguish between facts and opinions, ask yourself these questions:

• Does this statement give specific information about an event?

• Can I check the accuracy of this statement?

• Does this statement express someone's feelings, beliefs, or judgment?

• Does it include phrases such as *I believe,* superlatives, or judgment words?

2 Practicing the Skill

Read each statement below. Tell whether each is a fact or an opinion, and explain how you arrived at your answer.

(1) The Han dynasty ruled China from 202 B.C. to A.D. 220.

(2) The Han dynasty was a much better dynasty than the Qin dynasty.

(3) The Han divided the country into districts to be better able to manage such a large area.

(4) The government should not have encouraged support for arts and inventions.

(5) The Han kept very good records of everything they did, which helps historians today learn about them.

(6) Han rulers chose government officials on the basis of merit rather than birth.

(7) No other ruling family in the world can compare with the Han dynasty of China.

(8) Han rulers should have defended the poor farmers against the harsh actions of wealthy landowners.

3 Applying the Skill

Read one newspaper article that describes a political event. Find three statements of fact and three opinions expressed in the article.

Analyzing Library and Research Resources

Why Learn This Skill?

Imagine that your teacher has sent you to the library to write a report on the history of ancient Rome. Knowing how to choose good sources for your research will help you save time in the library and write a better report.

1 Learning the Skill

Not all sources will be useful for your report on Rome. Even some sources that involve topics about Rome will not always provide the information you want. In analyzing sources for your research project, choose items that are nonfiction and that contain the most information about your topic.

When choosing research resources ask these questions:

- Is the information up-to-date?
- Does the index have several pages listed for the topic?
- Is the resource written in a way that is easy to understand?
- Are there helpful illustrations and photos?

2 Practicing the Skill

Look at the following list of sources. Which would be most helpful in writing a report on the history of ancient Rome? Explain your choices.

(1) A travel guide to Italy today

(2) A guide to early Roman art and architecture

(3) A children's storybook about ancient Europe

(4) A history of ancient Greece

(5) A study of the rise and fall of the Roman Empire

(6) A book on modern republican ideas

(7) A biographical dictionary of ancient rulers of the world

(8) An atlas of the world

3 Applying the Skill

Go to your local library or use the Internet to create a bibliography of sources you might use to write a report on the history of ancient Rome. List at least five sources.

▲ Roman mosaic showing gladiators in battle

Analyzing Primary Source Documents

Why Learn This Skill?

Historians determine what happened in the past by combing through bits of evidence to reconstruct events. These types of evidence—both written and illustrated—are called primary sources. Examining primary sources can help you understand history.

1 Learning the Skill

Primary sources are sources that were created in the historical era being studied. They can include letters, diaries, photographs and pictures, news articles, legal documents, stories, literature, and artwork.

To analyze primary sources, ask yourself the following questions:

- What is the item?

- Who created it?

- Where did it come from?

- When was it created?

- What does it reveal about the topic I am studying?

2 Practicing the Skill

The primary source that follows comes from *Stories of Rome* by Livy. Livy was a Roman historian who lived from 59 B.C. to A.D. 17. Here he has written a story with a moral, or lesson to be learned. Read the story, and then answer the questions that follow.

Once upon a time, the different parts of the human body were not all in agreement. . . . And it seemed very unfair to the other parts of the body that they should worry and sweat away to look after the belly. After all, the belly just sat there . . . doing nothing, enjoying all the nice things that came along. So they hatched a plot. The hands weren't going to take food to the mouth; even if they did, the mouth wasn't going to accept it. . . . They went into a sulk and waited for the belly to cry for help. But while they waited, one by one all the parts of the body got weaker and weaker. The moral of this story? The belly too has its job to do. It has to be fed, but it also does feeding of its own.

Excerpt from *Stories of Rome*,
Livy, c. 20 B.C.

1. What is the main topic?
2. Who did the hands and mouth think was lazy?
3. What did the hands and mouth do about it?
4. What was the moral—or lesson—of the story?

3 Applying the Skill

Find a primary source from your past—a photo or newspaper clipping. Explain to the class what it shows about that time in your life.

Building a Database

Why Learn This Skill?

A database is a collection of information stored in a computer or on diskette files. It runs on software that organizes large amounts of information in a way that makes it easy to search and make any changes. It often takes the form of a chart or table. You might build databases to store information related to a class at school or your weekly schedule.

1 Learning the Skill

To create a database using word-processing software, follow these steps:

- Enter a title identifying the type of information in your document and file names.

- Determine the set of specific points of information you wish to include. As the database example on this page shows, you might want to record data on the imports and exports of specific countries.

- Enter the information categories along with country names as headings in a columned chart. Each column makes up a *field*, which is the basic unit for information stored in a database.

- Enter data you have collected into the *cells*, or individual spaces, on your chart.

- Use your computer's sorting feature to organize the data. For example, you might alphabetize by country name.

- Add, delete, or update information as needed. Database software automatically adjusts the cells in the chart.

2 Practicing the Skill

On a separate sheet of paper, answer the following questions referring to the database on this page.

1. What type of information does the database contain?
2. What related fields of information does it show?
3. The author learns that Canada also exports clothing, beverages, and art to the United States. Is it necessary to create a new database? Explain.

3 Applying the Skill

Build a database to help you keep track of your school assignments. Work with four fields: Subject, Assignment Description, Due Date, and Completed Assignments. Be sure to keep your database up-to-date.

| U.S. International Commerce | | | |
Country	Japan	United Kingdom	Canada
Exports to U.S.	Engines, rubber goods, cars, trucks, buses	Dairy products, beverages, petroleum products, art	Wheat, minerals, paper, mining machines
Value of Exports to U.S.	$128 billion	$35.2 billion	$232.6 billion
Imports from U.S.	Meat, fish, sugar, tobacco, coffee	Fruit, tobacco, electrical equipment	Fish, sugar, metals, clothing
Value of Imports from U.S.	$67.3 billion	$42.8 billion	$199.6 billion

Summarizing

Why Learn This Skill?

Imagine you have been assigned a long chapter to read. How can you remember the important information? Summarizing information—reducing large amounts of information to a few key phrases—can help you remember the main ideas and important facts.

1 Learning the Skill

To summarize information, follow these guidelines when you read:

• Separate the main ideas from the supporting details. Use the main ideas in a summary.

• Use your own words to describe the main ideas. Do not copy the selection word for word.

• If the summary is almost as long as the reading selection, you are including too much information. The summary should be very short.

2 Practicing the Skill

To practice the skill, read the paragraph below. Then answer the questions that follow.

Improvements in farming tools also helped farmers produce more crops. By 550 B.C., the Chinese were using iron plows. These sturdy plows broke up land that had been too hard to farm with wooden plows. As a result, the Chinese could plow more and produce more crops. Because more food could support more people, the population increased. During the late Zhou dynasty, China's population had expanded to about 50 million people.

1. What are the main ideas of this paragraph?

2. What are the supporting details?

3. Write a brief summary of two or three sentences that will help you remember what the paragraph is about.

3 Applying the Skill

Read a newspaper or short magazine article. Summarize the article in one or two sentences.

Evaluating a Web Site

Why Learn This Skill?

The Internet has grown to become a necessary household and business tool as more people use it. With so many Web sites available, how do you know which one will be the most helpful to you? You must look at the details, so you do not waste valuable time in Web searches.

1 Learning the Skill

The Internet is a valuable research tool. It is easy to use, and it often provides fast, up-to-date information. The most common use of the Internet by students is in doing research. However, some Web site information is not really accurate or reliable.

When using the Internet to do research, you must evaluate the information very carefully. When evaluating the Web site, ask yourself the following questions:

- Do the facts on the site seem accurate?

- Who is the author or sponsor of the site, and what is that person's or organization's reason for maintaining it?

- Does the site information explore a subject in-depth?

- Does the site contain links to other useful resources?

- Is the information easy to read and access?

2 Practicing the Skill

To practice the skill, find three Web sites on the Buddha and his teachings. Follow these steps and write your explanation.

1. Evaluate how useful these sites would be if you were writing a report on the topic.

2. Choose which one is the most helpful.

3. Explain why you chose that site.

3 Applying the Skill

If your school had a Web site, what kind of information would be on it? Write a paragraph describing this site.

The Buddha ▶

Understanding Cause and Effect

Why Learn This Skill?

You know if you watch television instead of completing your homework, you probably will not get a good grade. The cause—not doing homework—leads to the effect—not getting a good grade.

1 Learning the Skill

A *cause* is any person, event, or condition that makes something happen. What happens as a result is known as an *effect*.

These guidelines will help you identify cause and effect.

- Identify two or more events.

- Ask questions about why events occur.

- Look for "clue words" that alert you to cause and effect, such as *because, led to, brought about, produced,* and *therefore.*

- Identify the outcome of events.

2 Practicing the Skill

As you read the following passage, record cause-and-effect connections in a chart or graphic organizer.

Around 200 B.C., Mesopotamians were among the first in the world to blend copper and tin to make bronze.

Bronze brought many changes to life in Mesopotamia. For one thing, bronze was much harder than the copper products that were used until that time. Because it was harder, bronze made better tools and sharper weapons. This improvement in technology was a help to farmers, craftworkers, and soldiers alike.

Molten [melted] bronze was also easier to pour than the metals used earlier. Craftworkers were able to make finer arrows, ax-heads, statues, bowls, and other objects.

3 Applying the Skill

Look again at the chapter you are currently reading. Choose a major event that is described and list its causes.

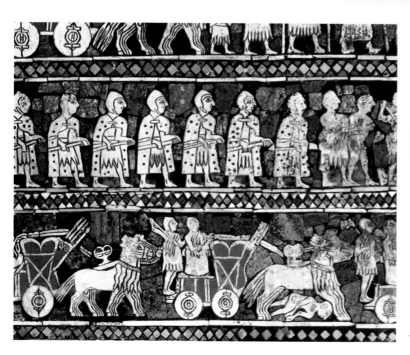

◀ The Royal Banner of Ur

Making Comparisons

Why Learn This Skill?

Suppose you want to buy a portable CD player, and you must choose among three models. To make this decision, you would probably compare various features of the three models, such as price, sound quality, size, and so on. By making comparisons, you will figure out which model is best for you. In the study of world history, you often compare people or events from one time period with those from a different time period.

1 Learning the Skill

When making comparisons, you examine and identify two or more groups, situations, events, or documents. Then you identify any similarities (ways they are alike) and differences (ways they are different). For example, the chart on this page compares the characteristics of two ancient civilizations.

When making comparisons, apply the following steps:

- Decide what items will be compared. Clue words such as *also, as well as, like, same as,* and *similar to* can help you identify things that are being compared.

- Determine which characteristics you will use to compare them.

- Identify similarities and differences in these characteristics.

2 Practicing the Skill

To practice the skill, analyze the information on the chart at the bottom of this page. Then answer these questions.

1. What items are being compared?

2. What characteristics are being used to compare them?

3. In what ways were the Phoenicians and Israelites similar? In what ways were they different?

4. Suppose you wanted to compare the two peoples in more detail. What are some of the characteristics you might use?

3 Applying the Skill

Think about two sports that are played at your school. Make a chart comparing such things as: where the games are played, who plays them, what equipment is used, and other details.

Phoenician and Israelite Civilizations

Cultural Characteristic	Phoenicians	Israelites
Homeland	Canaan	Canaan
Political Organization	city-states	12 tribes; later, kingdom
Method of Rule	kings/merchant councils	kings/council of elders
Main Occupations	artisans, traders, shippers	herders, farmers, traders
Religion	belief in many gods and goddesses	belief in one, all-powerful god
Main Contribution	spread of an alphabet	principles of social justice

Making Predictions

Why Learn This Skill?

In history you read about people making difficult decisions based on what they think *might* happen. By making predictions yourself, you can get a better understanding of the choices people make.

1 Learning the Skill

As you read a paragraph or section in your book, think about what might come next. What you think will happen is your *prediction*. A prediction does not have a correct or incorrect answer. Making predictions helps you to carefully consider what you are reading.

To make a prediction, ask yourself:

- What happened in this paragraph or section?

- What prior knowledge do I have about the events in the text?

- What similar situations do I know of?

- What do I think might happen next?

- Test your prediction: read further to see if you were correct.

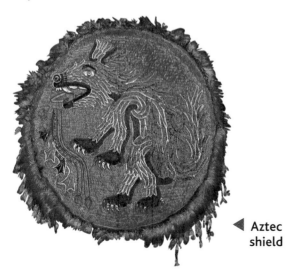

◀ Aztec shield

2 Practicing the Skill

To practice the skill, read the following paragraph about the Aztec Empire. Then answer the questions.

The Aztec of ancient Mexico built the strongest empire of any Native American group. They mined gold, silver, and other goods for trade. In building their empire, they conquered many other Native American groups. The Aztec fought their enemies using wooden weapons with stone blades.

In the 1500s, a Spanish army seeking gold heard about the Aztec and their riches. Led by Hernán Cortés, the Spaniards were helped by enemies of the Aztec. Armed with steel swords, muskets, and cannons, the Spaniards moved towards the Aztec capital.

1. Choose the outcome below that is most likely to occur between the Aztec and Spaniards.

   a. The Spaniards will avoid the Aztec altogether.

   b. The two groups will become friends.

   c. The Spaniards will conquer the Aztec.

   d. The Aztec will conquer the Spaniards.

2. Explain why you chose the answer you did.

3 Applying the Skill

Watch a television show or a movie. Halfway through the show, write your prediction of how it will end on a piece of paper. At the end of the show, check your prediction.

Drawing Inferences and Conclusions

Why Learn This Skill?

Suppose your teacher brought an artifact to class and a classmate exclaimed, "That came from Greece, didn't it?" You might infer that your classmate had an interest in Greece.

1 Learning the Skill

To *infer* means to evaluate information and arrive at a *conclusion*. Social studies writers do not always spell out everything in the text. When you make inferences you "read between the lines." You must then use the available facts and your own knowledge of social studies to draw a conclusion.

Use the following steps to help draw inferences and make conclusions:

- Read carefully for stated facts and ideas.

- Summarize the information and list the important facts.

- Apply related information that you may already know to make inferences.

- Use your knowledge and insight to develop some conclusions about these facts.

2 Practicing the Skill

Read the passage below and answer the questions.

Many Greek temples were decorated with sculpture. Greek sculpture, like Greek architecture, was used to express Greek ideas. The favorite subject of Greek artists was the human body. Greek sculptors did not copy their subjects exactly, flaws and all. Instead, they tried to show their ideal version of perfection and beauty.

1. What topic is the writer describing?
2. What facts are given?
3. What can you infer about Greek cities from the information?
4. What conclusions can you draw about how the Greeks felt about sculptures?

3 Applying the Skill

Read one of the biographies in this text. What can you infer about the life of the person described? Draw a conclusion about whether or not you would like to meet this person.

◀ Ancient Greek sculptures of Socrates (far left), Plato (middle), and Aristotle (left)

Recognizing Economic Indicators

Why Learn This Skill?

Every day, business and government leaders are faced with the challenge of trying to predict what will happen to the economy in the coming months and years. To help these leaders in making decisions, economists, or scientists who study the economy, have developed ways to measure an economy's performance. These ways are called economic indicators.

1 Learning the Skill

Economic indicators are statistics, or numbers, that tell how well the economy is doing and how well the economy is going to do in the future. They include the number of jobless, the rate at which prices rise over a period of time, and the amount of goods and services that are produced and sold. Each month, the U.S. Department of Commerce gathers data for 78 economic indicators covering all aspects of the state of the United States economy. The chart below lists some common terms for economic indicators that you may read about.

▲ Prices on the stock market often rise or fall based on changes in economic indicators.

2 Practicing the Skill

Start an Economics Handbook. Using a dictionary, look up each economic term listed on this chart. Write a definition for each term in your Economics Handbook.

3 Applying the Skill

Think about one of the countries you have read about in this text that has grown to be wealthy. Using the terms that you just defined, write a paragraph describing that country's wealth.

Economic Indicators

Term	Definition
Saving	
Income	
Expenditure	
Consumption	
Inflation	
Debt	
Gross Domestic Product (GDP)	
Interest Rates	
Credit	
Export	
Import	

Interpreting Political Cartoons

Why Learn This Skill?

Political cartoonists use art to express political opinions. Their work appears in newspapers, magazines, books, and on the Internet. Political cartoons are drawings that express an opinion. They usually focus on public figures, political events, or economic or social conditions. A political cartoon can give you a summary of an event or circumstance and the artist's opinion in a quick and entertaining manner.

1 Learning the Skill

To interpret a political cartoon, follow these steps:

- Read the title, caption, or conversation balloons. Most cartoons will carry at least one of these elements. They help you identify the subject of the cartoon.

- Identify the characters or people shown. They may be caricatures, or unrealistic drawings that exaggerate the characters' physical features.

- Identify any symbols shown. Symbols are things that stand for something else. An example is the American flag that is a symbol of our country. Commonly recognized symbols may not be labeled. Unusual symbolism will be labeled.

- Examine the actions in the cartoon—what is happening and why?

- Identify the cartoonist's purpose. What statement or idea is he or she trying to get across? Decide if the cartoonist wants to persuade, criticize, or just make people think.

2 Practicing the Skill

On a separate sheet of paper, answer these questions about the political cartoon below.

1. What is the subject of the cartoon?
2. What words give clues as to the meaning of the cartoon?
3. What item seems out of place?
4. What message do you think the cartoonist is trying to send?

3 Applying the Skill

Bring a news magazine to class. With a partner, analyze the message in each political cartoon that you find.

California Standards Handbook

GRADE 6

Dear Student and Family,

After you complete each chapter, take time to review what you have learned by using this handbook. **The California Standards Handbook** lists all of the California History-Social Science content standards covered in each chapter of the book. In addition, a brief review of the content and page numbers where the content can be found are included. Test your knowledge of each major standard by answering the questions that appear in each of the red boxes.

Remember, the importance of the knowledge and skills you gain this year will extend well beyond your classroom. After all, you learn about the worlds' history not simply to know names and dates, but to become a well-informed citizen of the United States and the world.

Contents

WH6.1

What Is the Standard? ➡ Where Can I Find It?

WH6.1 **Students describe what is known through archaeological studies of the early physical and cultural development of humankind from the Paleolithic era to the agricultural revolution.**	**Chapter 1, Section 1** covers standard WH6.1, including archaeological studies such as those by the Donald Johanson, Tim White, and the Leakey Family. (See pp. 122–31.)
WH6.1.1 Describe the hunter-gatherer societies, including the development of tools and the use of fire.	**Chapter 1, Section 1** When hunter-gatherer societies began using tools and discovered how to use fire, their lives began to change dramatically. (See pp. 122–26.)
WH6.1.2 Identify the locations of human communities that populated the major regions of the world and describe how humans adapted to a variety of environments.	**Chapter 1, Section 1** By using tools, fire, warmer clothing, shelters, and changing their diet, early peoples adapted to the changing environment. Humans developed early communities such as Jericho and Çatal Hüyük. (See pp. 122–26.)
WH6.1.3 Discuss the climatic changes and human modifications of the physical environment that gave rise to the domestication of plants and animals and new sources of clothing and shelter.	**Chapter 1, Section 1** The coming of the Ice Ages caused people to adapt, including developing new clothing. (See pp. 125–26.) **Chapter 1, Section 1** After the Ice Ages, people began to domesticate plants and animals and build mud-brick houses. They also began to specialize in different activities, including weaving cloth for clothes. (See pp. 127–31.)

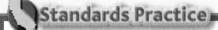

Standards Practice

1 **Because Paleolithic people hunted and gathered, they**

- **A** lived along rivers and lakes.
- **B** were always on the move.
- **C** settled in villages on plains.
- **D** built fortresses in mountain areas.

2 **Which of the following was a change brought by the farming revolution?**

- **A** Steady food supplies meant healthy, growing populations.
- **B** Warrior-kings founded city-states.
- **C** All people became farmers.
- **D** Different groups began using stone tools.

WH6.2

What Is the Standard? ➡ Where Can I Find It?

What Is the Standard?	Where Can I Find It?
WH6.2 Students analyze the geographic, political, economic, religious, and social structures of the early civilizations of Mesopotamia, Egypt, and Kush.	**Chapter 1, Sections 2 and 3** cover early civilizations in Mesopotamia, including the Sumerians, Akkadians, Babylonians, Assyrians, and Chaldeans. (See pp. 132–49.) **Chapter 2** covers the rise of Egyptian civilization, trade, hieroglyphics, temple building, and the civilization of Kush. (See pp. 152–95.)
WH6.2.1 Locate and describe the major river systems and discuss the physical settings that supported permanent settlement and early civilizations.	**Chapter 1, Section 2** The yearly flooding of the Tigris and Euphrates rivers created rich soil allowing for good agriculture and early civilizations. (See pp. 132–34.) **Chapter 2, Section 1** In ancient Egypt, the Nile River provided fertile farmland in the desert. (See pp. 156–62.)
WH6.2.2 Trace the development of agricultural techniques that permitted the production of economic surplus and the emergence of cities as centers of culture and power.	**Chapter 1, Section 2** New agricultural techniques arose, such as irrigation through building dams, channels, walls, and ditches. These led to the rise of cities, religion, writing, science and math. (See pp. 133–37.) **Chapter 2, Section 1** The Egyptians developed irrigation and other techniques to control Nile flood waters. (See pp. 159–60.) **Chapter 2, Section 1** Many different classes existed in ancient Egypt. (See pp. 163–70.) **Chapter 2, Section 2** Egyptians embalmed their pharaohs and built great pyramids as tombs so that the pharaohs would make it to the afterlife. (See pp. 165–70.) **Chapter 2, Section 3** The pharaoh Akhenaton tried unsuccessfully to make Egyptian religion monotheistic. (See p. 183.)
WH6.2.3 Understand the relationship between religion and the social and political order in Mesopotamia and Egypt.	**Chapter 1, Section 2** Mesopotamians built temples and held religious festivals to please the gods. (See pp. 135–36.) **Chapter 2, Section 2** The pharaoh was considered both king and god. (See pp. 165–70.)
WH6.2.4 Know the significance of Hammurabi's Code.	**Chapter 1, Section 2** Hammurabi's law code impacted many later peoples. (See pp. 138–41.)

What Is the Standard? → Where Can I Find It?

WH6.2.5 Discuss the main features of Egyptian art and architecture.	**Chapter 2, Section 2** Massive pyramids were built as tombs for pharaohs. **(See pp. 168–70.)** **Chapter 2, Section 3** During the Middle Kingdom, Egyptian arts blossomed. **(See pp. 178–80.)**
WH6.2.6 Describe the role of Egyptian trade in the eastern Mediterranean and Nile valley.	**Chapter 2, Section 1** Egypt began trading with Mesopotamia, which helped spread ideas and goods. **(See pp. 161–62.)** **Chapter 2, Section 3** During the New Kingdom, Egypt used trade and conquest to dominate the Eastern Mediterranean. **(See pp. 180–82.)** **Chapter 2, Section 4** Kush grew powerful through overland trade and trade along the Nile. **(See pp. 189–91.)**
WH6.2.7 Understand the significance of Queen Hatshepsut and Ramses the Great.	**Chapter 2, Section 3** Queen Hatshepsut was more interested in trade than conquest. **(See pp. 180–82.)** **Chapter 2, Section 3** Ramses the Great expanded Egypt's power through military expeditions. **(See pp. 184–86.)**
WH6.2.8 Identify the location of the Kush civilization and describe its political, commercial, and cultural relations with Egypt.	**Chapter 2, Section 4** During the 700s B.C., Kush conquered Egypt and styled its culture and government on Egyptian models. **(See pp. 189–91.)**
WH6.2.9 Trace the evolution of language and its written forms.	**Chapter 1, Section 1** The development of spoken language made it possible for people to pass on knowledge. **(See p. 126.)** **Chapter 1, Section 2** Mesopotamians wrote using cuneiform. **(See pp. 136–37.)** **Chapter 2, Section 1** Egyptians used papyrus and hieroglyphics to record history. **(See p. 160.)**

Standards Practice

1 **The Sumerian system of writing known as cuneiform was made up of**

A about 30 letters representing sounds.

B picture symbols representing objects, ideas, and sounds.

C characters that represented ideas only.

D wedge-shaped markings first used to track business deals.

2 **The kingdom of Kush was favorably located**

A along the Mediterranean Sea.

B in the Fertile Crescent between Syria and Canaan.

C along the upper Nile River south of Egypt.

D in the Congo River basin.

WH6.3

What Is the Standard? ➡ Where Can I Find It?

What Is the Standard?	Where Can I Find It?
WH6.3 Students analyze the geographic, political, economic, religious, and social structures of the Ancient Hebrews.	**Chapter 3** covers standard WH6.3, including the rise of the Hebrews in Canaan, the teachings and practices of the Jewish religion, the political leaders of Israel, and the ways Jews have protected their culture under foreign rule. (See pp. 196–227.)
WH6.3.1 Describe the origins and significance of Judaism as the first monotheistic religion based on the concept of one God who sets down moral laws for humanity.	**Chapter 3, Section 1** The early Israelites believed in one God who gave them commandments and made covenants with them. (See pp. 200–03.)
WH6.3.2 Identify the sources of the ethical teachings and central beliefs of Judaism (the Hebrew Bible, the Commentaries): belief in God, observance of law, practice of the concepts of righteousness and justice, and importance of study; and describe how the ideas of the Hebrew traditions are reflected in the moral and ethical traditions of Western civilization.	**Chapter 3, Section 1** The ancient Israelites practiced monotheism and held certain commandments to be given by God. These laws detailed concepts of righteousness and proper living and were recorded in the Hebrew Bible. (See pp. 201–03.) **Chapter 3, Section 1** Prophets arose who taught the Israelites about God and about a just society. (See pp. 206–12.) **Chapter 3, Sections 1, 2, and 3** The Israelites developed many concepts that are reflected in Western civilization. (See pp. 201–03, 210–12, 217–18, 220–23.) **Chapter 3, Section 2** While in exile, the Jews studied the Hebrew Bible to keep their faith strong. (See pp. 213–15.) **Chapter 3, Section 3** Jewish leaders focused on education and wrote commentaries on the Torah. (See pp. 220–23.)
WH6.3.3 Explain the significance of Abraham, Moses, Naomi, Ruth, David, and Yohanan ben Zaccai in the development of the Jewish religion.	**Chapter 3, Section 1** The Israelites believed they were descended from Abraham, who first settled Canaan. (See p. 201.) **Chapter 3, Section 1** Moses led the Israelites out of Egypt, and delivered the Torah and Ten Commandments. (See pp. 202–03.) **Chapter 3, Section 1** After Moses died, other leaders led the Israelites, including Joshua and Deborah. (See pp. 204–05.) **Chapter 3, Section 2** The two most important kings of Israel were David and Solomon. (See pp. 206–10.)

WH6.3

What Is the Standard? ➡ Where Can I Find It?

Chapter 3, Section 3 The biblical story of how Ruth remained loyal to Naomi inspired Jews. **(See pp. 218–19.)**

Chapter 3, Section 3 Johanan ben Zakkai established a school to teach the Torah. **(See pp. 222–23.)**

WH6.3.4 Discuss the locations of the settlements and movements of Hebrew peoples, including the Exodus and their movement to and from Egypt, and outline the significance of the Exodus to the Jewish and other people.

Chapter 3, Section 1 Moses led the Israelites in the Exodus, or escape from Egypt. **(See pp. 202–04.)**

Chapter 3, Section 1 Once the Israelites settled in Canaan, they began to conquer the neighboring regions. **(See pp. 204–05.)**

Chapter 3, Section 2 When the Chaldeans conquered Israel, they exiled most Jews into Babylon. **(See pp. 210–12.)**

Chapter 3, Section 3 The Persians allowed the Jews to return to Jerusalem. **(See p. 214.)**

Chapter 3, Section 3 Many Jews lived throughout the Middle East and the Mediterranean. **(See pp. 215–16.)**

WH6.3.5 Discuss how Judaism survived and developed despite the continuing dispersion of much of the Jewish population from Jerusalem and the rest of Israel after the destruction of the second Temple in A.D. 70.

Chapter 3, Section 3 The Romans destroyed the temple in A.D. 70 and exiled the Israelites from Jerusalem in A.D. 135. **(See pp. 220–22.)**

Chapter 3, Section 3 The Jews spread throughout the Middle East and the Mediterranean and preserved their culture and teachings. **(See pp. 221–23.)**

Chapter 3, Section 3 Jewish leaders focused on studying the Torah and the commentaries, such as the Talmud. **(See pp. 222–23.)**

Standards Practice

1 In the covenant, or agreement, between God and the Israelites,

A God promised the Israelites an eternal life if they followed his laws.

B God agreed to return the Israelites to Egypt if they prayed five times a day.

C God pledged to protect Israel's kings if the people obeyed his laws.

D God promised to return the Israelites to Canaan if they followed his laws.

2 Why was Ruth an important figure in Jewish tradition?

A As a queen, she saved the Israelites from persecution.

B Her political skills made her Israel's first female ruler.

C Her devotion to family provided an example for Jewish women.

D Her courage and bravery helped the Israelites escape from Egypt.

WH6.4

What Is the Standard?	→ Where Is It Covered?
WH6.4 Students analyze the geographic, political, economic, religious, and social structures of the early civilizations of Ancient Greece.	**Chapter 7** covers much of standard WH6.4, including the establishment of city-states and the rise of Athens and Sparta. **(See pp. 332–71.)** **Chapter 8** also covers standard WH6.4, including the importance of Greek literature, the rise of Alexander the Great and the spread of Hellenism. **(See pp. 372–415.)**
WH6.4.1 Discuss the connections between geography and the development of city-states in the region of the Aegean Sea, including patterns of trade and commerce among Greek city-states and within the wider Mediterranean region.	**Chapter 7, Section 1** Greece's first civilizations developed large trading networks. **(See pp. 336–40.)** **Chapter 7, Section 1** The mountains and seas surrounding Greece led to the rise of city-states. **(See pp. 341–42.)** **Chapter 7, Section 2** The growth of Greece depended on establishing colonies and trade throughout the Mediterranean region. **(See p. 343.)**
WH6.4.2 Trace the transition from tyranny and oligarchy to early democratic forms of government and back to dictatorship in ancient Greece, including the significance of the invention of the idea of citizenship (e.g., from Pericles' Funeral Oration).	**Chapter 7, Section 1** Many Greek city-states were run by their citizens, or members of the political community. **(See pp. 341–42.)** **Chapter 7, Section 2** Tyrants became unpopular as citizens wanted more rights. Most city-states became oligarchies or democracies. **(See pp. 344–50.)**
WH6.4.3 State the key differences between Athenian, or direct, democracy and representative democracy.	**Chapter 7, Section 4** Representative democracy in the United States differed from Athenian democracy in key ways, such as electing officials who make laws. **(See pp. 358–61.)**
WH6.4.4 Explain the significance of Greek mythology to the everyday life of people in the region and how Greek literature continues to permeate our literature and language today, drawing from Greek mythology and epics, such as Homer's Iliad and Odyssey, and from Aesop's Fables.	**Chapter 8, Section 1** Greek religious beliefs influenced festivals and actions. **(See pp. 376–78.)** **Chapter 8, Section 1** The Greeks wrote poetry and fables based on their religious beliefs. **(See pp. 379–81.)** **Chapter 8, Section 1** Greek literature has influenced readers for nearly 3,000 years. **(See pp. 379–81.)** **Chapter 8, Section 1** Greece made important contributions in drama. **(See pp. 382–83.)**
WH6.4.5 Outline the founding, expansion, and political organization of the Persian Empire.	**Chapter 7, Section 3** Persia created a large empire divided into local states called satrapies. **(See pp. 351–53.)**

What Is the Standard? → Where Is It Covered?

What Is the Standard?	Where Is It Covered?
WH6.4.6 Compare and contrast life in Athens and Sparta, with emphasis on their roles in the Persian and Peloponnesian Wars.	**Chapter 7, Section 2** Sparta maintained its oligarchy and developed a militaristic government. **(See pp. 346–47.)** **Chapter 7, Section 2** Athens created a democracy and focused on trade and culture. **(See pp. 348–50.)** **Chapter 7, Section 3** Athens and Sparta joined forces to defeat the Persians in the Persian Wars, but later fought the destructive Peloponnesian War. **(See pp. 354–57, 364–67.)**
WH6.4.7 Trace the rise of Alexander the Great and the spread of Greek culture eastward and into Egypt.	**Chapter 8, Section 3** Alexander conquered the Persian empire and spread Hellenism throughout southwest Asia. **(See pp. 398–402.)** **Chapter 8, Section 4** The Greeks spread their art, architecture, literature, theater, philosophy, and mathematics. **(See pp. 407–10.)**
WH6.4.8 Describe the enduring contributions of important Greek figures in the arts and sciences (e.g., Hypatia, Socrates, Plato, Aristotle, Euclid, Thucydides).	**Chapter 8, Section 1** Some of the great Greek writers include the dramatists Sophocles, Euripides, and Aeschylus. **(See pp. 382–83.)** **Chapter 8, Section 1** Greek ideas of art and architecture influence styles today. **(See pp. 384–85.)** **Chapter 8, Section 2** Greek philosophers tried to answer life's big questions. **(See pp. 393–96.)** **Chapter 8, Section 2** Thucydides was one of the first historians in the world. **(See p. 397.)**

Standards Practice

1 **Aesop wrote his fables to**

 A praise Greek military heroes.

 B teach Greeks about their past.

 C provide entertainment only.

 D teach a moral lesson.

2 **After becoming Macedonia's ruler, Alexander the Great**

 A began an invasion of the Persian Empire.

 B conquered all of the Greek city-states.

 C set up colonies in India.

 D agreed to peace with Carthage.

3 **How did geography influence early Greek government?**

 A City-states grew only in river valleys.

 B Mountains and seas separated independent city-states.

 C Greeks united under one central government.

 D Greeks lacked organized government.

4 **Cleisthenes was important to Athens because he**

 A helped Athens become a democracy.

 B made Athens a great military power.

 C set up a school for artists and writers.

 D took away the rights of farmers.

What Is the Standard? ➡ Where Is It Covered?

WH6.5 Students analyze the geographic, political, economic, religious, and social structures of the early civilizations of India.

Chapter 4 covers standard WH6.5, including India's first civilizations, Hinduism and Buddhism, the Mauryan empire, and the achievements of these people. **(See pp. 234–71.)**

WH6.5.1 Locate and describe the major river system and discuss the physical setting that supported the rise of this civilization.

Chapter 4, Section 1 The Indus River system gave rise to the Harappan civilization. India's monsoons and snowmelts helped the rise of agriculture. **(See pp. 238–41.)**

WH6.5.2 Discuss the significance of the Aryan invasions.

Chapter 4, Section 1 The Aryans brought new farming techniques, language, and metal tools and weapons. **(See pp. 242–45.)**

WH6.5.3 Explain the major beliefs and practices of Brahmanism in India and how they evolved into early Hinduism.

Chapter 4, Section 2 India's first major religion was Hinduism, which involved a universal spirit called Brahman. **(See pp. 246–48.)**

WH6.5.4 Outline the social structure of the caste system.

Chapter 4, Section 1 The caste system organized Indians into four classes. **(See pp. 243–45.)**

WH6.5.5 Know the life and moral teachings of the Buddha and how Buddhism spread in India, Ceylon, and Central Asia.

Chapter 4, Section 2 The Buddha's life and teachings created a new religion called Buddhism which spread throughout India to Central Asia. **(See pp. 249–53.)**

WH6.5.6 Describe the growth of the Maurya empire and the political and moral achievements of the emperor Asoka.

Chapter 4, Section 3 Asoka, the Mauryan Empire's greatest king, conquered almost all of India, then he converted to Buddhism and dedicated his life to Buddhism. **(See pp. 260–63.)**

WH6.5.7 Discuss important aesthetic and intellectual traditions (e.g., Sanskrit literature, including the *Bhagavad Gita*; medicine; metallurgy; and mathematics, including Hindu-Arabic numerals and the zero).

Chapter 4, Section 3 Under the Mauryan and Gupta empires, India built Hindu and Buddhist temples and shrines, wrote some of India's great literature in Sanskrit, such as the *Bhagavad Gita*, and developed algebra, and the zero. **(See pp. 264–67.)**

Standards Practice

1 Hinduism grew out of the

A teachings of the Buddha.

B spiritual ideals of the ancient Israelites.

C religious customs of many people over thousands of years.

D the Islamic conquests.

2 What kind of upbringing did the Buddha have?

A He was raised to be a farmer.

B He grew up in luxury as a prince.

C He was born into a wealthy family.

D He was the son of a Hindu teacher.

WH6.6

What Is the Standard? → Where Is It Covered?

WH6.6 Students analyze the geographic, political, economic, religious, and social structures of the early civilizations of China.

Chapter 5 covers standard WH6.6, including the geographic qualities that led to the rise of important Chinese civilizations, including the Shang, the Zhou, and the Han dynasties, and how people lived and what they believed. **(See pp. 272–307.)**

WH6.6.1 Locate and describe the origins of Chinese civilization in the Huang-He Valley during the Shang Dynasty.

Chapter 5, Section 1 China's first civilizations arose in the Huang He valley. **(See pp. 276–78.)**
Chapter 5, Section 1 The Shang dynasty developed the first Chinese language and the concept of honoring ancestors. **(See pp. 278–81.)**

WH6.6.2 Explain the geographic features of China that made governance and the spread of ideas and goods difficult and served to isolate the country from the rest of the world.

Chapter 5, Section 1 China is surrounded by vast mountain ranges such as the Himalaya to the southwest and the Kunlun Shan and the Tian Shan to the west. The Gobi Desert also covers much of China. These features helped isolate ancient China from most other peoples. **(See p. 278.)**

WH6.6.3 Know about the life of Confucius and the fundamental teachings of Confucianism and Daoism.

Chapter 5, Section 2 Confucius taught the importance of duty and filial piety. **(See pp. 287–89.)**
Chapter 5, Section 2 Daoists follow the teachings of Laozi, and believe people should give up worldly desires and follow the force that guides all things—the Dao. **(See pp. 290–91.)**

WH6.6.4 Identify the political and cultural problems prevalent in the time of Confucius and how he sought to solve them.

Chapter 5, Section 2 Confucius lived in a time when the government was struggling to run society and when many people were not following the ancient traditions. **(See pp. 287–89.)**
Chapter 5, Section 2 Confucius wanted to improve society through teaching people to do their duty, honor their parents, and do many other noble activities. **(See pp. 287–89, 292–93.)**

WH6.6.5 List the policies and achievements of the emperor Shi Huangdi in unifying northern China under the Qin Dynasty.

Chapter 5, Section 3 Emperor Shihuangdi united much of China under one dynasty. **(See pp. 294–97.)**
Chapter 5, Section 3 Shihuangdi created one currency, and built roads, a huge canal, and the Great Wall. **(See pp. 294–97.)**

**What Is the Standard?** **Where Is It Covered?**

WH6.6.6 Detail the political contributions of the Han Dynasty to the development of the imperial bureaucratic state and the expansion of the empire.	**Chapter 5, Section 3** Under the Han dynasty, the civil service exam created a government run by scholars. **(See p. 298.)**
	Chapter 5, Section 3 The Han rulers continued to expand the empire and ruled in a period of much peace. **(See pp. 298–300.)**
WH6.6.7 Cite the significance of the trans-Eurasian "silk roads" in the period of the Han Dynasty and Roman Empire and their locations.	**Chapter 5, Section 3** The Han dynasty also developed the Silk Road and began a trading network that reached much of Asia and the West, including Rome. **(See pp. 300–02.)**
	Chapter 5, Section 3 The Silk Road brought new goods and ideas to China. **(See pp. 300–02.)**
WH6.6.8 Describe the diffusion of Buddhism northward to China during the Han Dynasty.	**Chapter 5, Section 3** Buddhism reached China during the A.D. 100s. **(See p. 303.)**
	Chapter 5, Section 3 Buddhism began as an important religion in China after the Han dynasty collapsed. **(See p. 303.)**

Standards Practice

1 **Remains found by archaeologists show that the Shang dynasty may have**

A dug the Grand Canal linking parts of China.

B strengthened the Great Wall of China to keep out invaders.

C erected ziggurats to worship their gods and goddesses.

D built the first Chinese cities.

2 **Through his teachings, Confucius hoped to**

A encourage people to sacrifice to the gods.

B spread the idea that there is only one god.

C create a peaceful society.

D found communities of monks and nuns.

3 **What change did Emperor Qin Shihuangdi bring to China?**

A He allowed local officials to pass on their posts to relatives.

B He created one currency, or type of money, for the entire empire.

C He made Buddhism China's official religion.

D He used civil service examinations to choose officials.

4 **Why was the Silk Road important to China?**

A Merchants used it to carry goods west to the Mediterranean world.

B Caravans carried goods over it to Southeast Asia.

C It helped link all of the regions that made up China's empire.

D Chinese troops used it to conquer Tibet.

What Is the Standard? ➡ Where Is It Covered?

What Is the Standard?	Where Is It Covered?
WH6.7 Students analyze the geographic, political, economic, religious, and social structures during the development of Rome.	Chapters 9 and 10 cover standard WH6.7, including the rise of the Roman Republic and its transition to empire, its decline and fall, Rome's legacy, and the Byzantine Empire. (See pp. 416–95.)
	Chapter 11 covers the development and spread of Christianity, as well as how the Roman Empire and later European kingdoms adopted Christianity. (See pp. 496–525.)
WH6.7.1 Identify the location and describe the rise of the Roman Republic, including the importance of such mythical and historical figures as Aeneas, Romulus and Remus, Cincinnatus, Julius Caesar, and Cicero.	Chapter 9, Section 1 Rome arose in a key location on the Tiber River in central Italy. (See pp. 420–23.)
	Chapter 9, Sections 1 and 2 The republic became strong through a powerful military and shrewd rulers. (See pp. 423–30.)
	Chapter 9, Section 3 Major economic problems and political instability led to the rise of the dictator Julius Caesar. (See pp. 435–43.)
WH6.7.2 Describe the government of the Roman Republic and its significance (e.g., written constitution and tripartite government, checks and balances, civic duty).	Chapter 9, Section 2 Rome's government had a group of elected officials who held different responsibilities. (See pp. 426–31.)
WH6.7.3 Identify the location of and the political and geographic reasons for the growth of Roman territories and expansion of the empire, including how the empire fostered economic growth through the use of currency and trade routes.	Chapter 9, Section 2 As Rome expanded, it fought Carthage for control of the Mediterranean. (See p. 434.)
	Chapter 9, Section 4 During Rome's *Pax Romana,* good leadership, strong trade and good currency helped the empire grow and prosper. (See pp. 444–51.)
WH6.7.4 Discuss the influence of Julius Caesar and Augustus in Rome's transition from republic to empire.	Chapter 9, Section 3 Caesar's military abilities helped him defeat his enemies and become dictator. (See pp. 438–39.)
	Chapter 9, Sections 3 and 4 Caesar's grand-nephew Octavian defeated Antony in a civil war to claim the rule of Rome, and then established a long-lasting peace. (See pp. 440–41, 444–46.)

WH6.7

What Is the Standard? ➡ Where Is It Covered?

What Is the Standard?	Where Is It Covered?
WH6.7.5 Trace the migration of Jews around the Mediterranean region and the effects of their conflict with the Romans, including the Romans' restrictions on their right to live in Jerusalem.	**Chapter 11, Section 1** After the Romans conquered Judaea, they made the Jewish region a province. **(See pp. 500–01.)** **Chapter 11, Section 1** A Jewish rebellion led to the destruction of Jerusalem and the scattering of the Jews throughout the Mediterranean world. **(See pp. 500–01.)**
WH6.7.6 Note the origins of Christianity in the Jewish Messianic prophecies, the life and teachings of Jesus of Nazareth as described in the New Testament, and the contribution of St. Paul the Apostle to the definition and spread of Christian beliefs (e.g., belief in the Trinity, resurrection, salvation).	**Chapter 11, Section 1** Jesus of Nazareth preached that people should develop a relationship with God, and love and forgive each other. **(See pp. 502–05.)** **Chapter 11, Section 1** Early church leaders taught that people could gain salvation through Jesus, whom they taught was a member of the Trinity. **(See pp. 506–08.)**
WH6.7.7 Describe the circumstances that led to the spread of Christianity in Europe and other Roman territories.	**Chapter 11, Sections 1 and 2** Early church leaders spread the message of Christianity throughout the Middle East and into Europe, where an organization developed. **(See pp. 506–14.)** **Chapter 11, Section 3** Christian ideas were spread throughout Europe by missionaries. **(See pp. 515–21.)**
WH6.7.8 Discuss the legacies of Roman art and architecture, technology and science, literature, language, and law.	**Chapter 9, Section 2** The Roman legal system influenced the laws of the United States. **(See p. 431.)** **Chapter 10, Section 2** Roman literature, language, government architecture, and the spread of Christianity still influence us today. **(See pp. 462, 482–83.)**

Standards Practice

1 Which of the following practices did the Romans pass on to the world?

A the staging of plays
B the use of concrete in building
C the development of gunpowder
D the making of bricks

2 Jesus' parable of the Prodigal Son taught that

A people should carefully observe religious rituals.
B alms should be given at all times to the poor.
C God generously forgives those who turn from bad deeds.
D people should work for peace on earth.

California Standards Handbook Answer Key

The answers for the California Standards Handbook are listed below. Use this answer key to check your understanding of the material covered in the grade 6 social studies course.

WH6.1

1 B
2 A

WH6.2

1 D
2 C

WH6.3

1 D
2 C

WH6.4

1 D
2 A
3 B
4 A

WH6.5

1 C
2 B

WH6.6

1 D
2 C
3 B
4 A

WH6.7

1 B
2 C

Glossary

This glossary includes all the yellow highlighted and boldfaced vocabulary words from your text. Content vocabulary (those words highlighted in yellow in your text) are words that relate to history content. Academic vocabulary (those words **boldfaced** in your text) are words that will help you understand all of your school subjects. Academic vocabulary is shown with an asterisk (*).

A

* **access** to gain use of or have available (p. 318)

* **accommodate** to provide someone with something needed or desired (p. 428)

* **accurate** to be free from mistakes (p. 397)

* **achieve** to get something desired by effort (p. 399)

acupuncture Chinese practice of easing pain by sticking thin needles into patients' skins (p. 300)

* **affect** to make a change in or have an influence on (p. 248)

agora an open area in the Greek city-states that served as both a market and a meeting place (p. 341)

alliance agreement between people or nations to work together for assistance or protection (p. 320)

alphabet group of letters that stand for sounds (p. 205)

anatomy the study of body structure (p. 463)

anthropologist scientist who studies the physical characteristics and cultures of humans and their ancestors (p. 123)

apostle early Christian leader who helped set up churches and spread the message of Jesus (p. 506)

aqueduct a human made channel built to carry water (p. 448)

archaeologist scientist who learns about past human life by studying fossils and artifacts (p. 123)

* **area** a space of land (p. 249)

aristocrat a noble whose wealth came from land ownership (p. 279)

artifact weapon, tool, or other item made by humans (p. 123)

artisan skilled craftsperson (p. 136)

astronomer a person who studies stars, planets, and other heavenly bodies (pp. 147, 409)

* **authority** the right to give commands (p. 477)

* **aware** to have understanding or knowledge of something (p. 249)

B

barter to exchange goods without using money (p. 476)

* **behalf** to represent or support another person (p. 359)

Brahman in Hinduism, the universal spirit of which all gods and goddesses are different parts (p. 247)

Buddhism religion founded by Siddhartha Gautama, the Buddha; taught that the way to find truth was to give up all desires (p. 249)

bureaucracy a group of appointed officials who are responsible for different areas of government (p. 281)

C

* **capable** the ability to do something well (p. 448)

* **capacity** the ability to contain or produce (p. 421)

caravan group of traveling merchants and animals (p. 146)

caste a social group that a person is born into and cannot change (p. 243)

cataract steep rapids formed by cliffs and boulders in a river (p. 157)

* **challenge** to face difficulties (p. 432)

* **chapter** a new division of time in history or in a book (p. 423)

city-state independent state made up of a city and the surrounding land and villages (p. 135)

* **civil** an issue or problem between citizens of the same country or nation (p. 296)

civilization a society with cities, organized government, art, religion, and class divisions (p. 133)

clergy religious officials, such as priests, given authority to conduct religious services (p. 513)

* **code** system of principles or rules (p. 139)

* **collapse** to break down or cave-in completely (p. 189)

colony settlement in a new territory that keeps close ties with its homeland (p. 343)

comedy a form of drama in which the story has a happy ending (p. 383)

* **commit** to set a goal and perform the steps necessary to achieve it (p. 446)

* **community** a group of people with common interests and shared rights (p. 341)

* **complex** having many parts, details, ideas, or functions (p. 133)

* **concept** an idea or thought (p. 266)

* **conflict** strong disagreement (p. 383)

Confucianism a system of beliefs introduced by the Chinese thinker Confucius; taught that people needed to have a sense of duty to their family and community in order to bring peace to society (p. 288)

* **consist** what something is made up of (p. 136)

* **constant** occurring over and over again (p. 464)

* **construct** to build or put together (p. 184)

consul one of the two top government officials in ancient Rome (p. 428)

* **convince** to make a person believe or agree (p. 287)

* **core** the center or most important part (p. 143)

covenant agreement (p. 202)

* **create** to make (p. 204)

* **culture** particular form or style of a society (p. 339)

cuneiform Sumerian system of writing made up of wedge-shaped markings (p. 136)

currency a type of money (pp. 296, 450)

Dao the proper way Chinese kings were expected to rule under the Mandate of Heaven (p. 282)

Daoism Chinese philosophy based on the teachings of Laozi; taught that people should turn to nature and give up their worldly concerns (p. 290)

* **decade** a period of 10 years (p. 502)

* **decline** to move toward a lower level (p. 189)

deity a god or goddess (p. 167)

delta area of fertile soil at the mouth of a river (p. 157)

democracy government in which all citizens share in running the government (p. 346)

* **despite** in spite of (p. 436)

dharma in Hinduism, the divine law that requires people to perform the duties of their caste (p. 248)

Diaspora refers to the scattering of communities of Jews outside their homeland after the Babylonian captivity (p. 216)

dictator in ancient Rome, a person who ruled with complete power temporarily during emergencies (p. 429)

direct democracy system of government in which people gather at mass meetings to decide on government matters (p. 359)

disciple close follower of Jesus (p. 502)

doctrine official church teaching (p. 513)

domesticate to tame animals and plants for human use (p. 127)

*dominate to have control over someone else (p. 264)

drama a story told by actors who pretend to be characters in the story (p. 382)

dynasty line of rulers from the same family (pp. 162, 260, 278)

*economy organized way in which people produce, sell, and buy goods and services (p. 363)

embalming process developed by the ancient Egyptians of preserving a person's body after death (p. 167)

empire group of territories or nations under a single ruler or government (pp. 139, 209)

*enforce to make sure laws are carried out correctly (p. 347)

*enormous great in size or number (p. 489)

epic a long poem that tells about legendary or heroic deeds (p. 379)

Epicureanisma philosophy founded by Epicurus in Hellenistic Athens; taught that happiness through the pursuit of pleasure was the goal of life (p. 408)

*establish to put securely in place (p. 510)

*estate a large country house on a large piece of land (p. 436)

*estimate a guess based on evidence (p. 313)

excommunicate to declare that a person or group no longer belongs to a church (p. 518)

exile period of forced absence from one's country or home (p. 214)

*expand to increase in number, size, or amount (p. 483)

*expose to lay open (p. 313)

fable a short story that teaches a lesson (p. 380)

*feature shape or appearance of land or an object (p. 158)

filial piety children's respect for their parents and older relatives, an important part of Confucian beliefs (p. 286)

*focus center of interest (p. 201)

Forum open space in Rome that served as a marketplace and public square (p. 464)

fossil trace or imprint of a plant or animal that has been preserved in rock (p. 123)

*found to start or establish (p. 298)

*foundation the beginning of a system or building; the first layer (p. 441)

*framework basic structure of a building or organization (p. 365)

*generation a group of individuals born and living at the same time in history (p. 380)

glacier huge sheet of ice (p. 313)

gladiator in ancient Rome, person who fought animals and other people as public entertainment (p. 464)

*goal the object toward which effort is directed (p. 408)

gospel ("good news") the four accounts of Jesus' life, teachings, and resurrection (p. 513)

*grant to permit as a favor (p. 378)

guru a religious teacher and spiritual guide in Hinduism (p. 245)

Hellenistic Era period when the Greek language and Greek ideas spread to the non-Greek peoples of southwest Asia (p. 402)

helot person who was conquered and enslaved by the ancient Spartans (p. 346)

hierarchy organization with different levels of authority (p. 513)

Glossary

hieroglyphics a system of writing made up of picture symbols developed by the ancient Egyptians (p. 160)

Hinduism a religion that grew out of the religion of the Aryans in ancient India (p. 247)

icon Christian religious image or picture (p. 516)

iconoclast person who opposed the use of icons in Byzantine churches, saying that icons encouraged the worship of idols (p. 517)

ideograph a character that joins two or more pictographs to represent an idea (p. 280)

* **income** pay received from work done (p. 487)

* **individual** a single member of a group (p. 242)

inflation period of rapidly increasing prices (p. 476)

* **instruct** to give knowledge or information (p. 207)

* **internal** the inside structure of a community, government, or body (p. 357)

* **interpret** to explain the meaning of something (p. 280)

* **interval** space between things or time (p. 146)

irrigation method of bringing water to a field from another place to water crops (p. 134)

* **isolate** to be apart from others (p. 421)

* **issue** to distribute officially (p. 512)

* **item** a separate part of a group (p. 283)

karma in Hinduism, the good or bad energy a person builds up based upon whether he or she lives a good or bad life (p. 248)

* **labor** work that is physically hard (p. 164)

laity church members who are not clergy (p. 513)

latifundia large farming estates in ancient Rome (p. 436)

* **lecture** a talk given in front of a group for instruction (p. 408)

legacy is what a person leaves behind when he or she dies (p. 402)

Legalism Chinese philosophy developed by Hanfeizi; taught that humans are naturally evil and therefore need to be ruled by harsh laws (p. 291)

legion smaller unit of the Roman army made up of about 6,000 soldiers (p. 424)

* **legislate** to make law (p. 428)

* **link** to join separate things together (p. 282)

* **maintain** to keep control of a situation (p. 183)

* **major** great in number, quality or extent (p. 409)

mandate formal order (p. 282)

martyr person willing to die rather than give up his or her beliefs (p. 511)

messiah in Judaism, a deliverer sent by God (pp. 221, 502)

* **military** an army (p. 401)

missionary person who travels to carry the ideas of a religion to others (p. 519)

monastery religious community where monks live and work (p. 519)

monotheism the belief in one god (p. 201)

monsoon strong wind that blows one direction in winter and the opposite direction in summer (p. 239)

mosaic picture made from many bits of colored glass, tile, or stone (p. 490)

Glossary

Glossary

mummy a body that has been embalmed and wrapped in linen (p. 168)

myth traditional story describing gods or heroes or explaining natural events (p. 377)

nirvana in Buddhism, a state of wisdom and freedom from the cycle of rebirth (p. 249)

nomad a person who regularly moves from place to place (p. 125)

*__occupy__ to live in or take possession of something (p. 201)

ode poem that expresses strong emotions about life (p. 462)

oligarchy government in which a small group of people holds power (p. 346)

oracle sacred shrine where a priest or priestess spoke for a god or goddess (p. 378)

*__overseas__ across the sea or ocean (p. 340)

papyrus a plant of the Nile Valley used to make a form of paper (p. 160)

parable story that uses events from everyday life to express spiritual ideas (p. 503)

*__participate__ take part in an activity or gathering (p. 349)

paterfamilias ("father of the family") name for the father as head of the household in ancient Rome (p. 465)

patrician wealthy landowner and a member of the ruling class in ancient Rome (p. 427)

Pax Romana ("Roman Peace") long era of peace and safety in the Roman Empire (p. 445)

peninsula a body of land with water on three sides (p. 337)

*__period__ a portion of time in history (p. 166)

persecute to mistreat a person because of his or her beliefs (p. 511)

pharaoh all-powerful ruler in ancient Egypt (p. 166)

philosopher a thinker who seeks wisdom and ponders questions about life (pp. 360, 393)

philosophy the study of nature and the meaning of life; comes from the Greek word for "love of wisdom" (p. 393)

pictograph a character that stands for an object (p. 280)

pilgrim person who travels to a religious shrine or site (p. 264)

plane geometry a branch of mathematics that shows how points, lines, angles, and surfaces relate to one another (p. 410)

plebeian member of the common people in ancient Rome (p. 427)

polis early Greek city-state, made up of a city and the surrounding countryside and run like an independent country (p. 341)

pope the bishop of Rome, later the head of the Roman Catholic Church (p. 514)

praetor important government official in ancient Rome (p. 428)

*__predict__ a guess about what will happen in the future (p. 321)

*__principle__ law or fact of nature (p. 169)

*__promote__ to help grow or develop (p. 290)

prophet person who claims to be instructed by God to share God's words (p. 207)

proverb a wise saying (p. 209)

province political district (p. 144)

pyramid huge stone structure built by the ancient Egyptians to serve as a tomb (p. 168)

rabbi Jewish leader and teacher of the Torah (p. 222)

raja a prince who led an Aryan tribe in India (p. 243)

* recover to regain normal health or purpose (p. 280)

reform change that tries to bring about an improvement (p. 477)

regent person who acts as a temporary ruler (p. 491)

* region broad geographical area (p. 338)

reincarnation rebirth of the soul or spirit in different bodies over time (p. 248)

* reject to refuse to believe (p. 394)

* rely to depend on (p. 487)

representative democracy system of government in which citizens choose a smaller group to make laws and government decisions on their behalf (p. 359)

republic a form of government in which the leader is not a king or queen but a person elected by citizens (p. 423)

* require something that is necessary to do or to have (p. 248)

* reside to live in a particular place (p. 506)

* restore to put back into order or to fix (p. 179)

resurrection the act of rising from the dead (p. 505)

* revolution extreme complete change (p. 127)

rhetoric public speaking (p. 465)

* route established course of travel (p.146)

S

Sabbath weekly day of worship and rest for Jews (p. 214)

saint Christian holy person (p. 490)

salvation the act of being saved from sin and allowed to enter heaven (p. 508)

Sanskrit written language developed by the Aryans (p. 243)

satire writing that pokes fun at human weaknesses (p. 462)

satrap official who ruled a state in the Persian Empire under Darius (p. 353)

satrapies the 20 states into which Darius divided the Persian Empire (p. 353)

savanna grassy plain (p. 188)

schism separation (p. 518)

scribe record keeper (p. 136)

* secure to provide safety (p. 299)

* series a number of things arranged in order and connected by being alike in some way (p. 215)

* similar having qualities or position in common (p. 241)

sinkhole a place in the ground where the earth has caved in and water collects (p. 318)

social class group of people who share a similar position in society (p. 285)

Socratic method a way of teaching developed by Socrates that used a question-and-answer format to force students to use their reason to see things for themselves (p. 394)

* sole to be the only one in power; to be alone (p. 440)

solid geometry a branch of mathematics that studies spheres and cylinders (p. 410)

Sophist a professional teacher in ancient Greece; believed that people should use knowledge to improve themselves, and developed the art of public speaking and debate (p. 393)

specialization the development of different kinds of jobs (p. 131)

* status a position or rank (p. 425)

Stoicism philosophy founded by Zeno in Hellenistic Athens; taught that happiness came not from following emotion, but from following reason and doing one's duty (p. 408)

* structure materials arranged to form a building or statue (p. 168)

stupa Buddhist shrine that is shaped like a dome or mound (p. 262)

subcontinent large landmass that is part of a continent but distinct from it (p. 239)

Glossary

*successor the person next in line as leader (p. 445)

*survive to continue to exist or live (p. 516)

*symbol an item that represents an idea or a faith (p. 209)

synagogue Jewish house of worship (p. 214)

*task a piece of work (p. 125)

*technique a method used to accomplish a task (p. 461)

technology tools and methods used to help humans perform tasks (pp. 126, 159)

theocracy government headed by religious leaders (p. 252)

Torah the laws that, according to the Bible, Moses received from God on mount Sinai; these laws later became the first part of the Hebrew Bible (p. 202)

*trace very small amount (p. 216)

*tradition the handing down of information, beliefs, or customs from one generation to another (p. 380)

tragedy a form of drama in which a person struggles to overcome difficulties but meets an unhappy end (p. 382)

tribe group of related families (p. 201)

tribute payment made by one group or nation to another to show obedience or to obtain peace or protection (pp. 179, 209)

triumvirate in ancient Rome, a three-person ruling group (p. 438)

tyrant person who takes power by force and rules with total authority (p. 345)

*unify to bring together (p. 513)

vault a curved structure of stone or concrete forming a ceiling or roof (p. 461)

*version a copy of a writing which is in one's own language or style (p. 216)

veto to reject (p. 428)

*vision picture created by the imagination (p. 353)

*welfare doing well; having what is needed to live well (p. 166)

Zoroastrianism Persian religion founded by Zoroaster; taught that humans had the freedom to choose between right and wrong, and that goodness would triumph in the end (p. 353)

Spanish Glossary

This glossary includes all the yellow highlighted and boldfaced vocabulary words from your text. Content vocabulary (those words highlighted in yellow in your text) are words that relate to history content. Academic vocabulary (those words **boldfaced** in your text) are words that will help you understand all of your school subjects. Academic vocabulary is shown with an asterisk (*).

A

* **access / acceso** ganar uso de o tener disponible (pág. 318)

* **accommodate / acomodar** proporcionarle a alguien algo necesitado o deseado (pág. 428)

* **accurate / exacto** estar libre de errores (pág. 397)

* **achieve / lograr** obtener algo deseado por esfuerzo (pág. 399)

acupuncture / acupuntura práctica china para aliviar el dolor clavando la piel de los pacientes con agujas delgadas (pág. 300)

* **affect / afectar** realizar un cambio en o tener una influencia en (pág. 248)

agora / ágora en las primeras ciudades-estado griegas, un área abierta que servía tanto de mercado como de lugar de reunión (pág. 341)

* **alliance / alianza** acuerdo entre gente o naciones para trabajar juntos por asistencia o protección (pág. 320)

alphabet / alfabeto grupo de letras que representan sonidos (pág. 205)

anatomy / anatomía estudio de la estructura corporal (pág. 463)

anthropologist / antropólogo científico que estudia las características físicas y las culturas de los seres humanos y sus antepasados (pág. 123)

apostle / apóstol nombre dado a líderes cristianos que ayudaban a establecer iglesias y a difundir el mensaje de Jesucristo (pág. 506)

aqueduct / acueducto canal construido por el hombre para transportar agua (pág. 448)

archaeologist / arqueólogo científico que aprende acerca de la vida humana en el pasado estudiando fósiles y artefactos (pág. 123)

* **area / área** un espacio de terreno (pág. 249)

aristocrat / aristócrata noble cuya riqueza provenía de la propiedad de la tierra (pág. 279)

artifact / artefacto arma, herramienta u otro artículo hecho por humanos (pág. 123)

artisan / artesano persona hábil artísticamente (pág. 136)

astronomer / astrónomo persona que estudia las estrellas, a los planetas y a otros cuerpos celestiales (págs. 147, 409)

* **authority / autoridad** el derecho a dar órdenes (pág. 477)

* **aware / informado** tener un entendimiento o conocimiento de algo (pág. 249)

B

barter / trueque intercambiar bienes sin utilizar dinero (pág. 476)

* **behalf / de parte de** para representar o apoyar a otra persona (pág. 359)

Brahman / Brahman en el hinduismo, el espíritu universal del que todos los dioses y diosas son partes diferentes (pág. 247)

Buddhism / budismo religión fundada por Siddhartha Gautama, Buda; enseñó que la manera de hallar la verdad era renunciar a todo deseo (pág. 249)

bureaucracy / burocracia grupo de funcionarios designados que son responsables de diferentes áreas del gobierno (pág. 281)

C

*capable / capaz la habilidad para hacer algo bien (pág. 448)

*capacity / capacidad la habilidad para contener o producir (pág. 421)

caravan / caravana grupo itinerante de mercaderes y animales (pág. 146)

caste / casta grupo social en el que una persona nace y que no puede cambiar (pág. 243)

cataract / catarata rápidos empinados formados por precipicios y rocas erosionadas en un río (pág. 157)

*challenge / desafío enfrentar dificultades (pág. 432)

*chapter / capítulo una nueva división de tiempo en la historia o en algún libro (pág. 423)

city-state / ciudad-estado estado independiente compuesto por una ciudad y la tierra y aldeas circundantes (pág. 135)

*civil / civil un asunto o problema entre ciudadanos del mismo país o nación (pág. 296)

civilization / civilización sociedad compleja, con ciudades, un gobierno organizado, arte, religión, divisiones de clase y un sistema de escritura (pág. 133)

clergy / clero funcionarios religiosos, como los sacerdotes, con autoridad concedida para llevar a cabo servicios religiosos (pág. 513)

*code / código sistema de principios o reglas (pág. 139)

*collapse / colapsar echar abajo o derrumbarse completamente (pág. 189)

colony / colonia asentamiento en un territorio nuevo que mantiene lazos cercanos con su tierra natal (pág. 343)

comedy / comedia forma de drama en el que la historia tiene un final feliz (pág. 383)

*commit / comprometer fijar una meta y realizar los pasos necesarios para alcanzarla (pág. 446)

*community / comunidad un grupo de gente con intereses comunes y derechos compartidos (pág. 341)

*complex / complejo que tiene muchas partes, detalles, ideas, o funciones (pág. 133)

*concept / concepto una idea o pensamiento (pág. 266)

Confucianism / confucianismo sistema de creencias introducidas por el pensador chino Confucio; enseñó que las personas necesitaban tener un sentido del deber hacia su familia y la comunidad para llevar paz a la sociedad (pág. 288)

*consist / consistir de lo que está hecho algo (pág. 136)

*constant / constante ocurriendo una y otra vez (pág. 464)

*construct / construir edificar o juntar (pág. 184)

consul / cónsul uno de los dos altos funcionarios en la Roma antigua (pág. 428)

*convince / convencer hacer que una persona crea o esté de acuerdo (pág. 287)

*core / núcleo el centro o la parte mas importante (pág. 143)

covenant / pacto acuerdo (pág. 202)

*create / crear hacer (pág. 204)

*culture / cultura forma o estilo particular de una sociedad (pág. 339)

cuneiform / cuneiforme sistema sumerio de escritura compuesto de símbolos con forma de cuña (pág. 136)

currency / moneda sistema monetario (págs. 296, 450)

*currency / divisa un tipo de dinero (págs. 296, 450)

D

Dao / Dao manera apropiada en la que se esperaba que los reyes chinos gobernaran bajo el Mandato del Cielo (pág. 282)

Daoism / Daoism filosofía china basada en las enseñanzas de Laozi; enseñó que las personas debían volverse a la naturaleza y renunciar a sus preocupaciones terrenales (pág. 290)

*** decade / década** un período de 10 años (pág. 502)

*** decline / descenso** moverse hacia un nivel inferior (pág. 189)

deity / deidad dios o diosa (pág. 167)

delta / delta área de tierra fértil en la boca de un río (pág. 157)

democracy / democracia forma de gobierno en la que todos los ciudadanos participan en la administración del gobierno (pág. 346)

*** despite / no obstante** a pesar de (pág. 436)

dharma / dharma en el hinduismo, la ley divina que llama a las personas a realizar los deberes de su casta (pág. 248)

Diaspora / diáspora se refiere al esparcimiento de las comunidades de judíos fuera de su tierra natal después del cautiverio babilónico (pág. 216)

dictator / dictador en la Roma antigua, una persona que gobernaba temporalmente con poder absoluto durante emergencias (pág. 429)

direct democracy / democracia directa sistema de gobierno en el que las personas se congregan en reuniones masivas para decidir sobre asuntos de gobierno (pág. 359)

disciple / discípulo seguidor de Jesucristo (pág. 502)

doctrine / doctrina enseñanza oficial de la iglesia (pág. 513)

domesticate / domesticar domar animales y plantas para uso humano (pág. 127)

*** dominate / dominar** tener control sobre algún otro (pág. 264)

drama / drama historia contada por actores que pretenden ser personajes en la misma (pág. 382)

dynasty / dinastía línea de gobernantes de la misma familia (págs. 162, 260, 278)

*** economy / economía** forma organizada en que la gente produce, vende, y compra bienes y servicios (pág. 363)

embalming / embalsamado proceso desarrollado por los antiguos egipcios para la conservación del cuerpo de una persona después de muerta (pág. 167)

empire / imperio grupo de territorios o naciones bajo un mismo mandatario o gobierno (págs. 139, 209)

*** enforce / hacer cumplir** asegurar que las leyes se lleven a efecto correctamente (pág. 347)

*** enormous / enorme** grande en tamaño o número (pág. 489)

epic / epopeya poema largo que cuenta acerca de actos legendarios o heroicos (pág. 379)

Epicureanism / epicureísmo filosofía fundada por Epicuro en la Atenas helenista; enseñó que la felicidad a través de la persecución del placer era la meta de la vida (pág. 408)

*** establish / establecer** poner seguramente en su lugar (pág. 510)

*** estate / hacienda** una gran casa de campo en un gran terreno (pág. 436)

*** estimate / estimación** una evaluación basada en evidencia (pág. 313)

excommunicate / excomulgar declarar que una persona o grupo no pertenece más a la iglesia (pág. 518)

exile / exilio período de ausencia forzada de una persona de su país u hogar (pág. 214)

*** expand / expandir** aumentar en número, tamaño o cantidad (pág. 483)

*** expose / exponer** estar abierto (pág. 313)

Spanish Glossary

fable / fábula cuento corto que enseña una lección (pág. 380)

***feature / aspecto** forma o apariencia de la tierra o de un objeto (pág. 158)

filial piety / piedad filial el respeto de los niños para sus padres y parientes mayores, una parte importante de las creencias confucianas (pág. 286)

***focus / foco** centro de interés (pág. 201)

Forum / Foro espacio abierto en Roma que servía como mercado y plaza pública (pág. 464)

fossil / fósil huella o impresión de una planta o animal que se ha conservado en piedra (pág. 123)

***found / fundar** partir o establecerse (pág. 298)

***foundation / fundación** el comienzo de un sistema o edificio; la primera capa (pág. 441)

***framework / armazón** estructura básica de un edificio u organización (pág. 365)

***generation / generación** un grupo de individuos que nacen y viven en el mismo tiempo en la historia (pág. 380)

glacier / glaciar masa inmensa de hielo (pág. 313)

gladiator / gladiador en la Roma antigua, persona que peleaba contra animales y otras personas como entretenimiento público (pág. 464)

***goal / meta** el objeto hacia el cual se dirige el esfuerzo (pág. 408)

gospel / evangelio ("buena nueva") uno de los cuatro relatos sobre la vida, enseñanzas y resurrección de Jesucristo (pág. 513)

***grant / otorgar** permitir como un favor (pág. 378)

guru / gurú maestro religioso y guía espiritual en el hinduismo (pág. 245)

Hellenistic Era / Era helenista período cuando el idioma y las ideas griegas se esparcieron a los habitantes no griegos del suroeste de Asia (pág. 402)

helot / ilota persona conquistada y esclavizada por los espartanos antiguos (pág. 346)

hierarchy / jerarquía organización con diferentes niveles de autoridad (pág. 513)

hieroglyphics / jeroglíficos sistema de escritura compuesto por miles de símbolos gráficos desarrollados por los antiguos egipcios (pág. 160)

Hinduism / hinduismo sistema religioso que se originó a partir de la religión de los arios en la antigua India (pág. 247)

icon / icono imagen o retrato religioso cristiano (pág. 516)

iconoclast / iconoclasta persona que se oponía al uso de ídolos en las iglesias bizantinas, aludiendo que los iconos alentaban el culto de ídolos (pág. 517)

ideograph / ideógrafo un carácter que une dos o más pictografías para representar una idea (pág. 280)

***income / ingresos** el pago recibido por el trabajo hecho (pág. 487)

***individual / individuo** miembro individual de un grupo (pág. 242)

inflation / inflación período de incremento rápido de precios (pág. 476)

***instruct / instruir** dar conocimiento o información (pág. 207)

***internal / interno** la estructura interior de una comunidad, gobierno, o cuerpo (pág. 357) *interpret / interpretar explicar el significado (pág. 280)

*interval / intervalo espacio entre cosas o el tiempo (pág. 146)

irrigation / irrigación método para llevar agua de otro lugar a un campo para regar las cosechas (pág. 134)

*isolate / aislar estar aparte de otros (pág. 421)

*issue / emitir distribuir oficialmente (pág. 512)

*item / ítem una parte separada de un grupo (pág. 283)

karma / karma en el hinduismo, la energía buena o mala que una persona desarrolla según si vive una vida buena o mala (pág. 248)

*labor / labor trabajo físicamente duro (pág. 164)

laity / laicado miembros de iglesia que no constituyen el clero (pág. 513)

latifundia / latifundios grandes propiedades agrícolas en la Roma antigua (pág. 436)

*lecture / conferencia hablar frente a un grupo para su instrucción (pág. 408)

legacy / legado lo que una persona deja cuando muere (pág. 402)

Legalism / legalismo filosofía china desarrollada por Hanfeizi; enseñó que los humanos son naturalmente malos y por lo tanto necesitaban ser gobernados por leyes duras (pág. 291)

legion / legión unidad más pequeña del ejército romano, compuesta por aproximadamente 6,000 soldados (pág. 424)

*legislate / legislar hacer una ley (pág. 428)

*link / unir juntar cosas separadas (pág. 282)

*maintain / mantener tener control de una situación (pág. 183)

*major / mayor grande en número, calidad o extensión (pág. 409)

mandate / mandato orden formal (pág. 282)

martyr / mártir persona dispuesta a morir antes que renunciar a sus creencias (pág. 511)

messiah / mesías en el judaísmo, un salvador mandado por Dios (págs. 221, 502)

*military / militar un ejército (pág. 401)

missionary / misionero persona que viaja para llevar las ideas de una religión a otros (pág. 519)

monastery / monasterio comunidad religiosa donde los monjes viven y trabajan (pág. 519)

monotheism / monoteísmo la creencia en un solo dios (pág. 201)

monsoon / monzón en la Asia del sur, un viento fuerte que sopla en una dirección en el invierno y en la dirección opuesta en el verano (pág. 239)

mosaic / mosaico figura hecha con muchos trozos de vidrios de colores, azulejo o piedra (pág. 490)

mummy / momia cuerpo que se ha embalsamado y envuelto en lino (pág. 168)

myth / mito cuento tradicional que describe dioses o a héroes o explica eventos naturales (pág. 377)

nirvana / nirvana en el budismo, un estado de sabiduría y libertad del ciclo del renacimiento (pág. 249)

nomad / nómada persona que regularmente se mueve de un lugar a otro (pág. 125)

Spanish Glossary

O

*occupy / ocupar** vivir en o tomar posesión de algo (pág. 201)

ode / oda poema que expresa emociones fuertes acerca de la vida (pág. 462)

oligarchy / oligarquía gobierno en el que un grupo pequeño de personas mantiene el poder (pág. 346)

oracle / oráculo templo sagrado en donde un sacerdote o sacerdotisa hablaban a nombre de un dios o diosa (pág. 378)

*overseas / ultramar** a través del mar u océano (pág. 340)

P

papyrus / papiro planta de juncos del Valle de Nilo, empleada para hacer un tipo de papel (pág. 160)

parable / parábola historia que usa acontecimientos de la vida diaria para expresar ideas espirituales (pág. 503)

*participate / participar** tomar parte en una actividad o asamblea (pág. 349)

paterfamilias / paterfamilias ("padre de la familia") nombre dado al padre como cabeza de la casa en la Roma antigua (pág. 465)

patrician / patricio hacendado poderoso y miembro de la clase gobernante en la Roma antigua (pág. 427)

Pax Romana / Paz Romana era prolongada de paz y seguridad en el Imperio Romano (pág. 445)

peninsula / península extensión territorial rodeada de agua en tres lados (pág. 337)

*period / período** una porción de tiempo en la historia (pág. 166)

persecute / perseguir maltratar una persona a causa de sus creencias (pág. 511)

pharaoh / faraón rey todopoderoso en el antiguo Egipto (pág. 166)

philosopher / filósofo pensador que busca la sabiduría y formula preguntas acerca de la vida (págs. 360, 393)

philosophy / filosofía estudio de la naturaleza y significando de la vida; viene de la palabra griega que significa "amor a la sabiduría" (pág. 393)

pictograph / pictógrafo carácter que representa a un objeto (pág. 280)

pilgrim / peregrino persona que viaja para ir a un relicario o sitio religioso (pág. 264)

plane geometry / geometría plana rama de las matemáticas que muestra cómo se relacionan los puntos, las líneas, los ángulos y las superficies (pág. 410)

plebeian / plebeyo miembro de las personas comunes en la Roma antigua (pág. 427)

polis / polis antigua ciudad-estado griega, compuesta de una ciudad y las áreas circundantes y gobernada como un país independiente (pág. 341)

pope / Papa el obispo de Roma, posteriormente, la cabeza de la iglesia católica romana (pág. 514)

praetor / pretor importante funcionario de gobierno en la Roma antigua (pág. 428)

*predict / predecir** una suposición sobre lo que puede suceder en el futuro (pág. 321)

*principle / principio** ley o hecho de la naturaleza (pág. 169)

*promote / promover** ayudar a crecer o desarrollarse (pág. 290)

prophet / profeta persona que declara estar instruido por Dios para compartir Sus palabras (pág. 207)

proverb / proverbio dicho sabio (pág. 209)

province / provincia distrito político (pág. 144)

pyramid / pirámide inmensa estructura de piedra construida por los antiguos egipcios para utilizarse como una tumba (pág. 168)

Spanish Glossary

rabbi / rabino líder judío y maestro del Torá (pág. 222)

raja / rajá príncipe que dirigió a una tribu aria en la India (pág. 243)

*recover / recuperar volver a tener la salud o propósito normales (pág. 280)

reform / reforma cambio que intenta producir una mejora (pág. 477)

regent / regente persona que opera como un gobernante temporal (pág. 491)

*region / región amplia área geográfica (pág. 338)

reincarnation / reencarnación renacimiento del alma o el espíritu en cuerpos diferentes a través del tiempo (pág. 248)

*reject/ rechazar rehusarse a creer (pág. 394)

*rely / confiar depender de (pág. 487)

representative democracy / democracia representativa sistema de gobierno en el que los ciudadanos escogen a un grupo más pequeño para promulgar leyes y tomar decisiones gubernamentales en su nombre (pág. 359)

republic / república forma de gobierno en la que el líder no es un rey ni una reina sino una persona elegida por los ciudadanos (pág. 423)

*require / requerir algo que es necesario hacer o tener (pág. 248)

*reside / residir vivir en un lugar en particular (pág. 506)

*restore / restaurar volver a poner en orden o arreglar (pág. 179)

resurrection / resurrección acto de volver a la vida (pág. 505)

*revolution / revolución cambio extremo completo (pág. 127)

rhetoric / retórica hablar en público (pág. 465)

*route / ruta curso de viaje establecido (pág. 146)

Sabbath / sabbat día semanal de culto y descanso para los judíos (pág. 214)

saint / santo persona cristiana santificada (pág. 490)

salvation / salvación acto de ser salvado del pecado y aceptado para entrar al cielo (pág. 508)

Sanskrit / Sánscrito idioma escrito desarrollado por los arios (pág. 243)

satire / sátira escrito que hace burla de las debilidades humanas (pág. 462)

satrap / sátrapa funcionario que gobernaba un estado en el Imperio pérsico durante la época de Darío (pág. 353)

satrapies / satrapies los 20 estados en los cuales Darío dividió al Imperio pérsico (pág. 353)

savanna / sabana llanura cubierta de hierba (pág. 188)

schism / cisma separación (pág. 518)

scribe / escriba conservador de registros (pág. 136)

*secure / asegurar proporcionar seguridad (pág. 299)

*series / serie un número de cosas dispuestas en orden y conectadas por ser parecidas de alguna manera (pág. 215)

*similar / similar que tiene calidades o posición en común (pág. 241)

*sinkhole / cenote un lugar en la tierra donde la tierra se ha excavado y se recolecta el agua (pág. 318)

social class / clase social grupo de personas que comparten una posición semejante en la sociedad (pág. 285)

Spanish Glossary

Socratic method / método socrático método de enseñanza desarrollado por Sócrates que emplea un formato de pregunta y respuesta para forzar a los estudiantes a utilizar su raciocinio para ver las cosas por sí mismos (pág. 394)

*__sole / exclusivo__ ser el único en el poder, estar sólo (pág. 440)

solid geometry / geometría sólida rama de las matemáticas que estudia a las esferas y los cilindros (pág. 410)

Sophist / Sofista maestro profesional en Grecia antigua; creían que las personas deben utilizar el conocimiento para mejorarse a sí mismas, y desarrollaron el arte de hablar en público y el debate (pág. 393)

specialization / especialización desarrollo de diferentes tipos de trabajos (pág. 131)

*__status / situación__ una posición o rango (pág. 425)

Stoicism / estoicismo filosofía fundada por Zeno en la Atenas Helenista; enseñaba que la felicidad provenía no de seguir a las emociones, sino a la razón y de cumplir con nuestro deber (pág. 184)

*__structure / estructura__ materiales dispuestos para formar un edificio o estatua (pág. 168)

stupa / estupa templo budista con forma de cúpula o montículo (pág. 262)

subcontinent / subcontinente gran masa de tierra que forma parte de un continente pero está separada de él (pág. 239)

*__successor / sucesor__ la persona próxima en línea como líder (pág. 445)

*__survive / sobrevivir__ continuar existiendo o viviendo (pág. 516)

*__symbol / símbolo__ un ítem que representa una idea o una fe (pág. 209)

synagogue / sinagoga casa de culto judía (pág. 214)

*__task / tarea__ una parte del trabajo (pág. 125)

*__technique / técnica__ un método usado para cumplir una tarea (pág. 461)

*__technology / tecnología__ herramientas y métodos usados para ayudar a los humanos a realizar tareas (pág. 159)

theocracy / teocracia gobierno dirigido por líderes religiosos (pág. 252)

Torah / Torá las leyes que, según la Biblia, Moisés recibió de Dios en el monte Sinaí; estas leyes se convirtieron después en la primera parte de la Biblia hebrea (pág. 202)

*__trace / pizca__ cantidad muy pequeña (pág. 216)

*__tradition / tradición__ la entrega de información, creencias, o costumbres de una generación a otra (pág. 380)

tragedy / tragedia forma de drama en la que una persona se esfuerza para vencer dificultades pero encuentra un final infeliz (pág. 382)

tribe / tribu grupo de familias relacionadas (pág. 201)

tribute / tributo pago realizado por un grupo o nación a otra para mostrar obediencia o para obtener paz o protección (págs. 179, 209)

triumvirate / triunvirato en la Roma antigua, un grupo gobernante de tres personas (pág. 438)

tyrant / tirano persona que toma el poder por la fuerza y gobierna con autoridad total (pág. 345)

*__unify / unificar__ poner juntos (pág. 513)

vault / cámara estructura curva de piedra o cemento que forma un techo (pág. 461)

*version / versión una copia de un escrito que está en su propio lenguaje o estilo (pág. 216)

veto / veta rechazar (pág. 428)

*vision / visión impresión creada por la imaginación (pág. 353)

*welfare / bienestar haciéndolo bien; teniendo lo que se necesita para vivir bien (pág. 166)

Zoroastrianism / zoroastrismo religión persa fundada por Zoroastro; enseñaba que los humanos tenían la libertad de escoger entre lo correcto y lo incorrecto, y que la bondad triunfaría al final (pág. 353)

Spanish Glossary

A Gazetteer (GA•zuh•TIHR) is a geographic index or dictionary. It shows latitude and longitude for cities and certain other places. Latitude and longitude are shown in this way: 48°N 2°E, or 48 degrees north latitude and two degrees east longitude. This Gazetteer lists most of the world's largest independent countries, their capitals, and several important geographic features. The page numbers tell where each entry can be found on a map in this book. As an aid to pronunciation, most entries are spelled phonetically.

A

Actium [AK•shee•uhm] Cape on the western coast of Greece. 37°N 23°E (p. 454)

Aden Port city of the Red Sea in southern Yemen. 12°N 45°E (pp. 57, 60, 62)

Aden, Gulf of Western arm of the Arabian Sea, between Yemen, Somalia, and Djibouti. (pp. 51, 57, 60, 62)

Adriatic [AY•dree•A•tihk] **Sea** Arm of Mediterranean Sea between Italy and the Balkan Peninsula. (pp. 52, 54, 365, 421, 427, 449)

Aegean [ih•JEE•uhn] **Sea** Gulf of the Mediterranean Sea between Greece and Asia Minor, north of Crete. (pp. 51, 52, 54, 337, 354, 365, 370, 400, 510, 518, 524)

Afghanistan [af•GA•nuh•STAN] Central Asian country west of Pakistan. (pp. 48, 60, 62, 242, 400)

Africa Second-largest continent, south of Europe between the Atlantic and Indian Oceans. (pp. 49, 51, 56, 57, 58, 59, 72, 73, 74, 75, 115, 116, 125, 150, 232, 313, 329, 330, 342, 420, 421, 427, 432, 449, 454, 480, 510, 518, 524)

Alaska Largest state in the United States, located in the extreme northwestern region of North America. (pp. 48, 50, 64, 65)

Albania [al•BAY•nee•uh] Country on the Adriatic Sea, south of Yugoslavia. (pp. 52, 53)

Alexandria [A•lihg•ZAN•dree•uh] City and major seaport in northern Egypt in the Nile River delta. 31°N 29°E (pp. 56, 301, 400, 403, 406, 414, 449, 480, 486, 510,518, 524)

Algeria [al•JIHR•ee•uh] Country in North Africa. (pp. 48, 49, 58, 59)

Algiers [al•JIHRZ] Capital city of Algeria, largest Mediterranean port of northwestern Africa. 36°N 2°E (pp. 49, 58, 59)

Alps Mountain system of south central Europe. (pp. 51, 421, 427, 432)

Altay Mountains Mountain range in Asia. (pp. 51, 277)

Altun Mountains Range of mountains that are a part of the Kunlun Shan in China. (pp. 51, 277)

Amazon River River in northern South America, largely in Brazil, second-longest river in the world. (pp. 48, 50, 68, 69)

Amsterdam Capital of the Netherlands. 52°N 4°E (pp. 52)

Amu Darya [AH•moo•DAHR•yuh] Largest river of central Asia. (pp. 60, 61, 62, 63, 242, 252)

Andes [AN•deez] Mountain range along the western edge of South America. (pp. 50, 68, 69)

Angola [ang•GOH•luh] Southern African country north of Namibia. (pp. 49, 58, 59)

Antarctica Fifth-largest of the earth's seven continents; it surrounds the South Pole. (pp. 48, 49, 58, 59)

Antioch [AN•tee•AHK] Ancient capital of Syria, now a city in southern Turkey. 36°N 36°E (pp. 301, 510, 518, 524)

Anyang [AHN•YAHNG] City in northern China, was China's first capital. 36°N 114°E (pp. 276, 278, 306)

Apennines [A•puh•NYNZ] Mountain range that runs through Italy. (pp. 421, 427)

Appalachian Mountains Mountain system of eastern North America. (pp. 50, 64, 65, 329, 449, 486)

Arabian Desert Arid region in eastern Egypt; also called the Eastern Desert. (pp. 51, 133, 144, 157, 194)

Arabian Peninsula Great desert peninsula in extreme southwestern Asia. (pp. 51, 56, 57, 60, 62, 181, 301, 329)

Arabian Sea Portion of the Indian Ocean between the Arabian Peninsula and the subcontinent of India. (pp. 49, 51, 60, 62, 239, 242, 260, 264, 270, 301, 400)

Aral [AR•uhl] **Sea** Large saltwater lake, or inland sea, in central Asia. (pp. 51, 242, 301, 352)

Arctic Ocean Smallest of the earth's four oceans. (pp. 48, 49, 50, 51, 64, 65, 76, 313)

Argentina [AHR•juhn•TEE•nuh] South American country east of Chile. (pp. 68, 69, 71)

Asia Largest of the earth's seven continents. (pp. 51, 53, 54, 55, 56, 57, 58, 72, 73, 74, 75, 115, 117, 128, 133, 150, 233, 313 ,331)

Asia Minor Region of the ancient world, roughly corresponding to present-day Turkey. (pp. 51, 133, 144, 337, 342, 352, 400, 403, 414, 427, 432, 435, 448, 454, 480, 484, 486, 500, 510, 515, 518, 524)

Assyria [uh•SIHR•ee•uh] Ancient country in Asia that included the Tigris River valley in Mesopotamia. (p. 146)

Astrakhan [AS•truh•KAN] City in southern European Russia on the Volga River near the Caspian Sea. 46°N 48°E (p. 53)

Athens Capital of Greece, an ancient city-state. 38°N 23°E (pp. 52, 337, 342, 344, 354, 358, 365, 370, 376, 400, 406)

Atlantic Ocean Second-largest body of water in the world. (pp. 48, 49, 50, 51, 52, 54, 64, 65, 67, 68, 69, 72, 73, 75, 76, 128, 313, 342, 427, 449, 480, 486, 494, 510, 518)

Atlas Mountains Mountain range in northwestern Africa on the northern edge of the Sahara. (pp. 51, 58)

Australia Island continent southeast of Asia. (pp. 49, 51, 70, 72, 73, 74, 75, 128, 150)

Austria [AWS•tree•uh] Country in central Europe. (pp. 49, 52)

Azores [AY•ZOHRZ] Group of nine islands in the North Atlantic Ocean. (pp. 48, 50, 58, 59)

B

Babylon [BA•buh•luhn] Once the world's largest and richest city, on the banks of the Euphrates River in northern Mesopotamia. 32°N 45°E (pp. 132, 133, 142, 144, 146, 206, 213, 352, 398, 400)

Baghdad [BAG•DAD] Capital city of Iraq. 33°N 44°E (pp. 49, 57, 60)

Bahamas [buh•HAH•muhz] Country made up of many islands between Cuba and the United States. 23°N 74°W (pp. 48, 66, 67 70)

Balkan [BAWL•kuhn] **Peninsula** Peninsula in southeastern Europe bounded on the east by the Black and Aegean Seas, on the south by the Mediterranean Sea, and on the west by the Adriatic and Ionian Seas. 42°N 20°E (pp. 337, 484, 486)

Baltic [BAWL•tihk] **Sea** Sea in northern Europe connected to the North Sea. (pp. 49, 51, 52, 53, 54, 55)

Bangkok [BANG•KAHK] Capital of Thailand. 14°N 100°E (pp. 49, 61, 70)

Bangladesh [BAHNG•gluh•DEHSH] South Asian country bounded by Myanmar and India. 24°N 90°E (p. 242)

Barcelona City in northeastern Spain. 41°N 2°E (pp. 52)

Bay of Bengal Arm of the Indian Ocean between India and the Malay Peninsula on the east. 17°N 87°E (pp. 49, 51, 60, 62, 239, 242, 260, 264, 301)

Beijing [BAY•JIHNG] Capital of China. 40°N 116°E (pp. 49, 61, 63, 70)

Belgrade [BEHL•GRAYD] Capital of Yugoslavia. 45°N 21°E (p. 53)

Belize [buh•LEEZ] Central American country east of Guatemala. (pp. 48, 66)

Bering Sea Part of the North Pacific Ocean, situated between the Aleutian Islands on the south and the Bering Strait, which connects it with the Arctic Ocean, on the north. (pp. 48, 50, 64, 65, 70, 71, 76, 313)

Bhutan [boo•TAHN] South Asian country northeast of India. (p. 49, 242)

Black Sea Inland sea between southeastern Europe and Asia Minor. (pp. 49, 51, 53, 55, 56, 60, 62, 115, 301, 329, 342, 352, 365, 400, 403, 414, 427, 432, 448, 449, 454, 480, 486, 510, 518, 524)

Bombay Port city in western India, now called Mumbai. 18°N 72°E (pp. 60, 62)

Bordeaux [bawr•DOH] City in southwestern France. 44°N 0°W (pp. 52)

Borneo Third-largest island in the world, located in the Malay Archipelago in southeastern Asia. (pp. 49, 70, 301)

Brazil Largest country in South America. (pp. 48, 68, 69)

Britain Largest island in the British Isles. (pp. 48, 68, 69, 444, 460, 474, 480, 510, 515, 518)

Budapest [BOO•duh•PEHST] Capital of Hungary. 47°N 19°E (p. 52)

Bulgaria [BUHL•GAR•ee•uh] Country in southeastern Europe on the Balkan Peninsula. (pp. 9, 53, 400)

Byblos [BIH•bluhs] Ancient city of Phoenicia on the Mediterranean Sea, near present-day Beirut, Lebanon. 34°N 35°E (pp. 133, 146, 210, 226, 252)

Cairo [KY•roh] Capital of Egypt. 31°N 32°E (pp. 49, 56, 58, 59)

California State in the western United States. (p. 64)

Canada Country in North America north of the United States. (pp. 48, 64, 65)

Caribbean [KAR•uh•BEE•uhn] **Sea** Part of the Atlantic Ocean bordered by the West Indies, South America, and Central America. (pp. 48, 50, 64, 65, 67, 68, 69)

Carthage [KAHR•thihj] Ancient city on the northern coast of Africa. 37°N 10°E (pp. 421, 426, 427, 448, 449, 454, 486, 494, 524)

Caspian [KAS•pee•uhn] **Sea** Saltwater lake in southeastern Europe and southwestern Asia, the largest inland body of water in the world. 40°N 52°E (pp. 49, 51, 53, 55, 57, 60, 62, 115, 117, 133, 146, 242, 301, 329, 352, 400, 403, 449, 454, 480, 486, 518)

Çatal Hüyük [chah•TAHL hoo•YOOK] EarlyNeolithic community in present-day Turkey. (p. 122)

Changan [CHAHNG•AHN] Capital of China during the Tang dynasty, now called Xian. 34°N 108°E (pp.294, 295, 301)

Chang Jiang [CHAHNG JYAHNG] River in China, third-longest in the world;

formerly called the Yangtze River. (pp. 277, 278, 282, 301)

China Country in East Asia, world's largest by population; now called the People's Republic of China. (pp. 49, 60, 61, 70, 242, 277, 301)

Congo River River in Central Africa. (p. 58, 59)

Connecticut A state in the northeastern United States. (pp. 64, 65)

Constantinople [KAHN•STAN•tuhn•OH•puhl] City built on the site of Byzantium, now known as Istanbul in present-day Turkey. 41°N 29°E (pp. 301, 460, 474, 480, 484, 486, 494, 509, 510, 515, 518, 524)

Copan City in central America during the Mayan empire. 15N° 88W (p. 324)

Cordoba [KAWR•duh•buh] City in southern Spain. 37°N 4°W (pp. 52)

Corinth City of ancient Greece, southwest of the modern city of Corinth. 37°N 22°E (pp. 337, 365, 427, 432)

Corsica Island in the Mediterranean Sea. 42°N 8°E (pp. 342, 421, 427, 432, 449, 486, 494)

Costa Rica [KAHS•tuh REE•kuh] Republic in southern Central America. (pp. 48, 64, 65, 66)

Crete [KREET] Greek island southeast of mainland in the southern Aegean Sea. 35°N 24°E (pp. 53, 336, 337, 342, 352, 354, 365, 370, 403, 414, 427, 432, 486, 494)

Cuba Island country in the West Indies. 22°N 79°W (pp. 48, 64, 65, 67)

Cuzco [KOOS•koh] City in southern Peru. 13°S 71°W (pp. 68, 69)

Cyprus [SY•pruhs] Island country in the eastern Mediterranean Sea, south of Turkey. 35°N 31°E (pp. 49, 51, 52, 54, 56, 181, 210, 342, 352, 403, 414, 427, 432, 486)

Damascus [duh•MAS•kuhs] Capital of Syria. 34°N 36°E (pp. 56, 60, 146, 210, 226, 301, 510, 518)

Danube [DAN•yoob] **River** Second-longest river in Europe. (pp. 400, 427, 432, 449, 454, 480, 486, 494)

Dead Sea Salt lake in southwestern Asia, bounded by Israel, the West Bank, and Jordan. (pp. 51, 56, 133,157, 210, 226)

Deccan Plateau Region in India. (pp. 51, 239, 242)

Delhi [DEH•lee] City in northern India. 28°N 76°E (pp. 337)

Delos [DEE•LAHS] Greek island in the southern Aegean Sea. 37°N 25°E (pp. 358, 365)

Denmark Scandinavian country in northwestern Europe. (pp. 49, 52, 54)

East Africa Region in east Central Africa comprised of Burundi, Kenya, Rwanda, Somalia, Tanzania, and Uganda. (pp. 58, 301)

East China Sea Arm of the northwestern Pacific Ocean between the eastern coast of China and the Ryukyu Islands, bounded by the Yellow Sea and Taiwan. (pp. 51, 61, 63, 277, 278, 295, 306)

Eastern Desert Arid region in eastern Egypt, also called the Arabian Desert. (pp. 157, 194)

Edinburgh Capital city of Scotland. 55°N 3°W (p. 52)

Egypt Country in North Africa on the Mediterranean Sea. (pp. 56, 58, 59, 133, 144, 146, 189, 301, 342, 352, 400, 432, 444, 449, 454, 460, 474, 484, 486, 510, 518, 524)

El Salvador Central American country between Guatemala and Nicaragua. (pp. 48, 64, 65, 66)

England Part of the island of Great Britain lying east of Wales and south of Scotland. (pp. 48, 52)

English Channel Narrow sea separating France and Great Britain. 49°N 3°W (p. 52, 54)

Equator An imaginary circle that divides the earth into the Northern Hemisphere and the Southern Hemisphere; latitude of any single point on the Equator is 0°. (pp. 48-51, 58, 60-75)

Eridu [EHR•ih•DOO] Ancient settlement in Mesopotamia. 31°N 46°E (p. 133)

Estonia [eh•STOH•nee•uh] Republic in northeastern Europe, one of the Baltic states. (p. 53)

Ethiopia [EE•thee•OH•pee•uh] Country in East Africa north of Somalia and Kenya. (pp. 49, 58, 59)

Etruria [ih•TRUR•ee•uh] Ancient region on the Italian peninsula that was home to the Etruscans; area is now called Tuscany. (p. 421)

Euphrates [yu•FRAY•teez] River River in southwestern Asia that flows through Syria and Iraq and joins the Tigris River near the Persian Gulf. (pp. 60, 62, 133, 301, 329, 342, 352, 400, 414, 449, 454, 486)

Europe One of the world's seven continents, sharing a landmass with Asia. (pp. 50-55, 65, 72, 73, 74, 75, 128, 150, 232, 313, 329)

Florida State in the southeastern United States bordered by Alabama, Georgia, the Atlantic Ocean, and the Gulf of Mexico. (p. 64, 65)

France Third-largest country in Europe, located south of Great Britain. (pp. 48, 49, 52, 54)

Frankfurt Port city in west central Germany on the Main River. 50°N 8°E (p. 52)

Galilee [GA•luh•LEE] Region of ancient Palestine, now part of northern Israel, between the Jordan River and the Sea of Galilee. 32°N 35°E (pp. 510, 518, 524)

Ganges [GAN•JEEZ] Plain Flat, fertile area around the Ganges River. (pp. 239, 242)

Ganges [GAN•JEEZ] River River in India that flows from the Himalaya to the Bay of Bengal. (pp. 51, 60, 62, 238, 242, 260, 264, 270, 301)

Gaul Ancient Roman name for the area now known as France. (pp. 432, 435, 444, 449, 454, 460, 474, 480, 510, 515, 518)

Geneva [juh•NEE•vuh] City in western Switzerland. 46°N 6°E (p. 52)

Genoa City and seaport in northwestern Italy. 44°N 9°E (p. 52)

Germany Western European country south of Denmark. (pp. 49, 52, 54)

Ghana [GAH•nuh] Country in West Africa on the Gulf of Guinea. (pp. 58, 59)

Giza City in northern Egypt and site of the Great Pyramid. 29°N 31°E (pp. 133, 157, 165, 194)

Gobi [GOH•bee] Vast desert covering parts of Mongolia and China. (pp. 61, 63, 70, 217, 301)

Greece Country in southeastern Europe on the Balkan Peninsula. (pp. 336, 337, 342, 344, 352, 358, 370, 376, 400, 427, 432, 435, 444, 448, 454, 460, 474, 480, 509, 510, 515, 518, 524)

Gulf of Mexico Gulf on part of the southern coast of the United States. (pp. 48, 50, 64, 65, 66, 67, 314, 324)

Harappa [huh•RA•puh] Ancient city in the Indus River valley in present-day Pakistan. (pp. 238, 242, 270)

Himalaya [HIH•muh•LAY•uh] Mountain system forming a barrier between India and the rest of Asia. (pp. 51, 60, 61, 239, 242, 264, 270, 277, 301)

Hindu Kush Major mountain system in central Asia. (pp. 242, 264, 270)

Hispaniola [HIHS•puh•NYOH•luh] Island in the West Indies. 19°N 72°E (p. 67)

Hokkaido [hah•KY•doh] Second-largest island of Japan. 43°N 142°E (pp. 49, 61)

Honshu [HAHN•shoo] Largest island of Japan, called the mainland. 36°N 138°E (pp. 51, 61)

Huang He [HWAHNG HUH] Second-longest river in China, formerly called the Yellow River. (pp. 61, 277, 278, 282, 295, 301)

Huang He [HWAHNG HUH] Valley The Yellow River valley in central China. (pp. 61, 277, 278, 282, 295, 301)

Hudson Bay Large inland sea in Canada. 60°N 85°W (pp. 48, 50, 58, 59, 54, 65, 71, 72, 73, 74, 75, 76)

Hungary Eastern European country south of Slovakia. (pp. 49, 52, 73)

India South Asian country south of China and Nepal. (pp. 49, 51, 60, 62, 239, 242, 264, 270, 301)

Indian Ocean Third-largest ocean. (pp. 49, 51, 58, 59, 60, 61, 62, 63, 70-76, 115, 128, 233, 239, 242, 260, 264, 301)

Indonesia [IHN•duh•NEE•zhuh] Island republic in Southeast Asia, consisting of most of the Malay Archipelago. (pp. 49, 61)

Indus [IHN•duhs] River River in Asia that begins in Tibet and flows through Pakistan to the Arabian Sea. (pp. 239, 242, 260, 264, 270, 301, 400)

Ionian [eye•OH•nee•uhn] Sea Arm of the Mediterranean Sea separating Greece and Albania from Italy and Sicily. (pp. 337, 365, 370, 421)

Iran Southwest Asian country on the eastern shore of the Persian Gulf, formerly called Persia. (pp. 49, 57, 60, 62, 242, 400)

Iraq Country in southwestern Asia at the northern tip of the Persian Gulf. (pp. 49, 56, 57, 60, 62, 400)

Ireland Island west of Great Britain occupied by the Republic of Ireland and Northern Ireland. (pp. 48, 52, 515)

Israel Southwest Asian country south of Lebanon. (pp. 60, 62, 400)

Italy Southern European country south of Switzerland and east of France. (pp. 49, 52, 54, 342, 420, 426, 435, 444, 448, 449, 454, 460, 474, 480, 486, 494, 500, 509, 510, 515, 518, 524)

Japan Chain of islands in the northern Pacific Ocean. (pp. 49, 51, 61, 63, 70-1, 277)

Java Island of the Malay Archipelago in southern Indonesia. (pp. 49, 51, 61, 63, 70, 301)

Jeddah City in western Saudi Arabia. 21°N 39°E (p. 60)

Jericho Oldest Neolithic community, in the West Bank between Israel and Jordan. 25°N 27°E (p. 122)

Jerusalem [juh•ROO•suh•luhm] Capital of Israel and a holy city for Christians, Jews, and Muslims. 31°N 35°E (pp. 56, 60, 133, 144, 146, 200, 206, 210, 213, 226, 352, 486, 500, 509, 510, 515, 518, 524)

Jordan River River flowing from Lebanon and Syria to the Dead Sea. (pp. 56, 133, 210, 226)

Judaea [ju•DEE•uh] Territory in southwest Asia and a region of historic Palestine. (pp. 500, 510, 518, 524)

Judah [JOO•duh] Southern kingdom of ancient Hebrews in Canaan, renamed Palestine, (p. 146)

Kathmandu [KAT•MAN•DOO] Capital of Nepal. 27°N 85°E (pp. 60, 260)

Khyber Pass Mountain pass in western Asia connecting Afghanistan and Pakistan. 34°N 71°E (p. 238)

Kiev [KEE•EHF] Capital of Ukraine, on the Dnieper River. 50°N 30°E (pp. 49, 53)

Knossos [NAH•suhs] Ancient city on Crete. 35°N 24°E (pp. 336, 337, 370)

Korean Peninsula in eastern Asia, divided into the Democratic People's Republic of Korea (North Korea) and the Republic of Korea. (pp. 49, 51, 61, 63, 277)

Kunlun [koon•Lun] Shan Major mountain system in western China. (pp. 60, 61, 277)

Kyoto [kee•OH•toh] Ancient capital of Japan, formerly called Heian. 35°N 135°E (p. 61)

Kyushu [kee•OO•shoo] One of the four major islands of Japan. 33°N 131°E (pp. 49, 61)

Latium [LAY•shee•uhm] Region in west central Italy. (p.421)

La Venta City in central America during the Mayan empire. 17N° 94W (p. 324)

Lebanon [LEH•buh•nuhn] Southwest Asian country on the eastern coast of the Mediterranean Sea. (pp. 49, 56, 400)

Libya [LIH•bee•uh] North African country west of Egypt. (pp. 49, 56, 58, 400)

Lisbon [LIHZ•buhn] Capital of Portugal. 39°N 9°W (p. 52)

London Capital of the United Kingdom, on the Thames River in southeastern England. 52°N 0° (pp. 48, 52, 54)

Lower Egypt The northeastern part of present day Egypt (pp. 157, 181, 194)

Luoyang [luh•WOH•YAHNG] City in northern China on the Huang He. 34°N 112°E (pp. 276, 282, 301, 306)

Macao [muh•KOW] Region on the southeastern coast of China. (pp. 61, 63)

Macedonia [MA•suh•DOH•nee•uh] Country in southeastern Europe on the Balkan Peninsula. (pp. 337, 398, 400, 427, 432)

Madagascar [MA•duh•GAS•kuhr] Island in the Indian Ocean off the southeastern coast of Africa. 18°S 43°E (pp. 49, 51, 58, 59)

Mali [MAH•lee] Republic in northwestern Africa. (p. 49)

Marathon Village of ancient Greece northeast of Athens. (p. 354)

Massachusetts State in the northeastern United States. (pp. 64, 65)

Massalia [muh•SAH•lee•uh] Ancient Greek colony on the site of present-day Marseille. 44°N 3°E (p. 449)

Mediterranean Sea Inland sea of Europe, Asia, and Africa. (pp. 49, 51-56, 58, 59, 60, 61, 62, 63, 116, 133, 144, 146, 157, 181, 189, 194, 210, 226, 329, 330, 337, 342, 352, 365, 370, 400, 403, 414, 421, 427, 448, 454, 480, 494, 510, 518, 524)

Mekong [MAY•KAWNG] River River in southeastern Asia that begins in Tibet and empties into the South China Sea. (p. 301)

Memphis Ancient capital of Egypt. 29°N 31°E (pp. 156, 157, 165, 178, 181, 189, 194, 200)

Meroë [MEHR•oh•ee] Capital city of Kush. 7°N 93°E (pp. 187, 189, 301)

Mesoamerica [MEH•zoh•uh•MEHR•ih•kuh] Ancient region including present-day Mexico and most of Central America. (p. 64-67)

Mesopotamia [MEH•suh•puh•TAY•mee•uh] Early center of civilization, in the area of modern Iraq and eastern Syria between the Tigris and Euphrates Rivers. (pp. 133, 146, 352)

Mexico North American country south of the United States. (pp. 48, 64, 65, 66, 67, 71, 314)

Mexico City Capital of Mexico. 19°N 99°W (pp. 48, 64, 65, 66, 67, 71)

Milan City in northern Italy. 45°N 9°E (p. 52)

Miletus [MY•LEE•tus] Ancient Greek city on the Aegean Sea in present day

Gazetteer

Turkey. 35°N 27°E (pp. 337, 354, 365)

Mississippi River Large river system in the United States that flows southward into the Gulf of Mexico. (pp. 48, 50, 64, 65)

Mogadishu [MAH•guh•DIH•shoo] Capital of Somalia. 2°N 45°E (pp. 49, 58, 59)

Mohenjo-Daro [moh•HEHN•joh DAHR•oh] Ancient settlement in the Indus Valley. 27°N 68°E (p. 242)

Moluccas [muh•LUH•kuhz] Group of islands in Indonesia, formerly called the Spice Islands. 2°S 128°E (pp. 61)

Mombasa City and seaport of Kenya. 4°S 39°E (pp. 58, 59)

Mongolia [mahn•GOH•lee•uh] Country in Asia between Russia and China. (pp. 49, 61, 63, 277)

Morocco [muh•RAH•koh] North African country on the Mediterranean Sea and the Atlantic Ocean. 32°N 7°W (pp. 49, 58, 59)

Moscow [MAHS•koh] Capital of Russia. 55°N 37°E (pp. 49, 53)

Mount Everest Highest mountain in the world, located in the Himalaya between Nepal and Tibet. 28°N 86°E (pp. 51, 239)

Mount Olympus [uh•LIHM•puhs] Highest mountain in Greece on the border between Thessaly and Macedonia. 41°N 23°E (p. 337)

Mount Sinai [SY•NY] Part of a rocky mass on the Sinai Peninsula of northeastern Egypt. 29°N 33°E (p. 210)

Mycenae [MY•SEE•nee] Ancient city in Greece. 37°N 22°E (pp. 336, 337, 370)

Nanjing [NAHN•JIHNG] City in eastern China, capital during the Ming dynasty. 32°N 118°E (p. 61)

Napata [NA•puh•tuh] Ancient capital of Kush. 18°N 32°E (pp. 187, 189)

Naples City in southern Italy. 40°N 14°E (p. 52)

Nazareth [NA•zuh•ruhth] Ancient town near Galilee, now in northern Israel. 32°N 35°E (pp. 510, 518, 524)

Nepal [nuh•PAWL] Mountain country between India and China. (pp. 60, 61, 242, 246)

Netherlands [NEH•thuhr•luhnz] Country in northwestern Europe. (pp. 49, 52, 54)

New Carthage City and seaport in southern Spain on the Mediterranean Sea also called Cartagena. 38°N 1°W (pp. 427, 432)

Nile Delta The northern end of the Nile River in Egypt (pp. 133, 157, 181, 194)

Nile River World's longest river flowing north from the heart of Africa to the Mediterranean Sea. (pp. 49, 51, 56, 58, 59, 133, 144, 156, 157, 165, 178, 181, 187, 189, 301, 329, 194, 342, 352, 400, 414, 427, 432, 449, 486)

Nineveh [NIH•nuh•vuh] Ancient capital of Assyria, on the Tigris River. 26°N 43°E (pp. 133, 142, 144, 146)

North America Continent in the northern part of the Western Hemisphere between the Atlantic and Pacific Oceans. (pp. 48, 50, 64, 65, 72, 73, 74, 75, 128, 313)

North Sea Arm of the Atlantic Ocean between Europe and the eastern coast of Great Britain. (pp. 48-55, 76, 449, 454, 480, 518)

Norway Northern European country on the Scandinavian peninsula. (pp. 49, 52, 53, 54, 55)

Novgorod [NAHV•guh•RAHD] City in western Russia. 58°N 31°E (p. 49)

Nubia [NOO•bee•uh] Region in present-day Sudan on the Nile River, later known as Kush. (p. 157)

Olympia Site of the ancient Olympic Games in Greece. 38°N 22°E (pp. 345, 376)

Oman [oh•MAHN] Country on the Arabian Sea and the Gulf of Oman. (pp. 49, 57, 242)

Osaka [oh•SAH•kuh] City and port in Japan. 34°N 135°E (pp. 49, 61, 63)

Pacific Ocean The largest and deepest of the world's four oceans, covering more than a third of the earth's surface. (pp. 48, 50, 61, 64, 65, 66, 68, 69, 70, 71, 72, 73, 74, 75, 76, 128, 233, 277, 313, 314)

Pakistan [PA•kih•STAN] Officially the Islamic Republic of Pakistan, a republic in South Asia, marking the area where South Asia converges with southwest Asia. (pp. 49, 57, 60, 62, 242, 400)

Palenque City in central America during the Mayan empire. 16N° 93W (p. 324)

Palestine A historic region, situated on the eastern coast of the Mediterranean Sea. (pp. 444, 459, 489)

Paris Capital of France. 49°N 2°E (p. 52)

Pataliputra [PAH•tuh•lih•POO•truh] Capital of Maurya. 24°N 86°E (pp. 259, 260, 301)

Peloponnesus [PEH•luh•puh•NEE•suhs] A peninsula in southern Greece. 37°N 22°E (pp. 337, 344, 345)

Pergamum [PUHR•guh•muhm] An ancient city of northwest Asia Minor in Mysia, now Turkey. 39°N 28°E (pp. 403, 414)

Persepolis Ancient capital of Persian empire, now in ruins. 30°N 53°E (pp. 352, 400)

Persia The conventional European designation of the country now known as Iran. (pp. 301, 352, 400)

Persian Gulf An arm of the Arabian Sea in southwestern Asia, between the Arabian Peninsula on the southwest and Iran on the northeast. (pp. 57, 60, 62, 115, 117, 133, 146, 329, 352, 400)

Philippines [FIH•luh•PEENZ] Island country in the Pacific Ocean southeast of China. (pp. 49, 70)

Plataea [pluh•TEE•uh] Ancient city of Greece. 39°N 22°E (p. 354)

Plateau of Tibet [tuh•BEHT] World's highest plateau region, bordered by the Himalaya, Pamirs, and Karakoram mountain ranges. (p. 277)

Plymouth Town in eastern Massachusetts, first successful English colony in New England. 42°N 71°W (pp. 663, 691)

Poland Country in central Europe. (pp. 49, 51, 52, 53, 54, 55)

Po River River in northern Italy, the longest in the country. (pp. 421, 427, 432)

Gazetteer

Portugal A long narrow country on Atlantic Ocean, sharing the Iberian Peninsula with Spain. (p. 52)

Punjab [Poon•JAHB] **Plain** Area in northeast India between the Himalayan Mountains and the Hindu Kush. (p. 242)

Pyrenees Mountain range in southwestern Europe, extending from the Bay of Biscay to the Mediterranean Sea. (p. 432)

Quanzhou [chuh•WAHN•JOH] City in southeastern China. 25°N 111°E (p. 61)

Quebec [kih•BEHK] Capital city of Quebec Province, Canada, on the St. Lawrence River. 47°N 71°W (pp. 64, 65)

Red Sea Narrow, inland sea, separating the Arabian Peninsula, western Asia, from northeastern Africa. (pp. 49, 51, 56, 57, 58, 116, 144, 157, 181, 189, 194, 301, 329, 342, 352, 403, 449, 454, 486, 510, 518, 524)

Rhine [RYN] **River** One of the principal rivers of Europe, rising in eastern Switzerland. (pp. 52, 53, 54, 55, 449, 454)

Rhodes Island in the Aegean Sea. 36°N 28°E (pp. 427, 432)

Rio Grande [REE•oh GRAND] River that forms part of the boundary between the United States and Mexico. (pp. 48, 50, 66)

Rocky Mountains Mountain system in western North America. (pp. 64, 65)

Rome Capital of Italy. 41°N 12°E (pp. 52, 420, 421 426, 435, 444, 448, 454, 460, 480, 484, 486, 500, 509, 510, 515, 518, 524)

Russia Independent republic in Eastern Europe and northern Asia, the world's largest country by area. (pp. 49, 53, 55, 60, 61, 301)

Sahara [suh•HAR•uh] Desert region in northern Africa that is the largest hot desert in the world. (pp. 50, 51, 56, 58, 59, 189)

St. Petersburg Second-largest city and largest seaport in Russia, located in the northwestern part of the country. 59°N 30°E (p. 53)

Salamis [SA•luh•muhs] Island in eastern Greece in the Gulf of Saronikós. 37°N 23°E (p. 354)

Samaria Ancient city and state in Palestine, located north of present-day Jerusalem east of the Mediterranean Sea. 32°N 35°E (pp. 206, 210, 226)

Sardinia Island off western Italy, in the Mediterranean Sea. 40°N 9°E (pp. 51, 52, 421, 432, 449, 486, 494)

Sardis Ancient city of Asia Minor, now in Turkey. 38°N 28°E (pp. 352, 354)

Saudi Arabia [SOW•dee uh•RAY•bee•uh] Monarchy in southwestern Asia, occupying most of the Arabian Peninsula. (pp. 49, 56, 57, 60, 62, 400)

Scotland One of the four countries that make up the United Kingdom, the mainland occupies the northern part of Great Britain. (p. 52, 54)

Sea of Japan Arm of the Pacific Ocean lying between Japan and the Asian mainland; also called the East Sea. (pp. 49, 51, 61, 63, 277)

Sea of Marmara Body of water between the Black Sea and the Aegean Sea. (pp. 49, 51, 53, 55, 65, 57, 60, 62, 337, 354, 365)

Seine [SAYN] **River** River in northern France. (pp. 52, 54)

Seleucia [suh•LOO•shee•uh] Kingdom extending eastward from Asia Minor into what is now Pakistan. (pp. 403, 414)

Siberia Large region consisting of the Asian portion of Russia as well as northern Kazakhstan. (pp. 51, 61, 63)

Sicily [SIH•suh•lee] Largest island in the Mediterranean Sea off the coast of southern Italy. 37°N 13°E (pp. 51, 52, 342, 420, 421, 427, 432, 486, 494, 510, 518)

Sidon City and seaport in southwestern Lebanon on the Mediterranean Sea. 33°N 35°E (pp. 133, 210, 226)

Sinai [SY•NY] **Peninsula** An arid peninsula in north east Egypt (pp. 56, 210)

South America Continent in the southern part of the Western Hemisphere lying between the Atlantic and Pacific Oceans. (pp. 48, 50, 68, 69, 71, 72, 73, 74, 75, 128, 313)

South China Sea Arm of the Pacific Ocean, located off the eastern and southeastern coasts of Asia. (pp. 49, 51, 61, 63, 70, 277, 295, 301)

Spain Country in southwestern Europe. (pp. 48-9, 52, 54, 426, 427, 435, 444, 448, 449, 460, 474, 480, 484, 486, 494, 510, 515, 518)

Sparta City in ancient Greece and capital of Laconia. 37°N 23°E (pp. 337, 342, 344, 345, 354, 358, 365, 370)

Sri Lanka [sree•LAHNG•kuh] Country in the Indian Ocean south of India, formerly called Ceylon. (pp. 49, 51, 60, 62, 242, 246)

Stockholm Capital city and seaport of Sweden. 59°N 18°E (p. 52)

Strait of Gibraltar Narrow passage connecting the Mediterranean Sea with the Atlantic Ocean. 35°N 5°W (pp. 52, 54)

Strait of Magellan Channel between the Atlantic and Pacific Oceans on the southern tip of South America. 52°S 68°W (pp. 68, 69)

Strait of Messina Passage separating mainland Italy from the island of Sicily. 38°N 15°E (p. 421)

Sumatra Island in western Indonesia. 2°N 99°E (pp. 49, 51, 70, 301)

Susa Persian capital, in the region of southern Mesopotamia between the Tigris and Euphrates Rivers. 34°N 48°E (pp. 133, 146, 352, 400)

Sweden Northern European country on the eastern side of the Scandinavian peninsula. (pp. 49, 51, 52, 53, 54, 55)

Syracuse [SIHR•uh•KYOOS] The capital of Syracuse Province, on the southeastern coast of the island of Sicily. 37°N 15°E (p. 406)

Syria [SIHR•ee•uh] Southwestern Asian country on the east side of the Mediterranean Sea. (pp. 49, 56, 57, 60, 62, 146, 181, 400, 432, 484, 486, 510)

Syrian [SIHR•ee•uhn] **Desert** Desert of the northern Arabian Peninsula, including northern Saudi Arabia, northeastern Jordan, southeastern Syria, and western Iraq. (pp. 133, 210, 226)

Taiwan [TY•WAHN] Island country off the southeast coast of China, the seat of the Chinese Nationalist government. (pp. 49, 51, 61, 66, 63, 70, 277)

Taklimakan [TAH•kluh•muh•KAHN] **Desert** Desert in northwestern China. (pp. 51, 277)

Tarsus City in southern Turkey. 37°N 34°E (pp. 510, 518, 524)

Teotihuacán [TAY•oh•TEE•wuh•KAHN] Site in central Mexico that in ancient times was one of the largest cities in the world. 19°N 98°W (pp. 312, 314, 324)

Thar Desert Desert in northwestern India. (p. 270)

Thebes [THEEBZ] Ancient city and former capital of Egypt. 25°N 32°E (pp. 144, 178, 181, 189, 194, 337, 352)

Thermopylae [thuhr•MAH•puh•lee] Mountain pass in ancient Greece. 38°N 22°E (p. 354)

Tian [tee•AHN] **Shan** Mountain range in central Asia. (p. 60, 61, 277)

Tiber [TY•buhr] **River** River in north Italy. (p. 421)

Tibet [tuh•BEHT] Country in central Asia. (pp. 60, 301)

Tigris River River in southeastern Turkey and Iraq that merges with the Euphrates River. (pp. 60, 62, 133, 301, 329, 342, 352, 400, 414, 449, 454, 486)

Tikal Ancient mesoamerican city in present day Guatemala. (pp. 317, 324)

Tlaxcala [tlah•SKAH•luh] State in east central Mexico. (pp. 64, 66)

Tokyo Capital of modern Japan, formerly called Edo. 34°N 131°E (pp. 49, 61, 63, 70)

Troy Ancient city on the Aegean Sea destroyed during the Trojan War. 39°N 25°E (pp. 337, 342, 370)

Turkey Country in southeastern Europe and western Asia. (pp. 49, 56, 57, 60, 62, 400)

Turkmenistan [tuhrk•MEH•nuh•STAN] Central Asian country on the Caspian Sea. (pp. 60, 400)

Tyre [TYR] Town in southern Lebanon on the Mediterranean Sea. 33°N 35°E (pp. 133, 146, 210, 226, 342, 352, 400, 510)

Tyrrhenian [tuh•REE•nee•uhn] **Sea** Arm of the Mediterranean Sea between Italy and the islands of Corsica, Sardinia, and Sicily. (p. 54)

Ukraine [yoo•KRAYN] Eastern European country west of Russia on the Black Sea. (pp. 49, 53, 55)

Upper Egypt The area along the nile in central Egypt. (pp. 157, 181, 194)

Ur Ancient city in Mesopotamia. 32°N 47°E (p. 133)

Ural Mountains Mountain chain running from northern Russia southward to the Kirgiz Steppe. (pp. 55, 60)

Volga River River in western Russia, longest in Europe. (pp. 53, 55)

Wei He [WAY HUH] River in central China. (pp. 277, 278, 282)

West Indies Islands in the Caribbean Sea between North America and South America. (pp. 64, 65, 67)

Xian [SHYEHN] Capital of Shaanxi Province in China. (p. 282)

Xianyang [SHYEHN•YAHNG] City in northern China. 34°N 108°E (p. 295)

Xi Jiang [SHEE•JYAHNG] River in southern China. (p. 295)

Yagtze River [YAHNG•See] World's third longest river flowing through central China. (pp. 227, 278)

Yellow Sea Arm of the Pacific Ocean bordered by China, North Korea, and South Korea. (pp. 51, 61, 63, 277, 278, 282, 295)

Yucatan Peninsula Land mass extending into the Gulf of Mexico in present-day Southern Mexico. (pp. 66, 324)

Zambia Country in south central Africa. (pp. 58, 59)

Gazetteer

Italicized page numbers refer to illustrations. The following abbreviations are used in the index:
m = map, c = chart, p = photograph or picture, g = graph, crt = cartoon, ptg = painting, q = quote

Index

Index

Index

Index

Acknowledgements

Text

149 Excerpt from *Gilgamesh* by John Gardner and John Maier, copyright © 1984 by the Estate of John Gardner and John Maier. Used by permission of Alfred A. Knopf, a division of Random House, Inc. 288, 305 Excerpts from *The Essential Confucius*, translated and presented by Thomas Cleary. Copyright © 1992 by Thomas Cleary. Reprinted by permission of HarperCollins Inc. 291 Excerpt from "Higher Good Is Like Water" from *The Essential Tao*, translated and presented by Thomas Cleary. Copyright © 1991 by Thomas Cleary. Reprinted by permission of HarperCollins Inc. 428 Excerpt from *Virgil's Aeneid*, translated by Robert Fitzgerald. Translation copyright ©1981, 1982, 1982 by Robert Fitzgerald. Reprinted by permission of Random House, Inc.

Glencoe would like to acknowledge the artists and agencies who participated in illustrating this program: American Artists Rep., Inc.; The Artifact Group; Mapping Specialists, Ltd.; Ortelius; WildLife Art Ltd.

Photo Credits

Cover (bkgd)Getty Images, (l)Asian Art & Archeology, Inc., (r)Jeff Hunter/Getty Images; **077**(t)Dallas and John Heaton/CORBIS, (c)Jamie Harron/CORBIS, (b)Owen Franken/CORBIS; **078** (bl)Robert Landau/Corbis; (others)Getty Images; **079** Getty Images; **092** (l)Comstock Images, (c)AFP Worldwide, (r)Getty Images; **093** (t)Ron Sheridan/Ancient Art & Architecture Collection, (c)Katie Deits/Index Stock Imagery, (b)James King-Holmes/Photo Researchers; **094** (t)Scala/Art Resource, NY, (b)Nimatallah/Art Resource, NY; **095** (l)Michel Zabe/Museo Templo Mayor, (r)Museum of Ethnology, Vienna; **096** (t)American Museum of Natural History, (tc)Scala/Art Resource, NY; (bc)Chester Beatty Library, Dublin/Bridgeman Art Library, (b)Reunion des Musees Nationaux/Art Resource, NY; **098** NASA; **099** (t)CORBIS, (b)Lawrence Manning/CORBIS; **100** Mary Evans Picture Library; **101** (tl)Christine Osborne/Lonely Planet Images, (tr)Brand X Pictures, (bl)Frans Lemmens/Getty Images, (br)Michael Dwyer/Stock Boston/PictureQuest; **104** (t)Will Hart/PhotoEdit, (bl)The Newark Museum/Art Resource, NY, (bcl)Erich Lessing/Art Resource, NY, (bcr)Smithsonian Institution, (br)Robert Harding Picture Library; **105** (bkgd)Victoria & Albert Museum, London/Bridgeman Art Library, (inset)Archiv/Photo Researchers; **106** (t)Richard T. Nowitz/CORBIS, (bl)National Museum of India, New Delhi, India/Bridgeman Art Library, (bc)Asian Art & Archaeology/CORBIS, (br)David Hiser/Getty Images; **107** (l)Bettmann/CORBIS, (r)Scala/Art Resource, NY; **108** (l)Borromeo/Art Resource, NY, (r)Bibliotheque Nationale, Paris; **110** (t)MIT Collection/CORBIS, (b)Robert Harding Picture Library; **111** Ronald Sheridan/Ancient Art & Architecture Collection; **112** Matthews/Network/CORBIS Saba; **113** (t)Christopher Liu/ChinaStock, **113** (cl)D.E. Cox/Getty Images, (cr)Dan Helms/NewSport/CORBIS, (b)Tom Lovell/National Geographic Society Image Collection; **114** (t)Réunion des Musées Nationaux / Art Resource, NY, **114** (c)John Heaton/CORBIS, (b)Tom Lovell/National Geographic Society Image Collection; **115** SuperStock; **116-117** ©Worldsat International Inc. 2004, All RightsReserved, **116** (1)S. Fiore/SuperStock, (2)Scala/Art Resource, NY, (l)Giansanti Gianni/CORBIS Sygma, (c)Louvre Museum, Paris/Bridgeman Art Library, (r)Metropolitan Museum of Art, Rogers Fund and Edward S. Harkness Gift,1929 (29.3.3)/The Metropolitan Museum of Art; **117** (3)Sylvain Grandadam/Getty Images, (4)Timothy Kendall/Museum of Fine Arts, Boston, (5)Gary Cralle/Getty Images, (l)O. Louis Mazzatenta/National Geographic Society Image Collection, (c)SuperStock, (r)Bettmann/CORBIS; **118-119** Georg Gerster/Photo Researchers; **123** Morton Beebe; **125** Michael Holford; **127** American Museum of Natural History; **133** Hirmer Verlag; **134** Scala/Art Resource, NY; **135** (l)Nik Wheeler/CORBIS, (r)Michael Holford; **137** (l)Mesopotamian Iraq Museum, Baghdad, Iraq/Giraudon/Bridgeman Art Library, (r)Will Hart/PhotoEdit; **138** akg-images; **140** Réunion des Musées Nationaux / Art Resource, NY; **141** Louve, Paris/Bridgeman Art Library; **144** Boltin Picture Library; **145** Gianni Dagli Orti/CORBIS; **147** S. Fiore/SuperStock; **148** (t)Hirmer Verlag, (b)Pierre Vauthey/CORBIS Sygma; **149** Réunion des Musées Nationaux / Art Resource, NY; **152-153** Brian Lawrence/Image State; **155** Gianni Dagli Orti/CORBIS; **158** John Lawrence/Getty Images; **159** Erich Lessing/Art Resource, NY; **160** (l)Giraudon/Art Resource, NY, (r)Gianni Dagli Orti/CORBIS; **161**(tl)Caroline Penn/CORBIS, (tr)Kenneth Garrett, (b)Kenneth Garrett; **166** Sylvain Grandadam/Getty Images; **168** (l)Musee du Louvre, Paris/Explorer/SuperStock, (r)The British Museum; **170** John Heaton/CORBIS; **177** Doug Martin; **179** Gianni Dagli Orti/CORBIS; **180** (l)Smithsonian Institution, (r)file photo; **182** (l)CORBIS, (r)Metropolitan Museum of Art, Rogers Fund and Edward S. Harkness Gift,1929 (29.3.3)/The Metropolitan Museum of Art; **183** Erich Lessing/Art Resource, NY; **184** (t)Egyptian National Museum, Cairo/SuperStock, (b)Gavin Hellier/Getty Images; **185** (t)Michael Holford, (b)O. Louis Mazzatenta; **188** Egyptian Expedition of The Metropolitan Museum of Art, The Rogers Fund, 1930 (30.4.21)/The Metropolitan Museum of Art; **189** Timothy Kendall/Museum of Fine Arts, Boston; **190** Brooklyn Museum of Art, New York/Charles Edwin Wilbour Fund/Bridgeman Art Library; **191** SuperStock; **192** Egyptian National Museum, Cairo/SuperStock;**193** Bildarchiv Preussischer Kulturbesitz/Art Resource, NY; **196-197** Anthony Pidgeon/Lonely Planet Images; **199** Private Collection/Bridgeman Art Library; **201** Shai Ginott/CORBIS; **202** (l)North Wind Picture Archives, (r)Leland Bobbe/Getty Images; **203** (t)The Israel Museum, Jerusalem, (c)Stock Montage/SuperStock, (b)Laura Zito/Photo Researchers; **204** (l)Mary Evans Picture Library, (r)Charles & Josette Lenars/CORBIS; **207** Mary Evans Picture Library; **208** Bettmann/CORBIS; **209** Stock Montge/SuperStock; **214** (l)Richard T. Nowitz/CORBIS, (c)Bill Aron/PhotoEdit, (r)SuperStock; **215** Walker Art Gallery, Liverpool, Merseyside, UK, National Museums Liverpool/Bridgeman Art Library; **216** CORBIS; **218** Lawrence Migdale/Getty Images; **219** SuperStock; **221** (l)Paul Chesley/Getty Images, (c)Gary Cralle/Getty Images, (r)Dave Bartruff/CORBIS; **222** Peter Turnley/CORBIS; **223** (l)Richard T. Nowitz/CORBIS, (r) West Semitic Research/Dead Sea Scrolls Foundation/CORBIS; **224** Richard T. Nowitz/CORBIS; **225** The Israel Museum, Jerusalem; **228** (t)Erich Lessing/Art Resource, NY, (b)The Art Archive/British Library; **229** (t)Boltin Picture Library; (cl)Smithsonian Institution, (cr)Stock Montge/SuperStock, (b)CORBIS; **230** (t)Robert Harding Picture Library, (c)Seattle Art Museum/CORBIS; **231** (t)Robert Harding Picture Library, (c)Asian Art & Archaeology/CORBIS, (bl)Werner Forman/Art Resource, NY, (br)Boltin Picture Library; **232-233** ©Worldsat International Inc. 2004, All RightsReserved; **232** (t)Victoria & Albert Museum, London/Art Resource, NY, (bl)Christie's Images, London/Bridgeman Art Library/SuperStock, (bc)Vanni/Art Resource, NY, (br)Kamat's Potpourri; **233** (3)Robert Harding Picture Library, (4)Boltin Picture Library, (5) David Hiser/Getty Images, (bl)Hulton Archive/Getty Images News Services, (br) Charles & Josette Lenars/CORBIS; **234-235** David Cumming/CORBIS; **237** (l)Borromeo/Art Resource, NY, (r)SEF/Art Resource, NY; **240** (tl)Robert Harding Picture Library, (tr)Borromeo/Art Resource, NY, (bl)National Museum of India, New Delhi, India/Bridgeman Art Library, (br)Harappan National Museum of Karachi, Karachi, Pakistan/Bridgeman Art Library; **244** (l)Carl Purcell/The Purcell Team, (r)AFP Worldwide; **247** (l)Robert Harding Picture Library, (r)Borromeo/Art Resource, NY; **248** (t)SEF/Art Resource, NY, (b)Victoria & Albert Museum, London/Art Resource, NY; **249** Rajesh Bedi/National Geographic Image Collection; **250** Borromeo/Art Resource, NY; **251** (l)Archivo Iconografico, S.A./CORBIS, (r)Christie's Images, London/Bridgeman Art Library/SuperStock; **252** Sheldan Collins/CORBIS; **253** (l)AP Photo/J.A. Mills, (r)Bettmann/CORBIS; **258** Doug Martin; **261** Kamat's Potpourri; **262** (l)Robert Harding Picture Library, (r)Hugh Sitton/Getty Images; **263** (l)Ancient Art & Architecture Collection, (r)Hulton Archive/Getty Images News Services; **265** The British Library, London UK/Bridgeman Art Library; **268** Victoria & Albert Museum, London/Art Resource, NY;

269 Archivo Iconografico, S.A./CORBIS; 272 D.E. Cox/Getty Images; 275 (b)Giraudon/Art Resource, NY; 279 (t)Asian Art & Archaeology/CORBIS, (b)Asian Art & Archaeology/CORBIS; 280 Bridgeman/Art Resource, NY; 281 (t)Asian Art & Archaeology/CORBIS, (c)Asian Art & Archaeology/Corbis, (bl)file photo, (br)The Art Archive/Musee Cernuschi Paris/Dagli Orti; 283 file photo; 284 (l)Robert Frerck/Odyssey Productions, (c)Giraudon/Art Resource, NY, (r)Dennis Cox; 286 Lawrence Manning/CORBIS; 287 (t)Christopher Liu/ChinaStock, (c)Christopher Liu/ChinaStock, (b)Asian Art & Archaeology/CORBIS; 288 Chen Yixin/ChinaStock; 289 Vanni/Art Resource, NY; 290 (tl)Robert Frerck/Odyssey Productions, (tc)ChinaStock, (tr)Dennis Cox, (b)Giraudon/Art Resource, NY; 292 Keren Su/CORBIS; 293 Bohemian Nomad Picturemakers/CORBIS; 297 (t)ChinaStock; 298 Bibliotheque Nationale, Paris, (b)Robert Harding Picture Library; 299 (l)Ontario Science Centre, (r)Dean Conger/CORBIS; 302 (l)The Art Archive/National Palace Museum Taiwan, (c)The Art Archive/British Library, (r)The Art Archive/British Library; 304 Erich Lessing/Art Resource, NY; 308-309 Anna Clopet/CORBIS; 311 Gianni Dagli Orti/CORBIS; 313 file photo; 314 (l)Werner Forman/Art Resource, NY; (c r)Nathan Benn/CORBIS; 315 (l)Freelance Consulting Services Pty Ltd/CORBIS, (r)David Hiser/Getty Images; 319 Charles & Josette Lenars/CORBIS; 320 Gianni Dagli Orti/CORBIS; 322 (t)Boltin Picture Library, (b)Werner Forman/CORBIS; 323 Charles & Josette Lenars /CORBIS; 326 (l)Ancient Art & Architecture Collection, (r)Burstein Collection/CORBIS; 327 (tl)ChinaStock, (tr)Werner Forman/Art Resource, NY, (c)Bridgeman/Art Resource, NY, (b)Michel Zabe/Art Resource, NY; 328 (l)Scala/Art Resource, NY,(r)Ronald Sheridan/Ancient Art & Architecture Collection; 329 (t)Archives Charmet/Bridgeman Art Library, (c)Hagia Sophia, Istanbul, Turkey/ET Archives, London/SuperStock, (b)Scala/Art Resource, NY; 330-331 ©Worldsat International Inc. 2004, All Rights Reserved; 330 (t)Charles O'Rear/CORBIS, (c)Archives Charmet/Bridgeman Art Library, (bl)Scala/Art Resource, NY, (bcl)Scala/Art Resource, NY, (bcr)Sandro Vannini/CORBIS, (br)Robert Emmett Bright/Photo Researchers; 331 (3)Ric Ergenbright, (4)Sean Sexton Collection/CORBIS, (5)Richard T. Nowitz/CORBIS, (bl)Scala/Art Resource, NY, (bcl)Danita Delimont/Ancient Art & Architecture Collection, (bcr)Werner Forman/Art Resource, NY, (br)Scala/Art Resource, NY; 332 Vanni Archive/CORBIS; 335 The Art Archive/E.T. Archive; 337 Steve Vidler/SuperStock; 338 (t)Gianni Dagli Orti/CORBIS, (b)Nimatallah/Art Resource, NY; 339 (t)Alberto Incrocci/Getty Images, (b)Nimatallah/Art Resource, NY; 341 The Art Archive/National Archaeological Museum Athens/Dagli Orti; 345 The Art Archive/E.T. Archive; 346 Foto Marburg/Art Resource, NY; 347 (r)Michael Holford; 348 (l)Tom Lovell/National Geographic Society Image Collection, (r)Dan Helms/NewSport/CORBIS; 349 (t)Nimatallah/Art Resource, NY;350 Ronald Sheridan/Ancient Art & Architecture Collection, (b)The Brooklyn Museum, Charles Wilbour Fund; 351 (l)Mary Evans Picture Library, (r)Roger Wood/CORBIS, (c)Bettmann/CORBIS; 352 SEF/Art Resource, NY; 353 The Art Archive/Dagli Orti; 355 Bettmann/CORBIS; 356 Peter Connolly; 359 Steve Vidler/SuperStock; 361 (t)Scala/Art Resource, NY, (b)Vanni Archive/CORBIS; 362 Smithsonian Institution; 364 Nimatallah/Art Resource, NY ; 365 Gianni Dagli Orti/CORBIS; 366 368 Scala/Art Resource, NY; 369 Erich Lessing/Art Resource, NY; 372-373 Roger Wood/CORBIS; 375 Scala/Art Resource, NY; 377 (cw from top) (1)Bettman/CORBIS, (2)The Art Archive/National Archaeological Museum Athens/Dagli Orti, (3)The Art Archive/Achaeological Museum Tarquina/Dagli Orti, (4)Lauros/Giraudon/Bridgeman Art Library, (5)Lauros/Giraudon/Bridgeman Art Library, (6)The Art Archive/Archaeological Museum Venice/Dagli Orti, (7)Fitzwilliam Museum, University of Cambridge, UK/Bridgeman Art Library, (8)Giraudon/Bridgeman Art Library, (9)Peter Willi/Bridgeman Art Library, (10)Wolfgang Kaehler/CORBIS; 378 Mary Evans Picture Library; 379 James L. Stanfield/National Geographic Society Image Collection; 380 Alinari/Art Resource, NY; 381 Scala/Art Resource, NY; 382 (l)SuperStock, (r)Eric Robert/CORBIS; 383 (t)Erich Lessing/Art Resource, NY, (b)Mary Evans Picture Library; 384 (tl)Joel W. Rogers/CORBIS, (tc)Dave Bartruff/CORBIS, (tr)Vanni Archive/CORBIS, (b)Charles O'Rear/CORBIS; 391 Doug Martin; 392 393 Scala/Art Resource, NY; 394 (l)Mary Evans Picture Library, (cl)Scala/Art Resource, NY, (cr)Museo Capitolino, Rome/E.T. Archives, London/Superstock, (r)Reunion des Musees Nationaux/Art Resource, NY; 396 (t)SEF/Art Resource, NY; (b)Scala/Art Resource, NY; 399 file photo; 401 Robert Harding Picture Library; 402 (l)Yan Arthus-Bertrand/CORBIS, (r)Archives Charmet/Bridgeman Art Library; 404 David Lees/CORBIS; 405 Sandro Vannini/CORBIS; 407 Araldo de Luca/CORBIS; 408 Erich Lessing/Art Resource, NY; 409 (t)Eric Lessing/ Art Resource, NY, (bl)Bettmann/CORBIS, (br)Araldo de Luca/CORBIS; 410 (l)Scala/Art Resource, NY, (r)North Wind Picture Archives; 412 Museo Capitolino, Rome/E.T. Archives, London/Superstock; 413 Alinari/Art Resource, NY; 416-417 Roy Rainford/Robert Harding/Getty Images; 419 (tl)B. Wilson/Ancient Art & Architecture Collection, (tr)Erich Lessing/Art Resource, NY, (bl)The Newark Museum/Art Resource, NY, (br)The Newark Museum/Art Resource, NY; 422 Francis Schroeder/SuperStock; 423 (t)file photo, (b)Scala/Art Resource, NY; 425 Prenestino Museum, Rome/E.T. Archives, London/SuperStock; 427 Michael Holford; 428 Ronald Sheridan/Ancient Art & Architecture Collection; 429 The Art Archive/Archeological Museum Beirut/Dagli Orti; 430 North Wind Picture Archives; 437 (l)Scala/Art Resource, NY, (r)Time Life Pictures/Getty Images; 438 (tl)Archaeological Museum, Venice/E.T. Archives, London/SuperStock, (tr)Ronald Sheridan/Ancient Art & Architecture Collection, (bl)Louvre, Paris/Bridgeman Art Library, (br)Reunion des Musees Nationaux/Art Resource, NY; 439 (l)SuperStock, c)Museo e Gallerie Nazionali di Capodimonte, Naples, Italy/Bridgeman Art Library, (r)Mary Evans Picture Library; 440 Bettmann/CORBIS; 442 Nimatallah/Art Resource, NY; 443 Museo e Gallerie Nazionali di Capodimonte, Naples, Italy/Bridgeman Art Library; 445 Victoria & Albert Museum, London/Bridgeman Art Library; 447 Robert Emmett Bright/Photo Researchers; 448 (l)Roma, Museo Nazion/Art Resource, NY, (cl)Archivo Iconografico, S.A./CORBIS, (c)Archico Iconografico, S.A./CORBIS, (cr)Staatliche Glypothek, Munich, Germany/E.T. Archive, London/SuperStock, (r)Archivo Iconografico, S.A./CORBIS; 450 Ric Ergenbright; 451 (tl)B. Wilson/Ancient Art & Architecture Collection, (tr)Erich Lessing/Art Resource, NY; (bl)The Newark Museum/Art Resource, NY, (br)The Newark Museum/Art Resource, NY; 452 Bettmann/CORBIS; 453 SuperStock; 456-457 Picture Finders Ltd./eStock; 459 Giraudon/Art Resource, NY; 461 Nik Wheeler/CORBIS; 462 Bibliotheque Nationale, Paris, France, Giraudon/Bridgeman Art Library; 464 Pierre Belzeaux/Photo Researchers; 465 (t)Scala/Art Resource, NY, (b)Erich Lessing/Art Resource, NY; 466 Scala/Art Resource, NY; 467 (r)Giraudon/Art Resource, NY, (l)Stanley Seaberg; 473 Doug Martin; 475 CORBIS; 476 (t)The Newark Museum/Art Resource, NY, (c)The Newark Museum/Art Resource, NY, (b)The Newark Museum/Art Resource, NY; 477 Scala/Art Resource, NY; 478 (t)Hagia Sophia, Istanbul, Turkey/ET Archives, London/SuperStock, (b)C. Boisvieux/Photo Researchers, 479 Scala/Art Resource, NY; 481 Mary Evans Picture Library; 482 (l)Sean Sexton Collection/CORBIS, (r)Donald Dietz/Stock Boston/PictureQuest; 485 Stapleton Collection, UK/Bridgeman Art Library; 487 Scala/Art Resource, NY; 488 Andre Durenceau/National Geographic Society Image Collection; 489 (l)Giraudon/Art Resource, NY, (c)Brian Lawrence/SuperStock, (r)Ronald Sheridan/Ancient Art & Architecture Collection; 490 The Art Archive/Haghia Sophia Istanbul/Dagli Orti; 491 Ancient Art & Architecture Collection; 492 The Newark Museum/Art Resource, NY; 493 Scala/Art Resource, NY; 496-497 Richard T. Nowitz/CORBIS; 499 Galleria dell' Accademia, Florence, Italy/Bridgeman Art Library; 501 Nathan Benn/CORBIS; 502 (l)Reunion des Musees Nationaux/Art Resource, NY, (r)Scala/Art Resource, NY; 503 (l)Erich Lessing/Art Resource, NY, (r)Tate Gallery, London/Art Resource, NY; 504 Elio Ciol/CORBIS; 505 Louvre, Paris/Bridgeman Art Library; 506 The New York Public Library/Art Resource, NY; 507 Danita Delimont/Ancient Art & Architecture Collection;

508 Orsi Battaglini/akg-images; 510 Erich Lessing/Art Resource, NY; 511 Scala/Art Resource, NY; 514 Cott Nero DIV f.25v Portrait of St. Matthew/British Library, London/Bridgeman Art Library; 516 Scala/Art Resource, NY; 517 (t)Scala/Art Resource, NY, (b)Michael Holford; 519 C.M. Dixon/Photo Resources; 520 (l)Galleria dell' Accademia, Florence, Italy/Bridgeman Art Library, (r)PRAT/CORBIS; 521 Giraudon/Art Resource, NY; 522-523 Scala/Art Resource, NY; 527 (tl)Erich Lessing/Art Resource, NY, 527 (tr)Scala/Art Resource, NY, (b)Roy Rainford/Robert Harding/Getty Images; 537 Pierre Belzeaux/Photo Researchers; 542 Michael Holford; 544 Museum of Ethnology, Vienna London/Superstock, 545 (l)Scala/Art Resource, NY, (c)Museo Capitolino, Rome/E.T. Archives, (r)Scala/Art Resource, NY; 546 Tim Flach/Getty Images; 547 Jerry Barnett; 548-549 CORBIS; 548 (l)Picture Finders Ltd./eStock, (r)Sylvain Grandadam/Getty Images.

One-Stop Internet Resources This textbook contains one-stop Internet resources for students, teachers and parents. Log on to ca.hss.glencoe.com for more information. Online study tools include Study Central, ePuzzles and Games, Self-Check Quizzes, Vocabulary e-Flashcards, and Multi-Language Glossaries. Online research tools include Student Web Activities, Beyond the Textbook Features, Current Events, Web Resources, and State Resources. The interactive online student edition includes the complete Interactive Student Edition along with textbook updates. Especially for teachers, Glencoe offers an online Teacher Forum and Web Activity Lesson Plans.